AF709422

Reprints of Economic Classics

TARIFFS:

A STUDY IN METHOD.

Tariffs:

A Study in Method.

BY

T. E. G. GREGORY, B.Sc. (Econ.), Lond.,

Cassel Reader in Commerce in the University of London; some time Hutchinson Research Student of the London School of Economics and Political Science.

REPRINTS OF ECONOMIC CLASSICS

Augustus M. Kelley · Publishers

NEW YORK 1968

First Edition 1921
(London: Charles Griffin & Company Ltd., *Exeter Street, Strand, W.C. 2,* 1921)

Reprinted 1968 by
AUGUSTUS M. KELLEY • PUBLISHERS
New York, New York 10010
By arrangement with CHARLES GRIFFIN & COMPANY LTD.

Library of Congress Catalogue Card Number
68-20038

PRINTED IN THE UNITED STATES OF AMERICA
by SENTRY PRESS, NEW YORK, N. Y. 10019

TO

WILMA GREGORY,

AN APOLOGY

FOR MANY SILENT HOURS.

PREFACE.

1. The facts which have prompted me to write this book are simple. When, in the summer of 1918, I was asked by the authorities of the London School of Economics to prepare a set of Lectures upon Tariff Questions for the guidance of Consular students, I found to my very great surprise that the technical aspects of the subject had, so far as British writers were concerned, been almost completely neglected.[1] There were no text-books to which the enquirer might be referred, and it seemed to me very strange that a question which had agitated political parties for so long a time should not have resulted in a more complete survey from the angle of impartial comment. It was with the idea of in some degree filling the gap thus discovered that I first began to write this book. Later on, the attraction of the subject led me to extend the scope of the book somewhat, and to adopt a more critical attitude than I had at first intended. The line between description and criticism is always a thin one, however, but I have attempted, so far as was possible, to avoid that discussion of the fundamental rightness of free trade or protection, which has for the last twenty years provided the politicians with so much declamatory material. As I have more fully shown below, the ultimate questions are beyond the power of the economist to settle. He may, it is true, analyse the presuppositions in each case, and show that the

[1] An honourable exception is Mr. Higginson, whose "Tariffs at Work" is an interesting and illuminating introduction to the subject.

results contemplated are in dissonance with these assumptions, but he cannot directly attack the validity of political ideals, however little he may himself be in sympathy with them. I hope, therefore, that this book may be read, not with the aim of discovering the author's attitude towards "the Fiscal Question," but with the recollection of the true object of the study in view—namely, the examination of the technical problems which the existence of tariffs necessarily brings with it.

2. In writing this book, I have had to face two sets of difficulties. In the first place, it has not always been easy to differentiate between a critical survey of the ground and a mere description of the institutions actually at work, comparatively treated. Thus, I have had to resist the temptation to rewrite the tariff history of the nineteenth century, though the temptation to adopt a chronological basis was at times great. In certain cases, as in the treatment of the colonial tariff policy of different Powers, an historical description seemed unavoidable. But in general I have selected illustrations without overmuch reference to time and place, as it suited the general scope of the subject. I make no apology for the introduction of what may appear at first sight an excessive amount of illustrative material. Though tariffs represent, perhaps, the most plentiful result of economic legislation, the collation of *forms* appeared to be indispensable. There has been far too much talk of tariffs in the abstract in this country already. The only way of giving the reader a sense of the great complexity of the subject was to give him the opportunity of judging the "raw material" for himself. My main trouble was not the paucity of the material, but the necessity for selection.

3. The second difficulty was the question to what extent this book should deal with current topics of interest. I finally decided that it was desirable, as far as possible, to include matters of current concern. But I take this opportunity

of saying that it was not my intention to give a complete record of current events. Apart from the difficulty of doing so objectively, it would have been a departure from my main object, which was a description of tariffs in general. The current sources of information are easily accessible to all serious students, and my main effort has been to link up the present problems with tariff technology generally.

4. It is unnecessary at this stage to attempt to summarise the net results of the survey. One word may be permitted me however. The most casual reading of the book will be sufficient to justify the statement that there is no stage in the chain of events which leads from the legislative inception of the tariff down to the practical administration of its details which does not reveal unsuspected difficulties of choice between alternatives. The resolution of these difficulties is made easier by a consideration of the development of the tariff in the recent past. Without in any way committing oneself to the protectionist point of view, it is clear that if the United Kingdom ever adopts the principle of protection there are certain solutions which, on technical grounds, are not acceptable. Thus, the choice between specific and *ad valorem* duties has been, I venture to think, definitely determined in favour of the former. In the same way, there is simply no question as to the necessity for specialisation or differentiation between different grades of the same commodity. The naive idea of the uniform rate on simple categories, such as the "Tariff Reformers'" have so long been advocating, is quite untenable in view of the historical evolution through which the tariffs of other countries have gone. In the same way, I have tried to show that the demand for a "Scientific Tariff" involves very difficult questions of political and administrative expediency which cannot be shirked without possible disappointment to all concerned. Further, I have tried to show that the "unlimited" or "unconditional" form of the Most-Favoured-Nation Clause is quite capable of rational defence,

even on the assumption that in general a policy of protection is desirable.

5. One other remark in this connection may be permitted. At the moment of writing, there seems a growing agitation in favour of a "sliding scale" of duties in order to check "exchange dumping." The history of the sliding scale on wheat throws some light upon the difficulties of administering such a scale without increasing the very fluctuations it is desired to avoid. A fuller acquaintance with the past history of sliding scales would, I think, have modified the strength of the demand for their re-introduction.[1]

6. It is left for me to make grateful acknowledgments to Prof. A. J. Sargent, who has been good enough to read the whole book in MS., with the exception of the section dealing with Revenue Duties, and whose comments have been of the greatest value to me. Dr. Hugh Dalton has assisted the argument with criticism at several points. Those who know Mr. Headicar's grasp of the official and other literature stored in the Library of the School of Economics will realise what his help has meant in the accumulation of material. My thanks go to Miss H. Vernon-Jones for indexing the book.

TH. GREGORY.

THE LONDON SCHOOL OF ECONOMICS AND POLITICAL SCIENCE,
CLARE MARKET, KINGSWAY, W.C. 2,
February 21st, 1921.

[1] These difficulties have proved great enough to prevent the incorporation of the principle in the new Industries Preservation Bill, now passing its final parliamentary stages (August, 1921).

CONTENTS.

CHAPTER I.

CHAPTER I.—*Continued.*

CHAPTER II.

CHAPTER III.

CHAPTER IV.

CHAPTER V.

CHAPTER VI.

CHAPTER X.—*Continued.*

CHAPTER X.—*Continued.*

CHAPTER X.—*Continued.*

CHAPTER X.—*Continued.*

CHAPTER XI.

APPENDIX I.

APPENDIX II.

LIST OF ABBREVIATIONS EMPLOYED IN THIS BOOK.

B.T.J., ... *Board of Trade Journal.*

C.I.D., ... Colonial Import Duties, published by the Board of Trade.

Ec. J., ... *Economic Journal.*

F.I.D., ... Foreign Import Duties, published by the Board of Trade.

H.S.W., . . . " Handwörterbuch der Staatswissenschaften."

J. de Ec., . . . *Journal des Économistes.*

J.N.S., ... "*Jahrbücher für Nationaloekonomie und Statistik.*"

J. Pol. Econ. . . *Journal of Political Economy.*

Kelly, ... Kelly's " Customs Tariffs of the World " (1914 edition usually used).

Pallain, . . . Georges Pallain, " Les Douanes Françaises," 4 Vols., 1913.

P.P., ... Parliamentary Papers.

Q.J.E., . . . *Quarterly Journal of Economics.*

R.E.I., ... *Revue Économique Internationale.*

Schm. J., . . . "*Schmoller's Jahrbücher für Gesetzgebung und Verwaltung.*"

S.V.S.P., . . . *Schriften des Vereins für Sozialpolitik.*

T.N., ... Tariff Notes (published by the Bureau of Foreign and Domestic Commerce, U.S.A. Government).

T.S., ... Tariff Series (published by the Bureau of Foreign and Domestic Commerce, U.S.A. Government).

W.W.A., . . . " *Welt-Wirtschaftliches Archiv.*"

Z.S.W., . . . *Zeitschrift für Sozialwissenschaft.*

TARIFFS.

CHAPTER I.

Customs Areas, Customs-Making Bodies and Customs Law.

§ 1. It will not be necessary in the course of this work to devote very much space to what may be termed the antiquities of the customs, although we may occasionally require historical material for illustrative purposes. The object of the volume is the investigation of the scientific problems which arise from the imposition of charges upon goods passing across the frontiers of a country. When these duties are levied upon goods entering the country for consumption or further manufacture, they are described as import duties, when imposed on goods leaving the country they are described as export duties, when they are imposed on goods moving across the national territory to a destination outside that territory the duties are described as transit duties. These are the forms which are generally considered to be " true " customs duties to distinguish them from duties, also imposed on goods moving across the frontier, but imposed for purposes other than those for which customs duties are considered to be levied. These latter purposes are the collection of revenue, the achievement of specific ends for the standpoint of commercial policy or both these purposes together. In certain cases a small tax is imposed on all goods known as a " statistical " or " registration tax : " this it may be argued is a fee imposed for services rendered and not a duty properly speaking ; in other cases taxes or duties are imposed which vary not directly with some specific quality of the goods, but according to other circumstances—*i.e.*, the nature of the vehicle which has brought them to the frontier or the route the goods have taken. Such a differentiation, it may be argued, denies such duties the character of true customs duties.[1] This dispute is in the main a verbal one which need not detain us. From the technical point of view, no very clear line of distinction can be drawn, and we may, therefore, say that customs duties represent charges imposed upon, or incidental to, the importation, exportation, and transportation over a given area of commodities. The classificatory instrument in which such duties are embodied is generally described as the "Tariff," and the duties in question are indifferently spoken of as "Tariff Duties" or "Customs Duties."[2]

§ 2. It will not fail to strike the reader that "importation" and "exportation," "frontiers" and "national territory" are not terms that are entirely self-explanatory. The actual duties themselves are, or may be, very various and precise instructions have to be given as to how and when they are to be imposed. In this way there arises the necessity for a code of law, and a body of regulations which may be broadly described, with reference to a given country, as the Tariff or Customs Law of that country. But such a usage conceals a practical difficulty. The actual legislation of most countries draws a distinction between Tariff Law and Customs Law.[3]

[1] *Cf.* Pallain I., § 90, on the surtaxe d'entrepôt . . . "la surtaxe d'entrepôt n'est pas, à proprement parler, un droit de douane ; en effet elle ne presente pas ce caractère particuliér du droit de douane qu'est d'imposer la marchandise pour elle-même et selon le degré de main d'œuvre qu'elle a reçu." (The surtaxe d'entrepôt is not properly speaking a customs duty, as a matter of fact it does not possess the particular characteristic of a customs duty which is to strike the merchandise as such, and according to the quantity of labour which has been spent on it.) For the details of this tax, see below, p. 214 ; *cf.* also *op. cit.*, p. 70, note 4, for a further proof that the tax is not "properly speaking" a customs duty.

[2] Murray gives the following etymology for tariff ; Italian *tariffa,* "arithmetike or casting of accounts" (Florio) ; "a book of rates for duties" (Barretti) = Spanish and Portuguese tarifa, and Arabic ta'rif, notification, explanation, definition article. In its secondary technical sense it was first used in its Italian form : Murray quotes from a letter of 1592 to Lord Zouche and Johnson, *Dict.*, 6th edn., vol. 2, defines Tariff as a Cartel of Commerce, and quotes Addison, "This branch of our trade was regulated by a tariff or declaration of the duties of import and export." The French "douanes" is by Ménage drawn from the Greek δοχάνη (quoted Littré : Dict. de la Langue Française, Tome I., Pt. II., p. 1226, col. 2), on which Littre remarks, "tres-bonne étymologie, si elle rendait compte des formes espagnoles où *a-duana* paraît indiquer l'article arabeal : dès lors le mot se rattacherait à l'arabe addiuán (al dirán) maison ou lieu où se réunissent les administrateurs des finances pour le recouvrement des droits." The German "zoll" comes through the old High and Middle German Zol and old Saxon tolna and tol (*cf.* old English tolne and toll), from the Latin teloneum, toloneum, Customs House (Heyne Deutsches Wörterbuch 3, p. 1447 : Handwört. buch der S.W., 3rd edn., vol. 8, p. 1041). "Customs" is derived from Med. Latin "custuma."

[3] *E.g.*, Canada, South Africa, Germany (Zollgesetzgebung, Tarifgesetz-gebung) United Kingdom, etc.

Such a division of the subject matter finds its justification in the fact that Customs Law deals with importation and exportation of goods *in general*, and with the administrative regulations to which it is subjected, whilst the tariff law deals with the charges, and, in consequence thereof, the special regulations applicable to special classes of goods. Such a division finds a further justification in the *frequency of change* which the latter class of legislation is subject to as contrasted with the relative permanence of the general principles of the customs code. But in those cases where in principle all goods are liable to duty and only specified goods are exempt, the sphere of tariff legislation extends as widely as the sphere of customs legislation, at any rate so far as the goods themselves come into question.

At this stage, when we are seeking a preliminary acquaintance with our subject matter, we need not concern ourselves with these somewhat arid points, nor with the further distinctions between the "Legislative Tariff" and the "Official Tariff" which is imposed by the necessities of administrative convenience. Law and legislation involves a law-making body, and this again involves an area to which the laws themselves and any regulations flowing therefrom, relate. Our first task must, therefore, be to examine at some length the problems to which these considerations give rise.

§ 3. Let us begin by considering the question of territory. The tariff is a systematic ordering of the duties imposed on goods traversing, or passing inwards or outwards from, a given territory. It is a natural assumption that the territory in question is co-extensive with the national territory, in the sense that the area within which the authority of a given political Sovereign is supreme, is also the territory covered by those particular edicts of the Sovereign which we call "customs" or "tariff" law. But this natural assumption is invalid, and invalid on two grounds. Firstly, the law-making body for tariff purposes is not necessarily the same as the law-making body for other purposes. A country may in fact possess no law-making body for customs purposes at all. This is a point with which we will deal at more length in a subsequent section. Secondly, the national territory may be wider than the customs area, or, alternatively, the customs area may be wider than the national territory.

In this section we shall deal with the consequences flowing

from the second of these points: it follows that we must define the customs area and investigate the relationship between it and the national territory with some care.

We may define a national territory as any area subject to a common political sovereign: a customs territory as any area enclosed by a common customs line. Where the territory in question forms a geographical continuum, or where it is a geographically disparate but historically unified area, it seems natural that the boundaries of the State should also form the limits of the customs area, for quite sufficient reasons.

The first of these is the obvious convenience of collecting duties at the moment of passing the frontier, the second is the desire to bind the area together economically by affording the greatest possible facility for the movement of goods inside as wide an area as possible. But the process of consolidating territory under one common political sovereign has preceded historically the evolution of a unified customs area. On the other hand, whilst the tendency in modern times is to bind contiguous territory together into the same customs system, a process of exactly the opposite character has been going on if in the conception of national territory we include the colonial possessions of a country. Here, the tendency is towards dispersion and the creation of separate customs areas, a matter which will occupy us at greater length in a separate chapter.[1]

We must now turn to another set of circumstances. The states of the world have not been consolidated into distinct entities primarily with a view to the economic completeness of the result. Hence, we may get—

(1) "Fragments" of one state surrounded completely by the territory of another, whilst portions, or even the whole of an adjoining state may fit in economically and administratively more conveniently with its own territory.

(2) The economic relations between two states whether continuous geographically or not, may be so close that unity of administration and policy in customs matters may be thought desirable in one or other form; or it may be desired to bring such closer economic relations about.

---

[1] See below, Chap. viii., § 7.

In the last place the narrowly technical aspect of customs administration and commercial policy may require a differentiation of certain portions of a territory. There is generally a local "frontier trade" which requires separate treatment; there are what the French call "propriétés limitrophes"—*i.e.*, properties in adjoining customs areas belonging to nationals resident in its own customs territory; there is the necessity for taking safeguards against smuggling, which leads to a special régime in that portion of the territory nearest the frontier; finally, there is the important case of the "Free-port" district. All this class we may call "Inclusions or Exclusions on Administrative Grounds," and we may defer their treatment for the time being. The other cases we may range in the following order:—

(1) Countries with interior customs lines.

(2) Countries embracing the colonial area in the national territory (assimilation).

(3) Countries incorporating non-national territories (enclaves).

(4) Countries excluding portions of its own territory (exclaves).

(5) Customs unions between two or more countries.

§ 4. Countries with interior customs lines have now largely disappeared so far as the advanced economic nations are concerned, but the evolution of customs institutions in the past shows the situation very clearly. We may deal specifically with the United Kingdom,[1] France, and the late Austro-Hungarian Empire.

1. The Union of the Crowns of England and Scotland took place in 1604, but the legislative and economic union not until a century later (Act of Union: 5 and 6 Anne, chap. 8, art. 6, dealt with the customs arrangements.)

> "All parts of the United Kingdom should for ever have the same allowances, encouragements, and drawbacks, and be under the same prohibitions, restrictions, and regulations of trade, and liable to the same customs

[1] See the historical introduction to Sir T. J. Pittar's Customs Tariff of the United Kingdom from 1800 to 1897. Cd. 8706 of 1897. Quotations are drawn therefrom unless otherwise mentioned. It may be here added that internal freedom and a uniform external tariff were introduced in Prussia by the Finance Act of 1818—the first step towards the unification of Germany in the Zollverein.

> and duties on import and export; and that the duties and allowances in force in England when the Union commenced should take place throughout the whole Kingdom: but private rights belonging to particular persons were to remain safe and entire."

Very different was the position of the Irish customs under the Act of Union (39 and 40, G. III., c. 67). This Act placed the subjects of Great Britain and Ireland on the same footing as to encouragements and bounties in all places of the United Kingdom and its dependencies: swept away export prohibitions and bounties on trade from one area to the other, and in general provided for free trade between the two. But the Act did not create a united customs system, nor did it provide for absolutely free trade. On the contrary, apart from countervailing duties on excisable articles, regulations as to the treatment of dutiable goods imported *via* one and exported through the other, and exports moving in the same way, there were three separate sets of articles subject to duty.

(*a*) Special arrangements were made as to import duties on woollens, salt and hops, coals, calicoes, muslins, cotton twist, and yarns.

(*b*) A series of rates were laid down to which certain goods were to be liable on import into England from Ireland, and a further set of rates on imports from Ireland into England.[1]

(*c*) A further series of goods were to be charged for 20 years with an import duty of 10 per cent. in both countries on import from the other.

The English and Irish exchequers were united in 1816 by 56, G. III., c. 98, but this did not affect the customs situation, but the recommendations of the Commission of Enquiry appointed in 1821 led to an equalisation of the duties in the two countries by the Act 4, G. IV., c. 66 (2).

So far as the present position is concerned, the United Kingdom forms one whole. But, though by sec. 277 of the Customs Consolidation Act of 1876 (39 and 40, Vict., c. 36) the "Isle of Man shall be deemed and taken to be part of the United Kingdom for all the purposes of the Customs Acts," it has a separate tariff, and the said Act (secs. 278-283) had,

[1] For a list of these goods and the rates, see Pittar, *op. cit.*, pp. 55-58.

therefore, to regulate the movement of goods between this land and Great Britain and Ireland. (By sec. 283 imports of foreign goods into the island might be rationed).[1]

2. The French national territory on the mainland was first unified in 1791 by the Code des douanes of 6-22, August, 1791, sec. 1, art. 1, which lays it down that the tariffs decreed by the National Assembly shall be enforced "à toutes les entrées et sorties de la royaume." Certain exceptions exist in the case of free zones and administrative exclusions, but the main fluctuations of policy have occurred with regard to the islands of the coastland, including the important island of Corsica. In 1791 these islands were divided into assimilated and unassimilated; in the second case foreign goods imported thence had to pay duty on importation into continental France, but products of the islands themselves were free. The law of 4 Germinal An. II. prohibited foreign vessels from calling at these islands, but the crude products of the islands were free; manufactures could only be imported thence if it could be proved that local manufactures existed. Corsica was included by the terms of the Act, but in this case the law was not carried out, and consequently the island was treated as foreign territory. The present position is that some of the islands are completely assimilated, others only partially so, those unassimilated continuing to remain under the rules of the law of An. II. Corsica was assimilated to France by a law of An. XI., but the high cost of supervision again led to a change in 1808, when the island was again disassimilated. The customs service was re-introduced, and was modified by later laws, the system then created lasted until 1912. French goods and nationalised goods were admitted into the island free of duty; foreign products were admitted at special rates when imported direct, but Corsican products on their entry into France were subject to the rates of the *general* tariff with certain exceptions. The system created much dissatisfaction, and by the law of 8th July, 1912, assimilation was re-established.[2]

---

[1] Highmore, "The Customs Laws, including the Customs Consolidation Act, 1876," p. 204, *et seq.* Highmore points out that, for the purpose of the Inland Revenue Acts, the Isle of Man is not a part of the United Kingdom.

[2] Pallain I., §§ 201-210. Pallain warns against the assumption that the special régime of Corsica was the only or even the main cause of the malaise from which the island has suffered. Exaggerated views will simply lead to a demand for the re-establishment of the old privileges (*op. cit.*, p. 163, note 1).

Austria-Hungary.—There a double movement was in progress. (1) The incorporation of Austria and Hungary into one and the same customs area.

(2) The incorporation of outlying portions of the Empire into one or other of the main systems.[1] Both movements owe their inception to the energy of Maria Theresa, taking as her adviser Cobenzl, a Dutch "Staatsrat," in 1775. All the Austrian lands except the Tyrol, Hungary, the free ports and the free cities were included in the common customs area. Galicia was given a special tariff between 1778 and 1783, and was then incorporated; the Tyrol was incorporated at much the same time as the Italian provinces (1822-26). Fiume and Trieste were incorporated in 1791 (the free port districts remaining outside). After the system of "dualism" had been inaugurated in 1867, assimilation still went on: the small ports on the Croatian coast being incorporated in 1879, as were Dalmatia and Istria, and Brody on the Russian frontier.[2]

The relations between Austria and Hungary are much more difficult to describe. In the latter years of the 18th century the question was "allowed for decades to sleep in the archives of the Council and the Royal Chamber. The question was then taken up by the Hungarian estates in the three decades after 1802 and a settlement was fruitlessly asked for. Tired of the asking, Hungary in the last decade and a half (before the 1848 Revolution) took up more radical aims, and only then, in the hour of greatest need, did the President of the Chamber, Kubeck, revert to the old word. . . . But the bond of confidence between Vienna and the nation was broken, and no way for a peaceful solution was any longer open. The catastrophe of a Revolution and the victory of the Imperial arms had to prepare the way . . . in order that the absolute power of the conqueror should complete the programme and achieve by force over the heads of the citizens what their souls had yearned for through seventy-five years."[3] The unity of the customs régime was laid down in the constitution of 4th March, 1849, decreed by Imperial

[1] See Sieghart, "Zoll-trennung und Zolleinheit. Die Geschichte der österrichisch-ungarischen Zwischenzoll-linie" und Grunzel, Handelspolitik und Ausgleich in Oesterreich-Ungarn, 1912.

[2] An internal customs line still existed in the shape of a Tyrollese duty on grain. *V.* Grunzel, *op. cit.*

[3] Sieghart, *op. cit.*, p. 192.

Patent of 7th June, 1850, to come into force on 1st October, 1850.

The subsequent régime of dualism which dates from 1867 did not alter the facts of customs unity, but it profoundly altered the spirit. Unity of customs territory rested upon a ten-yearly agreement, the first concluded in 1867, known as the Ausgleich (the equivalent or compromise). The difficulties that this system caused are one illustration of the difficulties that a customs union may bring with it, and will be treated below.

§ 5. Assimilation of National and Colonial Régime. The country which is most closely wedded to this policy is to-day France. But traces of the system can be found even in the law of this country. Section 151 of the Customs Consolidation Act of 1876 enacts that—

> "The Customs Acts shall extend to and be of full force and effect in the several British possessions abroad, except where otherwise provided for by the said Acts, or limited by express reference to the United Kingdom or the Channel Islands, and except also as to any such possessions as shall by local Act or Ordinance have provided, or may hereafter, with the sanction and approbation of Her Majesty . . . make entire provision for the management and regulation of the customs of any such possession, or make in like manner express provisions in lieu or variation of any of the clauses of the said Act for the purposes of such possession." [1]

This is an assimilation of *customs law* and not of *tariff rates;* it might be possible equally to reverse the position.

The whole question of assimilation of tariff rates will be dealt with in the chapter on Colonial Preferences, to which the reader is referred for further details.

§ 6. We now come to the subject of customs "enclaves" and "exclaves," in which portions of the national territory

---

[1] Schedule A of the Customs Consolidation Act of 1876, in repealing the Customs Consolidation Act of 1853 (16 and 17 Vict. c. 107), expressly saves from repeal (*inter alia*) Sections 165, 166, 181, 182, 183, 185, 187, and 188 "so far as they relate to those of Her Majesty's possessions abroad in which other provisions have not been substituted by Local Act or Ordinance with the sanction of Her Majesty." Down to as late as 1855 the British Commissioners of Customs possessed Customs Establishments or at least Customs Officers in the British colonies. For an intensive sketch of this subject, see Appendix IX. (*c*) to the 1st Report of the Commissioners of Her Majesty's Customs, 1857, P.P. 1857, Vol. iii., p. 590 (p. 849 Report).

are incorporated in the customs area of another country, or *vice-versâ;* or the entire territory is so absorbed. It is difficult to distinguish this case from the further case which we have previously described as a "Customs Union" or "Customs Federation." Apart from the fact that a "Customs Federation" need not involve the abolition of an interior customs line between the two areas, we may, perhaps, point to the distinction of *spirit* which underlies the two cases. In the case of a customs union, a new super-national body is created, in which the contracting states all lose their original independence so far as customs affairs are concerned; in the case of the true "enclave" only the absorbed state or portion of the state does so. Such a distinction of spirit is also borne out by the facts of the case; such "absorbed" areas are generally small relatively to the area to which they are annexed.[1]

Such cases are not rare. We may point to two cases—Luxemburg and Monaco without in any way pretending to finality. Luxemburg was incorporated into the German Zollverein by treaty with the Netherlands signed on 8th February, 1842: after negotiations extending over a period of nearly three years.[2] In order to prevent the Dutch Government thereby obtaining a means of influencing the policy of the customs union, Luxemburg received no independent representation, being in fact represented by Prussia: the customs administration of Luxemburg was placed under the Prussian Ministry of Finance, which was also given the power to place a Prussian official at the head of the administration and to propose the controller at the chief customs offices and the chief frontier superintendents.[3] This arrangement continued until the signature of the Peace Treaty between the Allied Governments and the German Empire in 1919. Under that treaty the incorporation of Luxumberg in the German customs system ceases:[4] the country was given the choice

---

[1] This point is well brought out by Ashley, "Modern Tariff History," p. 7, speaking of the incorporation of the enclaves in the Prussian tariff system. "The policy of Prussia . . . was to take the absolute control of any Union which might be formed."

[2] Weber, "Der deutsche Zollverein," pp. 201-5, gives a good account of the negotiations, but see espec. Calmes, "Der Zollanschluss des Grossherzogtums Luxemburg an Deutschland," vol i. (2 Vols., 1919.)

[3] *Op. cit.*, p. 205.

[4] "Treaty of Peace with Germany," Part iii., Section ii., article 40.

of incorporation in the Belgian or French customs system, and since that time has chosen, after a plebiscite held for the purpose, to be incorporated into the French system.

The first convention with Monaco [1] relative to incorporation was signed on 9th November, 1865. Article 2 stipulated that "the French import and export duties, the navigation taxes as defined by French law, sealing and stamp duties, and in general the laws, ordinances, decrees, and regulations concerning the customs régime shall be applicable to the territory of the principality." The administration is in the charge of the French authorities.

Similar arrangements exist or have existed in numerous other cases. Thus the Austrian customs area included the small principality of Lichteinstein in virtue of arrangements concluded in 1852, 1863, 1876; whilst the German customs territory included the Austrian areas of Jungholtz and Mittelberg in virtue of arrangements made in 1868 and 1890.[2]

There is no difficulty in appreciating the economic advantages which follow such a policy of inclusion or exclusion respectively. It allows a territory to be associated with the area of which it forms a "natural" part: it reduces the cost of administration through cutting down the number of customs offices and officials, and it decreases the temptation to smuggling operations. The difficulties are entirely fiscal in character: such an incorporated area loses—if it is an independent area, such as Monaco—part of its revenue, and hence the adjustment of fiscal claims may present difficulty: a difficulty which arises also in the case of customs unions. Such difficulties have arisen—*e.g.*, in the case of Monaco: dutiable goods consumed in Monaco have paid duty elsewhere, and the question of the proper distribution of the proceeds has naturally led to difficulties.[3]

§ 7. We now come to the very important and difficult case of customs unions. Here it is necessary to premise that this phrase is used in contemporary discussion in a somewhat loose manner, and our first task must be to differentiate the various meanings which can be assigned.

---

[1] Pallain I., §§ 194-200.

[2] Havenstein, "Die Zollgesetzgebung des (deutschen) Reichs" edn. 1906, p. 5, note 1. Jungholz is incorporated into Bavaria in virtue of the Agreement of 1868, to which the Empire is not a party. For the exclaves, *vide op. cit.*

[3] For a full discussion, Pallain, *op. et loc. cit.*

The distinctions which can be drawn between different types of customs union must obviously turn upon the possible combinations of characteristics all of which are not inconsistent with the general idea of customs union. That general idea is the pursuance of a common customs policy by two or more independent countries. But what shall we describe as a common customs policy?

Two suggestions may be offered. The first is that any customs union requires as a *minimum* condition, freedom of trade between the two countries, the other is that a customs union requires as a minimum condition, a common external tariff. If these two minimum conditions are both present in a particular case we have this perfected form of customs union. Pursuing this line of argument we should have the following evolution of form :—

(1) Complete independence : both as regards duties against one another and as against third parties.

(2) Mutual reduction of duties : self-determination of duties against third parties.

(3) Mutual free trade with self-determination of duties as against third parties.

(4) Mutual reduction of duties with external unity.

(5) Mutual freedom of trade with external unity.

Here we have (with the exception of case (1) which represents the maximum of independence) a series of methods of closer union. What we have now to do is to decide which of them can be properly spoken of as falling into the category of "customs unions."

The easiest way of solving the problem is to call to mind the fact that besides "customs unions" there exist other forms of approach resting on the basis of treaty agreements between states all of which we may generically call "customs alliances." We may describe such treaty relations as "most-favoured-nation relations," "reciprocity relations," and "preferential relations." The essential point of distinction between the first and the latter two forms is that in principle the first is extensible to third states, the others are in principle exclusive.[1] A customs union, clearly falls into a group with

[1] We are not here concerned with the fact that those terms are themselves capable of more than one interpretation ; nor with the fact that the reasons for the adoption of preferential, reciprocal, or most-favoured-nation relations may

these preferential and reciprocal relations, and our task is really to indicate the specific further characteristics which a customs union must have as compared to mere reciprocity or preferential relations. The essence of the distinction between them lies in the fact that in a preferential or reciprocal scheme no *common* policy is pursued with regard to third states, whereas in a customs union there is. This requires us to ask how far "free trade" between the areas is a *sine quâ non.* The distinctions pointed to by political science supply us with a useful analogy. What we have really to deal with is the distinction between a Federal and a Unitary relationship in customs matters. We may state the position thus. Just as in a Federal State there is a common policy towards foreign states, although there may be considerable diversity of local legislation, so in a *Customs Federation* there is a common external policy in tariff matters, but this common policy is quite consistent with inter-state tariff duties. But the customs union proper conforms to the general conception of a unitary state, where there is uniformity of legislation all over the area, and where, from the customs point of view, there is complete freedom of trade.

So far we have been dealing with terminology. More important is the next investigation we have to make: the reasons which justify the policy of commercial union and the conditions necessary for the success of such a policy.

The reasons may be partly political, partly economic, but the first rest in essence upon the second. These latter may be summed up as follows:—

(1) The exploitation of the advantages of a larger economic area. The division of labour depends upon the extent of the market. Hence the wider the area for which

---

be very various. These reasons may be the desire to obtain counter-concessions, or they may be due to special geographical proximity or special political and historical ties, or all these factors in unison. What are described as "reciprocity" *duties* or "preferential" *duties* are merely differential rates accorded in consequence of the reciprocity or preferential relations subsisting. The relations *between* reciprocity, preferential, and most-favoured-nation policies are examined in the last chapter of this work. Of reciprocity resting on a geographical basis, the relations between Spain and Portugal are instances (this and similar cases can best be described as "erweiterter Grenzverkehr"—*i.e.*, "extended frontier relations"); the tariff relations between U.S.A. and Cuba are an instance of reciprocity based on political factors; the "reciprocity clauses" of the American Tariff Acts of the 90's of last century and the conception of reciprocity in some British Colonies illustrate the conception of reciprocity as an exchange of equivalents. All this is outside the immediate scope of this chapter.

production can be organised without needing to fear hindrances imposed by the tariffs of hostile powers, the cheaper can goods be produced. The consolidated area forms a wider market of which all the advantages of "international division of labour" hold good.

(2) The lessening of dependence on outside markets. Each producer has now a wider area over which to dispose of his goods freely, so that, even assuming that the scale of production does not increase, he can achieve the same economies of production as hitherto without fearing actual tariff changes hostile to him. The goods formerly distributed over a wider area can now be disposed of over a narrower one, by displacing there the products of hostile powers; the joint economy of the two countries is less dependent on external areas for the vent of products. Again, the wider the area the greater the chances that within the single customs sphere there will be found those particular commodities, natural resources and raw materials in which each area by itself was deficient, and, therefore, formerly dependent on foreign supplies. In other words, a customs union enables the ideal of "self-sufficing economic areas" to be at any rate approximately reached.

(3) Increased ease of commercial bargaining with third states. Since the whole area is now one from the standpoint of external commercial policy, foreign states are confronted by at once a more powerful bargaining entity, and a more tempting object of desire. For exclusion, relative or absolute, now means exclusion from a larger area: and the maintenance of an intransigeant attitude carries a heavier penalty with it. The customs union area is more powerful offensively and defensively, and is therefore able to win greater advantages for itself than the two separate states would have been able to do.

The political advantages which follow can now be easily grasped. They rest essentially on the assumption that closer economic unity spells closer political unity also. The closer relations which a free internal market afford are so valuable economically that political conditions will be adjusted so as to secure their continuance,[1] and thus there will be a political

[1] Weber, *op. cit.*, p. 462, § 6, vividly depicts the anxiety felt in all parts of Germany during the period anterior to the struggle between Prussia, Austria, and her South German allies, lest the war which was regarded as inevitable should disrupt the union. In fact, though the treaty basis of the Verein was necessarily ruptured as a result of the conflict, the system continued to function throughout the whole period.

drawing together on the basis of the economic alliance. Hence, it will pay to sacrifice immediate advantages in the political sphere in order to safeguard the economic union upon which the political alliance can be built up.

As against third states, it will help to remove that political dependence which tends to follow on the recognition by a state that its market is bound up with amicable relations with a given state.

The advantages of the customs union seem so obvious that it is not surprising that the idea of forming such a union between various countries should be one of the most persistent principles of 19th and 20th century economic and politico-economic writing and endeavour. The plans for the formation of such unions have been many: the achievements in this field, however, have been less than might at first sight be supposed to be the case.

The great historical achievement was the creation of the German customs union or Zollverein between 1818 and 1834. It has served as a text for innumerable sermons. It has served as the model for a projected British Empire customs union; for projected unions between Holland and Belgium, between Holland and Germany, between the States of Europe against American competition, and for a union which has of recent years attracted most attention of all, between the Central European powers—*i.e.*, the creation of a "Mittel Europa," consisting, in the most ambitious of these projects, of the Scandinavian countries, the former Central Empires,[1] the Balkan States, and Turkey. What have been the successes in this field?

There is an historical parallel to the German Zollverein in the shape of the former South African customs union,[2]

[1] These schemes have in part at least found their counterpart in the various proposals for customs unions, of which France was to be the buttress. Pan-Americanism represents a similar principle, this time with the United States as the central point. See Grunzel, "Economic Protectionism," pp. 29-34; Pentmann's "Die Zollunions-idee und ihre Wandlungen im Rahmen der wirtschaftspolitischen Ideen," Jena, 1919; V.S.P., vol. xc., 1900; Prof. Francke's "Zollpolitische Einigungsbestrebungen in Mittel-Europa," and for a very complete survey of the middle European customs union controversy, see esp. Battaglia's "Ein Zoll-und-Wirtschaftsbundniss zwischen Oesterreich und Deutschland," Vienna, 1917. The most complete survey up to the date of its publication seems to be Bosc's, translated into German in 1907, as "Zollalliancen und Zollunionen in ihrer Bedeutung für die Handelspolitik der Vergangenheit und Zukunft," which I have not been able to make use of.

[2] See below, Note 1, appended to chapter.

which preceded the formation of the Union of South Africa; there was at one time a chance that the Balkan States would form a union based on the actually negotiated union between Serbia and Bulgaria, which was broken down by Austrian opposition:[1] Norwegian-Swedish inter-state free trade finally broke down.[2] On the other hand, the U.S.A., Canada, Australia, and the late Russian Empire had become vast free trade areas, but in these cases political unity preceded or accompanied tariff unity. It is necessary, therefore, to go very carefully into the difficulties, as well as the advantages or supposed advantages, of such customs unions.

§ 8. We may begin with a quotation from the late Professor Schmoller. The German Zollverein "is really the one considerable exception to the historical law that political union tends to precede commercial union. The reason is simple: a common commercial and customs union is so very much conditioned by political tendencies to union, by uniformity in the conditions of power, by uniformity in the circumstances of political feelings and interests, that it is only under exceptionally favourable circumstances that a customs union of really independent states can succeed."[3]

We may divide up our discussion of the difficulties[4] associated with the formation of customs unions under the following heads:—

(1) **Financial.**—The division of the income from customs duties between independent states is always a matter of great

[1] This Serbo-Bulgarian Union was described in the R.E.I. for August, 1910, p. 332, *et seq.*, by A. Taranoff.

Serbia had felt herself tied to Austria as her main export area: Bulgaria had begun since 1894 to create a national industry, but required markets. The idea was taken up between 1902-4; conversations between the two States were held in 1904-5; the Customs Treaty was signed in July, 1905, to come into force on March 1st, 1906.

[2] Grunzel, *op. cit.*, p. 33. The arrangement lasted from 1874 to 1890, was then modified and finally swept away with the political union in 1905. Ever since 1825 there had been a differential rate for products imported on the land frontiers of the two States. The principles of the 1874 agreement were mutual free trade except with regard to sugar and sugar products, tobacco, brandy and spirits, and a few other articles on which the full duty was payable, abolition of the differential land duties. Each country maintained otherwise complete autonomy; the era being one of free-trade principle, it was hoped that a closer approximation in the tariffs would be brought about by the reduction of duties on both sides. Later on, as the effects of the system were felt to be unfavourable, opinion changed. See also Dr. Fahlbeck in V.S.P., vol. xlix., 1892, p. 319-320.

[3] In Schmoller's "Jahrbuch," 1916, vol. xl., p. 529.

[4] *Cf.* Schraut, "System der Handelspolitik und meist-begunstigung," 1884, Chap. x., pp. 115, *et seq.*

delicacy, and, even in the case of federal states where the sentiment of unity is stronger, has caused much heart burning.[1] The most obvious basis of division is population,[2] but this

---

[1] In the case of a federation it is possible to cut the knot by dividing the field of taxation so that the expenses of the federal government and the federating states can be met from different sources. But this solution is by no means ideal in all cases: where it is not easy to find alternative sources of revenue and where the expenses of the federal government are light as compared to its income from customs, where, moreover, the federating states desire to retain some financial control over the central government, the solution of dividing the field of taxation may give way to the policy of distributing, on some agreed basis, the proceeds of the customs duties between the various governments. In this case there is a clear analogy with the cases in the text.

The Australian Constitutional provisions are a case in point. By § 87 of the Act, for a period of ten years "of net revenue of the Commonwealth from duties of customs and excise, not more than one-fourth shall be applied annually by the Commonwealth towards its expenditure." The balance was to be paid to the States or applied to meeting the interest charges on transferred State debts. The principle of distribution for the period, first, before the imposition of uniform customs duties and then five years thereafter was to the effect that each State received the excess of *revenue collected in the State* over its proportional share of the Commonwealth expenditure (§ 89, 93, 94). Thereafter Parliament was to provide "on such basis as it deems fair, for the monthly payment to the several States of all surplus revenues of the Commonwealth." By the Surplus Revenue Act of 1910, § 87 of the original Act gave way to a new arrangement, by which for ten years, terminating on June 30th, 1920, or thereafter, until Parliament otherwise decides, the States were to be paid 25s. per head of population. (*Australian Official Year Book*, No. 8, pp. 32, 690.)

This does not complete the story. By § 95 of the Constitution, Western Australia was for five years given the special right of imposing duties "on goods passing into that State and not originally imported beyond the limits of the Commonwealth"; whilst by § 96 "financial assistance could be provided to any State on such terms and conditions as the Parliament thinks fit." Such grants have, in fact, been made to Western Australia and Tasmania, "in consideration of the sacrifices made by these States when yielding control of their Customs Revenue to the Commonwealth."

[2] The basis of population was generally chosen as the principle of distribution in the various proposals for unions and in the actual treaties of union in Germany from 1820 onwards. But when Frankfort-on-Main joined the union, in 1836, special concessions had to be made: the town's share of the revenues being about 4½ times the amount which a simple population basis would have yielded. (Weber, *op. cit.*, pp. 136, 137.) In the case of Hanover also a considerable concession was made, Art. 11 of the Treaty with Prussia of September 7th, 1851, laying it down that, though the contribution of Hanover to the common expenses should be in proportion to population, her share of the revenue should, after calculation on the basis of population, be increased by three-fourths, with a given maximum of increase per capita. (For the circumstances connected with this Treaty, etc., see Weber, *op. cit.*, Chap. xxv., esp. p. 293, *et seq.*) The Customs Union Treaty of 1833, Art. xxii., providing for a distribution of the revenue on the basis of population, arranged for a three-yearly census, and provided also that each state should include in its population "the population of such states as have acceded, or may yet accede, to the Customs Union by means of a treaty with one or other of the contracting states, guaranteeing an annual payment by the latter, as an indemnity for the share of the former in the common customs revenue." (*Commercial Tariffs and Regulations*, Part i., 1841, pp. 17-18.)

may not be in all cases a fair test: for the consumption of the taxed articles may be very different in different portions of the customs territory. Moreover, the distribution of the imports over the different frontiers may be very unequal in different parts of the area, so that the proportion of administrative cost to population, consumption, and revenue will be unequal.

(2) **Constitutional.**—The next problem is the form of the customs-making body. The alternatives are (*a*) a diplomatic conference with subsequent separate ratification by legislatures, (*b*) a new and directly elected legislature with exclusive powers in customs matters. The difficulty is to get agreement in the first case, to get a separation of the ground between "customs matters" and "non-customs matters" in the second.[1]

(3) **Administrative.**—There the problem is to get uniformity of administrative technique. The alternatives are—(1) The creation of a common service, amenable to the customs conference or parliament, and supported on the revenue from the duties.

(2) Each member of the union maintains its own service, but the principle of mutual inspection is set up.

(3) Each member maintains a separate service, but (*a*) one of them is given the right to inspect the service as a whole, (*b*) or a separate inspectorial service is set up for the control of all the states.

It will be fairly obvious that whatever solution is adopted, plentiful opportunity for friction remains. Whilst a common service provides for the greatest uniformity, it involves the maximum of interference with local sentiment: mutual inspection or inspection by a chosen member lends itself easily to constant recriminations, whilst a common inspectorial service, unless provided with powers of local interference

---

[1] The German Zollverein successively knew two forms: Customs Conference of Diplomatists representing fully Sovereign States was followed after the war of 1866 and the reconstitution of the Union, by a Customs Parliament and a Customs Council, in both of which bodies decisions were arrived at by majority vote. Weber (*op. cit.*, p. 471) points to the complete immobility which the older system had produced in the affairs of the League. In the new arrangements, also, Prussia was given a dominant position, which corresponded to the real position of affairs (*op. cit.*, p. 474). The whole question of customs-making bodies is separately discussed below. As a matter of fact, the first yearly session of the Customs Parliament of 1868 resulted in nothing being done, largely owing to the political ill-feeling between North and South.

can reveal defects, but cannot remedy them. To give such powers of interference is, of course, again to rouse the danger of wounding local pride.[1]

(4) **Economic.**—It is here that the really vital problems from our present standpoint begin to arise.

(a) *Opposition of Interests between different Groups within the Area.*—In each part of the area there are some interests likely to suffer from the proposed change. Thus, if one part is industrially strong but agriculturally weak, the other agriculturally strong but industrially weak, the agrarian interests in the one part and the industrial interests in the other will be inclined to oppose the union.

Three alternatives are open (1) to allow "intermediate" customs duties to be imposed in the interests of the weaker groups. (2) To sacrifice the weaker interests in the hope that free trade will stimulate inter-union division of labour, and thus ultimately cause a transfer of capital and labour to those industries which in each part of the joint area are best fitted to survive. (3) To provide for a gradual transition from one stage to the other by successive reductions of the interior duties.

It is here that we strike upon one of the logical difficulties of the situation. For, if the free trade argument (No. 2 above) is adopted, it is difficult to concede its applicability *inside*

---

[1] Two subordinate points require mention. The first is the difficulties of arranging a union between countries with different *currency* systems. Diehl, "Zur Frage eines Zollbündnisses zwischen Deutschland und Oesterreich-Ungarn," p. 36, brings forward the argument that a depreciated currency acts as a tax on imports and a bounty on exports. Consequently, if one state has a depreciated currency and the other members of the union have not, this one state will enjoy an advantage. It may be doubted whether either the premise or conclusion is necessarily always true. It is, however, quite obvious that the adjustment of claims between the various members of the union will be difficult unless those members whose currency is not depreciated can claim to be paid at par. This would probably force the state with the depreciated currency to demand payment of duties in gold or in paper equivalent of gold. Otherwise the tendency would be to import through that area, since the net duty payable would be less. This does not involve the assumption that the aggregate imports of the union would be any greater, but only that their geographical distribution between the frontiers would alter.

The second point is the difficulties caused if the excise taxes of the states forming the union are different. For if they differ, this involves countervailing duties between the states. This is a difficulty which customs unions share with federations, and even with unitary states where local excise taxes are imposed. These differences in excise taxes played an important rôle in the history of the Zollverein, and they also complicated the working of the S. African Customs Union. The right to impose countervailing duties remained under the German Imperial Constitution of 1871 (Art. 33).

the area and yet resist its applicability to trade *outside* the area: or, if the protectionist argument is adopted that weaker industries should be sheltered from outside competition, it is difficult to see why they should not be protected against internal competition, in both cases so long as the purely economic standpoint is adhered to. If the case for intermediate duties is granted, then again the difficulty arises; either the duty is sufficient, in which case the external tariffs are too high, or it is insufficient, in which case a protectionist should oppose the union.

The only approach to the problem which seems logically consistent is the one which asserts that the united area forms a "natural economic whole" with such balanced parts that though temporarily union is likely to result in difficulties to certain industries, yet the whole is naturally so fitted for self-sufficiency that in the long run the various parts will be complementary, and can meet the full needs of the population. A gradually declining intermediate duty will give the weaker industries time to adjust themselves, whilst protection against the outside world, just because the area is self-sufficing and complementary, can be safely maintained, and in the interests of national independence, *ought* to be maintained.[1] The question of the policy to be pursued under such circumstances, assuming that they exist, is beyond our subject, but it must be insisted that this argument assumes the self-sufficiency of the area: and this is a question of fact: and the further practical question arises as to whether the autonomous development of each part has not proceeded so far that, though an adjustment of interests might have been possible on the basis of complementary natural resources of the component areas, actual adjustment is no longer possible or desirable.

(b) *Opposition of Interests beyond the Area*—i.e., *as against Third States.*—It is not likely that both areas will have identical interests in importation from, or exportation to, third states. Consequently there at once arises the necessity of adjusting the interests of different parts of the union. The industrial areas will desire protection on manufactured goods,

[1] This imperative may, of course, be questioned: it does not follow that because a thing could be done, therefore it ought to be done. The purely economic side of the situation requires the further question to be answered; if it *is* done, will the economic advantages outweigh the disadvantages? But if the validity of the ideal of national independence is granted, purely economic issues are not necessarily the decisive ones.

free trade in foodstuffs and raw materials, the agrarian areas will desire the reverse.

Assuming that compromise is possible on the basic principles of the tariff policy to be pursued, important questions of detail still arise. Ought the *degree* of protection to be adjusted to the needs of the weakest or the strongest portions of the industrial or agricultural system of the joint area? If the weakest industrial area and the strongest agricultural area or *vice versâ* are situated in different portions of the joint area, ought agriculture desiring cheap imports of manufactures in return for exports of food to be sacrificed to the needs of the weaker industries, if these are threatened: ought the stronger industries to be deprived of their opportunities for export by retaliation on the part of third states owing to *their* food exports being threatened in order to protect the weaker agricultural areas?

If it be argued that the uniting states, in order to overcome these difficulties, should pursue, not a joint external policy, but a separate tariff and treaty policy, the resulting system will simply be one of internal preference or free trade. But, from whatever point of view regarded, considerable difficulties still remain. For one or both states may find that the grant of preference to the other has weakened its power of obtaining concessions from a third state; whilst it may equally be found that concessions to a third state have lowered the value of the preference or the free trade arrangement.

Difficulties may also arise in the interpretation of treaties, for should one of the parties have concluded most favoured treaties with a third state, is not this state entitled to these privileges? The answer may be made that a union abolishes the customs duality of the two states; consequently that most-favoured-treatment cannot be used by a third state to claim these rights. But this simply raises in an acute form the problem, what *is* a customs union? To admit the claim for a generalisation of these privileges is of course to reduce their value: but to refuse their extension is to risk retaliation. If the burden of any such retaliation hits one part of the union, whilst the preferences redound to the benefit of the other part, it is not likely that considerable friction will result.

Here, then, are many causes of possible friction. If these causes find an emollient in the shape of a strong national sentiment of unity, they are more capable of adjustment: if to them are added strong differences of political outlook, national sentiment, historical associations, they will prevent the union being successful or permanent. It does not follow that the existence of such a desire for political association will necessarily yield the requisite basis for union, but its absence simply emphasises the inherent economic difficulties.[1]

It is the merit of the already mentioned work of Dr. Pentmann's [2] to have analysed very fully the relations between the historical advocacy of the customs union principle and the political economic movements of the successive decades of the 19th and the 20th centuries. From this analysis it appears fairly clearly that the *practicability* of the customs union is bound up strictly with the principle of nationality: and that it was at the time when the free trade movement and the idea of national unity were mutually compatible that the union movement achieved its greatest success.[3] Historically the movement has found no firm basis but these two in combination: for Imperialism, though it desires a world state, is opposed to the subordination to the will of others which the give and take of a union requires: Imperialist States desire to control, and not to share control; whilst the National State, once founded on the basis of national sentiment, is averse to any movement interfering with the right of "self-determination," even in customs matters. Hence the customs union principle in the last third of the 19th century represented, in the main, reaction from the dominant ideals: it was the protest of free traders like Molinari against the growing exclusiveness of the Nationalist State, or of agrarians against over-seas competition, or of European industrialism afraid of the "American danger." [4]

---

[1] If Diehl (*op. cit.*, p. 12) says that "a zollverein is only then in place if the economic circumstances appear to warrant its purposiveness," and emphasises 'that the political . . . cannot possibly be decisive," he is not contradicting, but enforcing the argument in the text.

[2] See above, § 7, note, p. 15.

[3] Emphasised also by Jastrow, "Die mitteleuropaische Zollannäherung und die Meistbegünstigung," 1915, pp. 11, 12.

[4] Pentmann, *op. cit.*, pp. 125-9. If our author stresses the antagonism between the Imperial position and the standpoint of the supporters of the customs union by saying that the one represents "world economics and world policy," the latter "isolation and limitation to a geographically defined area" (p. 126), he is using the phrase Imperialism in rather a different sense than the sense he has himself assigned to it in a previous section (p. 97), when he defines it as "the effort of modern states to expand politically and economically by the aid of the power of the state,

§ 9. We are not without an illustration of the dangers to which a customs union may be exposed in the event of one or more of the members resenting the association. The history of the tariff relations between Austria and Hungary provide the illustration we require. Even had the war not destroyed the pre-existing relations subsisting between these two states, it is doubtful whether they would have continued in their old form after 1917.

The customs union [1] between Austria and Hungary was the result of an agreement first concluded in 1867 and celebrated under the name of the "Ausgleich" or compromise. The compromise itself rested on the Constitutional Laws of Austria and Hungary,[2] which divided the affairs of the Empire into two classes: (*a*) Joint affairs. (*b*) Affairs to be settled in common—*i.e.*, matters in which both parties retained independence, but which it was desirable to settle on a uniform basis. The conclusion of treaties was an affair of the first type, the tariff relations of the Empire was an affair of the second. On the basis of this constitutional position, it was inevitable that sooner or later the treaty powers would be involved in the tariff powers, and in fact it was very soon the policy of Hungary to identify the two matters. Tariffs were to be submitted to the two legislatures after an agreement had been reached as to their content by the appropriate Ministers of the two countries.

The history of this preparatory meeting of the Ministers itself shows some of the difficulties of the situation. We may quote Grunzel's statement.[3]

---

this expansion at the same time being directed primarily to the agrarian areas of the world outside Europe, with the object of attaining territorial sovereignity over these." There would seem to be territorial "limitation (Beschränkung)" here also. It is the difference in *spirit* that really distinguishes the "Colonial World State" from the "autonomously determined Customs Union."

[1] Grunzel, "Handelspolitik und Ausgleich in Oesterreich-Ungarn," 1912; P. Westphal, "Die Krise zwischen Oesterreich und Ungarn," 1906; Lájos Lang, "Hundert Jahre Zollpolitik"; Matlekovits, "Die Handelspolitschen Interessen Ungarns" in S.V.S.P., vol. xciii., 1901; Petritsch, "The Fiscal Question and the Experience of the Austro-Hungarian Empire," in Ec., J. vol. xiv.; Jarray, "Les Dispositions Économiques du Nouveau Compromis Austro-Hungrois," in R.E.I., 1908; Michels, "Die Zolltrennung Oesterreich-Ungarn," in Schmollers Jahrbuch, vol. xxxii., pp. 557-620.

[2] The text of these Acts will be found in Dareste, "Les Constitutions Modernes"; the Austrian Act will also be found in Dodd, "Modern Constitutions." It is to be noted that the two Acts are not in complete accord.

[3] *Op. cit.*, pp. 147-8; *cf.* Lang, *op. cit.*, pp. 208-211.

"In the compromise of 1867 the Hungarians agreed to the formation of such an organ, but attempted nevertheless to reduce its powers and position as much as possible, in order to prevent the development of a kind of centralised Customs Parliament therefrom, on the model of the German Zollverein. In this way there arose the institution of the Customs and Commercial Conference, composed of the respective Ministers of Commerce and Finance, and, in so far as relations with foreign countries came into account, of the common Minister of Foreign Affairs, or his representative. The compromise of 1907 added the two Ministers of Agriculture. It was further possible to call representatives of chambers of commerce from time to time, and since 1907 representatives also of agricultural corporations, who possessed no voting rights. The calling of the conference lies in the hands of either government, and, in consequence of a case of a refusal to attend on the part of Hungary, it was expressly laid down in the compromise on 1878 that attendance at the conference could not be refused. . . . "

The form of the union was declared in the first paragraph of the compromise. The two states were to be surrounded by a uniform customs wall, and should not impose on their mutual commerce any import, export, or transit taxes, but, whilst previously to 1907 the talk had been of "Austro-Hungarian Customs Territory" and the "Austro-Hungarian Customs Tariff," in the compromise of 1907, the phrase "treaty customs area" (Vertrags Zollgebiet der beiden Staaten der . . . Monarchie) was substituted; a change of title which was significant of a growing desire of Hungary to shake off the union altogether, for, as Jarray sums up the results of the 1907 compromise: "the second preoccupation of the negotiations . . . is the desire to make a clean sweep in 1917: from that time it is recognised that any economic treaty with a foreign power cannot be concluded for a period subsequent to that date without the constitutional ratification of each country, and that a single one of the two states may, at its desire, denounce the existing treaties. In their mutual economic relations, the final article of the Ausgleich does indeed pre-visage negotiations in 1915, but for the first time since 1867, as well in the actual compromises, as in those projected, one no longer finds 'la clause de la tacite réconduction,' the silence of the two governments is sufficient for Hungary to resume complete fiscal autonomy on January 1st, 1918. It is the preparation for this fiscal autonomy in 1918 which is the dominant preoccupation of the treaty as to the future."

The history of the negotiations to bring the successive compromises into being are in themselves proof of the difficulties of the situation. There have been five such Ausgleich periods—

1868-1878.
1878-1887.
1888-1897.
1898-1907.
1907-1917.

The story of the negotiations leading to the 1907 position will sufficiently illustrate what has just been said. An agreement had been reached between Austria and Hungary in 1896, but the political position in Austria led to the old agreement being continued by Imperial rescripts of 30th December, 1897, and 30th December, 1898; in Hungary the position was "extra-legal" (ex-Lex Zustand). A new agreement for the putting into force of the 1896 Ausgleich was arrived at, and was again put into force by rescript of 21st September, 1899. Hungary retorted with "Law XXX., 1899, which stated that a condition of autonomous territory had arisen, and that the community of customs territory would only be maintained through unilateral disposition on the basis of reciprocity until 1907. If a customs and commercial union had not been reached by 1903, international treaties extending beyond 1907 were not to be concluded. . . . Commercial treaties without determination date were to be denounced in the year 1903 at the demand of either state. Owing to these clearly defined dates, Hungary obtained a sharp hold upon Austria, which was pre-occupied with internal difficulties, and possessed a far greater interest in the undisturbed maintenance of commercial relations. . . ." [1]

A new agreement was arrived at in 1903, which was to come into force for ten years from 1st July, 1903. The most important feature was the new tariff, on the basis of which the new commercial treaties, which were to come into force on 1st March, 1906, were concluded. A new crisis arose over the attitude of the Hungarian Government in treating the

[1] Grunzel, *op. cit.*, p. 118.

tariff as a purely Hungarian one, and the Austrian Government withdrew the Ausgleich proposals of 1903 in protest. A new series finally led to the new proposals which were recognised to be only the prelude of complete Hungarian autonomy in customs policy.

So far we have been dealing with the external facts of the case, but how are they to be explained?

The answer is given by the fact that in both Austria and Hungary there are groups that did not see eye to eye in tariff matters. Hungary is still predominantly an agricultural state, in which industry is not as a whole in a position to compete against the higher developed industry of Austria. Austria again possesses an agricultural class whose interests are not identical with free trade with Hungary. Hence Hungarian agrarians are free trade and pro-union, whilst the reverse tends to be the case in Austria. In foreign trade matters, however, the interests of Hungarian agriculturists and Austrian manufacturers are opposed; for Austrian industry is faced by the superior competition of foreign (especially German) industry, just as Hungarian industry is faced with the superior competitive powers of Austria. Whilst the Hungarian agriculturalists support free trade inside the area, they also support free trade in manufactures outside the union territory, and find themselves opposed to the industrialists in so doing. Whenever the interests of these two groups are coincident, there has been greater ease in the relations between the two states. Thus, in the first Ausgleich period, there was no difficulty on this ground, because both sides expected a continuance of free trade. The trouble came in the second period, when the industrial and financial depression after 1873 turned the Austrian manufacturers in a protectionist direction; whilst the Hungarian farmers remained free trade.

In the third period, the rise of over-seas competition rallied the Hungarian to the idea of protection, and, therefore, made it easier to arrange for mutual concessions; thus the Hungarian law of 1899 demanded the creation of a tariff which should uniformly protect the agricultural and industrial interests of both states.[1]

Deprived of the right to protect industry directly against Austrian predominance, the Hungarian state adopted what

---

[1] Matlekovits, *op. cit.*, pp. 1-24; Grunzel, *op. cit.*, p. 115.

is now known as "administrative protection": they manipulated state powers to protect indirectly. The Austrians complained of acts inconsistent with the spirit of the union, for by means of preferential railway rates, restriction of state and municipal contracts to Hungarian firms, imposing registration taxes on Austrian goods, subsidising home industries by exemption from taxation, all the elements of differentiation were in fact present, and only the form distinguished them from the usual forms of protection.[1]

All these causes of irritation were, to conclude, exacerbated by the opposition of national sentiment in the two countries. This opposition is even given a predominant influence by Petritsch.[2]

Although Grunzel's reform schemes now only possess an historical interest, a word may be said of them, because the stipulations of the Treaty of Peace permit of their realisation under somewhat altered circumstances. He proposed to give both sides complete economic freedom; they might arrange their external tariffs as they wished, although he hoped that it would be possible to arrange a common tariff against third states; the essence of his scheme was that the two contracting states should grant each other preferential rates, lower than those which they granted to other "most favoured states." His belief was that neither side wanted complete separation, but desired only freedom to work out its customs policy unhampered by the necessity of complete free trade between the two areas. "The estrangement between the two states would not grow greater, for all experience teaches, that opposites are only stimulated by a forced community of resisting parts, but are mitigated by the clear sighted delimitation of spheres of interest.[3]"

---

[1] Matlekovits, in Ec. J. xvii., pp. 22-3, "The Ausgleich between Austria and Hungary."

[2] *Op. cit.*, p. 25. For a balanced judgment, see Michels, *op. cit.*, p. 568, "The development of the idea of customs separation is, therefore, mainly to be regarded as a concession to the independence idea in Hungary, against which Hungarian agriculture has not yet put its true economic interests in the balance, as a concession to the protectionist interests of those branches of Hungarian industry which do not yet dominate the home market, do not yet export to Austria, on the other hand, as a concession to Austrian agriculture, which, in part in revenge for the Hungarian idea of independence, wishes to see protection extended to Hungarian imports."

[3] *Op. cit.*, p. 227. The framers of the original Ausgleich "were caught by the free-trade fallacy that the natural productive factors were the decisive ones in economic activity, and overlooked the influence of the human mind, seeing in the two countries only partners and not also competitors."

Those stipulations of the Treaty of Peace with Austria, which permit the new state to negotiate preferential treaties with Hungary and Szecho-Slovakia without having to extend the lower rates so granted to the other Allied and Associated Powers, are only an application to the present situation of the principles laid down in 1912 by Grunzel.[1]

§ 10. **Non-Autonomous Tariff Areas.**—The essence of the idea of tariff autonomy is the free determination by the appropriate customs-making body of the state in question of what its tariff policy shall be. Hence, our classification of countries falling into this category must not be influenced by the possible secondary consequences which such a state of non-autonomy may carry with it—*e.g.*, low tariffs or no tariffs at all.

The difficulty in treating of this subject lies in determining what are the limits of self-determination in the making of tariffs, within which a country may be said to be really "autonomous." Most states conclude treaties with other nations regulating their tariff relations. For the duration of the life time of such treaties the country is tied in so far as its co-contractant is concerned, in the matters to which the treaty refers, and to the extent of such content as the treaty may possess. A country may even be bound in perpetuity by such a treaty, as France and Germany were by the treaty of Frankfort. Again, a country may have quasi-sovereign rights, that is, its general constitutional powers may include some tariff making rights, and yet the degree to which these rights are at any time exercisable, is dependent on its legal relations to some other state. Colonies may be in this position. Consequently, we are dealing with a group of countries which it is not easy to separate off sharply from countries possessing complete rights in the making of their own tariffs.[2]

---

[1] Treaty of Peace, Part X., Article 222. It is true that this clause only permits such arrangements for a period of five years, but it is obvious that if the new states desire to found a new Danubian Federation in the course of time, that their position *inter se* must be such as to allow them to grant each other special tariff reductions which other states should not be able to claim.

[2] The question whether a country has the right to frame its own tariffs is a very different thing to asking whether the tariff it actually has is suitable to its needs or not. This point arises especially in the case of colonies, whose tariffs may be adjusted to the local needs, without the tariff-making body being locally controlled. Where there is adaptation to what are considered the local needs, but the tariff is framed by a body not locally controlled (though it may be influenced by local *opinion*), we have what is known as "tariff personality." For a further discussion of this important point, see below, Chap. viii., § 7.

We may distinguish the following groups of cases :—

(1) Autonomous areas limited in some definite respects.
(2) Non-autonomous areas—
(*a*) " Open-door " areas.
(*b*) Dependent non-open-door colonies.

(1) *Autonomous Areas Limited in some Definite Respect.*—The most important instance of this type of limitation was imposed by sec. 11 of the Treaty of Frankfort of May 10th, 1871.[1] The essential portions of this section for our purpose are the following :—

> The Treaties of Commerce with the different states of Germany having been annulled by the War, the French Government and the German Government will adopt as the basis of their commercial relations the system of reciprocal treatment on the footing of the most-favoured-nation.
>
> Are included therein import and export duties, transit dues, customs formalities, the admission and treatment of the subjects[2] both nations as well as their agents.
>
> Shall nevertheless be excepted from the above rule the favours which one of the contracting parties has granted or may grant, by treaties of commerce, to other states than the following :—" Great Britain, Belgium, Netherlands, Switzerland, Austria, Russia. . . . The French Government nevertheless reserves to itself the right of levying tonnage and shipping duties (Droit de Pavillon) on German vessels and their cargoes, under the reservation that their duties shall not be higher than those imposed on vessels and cargoes of the above-mentioned nations." [3]

This clause was inserted in the treaty after the French delegates had refused to concede the demand originally put forward by Bismarck, that the tariff treaty of France with

[1] Oakes and Mowat, " The Great European Treaties of the Nineteenth Century," p. 283 ; May, " Le Traité de Francfort," Chap. xiii., pp. 236-247 ; Auguste Oncken, " L'Article onze du Traité de Paix de Francfort " in Revue de'Econ. Politique, V., pp. 585-603 ; Sartorious von Waltershausen, " Der paragraph Elf des Frankfurter Friedens," 1915. May and the last-cited author give further references.

[2] These words are omitted in the English text by Oakes and Mowatt. *Cf.* French text in Marten's " Recueil Général de Traités," new series, vol. xix., p. 693.

[3] The effect of the limitation is discussed below in connection with the Most-Favoured-Nation Clause, Chap. xi., § 11.

the Zollverein, concluded in 1862 and expiring in 1877 (it only came fully into force in 1866), should be prolonged for ten years as from the date of negotiations—*i.e.*, until May, 1881. Bismarck feared above all things a tariff war: "he would prefer to recommence the war of cannon rather than expose himself to a war of tariffs." The French above all things desired to be free to raise the customs duties and so finance the indemnity. Mutual most-favoured-nation treatment seemed to give both sides what they wanted—the French liberty, the Germans security. May explains Bismarck's negligence to extend the range of countries so enumerated in the treaty by the fact that "l'Allemagne n'avait pas de produits à importer qui pussent concurrencer ceux de ce pays. Elle n'avait donc rein à craindre de ce côté"—*i.e.*, Germany exports did not compete with those of these non-included areas, consequently concessions made by France did not directly matter to Germany.

What have been the practical results of this clause in the period between the two wars, by which it was respectively produced and abrogated? We may distinguish four periods.

(*a*) 1871-79. Until the conversion of Bismarck to a protectionist policy in 1879, France enjoyed the benefits of the liberal trade policy pursued by the German Government. "(Between) 1871-79 Germany continued her liberal economic policy. The treaties with England, Belgium, Italy, etc., guaranteed numerous easements of intercourse, which were generalised by the most-favoured-nation clause. In addition there were autonomous tariff reductions. This state of affairs was a very favourable one for France, inasmuch as she was in many cases no worse off, but rather better off, than in the preceding years." [1]

(*b*) In the second period, 1879-1892, Germany pursued an autonomous tariff policy on the whole, such treaties as she concluded being in the main simple most-favoured-nation ones without conventionalised tariff rates. France, therefore, gained nothing directly, since the German rates were not tied. Germany gained from any concessions made by France. Consequently in this period the main benefit accrued to Germany. In addition, the neutrals suffered, for France refused to extend to them privileges which she had also to

[1] Sartorious von Waltershausen, *op. cit.*, p. 113.

grant to Germany, whilst the greater the concessions made to gain admittance to the French market, the greater the benefit accruing to Germany also.[1]

(*c*) In the third period, 1892-1906, when the policy of Count Caprivi led to the conclusion of the Middle European Treaties by Germany in the nineties, whilst France swung over to the maximum-minimum tariff system, the boot was rather on the other leg, for France benefitted by the concessions obtained by Germany.

(*d*) In the fourth period, after the new tariff of 1902 in Germany, the position again altered, for the finer specialisation introduced into this tariff, and the introduction in some cases of categories of advantageously treated objects (on Belgian horses, Swiss cattle, etc.) which France could not produce, reduced the advantages of the extension to France of the concessions made in the conventional tariff to other countries.

Some evidence is furnished by the state of the balance of trade between the two countries. In the first period this was in favour of France, in the second of Germany, in the third of France, in the fourth of Germany again.[2]

The net effect of the clause cannot really be stated in terms of economics: its main effects have been political. It has stimulated the suspicion that Germany was preparing for France "an economic Sedan," and has, therefore, aided the protectionist reaction. Whether it would have been possible to have dispensed with any such clause altogether, is a very different matter: if we assume that *some* treaty relation was desirable in the economic interests of both countries, criticism must be concentrated upon the *form* of the clause rather than its *content*. The alternative would have been a terminable most-favoured-nation agreement, which would probably *not* have been withdrawn, just because it was terminable, and so dissociated from the humiliation involved in the permanence of paragraph XI. In that case, the de facto relations would have been the same, though the tariff relations of the two states would have been judged more au fond, and have been less coloured by political prejudice. It is possible to argue that had the clause not been permanent,

[1] Oncken, *op. cit.*, pp. 596-7; von Waltershausen, p. 17.

[2] Von Waltershausen, *passim*, who is, however, careful to warn against undue stressing of this factor.

Germany would not have pursued an autonomous policy after 1879. The fact that this policy had in any case to be abandoned proves that this step was inevitable. The only doubtful point at issue is the rapidity with which the change would have come about. The question involves a consideration of the importance of the French market to Germany: of the German market to France: of the growing political influence of the industrial party in Germany: and of the question, how far Germany could have obtained concessions from other countries which need not have been extended to France owing to the absence of any treaty relationship, and which would have compensated in part for any possible losses in consequence of such absence.[1]

One again finds that the victors have taken advantage of the situation to impose tariff conditions which limit the autonomy in customs matters of the vanquished. Broadly speaking, in the case of Germany and Austria the Allies have insisted on *non-reciprocal* most-favoured-nation treatment for a limited period of time. Thus, by the Treaty of Peace with Germany (Part X., Economic Clauses, § I., chap I., Customs Regulations, Duties, and Restrictions), the latter country by Arts. 264-267 grants most-favoured-nation treatment in regard to import duties, customs regulations, excise duties, export duties, export prohibitions, importation, exportation, or transit of goods, to all the Allied and Associated States; by Art. 269 the 1914 conventional rates must be granted "during the first six months after the coming into force of the present treaty," whilst "during a further period of thirty months after the expiration of the first six months, this provision shall continue to be applied exclusively with

[1] Von Waltershausen believes that the losses to the trade of both countries would in any case have made it impossible for them to have conducted trade on the basis of their general tariffs, whilst political factors would have prevented France from concluding anything but a simple most-favoured-nation treaty. . . . "I believe, therefore, that one must conclude that, if no permanent pure most-favoured-nation treatment had been insisted on in 1871, one would have had to renew it from period to period." Writing, in 1915, as he did, von Waltershausen wished in the treaty of peace to maintain a *provisional* clause of the same kind, but desired the definitive tariff relations between the two countries to be dependent on the outcome of the tariff negotiations between the Central Powers. For, in the event of their granting one another preferential rights, it was undesirable, by the previous concession of most-favoured-nation treatment to other states, to have to grant these preferences to other states also.

regard to products which, being comprised in section A of the first category of the German customs Tariff of December 25, 1902, enjoyed at the above-mentioned date (July 31st, 1914), rates conventionalised by treaties with the Allied and Associated Powers, with the addition of all kinds of wine and vegetable oils, of artificial silk, and of washed and scoured wool, whether or not they were the subject of special conventions before 31st July, 1914." These obligations determine by Art. 280 "five years from the date of the coming into force of the present treaty, unless the council of the League of Nations shall, at least twelve months before the expiration of that period, decide that these obligations shall be maintained for a further period with or without amendments." Bearing in mind that by Art. 26 of the Covenant of the League of Nations, decisions, except where otherwise expressly provided for, "shall require the agreement of all the members of the League represented at the meeting," the question arises whether these stipulations are such as to lead to unanimity on the part of the members of the council. Since these provisions are non-reciprocal, they obviously represent directly a valuable commercial privilege for the Allied and Associated Powers. For that very reason also they weaken Germany's powers of obtaining concessions from other and neutral countries, except on onerous terms, for neutrals will naturally point out that the value of concessions made to them by Germany will be much reduced by the large number of Allied and Associated Powers who will also benefit. Assuming that Germany finds it impossible to conclude *any* agreements with any neutrals, the value of the pre-cited clauses will be diminished for the Allies, also, and as neutral trade will suffer, the neutrals will hope to put an end to the preferential position of the Allies as soon as possible, for apart from the direct loss, they can no longer play off Germany against the Allies. Hence, in so far as the neutrals are represented on the council, the necessary unanimity is not likely to be obtained.[1], [2], [3]

---

[1] At present only *one* neutral State is represented on the Council (Art. 4)—Spain.

[2] For Austria, Part x., sec. 1, Chap. i., Arts. 217-221 of the Austrian Treaty.

[3] Separate stipulations regulate the position of Alsace-Lorraine, Luxemburg, and Poland (German Treaty, Art. 268).

(2) *Non-Autonomous Areas.*—(a) *Open-Door Areas.*[1]—The term "open-door area" is one of political and diplomatic origin, and one the exact use of which is still a matter of dispute.[2] Thus, the two authorities referred to in note (1) differ from one another as to the precise meaning of the term, Schilder including in the concept the idea of extra-territoriality, which Grunzel rightly rejects, for an area may be autonomous in its general jurisdictional powers, and yet be an open-door area, a state of affairs which Schilder himself points out as evolving in Siam.[3]

There are two, and two essential features only, which distinguish the open-door area. Firstly, the tariff autonomy of the area is limited by irrevocable treaties. Secondly, the content of such treaties is such as to throw open the trade of the area on equal terms to all trading nations or, at any rate, to the signatories. Such treaties may also stipulate for a low range of customs duties, but this is *not* an absolutely indispensable feature of the situation though an alteration of the duties cannot take place without general agreement of all the Powers with whom treaties have been concluded. It is necessary to emphasise that fact that the open-door area is only bound to the signatories of the treaties : to other states it is not bound, except it conclude special treaties with these, which are not necessarily based on the principle of equality.[4]

---

[1] The matters dealt with in this section have been dealt with by Schilder in his "Entwicklungstendenzen der Weltwirtschaft" (Chap. viii., also § 11 of Chap. v.). A somewhat less elaborate treatment will be found in Grunzel's "Economic Protectionism," Chap xi., § 3, "Customs Districts wholly or partly Dependent."

[2] An investigation of the leading text-books on international law will show that the phrase does not appear in the indices of any of them, an exception to the general rule being J. Basset Moore's "Digest of International Law," but the phrase there occurs in connection with the attitude of the United States towards the partition of China.

[3] *Op. cit.*, p. 319.

[4] Thus Turkey concluded special treaties with the Balkan States (Schilder, *op. cit.*, p. 283) ; China has concluded special treaties with Russia and India as to the land frontiers, whilst the open-door position of the Congo Basin, based on the Berlin Act of 1886, and the Brussels Act of 1890, has recently been modified by the Convention of Saint-Germain-on-Laye of the 10th September, 1919, which only grants equality of treatment to the Signatory Powers, and to the adhering powers ; the States which have a right to adhere being "States exercising authority over African territory, and other States, Members of the League of Nations, which were parties to either of the above Acts." Subject to the condition of equality, the "States concerned reserve to themselves complete liberty of action as to customs and navigation regulations and tariffs to be applied in their territories." Thus, those "enemy states," not members of the League of Nations, are ex-

But since the interest of the states trading with such areas is involved in their obtaining "open door" privileges, the number of such signatories as do conclude treaties conferring such rights tends to be large, and the larger their number the more difficult is it to cause any alteration in the contents of the treaty system.

The treaties inaugurating the régime may be of two kinds—(1) Treaties concluded by the state itself with each co-contractant separately. This is the position in China and Siam.

(2) Treaties concluded among the trading nations themselves, regulating the conditions under which one or more of them shall be given the right of territorial overlordship over the area in question.

The distinction just drawn points to a grouping of the open-door areas into two classes—

(1) The "older" open-door areas. Turkey, China, Siam, (Morocco, Tunis, and Tripoli, as well as Japan, were at one time in this position), with settled, even if backward, governments of their own.

(2) The "newer" open-door areas, representing either (*a*) areas taken over for colonisation or exploitation purposes by the Powers, such as the great belt of Equatorial Africa dealt with by the great Berlin Act of 1886, and the subsequent Act of Brussels of 1890.[1]

(*b*) Areas which, though in the past subject to full open-door rights, are on the way to being pure colonies, in which the open door now simply temporarily limits the rights of the possessing power for a determinate period (as, for instance, Egypt under the Anglo-French agreement [2] until 1934).

(*c*) Areas with settled governments of their own, but in which one or more of the Great Powers possess special political interests, such as Persia and Afganistan, the trading

---

cluded, and the revised convention removes the necessity for uniformity of rates throughout the area, upon which the original Act insisted, to the extent of proclaiming the right of each state to regulate these matters as it thinks fit. (See *B.T.J.*, 20/1/20, p. 155.) Cmd. 477 (Treaty Series, No. 18).

[1] Hertslet, "Commercial Treaties," vol. xvii., p. 65: vol. xix., pp. 304-5.

[2] Bernhard, "Handbook of Commercial Treaties," p. 338, *et seq.* "Declaration . . . respecting Egypt and Morocco." Art. IV. The declaration to remain in force for thirty years and, unless denounced one year in advance, for five years at a time thereafter.

rights to which areas were part of the settlement between the United Kingdom and Russia before the War.[1]

The whole position of open-door areas is essentially unstable. They may cease to be open to the trade of all nations in consequence of their becoming strong enough to throw off the shackles formerly pressing on them,[2] or because they are taken over by a colonising power which gradually emancipates itself from the obligations it has formerly incurred. With the intensification of imperialist claims in the last few decades this process of absorption went on on a large scale. The series of treaties which are liquidating the results of the Great War will, when they are completed, have parcelled out the whole available territory, with the exception of China and Siam, and possibly Abyssinia.[3]

---

[1] Treaty Series, No. 34, of 1907. As to Persia, preamble to Art. I.; as to Afghanistan, Art. IV. of appropriate portion of Convention. The position in Persia was distinctly equivocal, since the two Powers reserved for themselves distinct spheres of "economic penetration." For another instance of a similar attempt to reconcile the principle of special financial concessions with the open door, see the Agreement between the United Kingdom, France, and Italy respecting Abyssinia (T.S., 1907, No. 1), Arts. 6 and 7, by which concessions to French railway companies are made subject to equality of treatment of the subjects of the three Powers in the first instance, with a subsequent stipulation that "the three signatory powers agree to extend to the nationals of all other countries the benefit of the provisions . . . relating to equality of treatment as regards trade and transit." The whole conception of the open door is, in fact, difficult to maintain in view of the newer relations between "advanced" and "new" countries, which take the form primarily of financial, and only secondarily of trade intercourse. This economic fact is gradually leading—*e.g.*, in China—to the principle of a "right of entry" into any financial syndicate formed for specific purposes. Mr. H. N. Brailsford is entitled to the credit for the first thorough examination of the implications of these changing economic relations. *v.* "The War of Steel and Gold" and the "League of Nations," *passim*. On China, see Overlach, "Financial Control in China."

[2] This development has taken place in the case of Japan, and also in the case of those Balkan States which separated from the Turkish Empire by the Berlin Treaty of 1878 (Mowat, *op. cit.*, p. 332, *et seq.*; "State Papers, Domestic and Foreign," vol. lxix., p. 749); Bulgaria, Art. 8; Eastern Rumelia, Art. 20; Servia, Art. 37; Roumania, Art. 48; taking over, nevertheless, the open-door obligations resting on the Turkish territory, of which they were the heirs, whilst Greece had obtained full autonomy on the other hand. § 1 of the protocol of the Conference of London of 1830, *op. cit.*, p. 120.

[3] The position under the Covenant of the League is such as to add nothing to the body of principle already existing on the subject of the open door. By Art. 22, "Mandatory States" are to secure "equal opportunities for the trade and commerce of other members of the league," whilst a general obligation on the members is that they will "make provision to secure and maintain freedom of communications and equitable treatment for the commerce of all members of the league." Presumably this also applies to the colonies of members, but no definition is given as to what meaning is to be given to the term "equitable."

The question, therefore, arises whether the privileges conferred on trading nations by the régime of the open door are so great that a determined attempt should be made to prevent the gradual extinction of this régime altogether. This question was asked by Schilder and answered in the negative by him. It will be desirable to investigate this matter somewhat more closely.

Schilder's argument, briefly put, is that the open door is not worth having, because it is the price paid by the West for a continuance of inefficient government. It is only the backward states of the world that will consent to a continuance of the open door in their areas; as soon as they reach a higher stage of economic and political power, they cast the shackles off, as Japan and the Balkan States have done. It is true that the consequence is that these states thereupon attempt to protect their own industries, and to pursue an autonomous tariff policy, which will result in their favouring those states which are prepared to concede advantages to them. Similarly, when European Powers take over such areas as colonies, they try, as far as possible, to abandon the open door, and to favour their own nationals. But though, in both cases, the result is the introduction of inequality, there is still a net gain. This gain arises from the fact that these renovated states are, in the long run, much more valuable markets, owing to the increased productivity which results from the order, science, and stability of the new régime. Since an increase of productivity increases the purchasing power of the area in question, it is difficult to suppose that, indirectly at any rate, the whole body of trading nations will not gain.

This argument is only valid on the assumption that it is impossible to obtain the advantages of better government without abandoning the open door. It is, of course, perfectly true that modern and scientific methods are capable of increasing the resources of the areas in question, and that the result will be an increase of purchasing power. It is probably also the case that the advantages of stimulating productivity will outweigh the direct economic disadvantages of inequality in the terms on which various traders can compete. But this does not prove that it would not still be better to reorganise the productive conditions, without abandoning that feature of the open door which looms largest in the popular mind—the equality of all nations in the trade with the area.

It is impossible, within the limits of this work, to discuss whether the state of public opinion is such as to allow the continuance of open-door arrangements in areas which have assumed full rights of self-government, or which have fallen into the administrative sphere of a colonising power. In order to answer the question, it would be necessary to investigate the validity of the whole theory of protection, and a further investigation would be necessary into the political forces which at any moment determine the policy of Governments.

Discussion of the open-door areas has brought us to the point at which it becomes necessary to say a word as to another class of non-autonomous tariff areas, viz. :—

(b) *Dependent Non-open-door Colonies.*—" Colony " is a concept of political science, and there is, therefore, nothing in the status of a colony which necessarily implies that its tariff making powers *must* be subordinate, or even non-existent. But, though there is not this necessary logical filiation, there is the practical fact that in the overwhelming number of cases the colonial empire is not free to frame its own tariffs. The practical question is the degree to which a colony should be subordinate to the metropolitan power, and this is a question which is answered differently by different colonial powers at the same time, and differently at different times by all of them, and in different ways within one and the same system. The subject of the colonial régimes of the powers possessing colonies is dealt with in a later section, here it is only necessary to point out that the variety of type is greater than is usually supposed. In addition to the cases in which the colony has no autonomy at all, and those in which it possesses complete, or almost complete, freedom, there are the cases in which the tariff régime is *jointly* determined, so that the question here is as to the division of power. The wishes of the colony may as a rule be the decisive factor, or the wishes of the metropolitan area may come first, but the wishes of the colony in some degree be given satisfaction. Hence the possible grades of dependence are numerous.[1]

---

[1] See below, Chap. viii., p. 250, *et seq.*, for a further treatment of colonial problems.

NOTE I. TO CHAPTER I.

IT may be well to describe in some detail the growth of the South African Customs Union and the present South African position, which is complicated.

The first convention was one concluded between Cape Colony and the Orange Free State in 1889. To this arrangement British Bechuanaland adhered as from June 1st, 1890, and Basutoland after July 1st, 1891. An abortive conference between various South African territories was held in 1896: the Transvaal and Portuguese Governments were not included, and Natal refused unless all the South African Governments were included. A new conference was held in 1898. A new convention, coming into force on 1st January, 1899, was concluded between the Cape Colony, Natal, Orange Free State, as from 1st January, 1899. After the War a new convention was concluded in May, 1903—this time between the Cape Colony, Natal, Orange River Colony, Transvaal, and S. Rhodesia. Provision was made in this convention for the admission of any state or colony in South Africa or Central Africa having a civilised government. To this convention Swaziland adhered, 11th October, 1904, and Northern Rhodesia, 1st December, 1905. In March, 1906, a new conference was held at Pietermaritzburg, and a new convention concluded, coming into force on 1st July, 1906. The Transvaal notified her intention of leaving after 30th June, 1908, and a Pretoria conference was held in May, 1908. The Transvaal agreed to withdraw notice, and a new protocol to convention was added, coming into force on 15th August, 1908. After the formation of the South African Union, which absorbed the Cape, Natal, Transvaal, and Orange River Colony, new arrangements were concluded with the non-union territories by the South African Government. By an agreement with Bechuanaland (Col. Reports Annual, No. 696), dated 29th June, 1910, "it was arranged that in future all revenue in customs duty accruing to the protectorate should be paid into the union treasury, while the protectorate became entitled to receive annually a fraction of the total customs revenue of the union equalling that which the average customs receipts of this territory for the last three years bore to the sum collected under this head during the same period by the colonies and territories comprising the South African Customs Union." A protocol was added, 1st September, 1913, equalising the duties on spirits and beer in the union and in the territory (Report, 1913-14, Cd. 7622). A similar arrangement was concluded with Swaziland, dated 30th June, 1910. "Payments due to Swaziland are assessed on the proportion which the average of the collections for three years ended the 31st March, 1911, bears to the total customs collections of the union in each year (C. R. Annual, Swaziland, 1910-11, Cd. 5467).

The relations between the union and Northen and Southern Rhodesia are somewhat different. The tariff of S. Rhodesia is practically identical with that of the South African Union (Ord., No. 30 of 1914, and by O., No. 7 of 1915) and the Northern Rhodesian tariff is classified similarly to that of S. Rhodesia. But the position is complicated by the fact that—

(1) In virtue of the so-called Rhodes clause in *both* Northern and Southern Rhodesia (Art. 478, the S.R. O-in-C., 1898, amended by O.-in-O. of 10th August, 1914, and Clause 19 of the N.R. O.-in-C. of 1911, amended 1914).

> "No customs duties levied on any articles, other than tobacco in any form of intoxicating liquors of any kind, produced or manufactured, in any part of H.M. Dominions or in any British Protectorate and imported into Southern or Northern Rhodesia (as the case may be) shall exceed in amount the duties levied on similar articles from over-sea according to the tariff in force in the S.A. Customs Union at the date of coming into operation of the "Southern Rhodesian Order-in-Council, 1898, or the tariff contained in the Customs Union Convention concluded between the Colony of the Cape of Good Hope, the Orange Free State, and Natal in May, 1898, whichever are the higher."

(2) Northern Rhodesa is divided for customs purposes into two areas—

(*a*) The Zambesi Basin, where the tariff operative is, with the above-named exception, similar to that in the union.

(*b*) The Congo Basin, where in general the rate of duty is limited to 10 per cent. *ad valorem*, owing to the inclusion of the area in the open-door territory of the Berlin Conference of 1885. (On the points raised above, see C.I.D., 1914 and 1915: Official Year Book of the Union of South Africa, 1910-16, pp. 492-3; Cd. 1599 of 1903, Cd. 2977 of 1906.) It may be mentioned also that preferential relations exist under the Pretoria Convention of 1st April, 1909, between the Transvaal and the Mozambique Governments, an arrangement concluded in the first instance for ten years, and terminable thereafter at one year's notice. The convention provides for free importation into the Transvaal of all articles the produce of the Province, whilst it also equalises export duties on goods exported either *via* Cape or Natal ports or Portuguese ports, and applies similar treatment to imports.

A glance at a map will explain the differences in the attitude which have been described above towards union on the part of different provinces. The South African Union has been described as a railway union: it is equally true that the geographical pull exercised by the seaboard colonies on the landlocked ones should lead to a desire for union. The Transvaal, with an alternative port, is in a different position to the others, and has in the past taken up a somewhat intransigeant attitude.

A word may be said as to the position in Australia before the passage of the Commonwealth Act.

From a very early date in the history of the Australasian colonies the desirability of common action had been recognised, although, as events turned out, customs unity did not come into being until complete political unity was also achieved. In 1849 "the Lords of the Committee of Council appointed for the consideration of all matters relating to trade and plantations" reported to the Privy Council [1]—

> "There yet remains a question of considerable difficulty. By far the larger part of the revenue of the Australian Colonies is derived from duties on customs. But if, when Victoria shall have been separated from New South Wales, each province shall be authorised to impose duties according to its own wants, it is scarcely possible, but that in process of time differences should

[1] Correspondence on the Australian Colonies Government Bill, Parl. Pap. 1850, vol. xxxvii., pp. 74-5. For a general sketch of the Australian problem, see Egerton, "Federations and Unions in the British Empire," pp. 40-67; Wise, "The Commonwealth of Australia," Part ii., Chap. i.; and for the period 1860-73, esp.; Coghlan, "Labour and Industry in Australia," vol. ii., pp. 1136-85.

arise between the rates of duty imposed upon the same articles in the one and in the other of them. There is already such a difference in the tariffs of South Australia and New South Wales, and although, until of late, this has been productive of little inconvenience, yet with the increase of settlers on either side of the imaginary line dividing them, it will become more and more serious. The division of New South Wales into two colonies would further aggravate this inconvenience, if the change should lead to the introduction of three entirely distinct tariffs, and to the consequent necessity for imposing restrictions and securities on the import and export of goods between them. So great indeed would be the evil, and such the obstruction of the inter-colonial trade, and so great the check to the development of the resources of each of these colonies that it seems to us necessary that there should be one tariff common to them all, so that goods might be carried from the one into the other with the same absolute freedom as between any two adjacent counties in England. We are further of opinion that the same tariff should be established in Van Diemens Land also, because the intercourse between that island and the neighbouring colonies in New Holland has risen to a great importance and extent, and has an obvious tendency to increase. Yet fiscal regulations on one side of the intervening strait must of necessity check, and might perhaps, to a great extent, destroy that beneficial trade.

"If the duties were uniform it is obvious there need be no restrictions whatever imposed upon the import or export of goods between the respective colonies, and no motive for importing into one goods liable to duty, which were destined for consumption in another, and it may safely be calculated that each would receive the proportion of revenue to which it would be justly entitled, or, at all events, that there would be no departure from this to an extent of any practical importance.

"Hence, it seems to us that a uniformity in the rate of duties should be secured.

"For this purpose we recommend that a uniform tariff should be established by the authority of Parliament, but that it should not take effect until twelve months had elapsed from the promulgation in the several colonies of the proposed Act. . . . We should not, however, be prepared to offer this recommendation, unless we proposed at the same time to provide for making any alteration in this general tariff, which time and experience may dictate, and this we think can only be done by creating some authority competent to act for all those colonies jointly."

These predictions of future trouble if the tariff relations were not to be definitely settled *ab initio* proved correct: the opposition of interests between Victoria and New South Wales were to be a stumbling block to union for many a day.

British, as distinct from colonial, opinion was to pronounce itself in favour of customs unity at a later stage also: when, at the beginning of the seventies, the Australasian Colonies desired to grant each other preferential duties, the proposal was met at home by the counter suggestion of a customs union, this time, indeed, on the ground of the difficulties of the treaty position of the United Kingdom.[1]

Both in 1891 at the Sydney conference, and in the negotiations which, dating from 1897, finally led to the founding of the Australian Commonwealth the tariff problem played an important part, though policy as to free trade or protection was relatively less important than the technical point as to the *adjustment of revenue claims*,[2] and this led to some complications in the form of the constitution.

---

[1] See Lord Kimberley's dispatch, dated 19th April, 1872, quoted; Keith, "Responsible Government," vol. iii., p. 1171, *et seq.*, esp. p. 1177. "Customs unions which have hitherto, so far as I am aware, never been formed except between neighbouring communities have for their object the removal of the barriers to trade created by artificial boundaries and the establishment of a cheaper and more convenient mode of collecting the customs revenue of the united countries. But the formation of such a union does not, in itself, involve any question of protection to native industry, nor of inequality of treatment of imports from countries not belonging to the union. On the other hand, such reciprocity arrangements as the Colonies desire to conclude are not confined to the promotion of free intercourse between each other, but are intended to secure for the trade of the respective colonies special advantages, as against imports from other places, in return for corresponding concessions. . . . A Customs Union, while it would incidentally secure important advantages to native industry by the removal of all obstacles to internal trade, would do so without establishing the principle of preferential duties."

[2] Egerton, *op. cit.*, pp. 59, 65; see also sec. 8 of the foregoing chapter.

CHAPTER I.—*Continued.*

TARIFF-MAKING BODIES.

§ 11. WE now pass to the consideration of one aspect of the subject which recent currents of thought render more than usually important and interesting. This aspect concerns tariff-making bodies.

Two allied currents of thought impinge here to form a stream of ideas hostile to the traditional technique by which tariffs actually come into being. The first current draws a large part of its strength from the power of words on what a distinguished statesman has recently described as the "uninstructed mind," and takes concrete shape in the demand for a "scientific tariff." The second draws its strength from the suspicion that the tariff is capable of being turned into an instrument of private enrichment at the expense of the public, and that the process by which tariffs are enacted—through the instrumentality of the legislature—enables a possibility to be turned into an actuality through the corruption of the legislator: directly, as when corrupt bargains are made between powerful economic interests and individual politicians; indirectly, when the policy of governments is dictated by the necessity of safeguarding themselves from the attacks of powerful interests with allies in the press and the legislature itself, and on which they are dependent for the replenishing of the party funds. The suspicions alluded to lead to the demand for an "impartial" tariff-making body, for "taking the tariff out of politics."

§ 12. The demand for a scientific tariff comprehends this latter demand also, but it includes more than this. In this country the demand for a scientific tariff was, in the days before the War, based largely on the supposedly scientific character of the German tariff of 1902. Wherein its scientific character lay is not always clearly seen; the demand is to a large extent a mere worship of a phrase. It is only at the end of our present enquiry that we shall be able to answer the question, to what extent the term "scientific" can be applied to tariff making at all. But we may at this stage indicate the practical result to which these demands usually lead—what is desired is the creation of a "Board" or "Commission" in whose hands the creating of an impartial and scientific tariff shall lie.

We will begin our enquiry by discussing the traditional scheme—viz., the making of tariffs by legislative bodies.

§ 13. The making of a tariff involves two very dissimilar processes. A tariff is one and the same time an instrument of commercial policy, requiring, therefore, the accumulation of data and an ordered collection of facts bearing upon the matter in hand; and a body of law involving the general good, and, therefore, requiring the assent of the legislature. Here, then, we have the two fundamental facts of the situation. There must take place the collection of material bearing upon the end in view, and there must be a discussion of that end itself.

The political institutions differ in detail from country to country. One feature, however, is common to all countries with legislatures; legislation must be assented to by a majority of the representatives; if not an absolute majority of all the representatives, at least a majority of all the representatives actually voting. The practical problem resolves itself into getting such a majority at each stage of the progress of the measure; and from this point of view abstention from voting may be as important as voting itself. Further, no legislature can discuss or vote unless it has a project upon which to found its actions.

Finally, any discussion of the realities of the situation cannot avoid facing the blunt fact that the direct economic interest of particular groups *is* affected by the details of a tariff measure, and that it is, therefore, inevitable that business interests affected should strive to obtain what seems to them adequate, and to defeat what seems to them inadequate or opposed to their interests. Hence, whatever the tariff-making body may be, it must reckon with the propaganda of interested persons.

The acquisition of information may be undertaken by a government department, a select committee of the legislature, by an *ad hoc* commission or by the government organs, together with an advisory body. These methods are not exclusive of one another, they may all of them be adopted in sequence. But in countries with a permanent civil service, and with an executive government responsible for the inauguration of legislation, the government naturally seeks to utilise in the first instance the permanent machinery at its disposal. The great point is the adequacy of the information, and this may involve the public hearing of witnesses, the taking of confidential testimony, and so on.

It is obvious on reflection that the collection of information is a skilled process, in which the expert is necessarily at an advantage. Consequently the select committee of the legislature is liable not to pursue its inquiries with the same expertness as a government department, for it lacks the trained personnel which is desirable. But this general statement is subject to certain qualifications; wherever the information to be acquired is of a very contentious character—that is, cannot be clearly separated from issues of policy—it may be desirable to leave its collection in the hands of some political body, the departments of state being themselves called upon as witnesses in the dispute, which the collection of such information generally calls forth.[1]

§ 14. **The Framing of the Measure.**—The collection of information is a necessary preliminary to the drafting of the measure, but it must not be confused with the latter. The drafting of the measure and the collection of the requisite information may be separated or they may be joined, but, whatever machinery of drafting be adopted, here the first stage of the conflict between the "interests" concerned takes place. Whether it is a cabinet meeting discussing a new rate, or a Committee planning a new scale; pressure, direct and indirect, will be brought to bear upon the drafters. Consequently, it makes much less difference than is sometimes supposed, if the individual legislator is deprived of his right to propose amendments in the House: for so long as any group of men remain in whom discretionary authority resides, and on whom political influence can be brought to bear, the result will be that that pressure will be applied. In a centralised political system, where administrative policy

---

[1] The matters discussed in this section overlap with those discussed in the next, for the reason that the collection of information is only a preliminary to the drafting of the measure, and the collecting body may also be the drafting body. To discuss the collection of information apart from the drafting of measures involves, therefore, a certain amount of artificiality and overlapping. But it will be obvious that they are distinct functions, however much they may be associated with one another in practice. If it is permissible to use somewhat vague language, it may be said that the collection of "pure" knowledge is passing into the hands of experts, though the "contentious" knowledge may still be collected by non-expert bodies.

is in the hands of a cabinet, the issues on all points of less than first class will tend to fall into the hands of the minister in charge of the bill, and even where no cabinet system prevails, but the bill is in charge of a committee or some other group, whatever it may be called, the tendency will be the same—the decision tends to lie in the hands of a relatively few men.[1]

Hence, before ever the bill sees the light of day, a considerable amount of discussion, of compromise, of agitation, and counter-agitation will have taken place. Lord Morley has well described the immense responsibility and detailed work falling to the lot of a minister in charge of a tariff bill.[2]

So far, the matter has been dealt with analytically. Some illustrations may now be given of the actual system adopted in different countries.

Germany.—The German tariff of 1902 was the result of the collaboration of the organs of the government and an advisory committee. Since the German method seems to play a great part in the controversies on these subjects, it may be well to go into the matter fairly thoroughly. The preparations for the new tariff were begun in 1897 under Count Posadowsky, at first by the Imperial Treasury, and from July, 1897, by the Ministry of the Interior. In the collection of an "extraordinarily rich material" the department was assisted by the "Economic Committee for the Preparation and Consideration of Commercial Measures" (Wirtschaftlicher Ausschuss zur Zubereitung und Begutachtung Handelspolitischer Massnahmen), "for whose deliberations official secrecy was laid down. The composition of the economic committee and the resulting measures have become as much the subject of praise and satisfaction on the part of protectionists as the recipients of vehement attacks by free traders. In fact, the composition of the committee was intended to sanction a protectionist policy by the government (darauf angelegt, eine schutzzöllnerische Handelspolitik der Regierung zu sanctionieren), and to deprive all free trade scruples of the appearance of justification (allen freihändlerischen Einwendungen den Schein der Berechtigung zu entziehen). There were present on this body the leaders of

---

[1] See, for instance, the description of the "inner ring" which dominated the discussions on the Dingley Tariff in Beard, "Readings in American Government," p. 333, *et seq.*

[2] Morley's "Life of Gladstone," vol. i., p. 189, of edn. of 1908.

agriculture . . . in addition the trusted representatives (Vertraunsmänner) of the Central Verband der deutscher Industrieller, and the delegates of the German Handelstag, on which the Central Verband exercised a strong influence; each of the three corporations had sent five representatives, to which 15 had been added directly by the Imperial Chancellor. On the other hand, there were on the committee no representatives of the consumers, of the workers, of the small farmers (Kleinbauern), of the handicraft trades, or of the smaller manufacturers, and even the merchants and the export manufacturers complained that they were under represented. . . . For the determination of the height of the customs rates, which formed by far the most important theme of the discussions of the committee, a rich material, besides the utterances of the members, was collected. On the bases of all these desires (Zollwünsche) the government was to make up its mind, after there had been reached agreement in principle as to the road to be followed. In any case the new tariff was to contain higher rates than those considered necessary in the interest of the respective branches of industry, in order to have objects for bargaining available on the conclusion of new treaties. Although the representatives of the various groups of industries were not backward in asking for higher rates, it turned out that the government even asked on the committee if this or that rate ought not to be increased. The representative, Gothein, who was a member of the conference, summed up his impressions afterwards in bitter disgust. 'It seemed to him that on the committee he was in a robbers den for customs duties (wie in einer Animerkneipe fur Schutzzölle).'"[1]

This does not complete the story; the new tariff was subsequently considered by a conference of the chancellor and the representatives of the Federal States, and, finally, by the Federal Council, from July, 1901, to November of the same year; it was then submitted to the Reichstag, which appointed a committee of 28 to go over the ground again; this committee began its labours in December, and held 111 sittings revising the rates, which had already been to some extent altered by the Federal Council.[2]

---

[1] Hollander, "Der Deutsche Zolltarif von 1902" in Sch. Jahrbuch, 1913, pp. 844, 845, 846.

[2] Hollander, *op. cit.*, 1368, 1371.

The U.S.A.—The United States are the classical home of tariffs made by the legislature. There had been an *ad hoc* commission in 1882, but the general principle is that "hearings"—*i.e.*, the collection of information and the drafting of tariff bills—is in the hands of the Ways and Means Committee of the House of Representatives. But the committee hears the various government departments interested, and will in future have the advantage of the suggestions and the information collected by the Tariff Board.[1]

France.—The general principle is that the government frames the Tariff Act with the advice of the "Conseil Supérieur du Commerce et de l'Industrie," which framed the proposals of the years 1877 and 1890.[2] The Chamber of Deputies exercises a free right of revision through the Commission des Douanes in the first instance, and the initiative even can be taken by the Chamber. This was the case with the tariff revision in 1910.[3]

The United Kingdom.—The U.K. having a perfected parliamentary executive, the preparation of tariff projects is in the first instance in the hands of the Cabinet; but select committees of the legislature have been responsible in the

---

[1] The Commission of 1882 was appointed in virtue of an Act of Congress of 15th May, 1882. By sec. 2 of the Act, the President, with the consent of the Senate, was to appoint nine Commissioners from civil life; by sec. 3 it was the duty of the Commissioners "to take into consideration and to thoroughly investigate all the various questions relating to the agricultural, commercial, mercantile, manufacturing, and industrial interests of the United States, so far as the same may be necessary to the establishment of a judicious tariff, or a revision of the existing tariff upon a scale of justice to all interests, and for the purpose of fully examining the matters which may come before it." The report of the Commission was to be ready not later than the first Monday in December, 1882. The report of the Commission is printed as H. Misc., 47, 2nd Session, vols. ii. and iii. See also Taussig, "Tariff History of the U.S.," 6th edn., p. 231, and Stanwood's "American Tariff Controversies," vol. ii., p. 202, *et seq.*

[2] Ashley, "Modern Tariff History," 2nd Edn., pp. 379, 404. For the Conseil Supérieur, see U.S.A. Dept. of Commerce, Special Agents Series, No. 98, pp. 63-4. (Commercial Organisations in France). It meets upon the call of the Minister of Commerce, has the Minister as its President, and consists of four vice-presidents, six members by right who are the chief of the sections of commercial and industrial affairs and of technical education in the Ministry of Commerce, the general directors of the Customs and indirect revenue services, the chief of the section of political and commercial affairs of the Ministry of Foreign Affairs, the director of labour in the labour department, and last, 64 appointed members in two sections of 32 each, selected from presidents of chambers of commerce and from leading merchants and manufacturers.

[3] See Ashley, *op. cit.*, pp. 424-425, and Yves Guyot, "Les Procédés de la Commission des Douanes" in J. de Ec., 6th series, vol. xxii. (April, 1909), where the tactics and the policy of the Commission are sharply criticised.

past for important suggestions of policy—a classical instance is the Select Committee on Import Duties of 1840. This committee again drew its technical facts largely from official witnesses, such as Sir John Bowring, and its report is in fact a document dealing with *policy*, and policy, as already suggested, is more properly dealt with by a political body. The appointment in July, 1916, of a strong committee "to consider the commercial and industrial policy to be adopted after the War, with special reference to the conclusions reached by the Paris conference of the Allies" and certain specific matters connected therewith [1] may be taken as a more modern instance of the same kind: though this committee more closely resembles the Economic Committee of Germany so far as its composition is concerned—*i.e.*, it was not a select committee of the legislature. One of its proposals will occupy us further below.

We have now passed under review the methods of the great commercial countries, so far as the collection of information and the drafting of bills are concerned. The next matter is *the discussion in the houses.*

Sooner or later the bill must reach the whole house. Here the public process of amendment, if any, takes place, and at this stage the detail of the particular parliamentary procedure in force may affect the issue very much. If there is complete freedom of proposing amendments, the result may be very different to what it would have been if the only amendments in order were those *reducing* the rate,[2] or if the highest rate, whether the original rate or not, is put to the vote first.[3] Again, it makes a considerable difference whether each individual rate is put to the vote separately, or only the schedule or class to which the rate belongs, as seems to be the case in the United States.[4]

---

[1] For the full terms of reference, *v.* Cd. 9035, of 1918 (Final Report).

[2] As is the case in the United Kingdom, *on the assumption that a protective tariff will be assimilated, if such a tariff is ever to be introduced, to ordinary fiscal legislation.*

[3] As is the case in France, *v.* Pierre, "Droit Parlementaire," p. 949, "C'est le chiffre le plus élévé qui est mis au voix"; Supplement, pp. 82-3, "Lors de la revision du tarif général des douanes, en 1909, le principe que les droits les plus élévés doivent toujours avoir la priorité, lors même qu'ils auraient été propose par la Commission a été nettement confirmé. . . ."

[4] The fate of the German tariff was sensibly affected by the manipulation by the majority of the rules of procedure of the Reichstag. According to § 19, sub-sec. 2, the vote is to take place on each separate article in succession. The rule was silent as to annexes to bills, and the majority made use of this to propose an amendment

Other points affecting the fate of a tariff measure are the possibility of its amendment by a second chamber (as in France and the United States), a matter which in this country hangs together with the question whether it is a "money bill" or not; whether it is subject to closure, or has rights of precedence over other legislation. Enough will have been said to show that the influence of procedure is one of the elements which ought to be considered in judging of the fitness of legislatures to act as customs-making bodies, a question to which so high an authority as the late Professor Schmoller gave a pessimistic answer. The treatment of the tariff in the Reichstag, he declared, "was a new proof of the low capacity of large parliaments to bring good tariffs into being."[1]

§ 15. The first difficulty of the modern tariff is its technical complexity: the closeness with which it affects private interests and the impossibility of the individual legislator understanding the issues involved in each case. Hence, unintelligent voting. These are difficulties of a technical character.

The second main group of difficulties arises from the fact that without assuming that politicians are essentially dishonest, it is extremely hard, so long as the tariff remains a political issue, for politicians to avoid the *appearance*, and in some cases to avoid the *reality*, of dishonesty. A party is pledged to introduce a tariff or to revise an existing one. Two opposing interests bring pressure to bear: it may be in a perfectly honest way, by propaganda, deputation, and so on. Both groups must be conciliated if it can be done, assuming that both command a number of votes sufficient to turn the scale on a critical division. Or two groups are both dissatisfied with the amount of protection they receive: is it not perfectly natural that there will be log-rolling—*i.e.*, that the members most interested will agree to support one another? It may be answered that where the private member possesses only limited rights to move amendments, the public

---

to Article 1 of the Tariff Law, which deprived the minority, which was obstructing the passage of the bill, of any power to discuss the details of the rates. This action provoked violent opposition on the part of the parties of the left and their press, but the motion was carried, and is embodied in Art. 1 of the Act as it stands in the Statute book. The rates as fixed by the Commission were to be the rates embodied in the bill. For an American instance of juggling with procedure in order to affect the chances of a tariff bill, see Taussig, *op. cit.*, p. 232; and for a discussion of the relative effects of secrecy and publicity in the "tariff hearings," the same author, "How Tariffs Should Not Be Made," in *Am. Ec. R.*, vol. i., p. 20.

[1] Grundriss, vol. ii., p. 636, cited Hollander, p. 1425.

is protected: but this is not necessarily the case; for it is possible to bring pressure to bear before the bill is ever introduced: it is possible to threaten wrecking tactics: it is possible to influence public opinion. If the government or the party leaders give in, it is easy to accuse them of dishonesty: but is not compromise a lawful thing? And just because a tariff is a complicated thing, and it is never possible to say *exactly* how far a particular rate is justifiable or not, it is impossible to say if in consequence of pressure a particular rate is raised from *x*/- to *y*/- that there must be a corrupt bargain.

These are difficulties of a political character. The problem is to determine how far both types of difficulty are capable of minimisation.

The first solution which seems to carry most support at the present time is, as already suggested, the appointment of some board or commission. Before discussing this particular solution, it will be as well to ask how far the traditional machinery is capable of being overhauled.

It may be argued that where there is a strong party discipline, so that a member who votes against his party or his government can be held up to the moral obloquy of his constituents, the dangers of insubordination on tariff matters do not arise. The member will "vote straight," and the draft bill will not be assailed. This contention is in part true, but the extent of its truth must not be exaggerated. In the first place, the member may be pressing the interests of his constituents, and so far from resenting his votes, they applaud them. Secondly, as Professor Lowell has shown, even in the case of the English party system, the cohesion is often more apparent than real, and private remonstrances to the whips have replaced open opposition in the house.[1] Thirdly, where a system of protective duties is in force in a democratic country, the government itself must be prepared to concede the demands of those who supply it with funds for election purposes, and the party may, therefore, use party discipline not against, but to push a policy which a disinterested mind would reject.

The second solution is *publicity*.—Here we are on safer grounds: for knowledge will at any rate give the opponents solid ground upon which to base their arguments. But knowledge of what? No government can afford to allow its

---

[1] Lowell, "The Government of England."

own internal dissensions to be bruited abroad ; it is a sound political rule that where party dissensions are openly discussed the fate of that government is already sealed. One is left, therefore, with the demand that the grounds upon which the government or the party leaders have acted shall be made known. This is no doubt useful, but since the same facts may be perfectly capable of serving as the basis of more than one policy, according to the standpoint adopted, the real position is not changed in essentials.

A third solution is impartiality in the collection of evidence, and completeness of information. It has already been said that the collection of evidence is properly a matter for experts. The complexity of modern industrial life, and the great volume of facts to be mastered, makes it desirable that, whether the tariff be drafted by a cabinet or by a committee of the legislature, the information upon which they work should be put through the sieve of impartial criticism.

This, however, still leaves the matter in essence what it was ; an honest difference of opinion is still possible, and so also the suggestion of improper trafficking cannot be disproven by showing that the information upon which the traffic was based was impartially collected. To go a step further, and allow the rate to be fixed by an impartial person, or body of persons, is to take the matter out of the hands of the politicians altogether, and raises separate problems of its own.

We come then to the conclusion that so long as the traditional method is adhered to, the only real safeguard that the community possesses is a high moral tone in the tariff-making personalities themselves. But it must be confessed that the dangers referred to can never be entirely removed so long as the tariff affects private interests, and so long as these interests attempt to safeguard themselves against loss by political pressure. In the last resort, dependence must be placed upon public opinion in refusing to tolerate misdemeanours and a low moral tone among politicians. In this, as in so many other social and economic matters, there is no short cut to perfection. Some such short cut is found in the demand for a body which, itself impartial, will be able to elaborate an impartial and scientific tariff. Let us first of all ask whether a scientific tariff is a possibility at all, then whether such an impartial body is capable of meeting the demands of the situation outlined above.

§ 16. In what sense can a tariff be said to be "scientific?" We may put the matter very shortly by saying that whilst science may throw light upon alternative methods of achieving a result, the validity of the end to be attained is not a matter upon which administrative and economic science throws any light at all. This can be seen at once by reflecting more fully than is usually done on the case of the German tariff. In what ways is that tariff truly scientific? Firstly, it was drawn up with great care, and was the subject of detailed discussion by experts, with a general and special point of view. It embodies, therefore, a very careful classification, and a very finely adjusted differentiation between the different species of the same genius of article; it grades the duty so as to embody the general principle of "the protection of national labour" (Schutz der nationalen Arbeit), *in concreto* the more finished goods receiving heavier protection than the less finished. Here we have already passed over from what is scientific to what is only capable of scientific justification *so far as its technical form is concerned*, for the principle that "national labour" should be protected is, when all is said, a pure assumption, and though it may be possible to devise rates which in all cases mean the survival of the domestic industry under the pressure of foreign competition, it by no means follows that this is the only principle which ought to be adopted, or which could be adopted. Difficult as the problems of classification and differentiation are, they are at any rate definite: but the question of rate making is far less so, and involves assumptions as to the end to be pursued upon which science is directly incompetent to express an opinion. Once the end is given, the actual methods to secure the end are, as stated, capable of rational defence; they may be held to be the best methods of attaining that end: but the end itself is not a scientific matter at all.[1], [2]

---

[1] If a series of products, *a*, *b*, *c*, enter into the making of the article, the protection the article itself should receive must be based on the protection accorded these raw materials, plus an amount sufficient to compensate for any higher conversion costs as against the foreign competitor, or sufficient to offset any other differential advantages possessed by the latter. This is a question of fact and method; but the assumption is that existing industries represent the best distribution of the national capital and labour, an assumption which may legitimately be questioned.

[2] *Cf.* Professor Emery, quoted in "Scientific Tariff-Making," p. 116 (speaking of the tariff board of 1909), . . . "We had supposed that we were called to the

Let us now ask what an imperial body of commissioners can do. They can be given power to (1) acquire information, (2) suggest, on the basis of this information, what the tariff ought to be, (3) actually to be given powers of sub-legislation.

Now these are three very different types of activity, and raise issues of a very different character.

(1) The provision of information is a skilled task, but even here there is a limit to what an impartial body can do, if it is to avoid being dragged into the arena of party conflict. To supply information presupposes questions to which the information supplies an answer. Hence the responsibility

---

modest even if difficult task of accumulating information for the officers of the Government, and we are somewhat aghast to find that in some quarters there is being attributed to us an alchemistic power for good or evil. Many economic theorists have attempted to find the philosophers' stone by means of which prices could be made high for those who wish them high and low for all those who wish them low. It would be a fine thing if the farmer could always get \$2 a bushel for his wheat and the working man pay only \$1 a barrel for his flour. It would be a fine thing if the manufacturer could always get \$5 per yard for woollen cloth and the tailor could put 3½ yards of it into a suit of all-wool clothes and sell it for \$5 with a handsome profit. Strangely enough, some people seem to suppose that such things are possible by Government action, and to be inclined to hold any Government responsible which does not accomplish it. It is because of these exaggerations that we earnestly beg every intelligent man to take a reasonable view as to what any tariff board or tariff commission can do or cannot do."

See also p. 129, . . . "At this point we venture to make the general suggestion that in the consideration of so important an innovation as the one here contemplated the danger of being deluded by easy catch phrases should be constantly borne in mind. It is not uncommon to hear statements to the effect that the tariff question should have a 'scientific solution,' or that a tariff should be made 'purely a business question,' and 'be taken out of politics.' Such statements are serviceable when their meaning is really understood, but they are too often misleading. It is true that in the collection of facts for any purpose the scientific method is of the utmost value, but in dealing with the tariff problem scientific accuracy is impossible, and a scientific solution of the tariff question in the sense of a permanently perfectly just tariff, suitable to all times and places, is obviously a dream.

"It is also true that the question is a business question, in that it should be settled for the best economic interests of the country, and should 'be taken out of politics' in the sense that schedules should be adopted or rejected with a view to their effect on these economic interests, and not with a view to some political advantage in the play of party interests. On the other hand, the tariff is much more than a business question. It involves to-day, as it has involved through centuries in the past a great problem of economic policy regarding which there have always been and always will be differences of opinion. Even if accurate facts be established which receive the assent of every voter in the United States, there would still remain a fundamental divergence of view as to whether on the basis of these facts the industries of the country should be accorded no protection, moderate protection, or high protection. This is a fundamental problem, which must be settled by the popular will as expressed through its chosen representatives, and in this sense the tariff is inevitably one of the great problems of political contention."

for the framing of the questions is a delicate matter, for questions can be so framed as to bias the answer straight away. But framing the answer is not always any easier than framing the question. Inquiries involving issues of policy are not the most suitable for an impartial body, since no answer that can be given is incapable of being disputed.

(2) There is no such thing as a tariff rate which must be valid under all circumstances. Consequently any rate is based on certain assumptions: and the validity of these assumptions is always open to dispute. Hence, if it is left to a board to proceed on its own assumptions, it cannot avoid being attacked by those who reject the assumptions. If a board is to be given power to frame a rate for adoption or rejection by the legislature, it ought never to be left in the air as to what the underlying principles upon which it is expected to proceed are, but its activities in this case are always subject to difficulty. The safeguard is that the legislature can reject the rate; but then the board is attacked for suggesting the wrong rate; or the legislature is attacked for rejecting the right rate. In either case the board is involved in politics, and ceases to be impartial. Its decisions on technical grounds may be better than those of a legislature, but that will not save it from attack.

(3) To give the board power to enforce rates would be to endow it with legislative power. This involves, in the first place, an interference with the legislature's power of taxation: in the second place, it will concentrate upon the board the *whole* responsibility for the policy involved. It is absurd to expect that there will be no dissatisfaction with the legislation of the board, and that there will be no agitation on the part of interests adversely affected. Such agitation will be perfectly legitimate: the rates fixed by the board may be admirably devised to carry out a certain policy, *assuming a certain ideal to be the desirable one*, but it is never the case that complete unanimity will be reached on such a matter. Consequently, the board will be in politics, the personality of its members will become a matter of public concern on other grounds than their technical fitness for the post, accusations of favouring this group or that cannot be avoided: and the non-political nature of the board will be a danger rather than an advantage, for in the event of the board's rates being disapproved, it will be more difficult to change

the composition of the board than it would be to change the composition of a parliamentary majority.

§ 17. Our next task must be the examination of some current achievements and proposals in the field of impartial tariff boards.

(1) **The United States.**—There were special features in the American situation which merit a passing word. The tariff occupies a prominent place in the controversies between the two historic parties: the jealousy of the "executive" power has prevented the full growth of those governmental institutions in whose hands the initiative in these matters usually lies in European countries: the short period of time for which the House of Representatives sits, and the consequent haste with which the tariff revision has to be carried out, are prominent features of the situation.[1]

It was the late President Roosevelt who first urged the appointment of a tariff board, in a presidential message of 2nd December, 1902,[2] but what he wanted was a committee of "practical experts" whose rôle was conceived as distinctly subordinate to the Committee of Congress.

The first practical step was taken under the Payne-Aldrich tariff of 1909; in order to assist the President to determine whether undue discrimination was practised against the products of the United States (in which case a maximum tariff was to be imposed),

"To secure information to assist the President in the

---

[1] *Cf.* Emery, *op. cit.*, p. 120, ". . . if there were any board or group of Government officials in existence who had devoted themselves solely to the question of the industrial effects of the tariff for a period of twenty years, as is the case in Germany and Austria, such investigations would probably not be necessary. Such officials would already be sufficiently familiar in a personal and practical way with the facts regarding costs and competition in the different industries to be able to report or advise. No such body exists in the United States. . . ." This does not mean that there did not exist any department collecting information as to foreign tariffs. Since 1820 the American Treasury department had been collecting statistics as to foreign trade, whilst the State Department also maintained a Statistical Department, part of the duties of which department since 1842 had been the collection of tariff changes in the tariff systems of other countries. In 1903 there was founded the Department of Commerce, to which these two Departments were transferred, now forming the Bureau of Foreign and Domestic Commerce in the Department, with a separate Division of Foreign Tariffs. See "Department of Commerce, Condensed History, Duties, etc.," Washington, 1913, pp. 111-117.

[2] "Presidential Address and State Papers," Statesman Edn., vol. ii., p. 616. See also the Logansport speech of 23rd September, 1902, in "Scientific Tariff Making," pp. 80-82.

discharge of the duties imposed upon him by this section, and the officers of the Government in the administration of the customs laws, the President is hereby authorised to employ such persons as may be required (§ 2 of the Act)."

It is fortunate that we possess several statements by the chairman of the board created under the authority of this section, Professor Emery, regarding the manner in which the board interpreted its duties.[1] As we have already seen, Professor Emery was by no means uncritical of "easy catch phrases." The board under him proceeded on the assumption—

(1) That continuity of information was much more valuable than the making of special tariff reports in view of particular tariff acts. He, therefore, began on the making of a tariff glossary or dictionary, which could be kept up to date once it had been started (p. 131).

(2) That since the tariff theory of the party in power was that the tariff should compensate for differential costs of production, the immediate step to be taken was an investigation into costs of production at home and abroad, but too much was not to be expected even here (113, 121).

In the course of its existence the board prepared reports on Schedule K of the tariff (the wool duties), reports on Canadian Reciprocity, on pulp and newspaper print, and hoped to cover the whole tariff by the end of 1914 (*op. cit.*, 294, Tariff Committee's Investigation). The self-imposed restrictions[2] on the activity of the board did not save it from attack and destruction at the hands of the Democrats when they commanded a majority in Congress. It disappeared in 1912, the Democrats refusing an appropriation.

From then until 1914, nothing was done, but in that year

---

[1] The following page references are all to the volume, entitled "Scientific Tariff Making," published in 1913 by the "National Tariff Commission Association," a voluntary association carrying on the struggle for a permanent tariff board. It is a valuable survey of the details of American agitation, although it is sometimes wrong as to European details, and some of the contributions display a rather ingenuous attitude. See also W. S. Culbertson, "The Tariff Board and Wool Legislation," in *Am. Ec. R.*, vol. iii., p. 59, *et seq.*

[2] Culbertson says that the Board "never intended to go beyond reporting facts, and it persistently refused, under urgent political demands, to give even an opinion of what rates it considered equitable and just." Taussig's comment, in view of later events, is interesting ("History, etc.," 6th Edn., p. 424), . . . "The Tariff Board was a Republican device. However excellent its work—and no competent observer would deny that it had thrown much needed light on the industries which it investigated—a flavour of partizanship remained."

the passage of the Federal Trade Commission Act enabled a further step to be taken. By §6 (h) of that Act, the Commission was given power—

To investigate, from time to time, trade conditions in and with foreign countries where associations, combinations, or practices, of manufacturers, merchants, or traders, or other conditions, may affect the foreign trade of the United States, and to report to congress thereon, with such recommendations as it deems advisable.

In virtue of this Act, the Federal Trade Commission subsequently issued a report on South American Tariffs.

It required the mental revolution caused by the European War to bring into existence the present tariff commission. Title VII. of the U.S.A. Revenue Act of 1916, §§700-9 provides for the organisation and the powers of a tariff board. The board was to consist of six members, appointed by the President, by and with the advice and consent of the Senate, not more than three of whom were to belong to the same political party, members of different parties to alternate as much as practicable.

The functions of the new body were defined as follows :—

> By §702. To investigate the administration and fiscal and industrial effects of the customs laws of this country now in force, or which may be hereafter enacted, the relations between the rates of duty on raw materials and finished or partly finished products, the effects of *ad valorem* and specific duties, and of compound specific and *ad valorem* duties, all questions relative to the arrangements of schedules and classification of articles in the general schedules of the customs laws, and in general to investigate the operations of customs laws, including their relation to the federal revenue, their effect upon the industries and the labour of the country, and to submit reports of its investigations as hereunder provided.
>
> By §703. The commission shall put at the disposal of the President of the United States, the Committee on Ways and Means of the House of Representatives, and the Committee on Finance of the Senate, whenever requested, all information at its command, and shall make such investigations and reports as may be requested by the President or by either of said committees, or by

either branch of Congress, and shall report to Congress on the first Monday of December of each year hereafter a statement of the methods adopted and all expenses incurred, and a summary of all reports made during the year.

By § 704. The Commission shall have power to investigate the tariff relations between the United States and foreign countries, commercial treaties, preferential provisions, economic alliances, the effect of export bounties and preferential transportation rates, the volume of importations compared with domestic production and consumption, and conditions, causes, and effects relating to competition of foreign industries with those of the United States, including dumping and cost of production.

Later sections provide for the power to compel witnesses to attend, for the transfer to the Commission of the Cost of Production Departments in the Bureau of Foreign and Domestic Commerce, and for the fullest co-operation with other government departments, including the transfer to the Department of Employés of other Departments at the request of the President.

The chairman of the commission was the distinguished writer on economics and tariff history—Professor Taussig, of Harvard.

The work of the commission in the period of time that it has existed is already such, both in volume and in quality, as to indicate that it is likely in the future to become the most important source of detailed and critical tariff literature to which the student of tariff matters can turn. What it concerns us especially to notice is that the functions of the commission are primarily regarded as advisory.[1]

(2) **Australia.**—Under the Australian Inter-State Commission Act of 1912, there is appointed by § 4 a commission of three members "of whom one shall be of experience in the law. It shall be a body corporate, with perpetual succession, and a common seal, and capable of suing and being sued." The appointments thereto are, in the first

[1] For full details of the work of the Commission, see the Annual Reports, and the summary in the *B.T.J.* of 31/1/18, pp. 129-30, 20/3/1919, pp. 377-8, and 7/4/21, p. 369, *et seq.*

instance, for a period of seven years, every person so appointed being eligible for re-appointment. The Chief Commissioner is to enjoy a salary of £2,500 per annum, the others a salary of £2,000.

The main function of the commission is the regulation of common carriers, but, incidentally, by § 16 (Part III., Investigations), the commission "shall be charged with the duty of investigating, from time to time, all matters which in the opinion of the commission ought in the public interest to be investigated affecting—

(*a*) The production of and traffic in commodities.

(*b*) The encouragement, improvement, and extension of Australian industries and manufactures.

(*c*) Markets outside Australia, and the opening up of external trade generally.

(*d*) The effect and operation of any Tariff Act or other legislation of the Commonwealth in regard to revenue, Australian manufactures, and industry and trade generally.

(*e*) to (*h*). . . .

(*i*) Bounties paid by foreign countries to encourage shipping or export trade.

. . . .

(1) Other matters referred to the commission by either House of the Parliament, by resolution, for investigation.

By § 45 of the Act an annual report must be made, and this must be submitted to parliament; by § 49 hearings may take place in public or in private, "but it shall only take evidence in private where it considers that it is desirable in the public interest that the evidence should be taken in private." By § 50 the "Chief Commissioner may, by writing under his hand, summon any person to attend the commission at a time and place named in the summons, and then and there to give evidence and to produce any books, documents, or writings in his custody or control which he is required by the summons to produce."[1]

(3) *The Suggested Tariff Board for Special Industries in the United Kingdom.*—In 1918 the "Committee on Commercial and Industrial Policy" issued an interim report "on

[1] For details as to the Tariff work done by the Commission see Official Year Book of the Commonwealth of Australia, No. 11, pp. 1194/5.

certain Essential Industries." These are the industries which are now generally known as "key" or "pivotal" industries . . . "which . . . are essential to national safety as absolutely indispensable to important British Industries." (Report, p. 2, Cd. 9032). A second differentia of an essential industry was the being "supplied before the War entirely or mainly from present enemy sources or from sources under present enemy control." We need spend no time on the detailed proposals for the several products which come under this head, what concerns us is the general policy of the report.

The committee premise (1) that the qualitative rank of different industries may change from time to time, some industries may cease to be of great national importance, "and, on the other hand, new essential industries may emerge in the future."

(2) ". . . the causes which have rendered British trade dependent upon the present enemy countries for the supply of particular commodities are by no means uniform and the measures required to promote the various branches of industry involved may vary from time to time. The problem will also be affected as new economic and political conditions arise and changes occur in the international situation."

The report recommends the creation of a permanent board "charged with the duty of watching the course of industrial development, and of framing from time to time, when necessary, either on its initiative, or on the application of interested departments or persons, detailed schemes for the promotion and assistance of industries of the pivotal type. This organisation should take the form of a board of commercial and industrial experts, associated with whatever department of state is entrusted with the care of the commercial and manufacturing interests of the country, and represented in Parliament by the political head of the department. It should be a statutory body with a permanent chairman, and with power to appoint such secretarial and technical staff as it may from time to time require. It should issue an annual report of its proceedings, and such special reports as it may think expedient, which reports should be presented to Parliament; and it should be a statutory condition, that except upon recommendation, no state assistance by way of grant or subsidy should be given to any industry or branch of industry. It should work in close relation and co-operation with the department of Scientific and Industrial Research, and all other departments of the state interested in the development of industry, and it should always be cognisant not only of naval and military requirements as they affect industry, but *also of the current political relationship of this country, since changes in these respects may obviously bring to light fresh 'essential' industries.*"

The detailed functions of the board were to include (§ 31) investigation of price policy of state-assisted industries, investigation of the British character of assisted firms; regulations of import licenses, investigation of complaints that protection "by way of tariff or prohibition" had been improperly used, and complaints as to labour conditions in state-assisted industries.

The final report of the same committee (Cd. 9035) broadened somewhat the cases in which protection was given, but reasserted, even more emphatically than the previous report had done, what body it desired to place in charge of the delicate and difficult task of apportioning such protection. § 255 of the report says ". . . it is likely that the admission of the principle of protection, even for a limited and carefully considered list of industries, will give rise to a widespread demand for similar assistance from other industries which will exercise an amount of political pressure which it may be very difficult to resist. We accordingly recommend—

"(*a*) There should be established some strong and competent board to examine into all applications from industries for state assistance, and where a case is made out to frame proposals as to the precise nature and extent of the assistance to be given, whether by protective tariff duties or in other ways. The board, in our opinion, whilst working in co-operation with the Treasury and the Board of Trade, should be independent; it should not be charged with any administrative duties; it should report direct to the crown, and its reports should be laid before Parliament immediately on being made; and it should be its duty to place before Parliament its views as to any proposals for tariff legislation which it may not have itself formulated.

"The functions of the Special Industries Board, the establishment of which we recommended in our report on essential industries, might be merged in those of the board which we now recommend.

"(*b*) As a guiding principle for the work of the board (which should have full powers to call for evidence and to inspect books) it should be laid down that the industries for which state assistance of any kind can be given should be such as are of importance to the maintenance and development of the economic strength and efficiency of the nation, or for the supply of potential military requirements."

Sub-sections (*d*) and (*e*) of the same § 255 went on still further to define the principles on which the board was to proceed: protection was to be the last resort, and labour conditions in the industry were to be regulated and safeguarded.

The board has not yet come into existence: for our purpose it will be sufficient to ask whether the scheme thus outlined is a satisfactory one in view of what was previously said. The intent of the committee is excellent: the members do their best to avoid what is undoubtedly the danger in all tariff schemes—the real danger of political pressure. The only point to which criticism can legitimately point in the scheme in its final form is that the report does not sufficiently distinguish between the functions which are really political and those which are really scientific in nature. Thus, the choice of the industries to receive protection is ultimately a political matter; as will be realised the moment the phrase "economic strength and efficiency of the country" is investigated. In the absence of definitely evil social conditions in the industry, *any* industry can be said to form part of the nation's "economic strength," and the choice, so long as it has to be made on these grounds, involves a certain *ideal* upon which it is absurd to expect a "scientific" judgment, which will please everyone. The board may be in a position to review any questions as to the *how much*, as to the degree of urgency as between two definite cases: what it cannot do, as a scientific body, is to determine the validity of different national economic ideals.

The second point on which the report seems weak, is the non-realisation of the necessity of defining carefully the constitutional relations between the board and the political system. It is no doubt easy to draw analogies between such a board, and other quasi-independent bodies of commissioners, and to argue that the standing of the commissioners will be such as to cause their decisions to be respected. But this is only so if the board is confined to matters which are definitely objective in character, so long, in other words, as politicians take on their shoulders the political issues involved. So long as the board confines itself to definite issues of method and form, its decisions can be accepted even by those who as a matter of principle reject the whole policy on which they are based, provided such opponents can attack the policy of the government which, by accepting certain principles of national organisation, has invited the board to frame methods embodying these principles in definite forms: but the board definitely assumes political shape as soon as it evolves principles of its own, and will find itself in conflict with any government which refuses to accept these principles. It will then appear as if it were supporting the opponents of this government, and it will cease to be the impartial scientific body which the framers of the report evidently desired it to be. It is extremely desirable that the detailed proposals should emanate from a body which by its composition and permanency will command the respect even of the opponents of the Government, but nothing is gained by concentrating on such a body criticism for policy, which it will not be in a position to rebut without entering directly into the political field—the very last thing the framers of the report would desire, to judge by their statements.[1]

§ 18. We have now passed under review the areas to which tariffs apply, the bodies which create them, and the questions which a scientific treatment of these matters raises. Our next problem is an investigation of the technical nature of the tariffs themselves.[2]

---

[1] It may be noted that what is called the "Tariff Commission" in *Canada* is a group of Cabinet Ministers, touring the constituencies with a view to ascertaining public opinion.

The task of proposing changes is sometimes given to semi-official bodies, such as the Valuation Committees, which, in various European countries, establish the average values of imports. This method of delegation appears to obtain in Spain.

[2] I have not thought it necessary to rediscuss the problems which a diplomatic body as tariff-making authority raises. Those difficulties are best illuminated by concrete example: cases in point being the German and Austro-Hungarian conferences mentioned in the text above in relation to the whole issue of customs unions.

NOTE TO § 17, SUB-SECTION 3, p. 61.

Since the publication of the final report of the Balfour of Burleigh Commission we possess further schemes referring to the subject of a board of the kind suggested in the report. The text of the Government's Anti-dumping Bill, which was not proceeded with, contained proposals for the creation of a "Trade Regulation Committee" composed of the President of the Board of Trade, the Financial Secretary of the Treasury, the Under Secretary of State for Foreign Affairs, and the Secretary of the Department of Overseas Trade; certain important permanent officials and ten persons, "being members of the House of Commons, nominated by the House to be members of the committee." Subject to some slight exception, all orders made by the Board of Trade were to be submitted to this committee, its approval being necessary before the order thus made became valid. The second schedule to the Act set out the orders which required such sanction.

This was, it must be frankly stated, a thoroughly bad scheme, since it provided neither for the necessary freedom from political influence, nor for the presence of experts not in the service of the Government.

The bill introduced into the House of Lords by Lord Balfour of Burleigh himself follows closely the lines with which we are already familiar. The bill dealt partly with dumping, partly with state-aid to "Essential Industries," which the bill defined as being "industries supplying commodities which are essential to the national safety as being absolutely indispensable to important industries carried on in the United Kingdom, and which are entirely or mainly supplied from countries outside the United Kingdom" (§ 2 (3)).

Schedule 1 of the Act created a council of from five to nine members, with one member to act as chairman on appointment of the President of the Board of Trade, to hold office for five years. The duties of the council were to be—

(1) To watch the course of industrial development, and to advise the Board of Trade as to promotion and assistance of special industries.

(2) To examine proposals from government or private persons bearing on the subject.

(3) To issue an annual report.

CHAPTER II.

THE TARIFF AS A WHOLE—CLASSIFICATION OF TARIFFS.

§ 1. A FIRST glance at a collection of tariffs is apt to leave the student with no very clear idea of the principles upon which these are constructed. Yet certain broad differences may be observed, and it is the purpose of this chapter to examine and comment upon these, with a view of elucidating the respective disadvantages of each type.

§ 2. The tariff, in the first place, is a complex instrument usually laying down certain general principles of administrative policy, and at the same time providing the authorities who are to administer the law with detailed information as to the commodities and the rates which provide the subject matter of their duties. A clear line of distinction emerges according as the object is to impose restrictions on the outward movement of goods or on the inward movement of goods—*i.e.*, between import tariffs and import duties and export tariffs and duties—the phrase "tariff" in this connection implying primarily a systematic collection of such duties. It is possible to combine these groups into one and the same instrument or to provide separate instruments. *In fact* both import and export tariffs are combined in the same legislative instrument, although internally subdivision is of course practised. In the modern world the import list is of far greater importance than the export list, and in what follows in the next few chapters, the import tariff is primarily had in mind: a separate section will be devoted to export duties.

§ 3. It is usual to classify tariffs according as to whether they are revenue tariffs or protective tariffs. As a principle of classification this procedure suffers from the fact that a tariff may be intended both to raise revenue and to protect domestic capital and labour. Nevertheless it indicates an important point—viz., that a tariff which is intended primarily for revenue purposes does usually show some difference of form as compared to tariffs which either neglect the fiscal aspect or combine it with some other purpose. The *substantial* difference lies in the choice of the commodities selected, for there is no reason to suppose that the articles most fruitful of revenue must necessarily be those most dangerous to domestic capital and labour. This difference in practice manifests itself in the larger number of articles included in the protective or partly protective tariff, although the range of articles included is not necessarily a complete test of the purpose of the tariff, for it may be considered more desirable to impose moderate duties on a large number of articles rather than heavy duties on a few commodities, to proceed, to use a useful analogy, on the basis of the principle of *equal* sacrifice rather than on the basis of the principle of *minimum* sacrifice.[1] But if one asks wherein the difference of form consists, the answer to be made is that the revenue tariff is built up on the basic principle of a single rate on each commodity included in the tariff, whilst non-revenue tariffs or tariffs partly protective have as their basic idea the principle of more than one rate on each article included in the tariff. The normal rate per commodity in the revenue tariff is a single rate ; in the others, a multiple rate.

§ 4. Turning to the classification of types of tariffs based on the normal number of rates per article, one gets the following scheme :—

(1) Uni-linear or " single-line " tariffs, based normally upon the principle of one article one rate.

(2) Bi-linear or " double " tariffs, based upon the principle of one article two rates.

(3) Multi-linear tariffs, based normally upon the principle of one article three or more rates.

Such a classification as this seems at first sight so formal that no practical use could be made of it. And, in fact, the tendency in the discussion of classification of type has been rather to emphasise the political aspect of the matter—*i.e.*, to make the problem turn on the question whether the tariff

---

[1] That is, the *aggregate* loss of satisfaction may be less if a few articles only are dutiable, though this loss may be inflicted on a narrow circle of consumers, and these may suffer heavily : whereas it may be thought better to inflict a smaller but a more equal loss on a larger number of persons. *Cf.* taking a large slice of the income of a few persons with a small slice of a large number.

embraces only the decision of the autonomous legislative body which elaborates it, or contains externally determined elements as well. That is, the classification has turned on the autonomy of the tariff rates. Confused with this discussion is another on the form that the bi-linear tariff can take. Thus, Dr. Grunzel, [1] whose classification has been followed by Higginson [2] and Fisk,[3] speaks of "single rate tariffs" (Einheitstariff), which, "as coming into existence purely through internal legislation, are also known as autonmous tariffs." But, as he himself points out, Belgium, since 1868, has incorporated changes in the rates produced by bargaining into the single tariff, and this thus ceases to be purely autonomously determined. He goes on to speak of general and conventional tariffs and maximum-minimum tariffs, as two separate types. As a matter of fact the latter is, genetically regarded, an extension of the autonomony principle to the bi-lateral tariff. This has been clearly seen by van der Borght, who applies the phrase "double tariff" (Doppeltarif) to the maximum-minimum tariff. "Its nature does not depend upon the presence of two tariffs side by side, but in the circumstance that both tariffs have been determined by the autonomous legislature." It is clear, if autonomy is to be the classification principle, that the single tariff may or may not be an example of an autonomously created tariff, whilst the maximum-minimum tariff always is. But the addition of *this* principle of classification, though it draws attention to important aspects of the tariff, leads to difficulties as soon as one begins to get tariffs built up on the multi-linear principle. There is certainly a connection between the form of the tariff and the purposes which it is intended to carry out; but this connection leads rather to a parallelism of specialised forms within the lines set forth above, than to complete dissociation of each type from the others: [4] a parallelism which leads in practice to closer approximation than is generally supposed.

---

[1] System der Handelspolitik, p. 396, *et seq.*

[2] Higginson, Tariffs at work, p. 3.

[3] International Commercial Policies, Secs. 56-58.

[4] That is to say, whilst definite reasons can be assigned for preferring one of these two forms to the other, granted the desire to attain certain ends, yet at the same time these ends are themselves subserved under wider ends. The bi-lateral form of tariff is the technical response to these more general ends, within which there may be further specific differentiation.

The problem which has to be faced in practice is the necessity for making concessions, and yet the undesirability of giving the negotiators a perfectly free hand. The tariff as it leaves the hands of the legislator is the autonomous tariff. Now, a country may refuse to negotiate at all, or any concessions made as the result of negotiations may be completely generalised—*i.e.*, substituted *in toto* for the original rates. In either event there will only be a single line tariff. But within these extremes two other solutions are possible.

(1) Negotiations may take place on the basis of complete freedom, so that no limit to the reductions which might, under given circumstances be made, is present. When such reductions, or series of reductions, as negotiated with different countries and embodied in separate treaties are reduced to formal order, and are extended freely or in virtue of the most-favoured-nation clause to a large number of trading nations, there is consequently obtained a second tariff, the conventional tariff, which is so-called because all its elements are contained in different treaties; the autonomous tariff, which formed the basis of negotiations, still applying to countries with whom no arrangements have been concluded. In this way the bilateral tariff takes one particular form—that known as the general conventional tariff. The net effect of such an arrangement is to tie the contracting party for a series of years, in so far as the conditions stipulated in the conventions are concerned. Any changes which, on politico-economic grounds, may necessitate alterations in the tariff duties, can *only* produce changes in the conventional tariff, and can be applied to all countries only after the treaties then in existence have been denounced: a procedure which can only be effected as a rule after the elapse of a certain period of time, and which further involves a delay between the time of denunciation and the time at which the treaty ceases to have force.

(2) Again, negotiations may take place on the basis of granting to a power a reduction the extreme range of which is already laid down in the autonomous tariff itself. This explains van der Borght's use of the expression "double tariff" in this connection. The legislature fixes *two* rates as a normal practice, whilst in the previous case the legislators fix one rate and the diplomats another. In order to prevent concessions taking a course disastrous to what is conceived to be the interest of particular industries, the diplomatic

negotiations take the form only of concessions of this predetermined minimum. Now it is important to notice that, if the diplomatic instrument expressly guarantees *a definite* minimum rate, the freedom to change this rate during the duration of the treaty disappears as effectually as the freedom to change a conventional rate in the cases considered above. Hence, it makes a considerable difference whether the minimum rate in force at any time only is granted, whilst freedom to change this minimum is left unimpaired—*i.e.*, whether both rates *remain* autonomous or whether a *given* rate, which happens to be *the* minimum inscribed in the autonomous tariff, is granted. The maximum-minimum tariff at all times limits the reductions which may be granted, although it need not at all times allow this minimum to be varied as freely as the maximum can be varied. This latter point depends upon the terms of the treaties concluded, and on any legislative enactments defining the forms and terms of treaties to be adopted.

But in addition to these general and guiding principles the complications have to be dealt with. To both types of tariff there may be added rates based upon other principles and in such numbers as to virtually constitute a normal third class of rates. Finally, there are ways in which the two main types of bi-lateral tariff may be brought into closer touch with one another, so that the hard line of distinction becomes blurred in practice.

§ 5. Such a third class of rates may be represented by preferential rates granted by a mother country to its colonies, or a colony to a mother country and its sister colonies. If such preferential rates are sufficiently numerous—*i.e.*, if they tend to become "normal" in the sense of applying to a large number of areas and a large number of articles, such preference rates form collectively a preferential *system*, and the tariff in which they are included, a double rate or treble rate tariff. Such in fact is the Canadian tariff of 1907, which contains normally three rates—a general rate, an intermediate, and a preferential rate.[1] The general and intermediate rates

[1] The tri-linear tariff has now also been adopted by Australia. The 1920 Tariff Bill has three rates, a Preferential, an Intermediate, and a General Rate. It was stated by the Commonwealth Minister of Customs, on introducing the Bill, that the Preferential rates, in addition to being granted to the United Kingdom, might be granted in whole or in part to certain portions of the Empire. The intermediate

correspond to the maximum-minimum rates and the preferential rates applicable only to the United Kingdom, and certain portions of the Empire form a third class, also autonomously determined. In fact, however, the Canadian tariff is to some extent a fourth-rate tariff, since, in virtue of the French Convention Act of 1908, No. 28 of 1908, there exists a rate group of rates *lower* than the intermediate tariff rates, which, by virtue of the most-favoured-nation clause, have been extended to a wide group of countries.[1] By the creation of such a conventional group of rates the autonomous principle of the tariff is of course to some extent lost.

The position of preferential rates to colonies or granted by colonies to each other and their mother country is intermediate between the true normal rate and the rate which is clearly abnormal or exceptional.[2] These exceptional or differential rates will be treated in a separate chapter, and it seems advisable to postpone the discussion of colonial preferences also.

§ 6. Discussion of the conventional portions of the Canadian tariff brings one to the methods by which the two main types of bi-lateral tariff can be made to approach one another, remembering that one is the maximum-minimum, the other the general conventional tariff.

(*a*) The first method is for the countries adopting the maximum-minimum system, nevertheless to grant, as the result of negotiations, rates *below* the minimum fixed by the legislature in the original tariff.[3] In this respect the history of those nations which have adopted the maximum-minimum form of tariff is significant. Canada, as was seen above, has to some extent adopted this mixed form of tariff. The same is true of many of other countries as well. This form of tariff

---

rates might be used as a basis of reciprocity treaties, with foreign countries or with other portions of the Empire. Nevertheless the Commonwealth was precluded by the Bill from concluding arrangements with a Dominion or a foreign country if the "economic conditions" in such country or dominion "are substantially of a lower standard than those prevailing in Australia." See *B.T.J.*, 20/5/20, p. 690. The tariff as a whole is printed as a supplement to the *B.T.J.* for 22/4/20, without the text of the Bill, however.

[1] Colonial Import Duties, 1915 (Cd. 8094) Introductory Notes, pp. liv.-lv Statutes of Canada (10th Parliament) 7 and 8 Edw. VII., Vols. 1-2, 337-8 for complete list of French products enjoying the benefit of a Special Tariff.

[2] For the discussion of differential duties see Chap. 7; esp. § 2.

[3] Such conventional rates may nevertheless require the sanction of the Legislature in those cases where treaties involving a change in the law must be submitted.

was adopted first by Spain in the tariff of 1877, but the autonomy of both rates broke down in considerable measure during the discussion of commercial treaties.[1]

The same is true of Russia, Greece, and even France. As van der Borght points out the maximum rate in some cases really becomes a penal rate (Kampftarif), the effective rates for normal purposes being the minimum rate, and the conventional rate (Russia, Norway).

(*b*) The general conventional tariff may be modified by the insertion of minimum autonomously determined rates. This has been done in the case of the German tariff of 1902, coming into force in 1906. § 1 of the customs and of December 25, 1902, para. 2 runs as follows :—

In regard to the undermentioned cereals, the tariff duties shall not be reduced by way of convention to lower rates than are set forth in the following Schedule :—

Rye, 100 kilos, ...	5.00 marks.
Wheat and spelt, . . .	5.50 „
Malting barley, . . .	4.00 „
Oats, ...	5.00 „

The question of whether the inclusion of this provision changes the nature of the German tariff has been answered in the negative by a German commentator.[2] "It requires no further analysis" he says "to show that the provisions of § 1, para. 2 are completely different to those of the French double tariff. The organisation of our tariff system on the basis of the double tariff was expressly set aside in the bill on the ground of the overwhelming disadvantages of the system. The terms of § 1, para. 2 are on the contrary, as the Minister of the Interior expressed it to the Reichstag committee, 'a solemn explanation of the federated governments as to what they hope to support and carry in regard to greater protection of agriculture through higher duties on the conclusion of commercial treaties.' The terms of the legal enactments resting on the basis of the draft is according to this only an instruction to our negotiators which will lose its importance as soon as commercial treaties are concluded

[1] Van der Borght, *loc. cit.* A convenient summary of some of the matters discussed in his chapter will be found in the U.S.A. Monthly Commerce Reports, March, 1904.

[2] Trautvetter, Das neue deutsche Zolltarifrecht, p. 10.

with the countries relevant from the standpoint of cereal imports. Furthermore, this legislative provision, like any other, is capable of repeal. Had the wishes of the governments to carry the four minimum rates not been or only partially been realised, the consequent acceptance by the Federal Council and the Reichstag of an agreed tariff treaty—*i.e.*, of a new law—would have rendered the provision in so far nugatory as the new treaty went below the terms of the established minimum rates."

This quotation is useful as bringing out some of the difficulties attending the discussion of the classification of tariffs. It is of course quite true that the general form of the German tariff is unchanged by the inclusion of this one fixed rate, and it is also true that in so far as in negotiations the rate actually agreed upon is below the minimum fixed, and this departure is subsequently agree to by the Reichstag, that the tariff is in spirit a general conventional one. The decision turns upon the question as to what is really meant by the maximum-minimum tariff. The purely autonomous nature of this tariff is already departed from where the minimum rate is included in the tariff treaty as a binding rate, and this is the point referred to above when it is said that the matter will " lose its importance as soon as commercial treaties are included." In this sense of conventionalising certain rates, it is important to notice that France has consented to a modification of her claim to a purely autonomous tariff, even in quite recent years. Thus, by the convention of Oct. 20, 1906, between France and Switzerland, Art. 2 " the commodities of Swiss origin or manufacture enumerated in schedule B annexed to the present convention imported directly from Switzerland shall be admitted into France at the duties paid in the said schedule, all additional duties included. Articles not included in the said schedule will be admitted into France at the duties of the minimum tariff. In the event of one of the duties included in the said schedule B being raised, the new duty shall not be applicable to goods of Swiss origin or manufacture until twelve months after notification given to the Federal Government." [1] And although the French chambers refused to ratify the Franco-Swiss Convention of 1892, which would

[1] Pallain 4, p. 664. See also Franco-Russian Convention of 16-29 September, 1905, Art. 1, which conventionalises certain rates of duty on Russian goods mported into France. (Annex A to treaty.)

have reduced the rates on sixty-two articles of importance to Swiss producers, yet, after the Franco-Swiss tariff war of 1892-95, a new arrangement was come to comprising twenty-nine articles, "twenty of which the Customs Commission of 1892 had already accepted, so that, in reality, the convention of 1895 comprised only nine new articles." An examination of the detail, therefore, shows that in fact the two great types of bi-lateral tariff tend to approximate.

§ 7. So far only the principles have been examined, but the formulæ by which these principles are expressed in practice are well worthy of study.

(1) When the maximum-minimum system is examined, two methods of expression are found. In the first the normal procedure is to set out rates side by side on the schedule and to enforce their application by some general rule. This is the French system. Thus, the law of 11th January, 1892, which first introduced a complete maximum-minimum tariff into French customs practice, lays it down that—

"The general and minimum customs tariffs relative to imports and exports shall be established conformably to schedules A and B annexed to the present law. The minimum tariff may be applied to goods, the produce of countries where French goods enjoy corresponding privileges, and to which the minimum tariff is applied."

This passage must, however, be read in connection with a previous Act, that of 29th December, 1891, which prolonged certain treaties then in force "à l'exception de clauses portant concession d'un tariff de douanes applicable à des merchandises determinées," and then went on in Art. 2 to state that—

"The government is authorised to apply the minimum tariff in whole or in part to the products or merchandise of the countries which actually enjoy the conventional tariff, and who will consent on their side to apply to French goods most-favoured-nation treatment. This concession may not be accorded without reservation by the French Government of the right to determine by notification twelve months in advance."

What, therefore, is conceded is, as a Belgian commentator puts it [1]—"That France accords for a year the enjoyment

[1] Allard, La réforme Douanière en France: Ses conséquences pour le commerce France-Belge, 1909.

of her minimum tariff to those countries which grant her in exchange most-favoured-nation treatment: the law states also that France must give notice a year in advance to the country from which she has decided to withdraw the favour of her minimum tariff, but this obligation in no way implies that France should restrain herself even during the year from modifying as she desires the rates inscribed in this tariff." As has been seen this completely independent attitude has been somewhat modified in practice.

When one comes to examine the actual schedules, however, it is not the case that the rates laid down in the maximum and minimum schedules respectively are always different: the rate may be the *same* in both schedules. Moreover, the *number* of rates per tariff-unit or commodity is not always identical in the two cases: finally, there is not necessarily always a double rate—*i.e.*, there may be no minimum rate at all. Thus, some interesting side issues arise.

(*a*) The presence of duplicated rates need not occasion any surprise. Thus, in some instances—*e.g.*, raw materials—it is obviously desirable to maintain complete freedom of import, and, therefore, no differentiation is thought possible. But the inclusion of the free rate in the minimum column ties the country in question. Public policy again will explain why commodities injurious to health, or the subject of a state monoply should lead to prohibitions, which necessarily affect all countries. Thirdly, in the case of duties imposed primarily for revenue purposes, again similarity of rates is obviously the most convenient policy in general.

(*b*) When the French tariff of 1910 is carefully examined it will be noticed that in certain cases [1] the maximum tariff rate corresponds to more than one minimum rate—*i.e.*, that the minimum column is more specialised than the maximum. The reason for this is not far to seek. As will be shown in more detail in a later chapter, there is unanimity among all authorities on the point that specialisation considerably increases the protective effect of a tariff. The effect of this step is, therefore, to confine within narrower limits the benefits to be derived by the extension to other countries of the minimum tariff.[2]

---

[1] See for instance Nos. 524 and 536: on the other hand, No. 495 contains four rates in the maximum column and only one rate in the minimum.

[2] See, however, below (2) (*c*), p. 80.

(*c*) The French tariff of 1892 contained in the classes dealing with live animals, animal produce, farinaceous food, Colonial produce, and (to a very small extent) elsewhere a large number of rates which were only contained in the maximum tariff. At the same time the articles admitted free are mentioned in both cases. Now the *direct* effect of embodying the same rate in both schedules or embodying it in only the maximum is the same: no discrimination is practised. Nevertheless there is an important distinction: since, by excluding the given rate from the minimum column, no obligations of any kind are incurred, as against foreign countries. It is a reversion to the completest possible autonomy. An inclusion of a rate in the minimum column only still leaves the position as against countries not enjoying minimum tariff treatment completely free, but does to some extent hinder the position as against treaty countries, where a minimum rate, for however short a time, has been conventionalised.

The second form of maximum-minimum tariff is that in which only one column of rates is shown, and in which a general formula gives the treatment to be accorded to goods in the case not specifically treated. It is immaterial whether the minimum tariff rates are fixed and the maximum rates derived from these: or whether the maximum are fixed and the minimum derived therefrom. The United States Payne Aldrich tariff of 1909[1] may be cited as an example. The law enacts—

> "That on and after the day following the passage of this Act, except as otherwise specially provided for in the second section of this Act, there shall be levied, collected, and paid upon all articles when imported . . . the rates of duty which are by the schedules and paragraphs of the dutiable list of this section prescribed, namely:—
>
> (Here follow the duties.)
>
> "The provisions of the dutiable list and the free list of this section shall constitute the minimum tariff of the United States.

[1] Tariff Acts passed by Congress 1789-1900. H.D. Vol. 219, No. 671, 61st Chap., 2nd Sec., p. 700.

> "2. That from and after the thirty-first day of March, 1910, . . . there shall be levied, collected, and paid on all articles when imported into the United States or into any of its possessions . . . the rates of duty prescribed by the schedules and paragraphs of the dutiable list of section 1 of this Act, *and in addition thereto twenty-five per centum ad valorem: which rates shall constitute the maximum tariff of the United States.*"[1]
>
> (Hereupon follow the terms and conditions upon which the President is empowered by proclamation to admit the products of other countries under the terms of the minimum tariff.)

The same procedure is followed by Chile in the law of March 1, 1916, Act 23.[2]

> "The present tariff shall be regarded as the minimum tariff applicable to the products of countries which grant to imports from Chile most-favoured-nation treatment. The President of the Republic may apply the rates increased by 25 per cent. as a maximum tariff to products of other countries."

The Brazilian law of March 19, 1900, permits of a doubling of the minimum rate to form a maximum duty.[3]

An interesting example of both methods—*i.e.*, building up a maximum schedule from the minimum rate or the minimum rate by reductions from the maximum—appearing in one and the same instrument (itself constructed on the single rate basis as leading principle) is afforded by the U.S.A. Dingley tariff of 1897,[4] § 3. This section first empowers the President to negotiate for the conclusion of commercial agreements with countries producing and exporting to the U.S.A.,

> "Argols, or crude tartar or wine lees crude; brandies or other spirits manufactured or distilled from grain or other materials; champagne and all other sparkling

---

[1] Italics mine.

[2] T.S. No. 36.

[3] Kelly p. 899. It must be observed that the power in this and the preceding case is discretionary. Whilst we have thus a maximum-minimum tariff in form it is possible to regard these tariffs as single line ones with surtax powers. No use seems to have been made of the Brazilian clause.

[4] Tariff Acts, etc., p. 601.

wines; still wines and vermuth; paintings and statuary."

And in the event of these negotiations being successful, fixes a new scale of duties which shall thereupon and thereafter become applicable.

Furthermore, the section goes on to provide that if a government (or colonies of such government) "producing and exporting directly or indirectly to the U.S.A. coffee, tea, or quin, . . . or any such articles, imposes duties or other exactions upon the agriculture, manufacturing or other products of the United States, which, in view of the introduction of such coffee (etc.) into the United States, as in this Act hereinbefore provided for, he may deem to be reciprocally unequal or unreasonable, he shall have the power, and it shall be his duty to suspend by proclamation to that effect, the provisions of this Act relating to free introduction" of the articles aforesaid, and during such suspension a defined scale of duties shall come into operation.[1]

(2) The complications which have been discussed in connection with the maximum-minimum type of tariff find their analogies in the case of the general-conventional class. (*a*) The first difficulty is presented by the Belgian type of tariff in which conventional changes are substituted for the

[1] The introduction of the phrase "reciprocally unequal and unreasonable" suggests at first that the clause is intended to penalise countries which levy higher duties on the products of the United States than on those of other countries, that the penalty duties set up under the section are in fact duties resembling the European Surtaxes, a fuller treatment of which is contained in Chapter VIII, § 4, below. But this assumption is incorrect. The penalty duties were intended to foster reciprocity with the United States, that is, to lead to counter-concessions, and their application was not intended to be conditional on a comparison of the duties levied on American products and those of other countries, but on a comparison of the duties levied on the products of the United States, and those levied by the United States. The duties were, in other words, bargaining duties. The very similar list of articles included in sections of the Act of 1890 was introduced with the preamble "That with a view to secure reciprocal trade with countries producing the following articles," etc. For some analysis of the difficulties of this conception of unfairness in relation to the most-favoured-nation clause, see U.S.A. Tariff Commission Report, Reciprocity and Commercial Treaties, p. 421.

It may be added that the Tariff Act of 1897, from which this "argol clause," as it is usually called, is taken, conferred in section 4 a general power on the President to conclude reciprocity treaties, in which reductions up to 20 per cent. of the duties named in the tariff were to be permitted, and also allowed goods to be transferred to the free list, if they were the natural products of such countries but not of the United States, "or shall provide for the retention upon the free list of this Act during a specified period, not exceeding five years, of such goods, wares, and merchandise not included in said free list therein. . . ."

autonomous rate. Does this give one a true general conventional tariff? Reflection will show that this is not the case. There is certainly present the element of negotiation, which differentiates this tariff from the purely autonomous tariff, but since the changes are completely generalised, the tariff ceases to be a pure bi-lateral tariff. In *form* it is single line tariff, in *spirit* it *approximates* to the general conventional type, but must not be confused with the latter. Had it not been customary to confuse uni-lateralness with autonomy, no difficulty would have arisen, and the confusion primarily arose because of an insufficient appreciation of the variety of forms which the same general form of tariff can take.

(*b*) The true general conventional tariff must be a bilateral one, for the second line of rates is only the systematic formulation of the concessions obtained as a result of bargaining by a series of foreign countries. It naturally follows that (1) there is no need for a second rate to appear throughout the whole range of duties, since no country may have found it possible (or less probably) worth while to obtain a concession on some commodities; (2) the conventional rate need not be lower than the general rate, since a substantial gain is obtained even if the general rate is conventionalised, for this binds the country conceding the rate for a definite period of time; so that *stability* in tariff rates is assured even if no *reduction* can be obtained.

(*c*) An investigation of a general conventional tariff will also show that the *number of rates* per commodity in the two tariff columns do not necessarily agree. But in this particular case the effect of such greater specialisation will be very different from the effect in the maximum-minimum tariff type. Here the greater specialisations in the conventional column represent concessions obtained as a result of bargaining and, therefore, register a net gain to the country which has obtained them, whereas, in the former case the specialisation, being autonomously arrived at, is necessarily determined primarily in the interests of the home industries. Even in the case of the general conventional system, however, the increase in the extent to which specialisation is *ab initio* practised (*i.e.*, in the general tariff) has seriously reduced the advantages of the whole system to freer trade relations.

§ 8. There remains over a matter of the greatest importance and difficulty—a survey of the respective advantages and disadvantages of each type of tariff, the nature of which we have been investigating. We must, as far as possible, dissociate this discussion from the different question as to the advantages or disadvantages of commercial treaties as such—itself a matter of great difficulty. From the standpoint of this chapter we must regard the issue as a threefold one. (1) Considerations attaching to the standpoint of home industry and commerce. (2) Considerations arising from the nature of inter-state trade relations. (3) Administrative conveniences and inconveniences.

§ 9. From the standpoint of internal industry and commerce it seems as if the advantages were all on the side of the autonomous tariff, whether of the single or bi-linear type. For both of these types of tariff allow the legislature the greatest measure of liberty in fixing the degree of security to be afforded to home industry. And, moreover, in the absence of conventionally bound rates this protective effect can be varied at will: so that unforeseen events can be promptly responded to. M. Méline, the Frenchman most responsible for the introduction of the maximum-minimum tariff in France in 1892, thus expresses himself on this point—"What one had not foreseen, what one could not foresee in 1860, what one never can foresee when one ties oneself with treaties, is that in the course of their execution there may arise events which upset all the conditions of production, and which entirely destroy the efficacy of customs tariffs which are contained therein." [1]

Moreover, the adjustments can be made gradually. Since the legislature is at all times free to change a rate, it will not be necessary to alter violently the whole range of duties contained in a tariff, as is inevitably the case when the rates are conventionalised and the termination of treaties forces a revision of the whole scale. It must be confessed that this liberty of action is not always taken advantage of; the autonomous tariff of the U.S.A.[2] is generally revised as a whole, but here party rivalry plays the same rôle as a treaty does in other countries in producing a rupture in stability. The result is a paralysing uncertainty. So far from the autonomous

---

[1] R.E.I., *January*, 1907. "Les Traités de Commerce," p. 19.

[2] In fact the reciprocity element in the U.S.A. tariff policy has not been of great importance; in spite of the form which some of the tariffs have taken, it has in fact been really a single line one.

régime being more unstable, the exact contrary may be urged to be the case because changes need not be concentrated into a relatively short time, as, indeed, M. Méline expressly urges [1]—

"Her régime (*i.e.*, the French) . . . is not for all that one of commercial instability. We sustain the contention that it offers in reality, more real stability than the treaty régime . . . if our commercial conventions are theoretically only of very short duration, as a matter of fact they are renewed each year, and are consequently indefinite. . . . This is so true that we have not, since 1892, changed our economic system (written in 1907): the modifications introduced into our tariff do not exceed forty, unimportant for the greater part, and from which it is necessary to deduct five reductions. During this period, the principal countries of Europe have twice already placed in question their entire customs system and have altered it in respect of thousands of articles; to arrive at these alterations they have had to engage in negotiations which have lasted several years, delivering over industry and agriculture to an uncertainty which completely paralysed business. We ask in all sincerity, on which side do stability, continuity, and security for commercial transactions lie?"

Finally, under either form of the autonomous tariff, there is a greater degree of certainty for any one single industry or allied group of industries. They can bring pressure to bear on the legislature and obtain the protection they desire, without suffering anxiety on the score that what they have been granted will be swept away in whole or in part in the shape of concessions made to some other country—concessions the losses from which fall on them, whilst the benefits go to others.

§ 10. Inter-state commercial relations, however, are such that some concessions must generally be made to powers who have it in their hands to injure domestic industries by retaliation. Now this makes directly against the purely autonomously determined single-line tariff. A country having, by the adoption of this type of tariff, to offer concessions may indeed use other instruments than retaliation to bring pressure

[1] *Op. cit.*, p. 34.

to bear on unfriendly countries:[1] but its task would be greatly eased if it could maintain a measure of freedom in the fixing of its own rates and yet be in a position to offer a *quid pro quo*. This the bi-lateral autonomous tariff allows it to do. The practical problem then is to choose between a maximum-minimum tariff and a general conventional one. Both are flexible to some degree; which is the more flexible of the two? Which, in other words, is the better bargaining instrument? Now we must remember that flexibility is not the only desideratum of a good tariff, so that any answer given this question ought not to form the sole criterion. But, in fact it is very difficult to decide between the two.

There is, firstly, the purely technical problem of whether diplomatic negotiations proceed more easily when the full extent of the concessions available are known than when they are not known: when, in other words, the issue seems to depend solely upon the diplomatic ability displayed. It may be urged that the absence of a definite limit affords the diplomatist only illusory freedom. He is in any case bound to take note of the wishes of the home industrial and agricultural interests, and untoward concessions may lead either to a rejection of the treaty (or, if this is impossible, as it usually is, though, as in the case of the Franco-Swiss treaty in 1892, it is not unknown), to a weakening of the government, and the subsequent denunciation of the treaty at the earliest possible opportunity. Is anything lost, it may be asked, if instead of a diplomatic game of hide-and-seek being played, a frank avowal of the limits to which a country is prepared to go is laid down *ab initio?* In the hands of a skilful diplomatist there is even an advantage in being thus able to present a definite offer. There is considerable force in van der Borght's thesis[3] "that it is less the enunciation of the limits of the concessions than their too one-sided extent and their inelasticity which proves a hindrance to tariff negotiations." This still leaves us with the question of whether this *inner*

---

[1] As Schilder points out, "Entwick-lungs Tendenzen der Weltwirtschaft," p. 81, *et seq.*, direct diplomatic pressure whilst a tariff is in the process of elaboration may be as useful as subsequent bargaining. But, as the late Sir L. Malet used to insist, even an autonomously-determined revenue tariff provided certain opportunities for bargaining. See "Memoir of Sir L. Malet," p. 81*n*, 106*n*.

[2] This is now clearly grasped in the U.S.A.; also, see extract from 2nd Annual Report of the U.S.A. Tariff Commission, in *B.T.J.*, 20/3/19.

[3] *Op. cit.*, p. 443.

rigidity of the maximum-minimum tariff can be overcome? Our author thinks that neither of the two possible defects "is essential to the idea of a maximum-minimum tariff." It must be confessed that in this respect the general conventional tariff, which, even if it does not in fact allow all concessions, does oppose less effective barriers to any *single* concession, thus has a permanent advantage over the other. But as to the absence of effective inducement to counter concessions, it must be pointed out that the practice of raising the "general tariff rates preparatory to bargaining, virtually acts in the same manner as insufficient margins" between the maximum and minimum rate. We must beware in fact of attributing to a particular form of tariff a difficulty which is largely due to the general tendency towards such a raising of the tariff rates as to make negotiations difficult under any circumstances. Nevertheless on an impartial view, given an equal desire to negotiate, the general-conventional tariff seems on the whole to offer fewer difficulties.

But considerations of diplomacy are not the ultimately determining ones. It is significant that so few of the countries which have adopted the maximum-minimum tariff have been able to adhere to it strictly. This not merely applies to cases where, as in Brazil and Chile, the maximum rate is intended more as a penal surtax than as a true normal "general" rate—but also in cases such as those mentioned in § 6 of this chapter. The fact is that the ultimate matter is economic strength. In those cases where any economically weak or dependent country [1] with a maximum-minimum tariff, is bargaining with another power whose situation is more favourable in respect of conditions (*a*)-(*d*) below, whose power to retaliate is, therefore, also greater, concessions can be obtained by the latter, beyond the limits fixed by the tariff of the former, simply because, in the long run, the autonomy ideal of the former gives way to its economic necessities. It is true that even here, resisting power is not necessarily limited by economic strength, the psychological factor must be independently estimated. Nevertheless *in general* the fact

[1] Meaning by this (*a*) a country whose industries (including agriculture) are dependant on specialised areas of sale or (*b*) dependant for raw materials on a specialised source of supply, or (*c*) are on such a level of efficiency measured by cost per unit of output as to find sale in all areas difficult, or (*d*) are limited in their production to commodities for which there exist easily available alternative sources of supply or easily available substitutes.

remains that the bi-lateral autonomous tariff seems only applicable where the country adopting it offers a really valuable market. Here *any* difference in the tariff rates on the maximum-minimum scales is a consideration. Further, where a considerable loss is to be expected if all concessions were cut off, and where the country to whom concessions beyond the minimum are denied is unable to return to inflict proportional losses, then, in the event of a tariff war, though both sides will no doubt suffer, the loss falls more heavily on the latter. Under the conditions laid down, in the event of resistance being offered, therefore the maximum-minimum tariff of a country tends to be successful only against nations weaker than itself, or on much the same level of productive efficiency. In bargaining with a country stronger than itself, it represents merely a "first approximation" to the final result. The maximum-minimum tariff seems, therefore, a doubtful weapon for weak powers to use, and it by no means follows that a strong power will be unable to gain its ends without the use of it, as the case of Germany sufficiently attests.[1]

§ 11. On political grounds, the autonomous forms of tariff offer, as we have just seen, distinct advantages. From the administrative standpoint, a double-line or multiple-line tariff involves the creation of safeguards against the use by the exporters of a country not entitled thereto of the benefits of the lower tariff rates. In effect, such administrative difficulties are to some extent overcome by the extension to large numbers of third states of the advantages of the lower rates by means of most-favoured-nation clauses. Nevertheless an elaborate system of consular invoices, certificates of origin, and so on has had to be developed. In general one may say that the administrative difficulties increase more than in proportion to the number of rates in a tariff. Thus, the multiple tariff if applied to a first class commercial nation would offer very great difficulties in enforcement. The reason for this is not far to seek. A large proportion of the goods of modern export industries are themselves produced from raw materials and components

[1] Or with it, as the case of the threatened rupture between the U.S.A. and Canada after the passage of the Payne Aldrich Tariff of 1909 shows, though here political conditions in part explain the anxiety of the U.S.A. to come to a settlement. See O.D. Skelton in "Canada and its Provinces," vol ix., pp. 220-224.

not of indigenous origin. Hence the definition of the "country of origin" is an extremely vexatious matter. The larger the number of distinctions drawn—*i.e.*, the greater the number of rates—the greater the difficulties of adequate determination. Thus, the multiple tariff suggested for the United Kingdom, "Colonies, Allies, neutrals, and enemies," would offer considerable administrative difficulties (besides bearing no necessary relation to economic importance, and thus accentuating the difficulty of negotiating reciprocal concessions). These difficulties are not necessarily insuperable, but they are nevertheless real. From this point of view, the single-rate tariff is certainly the most advantageous. As we will have in a later chapter to deal with the devices which administrative technique has evolved, here only the problems which all differentiation creates need be noted.

CHAPTER III.

The Internal Form of the Tariff.

(1) Classification and Its Problems.

§ 1. In the previous chapter the external form of the tariff has been examined, and reasons were assigned for the divergencies of type which practice reveals. If we now turn our attention to the *internal* form of the tariff, we shall find divergencies to be much greater in this respect. Our first task must, therefore, be the reduction of these diverse forms to something like a consistent plan.

§ 2. Let us approach the problems of classification [1] by answering the question, what is the purpose of classification in tariff matters? First of all it is a guide to the inquirer as to where he is to find the commodity and its rate in which he happens to be interested. This is a minor, but still one object of classification: and one that, as it happens, cuts across other purposes for which classification is desirous. For the swiftest and most convenient classification from this point of view is simply an alphabetical enumeration of the commodities. Next comes the convenience of the legislator. Tariffs as legislative enactments undergo discussion, and hence there is considerable utility in grouping together rates or commodities between which there is some logical nexus, so as to facilitate parliamentary procedure thereon. It is quite obvious that an alphabetical classification is here by no means so obviously desirable as was the case before.

Lastly, the tariff represents an attempt to carry out certain objective purposes, of which the most important are the raising of revenue, and the achievement of certain industrial

[1] The problem of classification is generally treated as if it were a question of deciding under what rate a particular commodity is to be put (assimilation), or what the *precise meaning* of a given phrase (definition) is. These problems I treat separately in other chapters.

reactions deemed desirable in the national interest. Classification, it is obvious on reflection, must be governed by these purposes, and hence we are faced not with mere problems of arrangement as such, but with the adjustment of means to ends. Modern tariff classification acquires all its importance from this fact, and the point is not always clearly recognised that the classification actually adopted may be inconsistent with the objects which it is hoped the tariff will achieve.

§ 3. Under modern circumstances and in most countries the revenue aspect of the tariff falls behind the protective or industrial aspect. Now, if we ask what broadly this aspect involves, we get the twofold answer that a tariff is partly an instrument for safeguarding the home or internal market, partly an instrument by means of which the home market of some country is to be opened, or, at any rate, prevented from being closed. But the range of commodities is nowadays extremely great, and the divergencies of interest between different groups of producers and consumers have grown correspondingly. These forces have resulted in a growing need for complexity in the form of the tariff, and their technical expression is an extreme specialisation of commodities and a great multiplicity of rates.

The problems of specialisation will receive attention in a later chapter, when the factors making for specialisation, will again be examined in more detail. It is desirable to insist on the fact that growing specialisation—*i.e.*, an increase in the number of separately distinguishable or distinguished commodities *implies also an increase in the number of separately distinguishable rates.*

This, which is a matter of the greatest consequence, is not always clearly realised.

Anticipating somewhat, let us discuss a concrete case. At first sight it appears indifferent whether commodities are divided up into various classes, or whether a given number of rates are determined upon, between which the various goods are distributed. And so long as the number of classes either of rates or of goods are small, this is, on the whole, true [1]—in either case we get what is technically known as a "class rate." Thus, if we divide up all goods into foodstuffs,

[1] On other grounds there may be disadvantages, and in any case classification on the basis of rates will not yield the same tariff form as classification on the basis of articles.

raw materials, semi-manufactured articles, and completely manufactured articles rated at a given rate for each class, there could be four classes and four rates; or four rates completely exhausting all goods between them.

Now suppose specialisation to take place on a large scale: so that not only are different kinds of foodstuffs, etc., distinguished from one another, but elaborate specialisation on the basis of alcoholic content and so forth is adopted. It is quite obvious that we can no longer start with the rates and divide the goods up among them: on the other hand, to make this greater specialisation effective, rates must also become extremely specialised. In other words, that particular form of tariff which starts by classifying the rates and dividing up the goods among them is inconsistent with great specialisation: but so also is any other classification on the basis of the goods themselves which is influenced by a desire to limit the number of rates, in the supposed interest, let us say, of simplicity. It follows from this that whilst the absolute number of articles may, under such a scheme, be large, and whilst an increase in the number of rates will tend to greater possibilities of specialisation, yet each step towards *further* specialisation can only be at the expense of simplicity, so that the *limit to further specialisation* comes earlier with some classifications than it does with others.

§ 4. *One* test then of a tariff classification is the ease with which it permits of specialisation, but this is by no means the only question to be asked about classification. Let us revert for a moment to the division of commodities we have already mentioned into four groups—*i.e.*, foodstuffs, raw materials, semi-manufactured, and completely manufactured articles. It will be obvious on reflection that these categories really overlap—*i.e.*, that the division is made partly on the basis of *use*, partly on the basis of *finish*. It is obvious that considerable difficulty may be experienced in deciding whether some commodity is or is not a raw material, whether it is or is not a completely manufactured article. If the rates are class rates a decision on a point of this sort may make a great difference to the duty to be paid. If we think of the constant struggle of interests between the users of the particular commodity in question and the makers thereof, or the makers of substitutes therefor, it is obviously desirable that we should avoid, as far as possible, classifications which make the problem of assigning commodities to their appropriate category more difficult than in any case with the complexity of modern commercial life it is likely to be. This matter again will be resumed later.[1]

§ 5. A further point arises in the same connection. Ultimately, of course, one has to get down to the things themselves. But it is obviously convenient to sub-class the main divisions. As soon as we do this, we realise that some classifications require the same commodity by content to appear in two or more different groups. Again let us revert to the previous classification. Let us take such a commodity as wood. Imported in the shape of logs it would come under the raw material category, sub-category forest products, let us say. It would again, as dressed or sawn timber, come under the same category in the semi-manufactured group, and again under the same category in the completely manufactured group. Hence, to find *all* the possible rates to which timber in one form or another would be subject one would have to look in at least three different categories: whereas, were all the articles grouped under the basis of natural affinity we should look for it only once.

§ 6. These are difficulties of classification with which logicians have made us familiar. We now come to a subject of more technical nature. What is to be the *basis* of the classification in the sense of what we are to classify? The natural answer to give is to say "why, the commodities, of course." But this is just the difficulty. So long as we confine ourselves to large and undifferentiated items, there is no great difficulty, but this is exactly what modern tariff framers distinctly try to avoid. They specialise, and as soon as specialisation is adopted the question arises, are we to take the differentiated elements as the unit of classification, or shall we take the complex as the unit? If we build up on the former basis we shall treat each *rate* as a unit; on the later basis we shall take each associated complex of rates as the unit. Now this is a matter of some practical importance, as it may lead to wrong inferences being drawn. The tariff of Bolivia contained, in 1914,[2] no less than 3,587 separate tariff numbers

---

[1] It is to be noted carefully that the objection here raised is influenced mainly by the association of this particular classification with the idea of a uniform rate in the supposed interests of simplicity.

[2] Kelly, 1914, p. 864, *et seq.*

or units of classification: that of Peru contained 3,418 tariff numbers.[1] On the other hand, the U.S.A. tariff of 1913 contained only 657:[2] the German tariff of 1902[3] contained 946. Are we, therefore, entitled to draw the conclusion that these South American tariffs present a higher degree of specialisation than those of Germany or the United States? By no means; for, if we look into the matter we shall find that, whereas the South American tariffs associate one rate with one tariff number or unit of classification, those of Germany and the United States, on the other hand, treat the differentiated complex as one tariff entity or number. Hence, the number of ratings or units into which the tariff is divided for classification purposes is only a very rough guide to the degree of specialisation.

§ 7. If we cannot conclude from the number of "ratings" to the number of rates, neither can we conclude from the number of ratings to the number of separate articles enumerated. That this is so is due to the existence in many tariffs of so-called "blanket clauses" which lump together into one number a large collection of miscellaneous commodities, defined either by enumeration, unknown ("not otherwise provided for"),[4] and so on. An example from Canada may suffice:—

No. 453. "Telephone and telegraph instruments, electric and galvanic batteries, electric motors, dynamos, generators, sockets, insulators of all kinds, portable vibrators, such as Bee pedestal vibrators . . . adapted for scalp or body massage, electric douches, electric apparatus, n.o.p., boilers, n.o.p., and all machinery composed wholly or in part of iron or steel, n.o.p., and iron and steel castings, and iron or steel integral parts of all machinery specified in this item; boilers for hot water heating . . . 15 per cent., 25 per cent., $27\frac{1}{3}$ per cent." It is obvious that we are here merely dealing with a "class rate" incorporated into a tariff based in general upon a different principle.

§ 8. At this stage it will be best to turn from general principles to a consideration of classification in more detail.

---

[1] *Ibid.*, p. 1031, *et seq.* [2] *Ibid.*, p. 804, *et seq.*

[3] *Ibid.*, p. 337, *et seq.*

[4] Mr. J. H. Higginson, in his valuable "Tariffs at Work," p. 34, has been led into some ambiguous remarks on this point by not clearly expressing the distinction drawn above.

The subjoined table may help to give a survey of the whole position.

TARIFF CLASSIFICATION.

- Tariff Classification Based on
  - Rate
  - Article
    - Formal (Alphabetical)
    - Substantial
      - Material-Origin
      - Content
      - Use
      - Degree of Finish

      (With or without further sub-division and/or uniformity of rate within the class.)

§ 9. The two indispensable features of a tariff are a rate and an indication of the article or articles to which that rate is applied. But if we look at a modern tariff we shall find, as a rule, a good deal more than this. The units to which the various rates apply, whether these units are simple or complex, are generally numbered consecutively. Again, the principle of classification is generally made clear by the groups into which the articles are divided and again subdivided, being expressly enumerated and again arranged under differentia. In this way, by the creation of tariff numbers, tariff schedules, or tariff classes, reference is facilitated. But it is a mistake to think that these formal aids to the eye and the understanding are the *essence* of the classification. A real principle of classification may run through a tariff even though at first sight the tariff seems completely formless. Thus, the Argentine tariff containing 104 classes, nevertheless does not number the articles in these classes. On the other hand, whilst the Roumanian and Russian tariffs show consecutive tariff numbers, they do not show classes or sub-classes *formally*, although an inspection of the tariff will show in both cases that there is a principle of classification—*i.e.*, affinity of origin—running through them.

The next point, having uttered this note of warning against over-hasty conclusions, is to examine in more detail the scheme of classification set out above.

---

[1] In cases where a translation is being used, the greatest caution is necessary in drawing conclusions. An alphabetical arrangement in the original tongue may appear to be no classification at all in the translation—*e.g.*, Belgian Tariff.

§ 10. (1) **Classification on the Basis of Rate.**—This is one example, and a very interesting one, of the class rate. The basis is the rate to be paid, and the goods are distributed among the various rates. The result is, of course, that the degree of specialisation is limited because exact adjustment is impossible. But nevertheless a tariff built up on this basis may attain a fair degree of complexity, as witness the following article 2 of the Ecuador tariff of 1912 :—[1]

Art. 2. For the collection of import duties merchandise shall be divided into the following classes :—

1. Articles of prohibited introduction.
2. ,, free of duty.
3. ,, subject to 1 Centavos per kilo, gross weight.
4. ,, ,, 2 ,, ,, ,,
5. ,, ,, 3 ,, ,, ,,

—and so on, there being altogether 38 classes, with a flat rate for each class varying between 1 centavo and 60 sucres per kilo. "The method of dividing articles into classes and assigning to each class a specific rate of duty dates back to November 1, 1885 (law of August 22). At first only 8 classes were provided, but the number was increased to 9 in 1886, 11 in 1891, 15 in 1897, 17 in 1904, and, finally (in 1906), to 38 classes. With such increase in the classes the maximum rate of duty was raised." [2]

(2) **Classification on the Basis of Article.**—(a) *Formal Classification.*—Side by side with some obvious deficiencies the alphabetical classification offers some distinct advantages. It prevents the grouping together of commodities bound by a real affinity—at any rate if consistently applied—and it causes a maximum of dispersion from the standpoint of discussion. On the other hand, for practical purposes it offers the plain man what he wants—a short cut to the commodity he is interested in without more ado—and it is not inconsistent with great specialisation if that is thought desirable, nor with extreme simplicity of rates on the other hand. For a tariff

[1] Kelly, p. 986 ; T.S., No. 34, South American Countries, p. 194, *et seq.*

[2] T.S., No. 34, p. 196. See also "Customs Tariff of Venezuela" (Kelly, p. 1095), Art. 1, which provides for nine classes of rates, between which the commodities are divided : and "South African Customs Tariff Act," No. 26, of 1914 (Class III., 25 per cent. *ad valorem*, and Class IV., 3 per cent. *ad valorem*). For a reclassification of the South African Tariff based on articles and not on rates, see "Official Year Book of S.A." No. 1, 1917, p. 495. *et seq.*

based in principle on one rate only, such as is the Chinese tariff (which represents a uniform *application* of a 5 per cent. *ad val.* rate), the alphabetical form is indeed the obviously convenient form of classification. On the other hand, the Belgian 70 odd tariff numbers with a very much larger number of articles, which is also alphabetically arranged, contains some specialised rates.[1]

(b) *Classification on the Basis of Affinity.*—Before dealing with the examples of each class a short comparative discussion of these various types may be useful. Of the four, the degree of finish, which most nearly approximates to the formal or external pattern, appears to be the least desirable because, apart from the difficulties which are set up when it is associated with a class rate (which may make a classification question a very serious matter when the class rates diverge greatly), anything like an elaboration of degrees of finish may cause a great dispersion of ratings over the tariff, which seems to me to be undesirable. But as a principle of sub-classification *within* a schedule it may play a very useful rôle.

§ 11. When the other three are compared with one another, it is to be noted that—

(1) If the basis of material-*origin* is chosen, it is possible to combine together all the articles coming from the same parent stock, but there will arise the difficulty of articles containing two or more components; whilst articles of different origin, but serving the same end, will be grouped separately.

(2) For the greater part, classification on the basis of content will lead to much the same scheme as (1), but (*a*) it is possible, if *this basis* is chosen, to group together articles of dissimilar origin but common content—*e.g.*, margarine made of different raw materials, (*b*) classes of "mixed content" fit in logically with the classification, but, just as (1) above, it dissociates articles fulfilling the same end, but of different content—*e.g.*, iron bedsteads from wooden ones.

(3) If the basis of common purpose or use is adopted,

---

[1] The alphabetical classification was also the form adopted for the various tariffs of the German customs union. The basis of the system was the Prussian Tariff Law of 1818, which by § 6 formulated the principle of a single tariff rate on all commodities. The import tariff schedule, apart from the free-list class, divided up the dutiable articles into 67 groups alphabetically. (Text of Act in Jastrow, "Handelspolitik," vol. i. of "Textbücher zu Studien über Wirtschaft und Staat," p. 25, *et seq.*) In 1840 the Zollverein tariff contained 43 classes; it was "the simplest tariff on the Continent" (M'Gregor's evidence before the Select Committee on Import Duties, 1840). By 1902 the number of ratings had risen to 387, but the alphabetical basis was still retained.

articles of dissimilar origin will go together, but here there arises the possible difficulty of articles serving more than one end. This applies more particularly to the less specialised commodities.

(4) When any one basis is chosen as the general principle of classification, any one of the others can be made to serve as the principle of sub-classification within each main class.

(5) In practice it is hard to find a tariff based on one consistent principle, practical convenience being naturally considered more important than logical symmetry. Quite apart from the *general* scheme adopted, however, "marginal cases" have to be dealt with in special ways which require particular treatment in a later chapter.

Turning to the practical aspect, let us first see to what extent the tariffs of various countries are broken up into "classes."

§ 12. TABLE I.

Country.	No. of Main Classes.	No. of Sub-Classes.	Tariff Ratings.
Canada,	..	11	767
France,	4	34	654
Germany,	19	86	946
Italy,	..	19	472
Japan,	..	17	647
United States,	..	14	657

This table suffices to show the extraordinary diversity prevailing in the classification scheme adopted:[1] the tendency for the tariff ratings to reach an absolutely high figure is not necessarily accompanied by an equal growth in the number of schedules or classes. It is, moreover, extremely difficult to define precisely what the basis of classification in practice is.

The German tariff is clearly the most ambitiously conceived. Of it a German commentator says:[2]—"The tariff seeks to group commodities on the basis of economic affinity. This is achieved by placing together, so far as possible, the products of industries which are regarded as allied because they produce or use the same or similar raw products, or work up half-

[1] But, as is pointed out by De Leener, "L'unification des Régimes Douaniéres," in *R.E.I.*, vol. vi. (Oct., 1912), p. 62, there is a fair degree of unity due to conscious imitation of one country by another—*e.g.*, Greece has adopted largely the French basis, Austria-Hungary the German, "dans diverses de ses grandes parties"—*i.e.*, sub-classification. See also references given in above article to the Congre s at Mons in 1905.

[2] Trautvetter, "Das neue deutsche Zolltarifrecht," Berlin, 1905.

manufactured products made out of such raw material. In general the raw materials themselves are not to be found in the groups arising in this way. Rather do the vegetable and animal raw materials appear in the first, the mineral raw materials in the second section of the tariff. . . . If, therefore, the remaining sections—3-19—yield a picture of individual industries through a totalling up of all their products from the simplest to the most elaborated, yet, as a rule, raw materials would be sought there in vain. On the other hand, the first and second sections do not exclusively treat of raw materials." The German tariff is, therefore, ostensibly based, partly on degree of finish and partly on the use to which articles are put; the raw materials being specifically sub-divided on the basis of origin. The French tariff again follows on much the same lines. The French tariff is based on four main heads—"animal products," "vegetable products," "mineral substances," and "manufactures." But whereas, in the German tariff, the 19 main classes are really operative classificatory factors, the French tariff is really built up on the 34 sub-classes without further formal subdivision: of which classes 18-34 fall under the head of "manufactures." As might be expected with so large a number of classes falling outside the last caption, the line of division between manufactures and non-manufactures is somewhat arbitrary. Thus, the elaborate scales of rates for wire come under "class 17," metals, a subdivision of "mineral substances," whilst chemical manures (class 18 "chemical products") come under "manufactures." The basis of classification varies, either origin, as in the two previous cases, or common use, as in class 24, yarns, or class 25, "tissues." The extent to which the system adopted by these two tariffs is conveniently constructed can be tested, to some extent, by the degree of dispersion involved. Such a test is made difficult without elaborate analysis by the fact that the manufactured derivative is of course given very often a name which does not recall the original raw material: it is useless to look only at "wood" in the alphabetical index, for "furniture" may be a separate entry. In this particular case the French tariff shows "woods" in class 11, furniture in class 25, wooden houses in class 31; whilst in the German tariff there are only two classes—"forest products" and "manufactures of wood."

The Canadian and American tariffs (which very closely resemble one another) show more clearly the principle of associating the manufactured commodity with the raw material from which it derives. So for instance the Canadian tariff group 5, "pulp, paper, and books," group 8, "metals and manufactures thereof." Group 9, "wood and manufactures thereof" (which includes furniture, No. 519: but lumps in furniture of "iron or other material," and certain wire and other goods strictly belonging to group 8). Both tariffs, however, contain schedules built up on other principles as well—*e.g.*, U.S.A., schedule A, "chemical oils and paints" (internal arrangement alphabetical), which is based partly on content and partly on use or purpose; schedule H, "spirits, wines, and other beverages," which is clearly based on use. (These schedules form also groups 6 and 4 of the Canadian tariff, though their content is not the same.)

§ 13. It will be obvious from what has already been said that the construction of these tariffs is based upon somewhat conflicting principles. Further analysis reveals, moreover, the fact that the diversity of products has left a residuum of commodities which cannot be subsumed under any of the categories established, so that there emerges a class of goods presenting no further analogy with one another than the fact that it has been found impossible to classify them elsewhere.

Such "miscellaneous" classes are to be found in a large number of tariffs. As examples we might give the following:—

TABLE II.—"MISCELLANEOUS" CLASS.

Country.	No. of Class.	Official Description.
Australia, ...	XVI.	Miscellaneous.
Bulgaria, ...	XXX.	Manufactures and articles not enumerated in the above categories of the tariff.
Canada, ...	Group 11.	Miscellaneous.
France, ...	XXXIV.	Manufactures of various materials.
Italy, ...	XVIII.	Miscellaneous articles.
New Zealand, ...	XVI.	Miscellaneous.
Sweden, ...	XVI.	Articles not elsewhere mentioned.
Switzerland, ...	XV.	Articles not otherwise mentioned.
United States of America, .	Schedule N.	Sundries.

§ 14. It was pointed out in § 11 that if the basis of origin were taken, articles of mixed content would be difficult to classify, but that if the basis of content were taken, a class of mixed goods would fit logically into the texture of the tariff. Such classes are, in fact, to be found in a certain number of tariffs—*e.g.*, France, class XXI., "various compounds:" whilst classes such as "yarns" or "tissues," based on the idea of use, naturally make mention of commodities of mixed components. The problem of adjusting the *duty* on these mixed articles is a matter of the utmost complexity, as will be shown in detail in a later section.[1]

§ 15. The tariffs so far mentioned do not exhaust the variety of type which concrete reality presents. An interesting class not hitherto mentioned, combines classification on the basis of article with classification on the basis of *rate*. This can be done theoretically either by starting from groups of rates, and then associating under each rate articles possessing a degree of affinity in content, use, etc., or by classifying the articles on the basis of the affinity selected, and then sub-classifying them under the class rate which they will have to pay. Any example of the second of these alterations is afforded by the tariff of Costa Rica, which dividing the tariff into 10 classes, mainly on the basis of *content*, again subdivides the articles comprised therein on the basis of the rate to which they are subject. Such a tariff may be conceived of as consisting entirely of "blanket clauses" ranged under the principle of affinity. It shows also, what is important to remember, that there are no sharp lines of cleavage between the various kinds of tariff from the classificatory point of view; *in fact—i.e.*, starting from either end of the scale, it is possible to find intermediate types which partake in some degree of the nature of both. In the perfected tariff, the blanket clause represents a survival which is really inconsistent with the principle of specialisation upon which it is nominally based. From the standpoint of the class-rate tariff, such blanket clauses and their association with degrees of affinity represent a stage in the evolution towards higher specialisation.

[1] In Germany, see also Sub-class of Class I., "Products of the Food Industries not included in Nos. 1-197 of the Tariff"; Sub-class G of Class 4, "Chemical and Pharmaceutical Products not Elsewhere Enumerated." These classes represent an intermediate stage; they are miscellaneous, but confined to a definite range of commodities.

§ 16. In this chapter we have, however, only skirted the complexities of the subject. It has been assumed that the commodities or entities to be included in the tariff were given and we were merely considering the questions concerning their ordering or arrangement. But, in fact, we are not entitled to regard these entities as an unchanging number. What is the position of entities not expressly mentioned in the tariff? Are they free from duty or not? What is to be the position of mixed commodities? Again a most difficult problem is raised by the question, almost metaphysical in its bearings, of the relation of parts to wholes. All these are questions, which, although not purely problems of classification, stand in close relation to these. Again, what happens when a classification is disputed? This is a question of administration which will be reserved for a later stage. At the risk of prematurely disposing of some of the points raised, the others will form the subject of the next chapter.

[1] Kelly, p. 774.

CHAPTER IV.

THE INTERNAL FORM OF THE TARIFF.

(2) FREE GOODS AND PROHIBITED GOODS.

ASSIMILATION AND MIXED GOODS.

§ 1. WHEN goods cross the customs frontier of a country, two different views may be entertained as to their liability to pay duty. It may be held that in principle all goods whatsoever are liable to pay customs duties (unless specifically exempted), whether these goods have been expressly mentioned or not; whilst, on the other hand, it may be laid down that only goods expressly mentioned in the tariff, and those only, shall be liable to pay customs duty, whilst the rest are free without further question. It is in this way, that there is created the problem of the "non-enumerated goods" with which the first part of this chapter will be occupied.

§ 2. The first of these principles obviously springs from an attitude of mind specifically Protectionist, and we shall call it the Principle of Inclusion; the second from an attitude which cannot be classed as "free trade," though it has some analogies therewith; it may be termed the Principle of Exemption. But the bare setting forth of these two principles does not give one any clue to the treatment to which non-enumerated goods are in detail subject under the principle of inclusion, nor to the form in which the principle is enunciated in the tariff or customs law itself.

The *form* in which the principle is enunciated can take two main shapes—(1) The governing principle is formally expressed, with or without instructions as to the technical treatment to be applied, in the preliminary articles of the tariff or in the customs law as distinct from the tariff.

(2) The non-enumerated commodities may be treated

as a unity and classified under an appropriate class head in the body of the tariff itself.[1]

It will be obvious on reflection that these modes of expression are not incompatible with one another. A formal indication of the principle may be followed in the body of the tariff itself by a more detailed exposition of the treatment. Where the principle of exemption is followed, the formal statement of the principle is, of course, sufficient in itself, and no further statement is necessary (though the interpretation even here may be a very difficult matter). In the other case a formal statement always requires further elucidation.

The following scheme shows the possibilities of the case :—

Statement in Customs Law and Laws.	With or without.	Further statement in preliminaries to tariff.	With or without.	Statement in body of tariff.
		Further statement in body of tariff.		

Only the last link in the chain is really necessary.

We may conclude this aspect of the matter with a few illustrations. The two principles enumerated can be drawn from the laws of Switzerland and Holland respectively. In Holland,[2] the law of August 15, 1862, lays down—

" Art. 1. Under the name of import duty a duty shall be levied upon the under-mentioned articles when imported for home consumption. The import duty is set forth in the annexed tariff.

" Art. 2. No duty is levied upon goods not mentioned in Article 1 unless these goods can, according to their nature or destination, be classed under one of the headings of the tariff." In Switzerland,[3] on the other hand, the opposite principle prevails. By the federal customs law of June 25, 1893, Chapter I., Article 1.

" All goods imported or exported from Switzerland are,

[1] There is a third method which consists in classifying the non-enumerated goods within the classes to which they belong by affinity—*i.e.*, differentiating them *ab initio*. But this can be regarded as a particular case of the general principle just mentioned. See below, § 7.

[2] Kelly, p. 397; *cf.* Art. 3 of the German Vereinszollgesetz of 1869.

[3] " Die schweizerische Zollgesetzgebung, Textausgabe von Blumenstein and Gassmann," Zurich, 1918, p. 9.

with the exceptions laid down in this law, liable to duty at the rates laid down in the tariff law.

"The importation is free.

"(*a*) Of all objects which are designated as free in the tariff from time to time (jeweiligen), or made so in consequence of treaties with foreign powers."

In France, again,[1] the principle enunciated by the law of 6-22 August, 1791, still holds good—viz., that the only goods exempt from duty are those which the law specifically mentions.

In point of fact the majority of modern tariffs are based on the principle of inclusion, as inspection will speedily reveal. Reference may be made to Italy,[2] Art. 2 of Preliminary Dispositions of Tariff; Argentine, Art. 15 of Chap. IV., Law No. 4,933,[3]; Chile, Tariff of 1916, Art.[4] 2; Canada, Tariff of 1907, Tariff No. 711;[5] South Africa,[6] Tariff of 1914, Class VI., No. 193; U.S.A.,[7] Tariff of 1913, Class IV., No. 386. It will be noted that in some cases the principle is incorporated in the preliminaries to the tariff, in other cases it is included in the body of the tariff.

§ 3. Provided the principle is somewhere laid down, it seems to make very little difference whether it is formally expressed, or formally expressed with further directions, or expressed in the body of the tariff only without more ado. The point of convenience, however, carries some weight even in a matter of this sort. In France, for instance, the historical principle of treatment seems to have been questioned owing to lack of definite expression, as we learn from Pallain's lucid treatment of the matter.[8] This is, of course, a different matter to the *interpretation* of the rule, whatever it may be, by a court of law. For the student of customs institutions and for the inquirer into tariff regulations such a preliminary statement is, of course, a great safeguard against fruitless waste of time.

---

[1] Pallain I., § 76.

[2] Kelly, p. 449.

[3] F.T.C. Report, p. 107.

[4] F.T.C. Report, p. 149.

[5] Statutes of Canada, 1907.

[6] Act No. 26 of 1914.

[7] In the 1909 tariff this was No. 481. The present rate will be found, Kelly, p. 817.

[8] Pallain I., § 76, *et seq.* The *principle* is formulated by the law of 6-22 August, 1791, that the only goods exempt from duty are those which the law specifically mentions.

§ 4. What are the merits of either principle, looked at from the technical standpoint? Let us first of all remember the great difficulties that must be experienced in completing and enumerating all the possible varieties of goods that pass across the frontiers in view of the great complexity of modern commerce. A rule that only enumerated goods should be liable to duty, if strictly interpreted, fails to strike at least three important categories of products—(1) Substitutes, (2) absolutely new commodities, and, in certain cases at any rate, (3) commodities entered in a trade-name or category which bears no resemblance to those in the tariff, or the resemblance to which is disputed. It will be in most people's recollection that the courts had, in this country, great difficulty in defining the trade meaning of "sardine."[1] In some cases where the question at issue is the determination *under which rate* a particular commodity is to go, the exact description or use of which is in dispute, the problem is one of correct classification, but where no unenumerated clause exists and the commodity would escape the duty if it cannot be clearly shown to belong to the group of taxable articles, the problem is appropriate to our present enquiry. The case of new commodities explains itself; but the problem raised by substitutes is really no more difficult. The substitute may be a new commodity not previously known, or which, previously known, has not been mentioned in the tariff. To exclude it in either event would mean that the taxed commodity is not bought, and that the sale of the untaxed would rise.

§ 5. A strong case may, therefore, be made out for specific treatment of unenumerated articles. Is it possible to make out an equally strong case for the other principle?

It may be urged in the first place that certain administrative advantages are secured by the principle of limited protection or exemption. It leads to more careful definition and enumeration in the tariff, for the penalty for ambiguity is the freedom of the article. Secondly, it may be urged that the principle of treating new commodities as if the trade

[1] *Cf.* the following F.T.N., No. 23, pp. 64-65, Australia:—"An order issued by the Department of Trade and Customs, under date 9th July, 13, 1916, state that the term 'sardine' is not a generic expression which can be lawfully applied to any small fish prepared and packed in oil in tins, but can lawfully be applied only to the immature pilchard. In the case of canned fish imported into Australia on and after March 1st, 1917, the word 'sardine' may be used only as above indicated."

in them were fully established is undesirable on general grounds, since it has yet to be shown what specific principle of rating *ought* to be applicable to them. The case of substitutes is really similar (in those cases—namely, where, in consequence of newness, it has not been enumerated). Thirdly, it may be said that the general public is entitled to know what the duties are which it is called upon to pay, and the rule that unenumerated commodities should be liable throws far too much power in the hands of the bureaucracy, since whatever method of treatment is applied, a wide margin of uncertainty must necessarily exist.

§ 6. It must be carefully kept in mind that though views as to the proper fiscal policy to be pursued naturally affect the judgment as to the proper policy in this particular respect, yet that problem is one which is nearly independent of general principles altogether. It is a problem which arises within the limits of the general principle of protection, rather than an issue between the two schools of thought. When either the principle of customs duties for revenue purposes only, or the principle of protection for rigidly limited industries only is adhered to, the problem obviously does not arise in its broad form at all, although even here there are marginal cases—*i.e.*, doubts as to unenumerated commodities of the kind specificially taxed. The full force of the difficulty is only felt when the principle of protection in general is already accepted, and when the extreme complexity of modern commerce and the tendency to the specialisation of tariffs have to be adjusted to one another.

§ 7. So long as broad distinctions only were being drawn, extreme preciseness of definition was not perhaps essential. But at this point the question is forced on one, what is really meant by an unenumerated commodity? It is clearly a negative conception, but what is its precise connotation? Now a glance at any modern tariff will show that there are really three kinds of "unenumerated" commodities; the treatment of the second and third of which alone present any broad difficulty of treatment.

(1) There are commodities not specifically mentioned, but so explicitly associated with a definite sub-group or tariff unity that its treatment, once its nature is known, offers no difficulty.

(2) There are commodities not specifically enumerated but associated in the tariff with a *general* class heading.

(3) There are the commodities not specifically mentioned and *not* associated either with a specific or general class of goods in the tariff.

The following illustrations may serve to clarify the discussion :—

(1) Canadian Tariff of 1907: Group I. Animals, agricultural products, fish, etc.

No. 82. Grape wines; gooseberry, raspberry, currant, and rose bushes; fruit plants, n.o.p. trees, plants, and shrubs, commonly known as nursery stock n.o.p.

(2) Canadian Tariff, Group I., No. 133: All other articles, the produce of the fisheries n.o.p.

(" N.o.p. represents, and has the meaning of the words, " not otherwise provided for.")

(3) Canadian Tariff Group 11: Miscellaneous, No. 711. " All goods not enumerated in this schedule as subject to any other rate of duty and not otherwise declared free from duty, and not being goods the importation whereof is by law prohibited. . . .

" Provided that duty shall not be deemed to be provided for by this item upon dutiable goods mentioned as " n.o.p." in any preceding tariff item."

The distinctions attempted to be drawn will, I think, now be more concretely realised. Only the last two classes really enter into the question.

§ 8. Just as there are two principal standpoints from which to view the problem of unenumerated goods, so are there two main principles of treatment. They may be described as the principle of assimilation and the principle of uniform treatment. An illustration of each will serve again to make the position clearer. In the Canadian tariff No. 711, cited above, all the goods comprised within the number are dutiable at 15 per cent. or 17½ per cent. *ad valorem* according as they come under the British Preferential Tariff or the General Tariff. This is the principle of uniformity. So also in South Africa a 15 per cent. *ad valorem* duty shall be imposed upon—

All goods, wares, and merchandise not elsewhere charged with duty, and not enumerated in the free list, and not prohibited to be imported into the Union. . . .

The assimilation rule can be illustrated from the U.S.A. Tariff No. 386 ("Similitude" rule).

. . . That each and every imported article not enumerated in this section which is similar, either in material, quality, texture, or the use to which it may be applied, to any article enumerated in this section as chargeable with duty, shall pay the same rate of duty which is levied on the enumerated article which it most resembles in any of the particulars before-mentioned, and if any non-enumerated article equally resembles two or more enumerated articles on which different rates of duty are chargeable, there shall be levied on such non-enumerated article the same rate of duty as is chargeable on the article which it resembles paying the highest rate of duty. . . .

It would be wasted space to add to the illustrative material, which could be drawn from almost every tariff in the world.[1] In general the principle of assimilation has as wide a distribution as the principle of inclusion of which indeed it may be said to be the logical consequence. Sometimes both principles are incorporated in the tariff—viz., Sweden.

"Class XVI., Articles not elsewhere mentioned," contains the following numbers with the superscription as given—

ARTICLES WHICH CANNOT BE CLASSED UNDER ANY SECTION OF THE TARIFF.

No. 1,324.	Raw materials, . .	Free.
No. 1,325.	More or less manipulated,	15 per cent.

Here assimilation is clearly conceived to be the rule, whilst the principle of uniformity is laid down for the residual products.[2], [3].

---

[1] For further instances of assimilation, see Brazil, Prelim. Disp., Art. 13 (Kelly. p. 898); Mexico, Sec. C of General Regs. for Application of the Tariff ("Mex, Year Book, 1911," p. 405); Spain, § 22 of Disposition IV. Many of these tariffs also contain rules of the kind treated of in § 9.

[2] In Germany, according to § 3 of the Federal Customs Act of 1869, the principle of exclusion is laid down. In 1879, when the protectionist reaction had set in, it was proposed that this rule should be abrogated and that the principle of assimilation for non-enumerated goods should be adopted. This proposal was rejected. "The rule is of no material importance," for even before the last revision of the tariff only two commodities succeeded in not being brought under one or other head of the tariff. This result was achieved by the use of the power given in § 12 of the Federal Customs Act to issue an official tariff list (Amtliches Warenverzeichniss) for the right interpretation of the tariff, which, of course,

§ 9. The methods by which, in practice, assimilation is carried out can be dealt with more usefully in connection with the discussion on classification disputes in a later chapter. But it will be in place here to deal with the rules of assimilation applicable to complicated cases—viz., mixed goods.

What should be the treatment of commodities composed of more than one material? This is a question which, as a matter of fact can be, and is, answered in more than one way by the tariff makers of the world. It is possible to—

(1) Rate on the basis of each component *separately*, either according to value or to quantity.[4]

(2) Rate on the basis of the principal component only, either according to quantity or value, or some other test of importance.

It must be observed that the determination of the precise values and quantities may present very great administrative difficulties, but this can be overlooked for the moment in the search for principles. A few actual cases will suffice to show the principles adopted practically.[5]

U.S. Tariff of 1913, No. 386. " . . . on articles not enumerated, manufactured of two or more materials, the duty shall be assessed at the highest rate at which the same would be chargeable if composed wholly of the component material thereof of chief value, and the words 'component material of chief value' whenever used in this section shall be held to mean that component material which shall exceed in value any other single component material of the article; and the value of each component material shall be determined by the ascertained value of such material in its condition

---

is equivalent to conferring the right to assimilate. See Trautvetter, *op. cit.*, pp. 65, 107, *et seq.* On the position of substitutes mentioned in the text, see espec. § 139 of the Australian Customs Act.

[3] In those cases where the values of goods for purposes of customs taxation are established by Government (the so-called Official Valuation System), unenumerated goods are sometimes declared taxable at an uniform rate on the value assigned them by importers—*e.g.*, Argentina. This used to be the case in the United Kingdom, so long as official valuation was applied. See Book of Rates of 1660, " Goods inwards not rated to pay 5 per cent." *S.R.*, vol. v., p. 202.

[4] So far as can be discovered, this principle is not applied in any tariff as a *general* basis of assimilation, but " double taxation "—*e.g.*, sugar goods also containing alcohol—is to be found. And see also the surtax in the case of Brazil below; also German tariff note referred to in the same connection.

[5] For other instances, see Chile, Law of March 1st, 1916, Art. 2 (F.T.C. 149); Sweden, § 1 of Instructions (Cd. 5464, p. 84): in France the administrative practice dates from the ancien régime, a decision of the Conseil du Roi of 1760, first enunciating it clearly, Pallain I., § 76.

as found in the article. If two or more rates of duty shall be applicable to any imported article, it shall pay duty at the highest of such rates."

Spain—522 of Disposition IV.—"The assessment of duty on articles composed of two or more materials shall be subject to the following rules :—

"(*a*) In cases not provided for in the tariff, and when the value of the article is determined by the exterior material, the classification shall be made according to the corresponding number of that material.

"(*b*) Articles which, by reason of their nature and application, are composed of two different materials, as, for instance, tools, shall be taxed according to the weight of the predominant material.

"(*c*) When a mixture of different materials has been made in order to evade the payment of the rates paid by any particular number of the tariff on any article, as for instance, a mixture of flour and bran, of earth and a soluble chemical product, the duty of the material paying the highest duty shall be paid."

One more instance may be given, that of Brazil, which shows extreme specification of treatment.

Article 11 of Preliminary Dispositions.—"Wares manufactured or composed of different materials, not subject to special or fixed duties in the tariff or regulated by any particular provision shall be subject to the duties established for similar wares manufactured solely from the predominating material; in case of equality of materials, or of doubt as to the predominating material, such wares shall pay according to the most highly taxed material. Mixed tissues, with respect to which the special regulations established in the following article must be observed, are excepted :—

"MIXED TISSUES.

"Art. 12. Tissues visibly composed of different materials, for which no special duty is stipulated in the tariff, shall pay the duty of the most highly taxed component material, whatever be the proportion, except when all the threads of the woof and all those of the warp are composed of a material subject to the lowest duty, in which case a reduction of 10 per cent. will be granted.

"For tissues mixed with silk the following rules must be observed :—

"1. Mixed tissues in which all the threads of the woof or all those of the warp are of silk and the remaining threads of different material, shall pay the duties stipulated for similar tissues composed entirely of silk, with a reduction of 50 per cent.

"2. Mixed tissues with the warp and woof of silk, but in the warp or woof of which, or in both, there are visible tissues of any other material, shall pay the duties established for similar tissues composed entirely of silk, with a reduction of 20 per cent.

"No reduction, however, shall be granted to tissues of silk when in the warp or woof are found threads of a less highly taxed material in such an insignificant quantity that they do not alter the nature, importance, or value of the tissues.

"3. Mixed tissues with the warp and woof composed of other materials, but in the warp or woof of which or in both there are a few threads or mixture of silk shall pay the duties leviable on the most highly taxed material with a surtax of 30 per cent.

"4. Tissues of any material mixed with gold or silver, and not specially classed in the tariff, shall pay the duties leviable on plain corresponding tissues with a surtax of 20 per cent."

In these cases the search for the principle is lightened by its being laid down in the preliminaries of the tariff. In other cases an arduous investigation of the notes to the various tariff classes is required—*e.g.*, Germany (General Notes to Nos. 391 to 543 of the Tariff; number of threads to be basis of estimating "predominant material," Note (*a*)); Switzerland, note to Class VII. ("Mixed yarns, etc., are, unless otherwise stipulated, dutiable as articles manufactured wholly of the component material subject to the higher duty").

§ 10. But the choice as the basis of assimilation of the weight or value and highest rate of duty of one of the components does not, in fact, dispose of all the difficulties associated with the treatment of mixed goods. The point is briefly this, does the choice of the component of the predominant value or the predominant weight or paying the highest rate of duty involve payment on the basis of the weight or value of that component *as actually ascertained* or does it involve payment on the basis of the weight or value of the commodity *as a whole?* These two interpretations would obviously give one very different results. The Swiss rule enunciated above leaves no ambiguity, but, it must be confessed, that some of the precepts set forth are far from clear. In practice it is clear that the second alternative afforded the greater measure of protection, but it is clearly necessary from what is said that we have to distinguish between the process of assimilation (*i.e.*, subsumption under a given rate) and the process of imposition of duty, once assimilation has taken place.

It may be pointed out explicitly, what is sufficiently obvious, that the interpretation of these notes is a matter of great complexity. We may give as an instance an American case, Field & Co. *v.* U.S. (Court of Customs Appeals), T.D., 36,876.[1]

"Goods made by cementing with rubber a cotton cloth to a cotton and wool cloth, and goods made by cementing with rubber a cotton and silk cloth to a cotton and wool cloth, the rubber in each case, being negligible in value, are composed in chief value of cotton, wool, or silk, according to which represents the greatest value as yarn, plus its proportion, on the basis of quantity,of the cost of weaving and other expenses incurred in making the cloth and bringing it to the condition it had immediately prior to its combination with the other materials in order fo form the goods in question." [2]

Again,[3] "in determining which is the component material of chief value under paragraph 386 of a fabric with a warp yarn of wool and a weft yarn of mixed wool and mohair, the proportion of wool in the weft yarn should be added to that composing the warp yarn. The fact that the weft yarn is in chief value of mohair does not warrant the assumption for this purpose that it is entirely mohair." [4]

---

[1] See also Indian Sea Customs Act, 1878, § 21, "Goods whereof any article liable to duty under this Act forms a part or ingredient shall be chargeable with the full duty which would be payable on such goods if they were entirely composed of such article," or if there are two or more ingredients, then as if "they were entirely composed of the article charged with the highest rate of duty."

[2] Compilation of Customs Laws and Digest of Decisions Thereunder, Treasury Department Doc., No. 2780, 2 vols., vol. i., p. 878.

[3] *Ibid.*

[4] In the United Kingdom, the Schedule to the Customs Tariff Act of 1876 laid down that:—"Goods not prohibited to be imported into or used in Great Britain, composed of any article liable to duty as a part or ingredient thereof, shall be chargeable with the full duty payable on such article, or if composed of

When we turn to the next problem, which falls under the head of assimilation, we are dealing with a problem which requires very careful definition.

§ 11. It is the problem that may be described as "parts and wholes." A given commodity may be imported in parts; it may be imported as a whole. What ought to be the treatment of it when imported in the one form, when it is treated in a given way in the other? Note that this is a different problem to the one involved in the treatment of parts imported in bulk, or the treatment of wholes imported in bulk. The problem is this: if a given machine is imported in six complementary parts, how shall it be treated in comparison to the customs treatment of the machine as a whole? We may illustrate this kind of problem that has to be settled by a somewhat analogous problem concerned with the preferential treatment of commercial travellers' samples in Chile.[1]

"Samples of shoes consisting entirely of shoes for one foot only are no longer considered as samples of no value, since it was discovered quite recently that a commercial traveller was importing 300 shoes for one foot at one port and the mates to these 300 shoes at another port. When samples of single shoes now arrive in Chile they are cut and punched in such a manner as to destroy their commercial value."

Shoes are complementary commodities, just as are parts of a machine, and the importation in parts may lead to evasion of customs duties imposed on the complex as a whole. But against this must be set a possible loss to the "finishing" industries if an equal customs treatment leads to the com-

---

more than one article liable to duty, then with the full duty payable on the article charged with the highest rate of duty."

This was extended thus by § 7 of the Finance Act of 1901 :—7 (1). Where any manufactured or prepared goods contain, as a part or ingredient thereof, any article liable to any duty of customs, duty shall be charged in respect of any such quantity of the article as shall appear to the satisfaction of the Treasury to be used in the manufacture or preparation of the goods, and in the case of goods so containing more than one such article, shall be charged in a similar manner on each article liable to duty at the rates of duty respectively applicable thereto, unless the Treasury shall be of opinion that it is necessary for the protection of the revenue that duty should be charged in accordance with the Customs Act, 1876.

Any rebate which can be allowed by law on any article when separately charged shall be allowed in charging goods under this section in respect of the quantity of that article used in the manufacture or preparation of the goods.

[1] Introduction to T.S., No. 36, "C.T. of Chile," p. 12.

modities in question being imported in a completely finished condition. Any differential treatment calls for such an adjustment of the two rates as to leave some inducement, if this is thought desirable, to make use of the domestic finishing industry and yet not stimulate evasion.

Again, let us clear the situation by taking some actual examples.

In Australia, by § 140 of the Customs Act—

"(1) Whenever any dutiable goods are composed of two or three separate parts, any part, though imported by itself, shall, if so directed by the minister, be chargeable with duty at the rate applicable to the complete goods.

"(2) When the duty on the complete goods is specific or both specific and *ad valorem*, the minister may fix the proportionate rate of duty with which any part shall be chargeable."

In Spain, by § 23 of Disposition IV.—

"Whenever the administration is enabled to prove that with a view of evading payment of the duties provided in any number of the tariff, certain parts of any article or object have been presented separately at the same or different customs houses by one or several persons, the duties payable on the complete article or object shall be levied without prejudice to the surtax chargeable under § 6 of Art. 306 of ordinances."

In Mexico, by § C, Regulations for the application of the Tariff V. and VI.—

"When a manufactured object consisting of different articles described in the tariff or alphabetical list is presented in separate pieces, even united in the same package, and when, for each separate piece, a distinct declaration is made, such pieces shall be dutiable according to their respective rates, provided the weight can be ascertained.

"Scientific apparatus, such as barometers, thermometers, and other similar instruments fitted to manufactured articles, such as statues, candelabra, inkstands, clocks, etc., shall pay the duty based on the manufactured article of which they form an accessory."

§ 12. When a tariff is based upon the principle of inclusion it becomes necessary to determine what, if any goods, shall be admitted free of duty. The choice of these is, of course, determined by the relevant fiscal and economic motives, but in this chapter the problem at issue is the technical form in which exemption takes place. Here it becomes necessary to draw an important distinction between goods *contingently* free and goods *absolutely* free of duty. By goods contingently free are to be understood commodities which are normally liable to duty, but which, owing to exceptional circumstances are in certain cases freely admitted—*e.g.*, when imported, let us say, by settlers or a particular class of manufacturers. Such admission constitutes a differential treatment with a zero duty, and can be best examined in connection with differential duties of all kinds in a later chapter. In this chapter only the absolutely free goods and their treatment will be considered.

Two different methods of treatment are to be found in this connection. The first consists in distributing the free goods among the schedules to which they belong in virtue of the principle upon which the tariff is constructed. The second consists in forming a special class of commodities free of duty, or, as it is usually called, a "free list." The first is the more logical, since a freely admitted commodity is placed in a natural order with the goods with which it has affinity. On the other hand, a free list enables one to tell at a glance the total volume of commodities freely admitted. Nevertheless, when a tariff is built up on a logical order, one's natural impulse is to look at the appropriate schedule to see how a particular commodity is being treated. When the distribution of these two systems is enquired into, one finds that in the European tariffs the general principle of distributing of the free goods is generally adopted—among the countries making use of this arrangement being Bulgaria, France, Germany, Greece, Italy, Russia, Servia, and Sweden. Of the self-governing Dominions, New Zealand, Canada, and Australia adopt the same principle. On the other hand, South Africa (Tariff of 1914, Class V., Free), the United States (Tariff of 1913, Free List, appended to detailed schedules), and Newfoundland (Schedule B, "Table of Exemptions," in which both contingent and absolute free admissions are contained) show the other principle at work. It need hardly be said that these tariffs also show the principle of contingent freedom as well, but for reasons already given, the examination of this matter will be deferred.

§ 13. The last matter which requires a mention in this chapter is the subject of prohibitions. These have, during the

European War, become temporarily of great importance, but this is a phase which is now drawing to a close. Normally, the same distinction as in the case of free goods can be drawn—there may be contingent or absolute prohibitions. The contingent prohibitions again depend on special circumstances—*e.g.*, prison-made goods, the absolute prohibitions exclude importations of the article as an article under the totality of circumstances.

In practice the table or list of prohibited articles very often includes both descriptions of prohibitions,[1] whilst in some cases—*e.g.*, France and Roumania—the prohibitions are in fact inserted in the ordinary tariff schedules. The contingent prohibitions will be treated in the chapter dealing with differential duties: here one or two illustrations of absolute prohibitions may be given. In modern cases these absolute prohibitions are confined to a few commodities or substances deemed injurious on moral and social grounds, and no longer constitute, as prohibitions at one time did, an important political instrument.

In the U.S.A.[2] (3)—"All persons are prohibited from importing . . . from any foreign country any obscene book, pamphlet, paper, writing, advertisement, circular print, picture drawing, or other representation, figure or image on or of paper or other material, or any cast instrument, or other article of an immoral nature, or any drug or medicine, or any article whatever for the prevention of conception or for causing unlawful abortion, or any lottery ticket, or any advertisement of any lottery. No such articles, whether imported separately or contained in packages with other goods inhibited to entry shall be admitted to entry, and all such articles shall be proceeded against, seized, or forfeited by due course of law. . . . Provided that the drugs hereinbefore mentioned when imported in bulk and not put up for any of the purposes hereinbefore specified, are excepted from the operation of this sub-section."

Even here, it will be noticed, the element of contingency is not entirely absent. It is, in fact almost impossible to dissociate these two aspects of the matter.[3]

---

[1] See the U.K. Customs Consolidation Act, 1876, §§ 42-45.

[2] Tariff of 1913, Miscellaneous Provisions, G, § 1.

[3] Prohibitions of commodities which form an internal monopoly of the Government—*e.g.*, matches and tobacco in France—represent a form of contingent prohibition.

In the case of Canada, where the prohibited articles are contained in a separate schedule C, with consecutive numbers running from 1,201 to 1,212, the absolute prohibitions cover—

1,201. Books, printed paper, drawings, paintings, prints, photographs, or representations of any kind of a treasonable or seditious, or of an immoral or indecent character.

1,203. Coin, base or counterfeit.

1,204. Oleomargarine, butterine, or other similar substitutes for butter, and process butter or renovated butter.

1,205. Tea, adulterated with spurious leaf or with exhausted leaves, or containing so great an admixture of chemical or other deleterious substances as to make it unfit for use.

1,207. Animals suffering from any contagious disease.

1,208. Metallic trading checks in circular form.

1,209. Any goods (*a*) which, if sold, would be forfeited under the provisions of Part VII. of the Criminal Code. . . .

1,210 Posters and handbills depicting scenes of criminal violence.

1,211. Stallions and mares of less value than 50 dollars each.

The main examples of *contingent* prohibitions concern copyrighted commodities, prison-made goods, goods with fraudulent trade marks, goods liable to cause danger to the public health. As has already been stated, such contingent prohibitions are merely examples of a differential duty, and will be treated in connection with this subject.

CHAPTER V.

The Tariff Rate.

§ 1. The modern tariff maker has, as his first choice in the framing of the tariff rate, two great historical forms to draw upon. These are respectively known as the "specific duty" and the "*ad valorem*" duty. The literature dealing with their respective advantages and disadvantages is very voluminous, and attempts have not infrequently been made so to manipulate the actual form of the rate as to combine as far as possible the merits of both at one and the same time. Thus, we get the derivatives—"compound duties" and "alternative duties"—and, with a view to other issues also—"official valuation scales" and "sliding scales." To understand the purposes of these latter forms, we must first grasp the technical merits and demerits of the former.

§ 2. The specific duty is a rate imposed upon some definite and unvarying physical attribute or associated group of physical attributes possessed by the article made dutiable under the tariff. The duty may be based upon weight, superficial or cubical measure, specific gravity, tale or what not—the diversity of form will be dealt with subsequently in the chapter on "Differentiation." Here the important point to stress is the fact that the element selected as the basis of taxation is some attribute other than the *value* of the commodity in question. Inevitably there has been in the course of technical evolution a change in the attributes selected; the basis chosen has been more and more subtly determined. The all-important cause of this ever-increasing subtlety is the desire to discriminate between qualities and different areas as sources of supply, but for the moment our discussion of these points must be deferred.

§ 3. The *ad valorem* duty is, on the other hand, as the name implies, essentially a duty based upon the *value* of the commodity made dutiable under the tariff, and represents, therefore, a percentage on that value per unit of the commodity.

The *ad valorem* duty, therefore, does not allow escape from the necessity of choosing some definite physical unit—it is obvious that, as soon as we ask, upon *what* value the duty is assessed we must get some such answer as "value per ton, value per square yard," and so on.[1] Just because of this fact, as soon as for purposes of imposition of duty, an authoritative value is given to the commodity, we get a merging of the two forms: a fact which underlies the "official valuation" tariff, as will presently be more fully examined.

It follows from what has just been said that it is always possible to express an *ad valorem* duty in terms of specific duty and *vice versâ*. Thus, if the value of an article is £10 per ton, a duty of 10 per cent. *ad valorem* may be expressed as a specific duty of £1 per ton; and a specific duty of £1 per ton is equivalent to a 10 per cent. *ad valorem* duty.

Before proceeding to discuss the relative merits and demerits of these historical forms, an example of each may be given. Tariff No. 155 of the Australian tariff will serve as giving instances of what, in the remainder of this chapter, I shall call "simple" specific and *ad valorem* duties in contradistinction to the complex, differential duties with which the next chapter will deal—

No. 155.	(*a*) Rolled iron or steel beams, channels, girders, columns, trough and bridge iron and steel, not drilled or further manufactured, . . .	Per Ton. 17s. 6d.	25s. *ad valorem.*
	(*b*) Shafting, ...	12s.	17s.

§ 4. When we investigate the tariffs of the world we find that in so far as the principal trading nations are concerned, the specific duty has almost entirely displaced the *ad valorem* duty, except in the case of the United States of America. So considerable an extension of the principle among the leading commercial countries obviously calls for explanation. It is perhaps best to begin by pointing out that in a few cases the specific duty is not really applicable. This is the case in the commodities the value of which does not vary in any appreciable way with their physical qualities—pictures, old furniture, and such commodities the value of which obviously does not depend upon weight, superficial measure, and so on, but

[1] The fact that this does not necessarily appear in the rate as expressed in the tariff is due to the fact that the shipment as such is one of the value units which can be taken in practice.

upon "imponderables" which it is impossible to define in physical terms, are instances of the kind.[1]

(*a*) Specific duties, then, possess important administrative advantages and potentialities as compared to *ad valorem* duties. It is possible to grade the duty for slight variations in the physical constitution of the commodity—*e.g.*, threads per square inch in the case of textiles—and yet not present the administrator with insuperable technical difficulties in the way of assessment, though these difficulties are by no means negligible as the tariff rates become more specialised. *Ad valorem* duties do not present anything like the same capacity for specialisation. It is possible to grade a specific duty by varying the physical attribute chosen by as small an amount as $\frac{1}{100}$ of an inch—*e.g.*, in the case of wire, but it is quite impossible to specialise *ad valorem* duties in such a way that the percentage duty to be paid should vary for small changes in the value of the commodity without creating grave administrative difficulties, and offering great temptation to under-valuation and fraud. (But, as we shall see below, within the limits of a given percentage rate, the *ad valorem* duty is more elastic than the specific duty.)

(*b*) This brings one to the second administrative advantage which the specific duty has over the *ad valorem* duty. Any form of the latter involves a process of estimating what value should attach to the commodity in question. And it must be confessed that whatever process of valuation be chosen, the difficulties attending it are greater than those which present themselves when the activities of the customs officials are confined to the determination of physical attributes. But we must be careful to compare similar stages of development with one another; it is certainly true that if one compares the simplest form of *ad valorem* duty with the most advanced type of specific duty it might be difficult to say with which the advantage in this respect lies. All that is here said is that simple *ad valorem* duties involve greater difficulties than simple specific duties, and similarly at every point in the scale of complication.

(*c*) If specific duties have considerable administrative

[1] But see Alton and Holland, "The King's Customs," I., p. 175, for 18th century sliding scale in pictures, varying in size, and for duties on books by *weight*. This led to the malpractice of smuggling by interposing more valuable prints with the letterpress, *op. cit.*, II., p. 107.

advantages, they suffer from the fact that they easily lose their character of comprehensibility, and in this respect *ad valorem* duties have a distinct advantage. Everybody can understand that if a 20 per cent. *ad valorem* duty is imposed, prices in respect of the commodity in question will tend to fluctuate round a mean level 20 per cent. higher than before. In this advantage specific duties share, so long only as the duty is imposed on a physical attribute of a kind popularly understood. An increase in the tea duty of 3d. a lb. is quite recognised to mean that the price to the public will in all probability be raised by about 3d. But only an expert can tell what the effect on prices will be in the case of textiles assessed on the number of threads per square inch, or, in the case of liquids, assessed on specific gravity thereof, or what will be the precise effect of varying the duty according to some chemical element in high-speed steel. So far as high-speed steels are concerned, the experts may be left to look after themselves, but when articles of general consumption come into question, it is surely a serious defect from the politico-social standpoint that the estimation of what the duty will amount to should be subject to difficulties.

(*d*) If, in consequence of such considerations, the legislator deems himself bound to accept only simple specific duties, another serious difficulty presents itself. Simple specific duties are *regressive*—*i.e.*, they weigh more heavily upon the cheaper varieties or qualities than upon the dearer ones—*e.g.*, the proportion of the total price represented by the tax is greater in the case of cheap tobacco than in the case of more expensive tobaccos. When a purely revenue duty is being considered, it is clear that the maxim that taxation should be based upon ability to pay is being infringed. When the duty is intended to be protective, this regressive effect may or may not be considered desirable. It is clear that a flat rate has the result of protecting the less fine qualities *more* than the finer qualities, but judgment on this result depends on the object for which the duty was imposed. A simple illustration will show the *fact* of regression. Since a tax of 6d. per square yard of cloth worth—

1s. per yard	is equivalent	to an	*ad valorem*	tax of	50	per cent.
1s. 6d.	"	"	"	"	33⅓	"
2s.	"	"	"	"	25	"
2s. 6d.	"	"	"	"	20	"

to maintain an *ad valorem* rate of 25 per cent. throughout the range of qualities considered, the specific duty should be 3d., 4½d., 6d., 7½d. on the respective qualities. But a country [1] whose textile industries are just beginning to develop may find it desirable to levy a higher rate of duty on the inferior qualities, and this a uniform specific duty effects. The danger is that this concealed regressiveness is not perceived.

Complex specific duties are not subject to this factor of regressiveness to the same extent, for if attention is paid to that physical attribute which causes the commodity to be more valuable, it is possible to levy a higher rate on that variety which is in fact more valuable.

Ad valorem duties, being percentages of the values, are always directly proportional to value, and since values change with qualities, such a duty is not regressive, though it is not *progressive—i.e.*, it is always an equal proportion of the value, but not more than equal on the higher values.

(*e*) Closely connected with this fact of regressiveness is the further one that specific duties do not respond, as *ad valorem* duties do, to changes in the price level. Whether prices rise or fall 20 per cent. the ratio of the duty to the price remains the same with *ad valorem* duties, but changes in the specific duties inversely to the price movement. If the table of prices in the preceding section is taken to mean successive changes in the price of the same quality of cloth, this inverse movement can be clearly followed; as the price rises, the weight of the specific duty falls, as the price falls, so the weight of the specific duty rises. Whether this state of affairs is desirable or not is another matter, and requires careful examination.

A. **Rising and Falling Prices under a Revenue Duty.**—Let us take an *ad valorem* duty of 10 per cent. on a given commodity, say, wheat, and let us first assume, for the sake of avoiding complicating side-issues, that the whole supply is imported. Suppose the world price to be 50s. per quarter, and to rise by increments of 10s. per quarter to a price of 100s. Compare the consequences of an *ad valorem* duty to the effects of a specific duty of 5s. a quarter on wheat.

---

[1] See Bowring's evidence before Select Committee on Import Duties of 1840, qq. No. 818 and No. 819. "The principal disadvantage is that this system of levying duties uniformly by weight imposes the heaviest imposts upon the coarsest articles. . . . The only way to remedy that would be by classification, in which the element of value shall be introduced with the element of weight."

The price in the internal market would be—

Under an *ad valorem* Duty.	Under a Specific Duty.	Difference in favour of Specific Duty.
50s. + 5s. = 55s.	50s. + 5s. = 55s.	nil.
60s. + 6s. = 66s.	60s. + 5s. = 65s.	1s.
70s. + 7s. = 77s.	70s. + 5s. = 75s.	2s.
80s. + 8s. = 88s.	80s. + 5s. = 85s.	3s.
90s. + 9s. = 99s.	90s. + 5s. = 95s.	4s.
100s. + 10s. = 110s.	100s. + 5s. = 105s.	5s.

Given a certain class of consumers it is arguable that the specific duty yields a better result, since, although under the *ad valorem* duty, the consumer does not pay more than he did in proportion to the value of his *purchases*, he pays more in proportion to his *income*. Suppose, with a given income of £100, a householder buys 2 quarters of wheat a year. Under the *ad valorem* duty the amount represented by duty rises from $\frac{10}{2,000} = \frac{1}{200}$ of his income when wheat is 50s. per quarter, to $\frac{20}{2,000} = \frac{1}{100}$ of his income when wheat is 100s. per quarter. Now, since, in any case, a rise in the price of the commodity reduces the real ability to pay, it may be held that a duty which rises proportionately to a rise in the price of the commodity is undesirable, since the smaller the income the greater the proportion of the total income which goes in duty, and the greater the consequent sacrifice involved as compared with larger incomes, in those cases such as the one chosen, where differences in income tend to be greater than differences in the total amount of the commodity consumed. It follows that from the purely economic standpoint, the extra revenue which is obtained by means of the *ad valorem* duty is acquired at a sacrifice of utility greater than that which a transfer of the same amount not involving the effects analysed above would have had.

Now let us consider the position under *falling* prices. In this case the price in the internal market would be—

Under an *ad valorem* Duty.	Under a Specific Duty.	Difference in favour of *ad valorem* Duties.
50s. + 5s. = 55s.	50s. + 5s. = 55s.	nil.
40s. + 4s. = 44s.	40s. + 5s. = 45s.	1s.
30s. + 3s. = 33s.	30s. + 5s. = 35s.	2s.
20s. + 2s. = 22s.	20s. + 5s. = 25s.	3s.

The position is now reversed, and an *ad valorem* represents a smaller burden on the consumer than a specific duty would.

But since it may be held that a fall in price increases ability to pay, the case for the imposition of the *ad valorem* duty in this case is less strong, though, as between large and small incomes, the position is still unchanged.

These remarks have, however, been based upon the choice of a definite commodity, the demand for which is not proportionate to income, is socially unobjectionable and of the type known technically as "inelastic." Since, in general, elasticity of demand varies with the price level, it may be urged that in cases where there are social objections to the consumption of the commodity, the *ad valorem* duty is preferable to the specific, for, by raising prices more than the latter where prices are rising, it will assist to a greater extent in breaking down the demand for the commodity; whilst the specific duty is to be preferred on the same grounds when prices are falling.

B. **Rising and Falling of Prices under a Protective Duty.**—If, however, the duty is imposed not primarily for revenue but for protective purposes, is the position modified? We have here to take into account not merely the absolute amount of duty imposed, but also the deterrent effect which this amount of duty has on the volume of imports. In general, the lower the price in the country of export as compared to the country of import, the smaller the deterrent effect of a given amount of duty, since, even on the extreme assumption that the foreigner pays the whole of the duty, the greater the margin between price in the protected area and the selling price plus duty, and, hence, the greater also the profit. But the higher the price in the protected area, the less probability is there that the foreigner will bear the whole of the duty, since the higher prices are in the protected area, the greater are the indications of want, and the more freely will additional supplies be welcomed—*i.e.*, the higher will the demand-price for additional quantities be. When we are trying to follow the complications of this situation we are met by the further difficulty that the *ad valorem* duty can be assessed either on the basis of the internal price (as in the English corn-law legislation), or on the basis of export price of the country of origin (whether with or without cost of transport is immaterial in this connection from the standard of principle), so that we must deal with these alternatives separately, and then compare their effects.

In working out the problem, we are faced with 8 separate cases, of which only Nos. 1, 3, 5, and 7 are really of importance to us, since only under these circumstances is import likely.

(*a*) Duty Assessed on Internal Price.

1.	Rising prices at home	accompanied	by	falling	prices abroad.	Compared with the effects of a fixed specific duty.
2.	,, ,,	,,	,,	rising	,,	
3.	Falling ,,	,,	,,	falling	,,	
4.	,, ,,	,,	,,	rising	,,	

(*b*) Duty Assessed on Foreign Price.

5.	Rising prices at home	accompanied	by	falling	prices abroad.	Compared with the effects of a fixed specific duty.
6.	,, ,,	,,	,,	rising	,,	
7.	Falling ,,	,,	,,	falling	,,	
8.	,, ,,	,,	,,	rising	,,	

In all cases specific duties weigh more heavily when prices are falling, *ad valorem* duties when prices are rising. Let us first deal with rising prices.

Case 1.—When prices are rising at home, the higher the price, the smaller the sacrifice represented by a *fixed* duty to either consumer or foreigner. Hence, the protective effect of a specific duty gets less and less as the price goes up. Hence, as the price rises the consumer is more and more willing to pay the duty to get the foreign product which is (relatively and absolutely) getting cheaper: the profit, to the foreigner gets larger and larger, and the better the foreign harvest the worse the position for the internal producer under a fixed duty becomes. With an *ad valorem* duty assessed on the internal price the duty rises with the rise of price, and, therefore, postpones a given volume of imports till a higher price is reached than would be necessary to induce a similar volume of imports with a fixed duty, given a certain foreign price. But the deterrent effect even of an *ad valorem* duty assessed in this way decreases with every increase in the home price. Thus, taking a specific duty of 5s. per quarter, and an *ad valorem* duty of 10 per cent.,[1] a starting price of 100s., and a foreign price of 95s.—

At Home Prices of	The Specific Duty + the Foreign Price amounts to	The *ad valorem* Duty + the Foreign Price amounts to
100s., ...	100s.	105s.
105s., ...	100s.	105.5s.
110s., ...	100s.	106s.
120s., ...	100s.	107s.

[1] Duty assessed on home prices.

It is obvious from inspection (*a*) that it requires a home price between 105s. and 110s. with an *ad valorem* duty before the same volume of imports will be attracted as would be attracted by a home price of 100s. with a specific duty (*b*) that the deterrent effect of the *ad valorem* duty gets less as the home price rises, although in all cases the *ad valorem* duty is the more deterrent. But it may be argued that when prices are rising at home this is the time when the producer requires protection least, for in any case the shortage guarantees him his profits, whilst, alternatively, the consumer needs relief most urgently. The position of the producer, however, depends upon the causes inducing the rise. If it is due to failure of the harvest the question turns on whether the rise in the price is or is not sufficient to compensate for the fall in the volume of produce. But the high price may simply be due to the changes in the size of the population which is "pressing upon the means of subsistence." We have, therefore, to weigh possible gains to producers against losses to consumers. If we could suppose that the typical (or modal) income of the producers were less (without the extra gain resulting from protection) than the typical (or modal) income of the consumers, an increase of utility would result from the redistribution. In cases where production is carried on by small holders or proprietors such a profit might become of importance. (Nevertheless in practice the disadvantages attending high prices of wheat, etc., have led to the device of suspension by decree of government of the duties and their attempted automatic adjustment by means of "sliding scales," of which more will be said subsequently.)

Case 5.—When the duty is assessed on the foreign price, an *ad valorem* duty results in less and less protection, the better the foreign harvest since the lower import prices will be. There will, therefore, be a smaller deterrent effect than even a specific duty affords, and therefore, still less than an *ad valorem* duty assessed on home prices.

Cases 3 and 7.—When prices are falling at home, the *ad valorem* duties reduce the duty below the specific level whatever the mode of assessment. Hence, it can be argued that the protective effect is least when it is most wanted. Which will have the smaller deterrent effect? Imports will only continue if home prices are falling less rapidly than foreign, so that if the second method of assessment be adopted there is still less deterrence than with the first.

C. **Effect upon Revenue Collected.**—When the question is regarded from the standpoint, not of utility sacrificed or protection afforded, but of revenue collected, the following results emerge:—In a period of rising prices, specific duties tend to reduce the aggregate revenue as compared with the *ad valorem* duties, in a period of falling prices *ad valorem* duties tend to bringing less than specific duties would, *granted that the demand for the commodity is inelastic.* If the demand is elastic, a *rise* in price cuts off demand sharply, a fall in price stimulates demand, and, therefore, a lower duty per unit will not decrease the revenue when prices are rising so much as it would be reduced by a higher duty—*i.e.*, elasticity of demand makes for a specific duty in this case: whilst *falling prices* accompanied by an *ad valorem* duty will, under conditions of elastic demand, increase the revenue more than a specific duty would.[1]

(*f*) It follows, from the discussion in section (*e*), that a specific duty intended to be equivalent to a given *ad valorem* rate of duty requires constant adjustment as prices change in order to prevent its being more or less heavy than the *ad valorem* duty to which it is nominally adjusted would have been. The situation in China illustrates the difficulty very well. Ever since the Nanking Treaty of July 27, 1843, certain classes of imports have been subject to a uniform 5 per cent. duty, and since a revision of the specific rates into which the nominal *ad valorem* rates were converted has only taken place at long intervals, the 5 per cent. basis has not really been adhered to. The tariff of 1843 was revised by the Tientsin Treaty of 11th August, 1853, and the rates thereafter were not again revised until after the Boxer rebellion:[2] "Consequently the specific duties had become absurdly erratic. This was shown by the statistical secretary's list of values, issued by the customs in 1902, on which the latter accepted duties, pending the completion and publication of the new

[1] "There is an absolute limit to every duty beyond which an increase of it necessarily occasions a loss of revenue. In no instance is an increase of duty followed by an equal increase of revenue; but, on the contrary, the progress of the increase of revenue will be less and less, according as the duty advances, until there is no increase of revenue, but a falling off . . . there is nothing more easy of demonstration than that a diminution of revenue or an increase of taxation by an increase of revenue."—Sir H. Parnell, "Financial Reform," 2nd edn., pp. 41, 42. Parnell's remarks apply as aptly to a fixed duty with varying prices as to stable prices with varying duties.

[2] Chin Chu, "The Tariff Problem in China," p. 42 (Columbia University Studies, Whole No. 169).

tariff, which was to be based on the average values for three years—1897, 1898, and 1899. When the duties were fixed some forty years before, they were intended to represent an effective 5 per cent. on the value then current. How far they had drifted away, upward and downward, from this level can be seen by a cursory examination of the statistical secretary's list. On the first four pages, among the duties then paid, there were ups as well as downs from the 5 per cent. level. It appears that not a single article liable to specific duty on page 5 had paid as much as 5 per cent. The highest percentage was 3.85 per cent.; the lowest, 0.06 per cent. on imitation coral. On pages 6 and 7 there is further evidence of the heavy loss the Chinese revenue had been sustaining. On these two pages, with the exception of two or three articles which paid either a little above or below the 5 per cent. duty, all the rest paid far less than that rate; feather fans paying only 0.58 per cent. On pages 8 and 9 the story is repeated. Leather trunks were the articles on pages 10 and 11 which paid as much as 5 per cent., while rhinoceros horns got off with 0.04 per cent. This was the situation in which the Chinese tariff had been for many years. . . ." The rise in prices which was so marked a feature of the period after 1900 again affected the productivity of the tariff, with results that are graphically described by Sir R. Breden, formerly Acting Inspector General of the Chinese Customs. On the basis of 1912 imports the duty at 5 per cent. should have amounted in the aggregate to Hk, Tls. 21,189,858.[1] The total duties actually paid on import of general cargo (*i.e.*, exclusive of opium in both cases) was Hk. Tls. 14,275,564. It was only in 1918 that the Treaty Powers consented to the revision which the Chinese Government demanded.[2]

§ 5. A somewhat lengthy survey has shown that it cannot be said with absolute certainty which system is best adapted to meet all the demands which can be made in the search for the best possible tariff. The explanation of the remarkable success of the specific duty in ousting the *ad valorem* duty must be sought for chiefly in the difficulties which the administration of a complicated tariff based on *ad valorem* values brings with it. "Théroiquement ce systeme semble le

[1] Quoted *op. cit.*, p. 50.
[2] *B. T. J.*, 7/2/18; 7/11/18, and 6/2/19.

meilleur : en fait, il est entaché d'inconvénients profonds," says Professor Fontana-Russo.[1]

It now becomes necessary to discuss certain derivative methods of imposing duties, and to study their merits and demerits.

§ 6. **Mixed Duties.**—We have already seen that the great defect of specific duties is their regressiveness. If then *ad valorem* duties are associated in one and the same rate with a specific duty, a certain moderating influence is exercised in the lower ranges of quality and price. On the other hand, in the upper ranges in quality and price, such a mixed duty causes a certain increase of the duty (in consequence of the *ad valorem* portion), whilst preventing the absolute amount of the duty from rising as much as it would have done under a pure *ad valorem* duty. Whether prices rise or prices fall from the level to which the duties were originally adjusted, under the mixed duty the revenue remains steadier than under the *ad valorem* duty, and the regressiveness less than under the specific duty.

An illustration will suffice to make this clear :—

Let the specific and the *ad valorem* duties be adjusted to each other at a price of £40 per ton, and let a mixed duty yielding the same amount of revenue at this price be also elaborated. If the specific duty is £10 a ton, a 25 per cent. *ad valorem* duty will yield the same amount at this price, and so would a mixed duty of £5 per ton plus 12½ per cent. *ad valorem.*

	Range of Value per ton.	Duty collected under the Specific Duty.	Duty collected under the *ad valorem* duty.	Duty collected under the mixed duty.
	£20	£10	£5	(5 + 2.5) = £7.5
	30	10	7.5	(5 + 3.75) = 8.75
Adjustment level,	40	10	10	(5 + 5) = 10
	50	10	12.5	(5 + 6.25) = 11.25
	60	10	15	(5 + 7.5) = 12.5

Range of Value per ton.	Specific Duty equivalent to *ad valorem* duty of	*Ad valorem* Duty in all cases.	Mixed Duty equivalent to *ad valorem* duty of
£20	50 per cent.	25 per cent.	37.5
30	33⅓ "	25 "	29
40	25 "	25 "	25
50	20 "	25 "	22.5
60	16⅔ "	25 "	20.8

[1] Traité de Politique Commérciale, p. 491.

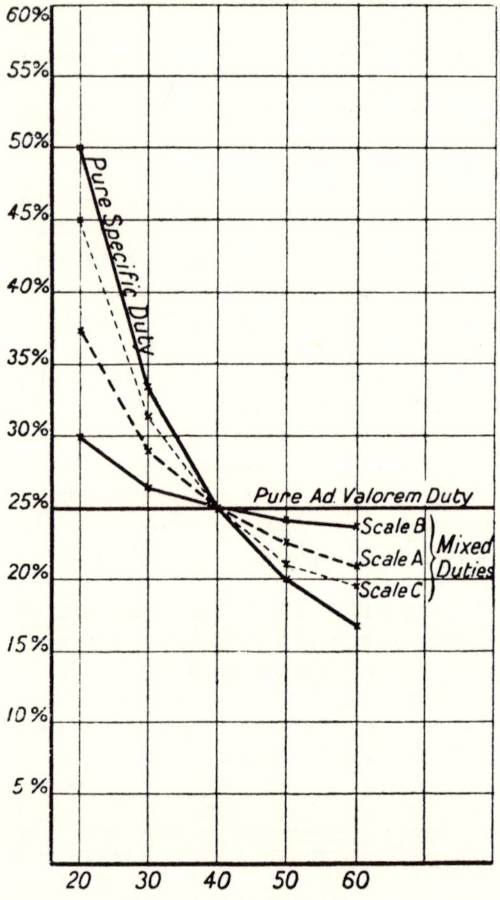

Chart 1.—*Ad valorem* equivalents of three Mixed Rates and a Pure Specific Ra adjusted to a 25 per cent. *ad valorem* duty at a given point.

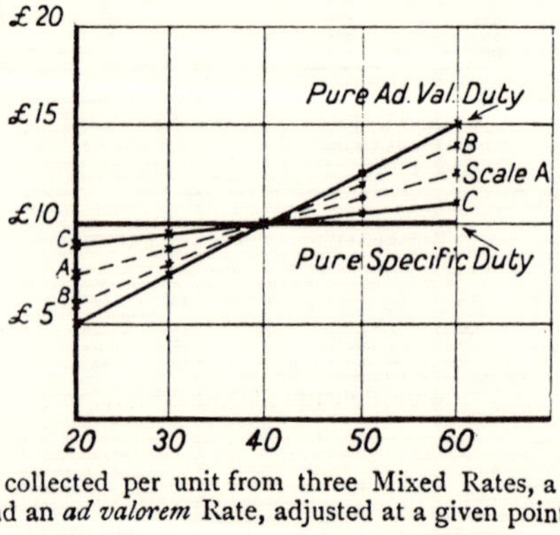

Chart 2.—Revenue collected per unit from three Mixed Rates, a Pure Specific Rat and an *ad valorem* Rate, adjusted at a given point.

It goes without saying that the quantitative distribution of the components of the mixed rate between specific and *ad valorem* portions affects the extent to which one extreme or the other—proportionate weight of duty or equality of revenue—is reached. This can be seen best by comparing on the accompanying chart the working of three different mixed scales as compared with a pure *ad valorem* duty and a pure specific duty. Scale A is the mixed scale chosen above; scale B is chosen on the basis of £2 per ton plus 20 per cent. *ad valorem;* scale C is selected on the basis of £8 per ton with 5 per cent. *ad valorem.* The greater the specific element the greater the regression and the steadier the revenue: the greater the *ad valorem* element the steadier the incidence of the rate, but the greater the fluctuation in the revenue.[1]

There is one fallacy in connection with mixed duties into which it is easy to fall. At first sight it appears as if a mixed duty were a method of differentiating the tax against the more expensive qualities without encountering the difficulties of classification and subdivision. But this is not the case. The specific portion of the duty will always make the total duty less on the higher priced articles than would have been produced by a pure *ad valorem* duty, as appears quite clearly from the following illustration :—

Range of Price.	Mixed Duty of £2 per unit + 20 per cent. (= 40 per cent. *ad valorem* on base price, £10).	An *ad valorem* duty of 40 per cent. would have yielded
£10	£4	£4
20	6	8
30	8	12
40	10	16
50	12	20
60	14	24
70	16	28
80	18	32

[1] The revenue and equivalent *ad valorem* rates under Scales B and C are as follows :—

Range of Value.	Scale B Duty.	Scale C Duty.	Equivalent *ad valorem* Rates.	
	Revenue.	Revenue.	Scale B.	Scale C.
£20	£6	£9	30 per cent.	45 per cent.
30	8	9.5	26.6 ,,	31.6 ,,
40	10	10	25 ,,	25 ,,
50	12	10.5	24 ,,	21 ,,
60	14	11	23.3 ,,	18.3 ,,

Such a duty, therefore, does not avoid the necessity of further differentiation.

The benefits of a mixed duty, such as they are, are not without accompanying disadvantages. It perpetuates all the disadvantages associated with the *ad valorem* duty from the administrative point of view, disadvantages which need not further be stressed at this point.

When we turn to the distribution of this type of duty, examples can be found in the tariffs of Canada,[1] South Africa,[2] U.S.A.,[3] New Zealand,[4] and France.[5]

§ 7. A much simpler device is constituted by the *alternative duty*. As we have seen, a specific duty is heavier with falling prices or inferior qualities: an *ad valorem* duty with rising prices or better qualities. If now an alternative be enforced, *both* an *ad valorem* and a specific duty be imposed, but only the heavier of the two collected, then the maximum revenue and the more protective of the two can always be enforced whatever the price level or the quality in question. When prices are falling, the specific duty will be applied; when prices are rising, the *ad valorem* duty comes into effect. An illustration is given by certain South African rates,[6] while other examples are afforded by Australia[7]:—

> No. 18. Confectionery, plain or fancy, of all kinds, compounded, made or preserved with sugar; sweetened cocoa or chocolate; honey, jams and jellies, etc., per lb., 2½d. (or 25 per cent. *ad valorem*, whichever duty shall be the greater).

The system in effect means that the specific duty is applied only to the cheaper or inferior qualities, an effect which could also be produced by differentiation and applying fixed rates to the lower qualities and *ad valorem* rates on the higher, as in the following American rate:—[8]

Sugar candy and all confectionery not specially provided for in this section—

---

[1] See Tariff of 1907, Nos. 23, 27, 104, 160, 161, 220, etc.
[2] See Tariff of 1914, Nos. 26, 27, 40, 44 (*a*), 47, 51, etc.
[3] See Tariff of 1913, Nos. 58, 185.
[4] See Tariff of 1907 (Kelly, p. 96, *et seq.*), Nos. 103, 104.
[5] See Tariff of 1910, No. 255*b*.
[6] Tariff of 1914. See §§ 4, 13, 16, 42, 44 (*b*), (*d*), etc.
[7] Tariff of 1914-17, Nos. 44, 94, 111, 114, 189, etc.
[8] Tariff of 1913, No. 180.

Valued at 15 cents per lb. or less lb., $0.02.
,, more than 15 cents per lb., 25 per cent. *ad val.*

An effect closely approximating to the spirit of the alternative duty is to be found in the provision inserted in several tariffs, by which a certain minimum value must be given to commodities dutiable at *ad valorem* rates, or, alternatively, that the minimum duty collected must be equivalent to a certain given *ad valorem* rate. An example of each class may be given, the one from Canada, the other from Sweden.

No. 592 of the Canadian tariff lays down *ad valorem* rates for certain classes of vehicles, and "finished parts of all articles in this item," and goes on—

> "Provided that for duty purposes the minimum value of an open buggy shall be $40, and the minimum value of a covered buggy shall be $50." [1]

In Sweden, Note 6 to Section XIII. A of the Tariff [2] provides that—

> Unless otherwise specially provided, the amount of duty payable on machines, apparatus, and parts thereof, which are chargeable by weight, must in all cases amount to at least 5 per cent. *ad val.*

§ 8. It was already pointed out in § 3 of this chapter that by assigning an official or authoritative value to a commodity and then levying an *ad valorem* duty, there was obtained a form of duty indistinguishable in its direct effect from a specific duty. We have now to examine this type of duty more closely than was then possible.[3] Firstly, duties levied after official valuation resemble specific duties in not responding to changes in the market values of commodities. The extent to which importers suffer or gain depends on whether the true market values are higher than official values or whether official values are higher than market values. In the first case they gain, in the second they lose. It is possible for government to meet the situation either by adjusting the values from time to time, raising them or lowering them as the case

[1] See also South African Tariff, No. 54, and the minimum quantities assigned in "General Note" to Class I. of tariff.

[2] Kelly, p. 634, col. 2.

[3] The actual administrative devices adopted will be examined in connection with Valuation Systems in a later chapter.

may be, or, leaving the values unchanged, to adjust the rates, lowering them when the official values are above market values, raising them when market values are above official values. The more frequently this is done the more elaborate does the administrative machinery require to be. The longer the official values remain unchanged the more out of touch with market conditions will the value be, to the detriment either of the merchants or the government. The experiences of China, with specific duties adjusted to a given *ad valorem* rate on a supposed market value form a case in point.

The degree to which official valuation tariffs are regressive depends upon the extent to which they are differentiated. In so far as blanket clauses or undifferentiated classes are laid down, the official duty acts in the same way as a specific duty, weighing more heavily on the cheaper units.

On the other hand, the official valuation system does not prevent considerable administrative inconvenience, since a large list of values may have to be established, which (whether by change of rate or change of the valuation) requires frequent alteration if the official values are to be kept in touch with real price movements. On the other hand, it allows the day-to-day administration to proceed more smoothly, since it relieves the customs authorities from the difficulties associated with the *ad valorem* system, but since the *ad valorem* rates may be converted into equivalent specific duties, this does not necessarily remove all difficulties in the ascertainment of the exact duty leviable, since specific duties may in themselves become highly differentiated. It is important to realise how closely both in form and spirit the official valuation system approximates to the specific system because it affects profoundly the judgment which one may pass on the whole idea. In form, there is a gradual change from the pure *ad valorem* duty to the pure specific duty, as the following duty perhaps shows more clearly than the previous discussion :—[1]

1. *Ad valorem* rates assessed on fluctuating values.
2. " " official values.
3. . . . . " with specific rates adjusted to given *ad valorem* values.
4. . . . . pure specific rate on quantity.

---

[1] This represents the *logical*, by no means the *historical* evolution, which very often starts with an official valuation system and goes on to a specific system without the pure *ad valorem* system being adopted at all, except for "non-enumerated" goods. This was the development in the case of the U.K.

As soon as stage 3 is reached, it is difficult to see any advantage in the official valuation duty over the pure specific duty, from which latter the former is only distinguished by being nominally equivalent to a given *ad valorem* rate of duty. If, however, the market values have fluctuated in either direction from the point at which they were when the official valuation was laid down, and a specific duty adjusted to a given *ad valorem* rate, this nominal equivalence is a mere sham. Brazil is a case in point. China we have already mentioned previously. The Brazilian duties are nearly all specific duties, but in the tariff there is a separate column of "ratios" giving what is supposed to be the percentage equivalent of the specific duties on an official valuation basis. But as a leading Brazilian expert has shown, the actual percentage equivalent of the specific duties on actual market values is in some cases enormously greater than these "ratios" would lead one to suppose.[1]

The official valuation system is, however, in spite of its defects, still in part or in whole applied to the imports of a considerable number of countries—India, Egypt, China, Uruguay, Argentina, Bolivia, and Brazil being amongst them. Their mention serves to show that the official valuation system no longer serves the need of great commercial communities. In spite of the official American opinion that "official valuation serves no useful purpose which could not be easily provided for in another way. On the contrary it tends to confuse the importer and to increase the complication surrounding the clearance of merchandise," [2] a recent American writer on the tariff recommends the system as a means of avoiding what he considers the still greater difficulty of a pure *ad valorem* duty.[3]

§ 9. A last form of tariff duty requires examination, which, in view of the claims made on its behalf, its historical importance, and the controversy which it has of late years aroused in academic and political circles in Germany is well worthy of study. This is the sliding-scale duty. Let us first examine its form and then the claims made on behalf of it.

---

[1] See the long analysis of Sr. M. Jansen Muller's Report in F.T.C. Report on Trade and Tariffs in Brazil, etc., pp. 65-73.

[2] *Loc. cit.*, p. 24.

[3] I. Newton Hoffmann, "Customs Administration under the 1913 Tariff Act," *J. Pol. Ec.*, vol. xxii., p. 868. This recommendation was supported before the Tariff Committee of the House of Representatives by the Treasury witnesses.

The form of the sliding-scale duty may be either *ad valorem* or specific—the essential point being that the amount of the duty should vary with current prices for the same grade of the commodity or the commodity as such. (In fact the sliding-scale, historically, is associated with only one group of commodities—various kinds of cereals—and we must, therefore, finally examine the question of whether defects alleged against its use are not influenced by this fact.) When the price is rising, since rising prices are unfavourable to the consumer, the duty on the commodity should be lowered; when prices are falling, since falling prices are unfavourable to the producer, the duty should be raised. By fixing a point below which the duty should never fall and a point above which it will never rise, it should be possible to fix the extreme limits of concessions to the consumer and the producer alike; the former never receives more than a certain mitigation of the burden, the latter is never allowed more than a certain amount of protection. But an upper and lower limit may equally well be provided by absolute freedom and absolute prohibition of import. In this way an extremely high price and an extremely low price lead to the maximum relief to consumer and producer respectively.

Before we enter into critical details, a couple of examples will serve to make the position clearer. The two English corn laws of 1822 and 1842 represent a simpler and more developed form respectively of the sliding-scale duty.

The Act of 1822 (3 G. IV., c. 60) allowed import of wheat from the British North American colonies when the price in the British market was 59s., and allowed foreign corn to enter when the price was 70s. or over. The scale then worked as follows:—

Corn from British North American Colonies.

	The duty should be per qr
If British prices were under 67s. per qr.	
,, between 67s. and 71s.	
,, at or above 71s.	
Other Corn.	
If British prices were under 80s. per qr.,	12s.
,, between 80s. and 85s.,	5s.
,, at or above 85s.,	1s.

Similar arrangements with different quantitative rates applied to wheat, meal, rye, barley, oats, and oatmeal.

The Act of 1842 (5 and 6 Vict., c. 14) allowed import at any time.

When home prices were under 51s. there was a flat rate of duty of 25s. per quarter on foreign corn. The duty then fell by 1s. for every rise in price of 1s. until the price of 73s. was reached: thereafter the duty was to be 1s. On corn from the British colonies, the duty was a flat rate of 5s. so long as the home price was under 55s., fell for every rise in price of 1s. by a similar amount until, at 58s., it was 1s., and remained fixed after that point.

Analogous arrangements existed for oats, barley, etc.[1]

What now were and are the claims advanced on behalf of the sliding scale? They comprise two sets of considerations:—

(1) By varying the duty according to the price level, a compensatory effect is produced which tends to prevent extreme fluctuations in the price level. For when prices rise, a greater import will follow in consequence of the lower duty, and this will reduce prices again. Again, a low internal price will cause the rates to rise, and this will check imports. Hence, the range of fluctuation will be less under a sliding scale than under a fixed duty. For under a fixed duty, adjusted to an expected average or normal price, there is no such compensatory effect. For either the duty is a fixed *ad valorem* one, in which case the higher the price, the greater the protective effect, thus causing a cumulative rise of price, or, in the event of falling prices, a cumulative fall of price: or the duty is specific, in which case, though there is greater ease in importation when prices rise and greater difficulty in importation when prices fall, yet the stimulus or check to import would still be facilitated if the duty were adjusted so as to be absolutely less as prices rose, and absolutely greater as prices fell.

(2) The conception of preventing extreme fluctuations is inevitably linked up with the conception of a normal price. The supporters of the sliding scale argue that such a normal or remunerative price can be maintained by the action of the sliding scale itself. For if the scale moves only slowly between the points forming the upper and lower limits of what is considered the "normal price," whilst, the further the price

---

[1] The history of the corn laws in the early 19th century can be followed in detail in the official history by Sir T. J. Pittar, already quoted.

moves away from these limits the easier or more difficult import becomes, there will be offered resistance to importation in precise proportion to the need for it. Thus, under the 1828 Act (9 G. IV., c. 60), between a 66s. price and a 69s. price, the duty rose or fell by 2s. a quarter for every 1s. fall or rise in price: after 69s. the rise or fall was more abrupt (although this principle was not carried out when the price was below 66s., when the duty rose or fell by 1s. for every 1s. fall or rise in the price).

How far are these claims justified? Here up to the present the balance of instructed opinion has been decidedly hostile. Prof. Diehl,[1] contributing to the German controversy an exhaustive analysis of British experience and British opinion between the years 1815 and 1846, opposes an extension of the system to Germany on the grounds that none of the objects which the sliding scale Acts intended to carry out were in effect achieved. But Great Britain is not the only country having had experience of the sliding scale. The French laws have been adversely summed up against in Amé's great work: [2] of other writers on "agrarian policy" it will be sufficient to mention Prof. J. S. Nicholson[3]—in this country, and Prof. Conrad in Germany; the former associating himself largely with Tooke's [4] criticism, the latter with Diehl.[5] The even more onerous regulatory policy of Portugal has also been made the subject of adverse criticism by an independent observer.[6] An examination of these hostile verdicts is, therefore, necessary.

1. The first criticism that may be urged against the sliding scale is that it is quite impossible for it to carry out its intended effects. At best the tariff is only one influence among many that settle the price of wheat at any given moment. The

[1] Diehl, "Ueber die Frage der Einführung beweglicher Getreidezölle," etc., in *J.N.S.*, iii. F, xix., p. 303, *et seq.* *In concreto*, Prof. Diehl points to the unanimity of opinion among the classical economists on the defects of the sliding scale, to the statistical evidence that great fluctuations were not prevented, and gives reasons for believing that the acts stimulated fluctuations; and investigates the evidence presented by contemporary pamphlet literature and the Parliamentary commissions of enquiry.

[2] Amé, Étude sur les Tarifs de Douane, ii., p. 73, *et seq.*

[3] Nicholson, "The English Corn Laws," pp. 92-3.

[4] T. Tooke, "History of Prices," vol. iii., pp. 20-49.

[5] Conrad, *S.V.S.P.*, No. 90, "Die Stellung der landwirtschaftlichen Zölle," pp. 160-6.

[6] Wagner, "Die Getreidezollpolitik Portugals seit 1888," in *J.N.S.*, iii. F, xx., p. 145, *et seq.*

effect produced by the tariff depends upon the extent to which it influences the supply on the market at a given moment, but even in this respect it is not the sole or even the predominant influence. A tariff cannot influence immediately the state of home or foreign supplies (although it may have helped in the past to influence a particular distribution of productive effort, and, therefore, the actual supply). Now consider a sliding-scale duty. Its special effects must depend upon the degree to which it influences the *rate* at which foreign supplies are drawn on, and it is hoped that it will influence this rate of import in the desired direction.

If now the assumption upon which the sliding scale rests be examined, it will be found to be this—that a given reduction or a given increase of duty will always affect the elasticity of supply, a given scale of demand prices being assumed, in such manner that the increased or decreased foreign supply, together with the home supply, will amount to an aggregate sufficient to produce the normal price. If, for instance, prices rise by a given amount, x/-, and consequently the duty falls by a given amount, y/-, the normal price being p/-, then the extra inducement to import will attract such a supply, and such a supply only, as will cause prices to fall again to the neighbourhood of p/-. If prices further rise by x^1/-, and consequently the duty falls by a further amount of y^1/-, it is assumed that the additional supply will be sufficient to bring the price down from $(p + x + x^1)$/- to p/-. Again, if prices fall by x/-, and consequently the duty rises by y/-, it is hoped that this will cause just enough of the amount which would be otherwise forthcoming to be cut off, to cause the price to rise again to p/-.

This completely mechanical assumption seems quite unjustifiable, whatever view be taken as to the incidence of the duty, as a concrete example will make clear. If the price is rising by 1s. a quarter and the duty falls by 1s. a quarter, profits will increase by 2s. for every shilling fall in the duty. If the price at home is 50s., and the duty 5s., the minimum price to the foreign seller is 45s. If, when the price at home is 51s. the duty is 4s., the minimum return to the foreign seller is 47s., and so on. What we are required to believe is that the deficiency which has resulted in a rise of price of 1s. will be just compensated by the additional supplies called forth by an extra 2s. profit: and the deficiency which results in a rise of price of 2s. will be just compensated by the additional supplies called forth by an extra 4s. profit. But if the elasticities of supply and demand are not the same, no such assumption is justified. Nor is there any necessary strict proportional relation between the amounts forthcoming at different profit levels, except that as the profit increases, the absolute amounts forthcoming will increase, so that the rate of additional inflow is not necessarily steady. Further, the price at home will be influenced not merely by the absolute amounts coming in but also by the amounts thrown on to the markets by those home growers or dealers who have been holding for the rise in price, and who now sell before prices get any lower. Under these circumstances there is no guarantee what the range of fluctuation may not be—the resulting price may be below the remunerative price in the end: so that the range of fluctuation may be as great under the sliding scale as under the fixed duty, although the mean may not be the same as it would have been under the fixed duty. (It may be argued that, at any rate, the mean will be lower under the sliding scale than under the fixed duty. But this overlooks that the sliding scale is intended to keep prices higher in good times, when, according to its advocates, an unremunerative price to the farmer results from the fixed duty. Therefore, there is no reason to suppose that over a series of years the average price is lower in the one case than in the other). There is, therefore, no reason to suppose that the price will necessarily be steadier under a sliding scale, and this argument is reinforced by a consideration yet to be mentioned. This is the fact that a sliding scale offers the greatest possible temptation imaginable to speculative manœuvres. For by buying up a part of the home supply at a time when high duties are still imposed, it is possible to force prices up, and thus admit corn at a lower duty; the extra profit made by the lower duties compensating for the losses made in "bulling" the price at first.[1] The risk attached to such a transaction is not necessarily great, for an anticipated shortage drives the price up rapidly owing to the inelasticity of the demand for wheat, and bull-buying thus tends to act cumulatively on prices. In this way an element of uncertainty occurs which is not present in the case of the fixed duty. We

[1] *Cf.* Lord Lauderdale's attack on the Sliding Scale in the Lords' debate in 1827, cited Smart, "Economic Annals of the xixth Century," i., p. 411.

are here not attacking speculation *in general*—what is being criticised is the effect of sliding-scale duties in stimulating a definite form of speculation, which, among other evil consequences, has that of increasing the difficulties of legitimate trade. For, if a speculative manœuvre is followed by heavy imports and a fall in price, the duty rises again, and consequently the conclusion of contracts for future delivery is made more difficult than it would be under a fixed duty, which gives in this respect a more certain basis of action. Hence, whilst " legitimate speculation " is made more difficult, and consequently prices are made less steady, a *spurious* speculation is encouraged, which still further adds to the resulting unsteadiness. If it is argued, as it is by the latest advocate of the sliding scale, that these dangers can be overcome by a carefully chosen form of sliding scale which only by slow degrees allows a greater measure of import, a fresh difficulty arises. Let us assume that a scale is drawn up, which will cause the transition from relatively high to relatively low duties to be only very gradually effected. This would certainly make speculative movements more difficult, because a given rise in price would only make a small difference to the duty. But the argument really defeats itself, because *the slower the transition, the more closely the duty approaches to a fixed duty.*

A word may be added as to the German controversy on the subject. In its first phase this controversy arose out of the agrarian crisis of the eighties and nineties of last century, and the negotiations for a new commercial convention with Russia at that time.[1] This period culminates with the destructive criticism of Prof. Diehl, which appeared in 1900. Interest has recently been revived by a publication emanating from Prof. Harms' Seminar at Kiel—Dr. Henningsen's " Die gleitende Skala für Getreidezölle," [2] which, together with Prof. Harms' laudatory introduction, has been sharply criticised by Diehl.[3]

---

[1] The details of the very various proposals can be found in Diehl and Conrad, as cited above and in Henningsen's book, mentioned in the text, pp. 94-107. The proposals range from a surtax varying with the depreciation of the rouble to Government monopoly of import in order to regulate prices and numerous suggestions for sliding scales.

[2] No. 99 of the Probleme der Weltwirtschaft, Jena, 1912.

[3] " Eine neue Verteidigung der beweglichen Getreidezölle," *J.N.S.*. iii. F, 102 Bd., p. 94, *et seq.*

Henningsen's main argument is that the failure of the sliding scale of the past was due, not to the choice of a defective principle, but to the choice of defective means. Apart from minor points—too abrupt changes from high to low duty point—the valuation systems adopted, etc., he sees the main error of the older systems in the fact that ". . . . the future duty was adapted to the price of the past, whereas in view of the intended price compensation, it would have been, above all things, necessary that the duty should be adapted to the prices of the period in which it should be applied. People constantly acted against this principle, in that they, on the contrary, adjusted the duty of the future to the price of the past. Through a mistake of this kind, there must very often have been produced the contrary of what was desired, because future prices could be completely the opposite of those preceding them" (p. 110).

Critically examined his argument seems at first blush completely to yield the whole position, for it is virtually tantamount to an admission that future prices are determined independently of the tariff, whereas the advocates of the sliding scale wish to adjust prices in the future by means of the tariff. But it is on reflection obvious that a duty adjusted to anticipated prices may, granted the general assumptions of the theory, compensate prices better than an absolutely fixed duty or a duty fluctuating with past prices.

But what *are* future prices? and how can they be determined? In answering this question, "the long-run price" and the "short-run" future price must be distinguished. We cannot say exactly what next week's prices are likely to be, but we can estimate what the general course of prices in the next few years is likely to be by taking a sufficiently broad view of prices in the past, for these reveal the underlying tendencies. To take a crude instance, the general level of prices was rising by about 2 per cent. per annum in the period before the war: it would have been quite safe to assert that they would probably have continued to rise by about this amount in the immediate future. But this is quite a different thing to asserting that in any particular year special causes may not be at work modifying the general situation: nor will it give one the slightest clue as to the probable course of day-to-day prices. Hence, our author proposes a triple sliding scale—(1) One—the basis rate—based on the average for the previous ten years and unchanged for five years.[1] (2) One based on day-to-day fluctuations—*i.e.*, on the difference between the actual price and the normal, ten year period price. (3) One based on seasonal fluctuations of a well-defined character. All three scales are, as will be seen, based on past prices, and the two latter have all the disadvantages associated with the older systems of sliding scales; the first is, of course, quite incapable of exercising an immediate steadying influence: it may possibly affect the mean price, but does nothing to prevent fluctuations about this mean. The practical difficulties in the way, are, as Diehl well points out, considerable, and Henningsen, himself, proposes a method of assessing the duty (fixing of rate after importation has taken place),[2] which would put importers into the most precarious of situations, and, therefore, add greatly to the instability of import.

We have still to deal with the question whether the defects of the sliding scale revealed by its working in the past are not due to the particular commodity to which it has been applied, and whether, in general, a more favourable result could not be anticipated. The great difficulty with regard to cereals is, of course, the fluctuating yield of the harvests which naturally tend to produce great fluctuations in price. Now, in the case of ordinary manufactured articles, fluctuations in price tend to compensate themselves rapidly. Since a rise in price will increase production and discourage consumption, and a fall in price discourage production and encourage consumption—a process of self-adjustment takes place with much less difficulty than in the case of wheat or other cereals, the annual supply of which forms a much less elastic *quantum*. A sliding-scale duty in order to correct temporary fluctuations is, therefore, less necessary in the case of manufactures, but, supposing it to be instituted, the same general effects are to be apprehended here also: high prices would be followed by low duties and reduced prices, followed by high duties and high prices again. And since the supply of manufactured goods is not to the same extent limited by "natural" causes, the fluctuations would tend to be more extreme since the elasticity of

[1] *Op. cit.*, p. 115, *et seq.*

[2] *Op. cit.*, p. 123. "If the system of elastic duties with changes at relatively short intervals is to be brought into complete working order, it will be necessary for the duty payable to be assessed and collected only at the termination of the period during which import takes place."

supply is greater than in the case of cereals. No change in attitude to be adopted toward the sliding scale therefore follows by widening the area of application.

But it is also obvious that a duty which is adjusted to the long-run price, to the "secular trend," is not in the same position, for such a duty does not respond to short-run changes in price. A duty consciously adapted to changes in the long period price is so far from being objectionable, that, as we saw, it is the contrary policy which evokes criticism. In all cases, however, changes in the tariff rate are a disturbing influence at the time of change, and the more frequent these changes are, the less desirable will the net effects of the tariff tend to be.

CHAPTER VI.

Differentiation and Specialisation of Commodities.

§ 1. In this chapter we at last arrive at the discussion of a question which, in some of its aspects, has already been touched upon lightly in several previous chapters. This is the problem of specialisation, which, it is safe to say, forms the keynote to the modern tariff problem. As a first approach to the technical complexities of the subject, we must deal with the causes which have made the matter one of such importance. There are two groups of causes, of very different import, which we shall have to consider. The first of these is the unsatisfactory character of the undifferentiated rate, from the narrowly technical point of view; the second comprises more particularly the diplomatic aspects of the matter as seen by the statesman and negotiator.

§ 2. The deficiencies of the simple *ad valorem* and simple specific duty have been so fully pointed out in the chapter on "Rates" that only a summary of the conclusions there reached is necessary in this place. The regressiveness of specific duties and the non-progressiveness (as distinct from proportionality) of *ad valorem* duties can be best overcome by the device of creating different price or quality levels, so that the rate varies with some specific change in quality or at different points in the scale of values. In this way the advantages of either type of duty can be obtained without incurring the specific disadvantages which follow if differentiation is not practised.

§ 3. Important as the above considerations are, they have probably played a smaller part in the transition from undifferentiated to differentiated tariff rates than have the diplomatic aspects of the matter. We have already seen that over a large area of the commercial world the type of tariff adopted is the "General Conventional," in the conclusion of which direct diplomatic negotiation plays a very considerable part. Now the manufacturers of different countries are very differently interested in the tariff; each group will be predominantly concerned in a relatively restricted number of specialities; for, under the influence of the international division of labour, the same commodity, though it may be produced in a considerable number of countries, will yet be specialised in a greater or less degree in each. If then it is desired to make concessions to a particular group of manufacturers in country A, all that it is necessary to do will be so to specialise the entries in the minimum tariff as to narrow the range of concessions to those groups in which country A is interested. The result will be that only the small group of manufacturers or producers in question will really benefit. Similarly, if it is desired to weight the scales *against* a particular group of producers in country B, in the hope of obtaining concessions from their Government, urged on by their fear of losses were these rates definitely to stand, all that it is necessary to do is to specialise the rates in the general tariff upon which negotiations will proceed. No country other than the one it is intended to alarm will protest, *ex hypothesi*, since the others produce a different grade or species of the commodity in question. Such specialisation represents an application of the principle of *divide et impera* to the conduct of tariff negotiations.

If, finally, the home manufacturing industrial group is particularly interested in the maintenance of protection for a particular range of grades, specialisation again enables this desire to be effectuated without difficulty. In the case of the general conventional system, if no country is particularly interested in that range of grades at the time the conventional tariff is being elaborated, the general tariff rates will not be challenged, and the specialisation will prevent competition in the future from becoming dangerous, whilst, if concessions with regard to that particular point are demanded, at any rate they can be sold at as high a price as possible in the shape of counter-concessions.

§ 4. Similarly, though the autonomous bi-linear tariff is not the subject of direct diplomatic bargaining, yet specialisation also plays an important rôle here. As was pointed out in Chap. II., § 2 (*c*), the greater specialisation introduced into the minimum tariff columns is "determined primarily in the interest of home industries." But since the benefits of the minimum tariff may be exchanged for the perfected conventional tariff, specialisation on both sides affects the issue here also; for an unfavourable specialisation in the general conventional tariff can easily lead to reprisals in the shape of a new specialisation introduced after a very short lapse of time in the autonomous tariff; whilst, contrarily, a favourable specialisation leads to the grant of the benefits of the conventional tariffs more easily.

§ 5. There seems no doubt that specialisation is a device which in effect seriously restricts the utility of the commercial treaty system. It is a device by means of which the principle underlying the European treaty system—uniformity of application—whether obtained by simple most-favoured-nation treatment or direct bargaining followed by the extension to any one prior contractant of the concessions granted to subsequent contractants—is superficially safeguarded, whereas, in fact, what is being practised is pure "reciprocity"—*i.e.*, a narrow offsetting of advantage between two contracting powers, the advantage of the arrangement to third parties being thus considerably diminished.

It is, of course, quite true that a third power enjoying most-favoured-nation treatment benefits by *all* the concessions made as the result of bargaining by another power with all its co-contractants. Nevertheless, since, in each case, a particular range of commodities was being considered, the sum total even of these concessions may yet leave out the special interests of the third power: although the probabilities are that it is likely to benefit by some, if not by all, the concessions obtained in this way. It is unnecessary to point out that the interests of different classes are not uniformly affected by increasing specialisation—whilst manufacturers suffer in so far as their special interests are not definitely considered, it may still remain true that the most-favoured-nation clause by providing for *uniformity* of rates (however differentiated these may be), irrespective of the origin of goods, leaves the trading classes of the community less adversely situated than might at first sight be thought to be the case. It still, however, remains true that the era of increasing specialisation, which reached its first high-water mark in the Central European powers in the nineties, was very critically regarded by authorities in this country.[1]

[1] See 7th Report of the Trade and Treaties Committee (C. 6641 of 1892) . . . "It is possible to minimise the benefits of the most-favoured-nation clause very materially by a careful tariff classification devised to favour the special produce of particular countries," . . . and Memoir of Sir L. Malet.

§ 6. How, then, is the process of differentiation achieved? It is important to notice that there are two *methods* and two *stages*. It would make exposition easier were the first of the methods exclusively associated with the first, and the second method exclusively associated with the second, stage of differentiation. This is largely, but, unfortunately, not completely, the case.

We may describe the methods of differentiation as "qualitative" and "quantitative," or, perhaps, more accurately as "differentiation by description" and "differentiation by measurement." In the first case the differentia are non-quantitative; they can only be described in verbal "roundabout" ways. Whenever an article is differentiated by being described as "polished," as having "superior finish" or other and similar qualities, we have differentiation by description. In the second case, some definite measurable quality or group of qualities or attributes are selected, and the quantitative variation in the degree in which these attributes are possessed serves as the basis of the differentiating process.

Now let us glance at the stages of specialisation. The first stage consists in elaborating the conception of a definite unit or "commodity," the second stage consists in differentiating or further specialising the commodity thus obtained. When the nature of this double process is fully grasped, it will be seen why, in the above paragraph, it was said that the first method tends to correspond with the first stage in the process, and the second method with the second stage. The statesman is confronted with a stream of goods possessing innumerable characteristics, and distinguished from one another by labels which have been affixed by trade custom and conventional convenience. His first task must consist in an attempt to make as precise as possible the meaning of these phrases, trade labels, conventional or habitual designations—to carve out a concept with which it is possible for him to work. In the overwhelming number of cases there is no difficulty in doing this—the broad natural differences between different types of articles serve to distinguish them one from another, and the first stage of the process is accomplished with no very great difficulty. What it is important to notice is, however, that (*a*) in some cases these trade labels and conventional designations are themselves subject to doubt and difficulty,[1] (*b*) that in most cases they are verbal descriptions referring to broadly conceived qualitative aspects of the commodity. These two circumstances at once justify the statement of coincidence with which we began and provide the reasons why it is not universally true. For in the effort to supplement the inadequacies of the conventional or trade designation, or in order to elaborate new concepts more suitable for his purpose, the statesman is driven on to quantitative standards of his own, although in the majority of cases he is at this point still confined to attempting qualitative and descriptive, rather than quantitative and measurable, definitions.

Here is how M. Méline describes[2] the use of qualitative definition as an instrument in the hands of the statesman; his examples are drawn from the German tariff of 1902, entering into force on March 1, 1906:—

"Si on veut, par exemple, faire des avantages à l'importation du bétail suisse au détriment des éleveurs français, on crée une catégorie spéciale à tarif réduit 'pour le bétail bovin de la région du haut plateau et des montagnes appartenant à la grande race tachetée ou à la race brune.' Sagit-il favoriser l'importation des chevaux pour la Belgique, l'Autriche et la Russie, on imagine de n'appliquer les droits du tarif conventionnel qu'aux animaux des races pures: flamande, brabançonne, ardennaise et norique. Pour les viandes, pour les conserves, pour le gibier, on crée une catégorie spéciale à droits très éléves pour les produits en vue d'une consommation plus fine, dénomination absolument arbitraire et fantaisiste qui paraît bien dirigée contre les produits français." The same tariff contains in addition some interesting quantitative definitions of what would at first sight be thought purely qualitative factors. Two definitions may be given—(1) the definition of the commodity "curbstone" (note to No. 685 of Tariff: Treaty with Sweden):—

> The conventional rates for curbstones shall also be applicable to such stones of this description as are not only plainly worked on both faces and on both the long

[1] It is hardly necessary to recall the controversy as to the meaning of the word "sardine"; as to what constitutes a trade name, see under *Trade Meaning of Tariff Terms*, in "Compilation of Customs Laws," etc., vol. ii., p. 1733, the American cases there cited.

[2] *Op. cit.*, p. 35.

> sides which remain visible after the stones are fixed in the ground, but which have also undergone a working on the third long side destined to be placed against the pavement, *to the extent that, on the upper edge of this side, as the result of the rectangular working of the top of the stone by striking away the projecting parts, a more or less even strip is produced, provided that the breadth of this strip does not exceed* 10 *centimetres*, or that, if the breadth be greater, it be proved that the stones are to be used as curbstones. (Italics not in original).

(2) Now let us compare this definition with a second one, that of "open-woven tissues" (note 2 to No. 405 of Tariff: Treaty with Switzerland):—

> The term "open-woven tissues" (under No. 408) includes, in addition to crape, only those tissues in which the space between the warp threads is as great as, or greater than, the thickness of the threads, and, similarly, the space between the weft threads is as great as, or greater than, the thickness of the threads. On the other hand, tissues in which such spaces do not occur, or occur only irregularly, in consequence of some defect in the weaving, are not excluded from treatment as close-woven tissues on this account. When thick and thin threads occur at regular intervals in the tissue, the thin threads serve to decide the width of the space. Finally, close-woven tissues in which open-woven strips or figures occur are to be treated as open-woven tissues. Tissues in which the spaces are completely closed by sizing are treated as close-woven. As close-woven tissues are also to be treated the smooth taffeta tissues known as "marceline" and "sarsenet" when they show at least 35 weft threads to the centimetre.

In these two instances we can see the quantitative aspect coming more and more in the foreground.[1]

§ 7. The purpose of the statesman may be achieved when he has thus succeeded in working out the concept of a separate "commodity" on whatever grounds this may be done. But it is possible to go a stage further and elaborate this concept

---

[1] *Cf.* Sweden; a distinction between *paper* and *pasteboard*, *F.I.D.*, p. 771. A commodity is paper "when weighing less than 350 grammes per square metre."

itself: the degree to which this is *necessary* being at least partly determined by the extent to which the concept of the commodity is itself specialised, for, if the definition is elaborate, the object aimed at, exclusion or inclusion of the products of a particular country, may have already been successfully reached. In certain cases, however, even with these elaborate definitions—and still more when the simpler trade categories are retained—a further sub-division comes or is thought to be desirable. In the first case, as well as in the second, quantitative definition is inevitable, for the possibilities of descriptive definition are exhausted in defining the commodity itself. Value is, if course, a quantitative aspect of the commodity, and where all else fails this form may still be resorted to. It follows from what we have been saying that (1) the degree to which different categories of articles are capable of elaborate sub-differentiation varies greatly; (2) that, to some extent, we must regard the two stages as alternative, an elaborate primary differentiation dispensing with the necessity for further specialisation, a simple primary differentiation leading to it.

§ 8. It is now time to turn to the detailed methods of specialisation which an examination of the tariffs of the present day reveals. And in this connection only the quantitative type of differentiation can be fully dealt with; specialisation by description does not lend itself to detailed analysis.

Let us remember that we began with four different types of duty—(1) specific duties; (2) *ad valorem* duties; (3) compound or mixed duties; and (4) alternative duties. We must now examine (*a*) the differentiation of the dutiable articles; (*b*) the differentiation of the rate; and (*c*) the types of differential scale which result.

§ 9. In dealing with the methods of differentiating the commodity it will be best to give references to actual tariffs and commodities, rather than spend time in verbal description. Among the methods adopted are to be found:—

(1) **Length.**—U.S.A., No. 363 (gloves).
France, No. 544 (sewing needles).
Brazil, No. 936 (musical boxes).

(2) **Breadth or Width.**—Spain, Nos. 361, 362 (carpets).
China (velvets and velveteens).
Brazil, No. 1,001 (bellows).

(3) **Thickness.**—U.S.A., No. 97 (marble—in block, rough or squared).
No. 329 (views of any landscape, scene, building, place, or locality in the U.S., on cardboard or paper, etc.).
France, No. 209*b* (hoop iron cold rolled).

(4) **Height.**—Italy, No. 411 (horses).

(5) **Diameter.**—France, No. 566 (tubes of iron and steel).
No. 567*b* (screws, eyebolts, strap hinges, hooks, bolts, rivets, etc.).

(6) **Cubical Content.**—U.S.A., No. 220 (packages of lemons).

(7) **Superficial Measure.**—U.S.A., Nos. 85, 86 (unpolished cylinder, crown, and common window glass).

(8) **Weight.**—Germany, No. 894 (steam engines, steam turbines, water-power machinery, combustion or explosion motors, etc.).
No. 907 (dynamos, electric motors, etc.).

(9) **Number.**—U.S.A., No. 345 (matches).
(For treatment of textiles—*i.e.*, threads per sq. inch, etc., see Commentary below.)

(10) **Miscellaneous.**—(*a*) *Age.*—Germany, No. 103 (cattle).
(*b*) *Altitude where raised.*—Germany, No. 103 (cattle). (Note 2.)
(*c*) *No. of Pipes.*—Brazil, No. 969 (organs).

(11) **Some Specific Quality.**

(*a*) *Resisting Power*—France, No. 561 (cables of iron and steel).
(*b*) *Specific Gravity.*—United Kingdom (beer).

(12) **Content of some Specified Element or Elements.**

(*a*) *Moisture.*—United Kingdom (tobacco).
(*b*) *Alcohol Content.*—U.S.A., No. 16 (chemical and medicinal compounds and preparations).
(*c*) *Acetic Acid Content.*—France, No. 172 (vinegar).
(*d*) *Manganese Content.*—France, No. 205 (cast iron).

(13) **Value.**—U.S.A, No. 119 (automobiles).
Germany, No. 100 (horses).

§ 10. This analysis, which does not pretend to be completely exhaustive of the variety of form to be discovered, will at least serve to show how different are the methods which even a cursory inspection reveals. Before proceeding further, a word or two of comment may be inserted here.

(1) Of the methods outlined above, it will be seen that the majority are quite simple and straightforward, requiring

only the simplest administrative care for their adequate functioning. The ascertainment of weight, length, breadth, height can obviously be performed quite easily. On the other hand, as we get to groups 11, 12, and 13, we get greater complexity, and consequently the need for higher administrative capacity, consequently also the introduction of technical instruments for the one ascertainment of the right class (polariscope for sugar; thread counter for textiles; hydrometer for alcohol). On the other hand, these more complex standards allow of a finer grading; an additional unit of duty can be charged for every additional degree of polarisation, of proof spirit, for small changes in the percentage of chemical content or in the number of threads. Perhaps the most interesting of all these methods of grading is the differentiation of textiles on the basis of thread content. The simple concept of number of threads per square inch or square millimetre, or whatever other unit of area be taken is really capable of many variations in practice, as the following three French examples will show, all taken from Class XXV. of the tariff :—

In the case of No. 382 the text runs—

> "Tissues of linen, hemp, and ramie, pure, plain, or figured . . . showing in warp and woof in a square of 5 millimetres, after division of the aggregate by 2." . . .

In No. 412 we have—

> "Brilliants or figured tissues, unbleached, containing in warp and woof in a square of 5 millimetres side."

In No. 416 we have for the article in question (bobbinet)—

> "Common—*i.e.*, with straight warp and single woof, containing in warp on a width of 25 millimetres."

When this system of thread enumeration is combined, as it is in the French, Swiss, and Brazilian tariffs, for instance, with duties varying not directly with the number of threads, but with the *weight*, a very complicated system is set up. To deal with the point here is to anticipate somewhat the subject-matter of a later section, but it will, nevertheless, be best not to break the continuity of the argument. Let us take the Brazilian system. No. 472 of the tariff runs—

> "Tissues, plain and twilled, not specially mentioned.

Basis 10 × 10 threads. . . . weighing per square metre" (thereupon follow the weight classes).

The result is that these weight classes only apply to the tissues containing the requisite number of threads; if there are fewer or more threads than the basis number, calculations are required before the proper weight category can be found. The Federal Trade Commission Report on the Brazilian Tariff[1] gives an instance of cotton prints weighing 8.5 kilos per 100 square metres, and containing 25 threads per square of 5 millimetres. "To ascertain item and rate applicable under paragraph 472 multiply the true weight per square metre (85 grams) by 20 (the 10 × 10 thread basis mentioned in caption of paragraph), and divide product by number of threads per square of 5 millimetres. Hence, $\frac{85 \times 20}{25} = 68$ grams, . . . and its weight per square metre that governs classification." The basis is 20 threads per square mm.; more threads than this reduce the tariff weight, less threads increase it—*i.e.*, the duty is standardised to a uniform thread content of 20 threads. The result is that the finer tissues gain, the coarser lose.

The Swiss authorities have deemed it advisable to include in the tariff itself the formula by which the weight category can be determined. Nos. 360-363 contain three weight classes per 100 square metres and two thread classes, and the commentary adds—To ascertain whether unbleached and creamed cotton tissues weigh 6 kilos. more or less, and more than 12 kilos. per 100 square metres, the following formula may be employed :—

k = the weight of the piece of tissue,
l = the length in metres, and
b = the width in centimetres of the piece of tissue.

$$\frac{k \times 10{,}000}{l \times b} = \text{kilogs. per 100 square metres.}$$

Remembering that 100 square metres = 10,000 square centimetres, there is no difficulty in following this formula; it is interesting mainly as an example of how differentiation robs the tariff of *obviousness* to the uninitiated. A more com-

[1] *Op. cit.*, pp. 45-46.

plicated instance is the following from the same tariff—notes additional to Nos. 405-413:—

"For the purpose of assessing duty on tissues presenting alternately close-woven and open-woven parts, the average number of threads is taken. This number is arrived at by counting the threads in warp and weft between two points which are regularly reproduced in warp and weft in the design of the tissue; by reducing this number of threads to the proportionate number in 5 mm. of the breadth of the design, and by adding together the results obtained for the warp and weft. In tissues woven of double or twisted threads, each single thread is separately counted. In the determination of the final result fractions of a thread are ignored."

(2) A second question which arises concerns the degree to which modern tariff makers appropriate for the purposes of specialisation the standardisations adopted by traders. As is well known, there is nothing more characteristic of modern business than the trend toward the setting up of standards, for the facilitation both of production and wholesale dealing. It would seem, therefore, peculiarly fitting that the trade standards should be taken over by tariff makers. Firstly, these standards tend to become international in character, and, hence, their inclusion in the tariffs of different countries would impart to these a character of uniformity which they at present greatly lack; secondly, their inclusion would greatly contribute to an easier comprehension by business men of the terms of taxation imposed.

Technically, of course, trade standards fall into one or other of the two types already described—they may be qualitative or quantitative. Here it is not a question of ascertaining the specific bases of the latter, but of whether they are included in the tariff as specific entities. If one investigates the matter, one finds that only to a relatively small degree is this the case. The two commodities where to some considerable degree trade standards have been taken over are yarns and sugar. In the case of yarns, there are two series of trade grades or numbers—the English numeration and the metric—in both cases resting on the length of thread contained in a given weight—and the English and metric standards thus derived are to be found in a large number of tariffs.[1]

[1] Strictly speaking, the numeration follows in the English system the number of "hanks" to the lb. avoirdupois, each hank containing 840 yards. The higher

So, for cotton yarns, see Russia, Sweden, Germany, Portugal, Spain, Switzerland, Greece, Bulgaria, and the United States, all of which show the English enumeration.[1] Belgium, France, and Italy base themselves on the metric system, though the French classification, being based on metres per kilogramme, is not directly translatable into the trade standards; the appropriate number being always half the grade of the tariff classification (*i.e.*, between 31,000-41,000 metres = between 15,500 and 20,500 metres per half kilogramme). Though these countries all adopt the English or metric numbers, they do not grade the duty in the same way: *cf.* Spain and Portugal—

Cotton yarns, single, unbleached—

	Spain.	Portugal.	
Grading.	Up to No. 15.	No. 1 to No. 40 inclusive.	The grading is clearly finer in the case of Spain than in the case of Portugal.
	No. 16 to No. 35 inclusive.	No. 41 to 60.	
	No. 36 to No. 50 inclusive.		
	No. 51 to No. 75 inclusive.		
	No. 76 to No. 100 inclusive.	No. 61 to No. 100.	
	No. 101 to No. 125 inclusive.	No. 101 and above.	
	No. 126 and over.		

In the case of linen yarns, the following countries adopt the English standards:—Russia, Sweden, Germany, Portugal, Spain, Switzerland, etc., but in the case of wool most of the previously mentioned countries adopt the metric system.

When we turn to the treatment of sugar we find that in the trade two systems of standardisation are in vogue—one based on colour (the Dutch standard), the other upon yield, the two being more or less brought into touch.[2] The numera-

the "count" or number, therefore, the finer the thread, for the greater the length of thread in 1 lb. of such yarn. The metric hank contains 1,000 metres, and the enumeration runs according to the number of hanks per half-kilo. (Oppel, "Die Baumwolle," p. 252.) These are the cotton bases; for worsted yarns the basis is the hank of 560 yards; for woollen yarns the local practice varies. (Clapham, "Woollen and Worsted Industries," p. 55.)

[1] The best source for following the discussion in the text is F.I.D., 1913; headings "Yarns and Thread" and "Articles of Food—Sugar."

[2] Of the 20 classes based on colour, under No. 7 corresponds to 67 % yield.

"	"	"	Nos. 7-10	"	80 %	"
"	"	"	Nos. 10-15	"	88 %	"
"	"	"	Nos. 15-18	"	94 %	"

See Sonndorfer, "Technik des Welthandels," pp. 128-9.

tion of the Dutch standard is to be found in a certain number of tariffs—Sweden, Portugal, Japan, and China, but, for the greater part, the modern tariff adopts yield (polarisation) without specific reference to the trade grades based on the same principle.

If we ask why greater use is not made of trade standardisations the main reason is to be found in the fact that, on the whole, trade grading refers primarily to raw or semi-manufactured articles, in which cases current fiscal theory postulates, as a rule, low or no duties: except where the revenue is an important consideration, as in the case of sugar. We are speaking here of quantitative standards: the trade names and grades of a qualitative kind are, of course, the necessary basis from which modern tariff standardisation has arisen.

§ 11. The differentiation of the *rate* can best be shown in diagrammatic form—

The rate may vary	(*a*) By equal absolute amounts per unit of assessment chosen.	Specific duties.
	(*b*) By unequal absolute amounts per unit of assessment chosen.	
	(*c*) By given percentage of value of article (1) equal and (2) unequal.	*ad val.* duty.
	(*d*) By given percentage *of duty* or by given addition *to duty*.	Both specific and *ad val.* duties.

We may now proceed to give examples of each type of rate variation.

(*a*) Germany—Tariff No. 454 (Textiles).—The rate varies from Mks. 90 on the lowest class, and then rises to Mks. 120 and Mks. 150 for the other two classes—*i.e.*, by an equal amount of Mks. 30.

(*b*) Germany—Tariff No. 440 (Cotton yarn, unbleached, single).—The rates for the classes run as follows:—Mks. 6, 8, 11, 14, 18, 22, 28, 34, 40—*i.e.*, there are four stages within each of which the rate rises by a different amount, increasing with the absolute amount of the duty.

(*c*) (1) Equal percentage rise, U.S.A., No. 265 (Lace).—Three classes on which the duty is 35, 40, and 45 per cent. respectively.

(2) Unequal percentage rise, U.S.A., No. 250 (Cotton thread not combed, etc.).—Eight classes, duty *ad val.*, 5, $7\frac{1}{2}$, 10-15,

17½, 20, 22½, and 25 per cent. Here there are two stages with a gap where the rate rises more rapidly. This case corresponds to (*b*) above.

(*d*) This case is the only one which may require any verbal explanation. It may be called "tariffication by reference," since the rates are only explicable by reference to some previous rate. Classes IV.-IX. of the Italian tariff abound in this method of varying the rate, and our illustrations will be drawn exclusively from these. Two instances may be given. The duties on single unbleached yarns (No. 162) fall into seven classes, increasing by unequal absolute amounts—viz., lire 18, 18, 30, 36, 45, 52, and 60. The duties on bleached yarns are stated to be (No 162*b*) "duty on unbleached yarns with an additional 20 per cent." The duty on plain tissues (No. 169*a*) falls into four main groups, sub-divided according to number of threads, so that there are twelve classes in all. Tissues, worked and damasked (No. 169*b*), are "dutiable as plain tissues, with an addition of 20 lire per quintal."

It will be noted that the adoption of one of these methods has by no means the same result as the adoption of the other. If the duties are increased by a given percentage of the original duties, the percentage increase in the second group of duties will be the same as the percentage increase in the original group; whereas, if the duties rise by a given absolute amount the given percentage rise will be *less* than in the original group of duties, because, on the higher ranges, the surtax will not be so great a proportionate addition as it is on the lower ranges of the original scale. Take—*e.g.*, of the duties on yarns above the 30-lire and 45-lire groups; they stand to one another as 2 : 3. The duties on the corresponding classes of bleached yarns will be 20 per cent. higher—*i.e.*, 36 and 54 lire respectively, and these also stand in the ratio 2 : 3. Now compare this result with one of the tissue groups. In the first of these classes the rate rises per quintal from 60 to 70 to 74 lire. The corresponding duties on worked tissues will be (20 lire surtax) 80, 90, and 94 lire. The first group stand to one another in the ratio 100 : 116⅗ : 123⅗; the second group in the ratio 100 : 112½ : 117½—*i.e.*, the first group rises more than the second. If it is intended to apply a surtax to a finer grade of commodity, therefore, this surtax does not entirely fulfil its purpose.

"Tariffication by reference" is applicable whether the original duties had been specific or *ad valorem*. Since the second duty varies with the first (although not necessarily proportionately as we have just seen), and since either form gives ultimately a quantitative basis to work upon, it makes no difference whether the first appears in the tariff as a percentage of value, an absolute amount, or a rate on some physical unity.

So far we have been examining solely the formal aspects of the matter. When we turn to the critique of these methods of rate variation, there is little that we can say at this stage. The various devices which have been analysed are to be traced back to the kind and degree of protection which it is desirable to impose on each grade of the commodity in question. Here it need only be pointed out that it is impossible to judge whether the duty is progressive by inspection of the rates alone except in the case of *ad valorem* duties. In the case of specific duties an increase in the amount of the duty tells one nothing unless one also knows the variations in value to which the article is subject. Nor can we judge directly from the changes upon which the specialisation turns what the changes in value are. A tissue with 54 threads to the square inch will no doubt be more valuable than one of the same species with only 27 threads, but whether the former is twice as valuable, or more, or less than twice as valuable we do not and cannot directly know. And without this knowledge the conclusions we can draw are very limited in scope.

§ 12. We are left with an examination of types of differential scale, as distinct from methods of differentiating article and rate. Here a preliminary word may be useful. It will, on reflection, be obvious that the choice of a particular method of differentiation is not necessarily decisive as to the actual basis of assessment of the duty. It may, for instance, be thought best to differentiate steel on the basis of chemical content, and yet levy the duty on the basis of value: the amount of the duty varying with the *change* of content, but not directly assessed *on* the basis of content. Hence, we at once get two main types of differential scale—(1) those in which the basis of classification is also the basis of assessment, and those (2) in which the basis of classification is not also the basis of assessment. The further details can best be seen when the position is put in diagrammatic form—

Basis of classification also basis of assessment of duty.	(1) *Ad valorem* scale—varying *ad valorem* rate with classification on *ad val.* basis. (2) Specific scale—varying specific rate assessed *on* the basis of classification.	(5) Mixed type. Compound scale—duty based partly on value, partly on physical attribute; classification either on value or specific basis, whether the latter is the same as the assessment or not.
Basis of classification not also basis of assessment of duty.	(3) *Ad valorem* classification with specific rates of duty. (4) Specific classification with (*a*) *ad val.* duties, (*b*) specific duties assessed on different basis.	

(1) *Purely* ad valorem *Scale.*—

U.S.A.—Tariff No. 260.—Stockings, etc., "all of the above, composed of cotton or other vegetable fibre, finished or unfinished."

If valued at not more than 70 cents per dozen pairs,	30 % *ad val.*
If valued at more than 70 cents and not more than 1 dollar 20 cents per dozen pairs, . . .	40 % ,,
If valued at more than 1 dollar 20 cents per dozen pairs, ...	50 % ,,

(2) *Specific Scale on Uniform Basis.*—

Germany—Tariff No. 432.—Tissues.

	Per 100 kilos. General Tariff.
Weighing more than 700 grammes to the square metre, ...	135 Marks.
Weighing more than 200 grammes and up to 700 grammes to the square metre, . ..	175 ,,
Weighing 200 grammes or less, ...	220 ,,

(3) Ad Valorem *Classification with Specific Duties.*—

Germany—Tariff No. 100—

	General Tariff.	Conventional Tariff.
Horses of a value up to 1,000 marks each (per head), ...	90	..
Horses of the Flanders and other breeds (pure pedigree stock), ...	..	50
Other, ...	..	72
Of a value of more than 1,000 up to 2,500 Mks. each	180	..
,, ,, 1,000 up to 1,200 ,,	..	72
,, ,, 1,200 up to 1,500:	..	..
Horses of the Flanders, etc., breeds, . ,,	..	75
Other, ...	..	120
Of a value of more than 1,500 up to 2,500 Mks. each,	..	120
Of a value of more than 2,500 Mks. each, .	360	..

This particular tariff number is interesting for more than one reason. It shows the finer grading of the conventional as compared with the general tariff rates which is characteristic of the general conventional system : shows also the descriptive differentiation at work in favour of certain breeds of horses (as to the significance of this we must recall M. Méline's article cited previously), and presents, what is important for us at this juncture, the very rare case of a specific duty accompanying an *ad valorem* classification.

Now let us see how this duty works out, assuming certain values for horses.

	Marks.	Rate under General Tariff.	Per cent. equivalent.	Rate under Conventional Tariff.	Per cent. equivalent.
Taking the value to be	1,000	90	9	72	7.2
	1,500	180	12	120	8
	2,000	180	9	120	6
	2,501	360	14.4	..	..

This result is certainly surprising : the per cent. *rate* of duty on horses worth 2,000 marks is less under the conventional tariff than the per cent. rate for horses worth only half as much ; and is the same for both under the general tariff. This result may have been intended (in the interest, perhaps, of breeders), but the scale is certainly regressive as between those two categories and only slightly progressive (under the conventional tariff) between the first and the second. The sharp rise comes with the last class ; owing to the absence of a conventional rating even treaty nations must pay the general rate, the percentage equivalent of which (14.4 per cent.) is just twice that of the lowest conventional rate, so that the rise is 60 per cent. under the general tariff and 100 per cent. under the conventional tariff, whilst the value has risen by 250 per cent.

(4) *Specific Classification with* (a) ad valorem *Duties.*—

U.S.A. Tariff No. 265.—Lace window curtains, etc., . . . made on the Nottingham lace-curtain machine, and composed of cotton or other vegetable fibre :—

Counting not more than 6 points or spaces between the warp threads to the inch, ...	35 % *ad val.*
Counting more than 6 and not more than 8 points or spaces to the inch, ...	40 % ,,
Counting 9 or more points or spaces to the inch, .	45 % ,,

Here a very small difference in the number of points or spaces makes a large difference in the rate of duty, which is, therefore, strongly progressive.

(4) *Specific Classification with* (b) *Specific Duty Assessed*

on another Basis.—France, Tariff Nos. 372-4. These numbers contain a large collection of rates upon woollen yarns of different kinds; the classification being based on length, the duty being assessed on weight. For combed wool, single, measuring to the kilogramme—

	General Tariff.	Minimum Tariff.	Difference.
40,500 metres or less, the rate per 100 kilos. is .	43	28	15
40,500 to 50,500 metres, ,, ,, .	56	36	20
50,500 to 60,500 metres, ,, ,, .	68	44	22
60,500 to 70,500 metres, ,, ,, .	81	52	29
70,500 to 80,500 metres, ,, ,, .	93	60	33
80,500 to 90,500 metres, ,, ,, .	105	68	37
100,500 and over, ,, ,, .	124	80	64

It will be noted that the duty rises in the minimum tariff column by equal amounts of 8 francs, whilst it varies somewhat unevenly in the general tariff column. Moreover, as the rise from class to class in the general tariff is greater than in the case of the minimum tariff, the relative incidence of the two values will diverge more and more as we ascend the scale towards the highest class: although, as we do not know the value scale, we cannot tell what the progressive rise of either duty will be, reckoned in percentages of the value of the commodity.

This type of differential scale is very common, since it allows of the choice of both a suitable differentiating element and a suitable basis of assessment. It is hence more elastic than type (2) examined above, for the two factors just mentioned need not necessarily be connected. At the same time since both factors are specific in form, they avoid difficulties as to valuation, which militate against other forms.

We may here examine a further case in which sub-classification is provided for. In this case the basis of the main and sub-classification and of the assessment of duty may all be different to one another, and if there is to be effective sub-classification the first two must be different. All three basis can be specific in character, but only two of the three can ever in the same case be *ad valorem*, of which only one can serve as classificatory principle, whether major or minor. This is obvious on reflection, for if the *ad valorem* principle were selected as classificatory basis for both classifications, there would not really be sub-classification.

An example of this type has already been incidentally

mentioned in § 11 (*d*), drawn from the Italian tariff: other illustrations may be obtained from the French and Swedish tariffs. Thus, in the French tariff, the various groups comprised under No. 412, "Brilliants or Figured Tissues," are first divided into classes according to weight per 100 square metres (7 classes): each class (except one) is divided into four sub-classes according to the number of threads in warp and woof in a square of 5 mm. side, and the duty is then assessed per 100 kilos. To give a Swedish example, No. 728 in the tariff: iron bars, rods, and coils are divided up according as to whether "the greatest dimension of the cross-section" is over 10 mm.: if this is not the case, the tariffication follows the rates for wire; if it is the case, the grading follows on the basis of thickness (3 classes), and the duty is assessed per 100 kilos.

(5) *Mixed or Compound Scales.*—We are finally left with the mixed or compound differential scale, which is, of course, only the compound duty applied to a differentiated article. In this type of scale the classification basis may be specific or *ad valorem*, the duty is in all cases both.

1. Here is a case of a mixed duty imposed on a specifically graded commodity—

U.S.A. Tariff of 1913—Tariff No. 16.—Chemical and medical compounds, etc., . . . immersed or placed in, or saturated with alcohol . . . and all alcoholic compounds not specially provided for in this section.

If containing 20 % of alcohol or less, per lb.,	$0.10 plus 20 % *ad val.*
Containing more than 20 % and not more than 50% of alcohol, ...	$0.20 plus 20 % ,,
Containing more than 50 % of alcohol, .	$0.40 plus 20 % ,,

2. In the 1909 U.S.A. tariff a large number of these compound scales were laid down. We may give an instance of an *ad valorem* classification.

U.S.A., 1909—Tariff No. 152.—Penknives, pocket knives, etc., . . . which have folding or other than fixed blades or attachments:—

Valued at not more than 40 cents per doz.,	piece, *ad val.* 40 %.
Valued at more than 40 cents per dozen and not exceeding 50 cents, piece, *ad val.*, .	40 % plus $0.01
Valued at more than 50 cents per dozen, and not exceeding $1.25, piece, *ad val.*, .	40 %, plus $0.05
Valued at more than $1.25 per dozen, and not exceeding $3.00, piece, *ad val.*, .	40 %, plus $0.10
Valued at more than $3.00, piece, *ad val.*, .	40 %, plus $0.20

3. Let us take another instance, No. 105 from the same tariff—

Spectacles, eye-glasses, and goggles, etc.		
Valued at not over 40 cents per dozen,	doz.	$0.20, plus 15 % *ad val.*
Valued at over 40 c. and not over $1.50	„	$0.45, plus 20 % „
Valued at over $1.50, . . .	„	50 % „

4. It will be noted that in the first two cases, the specific element changes, whilst the *ad valorem* remains constant; in the third case both change. It is also possible to leave the specific portion unchanged and to change the *ad valorem* portion, as is done in the following instance, tariff of 1909, No. 381 :—

Women's and children's dress goods, etc.		
Valued at not above 70 cents per lb.,	sq. yd.,	$0.11, plus 50 % *ad val.*
Valued at more than 70 cents per lb.,	„	$0.11, plus 55 % „

It will be interesting to compare the actual incidence of these duties with one another. We can only do this in the case of (2) and (3) where we know the duties assessed on certain ranges of value. Assuming in both cases values of 35 cents, 45 cents, 1.05, 1.50, 2.05, and 3.05 dols., what is the percentage equivalent of the compound duties actually imposed?

Value of Article.	Rate (2).	Rate (3).	Duty Payable. (2).	Duty Payable. (3).	*Ad valorem* Equivalents. (2).	*Ad valorem* Equivalents. (3).
35 c.	40 %	20 c. plus 15 %	14	25	40 %	71.4 %
45 c.	40 % plus 1 c. (12)	45 c. plus 20 %	30	54	66.6 %	120 %
105 c.	40 % plus 5 c (12)	45 c. plus 20 %	102	66	97 %	63 %
150 c.	40 % plus 10 c. (12)	45 c. plus 20 %	180	75	120 %	50 %
205 c.	40 % plus 10 c. (12)	50 %	202	102.5	98.5%	50 %
305 c.	40 % plus 20 c. (12)	50 %	362	152.5	118 %	50 %

A study of this table yields some interesting results.

(1) The regressive effect produced by the specific duty within the limits of any class subject to the same rate. As the value of the article rises within the group, since the compound rates do not as a whole move with the value, the proportionality of the *ad valorem* duty cannot prevent the percentage equivalent from falling, owing to the regressive character of the specific duty. Thus, with regard to the second of the selected rates, the equivalent falls from 120 to 50 per cent. owing to the fact that whilst the value has risen from 45 to 150 cents, the rates have remained unchanged.

(2) The second feature that may be pointed to is the

sharpness of the rise from one grade to another. Thus, a difference of 10 cents in the value in the case of the first selected commodity causes the duty to be more than doubled absolutely; or, to put the matter percentually, a rise in value of 29 per cent. raises the *ad valorem* equivalent of the duty by 66 per cent. In the case of the second commodity a 29 per cent. rise in value raises the weight of the duty by nearly 70 per cent., and more than doubles the duty payable absolutely. The result is of course greatly to increase the temptation to undervaluation, and this is a point which practical men like to emphasise. During the tariff hearings before the House of Representatives in the 1913 Tariff Bill, there appeared before the House Committee a certain Mr. Gerry, a practising attorney and an ex-customs official.[1] His evidence on this point is graphic:—

> "I think . . . that if you had a strict *ad valorem* duty it would be very much better in every instance than to have a sliding scale (*i.e.*, differential scale) where the rate of duty changes at different places, because, manifestly, the tendency is to undervalue. You cannot help it. There is always the tendency to shade the thing in some way. For instance, take the proposition of raw wool. It is brought in here, and if it is less than 12 cents a pound you pay 4 cents, if it is more than 12 cents a pound you pay 7 cents. You go out into China and Manchester and start in to buy wool, and your instructions are—'don't ship me any wool that is high-duty wool,' and your agent over there says—'I will do it.' But he is on a commission, a perfectly *bona fide* commission, and he goes out into the market. Suppose he cannot purchase this wool within the low duty limit: suppose he cannot do it. What does he do? He shades the duty, and the American importer does not know anything about the situation, and he is charged with fraud."

It is important to notice that though, in the case of specific graduation, there cannot be "undervaluation" in the direct sense, there can still be *adaptation* of the article to evade the tax scale, so that a sharp rise in the rate imposed on two

[1] "Tariff Hearings before the Committee of Ways and Means," vol. vi., 62nd Congress, 3rd session, 1912-13, H.D., vol. cxxxii., No. 1447, p. 6188, *et seq.*

successive specific grades will lead to deliberate evasion by keeping the commodity within the limits of the lower grade. The witness quoted above had an interesting tussle with the chairman of the committee, Mr. Fordney, on the question of fraud in relation to these acts of undervaluation and evasion, in the course of which the following dialogue occurred :—[1]

Mr. FORDNEY.—" Mr. Gerry, I will give you an illustration we had here the other day. A gentleman was talking on the subject of linoleum, and he showed what advantage had been taken of the Government. This linoleum is imported—I will be very brief, but I think this case will illustrate the point—it is made in yard widths.

" Under the Dingley law there was a rate of duty on linoleum 3, 6 and 9 feet wide, and there was another rate of duty on linoleum 12 feet wide. Now in this case the importer took advantage of the law without doubt, though the Supreme Court held there was no fraud committed. This importer ordered some linoleum, made in Japan, which was 11 feet 11¾ inches in width—just a quarter or a half inch under 12 feet, and he brought that in under the 3, 6, or 9-foot rate, which was considerably lower than he should have paid, because this linoleum was sold for 12-foot linoleum. When it came in, and was held up, the importer appealed from the decision of the collector of customs, and the case went to the Supreme court. The court held that the law said linoleum under 12 feet wide, and that when it was a quarter of an inch less than 12 feet it was under 12 feet, and, therefore, must be entered at the lower rate."

Mr. GERRY.—" There have been several cases along that line. In the case of . . . they brought in gun blocks at New York and the barrels at another port, as the duty on parts of guns was less than on completed guns. That case went to the Supreme Court, and the court held that there was no fraud, and that they had a perfect right to do just what they did do."

Mr. FORDNEY.—" But that was fraud."

Mr. GERRY.—" No; sir."

Mr. FORDNEY.—" I mean in the linoleum case."

Mr. GERRY.—" I beg your pardon, but I think it is a

[1]*Op. cit.*, pp. 6201-2.

proposition where congress, in the enactment of this tariff legislation, made a mistake in putting it that way."

Mr. FORDNEY.—" Linoleum never had been made between those widths—3, 6, 9, and 12 feet, and, in order to commit a fraud upon the Government or to evade the law and deprive the Government of the tax on that linoleum, they had it made a fraction of an inch under 12 feet wide in order to get the benefit of the 3-, 6-, and 9-foot rate, and it was sold in this country as 12-foot linoleum. To me that is absolutely clear, open, and above-board fraud."

Mr. GERRY.—" There was no misrepresentation: no advantage taken of the Government. You, yourselves, made the law, and the importer comes forward with linoleum measuring less than 12 feet in width. The same thing came up in the case of . . . on the question of the Dutch standard. The Tariff Act had been made to provide for the assessment of duty on the basis of the Dutch standard, which was the colour of sugar. That brought in sugar according to colour. The case went to the Supreme Court, and they held it was assessable on the basis of colour, and that there was no fraud involved."

§ 13. Deficiencies in the above two respects are, of course, not peculiar to the compound duty, and their discussion really leads to a general survey of the problems of differentiation and graduation of tariff rates. These are in important respects similar to the problems raised by the general question of graduated income taxation. In both the general and the special case we have to consider whether graduated or proportional taxation is the more desirable principle; in both cases we have to consider the *definition* of the taxable complex—"income" or "commodity;" in both cases we have to consider exceptions from the general rule—decided in the case of income by considerations of "fairness" or "equity" toward certain classes of income receivers, in the case of tariff rates by considerations of expediency and convenience, as well as by fairness to "consumers;" in both cases there is the question of how to avoid abrupt and sharp increases in the rate from class to class, and, connected especially with this last point, there is the question of the rate formula. Finally, though in both cases graduation may be desirable, the *rate of increase* of the tax must be taken into account, for otherwise the tax may become so onerous as to lead to the disappearance of the taxed commodity, whether income or article. In the case of protective duties this result may, indeed, be desired in particular cases, but so long as there is no general desire to prohibit foreign trade, the difficulty just contemplated must be taken into account.

In the case of income taxes, there exists a considerable critical literature on the problems just indicated. So far as the establishment of rate formulæ is concerned, no pretension to the requisite mathematical skill is here maintained. But it requires no great technical equipment to see that some, at any rate, of the scales examined in this chapter are defective when examined in the light of the above considerations.

But if there are analogies with the problems of the income tax, there are also important differences. In the case of income taxes, there is a "straight run" from the lowest to the highest incomes, and the position of the increase in the scale of quantity is the only point of *general* importance—the importance of "special adjustments" being concentrated very largely at the lower end of the scale. But in the case of tariff duties the importance of singling out for favourable or unfavourable treatment a particular class of commodity does not depend directly upon its place in the scale of values, but upon the qualitative aspects of the industrial and national situation at the time. Hence, the problem of graduation is much more difficult, since the presumed necessity for special measures in favour of, or against, a particular grade interferes with the construction of rate formulæ displaying a steady progressive trend. It may, therefore, seem as if the problem of graduated tariff rates is not capable of general discussion at all.

Nevertheless the existence of scales of the types we have been examining shows that the problem does exist. The "irregularity" due to special treatment of a particular grade can also be to some extent modified by the practice of "qualitative definition"—*i.e.*, the products of a particular country can be lifted out of the general group—it is only after qualitative differentiation has taken place that quantitative graduation occurs, within the limits of the definition thus provided. But this brings with it evils of its own: that of artificial constructions pilloried by M. Méline, whilst it may tend to postpone the very desirable step of greater international uniformity in customs definition, owing to the fear that with a uniform definition it may be impossible adequately to protect a particular range or grade of articles. The next difficulty which we have to face is the non-identity in some cases of the basis of classification and the basis of assessment. What is in general desirable is that the rates should be at least proportional to value, and in some cases progress with value. The case here has analogies to taxes intended to strike persons in proportion to their income, the tax being assessed on "objective" indications and not on the income directly.

So far as *proportional* taxation is concerned we may formulate the following proposition:—Since a flat rate assessed specifically is regressive in its incidence, to obtain an *ad valorem* equivalent proportional to changes in value a varying specific rate is required: increasing in amount as the value rises except in the event that it is *deliberately* intended to cause the cheapest varieties to be most heavily rated. An *ad valorem* duty, on the other hand, requires no variation in the rate or graduation of the commodity, if it is intended to be proportional and not progressive.

When we turn to the basis of classification of the commodity, we may lay down the following:—

(1) Negatively, the scale should, as far as possible, avoid wide classes.

(2) Positively, proposition (1) involves the choice as basis of classification of some continuous and significant attribute of the commodity in question.

(1) The avoidance of wide classes (grades containing many specimens all differing from one another) is based on the following ideas. If the duty is specific, the rate becomes regressive within the class. If the duty is *ad valorem*, progression becomes impossible as between members of the same class whose values may differ, whilst the wider the class the greater is the tendency for sharp rises from one class to another, if on the higher classes a much heavier rate is to be imposed than on the lower classes. Finally, if the duty is mixed or compound, this does not prevent the rate from becoming regressive as between members of the same class with lower and higher values.

(2) The reason why the scale should be based on some continuous and significant attribute of the commodity requires a little elaboration. By "significance" is meant the fact that variations in the value of the commodity are accompanied

by proportional variations, direct or inverse, in the quantity of the attribute, so that we may be sure that in grading the commodity on this basis, we are keeping in touch with the gradations in value, although, for administrative reasons, value itself is not chosen as the basis of classification. Value itself is, of course, the most *generally* significant attribute of the commodity. It follows that if the attribute chosen is to be significant of the value throughout, it must be continuous, that is, small changes in value are capable of being expressed in small variations in the chosen attribute. Otherwise, the formation of wide classes is more or less inevitable. It may happen that no such attribute is to be found, so that for the avoidance of wide groups the tariff maker is forced to choose between an inadequate physical basis and an *ad valorem* basis, which has difficulties of its own. In other cases, such a basis easily presents itself—alcoholic content and degrees of polarisation are cases in point. Colour (as in the case of the Dutch standard) is a deceptive basis as not being always significant of sugar content, and, therefore, of value.[1]

[1] For reasons already mentioned, the problems attending the construction of rate-formulæ are not discussed in this work. For a useful discussion of the general problems of graduated income and capital taxes, which present analogous difficulties, the mathematical reader may consult Edgeworth, *Ec. J.*, vol. xxix., p. 138, *et seq.*

NOTE I TO CHAPTER VI.

On Alternative Duties and Graduated Rates.

In a previous chapter the general question of alternative duties was discussed. Here it is only necessary to point to the fact that in certain cases the same principle can be found in the case of graduated duties.

In the case of Sweden, the notes to Section XIII. A, state that—

(6) . . . On machines, apparatus and parts thereof, for which rates varying according to the weight per article are fixed, the duty may in no case amount to less than the amount payable on the most highly taxed articles in the group with the next lower weight.

This constitutes a *minimum* rather than an alternative duty. A truer illustration is furnished by No. 135 of the 1909 American Tariff: iron or steel wire, round, grouped into three classes, on all of which specific duties are levied with the proviso that "all the foregoing shall pay duty at not less than 35 per cent. *ad valorem*." So also in the same tariff No. 314, "spool thread of cotton, crochet, darning and embroidery cottons, . . . three classes of specific duties with the proviso that 'none of the foregoing shall pay a less rate of duty than 20 per cent. *ad valorem*.' The same principle is applied to No. 357 of the same tariff, 'woven fabrics and articles n.o.p.f. in this section' where there are four classes with varying compound duties with the proviso that 'none of the foregoing articles or fabrics in this paragraph shall pay a less rate of duty than 50 per cent *ad valorem*.'"

NOTE II. TO CHAPTER VI.

Great Extension of Compound Duties.

The enormous rise of values which has accompanied the European War, by reducing heavily the *ad valorem* equivalent of the specific duties in force at the outbreak of the war; and secondly, the increased need for revenue and the necessity for economy in shipping and expenditure have all combined to increase very greatly the adoption of compound duties in the shape of surtaxes.

(1) As an instance of war legislation proper, we may cite the Canadian Act of 1915, "The Customs Tariff War Revenue Act, 1915," which provides, § 3, that—

> (1) There shall in addition to the duties of customs otherwise established by Schedule A to the Customs Tariff, 1907, and orders in council amending Schedule A, be levied, collected, and paid upon all goods enumerated, or referred to as not enumerated, in Schedule A, except as hereinafter provided, when imported into Canada or taken out of warehouse for consumption therein, the several rates of duties of customs herein specified:—

British Preferential Tariff.	Intermediate Tariff.	General Tariff.
5 per cent.	7½ per cent.	7½ per cent.

> (2) There shall be levied, collected, and paid upon all goods enumerated as being free of duty in Schedule A and in orders in council amending Schedule A, except as hereinafter provided for, when imported into Canada or taken out of warehouse for consumption therein, the several rates of duties of customs herein specified—

British Preferential Tariff.	Intermediate Tariff.	General Tariff.
5 per cent.	7½ per cent.	7½ per cent.

Some not very numerous exceptions follow.

(2) More striking perhaps were the changes in the French tariff which followed the closing of the war. A French Presidential Decree of June 14, 1919, provided for the imposition of *ad valorem* surtaxes on a very large number of articles, practically all numbers from No. 176 onwards being affected: leaving unchanged the position of foodstuffs,

animal substances, fruits and seeds, colonial produce, oils and seeds, etc. (Classes I.-XIV.: but including No. 23, wool of all kinds). The value on which the surtax was based was the declared value "of the goods at the place where and time when they are presented to the customs authorities, not including the import duty." The surtaxes ran variously from 5 per cent. *ad valorem* to 10, 15, and, in isolated cases, 20 per cent.

"A 'Report to the President of the French Republic is prefixed to the Decree, in which it is explained that the relaxation of the import prohibition régime . . . requires to be accompanied by an increase in the tariff rates of duty, since the tariff, owing to the general increase of prices, no longer represents the level of protection which its framers designed (*i.e.*, the *ad valorem* incidence of the duties is greatly reduced), and which is necessary if French industries are not to be overwhelmed by foreign imports as a result of the removal of the import prohibitions. Consequently, a provisional increase of the tariff duties is now introduced in order to re-establish the *ad valorem* incidence of the rates as far as possible on a pre-war basis, pending a general tariff revision, data for which are being collected and studied." [1]

The system outlined above lasted but a short time. A decree issued on July 8, 1919, "abrogates the decree of 14th June, by which *ad valorem* customs surtaxes were imposed, . . . and substitutes therefor a system by which the tariff rates of duty in respect of a large number of commodities are to be multiplied by a figure known as (the) 'coefficient of increase,' which is calculated in each case to represent the relation which the official valuation of the goods of 1918 bears to the corresponding valuation of 1919. The total duty leviable in respect of each category of merchandise covered by the present decree will thus be the ordinary tariff duty multiplied by the 'coefficient' which has been fixed therefor on the above-mentioned basis. Under the present decree in no case does the 'coefficient' or multiplier exceed 3, this figure having been adopted as a maximum for the provisional increase. An Inter-Ministerial Commission is to be appointed which will be charged with the periodical revision of the 'coefficients.'" [2]

---

[1] See Supplement to *B.T.J.*, 26/6/19.
[2] *B.T.J.*, 24/7/19, and Cmd. 273.

CHAPTER VII.

Differential Duties.

§ 1. The first question which requires treatment when the vast field of differential duties is reached, is the more exact delimitation of the ground. We have already seen in a previous chapter that it is incorrect to conceive of the normal rate per article as being necessarily a single rate only; and that, in fact, the more advanced commercial countries tend to replace the uni-linear by bi-linear and even more complicated tariffs.

From one point of view, even these normal rates can be spoken of as "differential." The "autonomous" rate, it may be said, is the only really normal rate, and even the autonomous rate where it is bi-lateral is differential in that the granting of the minimum rate is conditional, and the essence of a differential rate lies just in this point of the conditionality of its application.

To this attitude two objections may be made.

(1) It may be urged that, in fact, at any rate before the war, as between the leading commercial powers, the grant of the lower (conventional or minimum) rate to one another directly, or (through simple most-favoured-nation treaties) indirectly, was so much the rule, that the conception of the lower rate as a differential duty really loses its force. The exception, it may be urged, was the withholding of the favour, not the granting of it.

(2) That even if we admit that, in one sense, the bi-linear tariff is differential in one of its parts, yet when we speak of "differential duties," there is something more intended by the phrase than merely this.

Our task must be to find wherein this alleged difference consists.

§ 2. It would seem at first sight as if we could find the distinguishing characters of the differential duty in the excess or deficiency of the *number* of rates in the special case in which a differential duty is present, over the usual *number* of rates imposed in that tariff. Putting the matter quantitatively, if a^1, a^2 represent the normal rate in the tariff under discussion, then a *single* rate a, or the presence of a *third* rate a^3 would indicate the presence of a differential duty: as, for instance, in the case when, in a maximum-minimum tariff, no lower minimum rate is granted; or, to take the case of an additional rate, when in either type of tariff additional rates are imposed, either as a consequence of the desire to grant special favours or to express the reaction to exceptional circumstances.

This conception of the differential duty works very well so long as we are dealing only with the individual article or unit. But it suffers from the defect that it does not satisfactorily cover the following case:—Let us suppose *each* article to be dutiable at rates a^1, a^2, a^3, and yet let it be supposed that only one area of supply is either benefitted or prejudiced by the third of these rates. The normal rate is in this case made up of three separate components throughout, and yet the third component would be regarded as, what in fact it is, a differential duty. For that tariff, the third class of rates will be normal from the standpoint of *form*, but it will not be normal from the standpoint of *purpose*, for the object will be expressly to subject a *particular* source of supply to exceptional treatment.

The essence of a differential duty, then, we will define as *abnormality of purpose*. Hence, we may say that differential duties are rates intended to favour or prejudice the importation of particular goods, or grades of a given article, in a *special* degree, on grounds peculiar to those goods, or the circumstances attending their importation; or to favour or prejudice importation in a special degree on grounds peculiar to the *source* from which they come, or on both these grounds together.

§ 3. We may now proceed to classify differential duties more formally. One of the difficulties of the situation is that the specific titles which some of these duties have received have tended to obscure the underlying resemblances.

It will be noted that there is a general correspondence of form between the upper and the lower halves of the table, though, of course, the two halves represent opposite directions of purpose. It will, therefore, be best to take the components of the table in appropriate pairs.

- **Above Normal Rate.**
  - Discriminatory duties on particular goods.
    - (*a*) As being sold at unfair prices, or under unfair conditions. (Countervailing duties: anti-dumping duties.)
    - (*b*) As socially or otherwise undesirable.
    - (*c*) As imported indirectly or in non-national ships or by non-nationals.
  - Discriminatory duties on the goods of particular countries.
    - (*a*) For subjecting goods of the country of import to specially unfavourable treatment. (Retaliatory duties.)
    - (*b*) Imposed as a political measure without direct reference to economic conditions.

- **Normal Rate.**—(Which may itself be a complex phenomenon). . . .

- **Below Normal Rate.**
  - Preferential duties on particular goods.
    - (*a*) In consequence of monopolistic conditions inside the country of import.
    - (*b*) As socially or otherwise desirable. (Rebates.)
    - (*c*) As imported by methods approved of on national grounds.
  - Preferential duties on the goods of particular countries.
    - (*a*) As granting special favours to the importing country. (Reciprocity duties proper.)
    - (*b*) As being politically desirable without direct reference to economic conditions.
    - (*c*) As being colonies or mother-country. (Colonial preferences.)

§ 4. Anti-dumping, Anti-trust, and Countervailing Duties.—It is no part of the purpose of this work to enter into the very vexed question of "dumping," so far as the rights and wrongs of the matter are concerned. What we are here concerned with are the concepts underlying the various types of "countervailing" duty which the tariffs of the world reveal. We have in fact to deal with the three following types of duty or penalty :—

(1) Duties or penalties against bounties.
(2) Duties or penalties against dumping.
(3) Duties or penalties against "unfair competition."

Logically it is obvious that "unfair competition" is the widest of these concepts, and can be made to cover, without any stretching of language, the first two cases. And, in fact, the tariff treatment of these matters reveals that the legislator is moving away from mere anti-bounty or anti-dumping legislation towards a more comprehensive regulation of "unfair competition," in so far as this manifests itself in foreign trade, as well as generally. But for the moment let us deal with the first two of these points. What is the difference between a bounty-fed article and a dumped article?

(1) A bounty-fed article may be dumped, but a dumped article need not be bounty-fed. The essential fact about a bounty-fed article is, as the name implies, that upon the production or export thereof, a donation is paid to the producer, or the exporter. That donation may be explicit—as when the Government of a country deliberately stimulates the production of a commodity or its export by granting a premium based upon the quantities produced or exported: or it may be veiled, as when a government assesses a tax upon production and then grants a drawback—*i.e.*, repays upon exportation—an amount larger than the original tax it collected; or, by assessing the duty in such a way as to leave a very wide margin for improvements, and thus (if the goods are exported) practically giving the "infra-marginal" producers, or more efficient firms, a bounty in the nominal shape of drawback, varying with their efficiency. Or, again, a producer may sell abroad, instead of at home, and receive from a trust or cartel the difference between the home and the foreign selling price. This form of bounty may or may not be concealed, according to whether or not the trust or cartel publishes information on its action or not. These are the more obvious forms of bounty: when they take the shape of preferential railway rates or subsidies to shipping lines the connection between each individual shipment and the bounty becomes less and less close, and we then get into the region of the vague and the indefinite.

What is the effect of such measures? It is obvious that in so far as they tend to increase the attractiveness of foreign sales, they will increase the volume of exports. Now it is not necessarily the case that such shipments must be sold, as is commonly supposed, at prices which would be unremunerative to competitors or at prices which would be unremunerative to the sellers, were no such bounties granted. No business man will sell at unremunerative prices if he can get remunerative prices, and the question what price a bounty-fed article will fetch depends upon the volume desired, and the prices people are willing to pay, as well as upon the quantities sellers are willing to dispose of and the prices thereof. At a time of world shortage and consequent high prices a bounty-fed article will not necessarily be sold at unremunerative prices. The recipient of the bounty will then enjoy the high world price *plus* the bounty, and the tendency will be to divert from home consumption to export (if the bounty is on export only) until the rise in the home price and the fall in the world market will be sufficient to make it indifferent to the producer where he sells.

But as soon as production increases in consequence of high prices, world prices will fall, and, therefore, a different state of affairs as regards unremunerativeness is produced. As output goes on increasing and prices tend to reach cost of production level, the willingness of non-bounty-fed producers to sell further amounts decreases, but the willingness of bounty-fed producers to stop producing is only reached when world prices minus the bounty are less than their production costs. If bounty-fed producers stop just at the point when prices are on the margin of being unremunerative to *them*, their competitors will be selling at non-remunerative prices, and sales abroad, if the bounty is on export, will be "dumped sales" in one sense of that much-abused word, although they need not be unremunerative to the bounty-fed producer. Now let us complicate the matter by two further points. Let us suppose *first*, that in the country of production there is a tariff on the goods, which, when exported, are bounty-fed. What will be the effect? In the event of the bounty being granted for export only, internal prices will be higher than world prices to the extent at least of the bounty, and may be considerably higher. For the producer, when world prices are high, will earn the bounty over and above the world price by selling abroad, and will demand at least this amount more at home; and when prices are falling, he will always be at least that much to the good by selling abroad. For even in the event of the output being so large that prices are at cost, he can yet sell abroad at less than cost to the extent of the bounty. If, now, we assume *in the second place* that *competition is not free*, and the amount sold at home is consequently restricted, the price charged the consumer may rise considerably above the world price *plus* the bounty to an extent determined by the ease with which it is possible to "re-dump"—*i.e.*, buy at the world price plus costs of transport, and incur the duty involved.

We have now arrived at the conception of "dumping," but we must ask at this stage whether we have interpreted the position fairly. The reader will see that what we have been tacitly assuming is a uniform cost of production level. If now costs in the bounty-paying areas are *higher* than in the areas to which export takes place what is the position? In this case the bounty may merely compensate for the additional costs incurred at home. Hence, it follows, provided that the bounty is no greater than is required to compensate for these extra costs, that the country in question cannot sell at prices which will be unremunerative to its non-bounty-fed competitors, for when this country is selling at prices which bring it in less than cost, its competitors will still be selling at cost. The price at home, assuming a tariff and restricted competition, will still differ from world prices by the amount of the bounty (= difference in cost level), but the upper limit will be lower than before, for in this case foreign competition is advantageously situated, and will be prepared to take advantage of the situation more readily than was the case before, as soon as prices rise above the internal cost of production level.

(2) The importance of this difference between home and foreign price will become apparent in a moment. Let us now turn to "dumping" as such. The causes of "dumping" may be the presence of a bounty, the desire of manufacturers to keep up the aggregate volume of production at a time of depression, and consequent sales abroad at any price covering prime cost, the desire to oust rivals ("predatory competition," to use Prof. Foxwell's phrase), or any of these points together. There is universal acknowledgment that "dumping" is greatly assisted by tariffs and combination among producers. But when we look into the matter at all closely we find that it is extremely difficult to decide precisely what the essential nature of "dumping" is. An examination of current controversy will reveal that a large number of possible lines of action are all loosely described as "dumping." Let us take the following four cases:—

(1) Sale at prices below foreign market prices.

(2) Sale at prices with which competitors cannot cope.

(3) Sale at prices abroad which are lower than current home prices.

(4) Sale at prices unremunerative to the sellers.

If all these constitute cases of "dumping," what is the essential point in common which makes them cases of "dumping?" Is it the fact that the price must be unremunerative to the seller? Then only case (4) is "dumping." Or must prices be unremunerative to competitors? Then only case (2) is clearly "dumping." Or is the essence of "dumping" sale at prices below home prices? But both home and foreign prices may be remunerative, only the home price may be still more remunerative than the foreign price. It is, in fact, extremely difficult to provide an adequate definition of "dumping"—even so distinguished an analyst as Prof. Pigou does not provide us with a definition, keen as his analysis of anti-dumping legislation is.

(3) What, finally, can be said of unfair competition? In the wider sense of the word this covers a very wide area of ground—from the forging of trade marks to the importation of sweated goods. Some of the more important of the regulations against this type of action will be examined in another section. But "unfair competition" has also acquired a more specialised meaning when—*i.e.*, it has specific reference to "price discriminations." Here, as with "dumping," the point of interest to us is the legal definition and the measures proposed as a corrective.

§ 5. We must now turn to discuss these legislative definitions and measures.

(1) *Anti-bounty Clauses or "Countervailing Duties."*—So long as the government publishes the amount of the bounty, or so long as it is possible to measure the bounty, the legislator who desires to safeguard the position of the manufacturers of his own country has a fairly simple task before him. He can impose a duty varying in amount with the amount of the bounty against which it is a protection. In this case the foreign producer or seller, it is hoped, will pay the extra duty which will prevent him from decreasing the selling price by the amount of the bounty. The exchequer benefits, and the competition between non-bounty-fed and bounty-fed articles

is placed on a "fair" footing. It follows that there is no inconsistency in a free trader believing in the right to levy an anti-bounty duty—it may even be plausibly urged that it is his duty to support the enactment of such duties, as they will assist in the prevention of artificial means of diverting trade from one area to another.

We may quote some instances of anti-bounty legislation :—

In the United States Tariff Act of 1913, Section IV., paragraph E enacts that—

"Whenever any country, dependency, colony, province, or other political sub-division of Government shall pay or bestow, directly or indirectly, any bounty or grant upon the exportation of any article or merchandise from such country, colony, province, or other political sub-division of government, and such article or merchandise is dutiable under the provisions of this Act, then upon the importation of any such article or merchandise into the United States, whether the same shall be imported directly from the country of production or otherwise, and whether such article or merchandise is imported in the same condition as when exported from the country of production or has been changed in condition by manufacture or otherwise, there shall be levied and paid in all such cases, in addition to the duties otherwise imposed by this Act, additional duty equal to the net amount of such bounty or grant, however the same be paid or bestowed. The net amount of all such bounties or grants shall be from time to time ascertained, determined, and declared by the Secretary to the Treasury, who shall make all needful regulations for the identification of such articles and merchandise, and for the assessment and collection of such additional duties."[1]

In Japan, by Article VI. of the tariff of 1910—

"In respect of articles on which an export bounty is granted in foreign countries a customs duty of the same amount as the said bounty may be imposed by Imperial Ordinance in addition to the duty inscribed in the annexed tariff."

Other instances which may be cited are France (Tariff of 1910, Article 3); India (Indian Tariff Act of 1894, as

---

[1] For cases under this regulation and the substantially identical ones contained in the Acts of 1909 and 1897, see "Digest of Decisions," etc., vol. ii., pp. 1533-39. By G.A. 4524 (T.D. 21,501) the Board of Appraisers "may determine if there is export bounty or not, but if there is such bounty its estimate by the Secretary of the Treasury is conclusive."

modified, § 8), but the most important application of the principle of countervailing duties has been the international regulations of the bounties on sugar, which, to some extent at any rate, put an end to the interminable disputes and the bad feeling which this question had aroused.

(2) *Anti-dumping Duties.*—Certain theoretical points here require examination.

1. The first matter concerns the relative liability of a protectionist and a free trade country to exposure to "dumping." The first adequate analysis in this connection was made by Prof. Dietzel,[1] whose position has been usefully criticised and supplemented by Prof. Pigou.[2] Prof. Dietzel's position is that (*a*) high or prohibitive protection "undoubtedly obviates the danger" of dumping; (*b*) moderate protection "affords no security that the floods due to over production in other countries will not wash over the tariff wall." More particularly, since the tendency of a protective duty is to raise prices, whilst in free trade countries prices tend to be lower, "a free trade country is naturally protected against the danger of dumping. In protectionist countries, it is true, the duty *must* be paid, but if the price of the protected goods is higher by the amount of the duty than in the free trade country, the danger of dumping will be exactly equal in the protectionist and in the free trade country." To this line of argument Prof. Pigou offers two amendments :—

(1) Prof. Dietzel has overlooked the possibility that the imposition of even a moderate protective duty may, by affecting "the foreign country's normal export trade," contract "the scale in which it conducts the industry as a whole," and consequently affect the *magnitude* of the amounts dumped.

(2) Apart from the question of the influence of protective duties on the magnitude of the amounts dumped, the question is affected by the *type of duty* imposed. If the duty is *ad valorem* and not specific the danger of dumping is greater from the standpoint of the protected area than from that of the unprotected.[3]

Prof. Pigou's argument is, I venture to think, somewhat difficultly worded, and may be more simply stated thus—

[1] "Free Trade and the Labour Market," *Ec. J.*, 1905, pp. 1-11.

[2] *Op. cit.*, Prof. Dietzel on "Dumping and Retaliation," pp. 436-443.

[3] *Op. cit.*, p. 439, and, more shortly, "Protective and Preferential Import Duties," p. 75.

Suppose a country with a given cost level proposes to cut its price by a given amount, say from 90s. to 80s., or by 10s. If manufacturers sell their goods to a free trade country, if they wish to get in 80s. (Prof. Pigou's "receipts price"), they must sell at 80s., and can all sacrifice 10s. But what about the protectionist country? In that area prices will be higher than in the free trade area by about the amount of the duty, say 110s. to 100s. in the free trade area, the duty being a 10 per cent. *ad valorem* duty. In order to dispose of the product, the manufacturers pay the duty. The question is what price must they charge to get 80s. clear. The answer is simple. Let x be the price.

$$\text{Then } x - \frac{x}{10} = 80\text{s., or } x = 88{\cdot}8.$$

The duty will be 8·8s.: the price the manufacturers receive is 80s. Meanwhile prices have been reduced by 20s. in the unprotected area, but by 21.2s. in the protected. "Hence, for a like sacrifice of receipts price, he can reduce selling prices more in the protectionist than in the free trade country, and so other things equal can dispose of a larger part of his surplus there," [1] though this result depends on the duty being an *ad valorem* and not a specific duty.

The point for us is the warning that this passage contains as to the general conditions which a dumping duty ought to satisfy. Prof. Pigou, in another place, states that his argument is "of little practical interest," since it assumes the *ad valorem* duty to be assessed on declared values. The question is in what way can the duty be assessed to possess "practical interest?" Prof. Pigou, indeed, assumes the problem of differentiating between dumped and undumped cargoes of the same kind to be insoluble. By declaring at full price and then reselling at dumping prices *within*—*e.g.*, the customs limit of the United Kingdom, the importer renders prohibitive discriminating duties "upon cargoes intended to be dumped" nugatory. "The plan of imposing discriminating duties upon 'dumped' as distinguished from other imports of the same commodity must, therefore, be regarded as outside the range of practical politics."

---

[1] The price cut is *absolutely* greater in the protectionist area, but not *relatively* greater, being one-fifth in the free trade area, but slightly below this in the protectionist. But if we can assume greater elasticity at high than at low prices, the *effect* of the cut may be greater in the protected area.

The legislator may approach the problem of imposing duty on the "full prices" as distinguished from "dumped price" in one of two ways. The market price at time of purchase or export in the *country of export* may be taken as basis, or the market value at time of purchase or import in the *country of import* may be taken. If the latter basis be adopted, any import at a price lower than the domestic price would be "dumping;" if the former basis be adopted, only sale at prices differing from the domestic price of the country of export would be taken as "dumping." Whether this is a fair interpretation of "dumping" in the scandalous sense is another matter. Suppose this article is offered to all foreign countries at the lower price. Suppose, again, that it can be established that the lower price is still remunerative to the seller, who is merely taking advantage of trustification and tariffs in his domestic market to "milk" domestic consumers. We may answer these points as we will, the fact remains that the standpoint hitherto adopted for defining "dumping" in legal terms starts from the second plan we have outlined. In practice, the definition of "dumping" and the definition of "unfair competition" in the two cases stand in the relation of lesser to greater. In the case of Australia and the United States "dumping" is an integral part of the wider class of "unfair competition." Let us set out the definitions side by side [1] (see Table on next page).

So far we have been dealing only with the general conception of dumping. What are the provisos by which this general definition is hedged round?

I. **Canada.**— (i.) Only applies to goods of "a class or kind made in Canada."

(ii.) Certain goods specially exempt—

(*a*) Goods whereon the duties otherwise established are equal to 50 per cent. *ad valorem.*

(*b*) Goods of a kind subject to excise duties in Canada.

(*c*) Sugar refined in the United Kingdom.

(*d*) Binder twist or twine for harvest binders manufactured from certain fibres.

---

[1] A somewhat unsatisfactory summary is to be found in Cmd. Paper, No. 265, of 1919, "Summary Statement of the Legislative Provision for the Prevention of Dumping," which does not deal adequately with Australia. For further references see below.

Canada Act of 1904. § 19.	Canada Act of 1907. § 6.*	South Africa Tariff Act of 1914. § 8.	Australia Industries Preservation Act, 1906-10. Part III.	United States Revenue Act of 1916. § 801.
" Whenever it appears . . . that the export price or the actual selling price to the importer in Canada of any imported dutiable article, of a class or kind made or provided in Canada, is less than the fair market value thereof, as determined according to the basis of value provided in the Customs Act, such article shall " be subject to dumping duty.	" In the case of articles exported to Canada of a class or kind made or produced in Canada, if the export or actual selling price to an importer in Canada is less than the fair market value of the same article, when sold for home consumption in the usual and ordinary course in the country whence exported to Canada at the time of its exportation to Canada," the article is subject to special dumping duty.	" In the case of goods imported into the Union of a class or kind made or produced in the Union, if the export or actual selling value be less than the true current value of the same goods when sold for home consumption in the usual and ordinary course in the country from which they were exported to the Union at the time of their exportation thereto," the article shall be subject to special dumping duty.	Competition shall be deemed unfair if . . . (*e*) the imported goods have been purchased abroad by or for the importer, from the manufacturer or some person acting for or in combination with him or accounting to him, at prices greatly below their ordinary cost of production where produced or market price where purchased ; or (*f*) the goods are imported by or for the manufacturer, etc., and are being sold in Australia at a price which is less than gives a person importing them a fair profit upon their fair foreign market value or their fair selling value if sold in the country of production together " with charges to port of final shipment to Australia."	It shall be unlawful for any person importing or assisting in importing any articles from any foreign countries into the United States *commonly and systematically* to import, sell, or cause to be imported or sold such articles within the U.S. at a price substantially less than the actual market value or wholesale price of such articles at the time of exportation to the U.S. in the principal markets of the country of their production or of other foreign countries to which they are commonly exported " after adding charges " necessarily incident to the importation and sale thereof in the U.S.

* According to *The Manchester Guardian Commercial* Canadian Correspondent this definition is to be amended in the interests of greater stringency. See issue of 26/5/21, p. 840.

(iii.) Regulations made by the Minister of Customs may provide—

(*a*) For the temporary exemption from special duty of any article or articles, when it is established to the satisfaction of the Minister of Customs that such articles are not made or sold in Canada in substantial quantities and offered for sale to all purchasers on equal terms under like conditions, having regard to the custom and usage of trade.

(*b*) Any article when the difference between the fair market value and the selling price thereof to the importer as aforesaid amounts only to a small percentage of its fair market value.[1]

---

[1] Originally the regulations under (iii.) *b* allowed a difference of 7½ % (or 5 % in the case of some iron and steel products) before the duty came into operation. " New regulations were put in force on September 1st, 1914. The dumping duty was made applicable in all cases when the difference between the fair market value and the selling price of the goods to the importer should exceed 5 per cent. of their fair market value. The *entire difference* is taken into account for dumping duty purposes when exceeding 5 per cent. The dumping duty under the Customs Tariff applies without exemption allowance to articles of a class or kind made in Canada when admitted free of ordinary duties and also to round rolled wire rods of iron or steel.

The amount of any advance in the market value of goods between the time of their purchase by the importer and the date of their exportation to Canada is not subject to dumping duties, provided the goods have been exported in the usual course and the actual date of purchase is established to the satisfaction of the collector of customs by contracts or other sufficient documents produced for his inspection and attested. In computing the difference for customs-duty purposes between the " fair market value " in the country of export and the " selling price to the importer in Canada," the fair market value of goods is estimated on the usual credit basis, except when the article is universally sold in the country of export for cash only, in which case the fair market value is estimated on a cash basis. A *bona fide* discount for cash not exceeding 2½ per cent., when allowed and deducted by the exporter on his invoice, may be allowed in estimating the fair market value of goods for duty purposes. For example, hats sold for home consumption in this country (U.S.A.) for export at $100 on credit would be liable to dumping duty if sold to a purchaser in Canada on usual credit at $93, but would not be liable to dumping duty if sold to a purchaser in Canada for $93 cash. (Because, if 2½ per cent. be deducted from the credit price, the difference between that amount, $97½, does not differ by more than $5 from the Canadian selling value, which is $93 cash.) Machinery sold for home consumption in this country at $100 on credit, subject to 2½ per cent. cash discount, would not be liable to dumping duty if sold to a purchaser in Canada for $93 cash, as the difference does not exceed 5 per cent. after raising the cash price ($93) by 2½ per cent. to its credit equivalent. When the invoice shows that the purchased price is the same as the fair market value, but complaint is made or suspicion is aroused, a special agent of the Canadian Government makes investigation to ascertain the home market value. If the seller of the merchandise is in the United States, a special agent often goes to his place of business and asks to see his books, price lists, etc.

II. **Australia.**—The subject of dumping here is included under "unfair competition" which, by § 17 of the Act, "has in all cases reference to competition with those Australian industries, the preservation of which, in the opinion of the Comptroller-General or a Justice as the case may be, is advantageous to the Commonwealth, having due regard to the interests of producers, workers, and consumers," but by § 16 industries "shall not include industries in which, in the opinion of the Comptroller-General or Justice as the case may be, the majority of workers do not receive adequate remuneration or are subject to unfair terms or conditions of labour or employment." Further, by § 18 (2) "in determining whether the competition is unfair, regard shall be had to the management, the processes, the plant, and the machinery employed or adopted in the Australian industry affected by the competition being reasonably efficient, effective, and up-to-date."

III. **United States of America.**—(i.) The general proviso to § 801 is that such Act or Acts be done with the intent of destroying or injuring an industry in the United States or of preventing the establishment of an industry in the United States, or of restraining or monopolising any part of trade and commerce in such articles in the United States.

(ii.) Notice also the limiting condition that it shall be unlawful, *commonly and systematically*, to import at differential prices, etc.

IV. **Union of South Africa.**—(i.) Goods must be "of a class or kind made or produced in the Union." There is no other qualification, though § 8 (3) leaves the determination of such goods to administrative authorities.

We have now examined the qualifications surrounding the general principle of a special dumping duty. What are the penalties involved?

A Customs Department has accumulated a considerable mass of information in regard to the prices of many classes of commodities, and is often able to determine the fair market value of merchandise, but hearings are usually granted by the Commissioner of Customs to dissatisfied parties, and a special agent is sometimes sent to make additional investigations if there appears to be any ground for believing that the Customs Department has been misinformed as to the home market value of merchandise." F.T.N., No. 19: *cf.*, *B.T.J.*, 13/6/07; C.I.D., 1915, vols. lix.-lx., and Cmd. 265, pp. 3-4.

Canada.	South Africa.	Australia.	United States.
A special duty "equal to the difference between the said selling price of the article for export and the said fair market value thereof for home consumption," provided that the said special duty shall not exceed 15 per cent. *ad valorem* in any case.	A special duty "equal to the difference between the said selling price of the goods for export and the true current value thereof for home consumption as defined in this Act," provided that the special customs duty (or dumping duty) shall not in any case exceed 15 per cent. *ad valorem.*	After a judicial hearing by § 22 (2), "If the justice determines that the imported goods are being imported with the intent alleged and their importation should be prohibited either absolutely or subject to any specified conditions or limitations of any kind whatsoever, the determination when so published shall have the effect of a proclamation under the Customs Act, 1901, prohibiting the importation of the goods either absolutely or subject to those conditions or restrictions as the case may be; and in that case the provisions of that Act shall apply to goods so prohibited." But the Governor-General has power in part or whole to rescind the prohibition or any condition or restriction or limitation on importation imposed thereby, and the Justice's determination must be submitted to Parliament within 7 days after publication.	Any person who violates or contrives or conspires with any other person to violate this section is guilty of a misdemeanour and on conviction thereof shall be punished by a fine not exceeding $5,000, or imprisonment not exceeding one year, or both, in the discretion of the court. Any person injured in his business or property by reason of any violation of, or combination, or conspiracy to violate this section may sue therefor in the district court of the United States for the district in which the defendant resides or is found or has an agent, without respect to the amount in controversy, and shall recover *three-fold the damage sustained*, and the cost of the suit, including a reasonable attorney's fee.

The only country for which we have any records at all is Canada: in all the others no particulars are available as to the operations of the provision.[1] For Canada we have the following return:—

Years ended March 31st.	Total Import Duties Collected.	Dumping Duty Collected.
	$	$
1908-9,	48,059,792	47,722
1909-10,	61,024,239	54,796
1910-11,	73,312,368	53,912
1911-12,	87,576,037	86,354
1912-13,	115,063,688	88,963
1913-14,	107,180,578	92,426
1914-15,	79,205,910	68,296
1915-16,	103,940,101	69,143
1916-17,	147,631,455	91,715

In all these years the dumping duty collected is under $\frac{1}{1000}$th part of the total duties collected, and in the last year of all under $\frac{1}{1600}$th. No doubt since 1914 the war has made some difference, and this may account in part for the absence of any recorded particulars as to South Africa and the United States. But it is quite impossible to judge whether the results as recorded indicate the success of the measure or not. We do not know what amounts have escaped, and until we have an approximate idea we do not know how far evasion has been successfully practised. It may, in passing, be mentioned that the Canadian law has attempted to meet the difficulty pointed to by Prof. Pigou, of evasion by consigning instead of selling, by a special clause providing that "if at any time it appears to the satisfaction of the Governor-in-Council on a report from the Minister of Customs that the payment of the special duty by this section provided for is being evaded by the shipment of the goods on consignment without sale prior to such shipment, the Governor-in-Council may in any case or class of cases authorise such action as is deemed necessary to collect

[1] In New Zealand protection against the dumping of *agricultural implements* takes the form of bonuses to the manufacture of similar instruments in New Zealand (Act of 1905; the Agricultural Implement Manufacture, Importation, and Sale Act is now incorporated as Part I. of the Monopoly Prevention Act of 1908). No bonus was ever paid, only one case of complaint being raised and the claim to bonus was held to be unjustified. See Trust Laws and Unfair Competition, U.S. Bureau of Corporations' Report of 1915, p. 551.

on such goods or any of them the same special duty as if the goods had been sold to an importer in Canada prior to their shipment to Canada." This covers consignment generally, but hardly the case specifically raised by Prof. Pigou of sale at full price, and subsequent re-sale at a loss within the customs line, though power is given to amend entry, and "the deficiency paid upon the demand of the collector of customs" in those cases when "the full amount of any special duty of customs is not paid on goods imported."

(3) When we turn to "unfair competition" we find that we have only to deal with two countries—Australia and the United States of America.

The provisos in the Australian case we have already stated in the section on dumping, but "unfair competition" also includes—"Competition shall be deemed to be unfair unless the contrary is proved, if—(*a*) under ordinary circumstances of trade it would probably lead to the Australian goods being no longer produced or being withdrawn from the market or being sold at a loss unless produced at an inadequate remuneration for labour; or (*b*) the means adopted by the person importing or selling the imported goods are, in the opinion of the Comptroller-General or a Justice as the case may be, unfair in the circumstances; or (*c*) the competition would probably or does in fact result in an inadequate remuneration for labour in the Australian industry; or (*d*) the competition would probably or does in fact result in creating any substantial disorganisation in Australian industry or throwing workers out of employment . . ."

In the U.S.A., in addition to § 801 of the Act of 1916, § 802 states—

"That if any article produced in a foreign country is imported into the United States under any agreement, understanding, or condition that the importer thereof or any other person in the United States shall not use, purchase, or deal in, or shall be restricted in his using, purchasing, or dealing in the articles of any other person, *there shall be levied, collected, and paid thereon, in addition to the duty otherwise imposed by law, a special duty equal to double the amount of such duty:* provided that the above shall not be interpreted to prevent the establishing in this country on the part of a foreign producer of an exclusive agency for the sale in the United States of the products of said foreign producer or merchant, nor to prevent such exclusive agent from agreeing not to use, purchase, or deal in the article of any other person, but this proviso shall not be construed to exempt from the provisions of this section any article imported by such exclusive agent if such agent is required by the foreign producer or if it is agreed between such agent and such foreign producer that any agreement, understanding, or condition set out in this section shall be imposed by such agent upon the sale or other disposition of such article to any person in the United States."

That is, the agent may be tied, but not the user of the commodity.

With this clause we have arrived at the final point to be dealt with in this division—*i.e.*, the treatment of monopolies. If anti-dumping duties are imposed in the interest of producers, anti-trust clauses are introduced in the interest of consumers. A monopolist in foreign trade can be dealt with as in § 802 above—*i.e.*, his products can be penalised,[1] whilst a domestic monopolist can be threatened by mitigation of duty upon the goods competing with his.

Two cases may be cited as illustrations of the second type of anti-trust legislation. In Brazil, Art. 60, para. 2 of the tariff recites that—

". . . The government may also modify the rates of import duty, or even accord free admission, for such period as it may consider necessary, in respect of articles of foreign production which may compete with similar goods produced in Brazil by trusts." In Canada[2] under the tariff of 1907, § 12, and the Combines Investigation Act, 1910, § 21, whenever, as the result of a judgment of the courts or the holding of an investigation by the courts, or (under the latter Act) of a special board appointed for the purpose, "it appears, to the satisfaction of the Governor-in-Council, that with regard

[1] See also Part II. of the Australian Industries Preservation Act, "Repression of Monopolies," by which contracts made or combinations entered into in restraint of trade or tending to the destruction or injury of or with intent to destroy or injure any Australian industry, the preservation of which is advantageous to the Commonwealth, "in relation to trade or commerce with other countries or among the States," constitutes an offence punishable with a fine of five hundred pounds, or, in the case of a continuing offence, five hundred pounds for each day during which the offence continues, *v.* § 4 (1).

[2] A substantially similar clause had been introduced into the Tariff of 1897, but only one prosecution took place in regard to news printing paper in 1905. The result was a reduction of duty. Porritt, "Sixty Years of Protection in Canada," pp. 348-9.

to any article there exists any combine to promote unduly the advantage of the manufacturers or dealers at the expense of the consumers, and if it appears to the Governor-in-Council that such disadvantage to the consumer is facilitated by the duties of customs imposed on the article, or on any Pike article, the Governor-in-Council may direct either that such article be admitted into Canada free of duty, or that the duty thereon be reduced to such amount or rate as will, in the opinion of the Governor-in-Council, give the public the benefit of reasonable competition."

§ 5. **Articles Socially or Otherwise Desirable or Undesirable.**—In a previous chapter (IV., § 13) a distinction was drawn between absolutely free and contingently free goods, or absolutely prohibited and contingently prohibited articles. If we regard free and prohibited goods as representing the positive and negative ends of the duty scale we shall have no difficulty in placing these contingent prohibitions or easements among the other cases dealt with in this section, the essential point about which is that, owing to the conditions of time and place exceptional treatment is necessary.

(1) *Merchandise Marks Regulations.*—We will begin by examining certain regulations with which commodities must comply as a condition of importation. These form an integral part of a policy which has been described by Prof. Grunzel as "Administrative Protection"[1]—*i.e.*, "means have been sought for by which to place in the hands of the administrative authorities such control over the application of laws regulating economic activity that an actual, though of course not a formal, protection might be afforded to domestic production against foreign competition."

The object of legislating on the subject of merchandise marks is to prevent the fraudulent use of designs, marks, etc., of domestic manufacturers, and by insisting on a specific or general indication of origin to differentiate foreign goods as such from domestic goods as such.

A. In the U.K. the regulations contained in § 42 of the Customs Consolidation Act of 1876, bearing on the subject of merchandise marks, were repealed by § 19 of the Revenue Act of 1883, and these were in turn repealed by the Merchandise Marks Act of 1887 (50 and 51 Vict., c. 28), which, together

[1] Grunzel, "Economic Protectionism," p. 179, *et seq.*, espec. pp. 179-187.

with the Supplementary Act of 1891 (54 and 55 Vict., c. 15), constitute the general legislation on the subject.[1] The position is very complex. By § 16 of the Act of 1887—

" *All such goods and also* all goods of foreign manufacture bearing any name or trade mark being or purporting to be the name or trade mark of any manufacturer, dealer, or trader in the United Kingdom, *unless such name or trade mark is accompanied by a definite indication of the country in which the goods were made or produced are hereby prohibited to be* imported into the United Kingdom, and . . . shall be included among goods prohibited to be imported as if they were specified in § 42 of the Customs Consolidation Act, 1876."

What is the bearing of the phrase "all such goods?" This covers four classes of cases defined earlier in the Act, thus—

(1) Goods bearing any forged trade mark.

(2) Goods on which is falsely applied any trade mark or any mark so nearly resembling a trade mark as to be calculated to deceive.

(3) Any dye, block, machine, or other instrument for the purpose of forging, or of being used for forging a trade mark.

(4) Goods to which any false trade description is applied.

It is really this last clause which leads to the general necessity for clearly indicating the origin of *all goods*. A trade description means "any description, statement, or other indication, direct or indirect:—

"(*a*) As to the number, quantity, measure, gauge, or weight of any goods, or,

"(*b*) as to the place or country in which any goods were made or produced, or,

"(*c*) as to the mode of manufacturing or producing any goods, or,

"(*d*) as to the material of which any goods are composed, or,

"(*e*) as to any goods being the subject of an existing patent, privilege, or copyright, and the use of any figure,

---

[1] See Highmore, *op. cit.*, Part V. Appendix: Ham's "Customs Year Book," 1918, *s.v.*, "Marks," pp. 116-125.

word, or mark which, according to the custom of the trade, is commonly taken to be an indication of any of the above matters, shall be deemed to be a trade description within the meaning of this Act." By § 1 of the Act of 1891 "the customs entry relating to imported goods shall, for the purposes of the Merchandise Marks Act, 1887, be deemed to be a trade description applied to the goods."

A false trade description means a description "which is false in a material respect as regards the goods to which it is applied," and extends "to the figures, words, or marks, . . . whether including a trade mark or not, . . . as are reasonably calculated to lead persons to believe that the goods are the manufacture or the merchandise of some person other than the person whose manufacture or merchandise they really are."

We have thus three sets of cases—

(1) Forged or false trade marks, or instruments intended for forging or falsifying marks.

(2) "Colourable" trade marks unaccompanied by precise indications of origin.

(3) The generic class of "false descriptions,"

—all of which may lead to prohibition of import.

B. In addition to these *general* regulations special commodities are subject to particular regulations as to marks.

(1) Watches are dealt with specifically by § 7 of the 1887 Act.

(2) [1] Under the Margarine Act of 1887, The Sale of Food and Drugs Act, 1899, and the Butter and Margarine Act, 1907, the importation of margarine, margarine cheese, adulterated or impoverished butter, milk, cream, condensed, separated, or skimmed milk, and "any adulterated or impoverished article of food" to which, by order in Council, the terms of the section are made applicable if taking place without the article in question being imported in packages "conspicuously marked," renders the importer liable to a pecuniary penalty.

---

[1] Highmore, *op. cit.*, pp. 339, 343, *et seq.* Ham's C.Y.B., *s.v.*, "Sale of Food and Drugs Act and References to the Public Health Code," pp. 148-150.

We may give one further example of the same type—section N (F) of the 1913 American Tariff—[1]

1. "That all articles of foreign manufacture or production which are capable of being marked, stamped, branded, or labelled, without injury, shall be marked, stamped, branded, or labelled in legible English words, in a conspicuous place that shall not be covered or obscured by any subsequent attachments or arrangements, so as to indicate country of origin. Said marking, stamping, branding, or labelling shall be as nearly indelible and permanent as the nature of the article will permit.

"All packages containing imported articles shall be marked, stamped, branded, or labelled so as to indicate legibly and plainly in English words the country of origin and the quantity of their contents, and, until marked in accordance with the directions prescribed in this section, no articles or packages shall be delivered to the importer.

"Should any article or package of imported merchandise be marked, stamped, branded, or labelled so as not accurately to indicate the quantity, number, or measurement actually contained in such article or package, no delivery of the same shall be made to the importer until the mark, stamp, brand, or label, as the case may be, shall be changed so as to conform to the facts of the case.

"The Secretary of the Treasury shall prescribe the necessary rules and regulations to carry out the foregoing provision."

By § 2 of the above, any fraudulent violation, shall, upon conviction, lead to a fine not exceeding 2,000 dollars, or imprisonment for any time not exceeding one year, or both.[2]

(2) *Sanitary and Veterinary Regulations and Exclusions.*—Regulations made with a view to safeguarding the public health can quite easily be turned to protective uses by enforcing a greater standard of strictness than is the case with internal producers, or by prohibiting, permanently or temporarily, as part of public health policy, commodities or products without internal prohibition, or, alternatively,

---

[1] Clauses with more or less the same content have been incorporated into the various Tariff Acts from 1890 onwards. "Decisions," etc., p. 1539, *et seq*.

[2] For a further instance, see Australian Commerce (Trade Descriptions) Act, 1905, which follows the British model, C.I.D., 1915, xvii.-xxii.

without prohibiting internally produced commodities of a different kind with which these imports might compete. It is, of course, not always possible to prove the protectionist intent of such measures—more than once the British regulations have been suspected of such intent [1]—though in other cases the position seems less doubtful.[2]

As an interesting example we may give the United States regulations dealing with these matters in a summarised form :—[3]

Article.	Regulations in Force.	Authority.
Food and Drugs.	(1) Require special declaration on invoice. "The word 'food' includes all articles used for food, drink, confectionery, or condiments by man or other animals, whether simple, mixed, or compound. The word 'drug' includes all medicine and preparations recognised in the U.S. Pharmacopœia or National Formulary for internal or external use, and any substance or mixture of substances intended to be used for the cure, mitigation, or prevention of disease of man or other animals."	Act of 30/6/06.
	(2) Quantity of contents must be plainly and conspicuously marked in terms of weight, measure, or numerical count on the outside of the covering or container usually delivered to customers.	Do., as amended by Act of March 3rd, 1913.
	(3) Board of Agriculture to examine invoices of shipments of foods and drugs and "assistant appraisers and examiners will not allow invoices to pass finally from their custody until the invoices have been so examined."	Act of 30/6/06.

[1] Fuchs, "Trade Policy of Great Britain," p. 105, where some characteristic quotations are given, and (by implication) Grunzel, *op. cit.*, p. 181. Fuchs himself throws cold water on the idea, p. 105, "I have found little to confirm such a view"; p. 106, "In particular I have found it impossible from the material at my disposal to draw any conclusion as to how far the Government acted in good faith in the view it took from time to time with regard to the existence of cattle disease in other countries."

[2] Thus Grunzel, *op. cit.*, p. 183, points out that Austria-Hungary after an era of prohibition on sanitary grounds afterwards allowed limited import: this "involved public recognition of the commercial policy motive, . . . since it is inconceivable that the danger of infection could begin only when the import passed a certain mark."

[3] Customs Regulation of the U.S., 1915, Chap. ix.

Article.	Regulations in Force.	Authority.
Meat and Meat Food Products.	(1) The term " meat and meat food products for the purpose of these regulations shall include all imported meat and meat food products of or derived from any portion of the carcase of any cattle, sheep, swine, or goat, which are capable of being used as food by man, except such articles as organic therapeutic substances, meat-juice, meat-extracts, and the like, which are used only for medical purposes, and are advertised only to the medical profession." (2) Before being released from the custody of the Customs authority, all meat and meat-food products must be inspected and passed by inspectors of the Bureau of Animal Industry, Department of Agriculture. (3) Meat and meat food products imported into the U.S. must be accompanied by certificates of foreign official inspection, which must be delivered by the consignee or agent to the Inspector of the Bureau of Animal Industry.	Tariff Act of 1913. Note to Tariff, No. 545.
Animals and Hides.	(1) The importation of neat cattle and the hides of neat cattle from any foreign country into the U.S. is prohibited: Provided that the operation of this section shall be suspended as to any foreign country or countries, or any parts of such country or countries, whenever the Secretary of the Treasury shall officially determine, and give public notice thereof, that such importation will not tend to the introduction or spread of contagious or infectious diseases among the cattle of the U.S.; and the Secretary of the Treasury is hereby authorised and empowered, and it shall be his duty, to make all necessary orders and regulations to carry this section into effect, or to suspend the same as herein provided, and to send copies thereof to the proper officers in the U.S. and to such officers or agents of the U.S. in foreign countries as he shall judge necessary. (2) By T.D. 31,081, the landing of horses, asses, mules, sheep, goats, and swine from any of the countries of Asia and Africa at any of the ports of the U.S., the Territories or Dependencies thereof is prohibited. The landing of all animals from the Philippine Isles is similarly prohibited.	Tariff Act of 1913, § iv., para. H.

Article.	Regulations in Force.	Authority.
Viruses, Serums, and Toxins for the treatment of Domestic Animals.	Prohibited unless the importer holds a permit from the Department of Agriculture covering the specific product.	Act of March 4th, 1913.
Viruses, Serums, and Toxines for the Treatment of Man.	(1) Prohibited entry unless propagated in an establishment holding an unsuspended and unrevoked licence. The Treasury publishes a periodical list of establishments holding licences, the number of the licence, and the names of the several products produced. (2) Packages must be labelled or plainly marked with the name of the article, the name, address, and licence number of the manufacturer, and the time beyond which the contents cannot be expected to yield their specific results. (3) Samples must be sent to the Surgeon-General of the Public Health Service, and all importations will be detained pending examination.	Act of July 1, 1902.
Tea.	(1) The importation of any merchandise as tea, which is inferior in purity, quality, and fitness for consumption to the standards fixed and established by the Secretary of the Treasury in accordance with § 3 of the Act of 1897 is prohibited. (2) Tea until examined must be stored in special tea warehouses or other approved places; sworn samples may be submitted by importer or samples may be drawn by collector. (3) The examination " shall be made according " to the usages and customs of the tea trade, including the testing of an infusion in boiling water, and the " Read method with additions and modifications for the detection of artificial colouring and facing." Tea rejected by the examiner must be sent to the supervising tea examiner and appeal lies to a Board of three General Appraisers designated by the Secretary of the Treasury.	Act of March 2nd, 1897, amended May 16th, 1908, for low-grade tea to be used for chemical purposes only.[1]

[1] The Act is printed *in extenso* in " Decisions, etc.," vol. i., p. 1141, *et seq.* The Act provides in § 2 for the appointment each year of a board of seven members, " each of whom shall be an expert in teas," who shall prepare standard samples

The preceding statement (which by no means covers all the cases for which special regulations are laid down, even on public health grounds), may serve to illustrate a situation which can be more or less paralleled in other countries.[1]

(3) *Copyright Regulations.*—Two questions must be distinguished here: (*a*) the conditions under which copyright in literary or artistic products is awarded under the copyright law of a given country, (*b*) the conditions under which a given importation is held to be an infringement of such copyright, and, therefore, the customs regulations intended to check such importation. The position in the U.K. to-day is governed by § 14 (1)-(5) of the Imperial Copyright Act of

---

of tea, serving for one year, and removable at all times by the Secretary of the Treasury. By § 3 the Secretary of the Treasury, upon the recommendation of the Board, "shall fix and establish uniform standards of purity, quality and fitness for consumption of all kinds of teas imported into U.S.," samples of such standards to be deposited at certain specified customs houses, and dealers in tea shall be supplied with such samples at cost. "All teas, or merchandise described as tea, of inferior purity, quality, and fitness for consumption to such standards shall be deemed within the prohibition of the first section hereof."

[1] For U.K., see Ham's "Customs Year Book: Cattle," pp. 51-54; for other foods, see p. 148, *et seq.* Highmore, *op. cit.*, p. 312 (tea under Act of 1875): p. 343, *et seq.*, for agricultural produce. For South America, T.S., No. 34, p. 89, *et seq.*; p. 178, *et seq.*; p. 217, *et seq.*; p. 283, *et seq.*; p. 296, *et seq.* For France, see Pallain, vol. i., pp. 358-396. So far as cattle are concerned, the Government is authorised to prohibit entry or subject animals suspect to quarantine and prescribe at the frontier, without compensation, the slaughter of suspected animals (Laws of 1881, 1898, and 1905). These prohibitions or restrictions are issued by the Minister of Agriculture on the advice of the "Comité Consultatif des Epizooties," they may extend to all objects presenting the same danger. In addition, *at all times* import and export of cattle are subject to sanitary inspection of the cattle at the expense of the person concerned (déclarant). There are special regulations for (*a*) animals destined for breeding, grazing, or dairying, which are to be detained for forty-eight hours for the detection of tuberculosis: (*b*) animals for butchering purposes must be imported by special ports, and can only be sent to special places where there are public slaughter-houses under veterinary superintendence; (*c*) a large number of special cases—haulage animals, animals belonging to gypsies, circus proprietors, etc., racehorses, and animals intended for markets and fairs, and so on. There is a tariff of charges for inspection (Droits d'Inspection Sanitaires). Fresh or frozen meat is subject to sanitary examination; food containing borax or borac acid, fresh pork, whether frozen or not, from the U.S.A., fresh meat of horses, asses, or cross-breeds are a forbidden import. Salt pork from the U.S.A. is admissible under special conditions (forbidden altogether between 1881-1891); the import of river fish at times when the catch of the same is forbidden in France itself is prohibited; pharmaceutical products are subject to a special régime as to determination of duty (Tariff of 1910, No. 316); the import of saccharine or allied substances is prohibited, although it may be manufactured internally. Certain grades of mineral oil and certain plants are also subject to prohibition (*loc. cit.*, §§ 460-470).

1911, which, as Appendix IV. to the 1915 Edition of the Colonial Imports Duties shows, has been largely adopted throughout the Empire. By § 14 (1) copies made out of the United Kingdom of any work in which copyright subsists which if made in the United Kingdom would infringe copyright, and as to which the owner of the copyright gives notice in writing by himself or his agent to the Commissioners of Customs and Excise, that he is desirous that such copies shall not be imported into the United Kingdom, shall not be so imported.[1]

(4) *Prison Goods.*—Since articles produced by convict labour are held to be in a sense "sweated," their importation for sale in competition with the products of labour at normal rates is frequently forbidden. Thus, by § 52 (*d*) of the Australian Customs Act—

"Goods manufactured or produced wholly or in part by prison labour or which have been made within or in connection with any prison, jail, or penitentiary," are included among prohibited imports.

In Canada, by Tariff No. 1,206 (Schedule C) of the 1907 tariff "Prohibited Goods"—

"Goods manufactured or produced wholly or in part by prison labour, or which have been made within or in connection with any prison, jail, or penitentiary: also goods similar in character to those produced in such institutions, when sold or offered for sale by any person, firm, or corporation having a contract for the manufacture of such articles in such institutions, or by any agent of such person, firm, or corporation, or when such goods were originally purchased from or transferred by any such contractor."

Similar prohibitions are contained in the customs law of South Africa (Customs Management Act, 1913, § 23 (*d*); New Zealand (Proclamation of July 27, 1908); Newfoundland

---

[1] See also Ham's "Customs Year Book," *s.v.* Copyright. For the U.S.A., see "Decisions, etc.," p. 169, *et seq.* The position under the American Copyright Law of 1909 is that books and periodicals to be accorded protection must be printed from type set within the limits of the United States; the importation "of any article bearing a false notice of copyright when there is no existing copyright thereon in the U.S., or of any piratical copies of any works copyrighted in the United States, is prohibited" (§ 30). By § 31, during the continuance of the American copyright, *any* copies not produced in accordance with the manufacturing provisions of the Act are prohibited importation, *although authorised by the author or proprietor*, though there are certain exceptions to this rule.

(Schedule C to Tariff); the U.S.A. (Tariff of 1913, Sec. IV., para. 1)[1]; the U.K. (by 60 and 61 Vict., c. 63).

(5) *Rationing of Imports.*—Regulations and enactments having as effect a limitation of the total quantity which may be imported have received added importance owing to the exigencies of the European War, but similar regulations can be found in pre-war tariffs or commercial treaties. Thus, in the Canadian tariff of 1907 the quantity of raw sugar which may be imported under Tariff No. 135*a* is limited to " the extent of the quantity of sugar refined during the calendar year 1912 and 1913 by such refiners from sugar produced in Canada from Canadian beetroot," whilst, by Tariff No. 135*b*, raw sugar " when imported to be refined in Canada by any sugar refining company not engaged in refining sugar from the product of Canadian beetroot, to the extent of one-fifth of the weight of sugar refined from raw sugar by such refining company in Canada during the calendar year in which such raw sugar is imported." [2]

(6) *Tariff Rebates.*—A large number of tariffs allow of conditional free importation or conditional mitigations of the duty otherwise payable. We may divide these cases into four groups—(*a*) on account of some quality possessed by the article itself, (*b*) on account of the specific use to which the article is to be put, (*c*) on account of the individual by whom the import takes place, (*d*) special or exceptional circumstances. These various aspects cannot always be separated in practice, but they are nevertheless more or less distinguishable.

(*a*) Two cases can be mentioned in this connection—

1. Under the German Tariff of 1906 articles may be exempted from duty as being below a minimum standard of weight or value, or on which the duty, if levied, would be

[1] The exclusion of prison-made goods raises the whole question of how far the exclusion of sweated goods is (*a*) possible, (*b*) desirable. On this point, see S. and B. Webb, " Industrial Democracy," Appendix II., " The Bearing of Industrial Parasitism and the Policy of a National Minimum on the Free Trade Controversy," where (*n.* 1, p. 866) the device of a protective tariff is rejected, whilst the general argument of a " national minimum " is declared independent of the action of other countries (p. 869, *et seq.*). Apart from this, the question of definition would remain to be settled—a difficult matter, owing to the existence, not only of different wage-levels, but efficiency levels and " standards of life."

[2] For the restrictions under the Austro-Hungarian Treaties with the Balkans, see Grunzel, *op. cit.*, pp. 183-184. For the position in the U.K. at the end of July, 1919, see *B.T.J.*, 31/7/19, " Consolidated List of Import Restrictions."

below a given minimum amount. Thus, § 5 of the tariff enacts that—

The following goods are to be free of duty:—

(*a*) Articles sent by post from abroad, when the gross weight of such articles does not exceed 250 grms.

(*b*) All articles paying duty according to weight, when such weight is under 50 grms.

. . . Duties amounting to less than 5 pfennigs will not be levied, and higher duties only in so far as they are divisible by five, all surplus pfennigs being eliminated.

The Bundesrath may, in case of misuse of the provisions hereof, enact limitations affecting any specified goods or frontier limits.

The exemption may be restricted by the Bundesrath in case of finely-cut tobacco and cigarettes, and also tubes and small sheets of cigarette paper.

2. A much more important category is that of *Samples.*

We may begin with a few simple instances—

In Germany, by Art. 6 (10), there are included among the free goods—

"Sample cards and samples in cutting or patterns which are only fit to be used as such, except samples of alimentary or consumable articles, but including specimens and samples of coffee, cocoa, sugar, raw tobacco, and dried fruits imported through the post and weighing up to 350 grms."

By No. 1,774 of the Chilean Tariff of 1916 "samples of goods the duty on which would not exceed 2 pesos" are admitted free.

In Brazil, also, by Art. 2, § 1, "samples of no or insignificant value" are free. "By samples of no or insignificant value shall be understood fragments or parts of any kind of goods or merchandise in a quantity strictly necessary to reveal the nature, kind, and quality, provided that the duties leviable on each package do not exceed 1,000 reis." Moreover, the exemption is subject to "such bond being given as the Inspector of Customs or the Administrator of the Treasury may deem necessary."

These cases are already sufficient to show that the free importation of samples is usually subject to conditions; that the commodities themselves should possess no or little value is a precaution which is obviously necessary in the interests of revenue. The deposit of bonds for payments if the goods in question are sold or otherwise disposed of is a similar precautionary measure—the case of the attempted defraudation of the Chilean Customs Authorities which was mentioned in a previous chapter shows that an unlimited freedom of importing "samples" is provocative of fraud. Hence, the requirement that samples to be admitted as such shall be rendered useless for sale, although still retaining their value as instruments of display or advertisement. Thus, in France the general principle is that "samples without value" are admitted freely, but textile goods, such as ties, handkerchiefs, and so on—*i.e.*, "objets entiers" must be defaced "so as to destroy their use and deprive them of all value." In other cases, free admission for a period of six months is permitted, on the condition of deposit of the duty or the value of the article or bond given that the articles will be re-exported within the maximum period allowed, or that four times the duty or the value will be paid if re-exportation is not effectuated.[1] The position in the United States is that "samples solely for use in taking orders for merchandise (together with a group of miscellaneous articles imported for specific purposes) . . . may be admitted without the payment of duty under bond for their exportation within six months from the date of importation, and under such regulations and subject to such conditions at the Secretary of the Treasury may prescribe: provided that no article shall be entitled to entry under this section that is intended for sale or which is imported for sale on approval." [2]

(*b*) Rebates of duty on account of the use to which the commodity is to be put provide a very wide field from which to draw instances.

The Canadian tariff is particularly fruitful in cases of this kind. A certain proportion of "tariff numbers" provide that the rates laid down are applicable when the commodity in question is imported "by the manufacturers of . . . for

---

[1] Pallain, vol. i., § 321, *et seq.*

[2] 1913 Tariff, § 3, para. J (4). The position as regards samples *accompanying commercial travellers* is, in the case of the U.K. and certain reciprocating countries subject to agreement, providing for duty-free importation, the marking of the samples by the Customs, deposit of duty or bond therefor, and re-export within a maximum period of *twelve* months. See Ham's "Customs Year Book," 1918, pp. 152-153.

use exclusively in the manufacture of such articles in their own factories." The rebates thus granted are of two kinds. (1) The article is admitted at the lower rate fixed only under the condition laid down, otherwise it is presumably imported subject to the higher duty of the unenumerated clause: (2) if the article fulfils the condition it is admitted *free*, otherwise presumably it also is subject to the conditions of the unenumerated clause. A large number of special rates can be found in the various groups of the tariff (see especially Group II., the "miscellaneous" group), but in addition there is a special schedule B "of goods subject to drawback for home consumption." In the case of these goods, when they enter into cost of manufacturing certain articles (*e.g.*, No. 1,001, "oil, fuel, and other articles not machinery, when entering into the cost of binder twine manufactured in Canada") or when they enter into the manufactured article itself as a component thereof enjoy a rebate, the extent of the drawback being variously 99, 65, and 50 per cent. (17 out of the 21 cases receive the maximum drawback).

Similar conditions can be found elsewhere. Thus, in Germany, Art. 6 (12) of the tariff exempts from duty—

"Materials necessary for building, repairing, or equipping sea or river vessels, with the exception of cabin and galley requisites. This privilege does not apply to pleasure boats for river or lake navigation, which are subject to such special regulations as shall be issued by the Bundesrath."

§ 36 of Art. 2 of the Preliminary Dispositions of the Brazilian Tariff exempts from duty—

"Agricultural machines, . . . machines intended for central stations and component parts thereof, and exploitation materials for use in mines, imported direct by agricultural establishments or mining undertakers for their own use. Undertakings having imported apparatus and materials for any other use shall incur a penalty of double the duty fixed in the tariff.

"By exploitation materials are solely understood chemicals, explosives, metalloids, and simple metals, and necessary extracting and transport plant for mining purposes." Machines and materials for the improved manufacture of sugar also benefit.

Enough will have been said to draw attention to what may be called "rebates on industrial grounds." Other cases are imports intended for educational or scientific purposes and so on.[1]

(*c*) When we turn to rebates made on the ground of the special position of the importer we may distinguish three important cases. (It will be noted that the Canadian cases above could quite legitimately have been placed under *this* heading, but cases of this kind are now explicitly excluded.)

(1) Diplomatic privileges. In most tariff legislation provision is made for the exemption from tariff taxation of importations for their own use made by foreign ambassadors, and/or other diplomatic officials accredited to the country in question: together with articles imported for official use by foreign consulates, with or without the requirement of reciprocity.[2]

(2) The second case is that of goods imported by the government of a country itself. These goods need not be free of duty—in France, for instance, the rule that the king paid duty on imports for his own consumption " has passed . . . into modern legislation. Objects imported or exported on account of the government and the administrative authorities (Administrations Publiques) are liable to duty in the same way as those imported by way of trade or by private individuals.[3] But in a good many cases the opposite rule can be found, qualified or not as the case may be. The rule seems to obtain in most British colonies, whether self-governing or not: an instance may be given from South African legislation. Among the free goods are—

" Public stores imported or taken out of bond by and *bona fide* for the sole and exclusive use of the Government of His Brittanic Majesty and of any Government belonging to the Union; provided that a certificate is delivered to the Customs Authorities given under the hand of an officer approved by the Principal Officer of Customs setting forth that any duty levied on such public stores would be borne

---

[1] The most convenient survey to be had of the system of contingent free admissions is that contained in the Introductory Notes of the C.I.D., 1915, which covers only the British Empire, it is true, but gives a good idea of the principal cases involved.

[2] For France, see Pallain, § 317; Sweden, Art. 4 of Tariff; Italy, Preliminary Dispositions, Arts. 7-8: Spain, Disposition II. relating to Tariff, § 14. In the British Colonies such immunities are granted to the Governor and Consular Officers of Foreign Powers (see C.I.D., 1913, Introductory Notes).

[3] Pallain, *op. cit.*, n. 1, p. 278.

by the Government: and provided, further, that no portion of such stores used or unused shall be sold or otherwise disposed of so as to come into the possession of or into consumption by any persons not legally entitled to import the same free of duty without the consent of the Principal Officer of Customs, and the payment of the duties to him by the officer so selling or disposing of such public stores at the rate leviable at the time of sale."

In Sweden the exemption applies to "articles imported for the land or sea forces which are not manufactured in Sweden, or which cannot be obtained in Sweden in view of the necessity that they should be procured without delay." When such a right *is* accorded, the matter is not without difficulties unless the provision is carefully defined. What is a State? The matter seems simple enough in a unitary State, although even there there are local governing authorities, but how does the matter stand in a Federal State? Thus, in Australia [1] "the states have been made to pay heavily upon the railway materials they have imported, and this has been a cause of complaint by the State Commissioners. New South Wales secured a decision in the Supreme Court of the State that such duties were unconstitutional, but the Federal Government disregarded the decision. A High Court is provided for in the Commonwealth Constitution to decide questions of this sort or to refer them, if it pleases, to the Privy Council. But this court had not been organised, and the Federal authorities would not permit a direct appeal to the Privy Council as desired by the State. . . . Matters came to a crisis after the tariff of August, 1907, was imposed. This tariff levied a duty of 30 per cent (British manufacture, 25 per cent.) upon wire netting, which is extensively used in Australia for rabbit protection. The New South Wales Government had a large amount of such netting ordered for public use in protecting its crown lands and neighbouring properties from rabbit invasion when the tariff went into effect. The State authorities refused to pay the new duty—wire netting had previously been free or subject to but nominal rates—and

---

[1] The position is that:—(*a*) Articles imported by or being the property of the Commonwealth; (*b*) articles imported, or purchased in bonds, for the official use of the Governor-General, and declared as being for such official use; (*c*) articles imported or purchased in bonds for the official use of the State Governors and declared as being for such official use, shall be imported free of duty

seized by force the netting consigned to them. The Federal authorities appeared to have made no resistance, though, had they been informed beforehand of the design of the local government, there might have been an acute crisis. The matter is now in the way of compromise, pending a decision on the constitutional aspects of the question, and the duty on wire netting has been reduced by parliament." [1]

(3) The third class of case are goods accompanying, or intended for the use of immigrants. Thus, in Canada there is free admission under tariff No. 705 of the 1907 tariff for—

"Settlers effects,—viz., wearing apparel, books, usual and reasonable household furniture and other household effect: instruments and tools of trade, occupation, or employment, guns, musical instruments, domestic sewing machines, typewriters, bicycles, carts, waggons and other highway vehicles, agricultural implements and live stock for farm, not to include live stock or articles for sale or for use as a contractor's outfit, nor vehicles nor implements moved by mechanical power, nor machinery for use in any manufacturing establishment; all the foregoing if actually owned abroad by the settler for at least six months before his removal to Canada, and subject to regulations prescribed by the Minister of Customs: provided that any dutiable article entered as settlers' effects may not be so entered unless brought by the settler on his first disposal, and shall not be sold or otherwise disposed of without payment of duty until after twelve months' actual use in Canada."

Virtually, the same provision is in force in Newfoundland, but no similar provision is to be found in the other self-governing dominions. A clause with similar intents can be found in Brazil Preliminary Dispositions to Tariff, Art. 2, § 3. In Europe we may specify Italy Preliminary Dispositions, Art. 91, § 6; Germany, Art. 6, § 4; Sweden, Art. 4 ("old and used household articles and other effects when imported on behalf of persons immigrating from abroad, or persons who, having a domicile in Sweden, have resided abroad for at least one year, either uninterruptedly or with occasional intervals only, provided in all cases that the owner certifies in writing on his word of honour that the conditions specified as entitling the goods to free admission exist, that he, him-

[1] V. S. Clark in *Q.J.E.*, vol. xxii. (1908); Australian Economic Problems, vol. ii., "The Tariff," pp. 600-1.

self, has used the articles in question, that they are imported for his own use and not for trade purposes, and provided also that the customs office concerned find that they are not in excess of the requirements of the owner").

Closely connected are exemptions for "travellers' effects," which it is, of course, not always easy to distinguish from "immigrants' effects." An instance is No. 642 (Free List) of the U.S.A. Tariff of 1913—[1]

"Wearing apparel, articles of personal adornment, toilet articles, and similar personal effects of persons arriving in the United States.

"*Notes.*—(1) This exemption shall include only such articles as were actually owned by them and in their possession abroad at the time of or prior to their departure from a foreign country, and as necessary and appropriate for the wear and use of such persons, and are intended for such wear and use, and shall not be held to apply to merchandise or articles intended for other persons or for sale.

"(2) In the case of residents on the United States returning from abroad all wearing apparel, personal and household effects taken by them out of the United States to foreign countries shall be admitted free of duty, without regard to their value, upon their identity being established under appropriate rules and regulations to be prescribed by the Secretary of the Treasury.

"(3) Up to but not exceeding 100 dollars in value of articles acquired abroad by such residents in the United States for personal or household use, or as souvenirs or curios, but not bought on commission or intended for sale, shall be admitted free of duty."

(*d*) One other class of case falls within our present chapter. This is the class of temporary exemptions or impositions of duty made on grounds of special circumstances. Their inclusion is made difficult by the fact that Retaliatory Duties are in effect intended to be temporary and are yet excluded

[1] See also Germany, Art. 6, §§ 3 and 7; Italy, Art. 9, § 6. For the quantities of dutiable articles importable free by passengers into the United Kingdom, see Ham's C.Y.B., p. 46, § 9. The main exemptions are half a pound weight of manufactured tobacco and half a pint of spirits and cordials or perfumed spirits. In other cases the limit is value (not over three shillings, clocks, watches, and musical instruments) or duty payable (under one shilling "other dutiables"). To obtain exemption the goods must be duly declared and produced, and must be *bona fide* unconsumed stores of the passenger who brings them for personal consumption.

from consideration in this place, owing to the fact that they attach more to the country from which the goods come than to anything specifically peculiar to the goods themselves: also that a particular class of temporary exemptions—the so-called "Improvement Trade" exemptions—can be better dealt with in connection with drawbacks, warehousing, etc., in a subsequent chapter. But apart from these cases, several classes can be dealt with here.

1. **Seasonal Duties on Certain Commodities.**—In the German tariff there are some instances of this kind of duty. Thus, No. 23—potatoes, fresh, are dutiable—

From Feb. 15 to July 31, ...	At M. 2.50 or 1.00
Whilst from Aug. 1 to Feb. 14, . . .	Free

So also with fresh fruit.

Apples, Pears, and Quinces—

	General Tariff.	Conventional Tariff.
From Sept. 25 to Nov. 25, . . .	Free	
,, Nov. 26 to Sept. 24, . . .	2.50	
,, Sept. 1 to Nov. 30, ...	..	Free
,, Dec. 1 to Aug. 31, ...	..	2.00

The object of such seasonal duties is, of course, quite evident; it is protection for the producer during that part of the year when his competitive power is weakest, whilst, at the same time, it prevents the consumer being charged undue prices at the time when the supply is large.[1]

2. **Exemptions to meet Shortage of Domestic Supply.**—The right or power to suspend duties at times of natural shortness is possessed by numerous governments. The converse right is the power to suspend exportation at such a time, whilst the contrary proceeding is to suspend importation at times of great cheapness, so as to prevent an undue fall of price to the producer. The unison of all those points was, in fact, a feature of the English Corn Laws, and the same principle is still found to some extent in the existing Portuguese Corn Law.

We may now proceed to give some illustrative material.

(*a*) Import relaxations.

France.—(*a*) By the law of 29th March, 1887, Art. A, para. 2, "in exceptional circumstances and when the

[1] The tariff of the Austro-Hungarian Empire also contained similar duties (*e.g.*, Tariff of 1906: No. 37, Fruit not specially mentioned).

price of bread rises to a height menacing to the victualling of the public, the government, in the absence of the chambers, may suspend, in whole or in part, the working of the present act by a decree of the President of the Republic made at a session of the Council of Ministers (rendu en Counsil des Ministres). In this event, the measure taken by the government must be submitted for ratification immediately on the reunion of the Chamber." [1]

(*b*) In addition, by the law of July 12, 1906, the French Government possesses the right from the time of complete mobilisation of the army on the French continental frontiers, to suspend, in whole or in part, the duties on wheat (in grain or flour), salted meats, oats, barley, dried vegetables (beans and lentils). These suspensions do not require submission to parliament, a decree is all that is necessary, but the suspended duties are to be re-imposed as soon as possible.

In Switzerland, by Art. 4 of the Federal Customs Law—

"The Federal Council is entitled, in extraordinary circumstance, as for instance, in the presence of fundamental events (Elementarerignissen), etc., to allow such reductions in the tariff as seem to it suitable to the circumstances." [2]

Art. 35, para. 2 of the same law further defines the position—

" . . . Further, the Federal Council is empowered in exceptional circumstances, in particular in the event of dearness of foodstuffs (Lebensmittel), to temporarily effect requisite changes in the tariff.

"Under the circumstances previsaged in para. 2, the Federal Council is further entitled to take any measures which seem appropriate.

"Such dispositions have, however, to be reported to the Federal Assembly at its next meeting, and can only continue if the Federal Assembly approves thereof."

Since the Federal Council is empowered to take any measures that seem fit to it, it is entitled to prohibit export,

---

[1] No definition is given of what shall constitute exceptional circumstances; the law confers the right of suspending the duties in the absence of the Chambers "*dans les circonstances exceptionnelles de quelque ordre qu'elles soit,* qui entraineraient une hausse anormale et inquietante du prix du pain." Pallain, vol. i., pp. 10-11.

[2] Blumenstein and Gassman, *op. cit.*, pp. 15, 21. See also Customs Tariff, Arts. 4-5, p. 33.

or impose heavy export duties, for which there is in any case authority under Art. 28 of the Federal Constitution.

The only country normally maintaining a prohibition of import of "normal" foodstuffs so far as we are aware, is, or was, Portugal. As the tariff stood in 1914, the importation of corn was there prohibited, and the government fixed each year the quantities to be imported and the duties to be paid.[1]

3. In war time foodstuffs fall in line with other articles as involving the public safety. Hence, it is not surprising to find government empowered to prohibit the exportation of articles on these grounds. Since the export, or rather the prohibition of export, has become, in consequence of the European War, a matter of considerable interest, let us see what the position is in this country.

1. The original § 138 of the Customs Consolidation Act of 1876 was replaced by § 14 of the Customs and Inland Revenue Act of 1879, which enacted as follows :—

> 8. The following goods may, by proclamation or Order in Council, be prohibited either to be exported or carried coastwise :—Arms, ammunition and gunpowder, military and naval stores, and any articles which His Majesty shall judge capable of being converted into or made useful in increasing the quantity of military or naval stores, provisions, or any sort of victual which may be used as food for man ; and if any goods so prohibited shall be exported or brought to any quay or other place to be shipped for exportation from the United Kingdom or carried coastwise or be water borne to be so exported or carried, they shall be forfeited, and the exporter or his agent or the shipper of any such goods shall be liable to the penalty of one hundred pounds.

2. By § 1 of the Exportation of Arms Act, 1900, the Crown may prevent some of the above-named goods (excluding food) from being sent to any place or country in order to prevent their being used against the forces of the Crown.

3. During the war these powers proved insufficient. In consequence a series of Acts of Parliament and a whole host of statutory rules and orders thereunder have been enacted.

(*a*) By the Customs (Exportation Restriction) Act, 1914

[1] See the article by Wagner in *J.N.S.*, III., F, vol. xx., already cited.

(5 G. V., c. 2), the Arms Act of 1900 was made to apply "as if, in addition to the articles therein mentioned, there were included all other articles of every description."

(*b*) By the Customs (War Powers) Act, 1915 (5 G. V., c. 31), it is required, when export to a particular place or person, or a particular person at a particular place, is made a condition of a licence to export goods that "the person or place or both shall be inserted in all documents relating to the goods" (§ 4): and requires the exporter to prove that the goods have not reached an "enemy country," or that, if they have, "they reach such destination without his consent or connivance" if so required by the Commissioners of Customs and Excise.

(*c*) By the Customs (Exportation Restriction) Act, 1915 (5 and 6 G. V., c. 52), the powers conferred by the Acts of 1900 and 1914 "shall, during the continuance of the present war, include the power to prohibit the exportation of any article to any such country or place unless consigned to such person or persons as may be authorised by or under the proclamation to receive such article."

(*d*) By the Customs (War Powers (No. 2)) Act, 1915 (5 and 6 G. V., c. 71), proof must be given if and when required (unless security has been given by bond) that the goods "have not reached a person who is an enemy or treated as an enemy, or a country which is an enemy country or treated as an enemy country under any law for the time being in force relating to trading with the enemy."

(*e*) By § 15 of the Finance (No. 2) Act, 1915 (5 and 6 G. V., c. 89).

(1) *During the continuance of the present war and for a period of twelve months thereafter,*[1] the Treasury may, by order, authorise the Commissioners of Customs and Excise, during any period named in the order not exceeding three months, to refuse to allow the delivery of goods or commodities for home use from ships side or a warehouse on payment of duty in any cases where deliveries are demanded of amounts exceeding the deliveries which appear to the Commissioners to be reasonable deliveries in the circumstances.

[1] By § 13 of the Finance Act, 1919 (9 and 10 G.V., c. 32), "The powers of the Treasury under § 15 of the Finance (No. 2) Act, 1915 (which relates to the restriction on the delivery of goods from bond), shall be excercisable without any limit of time, and accordingly in that section the words, 'During a continuance of the present war and for a period of twelve months thereafter,' shall cease to have effect."

(2) This section confirms refusals of the Commissioners to allow such deliveries within one month before September 21, 1915.

This is not the place to give the history of the very complicated measures to which these Acts gave birth; they have been used as illustrative material.

§ 6. **Discriminations practised on grounds of method of import.**—Apart from the question whence goods are imported, the following points may be the subject of tariff treatment—the *method* of import and the *nature of the person* importing. These points now require discussion :—

(1) Tariff treatment of the method of importation covers, in general, preferences or discriminations as to the vehicles in which or by means of which importation takes place, and with preference or discrimination as to the route chosen for importation. In modern times these preferences and discriminations have taken the forms mainly (*a*) of favouring importation by national ships, and penalising import by non-national ships, (*b*) of making direct importation a favoured and indirect importation a penalised process. But there may be other cases as well.

(A) **Shipping Discriminations.**—Apart from the reservation of the coasting trade for ships of the country in question, and the granting of shipping subsidies and bounties on construction or mileage—both matters beyond the immediate purpose before us—modern tariff legislation works by increasing the duty payable on imports brought by foreign ships or by reducing the duty on imports brought into the country by ships of that country (including possibly its colonies). The 1913 U.S.A. Tariff Act contained both preferential duty and the penal duty based on these principles.

Sec. IV. J., para. 7, enacted "That a discount of 5 per centum on all duties imposed by this Act shall be allowed on such goods, wares, and merchandise as shall be imported in vessels built in the United States, and which shall be wholly the property of a citizen or citizens thereof."

Sec. IV. J., sub-sec. 1, enacted "That a discriminatory duty of 10 per centum *ad valorem*, in addition to the duties imposed by law shall be levied, collected, and paid on all goods, wares, or merchandise which shall be imported in vessels not of the United States, . . . but this discriminating duty shall not apply to goods, wares, or merchandise which shall be imported in vessels not of the United States entitled at the time of such importation by treaties or conventions or Act of Congress to be entered in the ports of the United States on payment of the same duties as shall then be payable on goods, wares, or merchandise imported in the vessels of the United States."

Sec. IV. J., sub-sec. 2, provided "That no goods, wares, or merchandise, unless in cases provided for by treaty, shall be imported into the United States from any foreign port or place, except in vessels of the United States, or in such foreign vessels as truly and wholly belong to the citizens or subjects of that country of which the goods are the growth, production, or manufacture, or from which such goods, wares, or merchandise can only be, or most usually are, first shipped for transportation. All goods, wares, or merchandise imported contrary to this section, and the vessel wherein the same shall be imported, together with her cargo, tackle, apparel, and furniture, shall be forfeited to the United States, . . .[1] The preceding sub-section shall not apply to vessels or goods, wares, or merchandise imported in vessels of a foreign nation which does not maintain a similar regulation against vessels of the United States." Such a discriminatory duty used to be part of the French navigation code under the name of surtaxe de pavillon[2] (and was, in fact, levied in the provision of the Navigation Act of 1660 (12 Chas. II., c. 18, § 5) that double aliens duty (for which see subsequent section) shall be payable on "any sort of ling, stockefish, pilchard, or any other kinde of dryed or salted fish . . . or any sort of codfish or herring, or any oyle or blubber made or that shall be made of any kinde of fishe whatsoever, or any whale fins or whale bones which shall be imported into England, Ireland, or Wales, or towne of Berwicke-upon-Tweed not haveing been caught in vessels truely and properly belonging thereunto. . . ."

(*b*) *Direct Importation.*—We may begin by quoting the

---

[1] By an Act of March 4th, 1915, "so much of Section 4 J." (of the Tariff Act cited above) "as imposes a discriminatory duty of ten per centum on all goods. wares, or merchandise imported in a vessel owned by citizens of the U.S., but not a vessel of the U.S. . . . are hereby repealed." This clause is strongly reminiscent of the English Navigation Act (12 Chas. II., c. 18, § 5), of which more will be said in a moment. The same clause has been substantially re-enacted since 1883 (Digest, etc., pp. 1552-3).

[2] On this surtax, abolished in 1866, see Amé, "Étude sur les Douanes," vol. ii chap. xix., and Pallain, vol. i., paras. 82-3.

famous clause of the Navigation Act of 1660 (§ 4), by which "nor goods or commodityes that are of foreign growth, production, or manufacture . . . shall be shipped or brought from any other place or places, country or countryes, but onely from those of their said growth, production, or manufacture, or from those ports where the said goods and commodityes can onely or are or usually have been first shipped for transportation and from none other places or countryes under the penalty of the forfeiture of all such of the aforesaid goods as shall be imported . . . as also of the ship in which they were imported."[1]

When we turn to modern illustrations a good many cases are to be found.

1. The discriminatory duty of 10 per cent. contained in the Tariff Act of 1913 is applicable also, and under the same conditions as to suspension by treaty, convention, or Acts of Congress, on goods, wares, or merchandise "which, being the production or manufacture of any foreign country not contiguous to the United States, shall come into the United States from such contiguous country," exception made "of such foreign products or manufactures as shall be imported

---

[1] This section of the Act was misquoted by Adam Smith in his celebrated discussion of the Navigation Acts in Book IV., Chap. II., of *The Wealth of Nations*. As every school-boy knows, Smith considered the Navigation Acts to be the logical consequence of one of the two justifiable cases of interference with foreign trade, not indeed because of the beneficial commercial effect which might follow, but because "defence is of much more importance than opulence" (W. of N., Cannan's edition, vol. i., p. 429). How far Adam Smith believed that the Navigation Acts achieved their aim is another matter. The terms in which he speaks of the Dutch in this very chapter are significant, and in the subsequent chapter on Colonies (*op. cit.*, vol. ii., p. 98) his argument distinctly minimises, if it does not completely negate, his previous remarks. The whole question of the Navigation Acts has been subject to somewhat reckless language both of eulogy and attack. Dr. Cunningham's views will be found modified in the later editions of his great work ("Growth of English Industry and Commerce: Modern Times," Part. I., 4th ed., 1907, p. 210, n. 2, "in the second edition of this book I felt justified in following the ordinarily received opinion (of the wisdom of the policy), but further consideration has caused me to modify my view"). For his views, see *op. cit.*, pp. 211-13 and 358-61. M'Culloch's note on the Navigation Laws (n. xii. to his ed. of the W. of N.) is still well worth consulting. Mr. J. M. Robertson's vigorous polemic ("Trade and Tariffs," p. 27, *et seq.*) largely follows him. On the other hand, the views that the Act were greatly injurious to the North American Colonies received a decided blow from Prof. Ashley ("Surveys, England and America," 1660-1760, espec. pp. 311-319). But Cunningham speaks of the "malign effects" of the Act, "not only on the Baltic trade, but on the sugar colonies, and also on the Royal revenue," although he goes on to say "that we are forced to suppose that in the opinion of experts it was serving its purpose, etc." (pp. 360-361).

from such contiguous countries in the usual course of strictly retail trade."

2. In France two such discriminatory duties are levied: (1) the Surtaxe d'Origine; (2) the Surtaxe d'Entrepôt, the first applicable to European, the second to extra-European products.

The Surtaxe d'Origine applies to European products imported elsewhere than from the country of origin, and enumerated in schedule D of the Tariff of 1892, supplemented by the laws of 30th June, 1893, 26th July, 1901, and 10th April, 1902.

As worked before the war, a fairly numerous class of exceptions to the rule existed—

(*a*) Russian goods loaded in German Baltic ports.

(*b*) Austro-Hungarian goods arriving from any German port or from Galatz or Odessa; petrol oils of same origin shipped *via* the Danube and loaded at Sulina directly for France.

(*c*) Cretan or Bulgarian products imported *via* Turkey in Europe.

(*d*) The Balearic Islands *via* Spain.

(*e*) Iceland or Faroe Islands *via* Denmark.

Finally, Amsterdam, Rotterdam, Flushing, Dordrecht, and Harlingen are treated as loading ports for merchandise from the States of the hinderland (" provenant des états limitrophes ").

The Surtaxe d'Entrepôt consists of the rules laid down in Schedule C of the Tariff of 1892, modified by the exemptions of one kind or another, particularly those of Schedule C of the Tariff of 1910.

The main exemptions are (*a*) as to areas—

Persian carpets, imported *via* Constantinople or Taganrog; products of Asiatic Russia imported from European Russia; products of Asiatic Turkey imported from Constantinople; products of the Canary Islands and of Spanish Settlements in Morocco imported from Spain; products of islands adjacent to Madeira imported from Portugal.

But, contrariwise, the duty applies to coffees and teas laden in Asiatic or African ports in the Mediterranean basin, even if they should be transported directly to France, unless accompanied by a certificate of the French Consul certifying that these goods have not been imported from a European country to the extra European country of origin.

(*b*) As to Commodities—Some important raw materials are exempted by the Tariff of 1910; of the more important are—

Wool in bales or skins from Australia, the Cape, or India; Indian cotton, tobacco, plumbago (Ceylon), jute, aloes, cocoa-fibre, and other vegetable filaments.[1]

3. The Spanish Tariff of 1911, entering into force on January 1, 1912, Schedule III., contains a list of surtaxes applicable to certain products "when extra European origin but imported from a European country either by land or sea. In case of voluntary trans-shipment in European ports, the duties established in this schedule will be levied." The articles in question are—petroleum (crude or refined), cocoa-nut and palm oil, indigo, raw cotton, manilla hemp, and agave, raw jute, untanned hides and skins (all last three exempt if only trans-shipped on through Bill of Lading), cocoa, coffee, cinnamon, cloves, pepper, and tea.

The question whether these surtaxes achieve their object, that of building up a local market, depends directly upon whether the cost *via* the old route plus the surtax is greater or less than the cost of direct importation. If the direct services are maintained as a purely commercial venture, the freights will probably be higher, and the cost of the raw material no less than it would have been if brought indirectly, since the purchaser has not the advantage of the wider market which such centres as London and Liverpool furnish. On the other hand, it is possible that such a surtax will merely accelerate what the normal developmental forces would in themselves have achieved—*i.e.*, the growth of the market generally serves to increase the possibility of direct importation owing to the fact that with a greater demand it will pay the specialised dealers and produce brokers to organise themselves, and for the shipping lines to run a direct service. Where this is not the case, the extra cost involved in buying the raw material directly rather than pay the surtax may be reduced by the granting of shipping subsidies, but, though this will maintain the competitive efficiency of the industry, it will, of course, throw a charge upon the national finances.

[1] Schedules C and D (rates and articles) can be found most conveniently in Kelly, p. 294. On the whole question, see Pallain, vol. i., paras. 87-91.

In so far as this procedure strengthens the national shipping and frees the national industry from dependence on foreign dealers there is a rational line of defence, but it is, of course, difficult to assess such a gain in terms of economics. So far as discriminatory taxes on imports brought in national ships are concerned, the direct effect is, of course, to encourage the national shipping industry. If the shipping costs of that country are above the level of those of its chief competitors, to an amount about equal to the gain to importers of the lower duties,[1] conditions are equalised, and the relative growth of the national shipping industry will be greater than would otherwise be the case, but the importer will gain nothing, since the higher freights compensate the lower duties. If the lower duties do not equalise or outweigh the greater cost of shipping, foreign ships will still be preferred.[2]

Two other cases may be briefly noted—

(1) Differential duties as between different frontiers.
(2) Differential duties as between importers of different nationality.

1. Where it is desired to favour importation by a particular route, or where, owing to the remoteness of domestic sources of supply from areas situated near a given frontier, these areas would suffer definite damage, it is possible to charge differential duties on different frontiers. Thus, under the tariff of the Austro-Hungarian Empire certain colonial products when imported by sea enjoyed a considerable reduction of duty—an incident, presumably, in the struggle between Hamburg and the Adriatic ports.[3]

In the German tariff as it was before the coming into force of the 1906 rates, several such rates existed, on salt and certain stones and stoneware. These were admitted free or at low duty rates when imported seawards, at higher rates when imported landwards. The salt differentiation which dated from 1879 was directed against French competition, the stone

---

[1] Or more correctly, if the absolute saving in duties is about equal to the absolute increased freightage involved in transporting a given amount of cargo in national rather than in non-national ships. Of course, a 10 per cent. reduction in duties cannot be directly compared with a 10 per cent. higher freight rate.

[2] But in both cases a statesman must reckon with the possibilities of retaliation, and the matter then becomes very complicated, and renders the advisability of the whole policy very uncertain.

[3] Cd. 2917, p. 1 (Classes I. and II.).

differentiation was made in favour of the local industries.[1] The same position—*i.e.*, differentiation between land and sea frontiers—was maintained by the Russian Empire before the last pre-war tariff, that of 1903 (coming into force on March 1, 1906), was promulgated, and was one of the factors contributing to the Russian-German Tariff War of 1893. One of the terms of settlement was that " Russia gave a pledge that for the future the discrimination hitherto existing between certain goods imported by land or by sea should cease ; and thus Germany obtained equality of treatment with England for her coal, coke, and iron." [2]

Differential land frontier duties exist also on the Chinese land frontiers.

2. A word must be said as to differential duties levied on the basis of the *nationality* of the importer or exporter. To our modern eyes the process of distinguishing between individuals and not between goods seems a reversal of the " natural " order of things.[3]

Differential treatment of goods rather than persons implies, however, the concept of a definite country of origin in a geographical sense, and the possibility of administrative measures for prevention of fraud. The " natural " desire to " make the foreigner pay " cannot always take the form therefore of differentiating against the country of origin or destination of the goods, but must content itself with penalising the *individual* engaged in buying, selling, or transporting them. Hence, the differentiation between " citizen " or " denizen," and the " alien " such as we find in the history of the English customs system, is a phenomenon which is explicable as the form which " protection " against the foreigner is likely to take in view of the economic conditions prevailing in mediæval England, when the merchant of another town was almost as much distrusted as the merchant stranger from beyond the seas. We find these differentiations in the little known fields of the town customs[4] and of the "semi-national

---

[1] Trautvetter, *op. cit.*, pp. 50-51.

[2] Cd. 1938. Reports on Tariff Wars between certain European States, p. 47. The Russian Government had, in the negotiations anterior to the Tariff War, already offered the same concession (*op. cit.*, p. 45).

[3] Not so unnatural as in 1914. The era of the " national " treatment of the alien seems in danger of being over.

[4] N. S. B. Gras, " Early English Customs System," p. 21, *et seq.*, esp. pp. 25-26.

customs," [1] as well as in the national customs system when the latter began to take definite shape. In the "Carta Mercatoria" of 1303 we have a "complete system of duties on all goods exported or imported by aliens." [2] Under such a system preferences would take the form of requiring merchants of a particular nationality to pay less than the usual aliens rates, or even than the denizen, whilst merchants of a penalised nationality paid more. Thus, in the late fifteenth century "tariff schedule" [3] which has recently been more than once reprinted, we find that on "cloth, without 'greyn' per cloth"—

	Customs	plus Subsidy.
Englishmen paid, ...	14d.	nil.
Spaniards paid, ...	14d.	,,
Hanse Merchants paid, ...	12d.	,,
Other Aliens paid, ...	33d.	12d.

The aliens duty survived almost to the nineteenth century, the last vestiges not being removed till 1874, even then with a reservation for certain rights of the City of London. The subsidy granted by Charles II., cap. 4, had, in addition to heavier aliens duty imposed on wines imported, still maintained a double export duty on goods exported by aliens. Moreover, by Rule XII., annexed to the Book of Rates, "The merchant stranger, who according to the Rates and Values in this Booke conteyned doe pay double subsidy for lead, tinne, woollen cloths, shall also pay double custome for native manufactures of wool or part wool, and the said strangers are to pay for all other goods, as well inwards as outwards, rated to pay the subsidy of poundage, 3d. in the pound or any other duty payable by Charta Mercatoria besides the subsidy," so that the minimum differential duty was 12d. in the subsidy for every £1 of value plus 3d. in the pound. But by 25 Chas. II., cap. 6, any clauses in any act or statute "As doe any ways concerne any custome or subsidie upon any of the native commodityes of this kingdome (except coales) or manufactures wrought or made in this kingdome, to be exported out of this realme payable by any merchant, alien made, denizen, or

[1] *Op. cit.*, p. 27, *et seq.*

[2] *Op. cit.*, p. 66, *et seq.*, and chap. xix. for Latin text and much new illustrative material. For translation, see Bland, Brown, and Tawney, "English Economic History Select Documents," pp. 211-216.

[3] *Op. cit.*, pp. 690-693. See also Williamson, "Maritime Enterprise," 1485-1555, table on p. 40, citing the 1811 ed. of Arnold's Chronicle, otherwise called the Customs of London. Ed. F. Douce.

other stranger or alien, over and above the custome and subsidie payable by His Majesties naturall born subjects . . . be hereby repealed." This still left some differentiation against the alien. In 1784 by 24 G. III., c. 16, "from and after the twentieth day of August, 1784, the duty commonly called the petty custom . . . and all other additional duties imposed by any Act of Parliament upon the goods of aliens or strangers born, over and above the duties payable by natural born subjects, except as hereinafter is provided, shall cease, determine, and be no longer paid or payable; any law, custom, or usage to the contrary notwithstanding; provided always . . . that this act shall not extend or be construed to extend to repeal or any wise alter the duties due and payable by any Act of Parliament upon goods inported into, or exported from this kingdom, in any foreign ship or vessel, nor to the duties of package or scavage, or any duties granted by charter to the Mayor and commonalty and citizens of the City of London."[1]

At the present day differentiation on the ground of nationality of the importer exists as one of the incidents of extra territoriality in—*e.g.*, China. The position there is that the customs are divided (though, so far as sea-borne trade is concerned, unilaterally administered since 1907) into the Maritime Customs and the Native or Regular Customs. Over the latter the Chinese Government has complete control, over the former, only the right of collection. The rates are fixed in consequence of a series of most-favoured-nation treaties with foreign powers, and, owing to the principle of extra territoriality, the foreigner in China is subject to his own laws and not to the legislation of China, the power of the Customs Department over the foreign importer is less than it would be in a European country. "This arises partly from the very considerable degree of protection accorded to foreign merchants by treaty, and partly from the fact that there is no competent tribunal before which a revenue case can be carried; the Chinese territorial courts are ruled out, the Consul is necessarily the advocate of this national, and the Commissioner of Customs is a party to the case."[2] The position results, in fact, in a considerable advantage to the foreigner,

[1] See also Alton and Holland, "The King's Customs," vol. i., p. 321.
[2] H. B. Morse, "The Trade and Administration of China," rev. edn., p. 381.

not merely as regards the direct customs duty payable, but in the further fact that "from the inland taxation, too, which presses so heavily on Chinese traders . . . his goods are exempted by payment of 'transit dues,' not exceeding a nominal $2\frac{1}{2}$ per cent. *ad val.*"[1]

Whenever distinctions are thus drawn between one group of individuals and another in respect to tariff advantages, whether in the rate of duty or in the regulations to which they are subject in the conduct of trade, it is almost impossible to prevent the favoured group from using their privileges as objects of pecuniary value to be traded in with the less favoured group. This was the case in 17th century England, and is the case to-day in 20th century China. In the Navigation Act, 12 Charles II., cap. 18, clause IX. recited that "for the prevention of the great frauds daily used in colouring and concealing of aliens goods," a large number of articles and goods imported from certain named areas were to be accounted foreign if imported in other than British ships. Precautions had to be taken in the pre-cited Act of 1784 "the better to prevent the said mayor and citizens from being fraudulently injured" by goods imported on aliens account from being entered as British. In China to-day, says Mr. Morse, "it would be unreasonable to expect that no foreigner would be found ready, for a consideration, to lend a corner of his flag to cover the nakedness of the poor Chinaman. Among the foreigners resident in China there is the same proportion of good, bad, and indifferent as among the same class in the home lands, and the mal-practice is common; but while the abuse of the flag provides a decent income to many among them, it causes great injury to the legitimate commerce of the countries from which they come, and disorganises the methods of administration, right or wrong, just or unjust, of the land in which they live."[2]

We now come to a group of differential duties, which, in view of their importance and the detail with which they require to be treated, can best be dealt with in a separate chapter. Our next task will, therefore, be to discuss colonial and other preferential duties.

---

[1] *Op. cit.*, p. 190. Chin Chu, *The Tariff Problem in China*, pp. 104-114. See also *China National Defence League* Pamphlets: *The World-Peace and Chinese Tariff Autonomy*.

[2] Morse, *op. cit.*, p. 191.

NOTE I. TO CHAPTER VII.

SINCE this chapter was written further measures have been undertaken, or have been attempted, in connection with dumping and unfair competition generally.

1. **Japan.**—An amendment to the Japanese Tariff Act of 1910 came into force on the 1st August of this year. Art. V. of the said Act is amended by the addition of an anti-dumping clause, which enacts that " if any important industry in this country is threatened with injury on account of the import of goods sold at an unfair price or the sale at an unfair price of goods already imported, such goods may . . . be charged with duties not exceeding the fair price of the goods, within the limits specified by " the commission set up to look into cases of dumping, in addition to the duties leviable under the Tariff Act. " In respect of goods specified under the provisions of the foregoing clause, which, having been already imported, are the property of, or in the possession of, a ' dumper ' or his agent, the surtax may be levied on such dumper or his agent, in accordance with the provisions of the foregoing clause, such surtaxes will be collected in accordance with the regulations for the collection of the national taxes." [1]

2. A very elaborate attempt to regulate dumping is contained in the abortive anti-dumping Bill which the British Government, in pursuance of its election pledges, introduced in the House of Commons in November, 1919, but which was not proceeded with. The Bill dealt with a variety of subjects, but, so far as our present purpose is concerned, the two points of interest are the regulation of dumping and the attempted restriction upon imports from countries with a depreciated currency.[2]

(A) *Dumping.*—The cases in which Part II. of the Act were to apply were defined as being the importation into the United Kingdom in substantial quantities and systematically

---

[1] *B.T.J.*, 9/9/20, p. 327.
[2] For the full text of the Act, see the *B.T.J.*, for 27/12/1919, p. 640, *et seq.*

of goods, or the offering of goods, or the apprehension that such sale or importation of goods is about to take place, if the importation or offer for sale is " at prices below the foreign value as defined by this Act." But the Act made it a condition that " the production or manufacture of similar goods in the United Kingdom is or *is likely* to be thereby adversely affected."

Though the Act does thus not cover the case of dumping where there is no British industry which could be injured by the importation, it did cover the cases of (*a*) goods produced in different countries (Art. 5 (3)), and the case of (*b*) goods imported in parts for the purpose of being assembled or made up in this country (Art. 6).

In analysing the working of the provisions, it is best to start with the conception of the foreign value of the goods. This was defined to be the price calculated *in sterling* " which at the date of the issue of the certificate to be issued by the proper officer as aforesaid was being charged for goods of that class or description in similar quantities for consumption in the country of production or manufacture, after deducting any excise or other internal duty leviable in that country, or, if no such goods are sold for consumption in that country, the price which, having regard to the prices charged for goods as near as may be similar when so sold or when sold for exportation to other countries, would be so charged, after deducting any such duty as aforesaid, if the goods were sold in that country."

The reader will notice that the foreign value is to be calculated in sterling. It was necessary consequently to give the authorities power to settle the rates at which foreign money was to be converted into English, and this power of conversion was given by Art. 5 (4) of the Act. The foreign value is the basic point.

We must now distinguish between the cases of import on or after sale, and the case of import before sale—that is, import on consignment.

The Board of Trade was given power to issue orders providing that such goods as the order might apply to should not be imported *unless*—

(1) The foreign exporter made a sworn statement stating the value and the origin of the goods.

(2) Such statement was certified by the " proper

officer"—*i.e.*, a British consular officer abroad, or, in the British Dominions, a person authorised by the Board.

(3) A declaration was made by the importer as to whether the goods have been imported on or after sale, or merely on consignment.

(4) The goods being imported on or after sale, the purchaser offered such evidence as the Board required as to the import price and the commissions, discounts, rebates, "or other advantage of any kind whether direct or indirect; . . . obtained by the purchaser in respect of the sale."

(5) The goods being imported on or after sale, the "importer before the clearance of the goods pays to the commissioners such sum as in the opinion of the commissioners is equal to the amount by which the foreign value of the goods exceeds the import price thereof."

Once such an order had been issued, the conditions of import *on consignment* were—

(1) Conditions 1 to 3 above.

(2) A declaration of the name and address of the person "at whose order and disposition the goods were held."

(3) The payment by the *vendor* to the Board of a "sum equal to the difference between the price at which the goods are sold and the foreign value of the goods," or, the provision of satisfactory proof that the lower prices at which the goods were being sold were due to depreciation of quality or other causes which the Board might validly accept.

It being quite impossible to carry out this part of the Act without powers of investigation, the Act gave the Board power to demand from the consignor that he comply with any requirements "as to storage, inspection, returns as to sales, production of books and documents, and the furnishing of information which may be made to him by the Board." Further, reasonable powers of entry, and the right to "inspect all books and documents relating to the business carried on by any such person" was conferred on officers appointed by the Board.

Those readers who are familiar with American practice

will recognise that here we have inaugurated the American system of Special Treasury Agents. So far as the American precedent serves, it is quite clear that the practice of demanding sworn consular invoices is an insufficient safeguard, and that the only resource is an inquisitorial system such as that demanded by the Act.

(B) When we turn to that part of the Act which deals with depreciated currency, we must again first begin with a statement of the conditions under which the Act applies. The Board might prohibit the importation "of any class or description of goods manufactured or produced" in a country, if it was satisfied

> "that there has been such a depreciation in the sterling value of the currency of any foreign country as, not being adequately compensated by increased cost of production in that country, is causing or is likely to cause sales in the United Kingdom of the products or manufactures of that country to take place in substantial quantities at prices substantially below those at which similar articles manufactured in the United Kingdom can be sold, *and that action under this provision is otherwise desirable.*" (Art. 9 (*c*)).

The Government was given power to grant licences without payment, or on payment of a sum "at a uniform *ad valorem* rate determined from time to time, and for periods of not less than three months in each case . . ." (Art. 10 (4).)

The powers conferred on the executive authority by this Act were obviously very wide: and it was thought better to associate an advisory committee, known as the Trade Regulation Committee, with the departments concerned. The committee was to be composed of ten persons nominated by the House of Commons, who had to be members of the House, the Parliamentary and Permanent Chiefs of the Board of Trade, and one Treasury representative. Draft orders were to be submitted to this committee by the Board of Trade, and were not to be proceeded with unless approved, except in emergency cases, but such emergency orders were to be provisional, and only to continue in operation for twenty-one days, and no longer. The committee might approve the draft order, with or without modification, as they thought fit. Finally, any question or matter arising out of the administration of this act might be referred to the committee by the President of the Board of Trade.

The Bill was so unpopular that it had to be withdrawn: and it is obvious that it would have involved leaving a great deal of discretion to the departments concerned, and also have involved considerable interference with the processes of private trading. It certainly made an heroic attempt to deal with cases of evasion of anti-dumping duty by consignment and subsequent resale. Whether the damage it inflicted by the interference it necessarily involved was greater than the good it would have done in checking cases of dumping is a matter upon which opinion will differ, and need not be discussed here. Its suggested treatment of the problem of depreciated exchanges can be attacked both from the standpoint of principle and from the practical view point. Theoretically, the checking of imports would certainly not improve the exchange of the country from which imports were prohibited; in fact, by making it difficult for that country to sell, it worsened its position. From the practical standpoint, the imposition of *ad valorem* duties which might not be changed for three months in effect was a confession of the impossibility of adjusting the penalty to the exact degree of guilt, and converted the whole scheme into a veiled system of import duties.

Lord Balfour of Burleigh's Protection of Special Industries Bill, introduced in the House of Lords in March, 1920, also contained a section dealing with the prevention of dumping. The Board of Trade was to be given power to prohibit the importation of goods, except under such conditions as it might ordain, if the "prices habitually charged by the consignor of any class or kind of goods imported into the United Kingdom," or the "prices at which imported goods of any class or kind are usually sold or offered for sale in the United Kingdom," or the "prices at which imported goods of any class or kind are usually sold or offered for sale in the United Kingdom, are less than the prices at which goods of the same class or kind are sold in the ordinary course of business in the country of origin."

3. Finally, it may be mentioned, as far as unfair competition is concerned, that in the Treaty with Germany, Art. 274-5 (introduced unto the Austrian Treaty as Articles 226-7), Germany undertook "to adopt all the necessary legislative and administrative measures to protect the produce or manu-

facture" of Allied countries "from all forms of unfair competition in commercial transactions."[1]

4. In addition to the legislation cited in the foregoing chapter, the Australian Tariff Bill of 1920 makes provision for anti-dumping duties. The Bill authorises "an addition, to the ordinary duty payable, of an amount equal to the difference between the fair market value of the same article when sold for home consumption in the usual and ordinary course of trade and free on board in the country whence and at the time it was exported to Australia, and the dumped price, except in cases where the difference amounts to 5 per cent. or less. With regard to subsidised freights, it is proposed to collect on goods landed in this way an additional duty of 5 per cent. on the duty otherwise payable. There is also a provision to meet the case of certain classes of goods that are sometimes imported at ballast freight rates."[2]

5. Under Title II. of the Emergency Tariff Act, which received the Presidential Assent on May 28, 1921, the United States has now introduced an anti-dumping system, apart from the measures treated in the text under the caption, "unfair competition." The penalties previsaged apply to cases of dumping when the Secretary of the Treasury finds "that an industry in the United States is being or is likely to be injured, *or is prevented from being established*, by reason of the importation into the United States of a class or kind of foreign merchandise, and that merchandise of such class or kind is being sold or is likely to be sold in the United States or elsewhere at less than its fair value." The Special Dumping Duty which under these circumstances becomes leviable is to be equal to the difference between :—

(*a*) The Foreign Market Value *and* the Purchase Price, or where there is no Purchase Price, the Exporter's Price.

(*b*) Where there is no Foreign Market Value, the difference between the Exporter's Price or the Purchase Price and the Cost of Production.

The definitions of these various terms are very lengthy, but in summarised form they are as follows :—

---

[1] So far as the protection of regional appellations is concerned, the treaty stipulated for reciprocity (Art. 274). For the details, see the clauses mentioned.

[2] *B.T.J.*, 20/5/20, p. 690.

The Purchase Price.—The purchase price of the goods plus packing ready for shipment—*i.e.*, the f.o.b. price, *plus* any export tax, drawbacks, and any taxes paid or remitted in respect of the goods, " by reason of the exportation of the merchandise to the United States."

Exporter's Sales Price.—Price of sale " by or for the account of the exporter," *plus* packing ready for shipment, but *less* (*a*) commissions due to sale in the U.S.A. ; (*b*) selling expenses in the United States ; (*c*) export taxes in the country of export, but with the *addition* of rebated or remitted taxation in the country of export.

The Foreign Market Value.—Wholesale market value in country of export *at time of exportation* for usual wholesale quantities and in the ordinary course of trade, " or, if not so sold or offered for sale for home consumption, then for exportation to countries other than the United States, including the cost of all containers and coverings, and all costs, charges, and expenses incident to placing the merchandise packed ready for shipment to the United States. . . ." (§ 205).[1]

6. As these pages pass through the Press, the House of Commons is discussing the Safeguarding of Industries Bill. This measure covers the problems of Key Industries, Dumping, and of Depreciated Exchange.

(1) So far as the Safeguarding of Key Industries is concerned, the Bill provides that on the goods named in the Schedule to the Bill, there shall be imposed *ad valorem* duties of $33\frac{1}{3}$ per cent. for a period of five years from the commencement of the Act. If these goods are dutiable otherwise, duties under the Bill " shall not be charged except in so far as the amount thereof exceeds the amount of those other duties." Goods consigned from, *and* grown, produced or manufactured in the British Empire are exempt. If dutiable goods form an ingredient of some other article, such article is not dutiable " if the compound is of such a nature that the article liable to duty has lost its identity."

The Board of Trade is given power to issue lists of goods dutiable under the Bill, and complaints as to improper inclusion or exclusion from such lists shall be remitted to a referee to be appointed by the Treasury, whose decision shall be final.

(2) There shall be referred to a Committee of " three persons

---

[1] *B.T.J.*, 2/6/21, pp. 621, *et seq.*

selected by the President of the Board of Trade from a permanent panel of persons appointed by him, who shall be mainly persons of commercial or industrial experience, any complaints that "goods of any class or description (other than articles of food and drink) manufactured in a country outside the United Kingdom are being sold or offered for sale in the United Kingdom :—

> (*a*) At prices below the cost of production thereof as hereinafter defined ; or
>
> (*b*) At prices which, by reason of depreciation in the value in relation to sterling of the currency of the country in which the goods are manufactured, are below the prices at which similar goods can be profitably manufactured in the United Kingdom ;

and that by reason thereof employment in any industry in the United Kingdom is being or is likely to be seriously affected.

If the complaint is substantiated, the Board may apply Part II. of the Bill to goods of that class, but no order of the Board may contravene "any treaty, convention, or engagement with any foreign power in force for the time being." Any Address by the House of Commons presented to the Crown within twenty-one days against such order shall void it, "but without prejudice to the validity of anything previously done thereunder."

Goods named in such order become liable to additional *ad valorem* duties of $33\frac{1}{3}$ per cent. But such a duty is not payable if it is shown that the goods have been sold at a price not less than the cost of production, whilst if the duty has already been paid, under such circumstances it becomes repayable, subject, however, to the production of a duly certified declaration, "stating the cost of production, at the date of the declaration, of the goods, and the country of manufacture of the goods." Goods partly manufactured in one country and partly in another, or undergoing different processes in different countries, are liable to duty in so far as any of these countries come under any order, unless it can be shown that "50 per cent. or more of the value of the goods at the time of export . . . is attributable to processes of manufacture undergone since the goods last left any country in relation to which such an order has been made." Here, again, the important point is the definition which is given to cost of production and value. The first is defined as :—

> (*a*) The wholesale price at the works charged for the goods of the class or description for consumption in the country of manufacture ; or
>
> (*b*) If no such goods are sold for consumption in that country, the price which, having regard to the prices charged for goods as near as may be similar when so sold or when sold for exportation to other countries, would be so charged if the goods were sold in that country ;

after deducting in either case any excise or other internal duty leviable in that country."

The value of the goods is the c.i.f. price—*i.e.*, the "price which an importer would give for the goods if the goods were delivered to him freight and insurance paid, in bond at the port of importation, and duty shall be paid on that value as fixed by the Commissioners."

NOTE II. TO CHAPTER VII.

THE DYESTUFFS ACT OF 1920.

TOWARDS the very end of the legislative session of 1920, the Government announced its intention of introducing legislation with the view of carrying out its pledge to afford assistance to the dye-making industry. As a result there was passed, in the teeth of powerful but unavailing resistance, the Dyestuffs (Import Regulation) Act, 1920 (10 and 11 Geo. V., ch. 77).

This Act prohibits the importation, for a period of ten years, except under licence, of "all organic dyestuffs, colours, and colouring matters, and all organic intermediate products used in the manufacture of any such dyestuffs, colours, or colouring matters shall be prohibited."

The prohibition shall not extend to the importation of such goods when wholly produced or manufactured in some part of the Empire, but this must be proven to the satisfaction of the committee set up under the Act.

To assist the Board of Trade in the grant of licences, there is set up an advisory committee of eleven persons. Of these eleven, five are to be persons "concerned in the trades in which goods of the class prohibited to be imported by this Act are used," three are to be representative of the manufacturers of such goods, and the last three are to be persons "not directly concerned as aforesaid." One of the impartial persons is to be chairman of the committee. Any applicant for a licence (which is to be non-transferable, and for the grant of which a fee not exceeding five pounds may be charged), may demand the withdrawal of a member of the committee whilst his application is being discussed, on the ground "that he is prejudiced, owing to the fact that such member . . . is . . . a trade competitor." In addition to the Advisory Committee on Licences, the Act contemplates the appointment of a second committee for the purpose of advising the Board "with respect to the efficient and economical development of the dye-making industry." [1]

[1] See also *B.T.J.*, 9/12/20, pp. 682-3.

CHAPTER VIII.

Retaliation, Reciprocity, and Colonial Preferences, Etc.

§ 1. **Retaliatory and Reciprocal Duties.**—The first point which requires discussion is the meaning to be assigned to these terms and their logical relationship. The policy of retaliation in its widest sense refers to any act of tariff policy (used in a broad sense) by which a nation counters a tariff policy of which it disapproves. The policy of reciprocity in its wider sense refers to any act by which a nation responds to a tariff policy of which it approves. Retaliation and reciprocity then alike refer to returning "like for like," only in the first case what is returned are unfriendly, under the second case, friendly acts.

In the history of the tariff controversy in this country in the last thirty years, the power to apply retaliatory tariffs has frequently been asked for—and as the ensuing discussion will show not inconsistently—even by those who in general maintained the free trade position. The essential point here is to ask in what sense we are to understand the meaning of this demand. There are two ways in which it may be interpreted which we must now analyse. Since retaliation is in all cases a policy of revenge for "unfriendly" actions, the two meanings of the term in this second and more technical use of the phrase turn upon the definition we choose to give of an "unfriendly" action.

Let us ask what are the possible acts against which retaliation is to be practised? For our purposes they divide into two classes—(1) Acts which on the part of the country which initiates them are intended in principle to affect all countries. (2) Acts which in principle are intended to affect only one country. Of course an act nominally general may, in fact, be aimed at a particular country, as we have previously seen in the case of differentiation. Nevertheless a broad line of distinction can be drawn between these two cases: the importance of the distinction lying in the very different retaliatory measures which become possible. In the first case the only retaliatory measure which can be applied is to raise duties where they have been in existence previously or to impose duties on articles hitherto free, with a view to a subsequent bargain, for, so long as the general relations between all the parties remain unchanged, no specifically unfriendly act can be alleged.

Let us take a case. Suppose that the view of the impending determination of tariff treaties a country passes a new tariff law by which duties are increased by 20 per cent. What reply can be made? All the countries most concerned will tend to raise their tariffs in order to maintain the same relative positions, but so long as all the countries generalise their tariffs the only countries which will suffer relatively are those which do not impose duties for protective purposes, *and* which do not have sufficient power in other ways to cause the grant to them of most-favoured-nation treaties by which they obtain subsequently any reductions agreed upon.[1] It is only when, on the basis of these general retaliatory measures, an alteration in the relative position begins to take place—*i.e.*, when reductions are made to some, but not to all, that specific retaliation takes place or at all justified. The aggrieved parties may then argue that they are being treated *less favourably* than other countries, and are entitled to enforce specifically hostile Acts. Such specific Acts generally follow the failure to arrive at some definite agreement on the future commercial relations of two countries,[2] and constitute the formal aspect of a "tariff war."

When the position is examined, *de facto*, the following complications at once arise:—

(1) The first point concerns bi-linear tariffs. The question arises whether the mere failure to grant the lower rates to a given power, constitutes such a specifically unfriendly act as to *justify* the taking of special retaliatory measures. Let us suppose a country with a bi-linear tariff. With countries A, B, C it maintains treaties by which the lower rates are granted, with countries D, E, F no such treaties exist. Now

[1] Even then they may suffer through inconvenient differentiations.

[2] I have used this phrase to remove the impression that an increase of duties is the sole ground for retaliation.

suppose that, on the determination of the existing treaty, C fails to come to an agreement with regard to a new treaty. The general tariff is thereupon applied to its products. Does this constitute a specifically hostile act, entitling C to special retaliation? It is certainly being treated less favourably than A and B, but not less favourably than D, E, and F. The argument that such a position as we have outlined constituted "treatment less favourable than that accorded to other countries," is logically not unassailable, but it seems to be the result to which historical experience points.

This question must, of course, be held apart from the further and entirely different question as to why an agreement is not arrived at. With regard to this second question the details of the negotiations which ended without result must be studied.

(2) Though the failure to conclude agreements may *justify* specific retaliatory acts, it does not in the least follow that it is desirable to enforce such acts—that is to say, no other consequences may follow but the enforcement on both sides of the higher rates of duty which in other cases have been reduced. A survey of the practice followed in recent tariff wars may, therefore, be of interest.

(*a*) In the Franco-Italian [1] tariff disputes, apart from shipping discriminations, Italy maintained surtaxes between 1888-1889: France between 1888-1892. Thereafter, until February, 1899, both sides maintained their maximum or general tariff against the products of the other.

(*b*) In the Franco-Swiss tariff war,[2] the Swiss imposed differential duties as from January 1, 1893: refused to pass the pending Convention as to Literary Property, refused to pass the additional article as to frontier regulations of the treaty of 23rd October, 1882, and raised difficulties as to commercial travellers, the enclave of Gex, and diverted their transit trade by railway regulations. The French only applied their maximum tariff, which has been assigned by Franke as the cause of their unsuccess. An agreement was concluded in July, 1895.

[1] On this dispute, see Cd. 1938, "Tariff Wars, etc.," pp. 6-38; Franke, "Der Ausbau des heutigen Schutzzollsystems in Frankreich," pp. 16-23; Ashley, "Modern Tariff History," pp. 394-7.

[2] The Swiss differential rates are given in Bajkic, "Die Französische Handelspolitik," 1892-1902. See also Franke, *op. cit.*, pp. 46-58; Ashley, *op. cit.*, pp. 408-10, and Cd. 1938, pp. 1-6 and p. 78, *et seq.*

(*c*) *German-Russian Dispute.*—Germany applied § 6 of Tariff Law of 1879 on August 1, 1893: Russia increased the duties of her maximum tariff by 50 per cent. differentially, and raised tonnage dues.[1] A new agreement was signed in February, 1894.

(*d*) *German-Spanish Dispute.*[2]—In May, 1894, both sides applied their maximum tariff. On May 25, 1894, Germany applied a 50 per cent. surtax on Spanish goods: in June, 1895 (in virtue of the law of 18th May, 1895), it imposed surtaxes of 100 per cent. on dutiable and 20 per cent. on free goods. From 1896-1899 a new *modus vivendi* on the basis of lowest autonomous rates regulated the commercial relations of the two countries; in February, 1899, new most-favoured-nation arrangements were concluded.

(*e*) *German-Canadian Dispute.*[3]—Canada, in virtue of § 5 of Ed. VII., c. 15 (Canadian Statutes), imposed a surtax of 33 per cent. upon German goods from November 28, 1903, to March 1, 1910. Germany imposed general tariff rates.

(*f*) *Roumanian-Austro-Hungarian Dispute.*[4]—The Austrian Tariff Act of 1882 gave power to impose surtaxes of 100 per cent. plus 15 per cent. on free goods. In June, 1886, in consequence of fruitless negotiations, Roumania applied her general tariff, Austria-Hungary retorted with surtaxes, which were not withdrawn until Roumania denounced all her treaties in 1890, as this removed the differentiation against Austria-Hungary. A new agreement resulted in December, 1893.

§ 2. When we turn to reciprocity we again find that the word has a general and a specific use.

In its widest use, it is applied in contradistinction to a policy of complete autonomy as implying any process by which tariff advantages are offset against one another. Thus, the

---

[1] Cd. 1938 (pp. 38-76). Ashley, *op. cit.*, pp. 92-99. The German surtaxes amounted to 50 per cent.

[2] Zimmerman, "Die Handelspolitik des Deutschen Reiches," 1871-1900, pp. 308-9; Ashley, *op. cit.*, p. 100.

[3] Ashley, *op. cit.*, p. 101; Porritt, "Sixty Years of Protection in Canada," pp. 413-416. For the causes of this dispute, which turned upon the question of the grant of the British preferential tariff rates in return for German conventional tariff, whilst Canada took the line that "this is a matter of purely domestic policy as distinct from foreign policy," and, therefore, would offer only most-favoured-nation treatment exclusive of these rates. See in addition Cd. 1,781 of 1904, "Copy of Canadian Sessional Paper containing Correspondence in Connection with the German Tariff."

[4] Grunzel, "Handelspolitik," p. 432.

conclusion of reciprocal most-favoured-nation agreements; the granting of conventional tariffs against minimum tariffs, bargaining for concessions which the contracting parties know will be generalised through most-favoured-nation agreements with other powers, all form instances of reciprocity in this wider sense of the term.

But there is a narrow connotation to the term, as expressing a particular type of bargaining policy. In this narrower sense attention is concentrated on one or both of the following conceptions :—

(1) The granting of exclusive right against exclusive right.

By "exclusive right against exclusive right" is not meant that subsequently no other country can have the same facilities extended to it, all that is meant is that extension to a third country is made conditional on that third country itself offering specific inducements deemed satisfactory. Hence, the claim that the conclusion of a most-favoured-nation treaty entitles a country to all the privileges which its co-contractant grants to any other country is not recognised by those countries that pursue a policy of strict reciprocity.

(2) The granting of equivalent right for equivalent right.

By this is meant that quantitatively the benefits gained must be equal to the sacrifice made. This is of course an extremely difficult point to adjudge, and we will defer the discussion of it to a later section.

§ 3. The next point which requires consideration is the logical relationship between retaliation and reciprocity. We may begin with a quotation from Professor Dietzel,[1] ". . . whosoever aims at the *permanent* establishment of tariff reciprocity, will also in consistency approve of the introduction of fighting duties, according to the circumstances, more or less frequently, in dealing with nations which impose exceptionally high import duties. The converse, however, does not hold good. He who grants that *here and there a tariff fight may be carried on*, does not at all need to allow that such fighting should be *reduced to a system.*"

"Prince Bismarck, for example, in the middle of the seventies, had in mind merely a policy of retort, but, so far as one can judge, would have refused a policy of reciprocity.

---

[1] Dietzel, "Retaliatory Duties" (English translation), p. 19.

At the present moment, too (written early in the century), Hicks-Beach, in England, wants merely a policy of retort: whereas Balfour seems to aim at one of reciprocity."

This subject is, however, capable of more detailed treatment.[1] We shall deal with it under the following heads :—

(*a*) *Relations between Reciprocity and Retaliation.*—It is fairly obvious that a general policy of retaliation is implicit in the acceptance of a reciprocity policy, however interpreted, although a policy of reciprocity does not establish the wisdom of retaliation in the narrow sense. If the co-contractants of a given country denounce the treaties concluded with them and raise their duties, a similar step must be taken by it against them, otherwise its relative bargaining position will suffer. It does not in the least follow that the best method of inaugurating new treaties based on reciprocity of concessions is to raise duties *ab initio*, just because of the ease with which this step can be imitated; but, though the country which inaugurates the higher duties may be mistaken, it would also be a mistake not to raise duties in return, since this would be probably regarded as a sign of weakness. So far we have been using "retaliation" in a wide sense. But in all cases a country pursuing a reciprocity policy must be in a position to exert pressure on such countries as refuse to enter into agreements, although it may not be expedient to use such power, initially. The commercial relations of the two countries may after rupture of negotiations be conducted on the basis of the maximum or autonomous rate, but this may provoke special measures on the part of the second country on the ground that it is being discriminated against if the first country simultaneously grants its minimum rates to a third country. If, finally, a country pursues a narrow policy of special concession, this may again provoke retaliatory acts, and requires ability to retort. As to the *wisdom* of retaliation *in specific cases* more will be said below.

(*b*) *Reciprocity and Tariff Autonomy.*—By "autonomy" is here specially meant the reservation in any tariff agreements

[1] If retaliation and reciprocity are both defined as "the policy of like for like" without further emendation, discussion as to the relationship between the two terms becomes a merely verbal one. Such an interchangeable use of the words is not unknown—*e.g.*, Grunzel, *op. cit.*, p. 429, when speaking of the application by two countries of maximum tariffs against one another, he says, "One of the States will soon find that this reciprocity worsens its position." (Der eine Staat wird daher bald finden, dass er bei dieser Reciprocität schlechter daran ist.)

which may be concluded of the power to raise the tariff rates at any time, or the refusal to concede a fixed rate for a specific time. The mere fact that the French Government has been able in the past to conclude commercial treaties on virtually this basis shows that it is not inconsistent with a policy of bargaining, but the experiences of the French Government also show that the maintenance of this attitude is not without difficulties.[1] It will be obvious, on reflection, that to ask for concessions without any time period being specified for the concessions offered, may at times seriously diminish the value of the latter; and make the conclusion of treaties with powers of an equal economic standing more difficult, or, alternatively, produce such a fear of upsetting any arrangement once reached with a country of this latter type, as virtually to produce the fixity of the "bound" tariff rate.

(*c*) *Reciprocity and a Policy of Pure Revenue Tariffs.*—There seems to be some doubt as to whether a country pursuing what is broadly a "free-trade" policy can pursue a policy of reciprocity. This misapprehension is partly due to a confusion between "free trade" and "autonomy" (although, as we have seen above, even autonomy is no barrier to tariff bargaining): partly to the belief that a country with revenue tariffs can offer no counter concessions: partly to the belief that a policy of revenue tariffs is inconsistent with differential rates. Neither of these last two assumptions is true. It is true that the area within which concessions can be offered is more limited, but this does not imply complete inability to offer any concessions.

So far as differentiation of the rate and a revenue tariff is concerned, the question we have to discuss is under what conditions of supply a differential rate will yield the same revenue as an undifferentiated rate would have done.[2] The answer is not very difficult. The conditions of supply

[1] "Although France succeeded eventually in making agreements with all countries of commercial importance and in securing most-favoured-nation pledges from most of these, she reached this end only after serious complications, which caused losses and left a permanent and somewhat adverse effect on her commercial relations. She did establish and maintain her autonomy in rate-making. The maximum tariff schedule stood essentially as a standardised warning. For the measure of autonomy which she gained, France paid by conceding a like measure to other countries, and she sacrificed guaranties of stability which the treaties of a former period had established." U.S. Tariff Commission, "Summary of the Report on Reciprocity and Commercial Treaties," p. 44. But see below, § 5.

[2] Pigou, "Protective and Preferential Import Duties," chap. i., § 11.

must be such that the elasticity of supply from the preferred source shall be such as to cause an expansion of supply from that area great enough to compensate for the lower duty charged by the larger volume against which it is charged, whilst the supply differentiated against must be inelastic enough to cause the volume not to fall off (in spite of a reduction of profit due to the lower price now prevailing in the importing country, or, in the event of this latter *not* being the case, that the elasticity of the preferred supply be such as to compensate both for the lower duty charged and the falling off of the supply from the area differentiated against.[1]

It may, of course, be a question of practical importance whether these conditions are likely or unlikely in any particular case. Here, we have been concerned only in the statement of the theoretical possibilities.

(*d*) *Retaliation and a Policy of "Free Trade*."—This is the second of the cases considered by Dietzel, and it will be observed that he carefully qualifies his statement. We may put the matter thus—a policy of retaliation is inconsistent with free trade if the object of retaliation is to oppose all but revenue duties. For, in that case, all, except those countries which maintain nothing but revenue duties will be retaliated against, and the policy of the country in question virtually ceases to be free trade, unless the efforts are *completely* successful, and becomes one of reciprocity with free-trade

---

[1] The questions discussed in the text really concern the consistency of reciprocity and a policy of tariff-for-revenue only. But if it be held (*a*) that a free-trade country should *never* impose any duty that will not yield a maximum of return, and that having arrived at the appropriate duty, having this object in view, it should not be suffered to alter it; (*b*) that, in fact, most countries simply raise their rates preparatory to a bargain, so that the net result of bargaining is to leave the duties what they would have been had no reciprocity been practised, then the *expediency* of a free-trade country pursuing such a policy may legitimately be questioned. If the first point alone is considered, we must weigh the possible gain by increased trade against possible revenue losses, in the second case we must follow Mr. A. W. Flux, who is arguing on the assumption that the position of the U.K. in fact prevents her from pursuing a policy of reciprocity, in the statement: "It will depend on the conclusion we form as to the extent to which other countries have been influenced by the tariffs retained by their neighbours, to check the raising of duties, whether an estimate of the loss of Great Britain places that loss at a magnitude great enough to be worth avoiding at the necessary price—namely, the retention of duties not desired for other purposes and hurtful in themselves." A. W. Flux, "Do Reciprocally Preferential Tariffs tend towards Free Trade?" in American Economic Association Publications, 3rd series, 1905, p. 346.

areas and protection against protected areas. There is in this case, therefore, the danger that the adoption of retaliatory duties will tend to their *permanent* use. It follows that for a free-trade country, not following a reciprocity policy, the main difficulty in the maintenance of retaliatory duties lies in the definition of the cases in which retaliation will be in order. The broader the considerations entitling a resort to this method of offence the more likely is it to become part of a wider policy of reciprocity.[1]

§ 4. **Types of Retaliatory Duty or Differential Surtaxes.**—Three points require notice here—

(1) The limitation or non-limitation as to the amount of the surtax and the scope of the surtax.
(2) Discretionary power, if any, granted to the executive.
(3) Any additional measures, if any, which are applicable.

A few illustrations may give an idea of the general position—

Canada.—Tariff Act of 1907, § 7.

" 1. Articles which are the produce or manufacture of any foreign country which treats imports from Canada less favourably than those from other countries may be subject to a surtax over and above the duties specified in Schedule A to this Act. Such surtax in every case to be one-third of the duty specified in the general tariff to the said schedule.

" 2. Any question arising as to any foreign country or goods coming under the operation of this section shall be decided by the Minister of Customs, whose decision shall be final.

" 3. The Governor in Council may make regulations for carrying out the purposes of this section, and may, by order in council, from time to time suspend the surtax from application to the goods of any country."

---

[1] It is interesting to observe that M'Culloch, probably the best representative of the pure free-trader, who was even bitterly opposed to the Cobden Treaty of 1860, gives a provisional assent to the doctrine of retaliation. See his " Political Economy," 4th edition, p. 162. " We would not, however, be understood as meaning, by anything now stated, to lay it down absolutely that restrictions, imposed for the purpose of retaliation, are always injurious to those who have recourse to them. This, certainly, has hitherto been their ordinary effect; but their policy depends wholly on circumstances," and so on, pointing to the necessity of weighing long-run gains with short-run evils, though there must be " reasonable grounds for concluding that the repeal or modification of the original prohibition will be brought about by the retaliation," otherwise " it would be most impolitic to embark in any such hostile course." For an objective discussion of the practical dangers of " retaliation " and a spirited attack on the implications of the word, see Smart, " The Return to Protection," chaps. xiii. and xiv.

France.—Tariff Act of 29th March, 1910, Art. 3.

"The Government may, by decrees issued in Council of Ministers—

"Apply surtaxes, not exceeding double the duties inscribed in the general tariff or not exceeding the value of the goods, to all or any goods from countries which may subject French goods to surtaxes or particularly high duties:

"Apply equivalent surtaxes to all or any goods from countries which may treat French products less favourably than the products of other states:

"In the two preceding cases, subject all or any articles which are free of duty in accordance with the tariff to an *ad valorem* duty not exceeding 50 per cent.:

"Saving treaty stipulations to the contrary, subject by way of reciprocity, any foreign goods to duties, taxes, or formalities identical with, or, as the case may be, similar to those which, in the country of origin, may be applicable to French goods:

". . . Take immediate steps, appropriate to the circumstances, in cases where measures enforced by foreign countries may be of such a nature as to restrict French commerce.

"Decrees issued in conformity with the foregoing paragraphs shall be converted into bills, and submitted for the ratification of the chambers, immediately if they are in session, and, if not, at the opening of the following session."

By Art. 4, "should French vessels be subjected in a foreign country to treatment less favourable than that accorded to vessels of other powers, the Government is authorised to levy on the vessels of such country entering French ports, or ports of a French colony or possession, and on the goods carried by those vessels, such duties or surtaxes as may be deemed necessary to countervail the prejudice suffered by the French flag."

Germany.—Tariff Act of 1902, § 10.

"Dutiable articles proceeding from states that treat goods or ships of German origin less favourably than those of other states may, in addition to the rate of duty given in the tariff, be subjected to a surtax of double the amount of this rate, or equivalent to the full value of the goods. Goods which are free of duty according to the tariff, may, in the above circumstances, be subjected to a duty of 50 per cent. *ad valorem.*"

Furthermore, if treaty rights do not prevent it, foreign goods may be subjected to the same duties and customs regulations as the foreign country in question imposes on German goods.

"The measures provided for above will be enforced by Imperial ordinance after the consent of the Bundesrath (Federal Council) has been obtained. Such orders are to be communicated to the Reichstag at once, or, if the Reichstag be not in session, when it next meets. They shall not be enforced, if not approved by the Reichstag."

Italy.—Art. 5 of the Preliminary Dispositions of the Tariff.

"Goods proceeding from countries in which Italian vessels and products are subject to a differential régime may be burdened with an increase of frontier duties up to 50 per cent. of the duty inscribed in the general tariff.

"In the case of goods duty free under the tariff, the same may be burdened with an import duty up to 25 per cent. of their official market value.

"These dispositions shall be issued, by Royal Decree, describing the goods liable to the surtax and the extent to which such increase of duty shall be applied.

"The decree in question must immediately be submitted to parliament to be converted into law."

Somewhat similar arrangements can be enforced in Japan (extra duties not exceeding in amount the value of the article),[1] and Switzerland.[2]

In discussing the U.S.A. form of the maximum-minimum tariff attention was drawn to § 3 of the tariff of 1897, which gave the President power to suspend the free entry of certain articles if the countries exporting these to the States imposed duties on American produce, which, in view of such admittance, were deemed "reciprocally unequal and unreasonable." As was there said [3] it is difficult to regard this clause as a pure retaliatory clause: it represents an instrument of bargaining rather than a pure instrument of retort. The 1909 Act, the clauses of which are also cited in the connection referred to "marked a distinct departure from the policy of seeking special favours by granting reciprocal concessions. Though, in form, the policy was that of the concession of a minimum tariff,

[1] Japanese tariff of 1910, Art. 5.
[2] Arts. 4 and 5 of the Customs Tariff Law of 10th October, 1902.
[3] See Chap. III., § 7.

virtually it amounted to a provision to impose maximum rates by way of penalty against unequal treatment of American produce."[1] The lower duties were after negotiation applied by proclamation[2] "to the countries comprising the entire commercial world; in no case was the maximum rate applied. In certain important instances, however, notably those of Germany and France, full equality of treatment was not extended to imports from the United States, and it would, therefore, appear that the Art. of 1909 did not provide a penalty method effective for the total elimination of all discrimination against American products in European markets." What we have to deal with here is, in fact, a bargaining provision rather than a differential surtax, and it is this latter which the report which has been cited recommends on the ground that—

"The method of additional duties is that which can be put into effect by the United States at once, without disturbance of its general tariff policy and without committing the country definitively as regards the permanent commercial arrangements which may be evolved as part of the coming international settlement. The necessary flexibility can be secured by leaving the actual imposition of additional duties to the discretion of the President, who shall act always in conformity with a stated general principle and subject to general limitations defined by statute. . . . It would seem indispensable that a considerable degree of freedom be left to the executive department. The restrictions within which that freedom shall be exercised must be prescribed according to the judgment of Congress. They may take the form of limiting that additions or penalties to stated *ad valorem* supplements to the existing duties, or to stated *ad valorem* duties (or equivalent specific duties) on articles appearing upon the general free list."[3]

There we do get the genuine differential duty in the form familiar from the European instances just cited.

§ 5. **Types of Reciprocity Powers.**—The general power to conclude reciprocity treaties with the limitations which may be imposed upon the executive forms part of the general subject of commercial treaties, and will be dealt with in that connection in a subsequent chapter. What will be examined

---

[1] Summary of Report, etc., p. 29. [2] *Ibid.*
[3] *Op. cit.*, p. 12.

here are the attempts which can be or have been made in the more accurate delimitation of the concessions to be offered and received—the measurement of concessional Acts. So far two types of measurement have been laid down in Tariff Acts—

(1) Sacrifice of similar duties for similar duties.[1]

Two instances can be cited from the 1913 U.S.A. tariff free list.

By No. 581, "potatoes and potatoes dried, desiccated or otherwise prepared, not specially provided for in this section" are free, but by a note appended—

> "Any of the foregoing specified articles shall be subject to a duty of 10 per cent. *ad valorem* when imported directly or indirectly from a country, dependency, or other sub-division of government which imposes a duty on such articles imported from the United States."

By No. 644, "wheat, wheat flour, semolina, and other wheat products, not specially provided for in this section" are free, but by a note appended—

> "Wheat shall be subject to a duty of 10 cents per bushel, wheat flour shall be subject to a duty of 45 cents per barrel of 196 pounds, and semolina and other products of wheat, not specially provided for in this section, 10 per cent. *ad valorem*, when imported directly or indirectly from a country, dependency, or other subdivision of government which imposes a duty on wheat or wheat flour or semolina imported from the United States."

(2) Sacrifice of equal revenue for equal revenue. By the New Zealand Act of 24th November, 1903—[2]

> "Where any country, being part of the British Dominions, reduces or abolishes or proposes to reduce or abolish the duty on any produce or manufacture of New Zealand, the governor may enter into an agreement with that country to reduce or abolish the duty on any article or articles the produce or manufacture of such country to an extent that the estimated revenue so

[1] It is important to notice that by "similar" duties is *not* meant duties *necessarily* identical in amount, though it *may also* mean this.

[2] Cited by J. W. Root, "Colonial Tariffs," p. 194.

remitted shall equal as nearly as possible the estimated revenue remitted by that country.

"Where any country, not being part of the British Dominions, reduces or abolishes, or proposes to reduce or abolish, the duty on any product or manufacture of New Zealand, the Governor may, subject to, or by virtue of treaty with His Majesty, negotiate with such country for an agreement with that country to reduce or abolish the duty on any article or articles the produce or manufacture of such country, to an extent that the estimated revenue so remitted shall equal as nearly as possible the estimated revenues remitted by that country."

Similar considerations may, of course, weigh with the negotiators in the conclusion of commercial agreements; thus, in the course of the German-Russian negotiations which ended abortively, "The German Government replied that a proposal, which secured to Russia reductions on four-fifths of her total export trade to Germany, with a consequent loss to that country of £1,250,000 customs revenue, and which accorded no alleviation to the German export trade to the Russian Empire . . . could not possibly serve as a basis for an agreement."[1] This passage serves well to show that even to a protectionist country the loss of customs revenue is by no means an insignificant factor.

It is obvious that of the two measures already discussed, the second measure is very much more important than the first. Under a system of international division of labour it is not at all likely that the import and export of the same commodity from each of the contracting countries to one another will so equal as to make identity of rates a matter of equal importance. Hence, the economic significance to the *importing* country (which may desire, and normally will desire, to profit its own industry) of such a demand on the part of the exporting country may well be much less than that of a demand for reciprocity with regard to different commodities, one of which it largely imports, and the other of which it largely exports. But when a country pursues a policy mainly or wholly influenced by considerations of revenue, the sacrifice involved in granting a concession—*i.e.*, the loss of revenue it will cause—is the *only* consideration, and the negotiations must be guided

[1] "Tariff Wars, etc.," p. 63.

by it, implicitly or explicitly, and even in a protectionist country a loss of revenue must be a serious matter, though its importance is secondary.

It must, however, be confessed that the whole question is one of great difficulty, and other tests which have been adopted are not entirely satisfactory.

By a present French law, of July 29, 1919,[1] the French Government has adopted what is virtually the policy of measuring reciprocal concessions by the absolute amount of the duty. The enactment which modifies the Act of 1892 runs—

> "The Government is authorised to negotiate with foreign countries, for an agreed period, concessions by way of reductions in the general tariff rates of duty, calculated as a percentage of the difference between the general tariff and the minimum tariff."

The reductions granted under these conditions may, in exchange for reciprocal concessions, be put into force provisionally by decree of the Council of Ministers. In such cases the agreements concluded must be submitted to ratification by the Chambers immediately if they be in session, or otherwise, at the beginning of the following session.

> The object of the law is "to give greater elasticity and to render it possible for the French Government to make concessions more nearly equivalent to the compensation obtained from the particular foreign country concerned. In the case of an article subject to a duty of 100 francs in the general tariff and of 50 francs in the minimum tariff, and in respect of which the Government had under the present law conceded in a commercial agreement, a reduction of say, 50 per cent. of the difference between the two tariffs, the rate of duty applicable would be 75 francs." [2]

[1] *Board of Trade Journal*, 14/8/19, p. 202.

[2] The interest of this new law is not exhausted by the facts already discussed. It represents virtually the adoption of a Tri-linear Tariff by the French Republic, since these rates will be intermediate between the maximum-minimum rates. Autonomy is still maintained, since the concession is a proportionate part of the difference between these latter rates, and the absolute amount of the duty will vary with changes in these rates, for the duty actually conceded = (minimum rate in force at any time) + (given percentage of the difference between maximum and minimum rate). Any change on the minimum rate will affect the absolute amount of duty payable, though the difference between it and the maximum may remain constant.

It is quite clear that the absolute reductions mutually conceded offer only a very rough guide to the real value of the concessions obtained. A given percentage reduction will make very much less difference to a strongly organised and efficient industry than it will to a poorly organised and inefficient one.

There remains the fairly obvious test of the relative volumes of foreign trade affected. This standard may, however, be interpreted in one of two ways. An equivalent concession may be regarded as meaning—(1) That the absolute amounts of trade affected on both sides are equal. (2) That the relative proportions of the total trade affected on both sides are equal. That is, the negotiators can off-set concessions affecting, say, £10,000,000 of exports on both sides: or they can offset concessions affecting one-third of the total exports whatever their amount on either side. Whatever alternative be the basis, it is in itself inadequate to test the value of the concession, for the *propulsive* effect must be considered as well—*i.e.*, the degree to which the given concession will stimulate trade.

This brings one to the centre of the whole question. From the purely economic standpoint the value of the concessions can be judged by the degree by which the annual net income of the two countries is increased in the aggregate, whilst the narrower question is the distribution of this increase between the two societies. In so far as the concessions stimulate the progress of the division of labour, and thus the efficiency of production in the two areas, the distribution of the surplus depends on the elasticities of demand and supply in the two areas. For, if the exports of the one are urgently desired in the second country whilst the exports of the other are less urgently needed, and at the same time alternative areas for the disposal of these exports are difficult to find, the equation of exchange will tend to the advantage of the first. Both will share in the benefits of the concessions, but one may gain to a somewhat greater extent than the other.

Such a test as this just discussed is not likely to be of very much use in actual negotiations, although as we shall see in the next section, the elasticity of supply and demand is a factor of importance even to the statesman. In each of the two contracting countries the interests directly represented are the exporters who will gain by the counter-concessions and the domestic producers who will, or fancy they will, suffer by the concessions necessary. Under these circumstances the final repercussion of the concessions on the aggregate national income is likely to be overlooked in the pressure brought to bear by the representatives of the particular industries affected, favourably or unfavourably, as the case may be.

§ 6. Our next task must be to attempt an evaluation of the policy of retaliation. On this question we must distinguish three schools—

(1) The anti-retaliatory school, which argues that retaliation *always* recoils on the heads of those who attempt to practice it.

(2) The school which argues that retaliation is always successful, or successful in the vast majority of cases.

(3) The moderate school, which includes the illustrious name of Adam Smith, to which the success or failure of the policy of retaliation depends upon the conditions under which it is undertaken.

(1) The position of the anti-retaliatory school is based upon the fundamental argument that it is impossible for one country to buy from another without selling to it directly or indirectly. Consequently any check to the flow of imports due to retaliatory duties diminishes to an equal degree the exports of the country practicising retaliation.

If, on the other hand, no check to importation takes place, owing to the inelasticity of the demand for the goods in question, the only effect will be that the price to the consumer will be raised, who is unable to pay as much for other things as he did before. The incidence of suffering is thus finally on the producers in those industries the demand for the products of which is thus deranged, and the retaliatory country is again the victim of its own policy.[1]

To this argument we owe an important correction by Professor Pigou,[2] which amounts to the statement that Pro fessor Dietzel, whose argument is summarised above, has overlooked two important points—(*a*) the effect of retaliatory duties in reducing the profits of producers owing to the necessity of their bearing part of the burden of these " in

[1] Dietzel, *op. cit.*

[2] Pigou, " Professor Dietzel on Dumping and Retaliation," *Economic Journal*, vol. xv., pp. 442-3.

the short run," (*b*) the fact that the duties by whomsoever paid flow into the "National Exchequer," and thus, other things equal, enable "an equivalent amount of other taxes to be remitted." If we to this add the possibility of the retaliating country compensating for any loss of imports by drawing these from an alternative source or diverting a portion of its own capital and labour (withdrawn from the export trade) to the production of the excluded or diminished imports itself, it seems at first sight as if the retaliatory school were completely in the right. But, as a matter of fact, if this last argument were completely true, it would prove too much. For if it is possible for the retaliating country to compensate for the loss in one direction by expansion in others, the same must necessarily be true in general of the country retaliated *against*, so that it would appear that alternatively neither side could be much injured by retaliation. A new investigation becomes necessary.

Let us first ask wherein the real loss from a retaliative war arises? It arises from the reduction in the aggregate income accruing to both countries through the additional impediment to the trade. If both areas have specialised their production in the expectation of normal trade relations, any new hindrances to trade which affect the exchange of goods consequently reduce the net income of both sides. To this standpoint it is no answer to say that both sides can make up the deficiency by stimulating their own production. For in so far as this enables the old output to be reached, it will still only be immediately at the cost of greater real effort, so that the per unit return to effort is less: whilst, in any case, it does not invalidate the point that with freer trade relations *and* the new level of energy a still greater net income could have been enjoyed. Hence, it must be acknowledged that immediately a trade war results in loss.

But because an aggregate loss is suffered it does not follow (*a*) that the loss may not be greater for the one side or the other—*i.e.*, that there may not be an unequal distribution of the burden. (*b*) That the loss may not be greatly reduced by the conscious efforts of both sides, or that thereby one side may not escape loss by this means to a greater extent than the other.

(*a*) The unequal distribution of the burden depends upon the elasticities of supply and demand in the two areas for the goods obtained from the other. Let us take an extreme case. Suppose an area A entirely specialised in the production of two commodities, X and Y, which we will suppose are also produced in other areas, O, P, and Q. In the case of a second country, B, X, and Y, are imported from A in return for commodities M and N, which are a natural monopoly. Let us suppose that there are no available substitutes for M and N, but that X and Y can be replaced without great difficulty.

Under such conditions it would still be true that the cessation of normal trade relations would cause the aggregate net income of both countries to be smaller than would otherwise be the case, but the loss would almost entirely fall on country A. If we ask the reason why, it lies in the ease with which the products of A can be dispensed with and the difficulties of dispensing with the products of country B. Hence, the demand in A for B's products is inelastic; that for A's products in B is elastic. On the other hand, the supply of B's products to A's market is elastic: whilst the supply of A's products to B's market is inelastic. Hence, in any trade war between A and B the chances are greatly in B's favour. For consumers in B can obtain the commodities X and Y in O, P, and Q, or dispense with them altogether, whilst consumers in A can only obtain M and N from B. Hence, the proper retaliatory policy for B to pursue is to impose differential import duties on X and Y from A, and differential export duties on M and N when exported to A. No doubt the diversion of the market would inflict certain losses also on B, but the losses of A would be much greater.

Hence, to quote an illustration from Professor Dietzel, a surtax imposed by Germany on Russian rye is much more dangerous to Russian agriculture than a differential duty on wheat: for the German market before the war was a very much more important factor for the Russian rye growers than it was for the wheat growers, for whilst the latter could substitute another market for the German market, it was considerably less easy for the former to find other areas for the vend of their products. On the other hand, the German consumer could substitute wheat for rye and non-Russian wheat for Russian wheat. We may add that a differential duty on German textiles or iron and steel goods would have been much more serious than a duty on German dyes, for the former could be much more easily replaced than the latter.

From the standpoint of the economist, therefore, the question which is of most weight is whether the balance of advantage with regard to these matters lies with the particular country he is considering or with its opponent. But the economist is not in a position to judge of certain other matters of almost equal importance. He is in a position to lay down the economic conditions—those which are likely to make for or against success on economic grounds: but he cannot judge of the *psychological* conditions in consequence of which, as Professor Pigou remarks, "the country which in a tariff conflict suffers the greater injury, will not necessarily be the one to yield." Nor can he forsee the *political* conditions by which the policy of retaliation must in any particular case necessarily be influenced. To judge of these matters, in a famous phrase of Adam Smith's, "does not perhaps belong so much to the science of a legislator, whose deliberations ought to be governed by general principles which are always the same, as to the skill of that insidious and crafty animal, vulgarly called a statesman or politician whose councils are directed by the momentary fluctuations of affairs."

CHAPTER VIII.—*Continued.*

§ 7. The next matter which requires our attention is the subject of Colonial Preferences—that is, reductions in tariff rates granted to the products of the Mother Country by the Colonies and by the Colonies to the Mother Country. In this connection we must take notice of the fact that the preferences in question may affect not only the *import* duties respectively levied, but also the export duties levied—that is, exports from the Mother Country to the Colonies or the Colonies to the Mother Country may remain untaxed in the country of export, whilst exports to, as well as imports from, other areas may be taxed.

Apart from "open-door colonies," whose tariff régime is fixed by international agreement, and where the questions discussed in this section consequently do not arise, we may divide colonies from the standpoint of tariff *form* into two classes—

(1) Those with assimilated tariffs.

(2) Those possessing, if we may take over a useful phrase from the French, "tariff personality."

In the first case the colony is in general subject to the same tariff as the Mother Country itself: in the second case the colony has a tariff devised in view of its own specific needs. Care must be taken to guard against confusing these concepts of assimilation and personality with those of *subordination* and *autonomy:* these latter distinctions refer to the tariff-making power and not to the tariff itself. It is true that a colony possessing complete tariff autonomy will not generally assimilate its position to that of the Mother Country: but the converse is not in the least true. A colony may possess no tariff autonomy or only autonomy in the very restricted sense that the local bureaucracy is responsible for the details of the tariff with a centralised veto, and yet assimilation may not be practised. On the other hand, a customs-making body truly representative of the colonies as well as of the Mother Country—say an "Imperial Tariff Parliament" of the British Empire—might yet adopt the idea of tariff assimilation. The decision to adopt one or other of these principles springs, in fact, from economic consideration which do not move completely parallel to the ideas underlying self government, although the acceptance of the principle of autonomy disposes to the idea of tariff personality more than the idea of colonial subordination does. The choice of assimilation or personality rests ultimately upon the acceptance of the view that in a definite sense Mother Country and Colonies *form one area.* From the standpoint of sentiment this may be accepted: from the standpoint of economic structure and need it is obviously open to destructive criticism. To this point we must later return.

When the idea of assimilation is accepted in its most complete form, the idea of a preference, together with the concept of "Mother Country" and "Colony," really disappears. There is, strictly speaking, only the national territory, wherever situated, and freedom of trade between the metropolitan and the overseas area is placed on the same footing as trade between two parts of the metropolitan area itself. But whether we describe the differential advantage as a "Preference" or not, it remains a differential advantage to traders, within the limits of the area, which can be directly compared to the differential advantages accorded by colonies with tariff personality to the Mother Country, if any such advantages are accorded at all.

§ 8. What we have now to do is to describe in some detail the relations existing in the tariff systems of the chief colonising powers.[1]

1. We may first deal with a country whose Colonial Empire has disappeared in consequence of the dispositions of the Treaty of Peace. Under the German law, as it existed before the treaty, German goods imported into the colonies enjoyed most-favoured-nation treatment, whilst "the products of the German colonies and protectorates may enjoy the customs reductions and reductions arrived at by treaty by means of a resolution of the Federal Council." (Tariff law of 1902, § 1, last paragraph.)

[1] A general oversight is given by H.C. Paper, No. 2969, of 1909, "Return showing the Fiscal Advantages at Present given by France, Germany, etc." Now somewhat out of date. See also J. W. Root, "Colonial Tariffs," 1906; and the references given in connection with the particular country mentioned.

2. In the case of Holland.—" No preference as regards customs treatment is accorded . . . to the produce of its colonies, or by Dutch colonies to the produce of the Mother Country."

3. Much more complicated is the position with regard to the French Colonial Empire. The situation varies as between (1) Algeria. (2) The " Assimilated " Colonies. (3) The " Non-Assimilated " Colonies. (4) The Protectorates of Tunis and Morocco. Corsica can be better treated under a different heading. For reasons of convenience we will begin with the assimilated and non-assimilated groups, the position of which, in principle, is governed by the Tariff Act of 1892.[1] It should be mentioned that under the influence of the Second Empire a liberalising movement had resulted in giving considerable freedom to the colonies : whilst in the eighties of last century, the " Forward Policy " of one school of thought, and the desire to make the colonies pay in view of the sacrifices which the new imperialism was entailing, united other schools with the first in an attitude of distinct reaction of which the clauses of the Act of 1892 are the witness. Art. 3-6 deal directly with the colonies. Art. 7 maintains the Algerian régime.

These Articles run as follows :—

> " Art. 3. The duties and immunities applicable to the products imported into the Mother Country from the colonies, the French possessions, and the countries within the protectorate of Indo-China, are fixed in conformity with Table E, appended to the present law.
>
> " Table E, above mentioned, does not apply to the following :—The French territories on the West Coast of Africa (except the Gaboon), Tahiti, and her dependencies, the French establishments in India, Obeck, Diego-Suarez, Nossi-Bé, and St. Marie de Madagascar. In all cases long cloths of French origin coming from the French settlements in India are exempt from duty. Exemptions or abatements (détaxes) can, in addition, be accorded to other natural or manufactured products proceeding from the said settlements, a list of such products

[1] On French colonial tariff policy generally, see Pallain, vol. i., pp. 169-237 : Girault, " The Colonial Tariff Policy of France " (Carnegie Peace Endowment Publication), with numerous references to other publications.

to be fixed by decrees of the Council of State for each possession. *The domestic products and manufactures which, on their importation into France, do not benefit by such exemption will be subject to the duties under the minimum tariff.*

"Foreign products imported into the French colonies and possessions and into the protectorate of Indo-China—with the exception of the territories enumerated in paragraph 2—are subject to the same duties as if they were imported into France.

"Decrees in the form of public administrative regulations, drawn up in accordance with the report of the Minister of Commerce, Industry, and the Colonies, and, after consultation with the Councils General or Administrative Councils of the Colonies, will specify the products on which, as exceptions to the preceding rule, special rules of duty will be levied.

"Paragraphs 1 and 3 of the present Article will not apply to each colony until after the regulation described in paragraph 4 has been introduced, but without this delay in any case lasting longer than one year. In any case the Government will have the power of at once granting the advantages of Table E, either entirely or in part, to such colonies as at present apply in their entirety the duties of the home tariff to foreign products, or who impose duties under that tariff on colonial produce coming from abroad.

"Art. 4. The Councils General and the Administrative Councils of the Colonies may also consult as to those exceptions to the customs tariff of the Mother Country which it may be deemed necessary to demand. The results of these deliberations must be laid before the Council of State, and action will be taken with regard to them in the same form as the regulations of public administration described in the foregoing article.

"Art. 5. *The products of one French colony imported into another French colony will not be subject to any customs duty.*[1]

"Foreign products imported from one French colony

---

[1] This rule applies, it should be carefully noted, whether the colony from which, and to which, the goods are sent is assimilated or non-assimilated.

into another French colony will be liable in this latter to the payment of the difference between the duties of the local tariff and those of the tariff of the exporting colony."

Art. 6 deals with the levying of the customs duties and the division of the " octroi de mer " (wharfage duties) which is beyond our scope.

The Act of 1892 gave the ground work; it is now necessary to deal with the details.

1. Schedule E, in addition to the treatment to be accorded to foreign products when imported into France *via* Algeria and the other colonies (in which latter case they were to pay *full* duty to prevent fraud),[1] imposed duties on sugar and its derivatives (to the full extent of the metropolitan tariff), and on cocoa, chocolate, coffee, pepper, and other spices, which were to pay half the duties of the metropolitan tariff. We may follow the fate of these duties.[2]

When, in 1900, the duty on coffee was reduced, and in 1908 the duty on pepper was raised, the absolute difference between the rate on foreign and colonial products was maintained. The introduction of two rates on colonial staples by the Act of 24th February, 1900, in place of the single rate theretofore existing, nominally increased the advantage accorded, whilst, in fact, the minimum rate was applied to foreign products, so that the actual advantage was less. But the whole matter is now unimportant. By the Act of 5th August, 1913, " beginning with 1st January, 1914, all colonial consumption staples proceeding from assimilated French colonies enter France free, with the exception of pepper, in regard to which there is no change." Sugar continues to be taxed, although the rate fixed has changed from time to time.

2. The list of " assimilated " colonies has also increased. In 1896 the Commores were added: in 1897, Madagascar, and the establishment of Nossi-Bé, Diego-Suarez, and Sainte-Marie.

3. The exceptions to the metropolitan tariff, which, by paragraph 3 of the above-cited law of 1892, were to be determined before the Act came into operation, relate especially to

[1] Pallain, vol. i., p. 224.
[2] Girault, *op. cit.*, pp. 105-107.

foodstuffs: live animals, rye, maize, and rice, fish salt, and vegetables enter free, or on payment of very low duty, in almost all the assimilated colonies. Coffee, tea, and spices enjoy in a certain number of the colonies a reduction of duty. Chemical fertilisers enter free in the sugar-producing colonies, coal enters free in the Antilles and Madagascar. As for manufactured products the reductions made in the French national tariff are much less numerous. The most important exception concerns the "sacks or casks which are used for the packing of colonial products."[1]

4. The non-assimilated colonies were put under the régime of the minimum tariff. Nevertheless sugar and sugar-derivatives have been put on an equal footing whichever type of colony they come from. The longcloths of India, which were exempted from duty, were rationed in 1904, so as not to compete too easily with the domestic cotton industry: and in 1906 the spinners and weavers thereof were put under strict supervision lest the conditions that only local thread should be used be broken. In addition a series of decrees freed or reduced the duties on products, such as palm oil, building wood, bananas, coffee in the bean, and vanilla coming from various parts of the French Colonial Empire in Africa.[2]

The Tariff Act of March 29, 1910, left this position substantially unaltered. The only clause concerning the colonies was Art. 7. This article—

> (1) exempted from the operation of the Act, importations into France from certain areas, including the colonies and protectorates, except in so far as the new tariff reduced duties in comparison with the old one:
>
> (2) altered the mode under which the exceptions previsaged in Art. 3, paragraph 3 of the Act of 1892 were to be decided upon, because the decision was henceforth to lie in the hands of the Ministers of the Colonies, Commerce, and Industry which made it more difficult to come to an agreement. The new rates were not to be applicable to foreign importations into the colonies,

[1] *Op. cit.*, p. 100, for this and other details.

[2] *Op. cit.*, pp. 116-17, and table, p. 7, of H.C. 296. In addition, the products of the New Hebrides enjoy uncertain privileges by the Act of July 30th, 1900, provided they are the products of French capital or labour (maize, coffee, cocoa, vanilla).

French possessions, and the protectorate of Indo-China until these exceptions had been decided upon, but the delay was not to be greater than one year.[1]

Colonial Export Duties.—These are not a very important feature. The fiscal duties and those levied in lieu of the tax on unimproved land seem to affect goods to all destinations; but there exist certain export duties in Indo-China which are differential, and which affect only products to non-French destinations. The fiscal duties levied in Madagascar were to be abolished by the end of 1914: in Gabon there are fiscal duties on ivory and india-rubber, duties on gold and ox hides in Guiana, and on ores in New Caledonia. The differential duties formerly levied in Indo-China were considerably reduced in 1908. In addition there exists a differential transit duty on foreign merchandise in Indo-China.[2]

We must now deal with Algeria and Tunis.

1. **Algeria.**[3]—From a very early period in the tariff relations between France and Algeria, the principle of assimilation has been adopted, the first step in this direction being taken by the ordinance of November, 1835, which admitted French products freely into Algeria, and applied French customs laws, etc., to it, although Algerian products continued to be treated as foreign products on their importation into France. This régime was further modified in 1843, and in 1851, when the principle of free admission of the products of Algeria into France was laid down, and when the last export duties on French goods destined for Algeria were abolished. Those articles not admitted free were dutiable at the rates of the metropolitan tariff. In 1863 these latter articles were subjected to most-favoured-nation rates, and full freedom was finally accorded by the law of 17th July, 1867. The same law (Part II.) established the principle that foreign products should enter Algeria free of duty, and the Act finally regulated the land trade of Algeria. The reaction first affected Algeria. By Art. 10 of the law of 26th December, 1884—[4]

---

[1] This delay was extended to 1st July, 1911, by the law of 30th March, 1911, and the decrees were promulgated on 30th June, 1911. Pallain.

[2] On the whole question. Girault, *op. cit.*, pp. 102-104.

[3] Girault, pp. 78-80. Pallain, vol. i., pp. 173-187.

[4] Text in Pallain, vol. iv., p. 317.

> Foreign products imported into Algeria shall be subject to the same duties as if they were imported into France.[1]
>
> Excepted from the foregoing disposition are the articles included in Schedule A to the law of 17th July, 1867, as amended by the law of 19th March, 1875.

The Act also abrogated certain concessions as to the improvement trade made applicable to Algeria by a law of 1863, and continued the land customs of the Act of 1867.

The exceptions comprise a very small number of commodities, the position as to which has been modified by laws of 1895, 1900, and 1903, including foreign sugars, coffee, spices, tobacco in leaf and rolled. These are subject to rates differing from those of the Metropolitan Tariff.

The relations of Algeria and the other French colonies [2] have had to be specially regulated by law. Algeria is not included in paragraphs 3-6 of the Act of 1892, and is not, therefore, a colony in the sense of paragraph 5, which lays down the principle of freedom of inter-colonial trade, nevertheless, in 1897 and in 1909, the Council of State laid down the principle that paragraph 5 was to be applied to Algerian trade with the colonies; in other words, Algeria was assimilated to the colonies. The Finance Act of 1910, on the other hand, assimilated Algeria to France by Art. 27, by which

> "colonial commodities, other than sugar and tobacco, produced by the colonies, the French possessions, and countries of the protectorate of Indo-China, shall pay in Algeria, under the same conditions the same duties as in France, with the exception that the special Algerian tariff shall be applied when that is more favourable. Tobacco produced by the above-mentioned territories is liable in Algeria to the tax inscribed in the local tariff; chemical matches from the same source shall pay the duty required by the national tariff in regard to matches imported on public account."

2. **Tunis.**—Tunis, though still outside the general French colonial system, shows traces of the favour with which the principle of assimilation is regarded.

(1) *Imports from France into Tunis.*—Until towards the

---

[1] "Cette expression de la loi doit être entendue dans le sens le plus large." P. I., p. 177—*i.e.*, it includes the surtaxes d'origine and d'entrepôt.

[2] Girault, pp. 119-122.

end of the nineties of the last century France was unable to exercise full liberty of action in Tunisian customs matters owing to engagements entered into by Tunis with foreign powers. The special stipulations made by Italy did not expire until 1905, and one reservation, made by the United Kingdom limiting the duty on cotton goods to 5 per cent. *ad valorem* on a c.i.f. basis, lasted till 1912 and six months to six months thereafter until denounced. But otherwise, by 1897, the way was clear for action, and in 1898 two decrees were issued regulating the customs tariff. A certain number of French and Algerian products hereby obtained a preference. Goods "nationalised" in France or in Algeria by payment of the tariff duties there imposed do *not*, however, enjoy these advantages.

(2) As regards imports from Tunis, the position is regulated by an Act of 19th July, 1890, amended by the Act of 19th July, 1904.

By the first of these Acts a certain number of Tunisian products (grain, olive oil, etc., horses, mules, cattle, and other animals, game and fowls, living or dead) were admitted free (Art. 1). Wines were to pay the lowest rates to which similar products of foreign origin were subject.

These concessions were subject to the conditions specified in Art. 4—*i.e.*, direct importation from defined ports by French ships. Viséd certificates of origin were necessary. Finally (Art. 5, D), the quantities to be so admitted each year were subject to the decree of the President of the Republic. The result was not altogether pleasing to French producers, since the higher price of grain in France encouraged the export of the entire Tunisian output, and the victualling of Tunis with foreign corn bought in bond. The result of the ensuing agitation was the passage of an amending Act, that of the 19th July, 1904, by which cereals and their derivates were to be freely admitted into France, without limitation of quantity, provided that similar foreign products were dutiable in Tunis at the rates of the French minimum tariff. The other formalities were to be continued, and all other Tunisian products were to be under the older law. But the régime of the Act of 1904 was, in 1907, extended to beans, so that a trend towards assimilation is observable.[1]

---

[1] Girault, *op. cit.*, pp. 132-133. For text of Acts, Pallain, vol. iv., pp. 356-357, 589-590.

3. **Morocco.**—Although the treaty of peace abrogates any special rights which the German Empire possesses in Morocco, this protectorate is still outside the regular customs régime of the French Colonial Empire.[1] Apart from the earlier treaties guaranteeing the continuance of the policy of the open-door in Morocco, there are certain special agreements on this point. The first of these is Art. 4 of the "Declaration respecting Egypt and Morocco" between France and the United Kingdom, by which for a period of thirty years, with subsequent renewals for five years at a time unless expressly denounced at least one year in advance, "the two governments, being equally attached to the principle of commercial liberty both in Egypt and Morocco, declare that they will not, in those countries, countenance any inequality either in the imposition of customs duties or other taxes, or of railway transport charges. The trade of both nations with Morocco and with Egypt shall enjoy the same treatment in transit, through the French and British possessions in Africa." By Art. II. any action taken by France in Morocco in view of her special interests in that country "shall leave intact the rights which Great Britain, in virtue of treaties, conventions, and usage, enjoys in Morocco, including the right of coasting trade between the ports of Morocco, enjoyed by British vessels since 1901."[2] The General Act of the Conference of Algeciras, Chap. V., regulated the customs régime of Morocco, and provided (Art. 95) for a customs valuation committee which was to nominate "twelve to twenty honorary members, resident in Morocco, whom it shall consult in connection with the regulation and whenever it may see fit. Such honorary members shall be chosen from the lists of prominent residents drawn up in the case of foreigners by the respective legations, and, in the case of Moorish subjects, by the representative of the Sultan," while the customs administration proper was to be supervised (Art. 97) by a permanent "Customs Committee," consisting of one delegate of the State Bank, of a Moroccan Special Commissioner, and "of a member of the Diplomatic or Consular Body nominated by the

---

[1] Girault, pp. 152-158; Cd. 3087 of 1906, *Despatches, forwarding General Act of the (Algeciras) Conference; Cd.* 1952 *of* 1904, *Anglo-French Agreement of* 1904. *Inclosure I., Declaration respecting Egypt and Morocco.*

[2] For an adverse criticism of this Agreement, see Aflalo, *The Truth about Morocco,* especially chap. ix.

Diplomatic Body at Tangier." Morocco, although not the only area under French control subject to the régime of the open door, is nevertheless the most important, and Professor Girault hopes that "the example of Morocco will no doubt show some years from now that the development of French commerce in the colonies is not dependent upon the application of the national tariff duties." [1]

The United States.[2]—The colonial tariff relations of the United States begin at the end of the nineteenth century with the annexation of Hawaii and the ceding of certain Spanish colonies to the States. With the important exception of the Philippine Islands, and with the less important cases of the Canal Zone and certain islands of the Samoa group, the United States pursues the policy of tariff assimilation.

> The preamble to the Tariff Act of 1913 lays down that "except as otherwise specially provided for in the second section of this Act, there shall be levied, etc., and paid upon all articles when imported from any foreign country into the United States or into any of its possessions (except the Philippine Islands and the islands of Guan and Tutuila) the rates of duty which are by the schedules and paragraphs of the dutiable list of this section, prescribed . . ."

A word may be said as to the position in each colony separately.

Porto Rico.—The Act of 12th April, 1900, provided that foreign goods were to pay the duties of the United States tariff, except coffee, which was to be 5 cents per lb. Exemptions also obtained for Spanish scientific and literary works (free for 10 years from April 11, 1899): and all books and pamphlets in the English language were to be free when imported into the island from the United States (§ 2). Until the 1st March, 1902, or until the establishment of local taxation laws by the local legislature, the goods of either country imported into the other were there dutiable at 15 per cent. of the duties imposable on foreign goods plus the payment of the local internal revenue

---

[1] *Op. cit.*, p. 155.

[2] For the U.S.A., see *Tariff Acts of the U.S.*, 1789-1909 (H.D., vol. cxxix, 61st C., 2nd session); *U.S. Customs Regulations*, chap. ix.; Root's *Colonial Tariffs*, passim.

duties, if any. On and after the earlier of these dates "all such merchandise and articles shall be entered at the several ports free of duty" (§ 3). § 49 of the same Act constitutes Porto Rico a customs area under the control of the Secretary of the Treasury.

Hawaii.—Reciprocity had existed with the Hawaiin Government since 1875, the U.S.A. Act ratifying the treaty being passed on 14th August, 1876, "each of the countries admitting free of duty various articles the products of the other, and neither country charging export duties on any of the articles which the other admitted free." After annexation, the Organic Act of 30th April, 1900, applied to the islands the customs laws and regulations of the U.S. Henceforth there were no customs duties, either import or export, between the two regions.[1]

Guan and Tutuila are islands not under the Treasury, but under the department of the navy. Exports from thence to the U.S. are admitted free, if certified to be the produce of these colonies, if uncertified, to be treated as foreign.

The Panama Canal Zone.—By the Act of 2nd March, 1905, imports to U.S. from the Canal Zone are to be subject to the same laws as imports from foreign countries. The customs administration of the Canal Zone is under the jurisdiction of the Department of War, and outward moving goods to the Zone are also treated as if they were going to a foreign country.

The Philippine Islands have a customs system different to that of the territorial U.S. or the assimilated colonies, and the policy with regard to trade between it and the U.S. is the result of slow evolution. The Act of 8th March, 1902, laid down the following principle in § 2 :—

> Imports into the U.S. from Philippines to pay in general as foreign goods, but goods the growth and produce of the Philippine Islands were to pay only 75 per cent. of the rates of duty aforesaid, less Philippine export duties: but articles on the free list of the U.S. tariff were to be exempt from Philippine export duties when imported into the U.S.

§ 8 of the Act applies the rates of the tariff of 1897 to imports from the Philippines. Otherwise the Act (§ 1) confirms the

---

[1] For these extracts, and for an elaborate discussion of the diplomatic difficulties created by the 1875 Treaty, see U.S.A. Tariff Commission, Report on Reciprocity and Commercial Treaties, pp. 104-121.

tariff laws passed previous to its enactment by the Philippine Commission.

The Philippine Act of 3rd March, 1905, revised the rates of import duty. By § 10 of the Act imports from the United States were dutiable at the rates laid down by the Act. Export duties on articles on the U.S. tariff free list were not to be levied on exports to the U.S., and duties imposed in the U.S. on Philippine goods were to be less any export duties there imposed.

A radical change was made by § 5 of the U.S. Tariff Act of 1909. All articles, the growth and produce of the Philippines or there manufactured out of materials furnished either by the islands or the United States, and not containing more than 20 per cent. in value of foreign material, were to be free of duty in the U.S., except—

(*a*) Rice.

(*b*) In any fiscal year, sugar in excess of 300,000 lbs.
filler tobacco in excess of 1 million lbs.
cigars in excess of 150 million in number.

In consideration thereof, "all articles, the growth, product, or manufacture of the U.S." shall be admitted to the Philippine Islands from the U.S. free of duty.

Such free admission was to be conditional upon the direct shipment thereof from the country of origin to the country of destination, including shipment in bond, through foreign territory contiguous to the United States. Such free imports were to be exempt from export duty in the Philippines and from excise duties imposable in the Philippines, but were to be subject to excise duties in the U.S. Foreign goods imported, as well as U.S. goods imported, into the Philippines were there to be subject to excise duty. Finally, foreign sugar and tobacco, in any form, were to pay on import into the Philippines "not less than the rates of import duty imposed upon sugar and tobacco in like forms when imported into the U.S."

The position was made still clearer by the Philippines Act of 5th August, 1909.

By § 12 "all articles, except rice, the growth, product,

or manufacture of the U.S. *and its possessions* [1] to which the customs tariff in force in the U.S. is applied, and upon which no drawback of customs duties has been allowed therein, going into the Philippine Islands shall hereafter be admitted therein free of customs duty when the same are shipped directly from the country of origin to the country of destination: provided that direct shipment shall include shipment in bond through foreign territory contiguous to the U.S. Said articles shall be as originally packed, without having been opened or in any manner changed in condition. . . ."

By § 13, articles, the growth and produce of the Philippines, going directly to the U.S. or *any of its possessions* shall be exempt from any export duties imposed in the Philippine Islands.

The Tariff Act of 1913 repealed the above § 13 and re-enacted § 15 of the 1909 Tariff Act with the exclusion of the limitation on the quantities of sugar and tobacco importable under that Act.

§ 10 **Portugal**.[2]—The general tariff policy in the Portuguese colonies, dating from the legislation of the period 1858-1892, is not assimilation, but that of granting very considerable preferences to Portuguese products: the general principle being that home products pay only 10 per cent. of the local tariff duties, though this rule is subject to considerable variations. In the Cape Verde Islands, according to Root,[3] the "national" products pay 20 per cent. of the local dues; in Portuguese India "goods and merchandise of national production, and goods nationalised in Portugal and the adjacent islands . . . will pay 50 per cent. of the duties fixed by the above table" (note to Tariff); in Portuguese East Africa, under the control of the Mozambique Company, national products pay 30 per cent. of the duty on foreign goods; in the islands of San Thomé and Principe, where the 10 per cent. rule holds, foreign goods imported *via* Lisbon in Portuguese bottoms pay 80 per cent. of the full duties.

In addition it is to be noted that there is free admission of mineral waters of national origin in the "Trans-marine

[1] This is an important step towards freedom of inter-Colonial trade.

[2] See J. W. Root, *op. cit.*, passim; Kelly, pp. 475-90; Marvaud, *La Mise en Valeur des Colonies Portugaises*, in R.E.I., January, 1912.

[3] *Op. cit.*, p. 74.

Provinces," and that the preference on tobacco is generally greater than 10 per cent., that on national wines sometimes more and sometimes less: whilst in most of the colonies certain national products obtain a preference of 100 per cent. of the duty by being put on the free list. Further, there are in certain of the colonies (San Thomé, Principe, Beira) what are practically surtaxes in the shape of "Municipal Imposts," which further differentiate in favour of national products.

The export duties, where they obtain, also differentiate between foreign ports and Portuguese ports or ports in Portuguese possessions: in one case at least they further differentiate according to whether foreign or Portuguese vessels are being employed in the export to foreign ports.

CHAPTER VIII.—*Continued.*

The Preferential System of the British Empire.

§ 11. The British preferential system is a difficult matter to describe. It has grown, as have other portions of the British Constitution, in response to the specialised needs of particular times and places, without very much attention having been paid in practice to the needs of the system as a whole. The root of the practical difficulties is to be found in the divergent attitudes until recently assumed by the Parliaments of the United Kingdom and those of the Self-Governing Dominions as to the value of a system of inter-imperial preferences. The result has been that in those portions of the Empire immediately subject to the influence of the Imperial Parliament, the development of differential tariffs has had to await a change in the attitude of the Imperial Parliament itself: a change of attitude which has been tardy in coming, and which even yet cannot be said to have completely expressed itself.

Before we deal with the technical aspects of the situation, a word must first be said as to the position in the self-governing dominions. In this connection two points require to be separately treated [1]—

A. The right of the colony to impose duties at all according to its own will.

B. The right of the colony to impose *differential* duties in favour of—

(*a*) Other colonies.
(*b*) The United Kingdom.
(*c*) Foreign countries.

A. Fiscal Differentiation from the United Parliament.—The stage at which a colonial legislature could impose its

[1] For an earlier study of this subject, see A. Todd, "Parliamentary Government in the British Colonies," pp. 222-234, 255-9; Keith, "Responsible Government in the British Dominions," vol. iii., chap. v., § 3, pp. 1114-22; § 5, p. 1140, *et seq.*; chap. vi., § 1, pp. 1158-83, and the references cited therein.

own system of tariff duties (though in one sense this had been reached by the North American Colonies before the Revolution) was not reached in the sense that the fiscal arrangements of the colony were throughout the expression of its own legislative will (free—that is, from concurrent legislation by the Imperial Parliament), until 1846, so far as the modern "self-governing colonies" are concerned. That Act, 9 and 10 Vict., c. 94, allowed the Canadian legislature to reduce or repeal duties imposed by Imperial Act. Later on, "the Australian colonies on their birth were given power to raise customs duties, subject, however, to the proviso that they should not be contrary to treaty, or differential, or imposed on goods for the use of the imperial forces in the colony. . . . In the case of the four South African Colonies no limitations were imposed in their powers with regard to customs duties when self-government was accorded, nor was New Zealand fettered in 1852, except by the provision that duties must not be contrary to treaty nor be levied on goods for the troops or naval forces. Newfoundland received the benefit of the Act regarding Canadian provinces of 1846."[1]

The first conflict occasioned by this policy occurred in 1859, when, in consequence of a new protective tariff imposed by the Canadian Government, the Home authorities, in the supposed interest of domestic producers, felt bound to raise a protest, though "leaving the Act to its operation." The Canadian Minister of Finance, Sir A. Galt, in a celebrated reply, retorted sharply that "it is . . . the duty of the present Government distinctly to affirm the right of the Canadian legislature to adjust the taxation of the people in the way they deem best, even if it should unfortunately happen to meet the disapproval of the Imperial Ministry. Her Majesty cannot be advised to disallow such Acts, unless her advisers are prepared to assume the administration of the affairs of the colony irrespective of the views of the inhabitants." Professor Keith sums up by saying that[2] "the rights of the case were distinctly with the Colonial Government, and that was the last attempt of the Imperial Government to address remonstrances in such a tone to the Canadian or other Colonial Government."

B. (*a*) *Inter-Colonial Differentiation.*—Inter-colonial pre-

[1] Keith, *op. cit.*, p. 1159.
[2] *Op. cit.*, p. 1164.

ferences first occasioned dispute in the seventies of last century. In 1870 the Australasian colonies (including New Zealand) desired to grant each other reciprocal free trade, but this desire conflicted with their constitutional régime. Precedents existed in the shape of certain Acts of Newfoundland and Prince Edward Island, dating from the year 1856: precedents which the Home Government in the subsequent controversy refused to regard as valid. The British Government took the broad free trade view in arguing its case with the colonial administrations concerned, but finally waived its objections, concurring in the view of the Chief Secretary of Victoria, " that no attempt can be more hopeless than to induce free self-governed states to adopt exactly the same opinions on such questions as free trade and protection which the people of England happen to entertain at that precise moment." [1] A step in the direction of inter-colonial preference was taken by an Imperial Act of 1873 [2] (36 and 37 Vict., c. 22), and the limitations were completely removed by an Act of 1895 (58 and 59 Vict., c. 3).

The only question now remaining is whether the grant of a preferential duty by one colony to another *must* be accompanied by the extension of the same privilege to similar products of the United Kingdom. On this Keith says—" It has recently been recognised by the Royal Commission which has suggested the basis for a reciprocity arrangement between Canada and the West Indies that any advantage extended to these Colonies by Canada shall be accorded gratis to the Mother Country. This . . . is in accordance with the

---

[1] For the full text of the Home Government's dispatches, see Keith, pp. 1166-1180.

[2] The enabling clause was thus worded, " The legislature of any one of the Australian Colonies shall, for the purpose of carrying into effect any agreement between any two or more of the said colonies, or between any one of more of the said Colonies and New Zealand have full powers from time to time to make laws with respect to the remission or imposition of duties upon the importation into such colony of any article the produce or manufacture of or imported from any other of the said colonies, or the produce or manufacture of or imported from, New Zealand. Provided always, that for the purpose aforesaid no duty shall be imposed upon, and no existing duty shall be remitted as to the importation into any of the Australian Colonies of any article, the produce or manufacture of any particular country which shall not be equally imposed upon, or remitted as to, the importation into such colony of the like article the produce or manufacture of any other country; provided further, that no duties shall be levied upon articles imported into any of the Australian Colonies for the supply of H.M. land or sea forces, nor shall any duty be levied or remitted contrary to or at variance with any Treaty or Treaties for the time being subsisting between Her Majesty and any foreign power."

principles laid down in regard to these negotiations as regards foreign powers by Lord Ripon in 1894, but it was not the principle adopted in the Act of 1873, which allowed the Colonies of Australia to shut out the Mother Country from any inter-colonial preference." [1]

(*b*) The right of the United Kingdom to receive special privileges from the dominions is no longer in dispute. As the Royal Commission just referred to puts it (para. 122)—"It may now be regarded as a settled principle that trade arrangements between parts of the British Empire are to be considered matters of a domestic character which cannot be regarded as discriminatory by any foreign power." This position has not been attained without a certain amount of strife: the granting to the United Kingdom of a preference was delayed for some time by the reluctance of the Home Government to denounce two treaties with Belgium and the Zollverein, dating from 1862 and 1865 respectively: and when preferential arrangements went into force in 1897 after the government had denounced these Treaties, a conflict was still to break out between Canada and the German Empire, owing to the exclusion of Canada from most-favoured-nation treatment by the latter country. This was done expressly on the ground that, as in consequence of these preferential arrangements, "Canada accorded to imports from Great Britain special customs advantages which she is not prepared to extend to imports from Germany, it naturally resulted from this situation that the Federal Council of the German Empire did not extend to Canada the most-favoured-nation treatment granted autonomously, and as an exception to Great Britain and the British Colonies and Possessions." [2]

Even at present there is a note of doubtfulness in the American attitude towards the claim that inter-imperial preferences are a "domestic concern." In the report of the U.S.A. Tariff Commission on "Reciprocity and Commercial

---

[1] Keith, *op. cit.*, p. 183. See Cd. 5369 of 1910, "Report of the Royal Commission of Trade Relations between Canada and the West Indies," par. 78 of Report: "It is, of course, a cardinal point in the policy of your Majesty's Government that any concession which is made to imports from the Dominion should also be extended to like products of the United Kingdom." This is not quite what is said by Prof. Keith, since he is speaking of Canada, and the report speaks of the West Indies. The ensuing agreement gave the U.K. the same privileges as the co-contractants, so the point is practically unimportant.

[2] Cd. 1781 of 1904. Correspondence in connection with the German Tariff.

Treaties," issued early in 1919, the Board says that—" It is to be noticed, however, in judging of the soundness of that contention, that British self-governing colonies possess tariff autonomy, and there is no British Imperial tariff system." [1] The appearance of the Dominions at the Peace Conference, and the inauguration of preferences by the United Kingdom, further complicate the matter.

(*c*) *Colonial Preference with Foreign Countries.*—The *locus classicus* on this subject is Lord Ripon's despatch, dated 28th June, 1895.[2] On the " question of commercial agreements between Her Majesty's Government and Foreign Powers in regard to their trade with the colonies " the following principles were laid down :—

(1) " It is obvious that a colony could not offer a Foreign Power tariff concessions which were not at the same time to be extended to all other Powers entitled by Treaty to most-favoured-nation treatment in the colony, . . . it is obvious that Her Majesty could not properly enter into any engagements with Foreign Powers inconsistent with her obligation to other Powers, and, before any Convention or Treaty can be ratified, therefore Her Majesty's Government must be satisfied that it fulfils this condition, and also that any legislation for giving effect to it makes full provision for enabling Her Majesty to fulfil her obligations, both to the Power immediately concerned, and to any other Powers whose rights under Treaty may be affected . . ."

(2) " Further, Her Majesty's Government regard it as essential that any tariff concessions proper to be conceded by a Colony to a Foreign Power should be extended to this country and to the rest of Her Majesty's Dominions. . . . Any tariff advantages granted by a Colony, therefore, to a Foreign Power would have to be extended to all Powers entitled by Treaty to most-favoured-nation treatment in the Colony, and Her Majesty's Government presume that no colony would wish to afford to, practically, all foreign nations better treatment than it accorded to the rest of the Empire of which it forms a part."

(3) " In regard to the other side of the question—namely, as to the terms which a colony seeks from a Foreign Power,

---

[1] Report cited, p. 414.

[2] C. 7824 of 1895 ; H.C., No. 1299, of 1910 : Keith, *op. cit.*, pp. 1119-1121.

the considerations mentioned appear to require that a colony should not endeavour in such a negotiation to obtain an advantage at the expense of other parts of Her Majesty's Dominions. In the case, therefore, of preference being sought by or offered to the colony in respect of any article in which it competed seriously with other colonies or with the Mother Country, Her Majesty's Government would feel it to be their duty to use every effort to obtain the extension of the concession to the rest of the Empire, and in any case to ascertain as far as possible whether the other colonies affected would wish to be made a party to the arrangement. In the event of this being impossible, and of the result to the trade of the excluded portions being seriously prejudicial it would be necessary to consider whether it was desirable, in the common interests, to proceed with the negotiations."

So far as a general preferential scheme within the Empire is concerned, it was not until 1917, under the influence of the Great War, that the Imperial Government agreed fully with the idea. On April 26, 1917, the Imperial War Cabinet settled upon a resolution, which was afterwards (but on the same day) approved of by the Imperial War Conference. The terms of the resolution, so far as it affects imperial preference, were as follows :—

"The time has arrived when all possible encouragement should be given to the development of Imperial resources, and especially to making the Empire independent of other countries in respect of food supplies, raw materials, and essential industries. With these objects in view this Conference expresses itself in favour of—

(1) The principle that each part of the Empire, having due regard to the interests of our Allies, shall give specially favourable treatment and facilities to the produce and manufactures of other parts of the Empire." [1]

The Government of the United Kingdom gave practical expression to the objects designated in the resolution by the preferential clauses of the Finance Act of 1919 to which reference will be made later. At the same time the Imperial Government has initiated a definite change of policy with regard to those portions of the Empire more directly under

---

[1] Cd. 8566 of 1917. Extracts from Minutes of Proceedings and Papers laid before the Conference.

its control. It has sanctioned differential export duties in the case of the West African Colonies, whilst the Government of India has entered upon the same path. All these measures will be discussed in appropriate detail in a later section. Our next step must be to examine the preferential systems of the self-governing dominions on the technical side.

(2) **Technical Aspects of the Scheme.**—The only method by which an intelligible idea of the preferential system can be obtained is to deal first with each part of the Empire separately.

Canada.—General Preferential Arrangements.—(*a*) The first Tariff Act, including a preferential section, was the Act of 1897, 60-61 Vict., c. 16. By § 17—

> "when the customs tariff of any country admits the products of Canada on terms which, on the whole, are as favourable to Canada as the terms of the reciprocal tariff herein referred to are to the countries to which it may apply, articles which are the growth, produce, or manufacture of such country, when imported direct therefrom, may then be entered for duty or taken out of warehouse for consumption in Canada at the reduced rates of duty provided in the reciprocal tariff set forth in Schedule B to this Act.
>
> "Any question arising as to the countries entitled to the benefits of the reciprocal tariff shall be decided by the Controller of Customs, subject to the authority of the Governor in Council.
>
> "The Governor in Council may extend the benefits of the reciprocal tariff to any country entitled thereto by virtue of a Treaty with Her Majesty.
>
> "The Controller of Customs may make such regulations as are necessary for carrying out the intention of this section."

The reductions contemplated in the above clause were specified by Schedule D to be as follows :—

> "One-eighth of the duty or levy" on and after 23rd April, 1897, until 30th June, 1898.
>
> "On and after the first day of July, 1898, the reduction shall in every case be one-quarter of the duty mentioned in Schedule A, and the duty to be levied

. . . shall be three-quarters of the duty mentioned in Schedule A."

Certain articles were, however, excluded.[1]

(*b*) Under this Act preferential treatment was extended to the "United Kingdom, British India (from 24th September, 1897), New South Wales, and various foreign countries."[2] It was, however, soon superseded by Act No. 37 of 1898, which, by § 2, substituted a new clause for § 17 above, and slightly varied the list of articles excluded from the 25 per cent. preference which Schedule D of the new Act still maintained. The new clause enacted that the preference should be extended to articles, the growth, produce, or manufacture of certain specified countries when imported direct into Canada from any such countries:[3] extended the benefits contingently to "any other British Colony or possession the customs tariff of which is, on the whole, as favourable to Canada as the British preferential tariff herein referred to, is to such colony or possession."

The provisos were that "manufactured articles to be admitted under such preferential tariff shall be *bona fide* the manufactures of a country or countries entitled to the benefits of such tariff, and that such benefits shall not extend to the importation of articles into the production of which there has not entered a substantial portion of the labour of such countries. Any question arising as to any article being entitled to such benefits shall be decided by the Minister of Customs, whose decision shall be final. . . . The Minister of Customs, with the approval of the Governor in Council, shall determine what British Colonies or Possessions shall be entitled to the benefit of the preferential tariff under paragraph (*e*) of sub-section 1 of this section. . . . The Minister of Customs may, with the approval of the Governor in Council, make such regulations as are deemed necessary for carrying out the intentions of this section."

---

[1] Wines, malt liquours, spirits, spirituous liquours, liquid medicines, and articles containing alcohol; sugar, molasses, and syrups of all kinds, beet or sugar-cane products; tobacco, cigars, and cigarettes.

[2] C.I.D., 1914, xlii.

[3] These countries were the United Kingdom, Bermuda, British Guiana, the British West Indies. According to C.I.D., 1914, vol. xliii., British India, Straits Settlements, Ceylon, New South Wales, were also accorded preferential treatment; New Zealand was accorded it from 26th February, 1904, and South Africa from 1st July, 1904.

The preferential system underwent certain changes between this date and the passage of the great tariff of 1907. In 1900 the Act 63 and 64 Vict., c. 15, § 2 amended the aforesaid Schedule D by enacting that "the reduction shall be one-third of the duty mentioned in Schedule A, and the duty to be levied . . . shall be two-thirds of the duty mentioned in Schedule A." The Act 4, Ed. VII., c. 11 (1904), enacted that, notwithstanding any thing contained in Schedule D to the said Act, the duty on certain articles was not to be less than the minimum fixed by § 16 or 17 of the Act: whilst § 18 of the Act allowed free import of molasses, "the produce of any British country entitled to the benefits of the British Preferential Tariff, when produced from sugar cane and imported direct by vessel from the country of production in the original package in which it was placed at the point of production, and not afterwards subjected to any process of treating or mixing."

(*c*) The Act of 1907 (6 and 7 Ed. VII., c. 11) greatly changed the system. The Act viewed the preferential system as a part of a wider system of general and intermediate tariff rates: it abolished the idea of a uniform preference, and treated each commodity as a separate entity.

The relevant sections of the Act are §§ 3 and 4. By § 3 a group of British countries were enumerated as enjoying the benefits of the preferential rates established by the Act, viz.:—

The United Kingdom, Bermuda, the "British Colonies, commonly called the British West Indies, British Guiana, British India, Ceylon, Straits Settlements, New Zealand, Cape Colony, Natal, Orange River Colony, Transvaal, Southern Rhodesia," and "any other British Colony or Possession admitted to the benefit of the British Preferential Tariff in Canada, in the manner hereinafter provided."

By § 4 (*a*) the Governor in Council might, by order, extend the benefit of the British Preferential Tariff to any British colony not named in § 3, and by 4 (*b*) "*withdraw* the benefit of the British Preferential Tariff from any British country (*other than the United Kingdom*) which has received the said benefit." Since the preference was specific, an extension of the intermediate tariff might, in certain cases, reduce the burden on British goods, and paragraph 4 (*c*) provided for such extension "in consideration of benefits satisfactory to the Governor in Council." The proviso was laid down (3 (*b*)) that "every manufactured article to be admitted under the British Preferential Tariff must be *bona fide* the manufacture of a British country entitled to the benefit of the British Preferential Tariff, and a substantial portion of the value of the manufactured article must have been produced by labour in one or more of such countries."

It must be noted that a certain number of articles, partly such as yield revenue, and therefore of a somewhat special kind, but also certain other commodities, receive no preferential reduction at all.[1]

We need not concern ourselves with changes in tariff details, but certain more important changes require a word of comment.

(1) The countries enjoying the benefit of the preferential tariff were largely added to by an Order in Council of 25th January, 1913, the areas named in the proclamation being—

Swaziland, Basutoland, Bechuanaland Protectorate, Northern Rhodesia, the Nyasaland, Uganda, East Africa, and Northern Nigerian Protectorates; the colony and protectorates of Southern Nigeria, Gold Coast, Sierra Leone, Gambia, Somaliland, Federated Malay States, British North Borneo, Sarawak, Brunei; Mauritius and dependencies thereof: the Seychelles and St. Helena, Ascension, Friendly Islands, Fiji, Falkland Islands, and British Honduras.[2]

(2) Reductions, consequential on the conclusion of tariff treaties by Canada, have, in certain cases, benefited the United Kingdom and other portions of the Empire. Thus, under the French Convention Act of 1908 (7 and 8 Ed. VII., c. 28) it is enacted by § 5 that—

> "The advantages so granted to France, Algeria, the French Colonies and Possessions, and the territories of the Protectorate of Indo-China by the said convention, shall extend to the United Kingdom and the several British Colonies and Possessions, so long as France, Algeria,

---

[1] See list C.I.D., 1914, p. cliii., of the non-revenue commodities, certain agricultural machinery, sail twine and canvas for sails, paints and colours, skelp-iron and steel stereotypes, electrotypes, celluloids, and bases for same, and textile machinery of a kind not made in Canada, seem the most important.

[2] Customs Memo. No. 1711 B, summarised in C.I.D., 1914, vol. xliii., and printed in full in the Canadian Department of Customs Publications, "The Customs Tariff, 1907, and the Amendments," edn. Dec., 1918.

> the French Colonies and Possessions and the said territories continue to be entitled to such advantages; provided, however, that nothing herein contained shall be held to diminish any advantage which the United Kingdom and British Colonies and Possessions now enjoy under the British Preferential Tariff."

The effect of this qualification is to open Canadian ports to goods originating in *any* British territory at rates which, in some cases, are more favourable than those originally accorded under the 1907 tariff.[1]

(3) Special arrangements were concluded between Canada and certain West Indian possessions in virtue of an agreement which received legal sanction by the "West Indian Trade Agreement Act," No. 56 of 1913.

The benefits of the Act were, by § 7, extended (*a*) to the original parties to the agreement—viz., Trinidad, British Guiana, Barbados, St. Lucia, St. Vincent, Antigua, St. Kits, Dominica, and Mount Serrat.

(*b*) To certain other colonies enumerated in Schedule D to the agreement "for the period of three years from the date on which the said agreement shall, according to its tenor, come into operation"—viz., Bahamas, Bermuda, British Honduras, Grenada, Jamaica, and Newfoundland.[2]

The agreement was to be in force for an original period of ten years, after which it might be terminated by any one of the parties thereto (in respect of such party) at the end of one year after the day upon which notice shall have been given by the party desiring such termination (Convention, § 8).

The tariff concessions granted were—

A. By Canada,[2] that on the goods enumerated in Schedule B to the Agreement, when such goods are imported direct into Canada from any British country, the duties shall be either (*a*) "at the rate of four-fifths of the several rates of duties, if any, imposed on similar goods when imported from any foreign country;" or (*b*) at the British Preferential Tariff

---

[1] For the extension of the intermediate tariff to other countries, either under most-favoured-nation clauses or special treaties, see C.I.D., 1914, pp. xlviii.-ix.: for the Japanese Convention of 1913, *ibid.*, p. 1.

[2] In the case of these areas, however, the concessions shall cease at the end of the period specified "as respects any of the said colonies which shall not have granted to Canada the advantages set forth in Section 1" of the Convention, on which see B above.

rates of the 1907 tariff or any amendments thereto, whichever shall be the lower rate.

B. By the other parties to the Agreement.[1] "On all goods enumerated in Schedule A, being the produce or manufacture of Canada, imported into any of the above-mentioned colonies, the duties of customs shall not at any time be more than four-fifths of the duties imposed in the colony on similar goods when imported from any foreign country; provided that on flour the preference in favour of Canada shall not at any time be less than 12 cents per 100 lbs."

The Canada-West-Indies Trade Agreement of 18th June, 1920.—The Agreement of 1913 is now about to be replaced by a new Treaty between the Canadian Government and the Governments of the Bahamas, Barbados, Bermuda, British Guiana, British Honduras, Jamaica, the Leeward Islands, Trinidad, and the Windward Islands. Jamaica, which kept out of the previous arrangement, has now, it will be noted, fallen into line with the other islands.

The Canadian Government promises—

(1) To grant a preference on all goods the produce or manufacture of the said islands, which are now subject to duty or will be so subject in the future, of at least 50 per cent. of the duties imposed on similar goods when imported from any foreign country.

(2) The exceptions to this rule are—

(*a*) Tobacco, cigars, cigarettes, or alcoholic liquors.

(*b*) The articles mentioned in Schedule A to the Agreement; sugar, on which there is a sliding scale of specific preference—cocoa beans, not roasted, crushed or ground (preference of 1.50 dollars), lime juice (10 cents per gallon), fresh limes (free against a general duty of 15 per cent. *ad val.*), arrowroot (1 cent per lb.), cocoanuts (per 100 free as against a general duty of 75 cents) cocoanuts, n.o.p. (preference 50 cents per 100), grape fruit (50 cents per 100 lbs.), rum (60 cents per gallon), onions (free as against a general tariff of 30 per cent. *ad val.*).

On the other hand, Canadian goods enjoy—

(*a*) In the case of Barbados, British Guiana, and Trinidad a preference of at least 50 per cent.

---

[1] United Kingdom products of the kind included in the Agreement enjoy any of the advantages reciprocally granted.

(*b*) In the case of British Honduras, Leeward Islands, Windward Islands, a preference of at least 33⅓ per cent.

(*c*) In the case of Bermuda and Jamaica a preference of at least 25 per cent.

(*d*) In the case of the Bahamas a preference of at least 10 per cent. of the duties imposed on similar goods when imported from any foreign country.

The exceptions are as follows :—

(*a*) All the islands except tobacco, cigars, and cigarettes.

(*b*) The Bahamas except also wines, malt liquors, liquid medicines, and articles containing alcohol.

(*c*) The articles mentioned in Schedule B to the Agreement are subject to definite specific preference :—

Flour (not less than one shilling per bag of 196 lbs. or per barrel).

Spirits (not less than 2s. 6d. per gallon), spirits, perfumed, unenumerated, potable, if not tested (preference of not less than 2s. 6d. per liquid gallon). Wine, beer, and ale (duty on Canadian product not to exceed four-fifths of full rate).

All the colonies, on giving six months' notice, may provide that the grant of these preferences shall be conditional on direct shipment or by way of one of the other colonies entitled to the advantages of the Agreement.

The Agreement goes on to provide for certain guaranteed shipping services, and for the effective control of freight rates on all contracts entered into with subsidised shipping lines.

The Agreement is subject to approval of the respective legislatures of the countries signing the Agreement, and is to remain in force for ten years, " and thereafter until terminated by twelve months written notice given either by the Government of Canada, or by the Government of any of the colonies aforesaid, but in the latter case the Agreement shall remain in full force and effect as to any of the other colonies which have not given such notice." [1]

Trinidad.—The *B.T.J.* for 9th December, 1920, contains particulars of the Bill proposing a new tariff made necessary in order to give effect to the Canadian-West Indies agreement. It proposes a new preference of 50 per cent. on the average on a very numerous class of articles, the preferential rates

[1] Art. 18 of the Agreement, published as Cmd. 864 of 1920.

in question applying " to goods the growth, produce, or manufacture of the British Empire." [1, 2]

South Africa.—The history of the South African Customs Union as such does not concern us here. From 1903 onwards provision was, however, made for imperial preference. By Art. III. of the Customs Union Convention of that year [3]—

" A rebate of customs duties shall be granted on any goods and articles, the growth, produce, or manufacture of the United Kingdom imported therefrom into the Union for consumption therein to the extent following :—

(*a*) In the case of goods and articles liable to customs duty under Class I., II., or V., a rebate of 25 per cent. of any duty chargeable thereon at an *ad valorem* rate, but of no other duty, and

(*b*) In the case of goods and articles liable under Class III. to duty at an *ad valorem* rate of 2½ per cent. a rebate of the whole of such duty.

Provided that the manufactured goods or articles in respect of which such rebate as aforesaid shall be granted, shall be *bona fide* the manufactures of the United Kingdom, and that in the event of any question arising as to whether any goods or articles are entitled to any such rebate as aforesaid the decision of the minister or other executive officer, in whom the control of the Customs Department immediately concerned is vested, shall be final."

By Article IV.—" A rebate similar to that for which provision is made in the last preceding article shall be granted in like manner and under like provisions to goods and articles the growth, produce, or manufacture of any British colony, protectorate, or possession granting equivalent reciprocal privileges to the colonies and territory belonging to the Union. . . ."

The Convention of 1906 [4] provided for preferences in the same terms as had the convention of 1903, but considerably

---

[1] See *op. cit.*, pp. 696-699. In the case of machinery there is imposed a duty of 5 per cent. *ad. val.* in the case of the General Tariff, whilst the same goods are free under the preferential tariff, certain animals, food products, cotton manufactures, manure, are also free under the preferential tariff and dutiable under the general tariff.

[2] For Trinidad, see further *B.T.J.*, 12/5/21, p. 533; for Honduras, *op. cit.*, 24/2/21 and 12/5/21; for St. Vincent, 24/3/21.

[3] Cd. 1599 of 1903. Draft Customs Union Convention.

[4] Cd. 2977 of 1906. Customs Union Convention.

altered the preference rates. In the case of Class I. the preference ceased to be uniform, but varied from article to article: in the case of Classes III., IV., and V., which fixed "class rates," of 25, 3, and 15 per cent. *ad valorem* respectively the preference was to amount to a uniform 3 per cent. in all cases, and in the case of Class II., which fixed a mixed rate of 15 per cent. *ad valorem* plus varying specific duties, with a minimum charge in all cases of 25 per cent. *ad valorem*, the duty reduction was also to be 3 per cent.

The Customs Tariff Act, No. 26 of 1914, again continued the general form of the preferences, and, whilst largely increasing the numbers of dutiable articles, also left untouched the preference rates which, therefore, remained in general as a 3 per cent. reduction to the United Kingdom and reciprocating colonies.

The benefits of the preferential rate had been extended to Canada on 1st July, 1904, to Australia (against special concessions) on 1st October, 1906, and to New Zealand (again in return for special concessions) on 1st January, 1907.[1]

Australia.—Australia maintains preferential relations with only two parts of the Empire—the South African Union and the United Kingdom.

Preferential relations with South Africa were first created by the Customs Tariff (South African Preference) Act, No. 17 of 1906. By § 2 of that Act "the dutiable goods specified in the schedule shall, when those goods are imported from and are the produce or manufacture of any of the British South African Colonies or Protectorates, which are included within the South African Customs Union, be in accordance with the rates of duty specified in the fourth column of the said schedule. Provided that nothing in this Act shall have the effect of imposing any duty on any goods which are free from or exempt from duty under the customs tariff, 1902."[2] The Customs Act of 1908, No. 7 of 1908, § 9, stated that it did not affect the validity of the 1906 Act, whilst the tariff

[1] It must not be forgotten that under the "Rhodes Clause" an additional rebate is payable on imperial goods imported into Northern or Southern Rhodesia.

[2] The Act granted a preference of 25 per cent. on the rates of duty contained in the C.T. Act of 1902 on butter, cheese, confectionery, fodder, hay and chaff, grain, jams and jellies, leather, machinery (agricultural, horticultural, mining, etc.), meats, fish, poultry and game, fresh, smoked, potted, or preserved in tins, preserved milk, timber. Other preferentially treated articles included fruits and vegetables, feathers, maize, spirits, tobacco, sugar, and wine.

resolutions of 3rd December, 1914, validated by the Customs Tariff Validation Act, No. 7 of 1917, did, in part, affect the articles included in the scope of the 1906 preferences.

A preference to the goods of the United Kingdom, was first granted by § 6 (1) of the 1908 Tariff Act, "the rates of duty set out in Schedule A in the column 'Tariff on Goods, the produce or manufacture of the United Kingdom' shall apply only to goods the produce or manufacture of the United Kingdom, which are shipped in the United Kingdom to Australia and not transhipped, or if transhipped then only if it is proved to the satisfaction of the collector that the goods have not since they were shipped in the United Kingdom been subjected to any process of manufacture." No. 13 of 1908, § 6 (i) A expanded this statement by enacting that "where in the said column no rate of duty is set out and the goods are not expressly declared to be free the rate of duty on the said goods shall be that set out in Schedule A in the column headed General Tariff."

The 1914 tariff did not affect the general scheme of preference, but considerably affected the details, by varying the rates. The Australian preference was based *ab initio* on the basis of treating each article as a separate entity, and consequently escaped altogether the earlier stage of preference history, in which the preference was uniform, either for all goods, or for classes of goods.[1]

[1] The effect of the new 1920 tariff is greatly to extend the preference to the United Kingdom, according to certain statistics presented by the Australian Minister of Customs on the introduction of the Bill. The number of items in previous tariffs, and in the proposed tariff, in which a preference of 5 per cent. and over is given, is as follows:—

Preference of—	1908/11.	1914 Tariff.	Proposed Tariff.
5 per cent.,	237	303	24
7½ "	4	3	..
10 "	10	120	367
12½ "	..	..	24
15 "	..	..	136
20 "	..	..	32
	251	426	583

—(*B.T.J.*, 20/5/20, p. 690.)

In estimating the value of a grant of preference, it is, of course, necessary to know, not only to what extent the manufacturer in the United Kingdom is advantaged in relation to his foreign rivals, but also the extent to which he can compete with the locally protected manufacturer. An increase of the duty, accompanied by a rise in the duty, may in the long run be no better worth having than a smaller preference, accompanied by a smaller absolute tariff wall.

New Zealand.—The Dominion of New Zealand maintains a reciprocity system with South Africa, but, in addition, grants a preference to all other parts of the Empire. Both policies were inaugurated by Act No. 78 of 1903—"The Preferential and Reciprocal Trade Act." The evolution of the general preference will be described first.

By §§ 2 and 3 of the Act *surtaxes* were imposed on the several articles named in a series of schedules "not being the produce or manufacture of some part of the British Dominions." In one case the surtax amounted to as much as the original duty (cement): the goods in schedule 2 paid a surtax of one-half of the original duty, the goods in the third schedule paid a surtax equal to 20 per cent. of the original duty. By § 9 (*i*) after 31st March, 1904, "no duty shall be leviable on tea grown in any part of the British dominions, except on tea in packets not exceeding 1 lb. in weight."

This system of surtaxes was expanded by the Tariff Act of 1907 (No. 15 of 1907). The general tariff was embodied in Schedule A. By § 5 of the Act a series of Schedules C, D, and E, defined the surtaxes, such that—

Goods in Schedule	D,	Part I.,	paid a surtax of	50	per cent.	Of the duty under Schedule A.
,,	D,	,, II.,	,,	,, 50	,,	
,,	D,	,, III.,	,,	,, 20	,,	
,,	E,	,, I.-II.,	,,	,, 20	,,	
,,	E.	,, III.,	,,	,, 10	,,	

whilst, by Part IV., "tea in bulk—viz., in packages of 5 lbs. or over, net weight of tea, paid 2d. per lb.

The tariff was consolidated by Act No. 35 of 1908, which is still the basis of the New Zealand tariff system, although it has since been modified in certain respects.

Schedule A contained the dutiable articles, Schedule B the exemptions or the "free list."

The surtaxes were as follows :—

Part C, [1] an amount equal to the amount of the original duty under Schedule A.

Part D (i) [2] and (ii), [3] an amount equal to 50 per cent. of the original duty under Schedule A.

---

[1] Cement, Portland and other structural and building cement.

[2] Basketware and wickerware, bicycles and tricycles, boots, shoes, clogs, candles, carriages, carts, drags, etc.; china, clocks, cordage rope and twine, earthenware, stoneware and brownware, fancy goods and toys, firearms, fish (potted), furniture,

Part D (iii), [4] an amount equal to 20 per cent. of the amount of the original duty under Schedule A.

Part E (i) [5] and (ii), [6] an amount equal to 20 per cent. of the original duty under Schedule A.

Part E (iii), [7] an amount equal to 10 per cent. of the original duty under Schedule A.

Part E (iv), duties of customs specified in the said sub-division of the said Part (*i.e.*, tea in bulk, 2d. per lb.).

By Part II. of the Finance Act, 1915 (No. 39), new rates were imposed on certain articles, some, among which, were treated preferentially.[8] By Part II. of the Finance Act, 1917 (No. 9), a further series of charges took place, partly in connection with the commodities already modified in 1915, but mainly in connection with textiles.[9]

§ 12 of the 1903 Act had enacted that "where any country, part of the British Dominions reduces or abolishes, or proposes to reduce or abolish, the duty on any product or manufacture of New Zealand the Government may enter into an agreement

---

glassware, hardware, hops, iron, iron pipes, jewellery, lamps, lawn mowers, musical instruments, upholstery.

[3] Bill-hooks, brooms, cartridges and cartridge cases, cars, waggons and trucks, electric batteries and cells, fish (dried, pickled, and salted), galvanised iron, heel plates and toe stiffeners, japanned and lacquered metalware, laces, leather goods, machinery, electric magic lanterns, mantelpieces, matches, stationery, cardboards, machines, n.e.i., boats, bags, textile or felt, granite, and other stone, etc.

[4] Biscuits, confectionery, chocolate, jams, jellies, etc.; iron sheets, lead piping, shot, paints, varnish, lacquers, soap, starch.

[5] Bicycle and tricycle fittings, gas engines, wrought-iron pipes, plain black iron, iron and steel cordage, motor engines for bicycles, printing paper.

[6] Butter cloth, canvas, cardboard boxes, castings for ships, iron boiler plates.

[7] Boots and shoes, artists' materials, cameras, ink (printing), anchors, chains, fire engines, machinery for dairying, mining, and gold saving, etc., metal wove wire and metal gauze; sheet zinc or iron, portable and traction engines, printing machines and presses, printing type and materials. Steam hydraulic pressure and vacuum gauges, indicators, surveyors' instruments, paints and colours, etc. Belting, binder twine, machinery (refrigerating, dredging, woollen mill, paper mill, rope and twine making, etc.). Steam engines and parts, engines and machines for mining purposes, etc.

[8] Fruits, preserved in juice or syrup, bicycles, tricycles, and the like vehicles. There was no differentiation as regards various classes of spirits.

[9] A 10 per cent. preference was granted on all articles n.e.i. made of textile, felt, or other piece goods, or of any combination of the same wholly or partly made up or manufactured and not being apparel or clothing either wholly or partly made up; drapery, flags, haberdashery, lace, and laces, n.e.i., ribbons or crape, wigs, textile piece goods, umbrellas, yarns.

A 12½ per cent. on apparel and ready-made clothing, n.e.i., feathers, furs and fur trimming, hats of all kinds, caps, hosiery, n.e.i., and a 20 per cent. preference on apparel made to order and for volunteer clothing.

with that country to reduce or abolish the duty on any article or articles the produce or manufacture of such country to an extent that the estimated revenue so remitted shall equal as nearly as possible the estimated revenue remitted by that country." This clause first bore fruit in 1906; by Act No. 63 of that year, power was given to the Governor to gazette a treaty with South Africa, and to make, by Order in Council, "such alterations in the existing New Zealand Tariff as in his opinion are necessary in order to give full effect to such Treaty." By Act No. 2 of 1907, the Treaty was ratified and confirmed, the said Treaty to continue in full force and effect until terminated by Order in Council. The Consolidating Act of 1908, § 8 provided that these arrangements were not to be affected—

> "Provided that, notwithstanding anything in the said schedule, no higher duty shall be levied on any goods the produce or manufacture of the said colonies than that which would be levied under this Act on the same goods if they were the produce or manufacture of other parts of the British Dominions." [1]

The special reciprocity arrangements were not affected by Act No. 21 of 1909 (§ 4), No. 39 of 1915 (§ 31), Act No. 9 of 1917 (§ 55).

Other Portions of the Empire.—In the legislative session of 1920 increased attention was paid to the dangers which might lurk in the attempt to force imperial preference on those portions of the Empire which did not possess full powers of self-government. This fear was prompted by the action of the Imperial Government in pushing forward the granting of preferential export duties in the West African Colonies, a matter to be considered in a separate section. On the 7th June, 1920, the Government, in answer to a question by Capt. W. Benn, stated that "an invitation to consider the practicability of preferential rates for goods of imperial origin has been addressed to all colonies and protectorates, except those which are precluded by existing international agreements from doing so, and a few others in which preference is already in force, or is from special circumstances inapplicable. Replies have been received so far from Hong Kong and Sierra

[1] The preferential rates cover feathers, fish, fruits, maize, sugar, tobacco (manufactured), tea, wines, and a 3 per cent. reduction of the duty on all other goods (except spirits).

Leone, in both of which preference is considered unnecessary; from Cyprus, where legislation on the subject has been passed," and from the West Indian Islands "in all of which the question is being considered."[1]

On June 16, in answer to a question "whether any colony or protectorate will be compelled to introduce preferential duties in its tariffs against the wishes of the non-official representatives of their respective Legislatures." the Government spokesman replied that "if any such case arises, the Secretary of State will consider the question with due regard to all the circumstances."[2]

It is, therefore, necessary to follow up the preferences in these non-governing areas.

(1) **Cyprus.**[3]—This colony granted by the Act, assented to on 4th May, 1920, preferences on the following commodities :—

(*a*) Musical instruments and parts thereof, locks and parts thereof, watches and parts thereof, cinematograph films, beer, ale, porter, and other malt liquors, cotton yarns and thread, cotton piece goods, matches, soap, woollen yarns and thread, woollen manufactures, earthenware and china, furniture, haberdashery and millinery, and dyes. In these cases the preferential rates were to be two-thirds of the full rate.

(*b*) Sparkling wines and other kinds of wine. The preferential rate to be $66\frac{2}{3}$ and 60 per cent. of the full rates respectively.[4]

(*c*) Spirits of all sorts, spirituous compounds, liquors, and cordials, 95 per cent. of the full rates.

(*d*) In the case of all other goods, the preferential rate was to be five-sixths of the full rate.

The grant covered all parts of His Majesty's Dominions outside Cyprus, "and any territories under His Majesty's protection, and includes India," whilst mandatory areas might be included by the High Commissioner by Order in Council.

Goods were not to be regarded as of imperial origin unless they contained such proportion of their value due to imperial

---

[1] Hansard, 7/6/20, col. 65.
[2] Hansard, 16/6/1920, col. 1262.
[3] *B.T.J.*, 10/6/20, p. 775.
[4] This closely resembles the list in the U.K. preferential scheme.

labour as the High Commissioner might by regulation prescribe.

(2) **Jamaica.**[1]—This Act (Tariff Amendment Law, No. 17 of 1920) provides for a duty of £10 for every £100 in value of cotton piece goods "when imported direct into this island from the United Kingdom, or when imported in accordance with regulations made by the Governor in Privy Council," and allows a preference of £1 13s. 4d. per cent. if the cotton goods in question be "made entirely of cotton grown within the British Empire."

Section 2 of the Act allows regulations to be made for the production of documents, for the manner of packing, "and the conditions governing the direct importation of such goods and their passage through another country," whilst § 5 allows this preference to be extended to any other portion of the Empire by resolution of the Legislative Council. In fact, by resolution of 15th June, the preference was extended to the greater portion of the Empire.

(3) **Malta.**[2]

The preferences provided in this Act are very numerous, they include—

Alcohol, beer, methylated spirits, tobacco, varnish containing spirits, arms and amunition, bicycles, chemicals, and apothecaries wares, unless containing alcohol, cutlery, and ironmongery, drugs, earthenware and chinaware, electrical goods, fancy goods, fruit, furniture, games and toys, glass and glassware, gold, silver, and instruments, iron and steel manufactures, jams and sugar preserves, jewellery, precious stones, lace, motor vehicles and parts thereof, photographic goods, pickles, sauces, and condiments (except tomato sauce and extracts of tomato), soap (except laundry), and stationery.

The greater part of these goods are given an *ad valorem* preference of 2½ or 5 per cent. The preference applies to all parts of the Empire, and the usual requirement of a given percentage of value added by imperial labour is laid down.[3]

Differential Export Duties within the Empire.—The matter which has of late attracted most comment is the steady develop-

---

[1] *B.T.J.*, 29/7/1920, p. 135.

[2] *B.T.J.*, 15/4/1920.

[3] All these preferences were inaugurated after the adoption of imperial preference by the United Kingdom, and the terms of the legislative instruments follow the British example closely.

ment of the differential export duty upon raw or semi-raw products of the Empire. Early in the war a Committee of Inquiry had been set up by the Colonial Office to investigate the trade in edible oils and fats. The trade had been allowed to fall largely into the hands of German traders and crushers, and evidence was forthcoming that German agriculturists had made themselves more familiar with the uses of the product for cattle feeding purposes than was the case with the British farmers. The committee came to the conclusion that in spite of the improvement in technique in the crushing mills in this country, the Committee " are convinced, from the evidence before them, that the bulk of the trade will revert to Germany in the absence of specific measures to the contrary. On this point the Committee are quite clear. The trade will not have become sufficiently rooted in this country by the end of the war to overcome successfully the competition it will then have to meet. The question before the Committee, therefore, is to decide what specific measure or measures can be suggested to establish and retain the industries in this country, having due regard to the interests alike of the native in West Africa and the consumer in the United Kingdom . . . the committee recommend the imposition at an early date in the several West African Colonies of an export duty of not less than £2 per ton on all palm kernels exported from British West Africa, the duty to continue during the war and for five years afterwards, and to be remitted on all kernels shipped to and crushed in any part of the British Empire. If a duty of £2 per ton be found insufficient to divert the trade to this country, the amount should be raised until the duty is adequate to effect its purpose, and this determination should be made clear from the outset.[1]

The foregoing proposal involves, let it be noted, no new departure in general principle. A similar differential charge has been imposed for some years in the Federated Malay States on exported tin ore, and it is understood that the same step as regards tin ore is contemplated in Nigeria." [2]

The duty here referred to is a duty on tin ore, equal to 70 per cent. of the duty on tin " exported under guarantees as the resident may require that it will be smelted in the colony

[1] Cd. 8247 of 1916.
Report, p. 22.

of the Straits Settlements or the United Kingdom." If "exported without such guarantees," there is to be an additional duty of 30 dollars per picul.[1]

The report of the committee was at once acted upon by the Government. Appended to the report, when it was issued to the public, was a copy of a dispatch to the Governor-General of Nigeria, and the Governors of Sierra Leone, the Gold Coast, and Gambia, signed by Mr. Bonar Law, endorsing the recommendation as "a practicable proposal which shall be adopted," and urging action in the shape of draft legislation "as soon as practicable." Since it was not certain that the suggested duty at the rate of £2 per ton would be effective, "it may, therefore, be expedient that power should be taken in the ordinance to modify the amount of the duty by order of the Governor in Council, which is a more expedient process than fresh legislation. . . ."

These proposals aroused great opposition in the House of Commons, and the matter was definitively raised during the discussion on supply (Colonial Office Vote) on 3rd August, 1916.[2] Naturally, the Malay States precedent played some part in the discussion, but the most novel departure was the attitude taken up by Sir H. Mackinder,[3] who boldly argued that "You have no right to apply your ordinary free trade theories which may be applicable to the ordinary highly civilised states in Europe to such territories as those vast countries, which are now more than half empty, and are of enormous wealth, in the centre of Africa. Those regions ought to be treated as an asset of the Empire. If they are so treated and developed with the help of our warlike expenditure, and expenditure in money and in life, if we keep the *pax Britannica* throughout vast areas of the world, by that expenditure we are entitled to treat those regions as being imperial estates." It is this conception of the colonial possessions subserving the needs of the United Kingdom, or, if the phrase be preferred, the rest of the Empire, which lend these proposals their interest.

The history of the proposed tax can be shortly stated. A differential duty on tin ore not smelted within the British

---

[1] C.I.D., app. vii. According to Mr. Bonar Law, this duty was first imposed in 1903. Hansard, vol. lxxxv., col. 586.

[2] Hansard, *loc. cit.*

[3] *Loc. cit.*, col. 573.

Empire, and equal to $3\frac{3}{4}$ per cent. on the value had been imposed in April in Nigeria.[1] By ordinance No. XLVI. of 1916 further duties of £2 a ton on palm oil, and £1 2s. 6d. on palm kernels were imposed, to come into effect as from 7th October, 1916, though only *half* the above rates were to be levied on the last two items until 31st March, 1917.[2] These last duties were not differential, and the proposed differential duty was not as a matter of fact enforced until the year 1919. By the Palm Kernels (Export Duty) Ordinance, 1919 (No. VII. of 1919), which was to come into operation "on such date as the Governor shall appoint, and shall remain in force for a period of five years from such date, when it shall cease to be operate, and shall stand repealed," such a duty was imposed, bond being given in lieu of duty "when palm kernels are exported to the United Kingdom or to a port elsewhere within His Majesty's Dominions or within a British Protectorate."[3] Finally, a notice in the *Board of Trade Journal* of 11th September, 1919,[4] states that "The Board of Trade have been informed by the Colonial Office that the Governments of Nigeria, Gold Coast, and Sierra Leone are taking the necessary steps to bring into force on 20th October an export duty of £2 a ton on palm kernels exported from those colonies to countries outside the British Empire."

Legislation on the same lines has recently been passed by the Government of British India. A recent notice states[5] that—

"The Board of Trade have received from the India Office copy of a telegram from the Government of India stating that a Bill passed the Council of India on the 17th September imposing an export duty on raw hides and skins at 15 per cent. *ad valorem* with a rebate of two-thirds of the duty on hides and skins exported to countries within the Empire.

"Rebate will be granted on the exporter furnishing a bond for the payment of the remainder of the duty. The bond will be cancelled on the receipt within a period of six months of a guarantee from a hides association or government official

---

[1] Bonar Law in Hansard, vol. lxxxviii., col 321, in reply to Mr. Molteno. (29/11/16.)

[2] Bonar Law, *op. cit.*; *B.T.J.*, 19/10/16, p. 218, and 21/12/16, p. 880.

[3] *B.T.J.*, 12/6/19, p. 757.

[4] P. 346.

[5] *B.T.J.*, 16/10/19, p. 486. For the conditions of the rebate, see *B.T.J.*, 13/5/20, p 662.

that the hides or skins have been delivered to a tanner for tanning within the Empire."

The United Kingdom.—The Finance Act, 1919, introduces imperial preferential rates in the case of articles subject to import duty. The quantitative aspects of the matter are dealt with in the second schedule to the Act, which lays down the following preferential rates :—

PREFERENTIAL RATES.

Goods.	Rate of Duty.
Tea, Cocoa, Coffee, Chicory, Currants, Dried or preserved fruit (within the meaning of § 8 of the Finance (No. 2) Act, 1915), Sugar, Glucose, Molasses, Saccharin, Motor spirit, Tobacco,	Five-sixths of the full rate.
Articles chargeable within the new import duties imposed by § 12 of the Finance (No. 2) Act,[1] 1915,	Two-thirds of the full rate.
WINE— Not exceeding 30 of proof spirit,	60 per cent. of the full rate.
Exceeding 30 of proof spirit,	66⅔ per cent. of the full rate.
Sparkling wine in bottles (additional duty),	70 per cent. of the full rate.
Still wine in bottle (additional duty),	50 per cent of the full rate.
Spirits,	Rates equivalent to the full rates as chargeable under this Act up to September 1, 1919.

[1] § 12 of this Act imposed duties of 33⅓ per cent. *ad valorem* upon motor cars, including motor bicycles and motor tricycles; accessories and component parts thereof; musical instruments, including gramophones, pianolas, and other similar instruments; accessories and component parts of musical instruments, and records and other means of reproducing music; clocks, watches, and the component parts of clocks and watches. In addition, there were imposed specific duties upon cinematograph films, whether in the blank, "positives," and "negatives."

The preferential rates came into force on and after 2nd June, 1919, and in the case of any other goods on and after the 1st September, 1919.

§ 8 (i.) of the Act lays down the *qualitative conditions* necessary for the enjoyment of the preference. In general it must be shown that the goods "have been consigned from, and grown, produced, or manufactured in the British Empire." The British Empire means "any of His Majesty's dominions outside Great Britain and Ireland, and any territories under His Majesty's protection, and includes India," and, by Order in Council, any future protectorate or mandatory territory "may be included within the definition of the British Empire for the purposes of this section, and this section shall have effect accordingly."

But "goods shall not be deemed to have been manufactured in the British Empire as aforesaid, unless such proportion of their value as is prescribed by regulations made by the Board of Trade, is the result of labour within the British Empire," and in the case of goods manufactured within the Empire largely from material "which is not wholly grown or produced in the Empire, the Board (of Trade) may, by order, direct that the preferential rate shall be charged only in respect of such proportion of those goods as corresponds to the proportion of dutiable material used in their manufacture which is shown to have been grown or produced in the Empire" (§ 8) (i). Goods manufactured in bond from preferentially produced material "shall to the extent to which they are shown to have been manufactured out of such material be charged at the preferential rate."

Towards the end of August, 1919, the Board of Trade issued regulations for the interpretation of the Act.[1] The proportion of their total value to be the result "of labour within the Empire" was fixed at 25 per cent.—except in the case of refined sugar, molasses, and extracts from sugar and manufactures where "no part of the goods shall be deemed to have been manufactured in the British Empire unless at least 5 per cent. of the total value of the goods is the result of labour within the British Empire." This low proportion was deliberately chosen, because the goods in question "are to a considerable extent manufactured in the British Empire

[1] *B.T.J.*, 18/8/19, pp. 281-284.

from material which is not wholly grown or produced in the Empire." Such goods enjoy the preference only in respect "of such proportion of those goods as corresponds to the proportion of dutiable material used in their manufacture which is shown to have been grown or produced in the Empire." The explanatory memorandum stating "the combined effect of the two rules being to allow preference where any of these articles are the result of an appreciable amount of Empire labour, but to confine it to the extent to which the finished article is the result of Empire material." What all this verbiage in effect amounts to is a provision whereby, in consideration of a qualification of the total remission of duty due to the working of the "proportion" rule, a less rigid standard of what is "imperial labour" is set up.[1]

§ 12. In the preceding sections we have passed under review the salient features of the chief colonial tariff systems of the world. A series of questions remain to be answered with the aid of analysis.

1. **Imperial Preference and the Ideal of the British Zollverein.**— To what extent can the Imperial preferential system be conceived as a first step towards a complete customs union against the rest of the world? In discussing this question it has usually been taken for granted that a common customs boundary must be logically accompanied by complete freedom of movement inside the customs area. But this is *not* logically necessary. It would not be inconsistent with the idea of an Imperial Customs *Federation* (though it would be inconsistent with a complete Customs *Union*) that a common barrier against foreign goods should be accompanied by the fact that inter-imperial trade was being subjected not only to revenue duties, but to true protective duties as well, just as the plans for a Central European Customs Union have recently recognised[2] the necessity for internal customs lines, at any rate in the immediate future. The possibility of a common tariff policy for the whole of the Empire must not be prejudiced on this score.

---

[1] Thus, if a consignment of sugar is worth £100 and only 5 per cent. is due to British labour, the preference will be paid on 5 per cent. of the value—viz., £5. Nineteen-twentieths of the consignment will pay at the full rate, the remaining one-twentieth will pay five-sixths of the full rate.

[2] That is, the idea was that of a federation changing gradually into a complete union.

We may regard the ideal of an Imperial Customs Union or Federation from the standpoint we are now taking as legitimately to be classified with systems of assimilated colonial tariffs. It is true that the "common tariff" would be "commonly" determined—*i.e.*, the idea of colonial political subjection to the pure will of the Metropolitan area would not be present, at any rate so far as the self-governing dominions are concerned. But a "common tariff" raises the fundamental point which the "assimilated" system raises—*i.e.*, in both cases the basic assumption is that the economic conditions in the colony and the metropolitan area are so far similar that the common tariff is not merely a technical possibility, but an economic desirability. This fundamental assumption will be investigated subsequently.

Meanwhile, it may be as well to point out that, logically, no reason exists for believing that a policy of Imperial preference is necessarily a first step towards a common economic policy in the sense of a completely unified tariff system.[1] On the contrary, the opposite is the case. Quite apart from the differences actually existing between the form of the preference in the different parts of the Empire, the *source* of the preference—*i.e.*, the original formulæ employed in Canada and New Zealand, for instance, shows that the idea of preference was closely allied in thought to the idea of reciprocity. Reciprocity, it is true, is based on the recognition of mutual gain from freer trade obtained by concession against concession, but this is by no means the same thing as recognition of an identical interest, but rather the reverse. There is parallelism, but not identity.

To put the two ideas in sharp and, therefore, somewhat inaccurate juxtaposition, it may be said that the supporters of the Zollverein begin with the assumption that whilst there may be differences in interest, these cases are relatively less important than those where the interests are identical, whilst the supporters of preference begin with the assumption that,

[1] *Cf.* Nicholson, "A Project of Empire," p. 258. "The system of preferences by the method of supertaxes must be regarded as a substitute for free trade within the Empire, instead of being a method by which it may be promoted. Judging by experience, preferential protection of this kind, like other forms of protection, would tend to be permanent owing to the creation of vested interests, and possibly to increase owing to the political power usually exercised by protected interests."

whilst each part of the Empire has predominantly different economic interests, there are also common interests to which a preference can give expression and free play. Even were this sense of common economic interest to go so far as to lead to complete freedom of trade within the Empire, this would not necessarily imply any approach to the ideal of a common Imperial tariff, for the step would be perfectly consistent with very different tariff policies in different parts of the Empire. If inter-imperial tariffs are not necessarily a barrier to a common extra-imperial tariff, neither is "free trade within the Empire" necessarily a step towards unification of Imperial customs tariffs.

The preceding argument does not, of course, assume the self-governing dominions to be, as things are, completely autonomous tariff areas. As will be clear from the terms of Lord Ripon's despatch, already quoted, some common ground is recognised to exist, and no one single area is allowed to narrow this ground for purely self-interested reasons. Concessions cannot be bought at the expense of other portions of the Empire, nor can concessions obtained remain unextended to other portions of the Empire. These conditions may, however, be made to imply more than is really the case. They are, in fact, only the extension to inter-imperial affairs of the principle of unconditional most-favoured-nation treatment. Thus, were Canada and Australia really completely independent nations, but maintaining most-favoured-nation treaties with one another, any concession granted by either to another power would in any case be extended to the other. A similar rule obtains under the present situation so far as concessions to foreign powers are concerned, though not as regards the concessions of either to the United Kingdom, which are *not* reciprocally granted.

The actual form of the preference leads to the same conclusion. It is, from inspection, clear that the utmost diversity of form prevails. This is only explicable and defensible if the standpoint of economic diversity of interest be taken. It may, of course, be legitimately questioned whether, in fact, so many divergent systems be necessary and whether a closer approach to uniformity be not possible. Nor is the discussion in the text intended in any way to prejudge other methods of arriving at Imperial unity, such as a close assimilation of legal conditions, and so on.

2. **Colonial Preference and a Pure Policy of Protection.**—The preceding discussion has raised in a direct form the question whether colonial preferences can be reconciled with a strict interpretation of the principle of protection of "Home interests," whether these interests be those of the colony or the metropolitan area. In the concrete the answer must necessarily turn upon the value of the preference and the interpretation of the phrase "interest." The acceptance of the protectionist standpoint involves the possibility of sacrificing the consumer's interest to that of the producer, and even if it be assumed that the security afforded the producer, and the economies of large scale production which a closed market affords him are capable of reconciling these possible antagonisms, a policy of protection for producers in any case involves some check to the flow of competing imports, whilst the grant of preference will quicken this flow. Hence, in so far as competing imports are concerned, a limit to the degree of preference is at once given, a protective policy being assumed. In so far as non-competing imports are concerned, the area of concession is at first sight wider. Here it is a question only of choosing between alternative sources of supply, and no *direct* limit of the degree of preference is afforded unless (*a*) revenue considerations come into question, (*b*) it is hoped to stimulate home production: so that the flow of imports can be held to be fatal to the prospects of a potential "infant industry."

Even here, however, an important *indirect* limit exists in the fact that a preferential concession may limit the extent to which concessions may be obtained from another area. This case presents no particular theoretical difficulties, since it is logically analogous to those cases in which the prior existence of unconditional most-favoured-nation treaties, or the suspicion that they will subsequently be granted, imposes difficulties in the negotiation of strict reciprocity treaties.

It may be argued that a method exists by which some of the practical inconveniences associated with the reconciliation of colonial preferences with extra-national treaties can be overcome. It may, for instance, be argued that a colonial preference is a domestic concern of the Empire which no foreign country has any business to inquire into. The force of such an argument depends, however, on the willingness of other Powers to accept it, or on the ability to enforce that point of view in case it is actively resisted. If the Foreign Power is weak in the special circumstances of the case, the argument will be accepted: if it is strong, there may be no difficulty in getting a tacit acceptance of the argument, *accompanied by the offer of a smaller concession than would otherwise have been the case.*

In any case, both the internal needs—*i.e.*, the pressure of domestic producers—and the external needs may lead to a situation in which preferences still exist, whilst their amount, relative to the duties imposed on non-preferential supplies, is a steadily diminishing one.[1]

3. **The Policy of Assimilation.**—We now come to the last point requiring discussion at this stage—the practicability and expediency of assimilation, in the sense of creating for a Colonial Empire a common uniform tariff against the rest of the world. This is a question, however, which affects not only the relations between colonies and their home country, but also, as already pointed out, the formation of customs unions or federations between independent States.

It might be thought sufficient to the point to the practical fact that the French policy of assimilation is rapidly losing ground in favour of the policy of differentiation. It is best, however, to approach the matter from the theoretical standpoint. The real difficulty is, of course, the fact that the economic situation, and, therefore, the needs of different portions of a widely scattered Empire are very diverse, and hence, if the tariff is to correspond to those needs, it must

---

[1] *Cf.* O. D. Skelton, "The Canadian Reciprocity Treaty," in *Ec. J.*, vol. xxi., p. 280. ". . . if the British tariff reformer complains that the negotiations with France and Italy and now with the United States have involved whittling down the British preference, he should reflect that were protection re-established in Britain, with an initial perference to Canada, negotiation with foreign countries to secure more favourable entry for British manufactures would inevitably result in whittling down the Canadian preference." As for the difficulty of reconciling protection with reciprocity and preference, *cf.* the following letter of Sir James Graham to Peel (dated 30/12/1842), "I wrote a memorandum a few days ago on the policy of a commercial treaty with the United States, under which Indian corn might be admitted duty free in return for a more favourable tariff as affecting the import of our more staple manufactures into America. . . . Stanley's despatch to Bagot (the Governor of Canada) is more strongly expressed than caution justifies. This may be considered as an engagement binding in honour, and if so, it must be fulfilled. But it will be found a very inconvenient and dangerous operation in the present temper of our agricultural supporters. It will excite as much opposition as a greater change, and it will not really effect the purpose of opening extensively the American market." Parker's "Life and Letters of Sir James Graham," 1792-1861, vol. i., p. 331.

be differentiated. The same applies, *mutatis mutandis*, to any attempted commercial rapprochement in the shape of a commercial union, where the parties thereto are on very unequal cultural and economic levels. Professor Grunzel has illuminated these points by his distinction between the customs area and the economic area, pointing out that even inside a geographically contiguous, politically unitary state the economic areas are not necessarily co-extensive with the customs boundaries.[1]

The greater the geographical dispersion, therefore, the greater the chances are that a common uniform tariff will be inapplicable, and that some parts of the area must suffer in consequence.

The argument may be put *a fortiori* thus—if, as in the case of such a geographically contiguous (and to some extent culturally uniform) area, such as Central Europe, the need for intermediate customs lines was felt to be a necessity, so much the more is this true of a widely scattered Colonial Empire. But geographical situation in part at least determines the relations to non-national areas, and, therefore, if the internal relations are such as to require some regard for local interests, the same must be equally true of external relations.

As has already been pointed out, internal freedom of trade need not be accompanied by homogeneity of external tariffs, and this disposes of those supporters of the idea of assimilation who desire a common external tariff because they desire a free internal market.[2] It may be argued that a common tariff would enable trade relations with other countries to be conducted on more advantageous terms.[3]

---

[1] Grunzel, "Economic Protectionism," p. 19, *et seq.*

[2] Professor Nicholson thinks that "internal free trade throughout the Empire, though possible without any customs union, would be promoted and strengthened thereby, and the benefits of real commercial union are too great to be cast aside on account of a literal interpretation of free trade . . . nor is there any reason to insist on the exact uniformity of the Imperial customs so long as the main ideas are realised. . . ." *Op. cit.*, p. 264. But "the negative argument (against protection) becomes overwhelming if we try to invent a complex and detailed protective system for the whole British Empire," (p. 265); also, we have to take account of geographical proximity, "trade with a near is more advantageous than trade with a remote country" (p. 267).

[3] This comes out in the "Central Europe" discussion—*e.g.*, Wolff, "Ein Deutschösterreichisch-ungarischer Zollverband," followed by Irresberger, "Das deutsch-oesterreichisch-ungarische Wirtschafts und Zollbündis."

There is some ambiguity in this view. It may be true that a customs union would have to meet with less opposition than a policy of preferential relations, *other things being equal.* But other things are not always equal—*i.e.*, it may be possible to follow an effective policy of preference, whilst a policy of federation or union might harbour so many oppositions of interest as to reduce its results in the conduct of negotiations below those which might have been produced by treaties, which assumed preference or reciprocity between the parties. These would now, of course, have to conclude separate treaties with third parties.

CHAPTER IX.

Valuation and Allied Problems.

§ 1. We have seen in a previous chapter that in the case of *ad valorem* duties there exist two possible systems of assessment—(1) on the basis of declarations furnished by the importer or his agent—*i.e.*, current "values"; (2) on the basis of values fixed by the administrative authorities themselves. But whichever system be adopted it will, on reflection, appear obvious that certain principles as to what constitutes "the value of a commodity" must be laid down. We may leave official valuation on one side for the moment and confine our attention to the freer system of declared values. If the importer is not to be allowed arbitrarily to select the basis of value he must be given directions as to three essential elements in the situation.

(1) As regards the place at which the goods are valued. The value of articles changes constantly across *space*. This is perfectly natural, because goods placed on a truck at the factory have not as yet incurred a whole series of marketing and transport expenses which must be met before they can reach the final consumer, by which time the value of the goods will have risen correspondingly. We must, therefore, investigate carefully the point in space at which the goods are supposed to be for valuation purposes.

(2) As regards the time at which goods are *valued*. The value of goods fluctuates from day to day according to the changing currents of demand and supply. Is the value for tariff purposes to be the value of the particular consignment at the time of purchase: the value of the particular consignment at the time of export or import (in which case the value will not be changed if the goods have already been sold, but will have changed if the goods are merely consigned for sale); or, is it to be the value of a *similar consignment* on the day of export or of import? In this last case, since time is a function of the movement of goods, changes in value may have taken

place in either direction which may considerably affect the tariff value of the parcel.

(3) As regards the *elements* which are to be included in the concept of value. There is first of all thè treatment of coverings. Goods cannot be sent without being packed, and the value of these coverings may be considerable. Ought the value of the article to include the value of the packings: or ought coverings and packings, if they have any value, to be treated as separate commodities? And what is the definition of a covering and a wrapping? As we shall see when dealing with specific duties, the whole question of the "wrapping" is one of very great complexity. Secondly, there comes the question as to whether *all* the elements (other than the value of packings) which at any point make up the aggregate value of the commodity are to be taken into account, or whether specific elements only are to be included, or, finally, whether percentual additions are to be made to cover these various "oncosts."

§ 2. Here then we have three sets of problems which may be answered in a considerable variety of ways. Their practical importance may, perhaps, be better realised if we take account of the fact that different answers given to these questions may very considerably affect the *amount of duty payable*. Hence, these points have more than a speculative interest. Let us take the case of a consignment of 1,000 tons of a commodity bought free-on-rail at £2 a ton and dutiable in the country of import at 5 per cent. *ad valorem*. If the valuation is to be made on the basis of time-of-purchase-price, the duty would amount to £100. If prices have risen to £3 a ton by the time of import, if the value at time of import is taken, the duty would be £150. Similarly with the other elements. A knowledge of the concerte conditions is, therefore, indispensable in a study of the incidence of customs duties, just as a study of what is meant by "taxable income" is necessary to an appreciation of income tax legislation.

Let us then summarise the position by means of a diagram. The basis of dealing in ordinary business intercourse is the wholesale market price—although this is a conception which itself requires closer definition, since its connotation may vary from time to time and from place to place. To this basis price there may be added (*a*) all or a selected series of "oncosts" up to the point of shipment, (*b*) all supplementary costs up to the time of landing, or a selected series of costs up to the time of landing. (*c*) Values of packing, or packing may be dealt with separately, and instead of actual oncost, in whole or in part, there may be percentual additions to value. We then get the following scheme :—

Market Value Basis.		Shipment (F.O.B.) Values.		Arrival (C.I.F.) Values.	
Time of purchase or Time of shipment or Time of actual import	+	1. Selected oncosts to port of shipment 2. Percentual additions to cover costs to port of shipment 3. Full value of costs to port of shipment	+	1. Selected costs to port of destination. 2. Percentual additions to port of destination. 3. Full costs to port of destination.	With or without inclusion of costs or value of wrappings

In practice only the f.o.b. and the c.i.f. bases seem to be known. The whole matter is, however, so complicated that it appears best to display the matter schematically as in the four following pages.

Other portions of the British Empire show methods which in part resemble and in part diverge from these types : Ceylon follows British India : Rhodesia follows South Africa : Papua follows Australia. In Zanzibar the basis is f.o.b. at port of shipment plus percentages varying with the area of origin *and* the types of commodity : in Uganda and East Africa the value is the local "spot" value at the time and place of importation : in Nigeria the basis is f.m.v. in principal markets whence and the time when the goods were directly exported : the Gold Coast colonies the value at port of shipment—"*i.e.*, invoice value, exclusive of trade discounts and of freight insurance and other charges."

§ 4. It will be noted that, cumbersome as some of these definitions are, they still leave a wide margin for dispute. What is the meaning in each case of export or exported directly ? What is the precise significance of time of export ? What is the meaning of "principal market or markets ? " All these points require ultimately some precise definition, since the valuation basis is affected by them. In a note at the end of this chapter we shall add a comment which may serve to show how difficult the whole matter is. At present all that need be done is to draw attention to the fact that it is only in connection with *ad valorem* duties that these difficulties arise—and this sufficiently explains their growing unpopularity.

Country.	Basis of Valuation.	Definition in Detail.	Source of Authority.
U.S.A.,[1] .	F.o.b.: wholesale market value, plus all costs to port of shipment. Packages included. Value to be based on time of exportation. Exception for special packages.	Whenever imported merchandise is subject to an *ad valorem* rate of duty based upon or regulated in any manner by the value thereof, the duty shall be assessed upon the *actual market value or wholesale price thereof, at the time of exportation to the U.S.*, in the principal markets of the country from whence exported, that such actual market value shall be held to be the price at which such merchandise is freely offered for sale to all purchasers in said markets, in the usual wholesale quantities and the price which the seller, shipper, or owner would have received and was willing to receive for such merchandise when sold in the ordinary course of trade in the usual wholesale quantities, *including the value of all cartons, cases, crates, boxes, sacks, casks, barrels (etc.) . . . whether holding liquids or solids, and all other costs, charges, and expenses incident to placing the merchandise in condition*, packed ready for shipment to the U.S., and if these be used for covering or holding imported merchandise, whether dutiable or free from any unusual article or form designed for use otherwise than in the *bona fide* transportation of such merchandise to the U.S., additional duty shall be levied and collected upon such material or article at the rate to which the same would be subjected if separately imported. . . .	Tariff Act of 1913, § 3, para. R.
Japan,[2] .	C.i.f.	Duty upon an article subject to *ad valorem* duty shall be levied according to the value thereof at the time of its arrival at the port of importation.	Customs Tariff Law, Art. 2, (Cd. 5150 of 1910, p. 3).

[1] But see now §§ 302-3 of the Emergency Tariff Act of 1921, *B.T.J.*, 2/6/21, p. 622.

[2] Quoted in Appendix II. to F.I.D., 1913, Cd. 7180, p. 1261. For an elaborate discussion of the decisions relating to the American definition, see "Digest of Decisions, etc.," vol. ii., p. 1425; and for decisions under earlier Acts, *Ibid.*, pp. 1426-54.

Country.	Basis of Valuation.	Definition in Detail.	Source of Authority.
Sweden, .	C.i.f.: cost of packing included. Time of purchase or if unpurchased (*i.e.*, consigned) place and time of despatch.	When the duty is fixed at a certain percentage of the value of the goods, such value shall in the case of goods imported in an undamaged condition be taken as the market price of the goods obtaining at the place and time of purchase—or, in the case of imported goods which have not been purchased, at the place of despatch at the time when the goods were shipped—with the addition in all cases of the full value of the packing, of insurance, freight, and other costs incurred up to the arrival of the goods, if conveyed by ship, at the port to which they are despatched or the port where they are unloaded from the vessel for further conveyance to their place of destination, and if they are otherwise conveyed, up to the first Swedish Customs House reached. In the case of articles which have suffered serious damage, only the decreased value which the articles are found to have at the place where declared for duty shall be taken into account.	Instructions to Customs Tariff Law, § 3 (Cd. 5464 of 1911, p. 85).
Netherlands,[1]	C.i.f. "current price in this country."	By the term "current price in this country" shall be understood the sum which it is considered may be charged on the day of the declaration for delivery by the first hand in the foreign country, minus the import duty according to the tariff. As regards merchandise to which the above provision cannot be applied, including such as from its nature, destination, or other reasons is less valuable to others than to those for whom it is intended, the value shall be fixed at the price of purchase from the first hand at the place of origin, plus the cost of packing, transport, insurance, and commission, whilst for separate portions of one article not in themselves constituting articles of trade, the value shall be fixed in proportion to the price of the whole article to which they are considered to belong.	Art. 12 of the Dutch Law of 26th Aug., 1822, as amended by the Law of 20th April, 1895.

[1] Note to Japan above.

Country.	Basis of Valuation.	Supplementary Detail.	Source of Authority.
British India,	C.i.f.: time basis, date of importation.	The wholesale cash price, less trade discount, for which goods of the like kind and quality are sold at the time and place of importation, or are capable of being sold, at the time and place of importation, without any abatement or deduction whatever, except of the amount of duties payable on the importation thereof, or where such price is not ascertainable, the cost at which goods of the like kind and quality could be delivered at such place, without any abatement or deduction, except as aforesaid.	§§ 29 and 30 of the Sea Customs Act of 1878.
Canada,	Fair market value. Time-basis, date of exportation.	Value for duty shall be the fair market value thereof when sold for home consumption in the principal markets of the country *whence and at the time when* the *same* were exported directly to *Canada*. Such market value shall be the fair market value of such goods in the usual and ordinary commercial acceptation of the term, and as sold in the ordinary course of trade, provided that a discount for cash for duty purposes shall not exceed 2½ per cent. and shall not be allowed unless it has been actually allowed and deducted by the exporter on the invoice to the importer.	Chap. 48 of the Revised Statutes of 1906, as amended by §§ 3, 4 of the Customs Amendment Act of 1907.
		Duty shall not be assessed on less than the invoice value in any case, *except on account of reduction in the fair market value of such goods between the time of their purchase by the Canadian importer and their exportation to Canada.*	
		Coverings when not included in invoice value of goods they contain are subject to special rates of 20 or 27½ per cent. respectively: otherwise they are dutiable at same rate of *ad val.* duty as the goods they contain.	Tariff Act of 1907. Tariff No. 710 as amended by the C.T. War Revenue Act, 1915 (affects rates only, not principle).

Country.	Basis of Valuation.	Supplementary Detail.	Source of Authority.
Union of So. Africa.	F.o.b. Time-basis, date of exportation.	For the purpose of estimating the amount of customs duty whenever levied on goods *ad valorem* and for the purpose of the declarations and oaths which may at any time be required by law or regulation in relation to the question of such duty the value for purposes of duty of those goods shall be taken to be the true current value for home consumption in the open market of similar goods in the *principal markets of the country from which and at the time at which* the goods were imported, including carriage to the port of shipment and the cost of packing and packages, but not including agents' commission when such commission does not exceed 5 per cent.; provided that in no case shall the value for purposes of duty, as in this section defined, be less than the cost of the goods to the importer at the port of shipment.	§ 7 of the Tariff Act of 1914. (Act No. 26 of 1914.)
Australia, .	F.o.b. Time-basis, time of shipment.[1]	When any duty is imposed according to value (*a*), the value shall be taken to be the fair market value of the goods in the principal markets of the country whence the same were exported in the usual and ordinary commercial acceptation of the term and free on board at the port of export in such country and a further addition of 10 per cent. on such market value.	§ 154 (*a*) of the Customs Act, 1901-16.
		The f.o.b. value includes freight charges up to port of shipment (or, if shipped through a second country), inland freight to frontier of first country, royalties, insurance, and (where stamps are affixed) inland revenue duties and royalties; but *excludes* cost of outside packages, commissions, brokerages, dock dues and export duties, overseas freight, etc.	Notice of 29/10/13 (but see orders No. 1169 of 1909 and No. 1421 of 1911, which modify position as to agents' commission).
New Zealand,	Fair market value, plus 10 per cent. Time-basis, time of export.	The value of goods subject to *ad valorem* duty shall be the fair market value thereof, when sold for cash in the ordinary course of business for home consumption in the principal markets of the country from which the goods were *exported*, at the time when they were so exported, with 10 per cent. added to such fair market value.	

[1] See Note (*a*) on p. 16 of *T.S.*, No. 37. " Customs Tariff of Australia." " The courts have held that in relation to the value for duty that the Customs Act requires that duty shall be paid on the fair market value for home consumption in the country of export at the time of shipment to Australia."

A word may now be added as to official valuation duties. What we have here to investigate is the methods chosen by the governments in fixing these values.

An interesting despatch [1] from the Indian Government, dating from the year 1860, well shows the kind of difficulties to which a government is exposed which attempts to assess values for taxation purposes. It appears that at that time each of the governments fixed its own valuations, and the main necessity was for uniformity: what concerns us is the difficulties experienced in arriving at a fair valuation. The Junior Secretary of the Board of Revenue in Bengal reporting to his government pointed out in the past the custom had been in arriving at a new valuation (which, according to the then custom, took place once in every three years) to consult the mercantile community: on proceeding to a new and independent valuation, the "Board regret to state that they found these articles of trade in which the more influential merchants are principally concerned, generally much undervalued by the Tariff Committee, while little attention appears to have been paid by them to the valuation on commodities, the tariff in which is for the most part confined to the small traders:" there were difficulties as to the price of basis, and the report then goes on to say that "the main and primary reason, however, why the valuations of the Committee differ from those of the Board is, that the interests of the merchants are antagonistic with those of the government."

Official valuation, then, whilst it may make less frequent the disputes between the administrative authorities and the mercantile community, certainly does not dispose of them absolutely. The conflict is merely concentrated by centring on the valuation list, instead of being the battle fought over time after time in the shape of valuation disputes on importer's declarations. The government is indeed in a difficult position: if it refuses all participation to the mercantile community[2]

[1] Copy of a recent despatch . . . from the Governor-General of India in Council on the subject of the valuation, etc., of imports for customs duties in India. *P.P.*, vol. lii., 1860, p. 187, *et seq.*

[2] It is interesting to find that what is described by Dr. N. S. B. Gras ("The Early English Customs System": Harvard Economic Studies, vol. xviii., Appendix C, p. 694) as "one of the earliest, if not the earliest books of rates that I have found," speaks of "a rate made of the prisys of allmaner of warys by the kynge counsell and by the advyce surveyors and cowntrowlers and costomers off the porte of London and the merchants adventerers of the same with other . . ." (15th July, 1507).

it is either running the danger of being out of touch with current price movements, and therefore of inflicting real injustice on importers, or, if it really can command adequate sources of information, it is really in a position to check importers' declarations and abandon the system altogether—the defect of which is that it is never in touch with actual prices for more than a short time, so that it inflicts losses either on the government or on the merchants.

In Egypt, "as regards certain articles . . . values for the purpose of assessing duty are established from time to time by agreements between the Egyptian Customs Administration and the principal merchants interested in the particular trade." In framing these valuation tariffs the prices ruling at the time in respect of the various articles to which they relate are taken as a basis; and, as the market is subject to fluctuations, the tariffs are fixed only for stated periods, and never for a period exceeding twelve months. The tariffs may be denounced either by the merchants (or any one of them) or by the customs administration, not less than fifteen days before the lapse of the period for which they were framed, but if not so denounced they are tacitly renewed from month to month.[1] This system, which allows interested parties to object, seems, on the face of it, to avoid many of the difficulties to which the rigidity of the valuation tariff exposes it, but it has also found its severe critic, on the ground that one person may override the wishes and views of the majority, and that the establishment of a value takes the form of a battle between merchants and officials. "The result is most often a compromise which satisfies nobody."[2] The same difficulties have made themselves felt in other countries—*e.g.*, Brazil. The leading Brazilian expert thus writes of the Revision Commission of 1897, on whose labours the present system still rests.[3] "The establishment of rates in our tariff did not and could not obey a sound unswerving judgment,

---

[1] C.I.D., 1915, p. 838. The present position in India is governed by the Sea Customs Act, 1878, by which "the Governor-General in Council may from time to time . . . fix for the purpose of levying duties, tariff values of any goods exported or imported by sea on which customs duties are by law imposed and alter any such values fixed by any Tariff Act for the time being in force." The revision now seems to be annual.

[2] E. Pegna. "Le régime douanier de l'Egypte," in *L'Egypte contemporaine*, No. 34 (November, 1917), p. 458.

[3] F.T.C. Report, p. 30.

based, on the one hand, on the result of calculations as to the nature, quality, and average cost of merchandise in the principal producing markets in the different countries, and, on the other hand, the result of extensive and profound study of conditions of existence and degree of development in the industries located in different regions of the extensive territory of the country. . . . Good will certainly was not lacking in the revision commission of 1897, nor in the sub-committees into which it was divided for special study of each schedule of the tariff, composed as it was of different representatives of the treasury, of commercial importing interests, and of national industries; but, given the diversity of interests represented, *questions in each case were resolved by a majority of votes or by agreement resultant of compromise by the interested parties through mutual concessions.* . . ."

§ 5. If a country has, for good or evil, adopted the pure *ad valorem* system, what measures can it take to safeguard the administration? There are two methods which constitute the first line of defence, which partake of the nature of control. A second line of defence is presented by primitive measures of various kinds, of which the most interesting is the right of "pre-emption." The rights of the administration, however, must not be allowed to override the right of the importer to be protected against unfair or undue exactions. Hence, we obtain an elaborate system of methods of appeal and redress, involving judicial process, the appeal to experts, the right of "abandonment," and so on.

Whether goods are liable to *ad valorem* or to specific duties, however, there is one subject of frequent dispute which is common to both these methods of assessment. This is the subject of the proper classification. In the case of countries with a single uniform rate of duty this problem does not arise. In the case of modern tariffs it is certainly a matter of great consequence. We may, therefore, deal with the question of disputes as one integral whole in a subsequent section of this chapter.

The two methods of control which come into question are the method of appraisement and the production of authenticated documents, or, to put the matter into simpler language, valuation by government officials, and authentication of documents by government officials. The method of appraisement in the strict sense is only required when *ad valorem* duties are imposed, although, of course, specific duties require an administrative staff: whilst authenticated documents occur or may occur in both cases, as we shall subsequently see.

§ 6. What, then, are the functions of the appraiser? We may confine ourselves to describing the American system in detail, since the U.S.A. presents the most interesting practical commentary upon the whole system of *ad valorem* duties.

The United States (including certain outlying dependencies) is divided for customs purposes into 49 districts. Among these 49 districts are distributed 16 appraisers and 19 assistant appraisers,[1] of which number the great port of New York absorbs one appraiser and 9 assistants. It follows that, in a large number of districts, the appraisement of merchandise is in the hands of an official who has other duties to perform as well.[2] In addition to the appraisers at the ports, there is a board of general appraisers with headquarters at New York, whose function will be apparent later.

What are the duties imposed by law upon the appraiser? They are defined in sections K and L of Section III. of the Tariff Act of 1913, which run as follows:—

K. "That it shall be the duty of the appraisers of the United States and every one of them and every person who shall act as such appraiser, or of the collector, as the case may be, by all reasonable ways and means in his or their power to ascertain, estimate, or appraise (any invoice or affidavit thereto or statement of cost, or of cost of production to the contrary notwithstanding) the actual market value and wholesale price of the merchandise at the time of exportation to the United States, in the principal markets of the country whence the same has been imported, and the number of yards, parcels, or quantities, and actual value or wholesale price of every one of them, as the case may require."

In Section L certain directions are given to the appraiser as to the approximate action to be taken in exceptional cases.[3]

The appraiser hence acts as valuer, and the question arises as to how far he is able to detect undervaluation. It is obvious

---

[1] "Reorganisation of the Customs Service." Presidential message, 4/3/13, 62nd C., 3rd session. H.D., vol. cxxxv., doc. No. 1450.

[2] "At ports where there is no appraiser provided by law, the return of the customs officer to whom is committed the estimating and collection of duties and who is designated as appraiser shall be deemed and taken to be the appraisement of merchandise." U.S. Customs Regulations, Art. 1121.

[3] See below, Note [1].

that the range of commodities is nowadays so great that a single individual would find it difficult to master more than the position as regards a few of them. In ports as large as New York, where the number of assistants is large, specialisation [1] becomes possible, but even with the best will in the world, an appraiser at a smaller port is thrown very much on his own judgment, and the wider the range of commodities the less trained in each particular direction can this judgment be. The matter, of course, becomes hopeless from the standpoint of the administration if there is collusion between the importers and the customs officials, and a lack of adequate technical knowledge and training is not compensated for by scrupulous honesty. In the previously mentioned Indian despatch one gets a vivid picture of the difficulties caused by lack of adequate training on the part of appraisers,[2] even under the official valuation system, and there seems no doubt that in many countries to-day the introduction of the appraiseership system would lead to great difficulties owing to the absence of the necessary administrative efficiency.[3]

As a matter of actual fact, the existence of a class of appraisers was not sufficient to prevent a series of grave frauds upon the revenue of the United States. "Millions of dollars in evaded duties were paid back into the Public Treasury during the four years' life of the Payne-Aldrich Tariff Act as a result of the vigorous and aggressive campaign against smuggling and under-valuation carried on by Secretary of the Treasury MacVeagh and Collector Loeb of New York." As a result of

---

[1] For a graphic description of the situation at New York, see Higginson, *op. cit.*, chap. iii., espec. pp. 51-65. Note that the appraiser *only* determines *market value* and not dutiable value. The estimation of dutiable value is the function of the collector. U.S. Customs Regulations, Art. 618.

[2] *Op. cit.*, p. 191. "The Board (of Revenue of Bengal) have been unable to ascertain from the head appraiser any intelligible account of the mode in which he arrived at his high valuation on some articles; his estimates appeared to be based upon the casual and, in all probability, exceptional prices of the day on which he made his valuations, rather than upon average prices. The Board in fact see much reason to apprehend that the knowledge possessed by the appraisers is very imperfect; and considering that they have no practical information of the prices of the English and local markets such as would be obtained by actual participation in trade, that they have only the most vague acquaintance with the proportions in which the qualities of the same class of goods are imported, and that in respect to the prices of many of the articles of commerce they have no knowledge, beyond what they may pick up from time to time in the performance of their duties, it is a matter of no surprise that their information should be most defective."

[3] *Cf.* F.T.C. Report, South America, p. 24, § 6.

this campaign there passed into the customs law of the United States a principle of great importance. This was the right to examine the books of importers. The frauds were largely detected by the activities of the "Special Agents" of the United States Treasury, who, having no positive data to go upon, practically won their victories by blackmail. "Usually travelling in pairs, the special agents would visit an importer's office and demand his books and papers. A refusal to deliver the documents was met with the threat that the man would be be arrested, and receive a great deal of undesirable publicity, resulting in an impairment of his credit and business standing. It might be said that in practically all of these proceedings the special agents were 'morally certain' that the man was guilty of wrongdoing, notwithstanding the fact that they lacked tangible evidence of any crime.

"The pressure thus brought to bear upon the suspected importer usually proved effective. In the first place, the importer being intimidated, became alarmed, and although advised by his attorney that the government agents had no legal right to the books .and papers, he felt that a refusal to produce them would be construed as an admission of guilt, and might lead to more serious trouble. Furthermore, importers feared publicity more than anything else, and not a few felt disposed to pay a large sum of money for alleged or actual evaded duties rather than fight for their rights in the courts." [1] This practice proved so successful that the Tariff Committee of the House of Representatives decided to embody the principle in the new tariff of 1913. Importers in, and exporters to, the United States who "shall fail or refuse to submit to the inspection of a duly accredited investigating officer of the United States, when so required to do, any or all of his books, records, or accounts pertaining to the value or classification of such merchandise, then the Secretary of the Treasury in his discretion, is authorised, while such failure or refusal continues, to exclude from entry any and all merchandise" sold or shipped by such persons, imported or consigned by or to them, respectively.[2] The Senate rejected these changes as far too drastic, but a compromise was reached in conference, the house para-

---

[1] These quotations are from I. Newton Hoffmann, *op. cit.*, *J.Pol.Ec.*, vol. xxii., p. 848, etc.

[2] See original clauses in Cd. 6774 of 1913 (U.S.A. proposed new C.T.), pp. 111-112.

graphs being restored, with the amendment to the effect that failure to produce books should be punishable, not by the exclusion of the merchandise from entry into the United States, but by the assessment of an additional duty of 15 per cent.[1]

The clause in question now forms paragraphs U and V of the 1913 tariff.[2]

Here then we have an additional means of control, which, under the existing U.S. system, is applicable not only to importers, but to exporters in foreign countries as well. How the system works with regard to the latter we shall see in a moment.

§ 7. Let us now examine the *second* method of control—the demand for the production of documents. The two documents which come into question here are the certificate of origin and the invoice. The first, as its name implies, has reference to the place of manufacture, and is, therefore, of primary importance when it is a question of imposing differential duties on the products of particular areas. The second acts as guide to the selling price of the commodity or of the value of the goods if no sale prior to consignment has been effected. It may, therefore, well be the case that invoices are required without certificates of origin, or certificates of origin without invoices (in those cases where the goods are subjected to specific duties, and the question of value is primarily of statistical importance), or that both may be required, in which case one and the same instrument may cover both aspects of the matter.

So far we have been dealing only with the documents, which may have to be of prescribed form; and of which more than one copy may have to be furnished. We have next to

---

[1] I. Newton Hoffman, *op. cit.*, p. 854. For the duties and position of the Special Agents, see U.S. Customs Regulations, Arts. 1129-1137.

[2] In addition, by paragraphs O and P powers are given to collectors and appraisers and the appeal bodies to be mentioned presently to "cite to appear before them and examine upon oath any owner, importer, agent, consignee, or other person touching any matter or thing which they . . . may deem material respecting any imported merchandise then under consideration *or previously imported within one year* and . . . may require the production of any letters, accounts, contracts, or invoices relating to said merchandise, and may require such testimony to be reduced to writing, and when so taken it shall be filed and preserved for use or reference until the final decision . . shall be made," the penalty of non-compliance to be a fine of from $20 to $500, and the loss of further rights of appeal, whilst false statements on examination lead to condemnation for perjury and the forfeiture of the merchandise or the value thereof.

deal with the process of authentication. Here we are faced with a large variety of forms of procedure. We may distinguish official acts of authentication and the affirmation of the correctness of the statement on the part of the individual. The official act of authentication may be accompanied by a declaration of correctness at the time: but this does not exclude the possibility that a further declaration may later be insisted upon, so that both the exporter and the importer may be bound by oath or declaration. Since the most usual form of authentication is that by the consulate of the country to which export takes place, we get the generic name for the class of viséd document—the "consular invoice." It may also happen that a declaration of correctness must be supplied with the invoice without any official act of authentication—*e.g.*, in the case of goods exported to the self-governing dominions from the United Kingdom under the conditions necessary for the enjoyment of British preferential tariff rates.

§ 8. The Tables on the three following pages, which have been drawn upon the basis of an official return,[1] may serve to show how these regulations as to documents work out in practice.

§ 9. The question at once arises as to how far such consular authentication acts as an effective check upon undervaluation, and to what extent business men regard the statutory declarations which they are required to make as binding on their consciences. The position as regards the consular verification is succinctly put in the evidence[2] given by Mr. J. F. Curtis, at the time Assistant Secretary of the U.S. Treasury, before the Tariff Committee of the House of Representatives in 1913:—

"The law provides for the beginning of a customs transaction at the time of shipment on the other side, where the shipper has to go before the Consul and make a declaration as to the correctness of his invoice, that he has put in the invoice all the necessary charges, and the Consul certifies on the invoice that he believes the statement to be true, and that certificate of the Consul now includes the certification that he believes the values are correct. Our consular force is nowhere near

[1] Cd. 5347 of 1910. "Memorandum showing regulations existing in British India, British self-governing dominions, . . . and in foreign countries in regard to certificates of origin other than sugar, the certification of invoices, etc."

[2] *Op. cit.*, p. 635.

Country.	Certificates of Origin required in what cases.	If One Form is required.	Invoices if and when required.	If to be Viséd or Attested.	Specific Regulations (if any) as to Goods or Countries.
Canada, . .	Goods desiring British preferential treatment.	Yes.	Yes. In all cases one form is required.	No.	Tea bought in bond in the United Kingdom. Special declaration in the case of animals.
Newfoundland, .	Required only for Greek currants and raisins and fish of British catch and cure: these being the only articles preferentially treated.		Yes, in all cases. Two forms of declaration prescribed for entry on invoice.	Attestation by owner, and if the owner is not the person entering the goods, the invoice must be verified by oath of importer or consignee.	
Australia, . .	Goods desiring British preferential treatment. Country of origin to be stated in *all* cases. Signature must be witnessed.	Yes.	Yes. In all cases.	Statutory declaration may be asked for.	Spirits, guns, goods suspected to be prison made, chemical steels and electro-dynamic goods.
New Zealand, .	Goods desiring British preferential treatment. Goods imported from South Africa, in case of tea imports.	Yes.	In all cases.	No.	Explosives, fruits and plants, animals and manures.

Country.	Certificates of Origin required in what cases.	If One Form is required.	Invoices if and when required.	If to be Viséd or Attested.	Specific Regulations (if any) as to Goods or Countries.
Union of South Africa.	Goods desiring British preferential treatment.	Yes.	In all cases.	No.	Second-hand clothing.
British India, .	Spirits delivered out of bond in U.K., if it is desired to avoid examination on arrival in India.	Yes.	May be asked for, and in practice are required to be produced.		
France, . . .	Required on certain articles to enjoy benefit of minimum tariff: the most important articles are hardened steel, wire of same, cattle and horses, raw iron, fats and oils, and certain colonial products.	Four methods of certification; certificates must be viséd by consular authorities unless issued by customs authorities; in case of reciprocity there is free consular certification.			
Japan, . . .	If goods are over 100 yen in value, certificate required, to be issued by Japanese Consul or local government or local chamber of commerce.	No special form, but must give specified particulars.			

Country.	Certificate of Origin required in what cases.	If One Form is required.	Invoices if and when required.	If to be Viséd or Attested.	Specific Regulations (if any) as to Goods or Countries.
Germany, .	Where differential treatment under the tariff is accorded, the importer must declare and, if required, must prove country of origin; and official certificate of origin may then be asked for, and the importer must guarantee by his signature for the correctness of the declaration.				Proof of origin must be given in cases of wine and fresh must of grapes, imported in barrels and tank waggons, if it is desired that rate of duty under Tariff No. 182 be applied.
Italy, .	Certificate necessary in general to secure most-favoured-nation duty under tariff: large class of minor exceptions.	6 forms possible; origin to be established by issuing authority and not by the actual shipper.			Imported meat must also have a certificate issued by an official sanitary authority.
U.S.A.,[1] .	Not generally required, necessary in case of goods imported from Philippines, in which case certificates must be viséd by customs collector or his deputy at port of shipment.		Where goods exceed $100 in value.	Consular visa necessary: declaration at time of visa and declaration at time of import.	Special measures in case of foods and drugs (Reg. 33 under Foods and Drugs Act of 30/6/06); viséd official certificate for imported meat.

[1] This is a summary of the position under § 3 of the Tariff Act of 1913. The original is too long to quote.

adequate to look into the correctness of the values given on invoices, and, as a consequence, the consular certificate on the invoice is to-day, while it is accepted at the smaller ports, where our appraising officers have no means of verifying or disputing it, regarded as almost absolutely worthless at the larger ports, because it carries no personal investigation by the Consul. . . . The ordinary practice is for the clerk in the Consul's office to stamp his name on it, and that transaction is done. If we had our Consuls really make an investigation we would have to quadruple the consular force; they simply have not the men to do the work now. We have in Europe (1913) six confidential agents of the Treasury Department who do the investigating work that theoretically should be done by the consular forces, and our number of agents is too small; it should be doubled, in my opinion. But while the Consul has any amount of time he chooses to take he can decline to consulate an invoice if he believes there is something wrong about it. But as a practical matter, unless we are conducting an investigation, and request the State Department to have an invoice held up, none of them is ever held up. The deputy stamps his name, receives the 2·50 dol. fee, and that is all that happens at the Consulate."

In South American customs practice also we are told that—

"Some of the countries of Latin America require, upon the viséing of the consular invoice at the port of origin by their consular representative, the payment of a consular fee which increases with the invoice value of the goods. Such consular fees are devised for raising revenue, and are an indirect way of increasing the tariff duties. Less attention should be given to this revenue feature of the consular service and more to making it an effective means of customs control in the port of origin. At the present time in practically all cases the Consul merely legalises the invoice, frequently with a rubber stamp, and seldom, if ever, verifies the value or does anything which would assist in the intelligent administration of the customs in his home country." [1]

On the question of the effectiveness of requiring declarations or affirmations of truth it is fairly obvious that this depends on the state of commercial morality on the one hand, the severity of the penalties for fraudulent declarations, and the

---

[1] F.T.C. Report, p. 27.

effectiveness of the supervisory service on the other. It is quite clear that an investigating service operating in a foreign country is at a great disadvantage as the Americans have discovered, since it is likely to encounter difficulties at every turn. The great war has, of course, interfered with the operation of the Special Agents Service in Europe, but even before this event the outlook was not encouraging.[1]

§ 10. We must now turn to the penalties which can be enforced against fraud, with special reference to the *ad valorem* system of duties.

We must distinguish between the act of undervaluation as such, and undervaluation accompanied by false declarations or fraudulent invoices.[2] Undervaluation may be the result of honest error, and must be considered by itself. The general punishment for fraudulent statements or acts is a fine, with or without imprisonment, together with (in some cases) forfeiture of the goods, or any of these punishments separately.

Under the South African Customs Management Act, 1913, Section III.—

"Any person who, knowingly, (*a*) produces any false invoice; (*b*) makes any false misrepresentation in regard to the country in which goods were grown, produced, or manufactured; (*c*) makes any false representation with intent to evade or contravene this Act or any law relating to the customs, shall be liable, on conviction, to a fine not exceeding three hundred pounds, or, to imprisonment without the option of a fine for a period not exceeding twelve months, and all goods in respect of which any false invoice is produced or false representation made, all goods imported, exported, or removed in contravention of this Act, or any such law, and all vehicles and animals used in the importation, exportation, or removal of the goods, shall be liable to forfeiture."

---

[1] I. Newton Hoffmann, *op. cit.*, p. 855, on the general question: *cf.* Higginson, *op. cit.*, p. 53.

[2] The word "declaration" has a general and a specific technical meaning. It may mean the verbal or written affirmation of the truth of statements or documents. But it may also mean the technical act of "declaring"—*i.e.*, furnishing information to the authorities on importation or entry. Hence a false declaration in the last sense may be accompanied by a false declaration of truth in the first sense. In what follows the context indicates what sense the word is being used in. When the British Consul at Rio de Janeiro reported on a new law for punishing discrepancies in declarations stated that "it is evident that the customs authorities are fully aware that false declarations are constantly being made and that steps should be taken to stop such practices," he is using the word in the second technical sense. A.S., No. 5049 (1911-12), p. 8.

In India, under the Sea Customs Act, 1878 (Chapter XVI.), the penalty for mis-description on bill-of-lading required under § 58 of the Act is a fine not exceeding 1,000 rupees, whilst for mis-descriptions on the bill-of-entry of various kinds (XVI., 37) the penalties are "that such packages, with the whole of the goods contained therein, shall be liable to confiscation, and every person concerned in any such offence shall be liable to a penalty not exceeding 1,000 rupees." In the United Kingdom (Customs Consolidation Act, 1876, 39 and 40 Vict., § 168) the "penalty on making false declarations, signing false documents, and untruly answering questions, and counterfeiting and using false documents" is a fine of £100. In the United States [1] "if any consignor, seller, owner, importer, consignee, agent, or other person or persons shall enter or introduce, or attempt to enter or introduce, into the commerce of the United States, any imported merchandise by means of any fraudulent or false invoice, declaration, affidavit, letter, paper, or by means of any false statement, written or verbal, or by means of any false or fraudulent practice or appliance whatsoever, or shall make any false statement in the declarations provided for . . . without reasonable cause to believe the truth of such statement, or shall aid or procure the making of any such false statement as to any matter material thereto without reasonable cause to believe the truth of such statement, or shall be guilty of any wilful act or omission by means whereof the United States shall or may be deprived of the lawful duties, or any portion thereof, accruing upon the merchandise, or any portion thereof" included or referred to in the above-mentioned documents, is liable for each offence to a fine not exceeding 5,000 dollars, and for imprisonment for a time not exceeding two years, and the merchandise liable to forfeiture.

---

[1] § 3, paras. G and H, Act of 1913. In the 1909 Act the imprisonment for false statement might include hard labour. § 28, sub-sec. 6 of that Act. Under-valuation as such is treated in para. 1. If there is established under-valuation there shall be paid "in addition to the duties imposed by law on such merchandise an additional duty of 1 per centum of the total appraised value for each 1 per centum that such appraised value exceeds the value declared in the entry." If, however, the under-valuation exceeds 75 per cent., "except when arising from a manifest clerical error, such entry shall be held to be presumptively fraudulent, and the collector shall seize such merchandise and proceed as in case of forfeiture for violation of the customs laws." The forfeiture applies "to the whole of the merchandise or the value thereof in the case or package containing the particular article or articles which are under-valued."

When we turn to the penalties for undervaluation as such, we find one or both of two methods enforced—the cited method of fines or surtaxes and the method of pre-emption. Let us deal with pre-emption. This is equivalent to hoisting a man with his own petard. The authorities, in other words, buy out the goods at the valuation put upon them by the importer himself. The motives for the action appear very clearly in the Australian legislation on the subject. § 161 of the Australian Customs Act states that—

"(1) For the protection of the revenue against the undervaluation of goods subject to *ad valorem* duties, any goods entered as of a specified value may, at any time before sale and delivery to a person who shall prove to the satisfaction of the collector that he purchased and took delivery in good faith and without any knowledge of the entry and subject as may be prescribed, be purchased by the customs at their declared value with an addition of £10 per centum on the amount of such value.

"(2) The purchase shall be effected by the seizure of the goods by an officer, and written notice of the seizure given to the owner.

"(3) The officer shall remove the goods to a warehouse or some place of security, and the owner shall thereupon be entitled to the purchase money.

"(4) The goods shall become the property of the King immediately on seizure, and shall afterwards be disposed of as may be prescribed, or as the collector may direct.

"(5) A refund, in whole or in part, of any duty paid on the goods may be made by the collector.

"(6) This section shall not limit or restrict any other power possessed by the customs relating to the goods."

Pre-emption is, in fact, a wide-spread practice. In South America "all the countries that levy *ad valorem* duties (in Brazil as well as in the four countries that have valuation tariffs) the customs authorities may take over goods believed to be undervalued at their declared value with an increase sometimes of 5 per cent. and sometimes of 10 per cent. . . . In Paraguay the provision takes a slightly different form. The importer of goods into that country if dissatisfied with the value fixed by the appraiser may 'abandon' the goods to the customs, demanding for them the declared value increased 10 per cent. In Bolivia, Brazil, and Uruguay both pre-emption and abandonment are in force—that is, the appraiser has the right of taking over goods believed to be undervalued, and the importer, similarly, if not willing to pay duties on the appraised value, has the right to demand from the customs authorities the declared value, increased 5 or 10 per cent." [1]

"Abandonment" of the Goods Acts in the opposite direction to pre-emption—it acts as a check on arbitrary valuation by the customs authorities. But, as we have seen, there is no necessity for both forms of check to be incorporated in the customs laws, although it is certainly the more logical procedure. In addition to the cases already cited, we may mention British India,[2] Egypt,[3] and Belgium,[4] where the system is combined with arbitration by experts. In France the system was in operation until 1881, when it was abolished.[5]

It does not require much argument to show that pre-emption as an administrative device falls very short of perfection. M. Orban sums up the matter neatly. The system has "all the effects (portée), and produces all the inconveniences of an expropriation: is the occasion of innumerable frauds: on the other hand, the realisation—that is, the re-sale of the goods by the customs is prejudicial to merchants." If the customs authorities have misjudged the value of the goods there may be a loss on realisation: if the goods are sold carelessly there may be a loss to the customs and injustice to the merchants generally, whilst there may be injustice to a particular importer if the customs officials are at all arbitrary in the exercise of their right to pre-empt.[6] In Belgium the system seems to have aroused much opposition.[7]

We come, then, to the other method of penalising under-

---

[1] T.S., No. 34, "Tariff Systems of S. American Countries," p. 22.

[2] Sea Customs Act of 1878, §§ 31-32.

[3] Pegna, *op. cit.*, pp. 454-6. In E. the right of pre-emption is combined with the right to demand payment in kind. "when the goods are homogeneous the customs retain 8 units out of every 100: if they are of different species or qualities, payment in kind is effected only in the case of the contested articles, at the choice of the customs in taking as basis the prices returned by the declarer (déclarant), when the difference between the declaration and the estimate does not exceed 10 per cent., the choice of the articles to be taken in kind belongs as to one-half to the merchant, and as to one-half by the customs. For indivisible objects—a piano, for instance—the customs pre-empt, in paying over the price declared, increased by 10 per cent."

[4] Higginson, *op. cit.*, pp. 66-69. Orban, "Législation douanière belge," §§ 26-27.

[5] Pallain, vol. i., § 107.

[6] *Cf.* Higginson, *loc. cit.*

[7] See, for proposals of change, Orban, *op. et. loc. cit.*

valuations—by the infliction of fines or surtaxes on the goods. A recent example of such legislation is afforded by § 49 of the South African Customs Management Act of 1913, which runs as follows :—

" If the value so ascertained and declared under any of the provisions hereinbefore contained relating to arbitration exceed by 15 per cent. and not by 30 per cent., the value originally declared by the importer, there shall be payable on the goods in addition to the amount of duty chargeable thereon, a penalty equal to such amount of duty.

If the value so ascertained and declared as aforesaid exceed by 30 per cent., and not by 60 per cent. the value originally declared by the importer, there shall be payable on the goods in addition to the amount of duty chargeable thereon, a penalty equal to three times such amount of duty.

If the value so ascertained and declared as aforesaid exceed by 60 per cent. the value originally declared by the importer, the goods shall be liable to forfeiture, but such goods may be released and delivered on payment of an amount equal to the full duty-paid value of the goods.

" Provided that nothing in this section . . . contained shall effect the forfeiture of goods for which a false invoice has been produced or the punishment for any false declaration made in connection with any such false invoice."

In Holland, the Law of April 20, 1895, as modified by the law of July 9, 1906, imposes the following penalties in § B—consequences of increased valuation—

" Art. 5. In case the declared value is increased in accordance with the fourth paragraph of Article I., the importer shall pay, in addition to the import duty on the amount to which the declared value has been raised, a penalty of five times the duty calculated on the difference between the latter amount and the value originally declared.

" Art. 6. The importer shall pay, in addition to the duty on the value fixed by the inspecting officials, the inspector or his deputy, the committee or the council, a penalty of ten times the duty calculated on the difference between that value and the declared value.

" Art. 7. If in the case referred to in the fourth paragraph of Article I. an increased declaration of value was offered to an amount which was not considered sufficient by the inspector or his deputy, and if, notwithstanding this, the value fixed by the final decision does not exceed that amount, the importer shall only pay, in addition to the duty on the value thus fixed, a penalty of five times the duty calculated on the difference between that value and the value originally declared."

The fourth paragraph of Article I., to which reference is made above, allows the importer to increase his valuation to an amount considered sufficient by the customs officials, so long as this increased valuation is deposited, in writing, before the official statement of disagreement with the valuation is lodged with the importer. The penalty varies, therefore, with the importer's willingness to amend his declaration, and the correctness of his statement in the first instance. If he is both incorrect in his original statement and unwilling to amend the penalty is twice as great.[1]

§ 11. It may at first sight appear as if difficulties of the kind we have just been examining could not occur when the duties levied are specified and not *ad valorem*. This is, however, a misconception of the actual situation. In the first place there are difficulties in establishing what is meant by the exact specific attribute chosen as the basis of assessment. Secondly, the same difficulties as to misrepresentation, falsification, and so forth can occur with specific as with *ad valorem* duties. We must deal with these matters separately.

The most universally occurring problem in the case of specific duties is the determination of the weight of the commodity. We have, on other words, the same situation as occurs in the *ad valorem* treatment of packages. Here again there are two extremes—the goods may be considered as including, for customs purposes, all wrappings, internal and external, or alternatively, all internal and external wrappings may be excluded, to be valued or weighed separately as the case may be, or to be admitted free of duty altogether. These two positions give one the true gross weight and the true net weight of the commodity in question. But a number of intermediate positions are possible which require careful explanation.

(1) There is, firstly, the possibility that, instead of deducting the *actual* weight of wrappings, a fixed allowance is made,

---

[1] Note that the Dutch practice penalises the *ex ess value* found; this is also the South American practice.

by the customs authorities, so that in the event of the true net weight being less than the gross weight minus the allowance the importer loses, unless he is given a choice of declaring or demanding either basis and conversely the customs loses unless it can demand either basis. In this way we arrive at the conception of a "legal weight."

(2) There is, secondly, the question of whether *all* the wrappings are to be included or excluded. We can easily imagine an intermediate stage, in which the outer wrappings only are excluded, and in this way we get the conception of demi-gross weight.

We may now combine the above two sets of points, and we get the following scheme :—

Goods may be dutiable on—

1. Gross weight—
   i.e., Goods plus Interior wrapping plus Exterior wrapping.

DEMI-GROSS WEIGHT.

2. Legal demi-gross weight—
   i.e., Gross weight minus Fixed allowance for exterior wrapping.

3. Real demi-gross weight—
   i.e., Gross weight minus Real weight of exterior wrapping.

NET WEIGHT.

4. Legal net weight—
   i.e., (*a*) Gross weight minus Fixed allowance for all wrappings exclusive of those specifically included by the tariff.
   (*b*) Gross weight minus Fixed allowance for all wrappings.

5. Real net weight—
   i.e., Gross weight minus Real weight of all wrappings.

With or without the right of either customs or importer always to ascertain actual weight.

With or without additional duties for wrappings excluded.

With or without special cases.

A word or two of comment may be added to this table. In estimating tares two special difficulties arise. The first is the difficulty of determining the meaning of "inner" and "outer" wrapping. In some cases it is almost impossible to dissociate the article from the immediate wrapper in which it is contained. Hence, in those cases where an importer may claim the establishment of the real weight—*i.e.*, dispute the official allowance, special conditions have to be laid down as to these immediate receptacles so as to make clear what is the connotation of the definition. Secondly, there is the difficulty that special wrappings of more than usual value may be employed, so as to evade duties altogether in those cases in which wrappings are free, or to cause them to be assessed at possibly lower rates by being associated with relatively inferior goods.

The logical course would seem to be to assess goods and wrappings separately. If the wrappings are included with the goods, then, if the wrappings are valuable, the customs may lose; if they are not, the importer loses because he pays on a heavier gross amount. If the two weight entities are separated, then, if the wrappings are valueless, nothing is lost to the importer, whilst, if they are valuable, nothing is lost by the customs. But both goods and wrappings may be of value, so that elaborate establishment of separate weights, etc., may hardly be worth while.

§ 12. The regulations tend, in practice, to be complicated: a simple outline covering a range of countries is given in the two following pages.

In Canada the position as to the treatment of wrappings is that "usual coverings, except receptacles capable of holding liquids, containing goods subject to a specific duty only not otherwise provided for . . . free.

". . . Receptacles capable of holding liquids when containing goods subject to a specific duty shall be charged with the rate of duty to which the same would be subject if imported separately, except when the coverings and the goods contained therein are rated together in the tariff item.

"Provided, further, that usual coverings designed for use other than in the *bona fide* transportation of the goods they contain shall be charged with the rate of duty to which the same would be subject if imported separately.

"Provided also that the term covering in this paragraph shall include packing boxes, crates, casks, cases, cartons, wrappings, sacks, bagging, rope, twine, straw, or other articles used in covering or holding goods imported therewith, and the

Table of Tare Allowances.[1]

Country.	General Principle.	Detail.
Russia, ...	Legal net weight.	Except where expressly stated in tariff. Calculated by deducting from gross weight a certain percentage for each article and each kind of packing by the official schedule of tare allowances.
Sweden, ...	Legal net weight.	Arrived at by weighing in gross without unpacking, and deductions made by general or special tare allowances. Importers may cause goods to be unpacked for the determination of net weight; so may customs with regard to solids and brandy and spirits, but not with regard to other liquid articles.
Belgium,[2]	(1) Real net weight.	*i.e.*, stripped of all packing if such weight is declared. This is compulsory as regards raw beet sugar and raw cane sugar not imported in coverings used in country of origin.
	(2) Legal net weight.	In all other cases. Gross weight with all recipients, wrappers, and packing whatsoever minus the fixed legal tare allowance. No tare allowance for containers which only imperfectly cover the goods.
Switzerland, . . .	Gross weight	Packing liable to same duty as goods contained therein, if enclosed in habitual packing used in commerce, except when evasion is attempted, when wrappings are dutiable as such according to weight and condition.

[1] F.I.D., 1913, Appendix I.

[2] For further details, Orban, *op. cit.*, §§ 22-23.

TABLE OF TARE ALLOWANCES—*Continued.*

Country.	General Principle.	Detail.
Germany,[1]	(1) Gross weight.	In case of articles dutiable by weight if duty does not exceed 6 marks per 100 kilos., or if the tariff expressly so provides.
	(2) Legal net weight.	Generally determined by deducting from the gross weight the percentage allowances for tare set out in the tariff. Duty is levied on the *actual weight* if (*a*) it is demanded by the importer, except in cases where this would cause inconvenience, *e.g.*, butter—(*b*) if the weight of the packing obviously differs to a considerable extent from the established. Certain groups of coverings and wrappings are always included in the net weight, except (in some cases) where the goods therein contained are dutiable at more than 50 marks per 100 kilos.
France,[2]	(1) Gross weight.	In case of some special articles, forced grapes and fruits, rough watch cases and watch fittings, and goods not dutiable at more than 10 francs per 100 kilos.
	(2) Real net weight.	Goods stripped of all packing, interior and exterior: certain special articles such as gold, platinum and silver, silks, coin, coffee, and generally on products dutiable at 10 francs or less per 100 kilos. *imported unpacked or in bulk.*
	(3) Legal net weight.	Levied in "cases where the party interested claims assessment of duty on the legal net weight (*i.e.*, gross weight minus legal tare allowance), or fails to demand at the proper time that duty shall be assessed on the real net weight." "Packing or receptacles serving as containers, coverings, supports, etc., for imported goods are in principle regarded as having a marketable value, and are consequently dutiable separately, except where the difference between the duty on the goods and the packing does not exceed 10 per cent. of the duty on the goods, and except where the duty on the goods is more than 10 fcs. per 100 kilos., and is levied on gross or demi-gross weight."

[1] "On importation of goods, receptacles commonly employed in trade are to be admitted free of duty" (Tariff Law, § 3).
[2] See "Décret relatif à l'application des droits inscrits au tarif d'éntree" of 27th August, 1911. Pallain, vol. iv., p. 847, *et seq.*

labour and charges for packing such goods, subject to regulations prescribed by the Minister of Customs."

§ 13. The second point with which we have to deal concerns errors and misrepresentation of the physical attributes of the goods. So far as *intent* is concerned, there is, of course, no difference between the two cases, so long—*i.e.*, as we are considering only questions of motive. In either case there may be error, or there may be a deliberate desire to evade the payment of duties. But the direction of misrepresentation or error is different in the two cases.

Error or fraud can occur either in the qualitative or quantitative description of the goods. Under quality is to be understood the nature of the commodity and the specific grade of fineness to which it belongs: under quantitative misdescriptions are included mis-statements as to the weight, number (and where value is a factor), value, and measure of the commodity. It need not be thought that any of these factors are self-evident, and that error, when it occurs, must be due to fraudulent intent. It is obvious that where the grade to which an article is assigned depends not on quantitative but on qualitative or descriptive bases, a legitimate difference of opinion may exist between the importer and the customs authorities. (Similarly, where the official *valuation* is based on qualitative differences an understatement of the value is again not necessarily indicative of fraud.) Goods may lose weight or gain weight on a voyage—*i.e.*, owing to the physical attributes of the commodity it may desiccate or absorb moisture, so that the invoice weight may differ from the weight declared by the importer. Under these circumstances it may be desirable for the authorities to allow a certain "tolerance"—*i.e.*, under or over-statements which do not exceed a certain percentage of error do not render the importer liable to punishment whether for mis-statement or for fraud.

It follows from what we have been stating that goods subject to specific duties require as careful an examination as goods subject to *ad valorem* duties, as will, indeed, be obvious if the reader will recall the elaborate devices for the differentiation of goods subject to specific duties which have been examined in a previous chapter.

The penalties which are enforced follow the lines of those imposed in the case of under-valuation in the case of *ad valorem* duties—*i.e.*, confiscation and surtaxes. The following summary of the French law on the subject, and the subjoined table representing the position in South America, will serve to show the situation better than any detailed description.

The position in France is still governed in the main by the basic Act of 1791, the "Code des douanes."[1] By Chapter II., Article 9, the following particulars are necessary when goods are being "declared":—

(1) "The quality, weight, measure, or number of articles subject to duty by weight, measure, or number, and the value when the goods are subject to duty according to their value. The place of loading and the destination, and, at ports, the name of the ship and that of the captain shall be given," and the marks and numbers of the packages, etc., noted in the margin of the declaration.

(2) Art. 18 of this law dealt with deficiencies on verification, and has been replaced by article 16 of the Finance Law of 28th December, 1895.

Art. 16. Article 18 of Chapter II. of the customs code of 6-22nd August, 1791, is modified as follows:—

"If the merchandise present (on examination) exceeds by more than 5 per cent. the weight, number, or measure declared, the excess shall be liable to the payment of the quadruple duty. For merchandise other than metals, dutiable by weight at 10 francs or less per 100 kilogrammes, the quadruple duty shall become due only if the excess is greater than 10 per cent. of the declared weight."

(3) Art. 20. All excess in the number of bolls, bales, cases, tuns, and casks declared shall be seized, for confiscation to be pronounced against them (pour la confiscation en être prononcée) with a fine of 100 livres (now 100 francs).

(4) Art. 21. If the declaration is false as regards the quality or species of merchandise, and if the duty evaded by this false declaration amounts to 12 livres (now francs) or more, the merchandise falsely declared shall be confiscated, and he making the false declaration shall be condemned to a fine of 100 livres (now francs). If the duty is less than 12 livres, confiscation shall not take place, but only the infliction of the said fine of 100 livres as surety for which the merchandise

---

[1] For text of this Act, see Pallain, vol. iv., espec. pp. 10-11. For commentary, see *ibid.*, vol. iii., pp. 430, §§ 29-32.

shall be retained. The said penalties shall not be enforced in case of theft or substitution legally proved.[1]

(5) Art. 22. In the case that, at the time of inspection (lors de la visite), the bolls, bales, cases, tuns, and casks are found to be less in number than those entered in the declaration, the masters of vessels, carriers, and those who have made the declaration shall be separately condemned to 300 livres fine for each boll, bale, etc., for the surety of which said fine the sea-going vessels, boats, carts, and horses, serving as transport, shall be retained, saving recourse, if it take place, of the captains and carriers against those who shall have made the declaration. There is no " pursuite sur le défaut " in case of theft or shipwreck after declaration made, proof being given.[2]

Now let us turn to South America.[3]

The question arises whether it is not possible for the importer to safeguard himself against the imposition of these heavy penalties. The answer is that if he has reason to believe the invoice, and/or his knowledge of the goods to be defective, he should, so far as the existing law gives him power to do so, voluntarily amend the statement. As will be seen in the case of Argentina such action may not lead to an entire release from penalty, but it certainly does reduce them.

We may now proceed to a somewhat wider investigation of this particular point.

---

[1] " There is not false declaration of species, but importation without declaration (punishable by a fine of 100 fcs.—Law of 16th May, 1863, Art. 9) when the declaration indicates a non-prohibited article when the examination shows that it is a prohibited one, and when the declared merchandise differs absolutely from the merchandise recognised by the service and this latter belongs to a class of mer chandise assimilated to prohibited merchandise." (For legal references, *op. cit.*, vol. iii., p. 431.)

[2] Pallain's comment on this regulation is instructive. " This rule presents a striking example of a fine having at the same time the character of a penalty (peine) and of a civil reparation. The packages entered on the manifest or on the declaration in detail, and not present (on examination) are regarded as having been introduced by fraud. Their introduction has caused the State a loss equal to the duties for which they were liable ; but one did not know the amount of these duties, firstly, because the entries in the declaration and the manifesto could not be checked, then because the manifest does not contain sufficient information for the liquidation of the duties. The legislator treats the law-breaker 'à forfait' ; the State does not claim the duties, but it demands a fine which disembarrasses it from the loss of these duties and will punish at the same time the law breaker, for the fine is well above the amount of the duties which a package of merchandise would normally pay in 1791, even the most heavily taxed. . . ."

[3] T.S., No. 34, p. 42.

Penalties for Inexact Customs Declarations.

[Penalty applied to excess, that is, appraised quantity or value above that declared.]

Countries.	Duty Involved.	Quantity.		Description—*i.e.*, Quality.		Tolerance,
		Weight.	Other.	Kind.	Quality.	
						Per Cent.
Argentina, .	..	Confiscation.	Confiscation.	Confiscation.	Double duty.	1 to 2
If corrected before appraisement.	..	Double duty.	Double duty.	Double duty.	2 % *ad valorem.*	2
Bolivia, . .	0-10 bolivianos	Double duty.	Double duty.	Double duty.	..	
	10-25 ,,	,,	,,	,,	Double Duty.	..
	25 plus ,,	,,	,,	Confiscation.	,,	..
Brazil, . .	0-100 milreis.	1½-5 % of duty.[a]	1½-5 % of duty.[a]	1½-5 % of duty.[a]	1½-5 % of duty.[a]	5[b]
	100 plus ,,	Double duty.[a]	Double duty.[a]	Double duty.[a]	Double duty.[a]	5[b]
Chile, . .	0-25 pesos.	,,	,,	,,	,,	..
	25-100 pesos.	,,	,,	Confiscation.	Confiscation.	..
	100 plus pesos.	Confiscation.	Confiscation.	,,	,,	..
Colombia, . .	..	20 % of duty.[c]	20 % of duty.[c]	Double duty.	Double duty.	10[d]
Ecuador, . .	..	Double duty.	Confiscation.	Confiscation.	,,	10
Paraguay, . .	..	Confiscation.	,,	,,	Confiscation.	5[e]
Peru, . .	5 soles—£5.	Double duty.	Double duty.	Double duty.	Double duty.	5[d]
	More than £5.	,,	,,	Confiscation.[f]	Confiscation.[f]	5[d]
Uruguay, . .	..	Confiscation.	Confiscation.	50 % of duty.	50 % of duty.	..
Venezuela, . .	..	Double duty.[g]	Double duty.[g]	([h])	([h])	5

[a] If there is evidence of fraud, confiscation and fine.
[b] In respect of respect of value.
[c] If quantity is under-stated at least 10 per cent., or over-stated at least 15 per cent.
[d] In respect to quantity.
[e] In respect to quantity. Tolerance in respect to description, only 3 per cent. (percentage of advance in value made by appraiser).
[f] If the duty assessed is less than five times that declared, double duty.
[g] If under-declaration affects more than two packages in a shipment, the fine is increased 25 per cent.
[h] Duty increased by percentage of under-valuation (compare U.S.A. above).

1. In the United Kingdom [1] "no alteration or addition, subsequent to the passing of the entry is to be allowed except by the surveyor upon a satisfactory explanation of the error being given, and, on the request of the merchant, written on the document. Invoices securely attached to the entries may be used as endorsements subject to the above conditions.

The surveyors may allow the amendment of entries without requiring a deposit when the goods are entered under a wrong denomination or omitted to be specified in the proper entry, and the amount of duty involved does not exceed 10s. to the prejudice of the Crown, but the statistical office is to be notified of the amendment at the time when it is allowed.

When liqueurs, cordials, mixtures, and other preparations containing spirits imported in bottle are entered in such a manner as to indicate that the strength is not to be tested, no amendment of the entry which would allow the goods to be tested after the account has been raised is to be permitted without the sanction of the board.

By B.O. 23rd August, 1872, in the case of free warrants requiring amendment for value or description of goods, the amendment is to be made by the surveyor, with whom discretionary power to allow or to refuse amendment, and to detain the goods rests." Further, by B.O.13, 746 of 1898—

"Free entries not to be amended by adding a number of packages to those already entered when the marks and numbers do not justify it. Further entry should be passed for additional packages."

In certain cases there may be amendment of the report which the master of every ship has to make within twenty-four hours after arrival from ports beyond the seas at any port in the U.K. by the Customs Consolidation Act, § 50, subject to the surveyor and officer stating that they are "satisfied with the report."

2. In France the original position taken up by the law was that no changes could be made in a declaration. The ordinance of 1687 stated that "those who shall have given or made their declarations cannot add or take away from it; and the truth or falsity of the declaration shall be judged by that which shall have first been declared." This attitude

[1] See Ham's Year Book, 1918: Vol. I., "Customs," under Importation Art. 46, and Report Art. 25.

was maintained, though in a modified form, by the Code des Douanes of 1791, Article 12 of which, after reciting the above text almost word for word, goes on to add "nevertheless, if, on the day of entry and before inspection (visite), the owners or carriers of the merchandise recognise some error in the declaration as to weight, number, measure, or value, they may rectify the said entries, in presenting again the same number, marks, and numbers of the articles as those stated in the entry, as well as the same *species* of merchandise. After this delay, the goods can no longer be received (in correction)."

The word day was originally interpreted narrowly as "the same day" (la journée même), and not as meaning "within a period of twenty-four hours," but this rule inflicted hardship on merchants, and the more favourable interpretation has now been adopted by the Administration itself.[1]

3. In the U.S.A. the position is stated thus in the customs regulations,[2] Art. 227 :—

"After an entry has been lodged in the custom house no change shall be permitted in the value thereof, except that the importer may, upon application to the collector, be permitted to amend his entry if it shall appear that the invoice or merchandise has not come under the observation of the appraiser." This applies to values in general, by Art. 1,021. "Collectors will make a preliminary examination of all import entries of merchandise, and, when found inaccurate and incomplete, either in the description of articles or in omitting to state proper quantities or values, or for any other error apparent on the face of the import entry, will require the correction thereof before the acceptance of the entry."[3]

§ 14. We now come to the last point which requires examination in this chapter—the settlement of disputes between the customs authorities and the importers. Disputes may take many forms, but those which we will examine here are disputes arising out of the valuation and classification of

---

[1] On the whole question, Pallain, vol. i., § 36.

[2] In referring to Act of 1913, § 3, para. 1, and Treasury decisions, 10,533, 22,543.

[3] This process of amending an entry must be carefully distinguished from the system of entry "by bill of sight." When an importer has no knowledge, or only slight knowledge, of goods consigned to him, he is obviously unable to declare or enter them without further investigation. Entry "by bill of sight" is a provisional entry of such particulars as are known to him, followed by a right to examine the goods in the presence of a customs official for the purpose of compiling a full entry thereafter. *Cf.* United Kingdom, C.C. Act, §§ 58-61.

merchandise. We have already seen something of the methods by which a deadlock can be settled—what are known as the methods of pre-emption and abandonment give customs authorities and importers alike an opportunity of putting the contention of their opponents to a decisive and practical test. Here we are concerned not with these points so much as with processes more or less of a judicial kind which may either be substituted for pre-emption or abandonment, or may be combined with them, so that these last form a reserve power drawn on only if all other methods of arriving at a settlement have failed. Of pre-emption and abandonment we have already seen something in a previous section, here it need only be stated that abandonment in practice is, perhaps, even more apt to be absurd than pre-emption. The danger is that goods will be entered at insufficient values in order that they may be abandoned and repurchased from the customs at prices which, even if higher than those entered, yet will be less than the same goods would have cost, *inclusive* of tariff charges in the normal way—for, since the goods are abandoned to the customs, the importer cannot be charged duties thereon.

"The abandonment of merchandise in the custom house," states an official Uruguayan report,[1] "frequently offers speculative ability a means of defrauding the Treasury. An individual imports a certain lot of parts corresponding to certain manufactured articles, and then requests entry, declaring an insignificant value for the supplementary parts, even though imported in large quantity. If the appraiser tries to increase the appraisement, the merchandise is abandoned. The customs service puts it up for sale at auction ; but naturally, there is no one so interested as the real owner—that is, the one who has in his possession the other parts, which, in connection with the abandoned parts, he can make into complete articles of commercial value. His speculation may result in his buying the abandoned parts for less than he should have paid as duty on them."

In general, to quote from the Federal Trade Commission report in the same connection[2] "the subject of abandonment and subsequent sale of undamaged goods at auction for less

---

[1] Memorandum relative al proyecto de tarifas de aduana, 1910: quoted T.S., No. 34, p. 278.

[2] F.T.C. Report, p. 99.

than the amount of duties and charges legally accruing should not be lightly dismissed as unimportant. If it is possible to place goods on the market at a price below cost plus customs duties and other fiscal charges, and if it is permitted to sell eventually to the highest bidder without regard to these, unfair competition obviously may exist under governmental approval, unconscious as this may be. The danger lies, of course, in the election of one importer to abandon goods, relying on an opportunity to have them subsequently bid in for what they might bring, and of another to clear at returned rates of duty plus other charges. The government, by permitting the entry of goods for consumption upon payment of less than the prescribed amount of duties, creates an undesirable inequality, loses revenue, and confesses that certain tariff provisions are unworkable, without affording uniformly applicable remedy to *bona fide* importers desiring to engage in the trade of articles too highly taxed."

§ 15. We must now turn to the subject of disputes as to valuation and classification. One more preliminary question occurs—is it possible by means of governmental action to reduce the frequency of these disputes? Since what is desired is the minimisation of friction, such governmental action should take the form of offering such information and advice as to reduce the chances of differing interpretations of a given tariff enactment. Two such methods are of great importance—the publication of an official tariff, and the furnishing of detailed advice.

(1) However described, as "tarif officiel," as in France and Belgium, "Gebrauchstarif" (working tariff), as in Switzerland, "Amtliches Warenverzeichniss" (official catalogue of goods), as in Germany, the primary object of the official tariff represents the systematic expansion of the text of the legislative tariff arranged so as to facilitate reference, incorporating as far as possible the official regulations, decisions, and decrees bearing on that text, and including, ranged under the appropriate tariff number or alphabetically, or in both of these ways, as many varieties and subspecies of commodities as possible.

The official tariff represents, in fact, a codification of customs tariff detail. It is not possible for the legislature to include all possible varieties of goods in detailed fashion in the tariff, and, as we have seen in a previous chapter, assimilation by the authorities plays an important part in tariff practice. In addition to this, it is obviously desirable to make known to traders the results of tariff disputes, in so far as they affect the classification of commodities. Hence, the compilations bearing the above titles, which are kept up-to-date by the publication in periodical journals, such as the *Board of Trade Journal*, the *Journal officiel*, the *Handelsarchiv*, and so on, of the most recent decisions and pronouncements.

The question we have so far been discussing must be carefully distinguished from the question of whether such an official compilation possesses any binding authority—*i.e.*, is in any dispute which arises between the customs authorities and importers to be regarded as possessing the same validity as the Legislative Act itself. In so far as the compilation merely embodies decisions arrived at in virtue of judicial processes or regulations or decrees issued by the customs authorities in pursuance of powers conferred on them by legislation, this point does not arise—the validity of the information contained in the guide depends upon the validity of the previous Acts. The point at issue arises when the customs authorities are bound by law to issue such a guide, when, consequently, there is legal authority behind the document itself. In that case is the guide to be regarded as a guide only or as a binding legal instrument in the absence of other decisions? This point has been discussed at some length in the case of Germany. Under the customs law of 1869, § 12, "for the proper application of the Federal Customs Law the official catalogue of goods shall serve." This contains in alphabetical order the individual commodities according to their commercial and other usual designations, and also designates the appropriate tariff number to be used in each case. The constitutional question is whether the official guide possesses the character of an "authentic interpretation of the tariff" or whether it is to be regarded as "in and for itself nothing but a pure administrative regulation (Verwaltungsvorschrift), an instruction for the customs officials?"[1] The constitutional point does not primarily concern us here:

[1] According to Trautvetter, *op. cit.*, pp. 107-115, who discusses the point at some length, the reigning opinion ("herrschenden Ansicht") of the jurists (including the distinguished constitutionalist, Professor Labaad) is for the latter interpretation from the strict standpoint of law, although *actually* "the real importance of the A.W.V. certainly goes much further."

the practical result of the two interpretations will, however, be very different. Were the guide to be regarded (in part or in whole) as law, disputes would be narrowed down to questions of *fact*—*i.e.*, to the question whether a particular article is or is not subsumed under a particular tariff number: if the official tariff is not in itself law, but only an expression of opinion on the part of the customs authorities, disputes can include questions both of law and of fact, for the decisions of the guide itself may be subject to dispute. The area of dispute can, therefore, be greatly widened. In Germany the congress of merchants was in favour of treating the goods catalogue merely as a "Hilfsmittel"—*i.e.*, as registering an opinion of the customs only, and thus not giving it the force of law, in spite of the difficulties which might thus be caused. The importance of the point at issue must not be exaggerated, it concerns only those commodities upon which no other previous decision has been taken. In all other cases the official tariff does not register a new decision, but incorporates principles otherwise arrived at.[1]

(2) The second method open to the government is to give information as to the rate which will be charged if a particular kind of commodity is imported. The German Tariff Law of 1902 contains a statutory enactment to this effect. Art. 2 lays it down that—

"An office shall be opened in every tax district, whose duty shall be to supply, on application, information as to the customs rates chargeable on any merchandise or articles imported into the German customs territory."

In this way legislative sanction is given to a system which

[1] In the case of Switzerland, the context leaves no room for doubt. Art. 2 of the Customs Tariff Law of 1902 states that "goods not mentioned in the tariff are to be referred to their appropriate position by the Federal Council. An official catalogue of goods shall be published and periodically issued." Hence the official tariff clearly has legal competence. In these cases where the executive possesses the power to issue binding orders the question loses its importance altogether, *cf.* § 25 of the Canadian Act of 1903; the Board of Customs is to have power "whenever any difference arises or whenever any doubt exists as to whether any or what rate of duty is payable on any class of goods and there is no previous decision upon the question by any competent tribunal binding throughout Canada" to "declare the rate of duty payable on the class of goods in question or that such goods are exempt from" and "any such declaration . . approved by the Minister of Customs . . . shall have the same force and effect as if such declaration or rate of duty had been sanctioned by statute," subject to appeal to the Governor in Council and the issuance of orders in council thereupon, also having statutory effect.

was in existence for some years before, being inaugurated by a decree of the Federal Council in 1898. Two important principles underlay the application of the decree, and, presumably, still govern the situation.

(1) The information given cannot be made the subject of complaint. If the importer is dissatisfied with the information given him, he can contest the interpretation by import and subsequent appeal.

(2) Should subsequent action by the advising authority or by a superior body lead to a situation unfavourable to the importer—*i.e.*, should the advice be found, in consequence of change of attitude in the interpretation of the law, to have misinformed the importer as to the rates to be charged, "no subsequent demand for higher duties on those shipments will be made which have already gone through all the necessary formalities at the appropriate customs office before the receipt of the new interpretation," and this treatment may even be extended for a period of three months after the change of interpretation, when proof is given that the importation is the consequence of contracts concluded in good faith before the publication of the intended change.

These privileges do not cover changes made in the law, in the official catalogue of goods or in the regulations made in the general executory devices: for these emanate from the central authorities, and the State authorities cannot overrule them without infringing the constitution.[1] (Somewhat similar arrangements exist in the Argentine and in Uruguay.)

§ 15. There are four possible methods by which valuation and classification disputes can be dealt with—

(1) By administrative process.
(2) By administrative court.
(3) By an ordinary court of the land.
(4) By arbitration by independent experts.

These methods are not exclusive, for they can be, and are, in fact, in many cases combined in one system: either as successive stages in a series of appeals, or by two methods being united at one and the same appeal stage—*e.g.*, the court must be guided by the opinion of experts, or a distinction may be drawn between valuation appeals and classification

[1] See on whole question, Trautvetter, *op. cit*, pp. 212-14.

appeals, and different methods may be adopted in the two cases.

The difficulty of making use of the ordinary law courts is explained by the extremely technical nature of the subject matter. Hence, a bias is at once given in favour of some other method of settling disputes. Again, in favour of the administrative process as against the administrative court is the elasticity which the absence of a judicial atmosphere gives. An administrative court, whilst it provides for expert review, tends to develop formalism and rigidity. Perhaps the most easy and simple of all the methods is that of arbitration by experts, but it is less easy of application in classification than in valuation cases.

In many ways the most elaborate system in the world is that of the United States, which may serve as an instance of combination of methods (2) and (3), though predominantly based on the idea of administrative courts. Case (1) is represented especially by Germany and Switzerland: a combination of(3) and (4) by France, whilst the method of calling in experts is very widespread in Europe and outside. We may begin by dealing with the four countries we have already mentioned, and turn to other illustrative material later.

1. Germany and Switzerland.—In Germany the position is governed by § 12 of the Federal Customs Law of 1869, which briefly enacts that—

"Complaints as to the application of the tariff shall, in individual cases, be decided by administrative process" (im Verwaltungswege).

In Switzerland, Art. 36 of the Federal Customs Law of 1893 and Art. 2 of the Tariff Law of 1902 lay it down that—

Appeals against the decisions of the inferior customs bodies as to the use (application) of the customs tariff shall be decided in the last instance by the Federal Council, if necessary after the hearing of the experts.

The executory decree of 12th February, 1895, further defines the position thus—

"§ 168. Appeals or complaints as to the treatment of dutiable goods are to be handed, together with all necessary information, to the executive of the respective customs areas (Direktion des betreffenden Zollgebiets), which shall deal with them in accordance with existing regulations or shall pass them on to the superior customs executive for further treatment.

"§ 169. Appeals in respect of customs treatment will, as a rule, only be considered when the articles in question are still under the control of the customs, or, in the case of proven irregular application of the tariff, on the condition that (the treatment of the) goods has been revised by the customs. Such claims as are made later than two months after liquidation, as well as those which are made in consequence of duty impositions based on the entry, but without official verification, shall not be admissible.

"Against decisions of the area executive appeal shall be made to the superior customs executive, to the customs department against the decisions of the latter, and against the decisions of the customs department to the Federal Council as court of last instance. The decision of the Federal Council shall be final.

"Unless appeals against the decisions of the lower authorities are made to the appellate authorities (Rekursinstanzen) within a period of twenty days from the communication of the disputed decision, the latter shall otherwise have force of law."

This system of administrative decision seems to have aroused much opposition in Germany, both among the mercantile community and the Reichstag: the Opposition demanding either administrative courts or trial before jury courts or other courts—whilst the congress of merchants has demanded a central imperial court "which should decide as to the application of the tariff after sworn evidence submitted by experts," somewhat on the lines of France, as we shall see later. Besides the objections to a judicial settlement of customs disputes already referred to, Trautvetter raises the constitutional plea that the administration of the customs is a matter for the individual states, with which a central court had no right to interfere.[1]

It will be noted that although the Swiss law provides for the calling in of experts to assist in the settlement of cases, the executory decree lays down no rules for this point. Unlike the German system, which leaves detail absolutely on one side, the Swiss regulations provide for a series of appeals, before the court of last instance is reached.

2. We now come to the United States, which provides

---

[1] *Op. cit.*, p. 211.

a very elaborate system. The stages in the process are appeals to a single general appraiser, to a court of general appraisers, from thence to the court of customs appeals, and, finally (in certain cases only), to the supreme court of the United States. The position varies as between valuation cases and classification cases, so that we will deal first with the courts.

In its present shape the system of administrative courts owes its origin to the Act of June 10, 1890: "An Act to simplify the laws in relation to the collection of the revenues."[1] By § 12 nine general appraisers were to be appointed by the President, with the advice and consent of the Senate, with a salary of 7,000 dollars a year, not more than five to be of one political party, and to have no other profession. In general their duties were to "exercise the power and duties devolved upon then by this Act, and to exercise . . . such other supervision over appraisements and classifications for duty of imported merchandise as may be needful to secure lawful and uniform appraisements and classifications at the several ports." Their duties were, (1) as single general appraisers, to hear appeals as to *valuation*, whether from importers or collectors, against the decision of the appraisers; (2) sitting as a court of three general appraisers, to hear appeals against the decision of the single general appraiser in valuation cases, and to sit as a court of *first* appeal in *classification* cases. In classification cases appeal lay from them on questions of law and fact to the "circuit court of the United States within the district in which the matter arises," and from thence, with the permission of the court, to the Supreme Court.

The changes made by the Tariff Act of 1909 so far as the general appraisership system is concerned we can leave on one side for the moment, since it is the system still in force: the main change came in replacing the circuit court by a new administrative court, the Court of Customs Appeals, and

---

[1] S.L., vol. xxvi., ch. 407; also Tariffs Acts, etc., p. 357. The "general appraiser" system dates from 1851, when an Act permitted the appointment of four appraisers, who were to be associated in appeal cases with one outside "discreet and experienced" merchant, so that a mixed court of *two* dealt with cases. As regards classification: in 1839 administrative appeal to the Secretary of the Treasury, and in 1857 appeal by administration *and* to the courts was allowed; before, under the 1839 Act, the two methods were exclusive of one another. See Fairlie, "Nat. Administration of the U.S.," pp. 102-4, and Goss, "History of Tariff Administration in the U.S. (up to 1890)," chap. iii., § 6.

providing for the professional representation of the United States Government.

(*a*) "That a U.S. Court of Customs Appeals is hereby created, and said court shall consist of a presiding judge and four associate judges appointed by the President, by and with the advice and consent of the Senate, each of whom shall receive a salary of 10,000 dollars per annum.

"It shall be a court of record, with jurisdiction as hereinafter provided for. . . .

"After the organisation of said court no appeal shall be taken or allowed from any Board of the United States General Appraisers to any other court, and no appellate jurisdiction shall thereafter be exercised or allowed by any other courts in cases decided by said Board of U.S. General Appraisers, but all appeals allowed by law shall be subject to review only in the Court of Customs Appeals hereby established, according to the provisions of this Act.

"The Court of Customs Appeals established by this Act shall exercise exclusive appellate jurisdiction to review by appeal, as provided by this Act, final decisions by a Board of General Appraisers in all cases as to the construction of the law and the facts respecting the classification of merchandise and the rate of duty imposed thereon under such classification, and the fees and charges connected therewith, and all appealable questions as to the laws and regulations governing the collection of the customs revenue; and the judgment or decrees of said Courts of Appeals shall be final in all such cases."

To some extent this power of finally disposing of questions has been reduced; by an amending Act, c. 267, of August, 1914,[1] to the codifying Act of 1911, in which the above sections of the Act of 1909 had been incorporated, appeal to the Supreme Court of the United States is permissible, in cases involving the construction of the U.S. Constitution, "or any part thereof, or of any Treaty made pursuant thereto, or in any other case when the Attorney General of the U.S. shall, before the decision of the Court of Customs Appeals is rendered, file with the court a certificate to the effect that the case is of such importance as to render expedient its review by the Supreme Court:" but § I. of the Tariff Act of 1909 dealing with rates was expressly excluded.

---

[1] S.L., vol. xxxviii., part 1, p. 703.

(*b*) § 30 of the Act provided that ". . . there shall be appointed by the President, by and with the advice and consent of the Senate, an Assistant Attorney General, who shall exercise the functions of his office under the supervision and control of the Attorney General of the U.S., and who shall be paid a salary of 10,000 dollars per annum; and there shall also be appointed by the Attorney General of the United States a Deputy Attorney General, who shall be paid a salary of 7,500 dollars per annum, and four attorneys, who shall be paid salaries of 5,000 dollars per annum each. Said attorneys shall act under the immediate direction of said Assistant Attorney General, . . . and said Assistant Attorney General, Deputy Assistant Attorney General, and attorneys shall have charge of the interests of the Government in all matters of reappraisement and classification of imported goods, and all litigation incident thereto, and shall represent the Government in all the courts and before all tribunals wherein the interests of the Government require such representation."

Here is, then, a sufficiently complex machinery: let us now see how it works.

(1) *Valuation.*—Appeal lies from the appraiser to a single general appraiser, whether the dissatisfied party is the importer or the collector. This constitutes reappraisement. Appeal lies from the single general appraiser to the Board of General Appraisers, which, § 12 of the Act of 1909 says, "shall be divided into three Boards of three members each, to be denominated respectively Board 1, Board 2, and Board 3. The President of the Board shall assign three general appraisers to each of said Boards, and shall designate one member of each of said Boards as chairman thereof, and such assignment or designation may be by him changed from time to time . . . each of the Boards of three general appraisers, or a majority thereof, shall have full power to hear and determine all cases and questions arising therein or assigned thereto . . . the decision . . . of the Board of three general appraisers, in all appraisement cases, shall be final and conclusive against all parties, and shall not be subject to review in any manner for any cause in any tribunal or any court. . . ."

(2) *Classification* cases go to the Board of General Appraisers as the court of first instance, thence to the Court

of Customs Appeals, and, in those cases specified by the law, to the Supreme Court of the United States.

How does this system work? In the first place, classification cases take up more time than valuation cases. Secondly, the Board tends to become judicial in character. Both these points come out in the evidence given by Mr. Curtis before the Tariff Committee of the House of Representatives [1]—

"The Board of General Appraisers began as a Board of Review under the Secretary of the Treasury. It has gradually grown away from that theory and become a court. The Board spends most of its time and effort in classification cases. While that is interesting business—studying what the language of a particular Act means as applied to a given piece of merchandise—it is not half so important as what that piece of merchandise is worth. When it comes to collecting the revenues of the Government the appraisal of the merchandise is far more important than the classification. Classification is merely a question of reading the statute and knowing what the merchandise is, in tariff language, by an accurate description. Appraisal is work where you have got to dig in and find out what have been the financial transactions concerning that piece of merchandise, and what have been the same type of transactions in the country of origin, because our statute, I think very properly, makes the tariff value of a piece of merchandise the foreign wholesale market value in the country of export.

"The Board spends more time on classification cases than on re-appraisement cases. They are only human in that. I think if I were in their place I would feel inclined to do that too. But they are slighting the real important part of collecting revenue from customs, and it is not proper to slight it."

The amount of work which the classification cases provides is certainly very great, and is out of all comparison to the number of re-appraisement cases.[2]

In this connection the Tariff Act of 1913 tried to check

---

[1] *Op. cit.*, pp. 6307-8.

[2] The latest figures I have been able to obtain are those for 1911 and 1912. In those two years the classification cases received were 121,187 and 96,099 respectively; decided were 66,419 and 120,801 respectively; and suspended were 51,524 and 9,256 respectively. The appraisements dealt with by single appraiser were 4,537 and 5,480 respectively; Boards of general appraisement were 1,468 and 1,670 respectively: and pending were 784 and 1,140 respectively.

the inflow of appeals by attempting to curb two presumed abuses of the system as it then was—the absence of any fees charged by the court, and the practice of lawyers in fighting cases on the "contingent fee" system—that is, charging their clients a fee only if the case were successful. The U.S. Treasury was strongly of opinion that both the absence of a protest fee and the "contingent fee" system led to an abuse of the whole system. The 1913 Act provides (paragraph M) for the deposit of a fee of 1 dollar for each *entry* in the case of valuation cases, and (paragraph N) for the deposit of a fee of 1 dollar with respect to each *protest*, in the case of classification cases, the fee to be returned in the event of the protest being sustained. The Government was defeated in its own administrative courts on the question of the interpretation of clause N, and, as the law then stood—*i.e.*, that a protest might cover more than one entry—seemed hardly likely to do much to check the stream of protests.[1]

The Act provides, as regards contingent fees (paragraph N) that "no agreement for a contingent fee in respect to recovery or refund under protest shall be lawful. Compliance with this provision shall be a condition precedent to the validity of the protest and to any refund thereunder, and a violation of this provision shall be punishable by a fine not exceeding 500 dollars, or imprisonment for not more than one year, or both."

3. **France.**—In France[2] disputes as to customs interpretation take place in the ordinary civil court—before the juge de paix, but the power of the judge is severely restricted by the necessity of employing and being guided by expert opinion. The essence of the French system is, therefore, "expertise"—the details now require to be examined.

Until 1881 valuation cases were decided by pre-emption in cases of suspected under-valuation, but since that year the procedure is the same for classification and for valuation cases. The practice of calling in experts dates from the 17th century (the ordonnance of 1687, titre I., art. 5, which speaks of "gens à ce connaissant)." The system was continued by Art. 2 of the decree of 5th August, 1810, and the law of 27th July,

---

[1] On this dispute and the findings, see I. Newton Hoffmann, *op. cit.*, p. 859. The test case was U.S. *v.* M'Coy Co. (T D 34,445), decided May 4, 1914.

[2] Pallain, I., § 105, and iv. passim, for text of Acts, etc., referred to.

1822, Art. 19. By that law "there shall be attached to the Ministry of the Interior (subsequently (1831) the Ministry of Commerce) three expert commissioners charged with resolving doubts and difficulties which may present themselves relatively to the nature (espéce), origin or quality of products, whether in the application of duties, bounties, or colonial privileges. . . . The ministry shall add, at each dispute, according to its nature, at least two merchants or manufacturers who shall have a consultative voice."

The system was greatly changed by the law of May 7, 1881, which, says Pallain, represents "une modification profonde . . . des ce moment l'expertise légale perd le caractére administratif, qu'elle avait au debut." By Art. 4—

"The two merchants or manufacturers added to the expert commissioners at each tariff dispute shall in future be appointed, one by the customs, the other by the importer (déclarant), and chosen from the list drawn up each year by the Chamber of Commerce of Paris. In the event of one of the parties refusing to designate its arbitrator, the choice shall be made from the same list by the civil judge of the canton in which the office of import is situated, at the request of the other party. *If the two experts agree, the commission of legal experts shall register their decision, which shall be final.* In case of disagreement, the commission . . . will assume the function of third arbitrator, and decide in the last instance."[1]

The tariff law of 1892 again modified the details by Art. 9. The list was in future to be drawn up each year "by the Ministers of Commerce, of Industry, and the Colonies and Finance after consultation with the chambers of commerce. These chambers shall transmit their proposals to this effect to the Ministry of Commerce each year. This list shall comprise persons possessing, either through practice of commercial or industrial operations, or by their technical knowledge of agriculture, commerce, or science, a special competence for the subjects in dispute."

For a long time, when the expert commissioners were deciding a case, they made a practice of calling in, in a purely consultative capacity, other experts who seemed to them to present special guarantees of competence, to advise on the

[1] Further, by Art. 2 of that Act, *value* was added to the subjects on which expertise was to be practised.

samples presented. This was condemned by a judgment (arret) of the highest civil court—the Cour de Cassation—a judgment rightly condemned by Pallain as "depriving the arbitrators of legitimate assistance.[1]

To sum up on the French system—

(1) On the four points in question the method of expertise is the sole process admissible, and the courts cannot substitute "their own judgment for that of the experts, nor have recourse to modes of proof other than legal expertise to decide in disputes of this nature which arise between the administration and the importers."

(2) But if these said points are not in dispute, the judge need not have recourse to expertise, and the process is only applicable to goods still in the hands of the customs.[2], [3].

We have now passed under review the appeal regulations of some great commercial countries: what is the position in the United Kingdom? There the law has incorporated with the principle of appeal to the courts an appeal to administrative settlement.

(1) By § 30 of the Customs Consolidation Act, "if any dispute shall arise as to the *proper rate of duty payable on any*

---

[1] "The experts cannot, whatever be their lights, know by themselves the totality of articles. If they are to decide with the sole help of the contradictory statements of the customs experts and the importer, they will be far from being able to decide."

[2] For exact details of the appeal to the court if the déclarant refuses arbitration, the sealing and despatch of samples, their weight, etc., see Pallain, note to § 108.

[3] The following comments of Pallain (notes 1 and 2 to I., p. 89) may interest the student of exact detail :—

"1. The experts have *not* to indicate the category of the tariff into which the product in question enters—which would constitute the solution of the question of law—but merely its nature, species, origin or value. The *judge* then decides if the terms of the decision of the experts proves the falseness of the declaration in a sense prejudicial to the Treasury."

"2. The judge is only tied by the decision of the experts when the question in dispute is relative to the basis upon which duty should be imposed (' qu'autant qu'il s'agit de contestations relatives à la base d'application des droits '). On the contrary, when it is a question of determining the value of articles serving to fix the amount of a *penalty*, the experts have no right to intervene ; it rests with the judge ' au fond ' to determine this value, after having sought advice, if necessary, in ordering a process of instruction according to the terms of the common law.

"In the same way, so far as duties *ad valorem* are concerned, the judge evaluates independently the amount of the freight which constitutes one of the elements of the value of the merchandise at the place where it is declared for the payment of duties.

"The judges are also not required to order an expert examination to verify the exactness of a customs declaration when their views are founded on the terms of the case itself, ' lorsqu'ils trouvent dans la cause les éléments de leur conviction.' "

goods admissible for home consumption, the importer or consignee, or his agent, shall deposit in the hands of the collector of the customs at the port of importation the duty demanded by such collector, which shall be deemed and taken to be the proper duty payable, unless an action or suit shall be commenced by the importer within three months after such deposit in one of His Majesty's courts of law at Westminster, Dublin, or Edinburgh against such collector, *to ascertain whether any and what duty is payable on such goods* . . ."

If the action establishes that an excess of duty was charged, the deposit shall be returned, or such part as represents the excess "with interest thereon after the rate of five pounds per centum per annum for the period during which the sum so paid or returned shall have been deposited; and shall be accepted by such importer in satisfaction of all claims in respect of the importation of such goods and the duty payable thereon, and of all or any damage and expenses incident thereto."

(2) In case any "dispute shall arise between any merchants or other persons, and any officer of customs, as to the seizure or detention of any ship or goods, or as to any apparently accidental omission, inadvertency, or non-compliance with the laws and regulations relating to the customs, the commissioners may determine such dispute as they may deem just, and if they find that penalty or forfeiture has been incurred, they may mitigate or remit the same."

(*a*) If the dispute has occurred in the *port of London*, the aggrieved person may demand to state his case to the commissioners personally, or demand a public inquiry, one of the said commissioners . . . "shall hear the matter in the presence of the parties, and of any persons interested or desirous of attending," evidence on oath shall be taken, the commissioner "reducing the same into writing in a narrative form, and shall lay the same, with his opinion thereon, before the Commissioners of Customs for their consideration; and such commissioners shall have the same power and authority for enforcing order during such enquiry as is vested in justices of the peace in petty sessions."

Any decision taken thereupon by the commissioners "in case any penalty or forfeiture shall be adjudged thereby, shall have the same force and effect as a legal conviction for penalties by a justice of the peace," unless within a week the person adjudged gives notice of refusal, in writing, when "the party against whom such order shall have been made shall have the same remedy by action at law as if no such order had been made."

(*b*) At the outports "the like inquiry shall be held by any collector or other person deputed for that purpose by the Commissioners of Customs, in the same manner in all respects, and with the like authority for maintaining order, as hereinbefore provided with reference to inquiries in the port of London." [1]

Cases in which arbitration or valuation by experts is decisive without the intervention of any legal or administrative authorities are South Africa (Customs Management Act, § 47): Sweden (instructions to be observed in applying the customs tariff, § 3): the consultation of experts is made obligatory by the administrative official having the final decision (with further appeal to the Superintendent of Customs) in the case in Chile (law of March 1, 1916, Art. 20). Holland [2] proceeds by administrative commission: Australia, in valuation disputes, makes use of experts (two appointed, one each by the contending parties, with a third appointed by the other two as arbitrator if there is disagreement).[3] We may end this chapter by giving the position in some other South American countries, summarised from the reports already cited.

Argentina.—Alternative methods: (1) appeal to commission of appraisers; or, where no such commission exists, to the collector; (2) where collector is also the original appraiser, cases go to arbitration before three disinterested persons, two selected, one by customs and one by consignee, the third chosen by the other two. Appeal lies from thence to the Minister of Finance.

Brazil.—Appeals go to the chief appraiser, who submits question at issue for advice to the tariff commission of every custom house appointed by the Minister of Finance. Appeal

[1] C.C.A., §§ 32-38. The only rules made in pursuance of the power conferred by § 38 as to these matters were those "set out in a general order of the Commissioners dated the 19th of November, 1853. The rules were framed with reference to the corresponding provisions in the C.C.A., 1853." Highmore, *op. cit.*, p. 44.

[2] Valuation law of April 20, 1895, as modified by law of 1906, and law of May 27, 1907.

[3] § 158 of the Customs Act, 1901-1910. Statutory rules, 1913, No. 346, §§ 112-122.

lies in certain cases—where the difference between the duties claimed by the customs and those on the basis of the importer's declaration exceeds a given amount—varying from custom house to custom house, to the board of arbitrators, which "consists of four experts appointed by the inspector of the customs, and they are obliged to serve under penalty of being deprived of all privileges granted by the customs laws. The proceedings are carried on under oath to act impartially, and all decisions must be reached by a majority vote. In case there is a tie vote the customs inspector is required to decide the question. The decisions of the Board of Arbitrators are not regarded as precedents for future action."[1]

In **Uruguay, Bolivia** and **Peru** also the use of experts forms a part of the procedure in some or all cases, whilst, in Colombia, the Customs Board, to which appeal must be made, has an outside member appointed by the House of Representatives.

For the settlement of valuation disputes the method of expertise certainly seems the most obvious and the "fairest" method. As far as classification is concerned, the case of France shows that even a great commercial country does not find it difficult to make use of the expert arbitrator in this connection, but here, perhaps, an administrative court constantly employed in the determination of the meaning of trade and tariff terms would seem to be better. At any rate, the foregoing analysis will have shown that there is no lack of variety in the institutions dealing with grievances, although, so far as valuation is concerned, one method seems to be predominantly employed.

---

[1] T.S., No. 34, p. 136.

NOTE I. TO CHAPTER IX.

On some Exceptions to the General Rule.

1. We have seen in the chapter above that, in a number of cases, the valuation basis is wholesale market value at the time of sale or export, with or without additions. It may, however, not always be possible to discover what the wholesale market value is, and there may be no wholesale market value at all. In these cases an alternative basis of valuation must be provided for the guidance of the appraiser.

In the United States the following, paragraph L of § III. of the Act of 1913, provides ways of escape :—

(*a*) When market value cannot be ascertained satisfactorily.

" When the actual market value, as defined by law, of any article of imported merchandise, wholly or partly manufactured, and subject to any *ad valorem* duty, or to a duty based in whole or in part on value,[1] can not be ascertained to the satisfaction of the appraising officer, such officer shall use all available means in his power to ascertain *the cost of production* of such merchandise at the time of exportation to the United States, and at the place of manufacture, such cost of production to include the cost of materials and of fabrication, and all general expenses to be estimated at not less than 10 per centum, covering each and every outlay of whatsoever nature incident to such production, together with the expense of preparing and putting up such merchandise ready for shipment, and an addition of not less than 8 or more than 50 per centum upon the total cost as thus ascertained ; and in no case shall such merchandise be appraised upon original appraisal or reappraisement at less than the total cost of production as thus ascertained."

(*b*) When there is no open market value.

---

[1] *I.e.*, the clause covers, not only *ad valorem* duties, but compound duties, and classifications based on value, even though the duty be specific.

" The actual market value or wholesale price as defined by law of any imported merchandise which is consigned for sale in the United States, or which is sold for exportation to the United States, and which is not actually sold or freely offered for sale in usual wholesale quantities in the open market of the country of exportation to all purchasers, shall not, in any case, be appraised at less than the wholesale price at which such a similar imported merchandise is actually sold or freely offered for sale *in usual wholesale quantities in the United States*, due allowance, *by deduction*, being made for estimated duties thereon, cost of transportation, insurance, and other necessary expenses from the place of shipment to the place of delivery, and a commission not exceeding 6 per centum, if any has been paid or contracted to be paid on consigned goods, or profits not to exceed 8 per centum, and a reasonable allowance for general expenses (not to exceed 8 per centum) on purchased goods."

2. In Australia, by § 160 of the Customs Act, 1901-10.

" Whenever it is difficult to determine the value of goods for duty, either because the goods are not sold for use or consumption in the country of production, or because a lease of the goods or the right of using the same is sold or given but not the right of property therein, or because the goods have a royalty imposed thereon, and the royalty is uncertain, or is not a reliable means of estimating the value of the goods, or because the goods are usually or exclusively sold by or to agents or by subscription, or are sold or imported in or under any other unusual or peculiar manner or conditions (of all which matters the minister shall be judge), *the minister may determine the value for duty of the goods.*"

NOTE II. TO CHAPTER IX.

On Some Definitions of Customs Terms.

Reference has already been made in the preceding chapter to the difficulties which may be associated with the definition of such terms as "import" and "export," "importer" and "exporter," and so on. In this note a few quotations from Tariff Acts and legal decisions are given which may go to show how the matter is dealt with textually and administratively. The following quotation may serve to show how important precision in definition may be. In one of the undervaluation cases in the United States the goods in dispute were in a bonded warehouse:—"The Government tried to seize the goods on the ground of fraud, but the importer resisted the attempt in the courts by holding that goods in bonded warehouse are not actually in the commerce of the country, and that before he presented the formal entry papers at the custom house there was no telling whether or not he would place the correct valuation on the goods."[1] On appeal, the Government won, but the experience led directly to a re-definition of the term "false entry" in the 1913 Act, which now includes a paragraph (§ III., paragraph 11) to the effect that "*The arrival within the territorial limits of the United States of any merchandise consigned for sale* . . . and the acceptance of a false or fraudulent invoice therefor . . . shall be deemed to be an attempt to enter such merchandise, notwithstanding no actual entry has been made or offered."

1. The words italicised in this quotation bring one directly to attempts to define the act of importation. By the South African Customs Management Act (§ 119) "import," "importation," or "importing" "shall mean to bring or the bringing of goods into the Union." This attempt to define, by reference to a territorial conception, of course raises the question of

---

[1] U.S. *v.* 25 packages of Panama hats (231, U.S. 358), quoted by I. Newton Hoffmann, *op. cit.*, p. 864.

what is meant by a country for customs purposes, and, as the American "Island Cases" show, this is by no means always a simple matter.

We may now turn to some American definitions[1] of the act of importation. An early American decision lays down that "the arrival of a vessel at her port of destination constitutes an importation." Quite consistent with this is the decision that "any importation is complete when the goods are brought within the limits of a port of entry with the intention of unloading them, and the right of the Government to duties accrues immediately upon importation. It is immaterial that before being unladen from the vessel the merchandise was lost overboard, so that the customs officers could not retain control over it."

2. *Importer* is defined in the U.K. Customs Consolidation Act, § 284.[2] "'Importer' shall mean, include, and apply to any owner or other person for the time being possessed of or beneficially interested in any goods at and from the time of the importation thereof until the same are only delivered out of the charge of the officers of customs," whilst in South Africa—

"Importer shall not include a person outside the Union who consigns goods thereto, but shall mean, in relation to goods, the person who actually brings the goods into the Union, or any person in the Union for the time being possessed of or beneficially interested in any goods at and from the time of the importation thereof."

In the United States, 1913 Act, § III., paragraph B, ". . . all merchandise shall, for the purpose of this Act be deemed and held to be the property of the person to whom the same is consigned, and the holder of a bill of lading duly endorsed by the consignee therein named, or, if consigned to order, by the consignor, shall be deemed the consignee thereof; and in case of the abandonment of any merchandise to the underwriters the latter may be recognised as the consignee."

---

[1] "Compilation of Customs Laws and . . . Decisions Thereunder," 2 vols., 1916. Importation defined, pp. 9, 11, 12, 1599, 1661, 1741. "In the case of the Algoma Central Ry. Co. *v.* Rex (1903), A.C. 478, it was held by the Privy Council, upon the construction of the Customs Tariff (Canada) Act, 1897, by which a duty is imposed upon foreign-built ships, that a ship was imported into Canada when it entered a Canadian port or harbour. Highmore, "Customs Laws," p. 45.

[2] See also definition in the Sale of Food and Drugs Act, 1899, § (1), (2). Highmore, *op. cit.*, p. 344.

3. *Time of Importation.*—A very full definition is given in the U.K. C.C.A., § 40—

"Such time shall be deemed to be the time at which the ship importing such goods actually came within the limits of the port at which such ship shall in one course be reported and such goods be discharged;" *but*, by the Finance Act of 1901 (1 Edw. VII., c. 7), § 7 (2)—"As respects the first levying or repealing of any duty of customs (including any duty imposed by this Act), the time at which the importation of any goods shall be deemed to have had effect shall be the time at which the entry of the goods under the Customs Act is delivered instead of the time mentioned in § 40 of the Customs Consolidation Act, 1876."

In the U.S.A. date of importation is defined (Customs Regulations, Art. 222: T.D. 26,219) in much the same way—

> "The date of importation is the date of arrival of the vessel at a port with intent to unload. In case the importing vessel enters two or more United States ports the date of importation will be the date of arrival of the vessel at the port at which the merchandise is landed . . ."

4. *Imported Merchandise.*—"*Every commodity having a value* brought within the limits of the United States is imported merchandise within the meaning of the customs law." [1]

5. *Country and Principal Markets.*[2]—"The term 'country' as used in the law, is to be regarded as embracing all the possessions of a nation however widely separated, which are subject to the same supreme executive and legislative authority and control.

"Merchandise imported from one country, being the growth, production, or manufacture of another country, will be appraised at its actual value in the principal markets of the country from which immediately imported. If it appears from the invoice, bill of lading, or other evidence that the merchandise was destined for the United States at the time of original shipment it will be appraised at its value in the principal markets of the country from which originally exported."

6. *Time of Exportation.*[3]—"For the purpose of ascertaining

---

[1] "Digest of Decisions, etc.," vol. ii., p. 1661.

[2] Arts. 576-577 of U.S. Customs Regs. based on a series of Treasury Decisions.

[1] *Op. cit.*, Art. 578.

the market value the appraiser shall consider the date on which merchandise actually leaves the country of exportation to the United States as the date of exportation, which date may be established by the date of sailing of the vessel from the foreign port as declared to by the master on entry or by a bill of lading showing the date of shipment certified by the American Consular officer.

"Merchandise shipped from an interior country, intended for exportation through the ports of another country to the United States is exported within the meaning of the law when it begins its journey to the United States from the interior place of shipment, and the time of exportation may be established by the date of the bill of lading, certified before an American Consular officer and noted on the certificate attached to the invoice, such consular certification to be accepted in the absence of conclusive evidence to the contrary."

NOTE III. TO CHAPTER IX.

Payment of Customs Duties.

There are several ways in which the general right of the Government of a country to determine the mode in which, and the time at which, taxes are to be liquidated affects the tariff position. By the regulations drawn up in these respects the severity of the rates established may be very considerably increased. This is especially the case with regard to the *mode of payment*—*i.e.*, the determination of the particular species of money in which the debt owing to the Government must be met.

There is no difficulty so long as the Government maintains effective parity between various species of coin—*e.g.*, between gold and silver or gold and paper. In either case the liquidation of customs duties in one only of these forms of money will not affect their incidence, although it may somewhat affect the convenience of the payee. For if there is effective parity or equivalence of value it should be possible *normally* to convert one species of money into another, and thus liquidate the debt in the particular form demanded—normally, because, if the Government, by heavy penalties, forbids the desired species to be bought at a premium, and this prohibition is effective through fear of consequences, there is no guarantee that the desired species *will* be forthcoming, and, as a consequence, the position is very different, amounting in extreme cases to a virtual prohibition of import. This is, however, only a special case of the general principle to which we now desire to draw attention—viz., that the emergence of a discount or a premium on the particular species of coin or money in which customs duties are by law payable will reduce or add to the height of the duty wall.

Let us first of all look at the situation from the standpoint of principle. Suppose a country in which gold is at a premium of 20 per cent. as compared with paper money, so that 100 gold units will purchase as much as 120 paper units of money. If the duties to be liquidated amount to 500 money units, it will make a great difference to the importer whether these money units are paper money or gold money units. Suppose they are gold. In that case to get the gold he will have to part with 120 paper units to buy 100 gold units, and to buy 500 gold units he will have to give $\frac{120 \times 500}{100}$ paper units = 600 paper units. In other words, the actual duties are 20 per cent. higher than the nominal amount owing to the premium on the species of money in which they are payable. Conversely, when the coin or other money in which the duty is payable is at a discount in terms of other forms of money, those who possess the latter find the actual weight, as distinguished from the nominal weight, of the duties diminished.

It follows that countries which have silver or paper currencies nominally worth so much gold, but actually below their nominal gold values can increase the burden of customs duties by the simple expedient of requiring that the customs duties shall henceforth be payable in gold—a fact which has largely been made use of.[1]

This device of demanding part or whole payment of customs

---

[1] *Cf.* explanatory note to the official translation of the Spanish tariff of 1906 states that :—

(2) In accordance with the law dated the 20th March last, promulgating the bases on which the revision of the former tariff was to proceed, it was enacted that all duties are to be levied in gold instead of in silver as hitherto. This provision is, of course, by itself equivalent to an increase in the tariff rates (Cd. 3066 of 1906). As for later legislation :—

" For the application of the law of December 24, 1912, to take effect on January 15, 1913, it has been decided that in payment of the customs duties in gold the following shall from that date be accepted for their full value :—

" Spanish gold coins ; gold coins of countries of the Latin-union, of the United Kingdom and Germany ; Bank of France or Bank of England notes.

" Drafts or cheques on Paris, London, or Berlin, provided they be payable respectively in francs, pounds sterling, or marks, and be duly guaranteed. Until further notice, and owing to the present monetary depreciation in relation to the par equivalent of gold at Brussels, the acceptance of drafts and cheques on that city is suspended. Payments amounting to less than 10 pesetas, and amounts on goods verbally declared by passengers may continue as heretofore to be settled in silver money with a surtax equal to the average price of the franc during the month preceding the month of payment." *Cf.* the position in China. The tariff is drawn up on the basis of the Haikwan tael, reckoned as equal to 2s. 5/16d. Rule I. appended to the tariff states that " imports unenumerated in this tariff will pay duty at the rate of 5 per cent. *ad valorem*, and the value upon which duty is to be calculated shall be the market value of the goods in local currency. This market value when converted into Haikwan taels shall be considered to be 12 per cent. higher than the amount upon which duty is to be calculated." This reduction has reference to the question of whether duty has been included in price or not, since in the case of c.i.f. contracts without duty there is no reduction : the point for us is the con-

duties in the form of currency appreciated or depreciated in relation to other forms makes the calculation of customs duties at times an exceedingly complicated matter. To show the degree of complexity which may be attained, the case of Brazil will be examined at some length. Our standpoint will be found somewhat different to that of the American report in which the material facts can be most easily found.[1]

The currency of Brazil is paper, which the Brazilian authorities assess in terms of foreign (gold) currency at the fixed rate of one paper milreis to twelve pence. The gold milreis is worth at par 27 pence. Of the total debt owing to the customs, a given percentage must be liquidated by purchasing, not gold, but gold drafts or "vales" at the Banco de Brésil, the price of the vale being fixed by the bank each week "in accordance with the average exchange rate of the paper milreis for the preceding week." Up to 1905 the regulations fixed the proportion payable in gold at 35 per cent. of the total duty: in that year the proportion was raised to 50 per cent. unless for 30 consecutive days the rate of exchange for paper milreis was less than 15d. (later 16d.). In 1914 the fall of exchange rates led to a return to the old proportion of 35 per cent., and, in 1916, this was again changed to 40 per cent.[2] What we have now to do is to follow out the working of these regulations in detail.

(A) When the real exchange value of the paper milreis is greater than 12d.—*e.g.*, when it is worth, say, 16 pence in reality, the fixed rate of exchange increases the burden of the duty; when the real value of the milreis is less than 12d., say, 8 pence, then the fixed rate of conversion reduces the burden of the duty.

---

version into a given currency, which may raise or lower the duty according to the value of the local currency.

As to general regulations as to mode of payment, *cf.* the following:—United Kingdom, Customs Consolidation Act, § 17, "All duties, rates, charges, and drawbacks . . . shall be paid and received in every part of the United Kingdom in British currency." In *Germany*, in so far as exceptions have not been made for import certificates, duties are payable in German imperial currency according to the specifications of the mint law. (Trautvetter, *op. cit.*, p. 209.)

For some details as to Italy, see Fontana-Russo, *op. cit.*, § 110, especially pp. 511-12. Other countries which have maintained the obligation to pay in gold at a time of depreciation of the currency are Russia, Austria-Hungary, and the United States during the Civil War period.

[1] T.S., No 34, pp. 116-19.

[2] These figures and the context must now be regarded as purely illustrative; for the latest information as to Brazil see Note IV. to this chapter.

For instance, £10,000 worth of goods, paying 5 per cent. *ad valorem*, pay—

(1) At the fixed rate of 12d. per paper milreis, . £500 or 10,000 milreis.

If the actual rate were adopted—

(2) At the rate of 16d. per paper milreis, .	£500 or 7,500 milreis, or 25 °/₀ less in milreis.
(3) " 8d. " .	£500 or 15,000 milreis, or 50 % more in milreis.

(B) But we have also to take into account the conversion of paper milreis into gold milreis to the extent of 40 per cent.

Suppose the paper money debt to be 10,000 milreis as above. Under the 40 per cent. rule he must change 4,000 paper milreis into gold milreis, and the question is, as to what this will cost him. The gold vale is nominally worth 27d., the gold value of the paper milreis may be 27d. or less. Suppose it to be had at 16d. Then one paper milreis will only buy 16/27 of a gold milreis. The importer must, however, buy 4,000 gold milreis. His total payment in paper milreis will be—

Under actual conditions when the milreis is worth 16d. per milreis, and the paper debt is first calculated on the basis of one paper milreis being worth 12 pence	6,000 plus 27/16 (4,000) or 12,750 paper milreis.
Whereas if before conversion into gold he had been allowed to calculate the paper debt at the actual exchange value of the paper milreis he would have paid	6/10 (7,500) plus 27/16 (4/10 of 7,500) = 4,500 plus 27/16 (3,000) or 9,562.5 paper milreis.

Or, as things are, he pays an additional amount due to—

(1) Conversion into gold of . . . 2,750 paper milreis.
(2) Conversion into gold at a different rate to conversion into paper of . . 3,187.5 paper milreis.

Under actual conditions, when the paper milreis is worth 8d. per milreis, an importer pays on a paper debt of 10,000 milreis	6,000 plus 27/8 (4,000) = 19,500 paper milreis.
Whereas if there were conversion throughout on the bases of the actual exchange value of the paper milreis he would pay	9,000 plus 27/8 (6,000) = 29,250 paper milreis.

Or, as things are, he pays an additional amount due—

(1) To conversion into gold of . . . . 4,500 paper milreis.

But he gains by

(2) Conversion into paper at a different rate to conversion into gold of . . . . 9,750 paper milreis.

We may now proceed to sum up as to the effects of the Brazilian system of converting into gold a fixed proportion of the paper debt due.

So long as the paper milreis is worth less than the gold milreis, to change from the former to the latter is in effect to raise the duties: and the rise in the duties is greater the greater the percentage to be converted, and the greater the premium on gold. If *all* the paper debt had to be converted, and the gold milreis were worth twice the amount of the paper milreis, the duties would be doubled: under the same conditions, if only 4/10 of the debt has to be converted, the extent of the rise would be 40 per cent.

This still leaves us with the cumulative effect of both aspects of the present system. The effect of the gold conversion is always to raise the weight of the duty, so long as paper is below gold in value. The effect of the customs exchange rate is sometimes to increase and sometimes to diminish the burden of the duty, according as to whether the customs rate is below or above the actual exchange rate. The two parts of the system may co-operate in raising the weight of the duty, or may, to some extent, counteract each other—*i.e.*, when the exchange rate actually is below the customs conversion rate, when the extent of the total rise is mitigated.

A somewhat curious arrangement exists in Bolivia (report cited, p. 24). "Bolivia has recently passed a law requiring the payment of a portion of the import duties in vales. In 1916 20 per cent. of the duties are to be paid by this means, and in subsequent years 50 per cent. until the issue is cancelled. Since the vales were placed on sale at a discount from their face value, this measure represents in effect a reduction in the import duties for payment in advance." [1] The report does

[1] So far as time of payment is concerned, the question is whether—apart from warehousing under bond—the entry of goods must lead to immediate payment of duties or not. The determination of the moment at which duty is payable must be distinguished from the determination of under what conditions an obligation to pay duty arises. The obligation to pay duties arises with and from importation, however defined, when the article in question is liable to duty; but the liquidation of the duty arises on the conclusion of determinate acts, and may be postponed for a determinate period. In general the position seems to be that goods can only be released for home consumption after payment of duties thereon, *cf.* U.K. Customs Consolidation Act, § 56. But in some cases at least entry for home consumption is not necessarily made the occasion for immediate payment of duties. In Germany, under § 12 of the Customs Tariff Law of 1902:—

"Credit may, on application, be given for the maximum limit of three months,

not state whether deferred payment is possible, and it seems at least as likely that the discount is an attempt to prevent this method of payment from becoming too onerous.

---

subject to sufficient security being furnished and upon compliance with the regulations framed by the Bundesrath.

"This credit does not apply to the payment of duties upon cereals, pulse, colza, and rape seed, or derivatives thereof produced by milling or malting. If such products are deposited in a public bonded warehouse or in a private warehouse (whether the latter be jointly locked by the customs or not), the duties credited for the storage term shall, if the goods enter consumption, bear interest at 4 per cent. for the full term of storage, according to rules to be issued by the Bundesrath."

It will be noted that certain agricultural products and derivatives are excluded and the evasion of the law through warehousing under bond made impossible by ante-dating the date of obligation by the addition of an interest charge. This was done in the supposed interest of agriculture, and the purchaser of internally produced articles of the kind in question, since these in paying for their purchases really pay the duty in paying the higher price. The regulations contained in the Act, otherwise merely give the seal of imperial legislative approval to measures which had existed from the early days of the Customs Union, but which had hitherto been regulated by each State separately—though owing to the general adoption of the Prussian law of 1828 there was in fact uniformity.

It will be noticed that the importer cannot demand credit as of right (Rechtsanspruch); it is a privilege optionally granted by the authorities. (Trautvetter, *op. cit.*, p. 190, *et seq.*)

In addition, the following instances may be cited:— . . . "Duties must be paid in cash in all South American countries except Ecuador, Colombia, Paraguay, and Uruguay. The acceptance of a note for the payment of duties is said to be the usual custom in Ecuador. Limited credit is allowed to customs brokers in Uruguay; under a blanket bond, payment in Colombia may be made within 15 days after the removal of the goods; and in Paraguay, as a temporary measure in view of the reduction of the limit for customs storage, a note with indorsement is accepted. Formerly credit was allowed in other countries (of South America), but the practice has gradually been discarded." (Report, etc., p. 44.)

NOTE IV. TO CHAPTER IX.

The Post War Situation in Europe and the Payment of Customs Duties.

The interest which regulations of the kind analysed in the previous note have, for the student of tariff matters, been greatly increased by the collapse of European currencies as a consequence of the war. This decline in the value of currencies has in effect reduced the weight of the tariff walls very considerably, for so long as payment can be made in depreciated paper, and the rate of duty remains unaltered, the actual burden of the duty declines in proportion to the depreciation.

It has consequently become necessary for the various States to amend their tariff laws in order to make the actual rates correspond more closely to the actual value of money. We have already had occasion to mention the " coefficients " of increase introduced by the French Government,[1] and the French case is only one among many.

The necessary reform has taken two main shapes, the ultimate effects of which are the same. It was possible to alter the rate of duty, or it was possible to define the coin in which the duty was to be paid. If payment in gold is demanded, the effect is to raise the duty in correspondence with the fall in the gold value of the currency, and thus allows the Government to raise the duty, without directly altering the rates in the tariff.

The following analysis does not pretend to exhaustiveness, since the situation varies almost from week to week.

Germany (*B.T.J.*, 25/12/19, p. 709).—Law of 21st July, 1919, provides that the duties should be paid in gold. " Under §§ 1 and 2 of the proclamation issued thereunder, when payment of such duties was made in paper money, the duty was to be increased by an agio (Aufgeld) to be fixed in

[1] See above, Chap. VI., Note II.

accordance with the value of the mark. Proclamations were issued week by week. . . ." Temporary powers of suspension given to Finance Minister by the law of 8th December, 1919.

Austria (*B.T.J.*, 19/6/20, p. 777).—" A decree of the Austrian Minister of Finance, dated 18th May, provides that, as from 28th May, Austrian customs duties when paid in bank notes have to be paid at *twenty* times the rate inscribed in the tariff. Prior to the enforcement of this measure, payment could be made in banknotes at *six* times the nominal rates."

Italy (*B.T.J.*, 22/4/20, p. 558).—" By decrees of 25th November, 1917, and 30th June, 1918, it was provided that sums payable in gold in respect of customs duties might be paid direct to the customs in paper currency . . . with the addition of 50 per cent. to the amount payable.

The *Gazetta Ufficiale* (Rome) for 8th April contains a decree, dated 6th April, which provides that, from the date of publication of the decree, the amount payable is to be increased by 100 per cent. when paper currency is used."

Portugal (*B.T.J.*, 1/1/20, p. 25).—Decree No. 6,263 of December 2, 1919, in its first article provides that—

" The Government is authorised to double the present import duties and surtaxes on all the articles annexed to decree No. 5,612 of 10th May, 1919, and to include in that schedule goods and merchandise which are not indispensable for the preservation of life and the development of national industry.

" The duties which are leviable or shall become leviable on the goods or merchandise to which this article refers, shall be paid in gold, the conversion being made by taking the value of 50 per cent. of the same duties in pounds sterling at the rate of the day, and the remaining 50 per cent. at the par rate of 4½ escudos for each pound.

" The payment of the duties may be made in currency or by means of the guias ouro referred to in Decree No. 4,133 of 18th April, 1918."

Roumania (*B.T.J.*, 3/6/20, p. 748).—Decision of April 20 decreeing the collection of customs on a gold basis, such duties, when paid in paper, to be collected at five times the rates prescribed in the Roumanian tariff.

Brazil (*B.T.J.*, 8/4/20, p. 498).—" H.M. Commercial Secretary at Rio de Janeiro reports that the Minister of Finance has issued a ruling to the effect that as the rate of exchange on London does not express the relation between English gold currency and Brazilian paper currency, and as the proportion of the customs duties to be paid in gold (55 per cent.) should be collected either in gold or its exact equivalent in paper currency, the sale price of the 'vales' shall be calculated as from 8th December last, on the basis of the New York rate of exchange instead of on the sterling rate. The gold 'vales' must be purchased in exchange for paper at the Banco de Brazil, which every week fixes the rate in paper at which it will sell these 'vales,' in accordance with the average rate of New York on Rio de Janiero for the preceding week. . . .

"The measure was introduced in order to increase the Federal Customs Revenue, and the difference in exchange thus realised involves an increase of from about 20 per cent. to 22 per cent. on the proportion of duties payable in gold, or an increase in the total duty of about 12 per cent."

Poland (*B.T.J.*, 29/1/20).—A new customs tariff came into force on the 10th January, 1920. "The rates of duty scheduled in the customs tariff are payable in gold marks, but the British Acting Commercial Secretary at Warsaw reports that for the present three paper marks are accepted as the equivalent of one gold mark." This ratio was increased to 10 paper marks on the 20th February, whilst, on certain articles of luxury the duties were to be collected exclusively in gold coin. (*B.T.J.*, 29/4/20, p. 592).

Czecho-Slovakia (*B.T.J.*, 27/5/20, pp. 718-9).—The Board of Trade reports on the new tariff, that "some of the rates in the tariff are quoted in francs, and others in Czech kronen. In cases in which duty is leviable in francs, the amount can either be paid in francs or in Czech kronen at the rate of 3.2 kronen to the franc. In the case of duties leviable in kronen, some are specified in the tariff as payable 'with surtax,' and some as payable 'without surtax.' In the cases where duties are payable 'without surtax' payment of the relevant duties may be made in paper money, but in most cases the duties fixed in kronen are payable 'with surtax,'—*i.e.*, a surtax of 200 per cent. of the nominal duty is levied when duties are paid in paper (in virtue of an ordinance of 28th January, 1919). This surtax (for payment in paper) is also levied on the amount of incidental expenses incurred in handling the goods, weighing charges, etc."

These rates were changed as from May 10, henceforward—

1. " Duties hitherto levied in francs are now payable in Czech kronen plus a surtax of 500 per cent.

2. " Duties hitherto levied in Czech kronen plus a surtax of 200 per cent. are now subject to a surtax of 300 per cent.

3. " Duties hitherto levied in Czech kronen without surtax will not be subject to a surtax of 100 per cent." (*B.T.J.*, 10/6/20, p. 777).

Hungary (*B.T.J.*, 10/6/20, p. 778).—Surtax on customs duties paid in paper raised to 1900 kronen for every 100 kronen payable as duty, as from June 1, 1920.

Belgium.—According to the *B.T..J.* of June 24, 1920, p. 842, *et seq*, the Belgium Government has adopted the French system of coefficients of increase on articles subject to specific duty. The Act came into force on June 10, 1920.

CHAPTER X.

Some Alleviations of the Protectionist Régime.

§ 1. The system by which the manufacturers and producers of a particular country obtain safeguards against foreign competition leads in practice to certain alleviative measures, intended, so far as possible, to reconcile the existence of protection with advantages which a freer trade system only can secure. The demand for these advantages comes in the first instance from the traders, who seek the utmost freedom of movement for goods, and who are in opposition in this regard, not only to the manufacturers, but also to the fiscal authorities, if these latter limit the freedom of movement of goods in the interest of the revenue. Further, the general interest of manufacturers to protect themselves against foreign competition does not prevent frequent conflicts of interest among themselves. Some articles they will desire to obtain freely, and will be opposed in so doing, by the domestic producers of some competing products. The exporting industries, for instance, whether or not desirous of securing the home market for themselves by means of duties, are also anxious to secure their share of the trade of other areas, a desire which may be imperilled if the cost of their raw materials is higher than that of some competing centre, owing to protection having been granted to the producers of some competing product, or to the producers of the raw material itself, if it is produced at home. In either case, the result is the same so far as prices are concerned. Again, those industries which perform a service on materials which are already worked up in the final form (but are not in their final state of finish), are interested in obtaining these semi-finished materials wherever they can be got, while the industries which prepare the form are desirous of excluding competing products. It is the international economic relations, therefore, which, both on the side of trade and manufacture, press for some mitigations of the rigour of the protectionist system. Some other instances in which the international factor is operative, though these cannot be strictly included under the cases already mentioned, work in the same direction. What we must next do, therefore, is to classify the forms of relief.

§ 2. A simple form of classification at once suggests itself. The alleviations introduced could be divided into those which are intended to assist trade, and those which are intended to reconcile the conflicting interests of manufacturers, and so on. Such a classification would, however, be defective, inasmuch as arrangements might subserve both purposes simultaneously. It seems better to delve deeper into the matter, and to search for some better principle of division.

The principle on which these alleviations are in general based may be formally stated thus—

Whenever the article imported is intended for consumption within the country of import, directly as a finished product, or indirectly in the form of a finished product of which it forms a part, the article shall be dutiable, *unless* it can be shown (*a*) that the source of origin of the goods is "nationalised" by ownership though not by situation, or (*b*) that the free importation of the goods represents merely an offset against an export of national origin; whilst, if the goods are intended for foreign consumption, the goods shall either not be taxed at all, or, if a tax has been imposed, that tax shall be returned in whole or part on re-exportation.

This formula does not quite cover the ground, but this is simply due to the fact that no clear line of distinction can be drawn between the cases covered in this chapter and those cases of free importation into the customs area, which were investigated in a previous chapter.

The essential fact is, however, brought out in the formula. Free importation in the cases covered by this chapter is dominated by the international trade and commercial situation, certain special instances apart.

The details of the methods will occupy us for the remainder of the chapter.

§ 3. We may distinguish three leading principles of organisation—

A. *Exclusion from the Customs Area*—

1. Free ports and free districts.
2. Bonded warehouses.
3. Manufacture in bond.

B. *Duty Free Movement into and out of the Customs Area*—

4. Improvement trade.
5. Frontier improvement trade.
6. " Propriétés Limitrophes."

C. *Payment with Subsequent Repayment, and Compensatory Trade*—

7. Import certificates.
8. Drawbacks.

A word may first be said as to the principle of division adopted. It will be seen that the three groups represent increasing degrees of association of the goods to be preferentially treated with the usual machinery of taxation. But it must not be implied as meaning that the customs organisation is only brought into requisition in the case of the two last groups. Within the first group itself there is an important division to be made, according as to whether the operations take place under the supervision of the customs organisation or not. Further, it must again be emphasised, the line of division between the subgroups is difficult to draw, and too much importance must not be placed on them.

CHAPTER X.—*Continued.*

Free Ports and Bonded Warehouses.

§ 4. Free ports and warehouses represent the methods whereby the transit and commerce of a country can be relieved from some of the defects of protection. But there is an important difference in the degree to which they are free from administrative control. Free ports and warehouses, alike, do not form part of the customs area, in that they represent areas in which goods, the free circulation of which is dependent on payment of duty, are exempt from the payment so long as they do not traverse the limits of the area in question. But whilst the essence of the idea of the free port is to relieve from the obligation of *customs supervision* as well as the payment of customs duty the relief afforded by the bonded warehouse is confined to the latter alleviation *exclusively;* in fact, *the condition* of relief from the immediate payment of duty is the submission to an increased degree of control by the customs—a submission which is marked by the necessity of giving bond to the customs for the due observance of the regulations imposed by the law.

The essential factor to the lay mind about bonded warehouses is the facility they afford for *storage.*

Goods only pay duty as and when they are withdrawn for home consumption. This is an important feature, but it is only side of a much wider advantage. *Since* goods only pay *if* they are withdrawn for home consumption, it follows that if they are withdrawn for re-export, the bonds entered into are simply cancelled. Hence, the bonded warehouse represents a method of attaining security from the standpoint of the customs authorities, and yet allowing the growth of a transit trade. It is this feature which should be emphasised in the bonded warehouse system.

How, then, does the free port stand in relation to the bonded warehouse? The answer has already been given. In so far as the free port frees the goods from *all* customs control, the degree of disposability is raised to a maximum.

From storing dutiable goods to manufacturing goods out of dutiable materials is a short step in theory, but a somewhat longer step in fact. The main fact about manufacturing in bond is that the removal of the goods without the cognisance of the customs authorities constitutes a breach of the bond: but a bonded warehouse is not necessarily the seat of bonded manufacturing. One of the difficulties of the subject, as we shall see in detail below, is the delimitation of the processes which are not considered as manufacturing, and which are, therefore, to be allowed in an ordinary bonded warehouse, from those which are regarded as manufacture, and which, as involving special risks, have to take place under special conditions. The distinction between manufacturing and warehousing is the difference between static and dynamic processes: the feature of customs supervision is the same. Just as warehousing in a free port is distinguished from warehousing in a bonded area by the absence in the former case of customs supervision, so manufacturing in a free port area takes place without the presence of customs officials.

Let us now turn to the detail of the subject.

§ 4. A free port or free zone is defined by the American Tariff Commission [1] as "an isolated, enclosed and policed area, in or adjacent to a port of entry, without resident population, furnished with the necessary facilities for lading and unlading, for supplying fuel and ships' stores, for storing goods and reshipping them by land and water; an area within which goods may be landed, stored, mixed, blended, repacked, manufactured, and reshipped without the intervention of customs officials. It is subject equally with adjacent regions to all the laws relating to public health, vessel inspection, postal service, labour conditions, immigration, and, indeed, everything except customs."

Such a definition is substantially accurate, in so far as it details the functions and characteristics of actually existing free ports, as they are known on the Continent of Europe. It suffers, however, in the two following respects—

1. There are cases in which a free port does support a "resident" population, and, historically, this case is very

[1] "Free Ports and the Re-export Trade," in *B.T.J.*, 1/5/19, p. 565, *et seq.* This article represents a summary of a report of the Commission.

important. Nor are such cases unknown at the present time—the free ports of the East, such as Singapore, Aden, Hong Kong, are of this type, in which the exclusion from the customs area affects the whole site as well as the technical "port." [1]

2. The definition does not cope with the technical details surrounding the administrative conception of the free port areas. There are, *e.g.*, in the German Customs Law of 1869 two sections dealing with free port areas. Under § 16 of the Act, certain areas can be excluded from the customs line, "where circumstances require it." This covers the case of the free port proper, which is definitely excluded from the customs area. But, in Chapter XIII. of the same Act, which deals with warehousing, there occurs a further clause, Article 107, which allows of the creation of "free warehouses" (Freie Niederlagen), which are expressly declared to be treated as foreign territory. The confusion is made still worse by the terminology of § 97 of the Act, which includes the free port among the examples of "general warehouses," whilst the general warehouse class is not excluded from the customs area at all. When Bremen entered the customs system by the Act of 31st March, 1885, the port of Bremen was not constituted a full free port but only a "free district" in the sense of Art. 107 of Customs Act. Through federal decision of 17th April, 1902, the Freibezirk (free district) of Bremen was constituted an exclave in the sense of § 16 of the Federal Customs Law, with the limitation that industrial works, apart from the equipment and the repair of ships, should not be allowed.

The legal difference between a free port and a free district now consists in this: "whereas in a free district only the lading and unlading of ships, as well as the warehousing, repacking, and mixing of dutiable goods takes place without customs control, in a free port a working up may also take place;

---

[1] *Cf.* Ehrenberg, article "Freihafen," in *H.S.W.*, vol. iv., pp. 449-451, who divides free ports into three groups, "free-port towns," "free-port areas," "free districts." The only remaining free-port town in Europe is Gibraltar. The earliest of this type of free port was Livorno (1547), followed by Genoa (1575), Naples (1633), Venice (1661), Marseilles, Gibraltar, Port Mahon, Treiste and Fiume, Ancona, and Messina. The Hanseatic towns only became free ports contemporaneously with the development of the German Zollverein. The growth of national sentiment on the one hand, the development of administrative technique on the other, are responsible for the gradual replacement of the first by the second type of free port. The free town will only remain, as Ehrenberg says, "in small States without a Hinterland, in isolated places serving transit trade, and especially in half or wholly uncultivated countries." . . .

residence is, however, in both areas confined to the supervisory staff and is not general. . . ." [1]

We can now see the rationale of § 107 of the Customs Act a little more clearly. The "free warehouse" is so-called because it represents only a warehousing port, and not a warehousing and manufacturing port free from all customs control: whilst a free port combines both qualifications, in the technical German conception. Hence, if we decide to treat of manufacturing as an essential feature of the free port, we must follow Ehrenberg in distinguishing a third type of free port, whilst, if we use the free port as a general term, we must exclude manufacturing as a necessary attribute of all free ports.

The question of whether free port facilities *ought* to include the right to manufacture is, of course, another matter: and brings us directly to the advantage of the system of free ports as such. The great attraction is the absence of restrictions, and this is a matter the importance of which naturally varies with the character of the restrictions actually in force. But it will, on reflection, be obvious that the trader and shipowner are usually more interested in economy of time than the manufacturer. Accordingly, the American report tends to stress the mercantile rather than the manufacturing advantages: the greatest advantage it sees in the free port area would be in "freeing the transhipment trade from the unsettling effects of tariff changes." The advantages to the manufacturer depend on the facilities it offers for the use without restriction of dutiable foreign raw material in articles intended for export when completed, and the degree to which manufacture in bond and drawbacks are inadequate to allow him to compete successfully. The advantages in this respect are described as "less important, . . . but not altogether insignificant." It may be mentioned, as a commentary on this attitude, that Wiedenfeld, in his study of the European ports, describes the free port industries of Hamburg in somewhat disparaging terms, ". . . only a few industrial works have grown up in the Hamburg free port, which do not constitute an essential feature in Hamburg's economic structure." [2]

America is not the only country in which a vigorous

---

[1] Wiedenfeld, "Die Nordwesteuropaischen Welthäfen," p. 158.
[2] *Op. et loc. cit.*

agitation for free port facilities is being conducted. For the French agitation, see " Les Zones Franches," by the Marseilles Chamber of Commerce, which represents the point of view of the local interests. That the absence of free port facilities is not an absolute barrier to the growth of an enormous transit trade, the history of the United Kingdom before the days of free trade testifies.

§ 5. When we turn to warehousing, a preliminary point arises. We must distinguish between warehousing and storing, for the former has acquired a technical meaning. Free goods as a rule cannot be warehoused, but, of course, they can be stored. The point simply is that warehousing from the customs point of view is the storage of goods under customs supervision, which is intended to subserve the convenience of the person warehousing, and so devised as to safeguard at the same time the right of the customs to revenue should the goods eventually pass into the customs area for consumption.

The first point which strikes one in investigating the warehousing system of Europe and the U.S.A. is the variety of types of warehouses with which we have to deal. This variety arises from two main points—

(1) The authority responsible for providing the warehouse or entrusted with the operation of the system.

(2) The functions which the several types are intended to carry out.

These two aspects go together: it is usually found that the competence of the warehouse varies with the nature of the authority responsible for it. By competence is to be understood a complex of conditions—length of time for which warehousing is permitted, the nature of the articles which may be warehoused, the security which may be asked for in the interests of the revenue, the nature of the operations which may be carried on in the warehouse, the degree of supervision over these operations which the customs may deem necessary, the number of times that the contents of the warehouse must be inspected to check the books kept—these all form possible instances of differentiation.

Before we describe the systems adopted by different countries, a few words of general explanation may not be out of place.

§ 6. **Warehousing Period.**—In contradistinction to the United Kingdom, the period of time during which warehousing is permitted is in the most cases (including the rest of the Empire) limited. The idea seems to be that commercial necessity cannot require a period of warehousing of indefinite extent: if, at the end of a few years, the goods still remain undisposed of, no useful purpose will be served by allowing them to remain any longer: on the contrary, such undisposed goods consume warehouse space, and the customs are deprived of the revenue which might accrue, if the goods were cleared for home consumption. Consequently, if at the end of the period the goods are not voluntarily taken up and either cleared for re-export or home consumption, then the customs or warehousing authorities have power to dispose of them; refusal to take up the goods being regarded as a case of abandonment. [1]

In India (Indian Sea Customs Act, 1878, § 103) "any goods warehoused may be left in the warehouse, in which they are deposited, . . . till the expiry of three years after the date of the bond executed in relation to such goods . . . The owner of any goods remaining in a warehouse on the expiry of such period shall clear the same for home consumption or shipment in manner hereinafter provided." In South Africa (Customs Management Act, 1913, § 65 (i)), "all goods warehoused or re-warehoused shall be duly cleared, either for exportation or home consumption or otherwise dealt with in accordance with the provisions of this Act or of any law relating to customs, within five years from the date of their first importation into the Union," with the proviso that if at the end of two years from the date of importation the balance of goods remaining in the warehouse, and the duties thereon do not amount to £10, the goods must be cleared and the duties paid. By § 65 (ii), "if any such goods be not so cleared, the commissioners may cause the same to be sold, and the proceeds to be applied, first to the payment of duties, next to the warehouse rent and other charges, and the overplus, if any, to be paid to the proprietor. Provided that the commissioner or other proper officer of customs may, if he thinks fit, grant further time for any such goods to remain warehoused.

---

[1] The period of time permitted varies with the type of warehouse, and will be dealt with below in that connection as regards certain countries. Belgium is also an exception—see below, § 13

§ 7. **Nature of the Articles which may be Warehoused.**—Apart from the question of the limitation of different articles to warehouses of different classes, a distinction which is due in the main to considerations of revenue security, the physical nature of certain commodities make them unsuitable for warehousing, owing to their rapid deterioration if stored, to the danger involved, or to the harm thay may inflict through offensive odour, evaporation, etc., to other goods. Such goods are either not warehousable at all or only to be warehoused under special precautions.

§ 8. **Security.**—When the question of security or bond required is reached, it is essential to distinguish between two cases—

(*a*) Bond which may be required of the warehouse keeper, for seeing that dutiable goods are not allowed to infringe the requirements of the law.

(*b*) Bond which may be required of the owner, or the representative or agent of the owner, of the goods, that he will observe the conditions of the law—*i.e.*, not remove the goods without entry and payment of the duties if they are removed for home consumption.

These are obviously concurrent liabilities : but the general phrase "bonded warehouse" conceals the fact that there may be two parties concerned on the bond required.

It is not necessarily the case that bond will be asked for from *both* parties ; it may be held that the liability of the warehouse keeper is a sufficient safeguard : whereas, if the warehouse authority is a public body or the State itself, it may be deemed desirable to obtain bond from each separate person depositing goods.

It will be noted that the system of obtaining bond for the amount of the duties accruing on the goods represents a much more onerous method than the system of merely bonding the warehouse keeper, and the latter is, therefore, to be preferred from the standpoint of trade facilities.

§ 9. **Operations in Bonded Warehouses.**—Some degree of manipulation is generally required, if only to prevent deterioration of the commodity, and the person depositing may even be required to carry out such manipulations on this ground. But, generally speaking, the distinction between manufacture in bond and warehousing in bond lies in the fact that in the bonded warehouse the essential character of the goods deposited may not be changed. In order to prevent these operations from becoming the occasion for surreptitious removals of dutiable goods from the premises, it is generally required that such operations shall take place only in the presence of accredited customs agents.

A special case is removal from the warehouse for the purpose of effecting some alteration which cannot be carried on in the warehouse, with the intention of re-warehousing. If bond has not been given before, it is obviously in place here, as it is also in the case of removal of goods from one warehouse to another.[1]

§ 9. **Customs Survey.**—A record of goods warehoused is obviously necessary: and, in fact, warehouse receipts have considerable importance in general commerce as documents upon which transactions may be financed.

It follows that the state of the books at any time should correspond with the contents of the warehouse in detail: and, to retain a check on the warehouse books, it is usual to provide for periodical surveys by the customs authorities, the frequency of which will naturally vary with the type of goods and the type of warehouse.

§ 10. We will now pass under review the warehousing arrangements of a few leading trading nations, and will begin with the—

United States.—In the States, apart from two classes of warehouses for manufacture in bond, of which we shall speak later, there are the following five classes:—[2]

Class 1. "Public Stores," owned or leased by Government for goods undergoing appraisal. Such portions of these warehouses as are used for seized or unclaimed goods are known as "general order" stores.

Class 2. Importers' private warehouses for the storage of goods owned by the proprietors of the warehouse.

Class 3. Bonded warehouses for the general storage of

---

[1] Removal from warehouse for repair or other operation may be regarded as a special case of the improvement trade. The practice is sanctioned in the case of the United Kingdom by § 96 of the Customs Consolidation Act:—

"The Commissioners of Customs may permit any goods to be taken out of the warehouse without payment of duty for such purpose and for such period as to them may appear expedient, and in such quantities, and under such regulations and restrictions, and with security by bond for the due return thereof of the payment of the duties thereon, as they may direct or require."

[2] See Customs Regulations of the U.S.A., Chap. xv.

imported goods, but seized or unclaimed goods may be stored therein if necessary.

Class 4. Bonded yards and sheds for the storage of heavy and bulky articles which are to be exclusively devoted to this purpose.

Class 5. Bonded bins or parts of buildings or elevators for the storage of imported wheat.

(If bonded for the exclusive use of proprietors goods, to be also known as importers' private warehouses—*i.e.*, they are regarded as falling into Class 2.)

The two remaining classes are bonded manufacturing warehouses, which fall outside the immediate scope of this section.

The general period of warehousing in the States is three years; by Article 804 of the regulations, "imported merchandise on which the duty has not been paid remaining in bonded warehouses beyond three years from the date of importation is abandoned to the Government, and becomes subject to sale. Such merchandise can not be exported with benefit of drawback without payment of duty." But the regulations are very complicated, and cover, in addition, the following cases:—

1. Unclaimed merchandise taken possession of by the collector. These are to be placed in Class 1 warehouses. If no entry follows within one year, the goods are to be sold within one year of date of importation.

2. Goods in general order warehouses may be re-exported if they have remained in G.O. for less than one year, if the intention of re-export is clear from the invoice and the bill of lading. Otherwise they may only be re-exported upon entry and appraisal and the payment of duty.

3. *Duty paid* merchandise entered for warehouse remaining in public store after the expiration of the bonded period will be treated as abandoned to Government, as is the duty paid or free merchandise remaining after one year of importation for which delivery permits have been issued. Further, "merchandise entered for warehouse, duty paid, and remaining in bonded warehouse beyond three years, and other duty paid or free merchandise for which delivery permits have been issued remaining in such warehouse at the expiration of one year from the date of importation, will be delivered to the warehouseman. . . . No application for remission or

refund of duty on account of casualty occurring after the expiration of three years from date of importation will be entertained."[1]

The warehouseman is the bonded proprietor of the warehouse, or the occupier thereof, and, since the goods have paid duty, the interest of the Government ceases. The warehouseman presumably knows the whereabouts of the owner, and can hand the goods on to him, at the same time that the possession of the goods constitutes security for any warehouse charges resting on the goods. It is to be noted that, by Art. 731 of the regulations, the "Government will not compel a warehouseman to deliver bonded goods, . . . and any question of infringement of private rights by the warehouseman must be left to parties in interest."

The obligations resting on the warehouseman are as follows:—The building proposed as warehouse must be approved by a board of insurance underwriters, or by the officers of two or more insurance companies, and must, in addition, be approved of by the department after inspection. The bond shall be executed "in such penalty and with such security as the collector may deem proper" (Art. 711). Storekeepers are appointed by the administration at the expense of the warehouseman, and accommodation on the premises must be provided for them. Storekeepers must keep an account of receipts and deliveries; when "a delivery is made it shall be noted opposite the record of the withdrawal permit in such manner as to show at all times the quantity of goods remaining in store. Storekeepers will record all permits on the credit side of the account, and return them daily to the collector. They will also make daily returns to the collector of goods received . . . and of partial deliveries of permitted quantities. . . . All delivery reports must be certified by the warehouseman as correct" (Art. 743). But in America the importer, as well as the warehouseman, enters into bond with the Government, the rule being, by Article 244, that the collector, after the duty has been estimated, "will take a bond . . . in double the amount of the estimated duties."

The following goods are not enterable for warehouse:—Free goods (unless in packages containing dutiable goods),

---

[1] U.S. Customs Regulations, Art. 806.

perishable goods, and explosives. Merchandise may not be withdrawn from warehouse in a quantity less than the entire package or one ton (Art. 242); the same limits apply to entries.

The operations permitted on application are defined by Articles 725-727 of the code, they include the examining, sampling, and repacking of merchandise under the supervision of the storekeeper. Finally, "inventories" of merchandise in bonded warehouse are to be taken whenever the collector "has reason to believe that irregularities exist" (Art. 744).

The American Tariff Commission, which, as we have already seen, has supported the idea of free ports, has also proposed changes in the existing warehousing, as part of a comprehensive modernisation of the Customs Administrative Law of the United States. Among the matters in which the Commission desires to see improvements are the following:—

The amendment of the bonding system: the bond which is required for goods entered for warehousing is to be dropped "as entirely unnecessary, as the Government retains possession of the merchandise until duties are paid:" whilst the scope of the law as to manipulation is also to be widened, "manipulation of any kind short of manufacture is provided for in the draft. For orderly procedure, and to assure equal treatment, permission of the Treasury is required." [1]

§ 10. **France.**[2]—Previous to the Revolution there were both free ports and warehousing facilities. Goods intended for colonial trade were allowed to be warehoused by edicts of 1664, and arrêts of 1668, 1670-1671. Warehousing facilities were extended to all goods by an ordnance of 1687, but this was withdrawn in the next year, the only goods then exempted being salt beef, lard, butter to be re-exported to the colonies, as well as foreign goods intended for the Guinea trade.

The revolution suppressed the free ports; the warehousing system was retained for the colonial trade, opened for the Indian and Levant trades, and extended to tobacco and cereals.

The present system dates from the law of 8 Floreal, An. XI.; applied at first to dutiable goods only, it was

---

[1] Reprint of the Commission's summary of the proposals of its draft Bill in *B.T.J.*, 12/12/1918, p. 738, *et seq.*

[2] Pallain, *op. cit.*, vol. i., pp. 517-50, and vol. iv. passim.

extended in 1832 (law of 9th and 27th February), to goods the import of which into France was prohibited, the same Act further authorising the creation of warehouses in the interior and at those frontier towns which would bear the cost of these establishments.

The French law divides warehouses into two great classes—

(1) Entrepôts réels.
(2) Entrepôts fictifs.

The essential distinctions between these two classes may be summed up thus—

(1) The entrepôt réel is under joint lock of the customs and the warehouse authority, which may be a public body, such as the municipality or a joint stock company or other concessionary. The entrepôt fictif is a private warehouse. Entry for warehouses of the second type must be in two names, that of the importer and that of a surety previously accepted by the customs collector (Receveur).

Entrepôts fictifs cannot receive prohibited goods, and only such dutiable goods as may be allowed at the time that the warehouse is established.

Entrepôts réels may receive all dutiable goods, and usually also receive all prohibited goods, though this is not always the case. There is a class of entrepôts réels which may only receive special classes of goods, the entrepôts speciaux.

The general rule is that only dutiable or probihited goods are warehousable—a rule to which there are certain minor exceptions. The period of warehousing is three years in the case of entrepôts réels, one year in the case of entrepôts fictifs, except in the case of cereals, which are warehousable for two years, the period running from the date of entry in the warehouse books, but it is open to the warehousekeepers to extend the period of warehousing in every case in which the interests of commerce demand it, and in which the goods are in good order: provided also, that in the case of warehousing in entrepôts fictifs, the surety remains good. In Marseilles the period of warehousing under the régime fictif is two years.

There are wide differences in the operations which may be carried on in the two types of warehouses. In the entrepôts fictifs no operations except those necessary to prevent the deterioration of the goods are permitted: with the permission and under the supervision of the local customs authorities. There are, however, some exceptions to this rule; coal briquettes may be manufactured, and marble may be worked, and at Marseilles oil may be pressed.

In the entropôts réels, no operations may take place without the permission and the supervision of the customs authorities, but the range of such work is wider than in the other case. The limitation in the case of these warehouses is that the operation must not be of such a character that the weight of the commodity is altered. The mixing of goods of different qualities may also take place under control, but this does not cover the mixing of wines, though it covers other alcoholic liquids, provided that the containers are not marked with French marks of origin.[1]

A word may be said, finally, in elaboration of the concepts of the various types of warehouses of which we have already spoken. The right of creating entrepôts réels belongs to the town, which has to provide the necessary building; where the building, which must be an isolated structure, has been erected in the past as the result of the mandatory terms of the law, the expense of supervision is borne by the State. The town may cede its rights: the local chamber of commerce may take over the obligations by means of the creation of a special joint stock company. If the warehouses are full, goods may be warehoused in private warehouses in portions specially set apart, under double lock, the goods themselves being entered under bond.

The entrepôts fictifs exist normally in (1) ports open to colonial trade, (2) in warehousing ports for those articles named in an ordnance of the 9th January, 1818.[2]

In addition to these goods the following articles are admissible to the entrepôt fictif:—

(*a*) The articles named in the Act of the 8 Floreal, An. XI., Arts. 14 and 15. The Act refers to the "provisions and products liable to the duties described in the tariff as consumption duties" (Art. 14), and "the seven species of French colonial products named in tariff schedule No. 1." [3]

---

[1] For the operations with coffees and feeding stuffs, see Pallain, pp. 532-3.

[2] For the many articles covered by this ordinance, see Pallain, vol. i., p. 538. The list includes roofing slates, oars, brooms, building and other wood, bricks, hemp, cotton-wool, empty casks and barrels, marble, skins, and soda.

[3] Text in Pallain, vol. iv., p. 57.

(*b*) Guano, rice, goods which, though free if directly imported in virtue of the tariff, are liable to the surtax d'entrepôt or the surtaxe d'origine; oil, in all places where a fictif warehouse legally exists, and in other places in virtue of special regulations; pig iron and iron in bars; foreign silk cocoons; furniture woods. Special exemptions exist for Marseilles. In the channel ports, brandies, currants, and tea may be warehoused under double lock (Entrepôts speciaux).

§ 12. **Germany.**[1]—We have already seen something of the intricacy of the German law on the subject of warehousing in connection with our discussion of free ports. The Customs Act of 1869 divides the warehouses up in the following classes:—

A. Public warehouses.	1. General and limited warehouses.	
	2. Free warehouses.	
B. Private warehouses.	3. Private transit warehouses.	May be under customs lock.
	4. Private partitioning warehouses. (Private-teilungslager).	
	5. Private credit warehouses. (Private-kreditlager).	

We have already seen that the free warehouses are not logically warehouses at all, but species of free ports, and that the inclusion of free ports in the defining clause of the "general warehouses" is equally indefensible on logical grounds. In dealing with the remaining classes we have really to deal with three cases, the public warehouses, the private warehouses not under joint lock, and the private warehouses under joint lock.

1. *Public Warehouses.*—The distinction between the general and the limited warehouses lies in the length of time during which warehousing is permitted. In places in which no general warehouses exist, where there is need for warehousing facilities, and where there is the appropriate space, these limited warehouses may be set up, in which goods may as a rule only be warehoused for a period of six months. In the general warehouses the period is five years (the administration may grant exceptions). Only dutiable goods can be entered, provided they are not goods excluded by special regulations under which, by virtue of the Act, such warehouse is to be

[1] See chapter of the Act, "of the warehousing of non-duty paid goods," in Havenstein's edition, pp. 82-91, and Tariff Act of 1902. p. 208, *et seq.*

governed. The warehouses can as a rule only be used by persons resident in the locality; others must employ a resident, though, if the consignee of the goods is not to be found, or the goods are refused by him, they may be entered in the name of the consignor.[1]

By § 4 of the warehousing regulations explosives, goods liable to rot, goods liable to combustion, goods suspected of infection are not warehousable. By Article 97 of the Act, it is the duty of the local community, or of the local business community (Kaufmannschaft) to provide the necessary facilities, if the State has no buildings available, and the facilities are desired.

Article 101 regulates the manipulation of goods in the warehouse; the owners or others having control of the goods are free to undertake, under the supervision of the customs authorities, the partitioning, sorting, cleaning, re-packing of goods, and other acts consistent with the idea of warehousing, provided suitable facilities are available therefor. The warehousing regulations require that the customs authorities are informed in writing beforehand of each act of unpacking, and the wrappings are dutiable on their exit from the warehouse. The taking of samples is permissible, as also the display of goods for inspection, but not for sale.

The payment of duty on the goods takes place on the basis of the weights and quality of the goods on entry. Unless a special application is made to pay duty on the basis of the weight or condition at clearance, no appraisement is necessary on clearance. The only exception is when the goods are taken out in instalments. But the general rule only applies when the goods are cleared for consumption; if they are intended for re-export, the clearance weight is taken, unless the period of warehousing has been less than three months, or the goods are of such a kind as do not suffer from loss of weight. In those cases, in which the weight of the goods has diminished, in consequence of re-packing or through unforseen circumstances, or in which it may be assumed that the reduction of weight ascertained at clearance has legitimately occurred through desiccation, evaporation, or ordinary leakage, the clearance weight constitutes the basis, in so far as the entry weight is not demanded by the person clearing. If the

---

[1] Havenstein, note 1, p. 84.

suspicion prevails that a portion of the goods has been surreptitiously removed from the warehouse, the entry weight is to be the basis. Goods which have completely spoiled and become useless during the warehousing period shall be free of duty, and are to be destroyed under customs supervision.[1]

The treatment of goods the ownership of which is unknown, and of the goods uncleared at the end of five years is dealt with in Article 104 of the Act. If goods have been warehoused for a year, and their owners and others disposing over them are unknown, they shall be exactly advertised on two occasions in public journals, at an interval of at least four weeks, and if, on the expiry of six months thereafter, no claim to the goods is made, the warehouser shall be entitled to sell them to the highest bidder. The proceeds, after deduction of the advertising and sale costs, the duties accruing on the goods, any expenses incurred in maintaining the goods, and the warehousing charges, shall be kept for six months, and if at the end of that time they are not claimed, shall go to the State. A more rapid procedure is allowed in the case of goods liable to quick deterioration (para. 2 of the article). In the case of uncleared goods, if the owner is known, and he has not obtained the right exceptionally to warehouse beyond the legal term, he is to be asked to remove his goods within a period which is not to exceed four weeks. If he does not conform to this request, the goods are to be sold publicly, and the proceeds are to be placed at his disposal, after the deduction of the expenses and the duties to which the goods are liable.

2. *Private Warehouses not under Customs Lock.*—The position of these is regulated by § 108 of the Act. The distinction between the three classes is indicated by their names—the transit warehouses are intended for the receipt of goods which are to be re-exported: the credit warehouses for the reception of goods intended for home consumption at some future date, whilst the partition warehouses are those in which goods are intended to be re-packed. The essential facts relating to these groups can best be followed from the subjoined quotation from Havenstein [2]—

---

[1] Article 103 of the Act (Clearance from Warehouse).
[2] *Op. cit.*, p. 89, note 2 to Art. 108.

"The private credit warehouses hamper their owners least: any kind of goods can be brought to them, though they must, as in the case of all other public and private warehouses, be notified; re-packing, division, working up are, indeed, only permitted to the same extent as in other private warehouses without joint lock—that is, the goods may not thereby receive such a new form as would entail a new designation or bring them under another section of the tariff—but all these acts are freed from any sort of notification to the authorities. Against this must be set the unconditional payment of duty on the basis of the entry weight, and the restriction of the credit period to six months. The private partitioning and transit warehouses grant a warehousing period of five years. The distinction between these two classes is really only nominal; because goods can be cleared for transit from the partitioning warehouse, and need not, in fact, be cleared from the transit warehouse. . . ."

3. *Private Warehouses under Customs Lock.*—If the warehouses of the first two named classes are put under the joint lock of the customs, then, according to Article 108 of the Act, they are assimilated to the rules of Articles 101 and 103 of the Act. Consequently the rules as to manipulation and the assessment of duty on the clearance weight apply to them as to the public warehouses. They even possess the advantage that, although the actual operations undertaken require the presence of the customs staff, they need not be notified in advance to the customs authorities as is the case with the public warehouses.[1]

The private warehouses without lock are restricted both as regards the articles which may be deposited in them, and as to the persons who open them. According to §§ 2, 3, and 11 of the regulations the only persons entitled to the privilege are industrialists, who keep business books in a regular manner, who are resident in the locality or are represented there and who possess the confidence of the administration; the permission is recallable, and is recalled at death or in the case of bankruptcy, although it may be transferred in these cases to the heirs or the creditors.

The goods which may be warehoused are those the duty on which falls below a given amount (as a rule 3 marks per

---

[1] Havenstein, p. 90.

100 kilos. or 6 marks with the permission of the financial authorities), or which are contained in the list published in the official journal (*Zentralblatt für das Deutsche Reich*). The list includes colonial products: cheese, rice flour, sago, and tapioca; olive and other oils; hard soap, iron tubes, and a few other commodities.

But this list is capable of increase, and, in particular, the Tariff Act of 1902 made important changes in this respect. By Article 11 (1) of this Act pure and mixed transit warehouses without customs lock were allowed for a series of commodities. Three cases were contemplated by the Act—

1. Pure transit warehouses (that is, warehouses intended exclusively for goods for re-export) may be set up for rye, wheat, spelt, oats, barley, buck-wheat, pease, rape, and colza. These are to be without joint lock, the manipulation and re-packing of goods therein is to be unrestricted, and need not be notified to the authorities; the warehoused goods may be mixed with domestic products, with the stipulation that the volume of goods cleared for export shall be written off from the contents thereof in foreign wheat at any time, but are otherwise to be treated as domestic. The result is that if at any time the volume of exports exceeds the mass of warehoused foreign goods the balance is treated as if the excess were due to export of domestic products, from which it follows that export certificates are to be given for this excess, which, as we shall see in a later section of this chapter, has important consequences.

2. "For goods of the kind indicated, which are partly to be exported, partly imported into the customs interior, there may further be created, in so far as a pressing need therefor can be recognised, similar warehouses with the further stipulation, that goods cleared from thence into the free circulation of the customs area, shall be written off duty free from the contents of the warehouse, in so far as these goods do not exceed the content of the warehouses from time to time of domestic products, but for the rest are to be treated as of foreign origin (mixed transit warehouse). The Federal Council is to determine at which places such warehouses are to be authorised."

The result is that an excess of imports over the volume of domestic products remaining in the warehouse at any time is dutiable.

3. For cereals *not* included in the list already mentioned, and for dutiable oligeanous fruits, intended exclusively for sale abroad, the Act allows the creation of transit warehouses without customs lock, "in which the treatment and repacking of the goods is to be permitted without restriction and without notification, as well as their mixing with domestic products, with the stipulation, that on the export of these mixed goods, the proportion of foreign goods contained in the mixture shall be regarded as the duty free export *quantum*. For goods of this sort, intended partly for export, partly for sale in the customs area, such warehouses may also be permitted."

The result of these arrangements is that the exporter remains liable to the customs for the foreign products remaining in store, and is not allowed to offset domestic products exported, against foreign products that he chooses to import.

These measures are the result of the pressure of the agricultural interests on the German Government, and are integrally connected with the import certificate method of which mention has already been made, and which is further discussed below, § 19.

§ 13. **Belgium and Switzerland.**—We may now deal in rather less detail with two other countries, and finish by saying a word as to the position in the United Kingdom. The Belgian law on the subject divides warehouses into three classes—

Entrepôts publics.
Entrepôts privés—(*a*) Entrepôt fictif.
(*b*) Entrepôt particulier.

The main distinction between the general and the other classes is the fact that the right to the erection of the latter classes is granted to individuals at the discretion of the authority, and is confined to given classes of goods. The distinction between the latter classes *inter se* lies in the nature of the control. The entrepôt particulier is under the double lock of the customs and the private warehouser, to whom the right has been granted, whilst the entrepôt fictif, although open to customs inspection, is not under double lock.

The general warehouse, on the contrary, is entirely in the control of public authorities. But the distinctions alluded to refer more to the régime than to the buildings, for private warehouses may be formed out of portions of the public warehouse, though separated from the latter. The law of 31st March, 1828, had created a special type of warehouse known as the "entrepôt dits de libre re-exportation," intended to assist the transit trade, a type which was retained by the basic law of 4th March, 1846, until the creation of the free ports contemplated by the Act had come about. These transit warehouses were suppressed by the Act of 1st May, 1858, although the free ports have never been actually established.

All articles are warehousable in the general warehouses, except those likely to injure other commodities, live animals, gunpowder, arms, and munitions (the latter may be sanctioned by the Government). In addition, the special regulations drawn up for each warehouse may exclude certain goods, though the regulations contain provisions by which articles not excluded by the law itself, may be warehoused *en succursale*, under conditions approximating to the regulations for the entrepôts particuliers.

Manipulation is permitted with the following limiting conditions :—

The goods cannot be exposed for sale, the mixing in the same package of goods subject to the different rates of duty is not permissible, nor re-packing in such a way as to change the basis of assessment. The operations have to be notified, although the customs personnel need not be employed to carry out the operations. In addition to the operations allowed in the warehouse itself, the law allows the warehoused goods to be temporarily cleared and re-entered, after undergoing a process of improvement ; bond being demanded, and the goods being ultimately dutiable at the higher rates accruing on the improved article.

There is no limit to the warehousing period, but the provisions as to the taking stock of the warehouses are mandatory. The general warehouses must be inspected at least once a year, the entrepôts particuliers also, except if they contain liquids, when they are surveyed once a quarter, whilst the entrepôts fictifs are surveyed once a quarter at least.[1]

In Switzerland the customs law of 28th June, 1893, allows the creation of warehouses, where it appears desirable in

[1] For the whole of the points raised in this section, see Orban, *op. cit.*, pp. 149-181.

the interests of commerce (Article 16), whilst the detailed regulations constitute Chapter 4 of the Executory Order of the same date.[1]

The warehousing period is very short; apart from special conventions, goods may not be warehoused for more than twelve months. The usual exclusions obtain (Article 85); as a rule no manipulations beyond those necessary for the preservation of the commodity are allowed, though the authorities may allow exceptions: goods deteriorating in the warehouse must be restored by the owner, in default by the customs at his expense. If the goods are still likely to damage other goods, they must be disposed of within a short time (Article 27). Goods which are refused by the consignee, or which are not removed after the period of twelve months has expired, or the ownership of which is not known, may be sold by the authorities.

In the United Kingdom[2] the business of warehousing is now exclusively in the hands of private persons, and corporations, who desire to make a profit thereon, or who store their own goods under bond. The power of appointing warehousing ports rests with the Lords of the Treasury (Customs Consolidation Act, § 12), whilst subject to their directions the Commissioners of Customs and Excise "may, by their order from time to time, approve and appoint warehouses or places of security in such ports and places, and direct in what different parts or divisions of such warehouses or places and in what manner, any goods and what sort of goods may, and may only, be warehoused, kept and secured without payment of duty upon the first entry thereof or for exportation only, in cases where the same may be prohibited to be exported for home use. . . ." The proprietor or occupier of every warehouse ("except existing warehouses of special security in respect of which security by bond has hitherto been dispensed with"), after the approval of the premises, "or some one on his behalf, shall, before any goods shall be warehoused therein, give or procure to be given security by bond, or such

[1] Blumenstein and Gassman, *op. cit.*, pp. 74-80, Arts. 81-102 of the Vollziehungsverordnung.

[2] See, for the details connected with warehousing in the U.K., Ham's "Customs Year Book, Warehousing Supplement." Some notes on the history of warehousing will be found in Higginson, *op. cit.*, pp. 129-31, based on 2nd Report of the C. of Inquiry into Customs and Excise, dated 3rd October, 1818.

other security as the Commissioners of the Treasury or Customs may approve, for the payment of the full duties chargeable on any goods which shall at any time be warehoused in any warehouse duly approved by them for that purpose, or for the due exportation thereof" (C.C.A., § 13). By Article 15 the Treasury and the Commissioners have power to revoke or alter any such warrant or order made by them.

The detailed treatment of warehousing in the Customs Consolidation Act is to be found in §§ 76-99 of the Act. A word or two may be said as to the warehouse itself as a preliminary. This is defined by § 13 of the warehousing code as "a secure place approved by the Board for the general service of the public for the deposit of goods liable to duty of customs or excise without payment of duty. The term includes general warehouse, bottling warehouse, re-packing warehouse, and vault, except when any of these are specifically named." The warehouse must be constructed of stone, brick, or concrete: its doors must open into the street or public way, "so as to be at all times accessible for the examination of the locks and fastenings without passing through other doors or gates." Duty paid goods must not be deposited "in objectionable proximity," the openings, such as windows, must be secured against the possibility of easy theft, windows in adjoining premises overlooking the roof of a proposed warehouse must be reported on by the surveyor or supervisor: "suitable office and other accommodation must be available for the customs officers in charge of the warehouse." "The provision of such accommodation may . . . be made a condition of the approval of any warehouses, and failure to maintain in proper order the accommodation required may entail the withdrawal of the privileges granted" (Code 53). By Article 59 of the code, "bond to secure the duty with one or more sufficient sureties must be given in the penalty of £3,000, or a larger amount, at the discretion of the Board, for a general warehouse or vault, and in the penalty of £1,000 for a bottling warehouse when separate and apart from a general warehouse." The minimum size of a warehouse is to be 5,000 superficial square feet (Code 61).

Goods are liable to forfeiture unless, in addition to a proper record of the goods themselves entered in the landing book, the place of warehousing is notified (C.C.A., § 77): all warehoused goods must be deposited in the original packages, unless they are such goods "as are permitted to be skipped [1] on the quay, or bulked, sorted, lotted, packed, or repacked in the warehouse after the landing thereof, in which case they shall be deposited in the packages in which the same shall be when the account thereof is taken by the proper officer," any alteration in the packages, or their removal from the space in the warehouse in which they are deposited, shall lead to a forfeiture of the goods (C.C.A., § 79).

By § 81 of the C.C.A., it is incumbent on the occupier of every warehouse "to stow the goods warehoused therein so that easy access may be had to every package and parcel thereof," and for every act of negligence in this respect he is liable to a fine of £5. The warehouse keeper is required to be able to produce any goods deposited in the warehouse and not cleared from thence at the request of any officer of the customs. Failure to warehouse after due entry for warehousing, or concealment of goods in, or clandestine removal of goods from, a warehouse, or transference from one package to another, "for the purpose of illegal mixing, removal, or concealment" shall lead to the forfeiture of the goods (§ 84). By § 64 of the code, based on §§ 85 and 97 of the Act, "it is illegal for the proprietor of goods, or warehouse keeper, by himself, or by any person in his employment or with his connivance, to open or gain access to any warehouse, except in the presence of an officer acting in the execution of his duty; or to abstract goods from any warehouse."

The operations which may be carried on in a bonded warehouse are defined by § 95 of the Act—

> "With the sanction of the Commissioners of Customs, and after such notice given by the respective importers and proprietors, and at such times and under such regulations and restrictions as the Commissioners of Customs shall from time to time require and direct, it shall be lawful in the warehouse to sort, separate, and re-pack any goods, and to make such alterations therein as may be necessary for the preservation, sale, shipment, or disposal thereof, provided that such goods be re-packed

---

[1] This is a technical phrase, which, according to Highmore (*op. cit.*, p. 82), "means the transference of goods from one package to another for the purpose of ascertaining the 'tare' of the package or for repairing the package."

in the packages in which they were imported, or in such other packages as the Commissioners shall permit (not being less in any case, if the goods to be exported or to be removed to another warehouse, than is required by law on the importation of such goods); and also to draw off British spirits into bottles for home consumption, or wine or spirits into reputed quart or pint bottles, or bottles or flasks of such smaller size as the Commissioners of Customs may see fit, for exportation only; and to draw off and mix with any wine spirits, not being British flavoured or compounded spirits, and not exceeding the proportion of 10 gallons of spirits to 100 gallons of wine, provided that if the wine so mixed be raised thereby to a greater degree of strength than 40 per cent. of such proof spirit, such wine shall not be admitted for home consumption; but wine in bond may be fortified to a greater degree of strength for exportation only, if it appear to the said Commissioners to be necessary for its preservation; and also to fill up any casks of wine or spirits from any other casks of the same respectively secured in the same warehouse; and also to rack off any wine from the lees, and mix any wines of the same sort, erasing from the cask all import brands, unless the whole of the wine so mixed be of the same brand; and also to take such samples of goods as may be allowed by the Commissioners of Customs, with or without entry, and with or without payment of duty, except as the same may eventually become payable as on a deficiency of the original quantity; and after such goods have been so separated and re-packed in proper or approved packages, the Commissioners of Customs may, at the request of the importer or proprietor of such goods, cause or permit any refuse, damage, or surplus goods occasioned by such separation or re-packing, or, at the like request, any goods which may not be worth the duty, to be destroyed, and may remit the duty payable thereon." [1]

One further point remains: the treatment of goods which have become damaged or spoilt in the course of warehousing. Duties may be remitted or returned on—

---

[1] For further references as to wine and spirits, see Highmore, pp. 89-91, and Ham, *s.v.*, " Wines and Spirits."

(1) Goods lost or destroyed by unavoidable accident, either on ship board or in removing, landing, or receiving into the warehouse, or in the warehouse (C.C.A., § 87).

(2) In general duties are to be paid according to landing account, "except as to the following goods viz. :—Tobacco, wine, spirits, figs, currants, and raisins, the duties whereon, when cleared from the warehouse, shall be chargeable upon the quantity of such goods, acsertained by weight, measure, or strength at the time of actual delivery thereof, unless there is reasonable ground to suppose that any portion of the deficiency or difference . . . has been caused by illegal or improper means."

(Extended to sugar and molasses by the Revenue Act of 1903) C.C.A., § 98.

(3) "No duty shall be charged in respect of any deficiency in goods entered and cleared from the warehouse for exportation unless the officers of customs have reasonable ground to suppose that any such deficiency, or any part thereof, has arisen from illegal abstraction" (C.C.A., § 99).

(4) "If any goods duly entered for delivery from the warehouse for removal or exportation shall be lost or destroyed by unavoidable accident, either in the delivery from the warehouse or the shipping thereof, the Commissioners of Customs may remit the duties thereon" (C.C.A., § 116).

§ 14. We have now surveyed the warehousing practices of a fair number of countries, but a further problem remains for discussion. Goods entered for warehousing may not be cleared for a considerable period of time. In the interval the rate of customs duty payable thereon may have changed considerably. Ought the goods, if and when cleared for home consumption, to pay the duty as it was at the time of entry for warehousing, or the duty as it is at the time the goods are cleared? This problem, is, as a matter of fact, only one of a number of cases which raise the same point. If the rate of duty changes, for instance between the time a vessel reports to the customs authorities and the time the goods are entered for immediate consumption, ought the rate to be the rate at the earlier or the later time? These questions will be discussed in a note to this chapter, our immediate problem is to discuss the bonded manufacturing system.

§ 15. We have already pointed out that (*a*) no very clear line can be drawn between processes which are, and those which are not to be included under the conception of manufacturing: (*b*) that just as there are the two alternatives of warehousing in a free port and in a building under customs supervision, so there is the alternative of manufacturing in a free port or manufacturing in a bonded warehouse. The difference between these two systems is thus already indicated; in the case of the free port the customs authorities are only cognisant of the products as they pass the customs frontier, in the case of the bonded manufacturing system the essential feature is the postponement of payment of duties at the cost of customs supervision of the stores on hand of dutiable materials and finished products.

In the United States the sixth and seventh classes of warehouses are described in the regulations as—

> "Warehouses for the manufacture in bond, solely for exportation, of articles, made in whole or in part of imported materials or of materials subject to internal revenue tax; for the manufacture for home consumption or exportation of cigars in whole of tobacco imported from one country; also for the storage and cleansing of imported rice intended for exportation," and as "warehouses for smelting and refining imported ores and crude metals for exportation or domestic consumption."

It will be noted that the conditions on which manufacture in bond is permitted vary a good deal from case to case; sometimes the nature of the material, sometimes the area of sale is restricted. These regulations attempt to summarise the provisions of the Tariff Act, paragraphs M and N of § IV., though the manufacture of rice in bond goes back to 1874.[1]

The essence of the system is extremely simple: the manufacturer must account to the authorities for every amount of dutiable material used by him. This is achieved in two ways, first, the dutiable material used must be stored apart in rooms "separated from the remainder of the premises, and secured by customs locks, to be used exclusively for the

[1] For the detailed regulations, see Customs Regulations of the U.S.A., Arts. 747-800.

storage and keeping of all imported merchandise, and of domestic spirits,[1] or other materials subject to internal revenue tax transferred into such warehouse for manufacture. A like compartment will be provided, which shall be used exclusively for the storage and keeping of merchandise or articles manufactured" (Art. 751). The second step taken is very strict control over the details of manufacture, by requiring the production of exact formulæ of manufacture. It consequently becomes easy to estimate the amount of product which ought to be turned out from a given amount of raw material entered to the warehouse in question. Further, by requiring the manufacturer not to depart from the formula which he has submitted, the checking of the quantities actually used in manufacture is simplified.

Under § 89 of the Australian Customs Act, 1901-10, and under regulation 70 of the Customs Regulations—

> "Manufacturing may be carried on in a manufacturing warehouse under and subject to these regulations—
>
> (*a*) Imported and manufactured goods may be used in the manufacture.
>
> (*b*) Australian and imported goods shall, until used, if the collector so directs, be kept separate from each other.
>
> (*c*) All operations shall, subject to these regulations, be conducted in such manner as the Comptroller directs.
>
> (*d*) The manufacturer shall keep such books and accounts, and render such returns as the Comptroller directs.
>
> (*e*) The labelling and marking of the goods manufactured shall be subject to the approval of the collector.
>
> (*f*) The collector may make such allowances for waste as he deems just, subject to the approval of the Comptroller.
>
> (*g*) The goods manufactured shall be subject to the control of the customs until delivery for home consumption or until exportation."

Article 71 of the regulations deals with the articles which may be manufactured in bond for home consumption, Article

[1] This was before the days of Prohibition.

73 with those which may be so manufactured for export: whilst Article 72 contains some interesting regulations as to the duties to be imposed on goods so produced.[1]

---

[1] The conditions are as follows:—Articles free of duty, if imported, are also free if manufactured in this way. It may be asked why in this case the goods should be produced under bond. The answer is that the raw materials may still be dutiable though the finished product need not be—though such a case would indicate extremely bad tariff-making.

Secondly, if the duties on goods used in a manufacturing warehouse for the manufacture of articles for home consumption, after due allowance for waste, total less than the import duty on the finished article, then the finished article may be cleared for home consumption on payment of such total. In other cases the finished article shall be dutiable as if it had been imported in its finished state. But no finished article subject to duty of excise shall be cleared for home consumption without payment of such duty.

Thirdly, the article, if containing spirits, shall be dutiable with the customs duty if the spirits are foreign, but if the spirits used are Australian, the duty shall be equal to the excise duty plus the customs duty on the other dutiable ingredients *or* "an amount equal to the import duty on the finished article," though "if the duty chargeable" under the second alternative "be less than the excise duty on the spirit contained in the article, the goods may be delivered for home consumption on payment of such excise duty."

CHAPTER X.—*Continued.*

The Improvement Trade.

§ 16. In the case of the continental countries, although the principle of bonded manufacture is known—it was, for instance, adopted by the signatories to the Brussels Sugar Convention, and occurs in other excise regulations—yet, so far as the working up of *imported* materials is concerned, the more important device is the free admission of products for free working up or improvement—the system, in other words, of the "Improvement Trade" or "Admission Temporaire." It is with the problems of this system that we must next deal.

We may describe the improvement trade as consisting in the free admission of materials or semi-manufactured articles into the customs area of a country with a view to subsequent re-exportation in a more finished state, or in the exportation of goods with free re-admission in a more finished state later on. But this definition conceals a difficulty which it is well to face at the outset of our inquiry. It is possible for the customs authorities to maintain two attitudes: and these two attitudes lead, or may lead, to very different results in practice, so far as the *nature* of re-exportation is concerned. There may be insistence on the maintenance of *identity throughout*—that is, the goods exported must be shown to be the goods originally imported if the payment of duty is to be avoided, and this provision may lead to seals and other external marks of recognition being affixed to the goods by the customs authorities themselves, or to a prohibition of the improvement trade in these articles of processes in which no such proof is possible. Or there may be only a demand for *equivalence:* for a given amount of goods imported, a given amount must be shown to be exported or the duty accruing on the imported goods will become payable, but strict proof of identity will not be demanded. So long as the imports and the exports balance, and so long as the goods are of a character that cannot be produced at home at all in their entirety, so that substitution is impossible, there is no real difference between the first and the second types, except as regards the customs formalities required; but the matter becomes very different if what is imported is retained in the country, and what is exported is an article entirely of domestic origin, and not a true re-export at all. Consequently, when the latter state of affairs arises, we have really to deal with a new kind of trading altogether, the disadvantages and advantages of which must and will be separately discussed under the section "Compensatory Trade Systems." The compensatory trade systems arise historically from the improvement trade, but lead too far away from the improvement trade to justify their being indiscriminately jumbled up with the latter.

The reader will see that in § 3 of the chapter the improvement trade has been subdivided into two sub-classes, the improvement trade and the frontier improvement trade. The justification for this step cannot be found in any logical difference: the reason for the distinction arises on administrative grounds. The customs laws of a good many countries make this distinction, though, as will be obvious on reflection, there is really no difference between re-export or re-import after improvement, if the process takes place within a defined distance from the frontier, or if it takes place at any other spot within the country, though this is the essence of the administrative distinction. The explanation lies in the administrative necessity of a different régime in the districts immediately abutting on the frontier (rayon frontière), which is usually reflected in the volume of customs control deemed advisable, and, on the other hand, in the difficulties which frontiers create for the inhabitants of frontier regions, whose economic affiliations are in large part affected by local considerations. But the nature of the improvement trade as an economic fact is not affected by these administrative difficulties, although a description of the customs régime cannot help adverting to them.

The customs laws of various countries make further distinctions to which it is necessary to refer in passing. There is, firstly, the distinction between the autonomous improvement trade and the conventional, which refers to the nature of the instrument by which the trade is regulated—the conventional trade referring to such trade as has been the subject of a convention between two countries. There is, further, the distinction between the active and the passive improvement trade, a distinction relating to the question whether the goods are first imported and then re-exported (active trade), or first exported and then re-imported (passive). Further, there may be drawn a distinction between transit improvement trade and other forms of improvement trade, the transit trade referring to those cases in which the goods are not re-exported to the country of export, but go on to some third country. But these definitions add nothing to the fundamental concepts of the improvement trade itself.

What is at once more important, and more difficult, is the conception of improvement *per se*. At what point is one to stop in the free admission of products; that is, at what point does the improvement trade cease to be a mere alleviation of the difficulties of a protectionist régime, and become an indirect method of re-introducing free trade? The usual difficulty in practice is the existence of competing interests, one of which benefits, the other of which suffers from the existence of this traffic. Hence, there are two ways of limiting the improvement trade: one is to define the nature of the processes in such a way as to avoid inflicting injury on a competing home industry by enumerating the processes which may be allowed, the other is to avoid any enumeration and simply enacting that proof of *necessity*—*i.e.*, the absence of equal facilities at home in the case of passive trade, or the absence of injury to domestic producers of the imported material in the case of the active trade—must be given, either in each individual case or as regards a particular class of operations.

We will again attempt to make the subject clearer by dealing with the arrangements in force in different countries. This time we will begin with Belgium.[1]

(*a*) *Active Improvement Trade.*—Article 4 of the law of 12th July, 1895, modifying the law of 4th March, 1846, allows the Government to permit the free importation of goods destined to be worked up in the kingdom, "sans caution de droits."[2] To this permission the tariff has added the cases of repairing and finishing, but only when these articles are capable of being furnished with seals, marks, or stamps by the customs. The importation takes place "sous caution de

[1] See Orban, *op. cit.*

[2] "Without bond."

droits," [1] and the period must not exceed a period of six months. Failure to re-export within the defined time, or the absence of customs marks intact leads to the definitive collection of the duties.

(*b*) *Passive Improvement Trade.*—The law of 29th March, 1873, authorises the Government, under certain circumstances, to allow the free re-importation of goods sent abroad, there to undergo improvement, "subir une main-d'œuvre," when this improvement cannot conveniently take place in the country itself, and this right may even be extended to foreign goods which may be sent abroad for repair and improvement. The goods in question must be marked with seals, signs, stamps, or special instruments prepared at the expense of the person interested. The customs, in order to assist themselves in the maintenance of the principle of identity, are to take samples of the goods in as many cases as possible. Export and re-import must take place at the same customs office, which must be a warehousing port or an office open to receive imports by railway. The export certificate must give an exact description of the goods, and the value must be stated in the case of goods liable to customs duty on an *ad valorem* basis. The document is only valid for one year. Import duties are payable, if on re-import, the goods fall under a new customs rate, or if the customs authorities estimate an increase in the value, weight, or volume of the goods; the duty being payable, in the case of goods which do not become reclassified, on the increase of volume, weight, or value: if the goods have fallen into a new tariff class, the duty payable is the difference between the duty which the goods would have paid in their state on exportation, and those which they ought actually to pay if they represented a completely new importation.

In the case of Switzerland, the student of customs legislation enjoys the advantage of being able to study a very careful classification and definition of what is meant by the improvement trade. Article 6 of the 1902 tariff law states that the Federal Council is empowered to permit this traffic, these ameliorations to be allowed "if particular interests of industry demand it, and there are no overwhelming counter interests, as well as under the condition that the essential

[1] "With bond."

nature of the goods is not altered thereby." This permission has led to the very elaborate "Regulativ" of 8th March, 1907.[1]

The decree in question, in so far as it is dealing with the autonomous trade, defines both the articles and the processes, and defines these things separately for the active and the passive trade, so that there is not necessarily coincidence. The articles are classified under the processes. The list is far too long to quote, but one of the sub-groups may be given for illustrative purposes.

In the transit improvement trade there is allowed the washing, singeing, clipping, teasing, fulling, cutting, bleaching, calendering, unoiling, cleansing, sorting, steaming, dyeing, mercerising, re-dying, printing, re-printing, winding, reching, starching, polishing, rolling, pressing, embossing, shrinking, steeping, decorating, etc., of cotton, cotton yarns, cotton satinette, rough and smooth silk, raw and coloured silk and half silk ribbons, woollen yarns, woollen and half woollen clothes: straw and straw plaiting.

In order to enjoy the benefits of the improvement trade, application has to be made by the firm interested, permission applying until further notice. The period of time within which re-export or re-import must take place is twelve months, though extensions of time may be granted (Art. 4). Application for free clearance certificates must be accompanied by samples and an exact technical description of the goods (Art. 5). These clearance certificates can only be granted in the case of goods which can be identified by description or by customs marks. Hence, the principle of identity is fully safeguarded.[2] In addition, the customs authorities are empowered, in the event of new additions to the list of improvement trade processes, to issue the appropriate regulations (Art. 6). The authorisations of the department are to be investigated once a year at a Conference, to which experts interested in the improvement trade, as well as impartial experts, are to be invited to participate (Art. 7).

In addition to the provisions of the autonomous code,

---

[1] Blumenstein and Gassman, *op. cit.*, pp. 105-148, which, together with its appendices and supplementary departmental regulations contains a complete oversight of the autonomous and the conventional improvement trade.

[2] Executory decree of 1893, § 112.

the treaties with Germany,[1] Italy,[2] and Austria [3] all contain provisions with regard to the improvement trade.[4]

The next Country we will investigate is *Germany.*[5] The improvement trade has occasioned much difficulty in the internal history of the Zollverein in the days before the Empire, and also in the trade relations of Germany and Austria. A very complete analysis of these difficulties will be found in the article of Dr. Benno Schmidt, mentioned in the foot-notes, but as these difficulties are now a matter of ancient history, they need not occupy us here.[6]

The basis of the system in Germany is § 115 of the Customs Act of 1869, which states that "articles imported with the intention of re-export, and destined for working up, perfecting, or repair, can be freed from import duties. In certain cases it is also permissible to export objects for defined purposes, and to return them in a perfected form."

The question of the maintenance of identity has, as already remarked, caused a good deal of trouble ever since the formation of the customs union: the present position is still governed by the general rules adopted at the customs conference of 1859. In that year it was decided that the obligation of identity might be waived "in those isolated cases in which the condition of a specific determination of identity through the marking of goods does not appear possible, but in which the need for customs modification is proven, and a misuse thereof to the disadvantage of the revenue can be avoided by means of other measures, after a careful examination

---

[1] Treaties of August 10, 1869; December, 1891, and 12th November, 1904 (*op. cit.*, pp. 111-5, 111-27). For a sketch of the improvement trade relations of Germany and Switzerland, see Benno Schmidt, "Zur Geschichte des Deutschen Veredelungsverkehrs," in Z.S.W., vol. xxvi., pp. 59-100.

[2] Treaty of 13th July, 1904.

[3] Treaty of 9th March, 1906 (*op. cit.*, p. 115).

[4] In pursuance of these treaties, the Swiss Government issued further decrees of 13/1/06 (Germany); 15/6/08 and 1/10/08 (Austria).

[5] Benno Schmidt, *op. cit.*, and Havenstein, under the appropriate sections of the Act of 1869. Further, see the Treaties with Switzerland, already mentioned.

[6] The main difficulties were (1) The delimitation of the improvement trade. (2) The reconciliation of the conflicting interests of the North and South: Prussia was first opposed to a liberal interpretation in 1833 and then herself desired the extension of the traffic, only to find the South hostile in 1851. (3) The question whether the States, if they went beyond the processes recognised in the successive treaties, were to be forced to bear the loss of duties thereby occasioned, or whether these losses were to be borne by the common exchequer of the Union.

of all the circumstances."[1] The same conference laid down the following detailed regulations :—[2]

A. In the case of cloths which have been imported from abroad for the purpose of washing, bleaching, fulling, printing, or dyeing with the intent to re-export them in an improved form, or which are exported with a like object and the intent to re-import them, if, on re-export or re-import, differences of weight are established, these shall not lead to the charging of customs duty, in so far as the same number of pieces are present, and the identity marks which are affixed at both ends on import or export are found intact.

B. In the case of other goods, differences of weight, arising from repairs, are to be exempt from duty if the difference is small. But in the case of re-exported goods it is understood that a reduction of customs duty can only be granted to the aforesaid goods, if the same are not altered by the improvement in such a way as to be unrecognisable as the imported goods on their being exported.[3], [4]

In the active trade the renewing of individual parts is treated as repair according to the circumstances. Re-export need not be *via* the original office. If the goods are not re-exported within the determinate period of time laid down, the goods are dutiable at the rate applicable at the time of original entry.

The position of individual species of goods is regulated by special regulations: among the articles so regulated are Wheat, Rice, Tapioca, and Arrowroot, Rice for the manufacture of Starch, Cocoa, Beeswax, Japan Wax, Paraffin, Tobacco Stalks, Unworked Tobacco Leaves, Tobacco Waste,

---

[1] Cited, Schmidt, p. 857.

[2] Cited, Havenstein, p. 103, note 11.

[3] The idea is, of course, to prevent surreptitious importation by reducing the weight of the re-exported article.

[4] The elaborate nature of these regulations shows that the improvement trade sometimes comes very near to being a case of manufacture under bond. This is especially the case in Germany. Under the terms of Annex A to the Zollverein Treaty of 1867 arrangements were come to in respect to crude iron and scrap iron (including scrap steel), which assimilated the treatment of these materials in the way of improvement trade to the case of warehousing under joint lock. Since that time, various decrees of the Federal Council have materially lightened the burden of maintaining identity, by allowing the mixing of imported with domestic iron, but the general principles of the 1867 agreement seem to be still in force as regards this particular commodity. The point is raised here in order to show how elastic the conception of improvement trade can be. *Cf.* Havenstein, pp. 100-101.

Spices, Almonds, Raw Coffee, Roasted Coffee, Figs, Nuts, Straw, Bast, Silk and Half Silk "Lazets." Materials for shipbuilding are regulated by the Shipbuilding Order issued by the Federal Council in 1906. In 1891 the import of mineral oil intended for the manufacture of vaseline or vaseline oil was freed from the payment of customs duty: the customs free import of iron billets for the manufacture of telegraph wires is also allowed, on proof of the export of the said wire: and the same applies to the importation of malleable iron bars for the manufacture of horse-shoe nails, provided the bars are not mixed with domestic iron.

By Federal decision of 12th December, 1889, the wrappings in which goods intended for re-exportation are packed, are to be treated as separate articles, which are dutiable unless also re-exported.

A word may also be said as to the conventional improvement trade relations. Improvement trade relations with Switzerland have always been important for the South German States, whilst Prussia was, from a relatively early time, interested in the linen trade with Bohemia and Austrian Silesia, and in the west with the Netherlands. Of these relations only those with Switzerland have continued to be the subject of commercial conventions to our own day: the treaty regulations with Austria breaking down in 1883, in part as the result of the Austrian resentment at the abuses which the trade had brought with it—*i.e.*, firms would buy raw material, pay duty on it as such, re-export it and get it worked up and re-import the product free of duty in the course of the improvement trade, thus obtaining a finished object at the cost of the duties on the raw material.[1]

The German-Swiss improvement trade concerns a wide range of processes and articles, Article 6 of the treaty of 1891-1904 referring to silks of all kinds, yarns, and cloths, hides and skins, objects intended to be lacquered, painted, or polished, "other goods intended for improvement, working up, or betterment, . . . if the essential nature" of the goods remain unchanged, other goods exported to Switzerland and to certain districts for the purpose of being embroidered, and satins, plush, and similar products exported

[1] *Cf.* Schmidt, *op. cit.*, p. 894, ". . . Missbrauch Deutscher Industrieller . . . rohe Ware zu beziehen, sie als solcher zu verzollen, um sie wieder im Veredelungsverker in das Ausland gehen, und an sich abfertigen zu lassen."

from Germany into Switzerland are also mentioned in this article. In all these cases the maintenance of identity is required, and proof that the articles that are thus sent are the product of the country of dispatch may also be asked for. The general principle of the methods of control is that "they shall be reduced to the least compactible with the purpose intended" (Art. 5 B of the Protocol). The 1869 treaty, which is still in force so far as its improvement trade clauses are concerned, refers, in part, to the same articles, but, in addition, mentions bells and type for recasting, straw for weaving, etc. This treaty defines carefully the formalities necessary as regards the weighing of goods, and lays down the principle that small differences in the imported and re-exported goods shall not be a cause for the imposition of duty. It may be noted that in the later treaties the period for re-import and re-export is twelve months, and that the treaty expressly allows the division of cloths imported into one of the contracting countries for dyeing and printing (Protocol 5 G).

The last country which we will investigate is *France.*[1] It is in France that the conflict between the principle of identity and equivalence has been particularly sharp, and it cannot be said that the principle of identity has completely carried the day, although it is now the rule.

The improvement trade dates from 1836, the law of 5th July, 1836, stating that "Royal Ordinances may authorise, with power of revocation in cases of abuse, the temporary admission of foreign products, on condition of re-exportation or replacement in warehouse within a maximum period of six months, and of the fulfilment of the formalities and conditions which shall be laid down."

The intention of this Act was clear, the underlying principle was to be that of identity, and, as Pallain puts it, the improvement trade was regarded as one form of the system of manufacture under bond: "L'Admission temporaire ne devant être, en quelque sorte, sous un autre nom, dans l'esprit du legislateur de 1836, qu'une manipulation en entrepôt, devait necessairement être soumise à la condition de la ré-éxportation a l'idéntique." Until 1850, as a result, all goods entering in this way, had either to be marked with seals, or, if this was not possible, the raw materials were

[1] Pallain, pp. 550-672.

submitted to manufacture in bond (soumis à l'exercise et au recensement de la douane).

The first breach in this system was made in 1850, when the régime of equivalence was set up in the case of wheat flour: when millers were allowed to export flour either from imported or domestic wheat, provided that the customs ratio between the imported quantity and the flour to be extracted were adhered to. In the following year the system was extended to iron intended for the manufacture of machinery, and was generalised for all metals by decrees of 17th October, 1857 and 15th February, 1862. The system was violently attacked by those iron districts which thought themselves victimised in the way we shall afterwards discuss in detail and the same complaints were rife with regard to the milling of wheat. The result was that after 1870 the system began to be changed. So far as iron was concerned, the new principle adopted was that of the "transport à l'usine;" the importer was no longer allowed to dispose of his products to another person, by means of transferable import certificates, but this still allowed him to maintain equivalence between the imported and exported goods. In the same way the decree of 1870, and the subsequent decree of 1888 no longer allowed the substitution of one kind of export for another—*i.e.*, it was no longer allowed to import iron made by the use of charcoal "fer au bois," and to export coke iron instead, "fer au coke." But Pallain insists that it is still possible for the manufacturer to substitute for the better quality imported a worse quality exported. "Perfect identity could only be obtained by manufacture in bond, which would be onerous for the Treasury and the manufacturer alike."

In the case of wheat flour, a decree of 1873 established a zone system, and required re-export within the zone, but this injuring the millers, the system of equivalence was again resorted to by decrees of 1896 and 1897. This again proved unpopular, and led finally to the law of 4th February, 1902, by which the transport à l'usine was adopted in the case of wheat milling also, though it follows in this case too that there is not thereby secured a full measure of identity.

Changes have taken place also in other directions: the discretionary power of the Government to allow products the benefit of admission temporaire was resented, though no change took place before the Tariff Act of 1892. Article 13 of this Act altered the Act of 1836, by laying it down that the benefit of admission temporaire should only be accorded in virtue of legislation, after advice given by the Consultative Council of Arts and Manufactures, except in the following cases :—

1. Requests for the introduction of objects for repairs and experiments.

2. Requests for the introduction of objects presenting an individual and exceptional character, not capable of being generalised.

3. Requests for the introduction of sacks and coverings for refilling.

With certain few exceptions the decisions already in force were maintained. The Act itself added to the number; the revision of the tariff by the Act of 1910 still further increasing the list.[1]

Apart from the special regulations affecting the metals [2] and cereals in the improvement trade, the general position is as follows :—

(*a*) The improvement trade is now only applicable to specific articles in virtue of law or of Government decree, so far as articles admitted prior to 1892 are concerned, or those in cases mentioned in the Act itself.

(*b*) In general, the articles admitted, require the "Garantie d'une soumission cautionée"—*i.e.*, bond.

(*c*) Articles can only be sent to the destination in view of which they have been admitted, and which is stated in the bond. The importer assumes two obligations—

(i.) The obligation of working up the commodity.
(ii.) Re-exporting the finished production in the specified period.

(*d*) The articles admitted to improvement can be imported in the ships of all nations, and from any port, whether in the

[1] Act of 1910, Art.

[2] Apart from the question of transport à l'usine (which is now obligatory in all cases except cast iron (fontes de moulage)), the right to import metals for improvement is confined to iron-masters, machine constructors, and metal workers, who have a special credit opened to them on demand, which must be sanctioned by the departments of Finance and Commerce, after advice given by the Consultative Council of Arts and Manufactures. The credit may be used at any time within a period of three years.

country of origin or not. But there are some minor exceptions to this: some articles (sugar intended for the manufacture of chocolate, for refining, and the making of sugar preparations) must be directly imported from non-European sources, whilst cereals of non-European origin indirectly imported must pay the surtaxe-d'entrepôt.

(*e*) The period of re-exportation is six months from the date of importation.

(*f*) Warehoused goods, after undergoing improvement, are in the same position as other warehoused goods. If these goods are subsequently entered for home consumption, they pay only the duty on the raw material, and according to the rates in force at the moment of clearance. This general principle was laid down in the arrêt of the Cour de Cassation of 27th June, 1870. There are, however, some exceptions to this rule of no great importance.

(*g*) Products, manufactured under the régime of improvement, and exported to the French Colonies, are free or dutiable according to the local tariff on French products. Exports to Corsica or to Algeria, however, do not count as an export, and, therefore, do not clear the account.

When applying for the right to import metals the parties interested must produce a detailed statement of the quantity of the metals of which they demand the temporary admission. This statement must specify exactly in the case of crude iron, if it is forge, pig, or cast iron: in the case of worked iron, whether it is coke iron or charcoal iron that it is desired to import.[1]

The countries mentioned are not, of course, the only ones in which the improvement trade is permitted.[2] But what we have already described will be sufficient to convince the reader that the matter is not devoid of considerable difficulties. Apart altogether from the ease with which the

---

[1] For the very technical questions relating to the cereals, see Pallain, I., pp. 590-614. Pallain's work contains an exhaustive survey of the rules relating to all the articles eligible for the improvement trade.

[2] For other cases, see Spain: Preliminary Dispositions to Tariff, Disposition Third (linen yarn, cattle imported for pasturage, cocoa-nut pulp, copra, etc.); Sweden, Tariff, Preliminary Dispositions: Art. 8 grants exemption from duties "for short periods of fixed duration" for (1) dutiable goods which are imported to be repaired or completed in Sweden and are intended for subsequent re-exportation; (2) goods intended to be tested and then re-exported. Period not to exceed twelve months and six months respectively. There must be no reasonable doubt as to the identity of the imported and exported article.

improvement trade slides over to the system of compensatory trade, if the method of equivalence is allowed, and apart from the judgment which must be passed on the latter kind of trade—the improvement trade, as we have seen, raises problems of principle and practice. Yet the events of the present time seem destined to give the trade an importance it has hardly had since the consolidation of the national states of Europe provided areas of considerable extent in which trade could freely take place. Owing to the fall in the value of the monies of the Central European Powers, they are unable to purchase goods on the world market, and are dependent on working up the products of other owners if their factories are to be kept going. Hence, the improvement trade may have a brilliant future before it: though it must be recognised that from the standpoint of the revenue system of these impoverished countries, there are disadvantages, since obviously the vitality of the trade depends upon the freedom from the imposition of duty.

CHAPTER X.—*Continued.*

"FRONTIER TRADE."

§ 17. WHEN we turn to the Frontier Improvement Trade we meet with no new principle, but only the application of the ideas we have already discussed to a particular set of circumstances. An illustration or two may suffice to make the matter clear.

In Switzerland Article 138 of the Executory Decree, basing itself on Articles 5 and 7 of the Customs Law, defines the matter as follows:—

"In the ordinary course of the *small frontier trade*, objects which are brought by the inhabitants of the frontier zone of 10 kilometres to the inhabitants of the same zone in the neighbouring State for repair, improvement, or working up, or *vice-versâ*, and which, having been repaired, improved, or worked up, are re-imported into the frontier zone of the country of origin within the defined period of time, shall be free of duty, in so far as reciprocity is maintained by the State in question.

"This refers in particular to repairs to clothing and shoes, which private persons in one frontier zone have performed for them by artisans in the other zone for their own direct benefit: to rough wood to be sawn: wheat to be milled, etc., given to foreign workmen in the normal course of trade, even if the raw material is itself of Swiss origin.

"For the rest, as regards the extension of the zone, as well as the various processes, there is reserved the right of separate arrangements with individual countries."

This passage, it will be noted, deals only with one aspect of the subject: small *commission* trade. The regulatory decree of 8th March, 1907, deals with the frontier trade in general. § 111 includes, under the "Frontier Trade," *all* the articles and processes included under the active improvement trade, "under reservation of reciprocity and the possible stipulations of commercial treaties, special conventions, etc.," and then goes on to add a large number of other processes, such as grinding of bones, wood gall, apples, etc., sawing, cutting, planing of wood, pressing of fresh fruit, curing of fish, milling, threshing of cereals, etc., salting of cheese, cutting, counting, printing, blackedging of paper, and various processes in connection with textile products.

In addition, the Swiss *law* separately regulated the "small" frontier traffic. Article 3, sub-section O, of the Customs Law allows the free import of "milk, eggs, fresh fish, snails, fresh field and garden produce, in so far as these products are intended for the market or hawking, and are carried by the supplier into Switzerland, or are only conveyed by small hand-carts. In any case, the observance of the legal frontier route (Zollstrasse) and declaration at the frontier office is obligatory in these cases."[1]

Very much the same sort of arrangement exists in Sweden as regards the small frontier trade as in Switzerland. Under Article 8 of the preliminary dispositions of the tariff, articles brought by the frontier population from Norway or Finland to undergo some process of improvement in Sweden, such as bleaching, dyeing, tanning, spinning, weaving, etc., or for repair, are admitted free of duty, provided there is compliance with the detailed regulations of the customs authorities, or, in special cases, of the customs authorities at the frontier. The passive improvement trade is also allowed in this connection. In Germany, under § 116 of the Customs Act, "in respect of the small frontier trade, special concessions may be made according to the local circumstances." The detailed regulations under this head are very similar to those in force in Switzerland.

§ 18. We are now left with the third of the alleviations which come under the second of our headings—viz., the case of the "propriétés limitrophes." The reason for this alleviation is quite simple. The frontier may cut a particular estate into two halves; shall the cultivator be forced to pay duty if he imports the produce of his fields into the customs area of the country in which the smaller portion of his estate lies? Or a rectification of the frontier takes place, by which an estate is separated from the village or hamlet in which the proprietor lives: how are the products of the estate to be treated by the country of residence?

---

[1] Blumenstein and Gassman, *op. cit.*, p. 12.

We may regard the actual concessions made in these cases as among the survivals of the system in which the basis of levying customs duty was the individual and not the goods which accompanied the individual directly. Thus, the following cases are recognised in the case of Switzerland :—

Customs Law, Article 3, sub-sections *m* and *n*—

"(*m*) Goods, animals, and machines which are exported by inhabitants for use (Bewirtschaftung) in foreign territory, on estates which are yet not situated more than 10 kilometres from the frontier and are re-imported within a defined period of time into Switzerland; in the same way the same articles, which are imported by foreigners into Switzerland for use on estates which are not more than 10 kilometres from the frontier, and remain only a short time in Switzerland; but in the latter case only if and to the extent that reciprocity is practised by the respective foreign country.

"(*n*) The crude products of the soil of such estates, situated on foreign soil within 10 kilometres from the frontiers, as are cultivated by inhabitants of the Commonwealth (owners, possessors of the usufruct, or tenants), whether in person or by third persons on their behalf."

By treaties with Germany and Austria the limits in respect to these frontier arrangements have been increased to 15 kilometres.

In the case of France, the arrangements are much more complicated. The basis of the French position is the ordinance of 13th October, 1814, which provides for freedom of export by foreigners of the products of their lands situated within a defined distance from the frontier, on condition that French owners of lands situated on their side of the frontier be given reciprocal rights. But free import into France, which, though not at that time the most important aspect of the situation, has now, with the cessation of export duties or prohibitions, usurped the predominant place in interest, is only permissible on two conditions—

(*a*) The right is restricted to estates which were French at the moment of the delimitation of the frontier.

(*b*) These estates must have remained in the hands of the French owners who were in possession at that time, or have been transferred to Frenchmen, the actual owners by bequest, and these legatees must be heirs in the direct line.

In the case of exports the condition of possession at the time of the delimitation of the frontier is not required; all that is asked for in this case is that the products are the harvests of territory actually cultivated by foreign owners or by foreign cultivators. Every change of proprietorship requires a re-affirmation of the right at the customs office. Each year the owners of the lands have to file at harvest time a declaration indicating the type of culture applied to each part of their lands, and the approximate quantities of products they propose to import or export, as the case may be. The cereals and other products of the earth have to be imported or exported in the form in which they are habitually raised from the soil, and, with the exception of wines, the period of free movement is limited to the period 1st June to 15th November, so far as imports are concerned, though, in the case of exports, the period is extended to the 1st April next following.

In addition to the autonomous law on the subject there are conventional regulations affecting the various frontiers, but these arrangements are by no means uniform, nor are they subject to the most-favoured-nation rule.[1]

§ 19.[2] We must now pass to the last of our divisions, treating of drawbacks and of compensatory trade. And, as the latter is historically connected with the improvement trade, we will begin with this subject.

The actual French law, by insisting on the obligation of transport to the place of manufacture, both in the case of metals and of wheat, has now placed strict limits to the degree to which substitution can be practised. But the German system of import certificates supplies us with an excellent illustration of the working of compensatory trade. In Germany, as in France, the system of compensatory trade grew up in connection with the improvement trade, and, in the controversies in connection with the system, writers generally discuss it under the title "Abschaffung des Identitätsnachweises" (abolition of proof of identity).

---

[1] On the whole subject, Pallain, I., pp. 137-152.

[2] On this section, see generally, Grunzel, "Economic Protectionism," pp. 206, 216, *et seq*; Lexis, art. "Identitätsnachweises," in *H.S.W.*, 3rd edn., vol. iii.; Pallain, *op. cit.*, pp. 556-65; Beckmann, "Einfuhrscheinsysteme," in Abhandlungen der Badischen Hochschulen, 1911; same author in *J.N.S.*, 1914, art. "Getreide ausfuhrverguetung und nationale Futterbeschaffung"; G. Michel, art. "Acquit-à-Caution" in Say and Chailler Nouveau Dictionàire d'Economie Politique, vol i.; Hausser, "Les Méthodes Allemandes d'Expansion Economique."

Previous to 1878 the only system in force as regards agricultural products was that of strict identity, which applied to the transit warehouses, whether these exported only foreign wheat, or were mixed warehouses, in which foreign and domestic wheat was mixed for exporting purposes. Under this system, the customs and the warehouse keeper kept running accounts, at periodical intervals the account was struck, and the importer was liable for every excess of his imports of wheat in the period over the amount of foreign wheat re-exported. These balances excluded the amount of domestic wheat which might have been exported, the account concerned only the dutiable foreign wheat, and the system was, therefore, of strict identity so far as the person importing, the place of import and export, and the species of imported and exported wheat was concerned.

The first breach in this was made in the interest of millers, who, from 1879 onwards, were allowed to re-export flour made from foreign wheat, under a drawback system. The amount of wheat so converted was often difficult to determine, as the flour actually was of mixed origin: consequently the Act of 23rd June, 1882, allowed millers to import duty free an amount of foreign wheat equal to the amount of flour exported, the amount being based on certain estimates of yield, but this amount of free import was to take place irrespective of whether or not the flour was actually made from foreign wheat, domestic wheat, or a mixture of the two. "The proof of identity was set aside for milling so far as nature and origin of the wheat was concerned, but was retained for the person and the place of export." [1]

The first breaches in the system were, therefore, in the interest of the millers. But when, in the eighties, the agricultural depression set in, the agrarians demanded an extension of the system. They had the option of selling at low world prices outside the area, but inside the customs area they were forced to lose part of the possible gains by the high cost of transport between east and west. At first the attempt was made to satisfy the agrarians by lower railway rates, the so-called "Staffel-tarife," or sliding scales, but this proved unpopular in the west, both with traders and with local growers. Consequently, in 1894, a new system was introduced of granting

---

[1] Beckmann, *op. cit.*, p. 35.

import certificates on the export of wheat, the exact grounds for which we shall examine later on. The certificates were granted on a minimum of 500 kg. of grain being exported; they could be used in the duty-free import of an amount of grain equal to the amount exported, thus giving the holder the right to save the amount of customs duties accruing on this amount of grain. These certificates were valid for a period of ten months: in the first four months they could only be used in the import of grain, in the next two months for grain or other products, in the last four months for other products only—wood, southern fruits, spices, salted herrings, raw coffee, cocoa beans, cocoa husks, caviare, olives, mussels or shellfish, lobsters, turtles, tea, olive oil in casks, cotton seed oil, train oil, and fat, petroleum and mineral lubricants.[1] A feature of the situation was that though the certificates were valid when given in lieu of the duties accruing on the articles enumerated, they could not be used for any species of wheat other than that for which they had been granted.

The Tariff Act of 1902, Article 11, sub-sections 1 and 6, left the main outlines of the system as they were, but an important change was made by allowing the inter-changeability of the various grain products *inter se*, though this concession was accompanied by the cutting down of the period of validity to a period of six months.

The same Act reduced the concessions to the traders by abolishing the postponement of duty payment in the case of the agricultural products named in § 12 of the Act, and requiring payment of 4 per cent. interest in the case of warehoused goods of these classes. Thus, the certificate system was extended in the interest of the agrarians at the time their foreign competitors were being subjected to new burdens.

The reaction against the agrarians in the years just before the war left its marks on the import certificate system also. After an inquiry in 1910 the Federal Council restricted the validity of the certificates to three months instead of six, and limited their availability for duty paying purposes to agricultural products.

We have so far been explaining the technique of the system, our next business must be to examine the case for the import certificate.

---

[1] Lexis, *op. cit.*, p. 578.

The basic idea of the system of compensatory trade is, as has already been explained, that the net balance of imports and exports is unaffected by the substitution of the freely admitted imports for domestic products in the re-exportation stage. For, it is argued, if in consequence of the free admission rights, imports increase, yet, since the *condition* of such free admission is a corresponding export, exports as a whole are increased to the same extent as the imports, consequently the balance of imports and exports is unaffected. It makes no difference to this fundamental principle how the traffic in import certificates is actually conducted. The imports admitted free under the system may be imported by the first holder of the certificate (that is, the exporter), and sold by him for the current price, his profit being the difference between the domestic price (which will be higher than the world price in consequence of the duty) and the buying price. The certificates may, alternatively, be sold by the first holder to some one else, who uses them to import goods, liquidating his debts to the customs by handing over these certificates.

The fact that, under the system of import certificates, the balance of imports and exports remains the same, even if true, is not, of course, a justification of a system which seems at first sight as aimless as a kitten chasing its own tail. We must, therefore, seek to discover the reasons which have led to the acceptance of the system in part or in whole in France and Germany.

Compensation over Space.—The first argument in its favour is that it enables the concentration of imports from and exports to the geographically best situated areas to take place, without the principle of protection having to be given up.

Let us take the following case:—A and B are two areas in the same country in which there is respectively a deficiency and a surplus over local demand. Let us further suppose that the two areas are separated by a distance of x miles, which raises the cost of transport to such a point that from the standpoint of buyers in A, it is immaterial whether they buy the amounts needed to cover their deficiency abroad or in B. In that case, consignments from B in area A will cost as much as foreign goods, whilst the producers in B will only get the local price in A minus the cost of transport. Since there is a surplus in B the price there will fall, whilst in A the price will be the world price plus the duty, so that any local producers will get more than the producers in B, assuming the cost of production to be uniform all over the area. In area A protection will be effective, in area B it will be ineffective, owing to the surplus. If, now, the exporters in B are given the right to import free a quantity corresponding to the amount they export, and sell this amount, or the right to it, to importers in A, what will be the result? Since in A the price is determined by the local shortage, the importers will buy the certificates at the full amount, the exporters in B will sell their products at the world price and get into the bargain the value of their certificates, so that in both areas the price will be the world price plus the duty, for even in B the local producers will no longer sell at home, but will sell abroad in order to get the right to sell import certificates. From the national standpoint, there will be more exported, but this is compensated for by heavier imports into A, whilst the costs of transport from B to A are avoided.

This is the historical case on which the German arrangements are founded. Owing to the heavy cost of transport from the Eastern wheat areas to the Western industrial areas, the latter imported from abroad, consequently paid the world price plus the duty. In the wheat growing East, there was a surplus, which could not be disposed of in the West except at prices no more remunerative than world prices owing to the cost of transport. Prices in the East were lower than prices in the West. The introduction of the certificates led to the equalisation of prices all over the area, and meant that the home price all over the area tended to be world price plus the duty.

Compensation over Time.—It is argued by the supporters of the system that the adoption of import certificates enables the producers always to get the protection which the law allows them in spite of periodicity in the production of the commodity. For (let us take wheat) the price tends to be depressed immediately after the harvest; the prices which the producer then obtains will not be greater than the world price owing to the superfluity of the product at the moment. The lower prices stimulate consumption at the lower prices, and then, when the shortage arrives, wheat is imported to make up the deficiency. If import certificates are given, then the farmer will export after the harvest, so that the home price will rise to the world level plus the duty more rapidly;

when later import takes place, owing to the depletion, the farmer sells his certificates, so that on the whole of his crop he obtains the world price plus the duty. In this way he gets the protection the law intends him to obtain.

Compensation over Qualities.—If the local taste prefers a quality that cannot be produced in the area in question, the protection given will to some extent be nugatory. A smaller quantity will always be consumed or a worse price be given. The domestic crop is exported and sold at the world price abroad. The exporter will get import certificates which he can sell to the importers of the preferred article. Thus, the price of the domestic article will rise in the home market to at least the world price plus the duty, and the producer will get the protection that he has been promised. More of the domestic product will be consumed abroad and less at home, but this is offset by greater imports of the preferred article.

Compensation over Different Articles.—This last argument can be expanded. If certificates given for one quality of article can be used in the payment of duties on a different grade, why should not the certificate given for one article be used in the payment of duties on an entirely different one? If one can use import certificates given because one grade of wheat has been exported in payment of imports of another grade of wheat, why should not wheat certificates be used in the payment of duties on the importation of rye or, indeed, any other article freely chosen?

There will, it is true, under this system, be no longer any pretence that there is a balance of imports and exports which the system leaves untouched, if the word balance be used at all strictly, but it can still be argued that imports and exports as aggregate values will retain the same relation to one another.

§ 20. Our next task must then be to analyse these arguments critically. In order to do this, we must first make a distinction between the par or customs value of the certificate and the actual market value. A certificate has a par or customs value, which is measured by the amount of duty it will meet: and a market value, which is measured by the amount which a purchaser will give for it if the holder desires to part with the certificate for cash. This market price will never exceed the value of the duties which presentation of the certificate will remit, but it might be the case that the actual value in the market will be less than this: the theoretical lower limit of the market price being zero.[1]

It is this possible difference between the par and the market value of the certificate that we must watch. Suppose there is to be such a difference, what will be its effect?

It may, however, be argued that such a difference between the par and the market value can never arise, for it overlooks the main point on which the whole system is based, that every additional export will necessitate an additional import, so that the demand is increased in proportion as the supply of certificates increases. But this argument is not universally true. It is only true on the assumption that the volume of home production and home demand are absolutely fixed—*i.e.*, on the assumption that we may safely neglect the possibility that the introduction will alter the amounts produced and consumed in the aggregate. In other words, we must take into account the elasticity of the supply of the domestic product, and the elasticity of the home demand at different price levels. We have already seen in the case of sliding scales how important it is to take account of elasticity in the analysis of these matters.

§ 21. There are cases in which the influence of the certificates will work permanently in one direction, and that a direction unsought for by the authors of the system. Let us notice that the price of the certificate will vary according as the area of substitution is large or small. The longer the period of time for which the certificates are available, the larger the area of space over which they are valid, and the larger the number of articles, customs duties on which can be paid by means of them, the higher the market value and the closer the approximation of the market value of the certificate to its par value. So much is surely common sense: even if, on the whole, the supply of certificates causes the demand for them, there may still be temporary maladjustments, and these will affect the price less and less, the more extensive the area over which the certificate can be used, using area to cover temporal as well as spatial relations, and including the interchangeability among goods.

So long as the articles, the import on which can be met

---

[1] Whenever there is such a difference the purchaser will virtually buy the goods at less than the rates of duty inscribed in the tariff.

by the presentation of certificates, *must be the same as those exported*, the value of the certificates will only approximate to their par value, so long as, for any reason, the volume of imports exceeds the exports or is no smaller than the volume of the exports. But as soon as the exports exceed the imports, the value of the certificates will fall: and will fall more and more the greater the excess of exports over imports. It follows that in the case of a country in which there is already an excess of domestic production as a whole over consumption as a whole, and in which the surplus is exported, the certificate system will have less and less effect in stimulating exports, so long as the certificate can only be sold to meet imports on a similar produce, because there will be more sellers than buyers, and the price of the certificate will represent a smaller and smaller gain. So also in the case of certificates valid for only a short period of time: the greater the excess of exports over imports in that time, the greater the offer of certificates, and the less will holders of them obtain, consequently the less and less effect will the system in general have in stimulating exports.

But if the certificates are capable of being used in payment of customs duties on articles *other than those* exported, even though there is an excess of the exports over the imports of the particular articles exported, the value of the certificates will remain high. In this case exporters can always reckon on the full or nearly the full par value of the certificates being obtained, and there is no longer any guarantee that the increased exports will be compensated by just enough increased imports to avoid the geographical and temporal disadvantages of which previous mention was made. Under the conditions supposed, just because the value of the certificates will approximate to par, it may pay to export a commodity which would not have been produced otherwise at all—*i.e.*, the export price plus the market price of the certificate may produce a redistribution of the relative profitableness of different forms of enterprise. In other words, the price of the certificate in the market may represent an export bounty to the exporter, which bounty is ultimately paid by the State in the shape of the loss of customs duties on the articles which are imported by means of the certificates. An actual case may make the matter clearer. The tendency of the import certificates was, in East Prussia, to stimulate the production of rye at the expense of wheat, in spite of the fact that wheat is replacing rye as an article of domestic consumption, and that the import certificates were originally intended to prevent the falling off in the production of wheat.

Apart altogether from the influence of the import certificate, there are reasons why rye should compete successfully with wheat. Wheat demands intensive cultivation to realise the maximum profit, rye does not: "medium or moderate cultivation results in low profits in the case of wheat culture. It is the opposite with rye; already under moderately intensive cultivation it brings in high net gains;"[1] in other words, though the absolute amount of profits may be higher in the case of wheat than in the case of rye, the highest profit in the case of rye can be obtained from a smaller amount of capital than in the case of wheat. Since, in both cases, under the import certificate method, the same par value can be obtained, so long as the certificates are valid for a large number of articles, there is a temptation to resort to rye; for this will reduce the amount of capital required by the cultivator to a greater extent than in the case of wheat. From the standpoint of imports, the rye exported will certainly require some additional wheat imports, but, in so far as the rye exports create certificates which are not used for cereal imports at all, there need be no additional import. Exports in this case can increase faster than imports, and the import certificate approximates to an export bounty.

§ 22. The case we have just examined is one in which the exports increase without a corresponding increase in the imports. Is it possible to find cases in which the imports will increase without a corresponding increase in the exports?

A simple case at once suggests itself. If the exports consist of high grade goods, paying a given rate of duty, then, if the certificates are exchanged for low grade goods, paying a lower rate of duty, the imports will grow at a greater rate than the exports. Thus, if the certificates received from goods which are dutiable at £1 per ton are used not for the import of similar goods, but for goods dutiable at only 5s. per ton, for every ton exported, 4 tons can be imported at the same cost in customs duty.

Further, if at any time, there is a failure to synchronise

---

[1] Beckmann, *op. cit.*, p. 138.

supply of certificates with the demand for them, they will fall to a discount. This discount will result in more being imported than would otherwise be the case. For, if the importer buys for £10 what will enable him to meet £20 in customs duties, he will obviously lose a profit of £10 unless he imports more. Lower prices here, as generally, will stimulate further purchases. Of course, such a possibility of extra profit will lead to the discount being temporary, for the rush to take advantage of the discount will raise the price of the certificate again.

To this deduction that such a discount tends to be temporary, there is, however, an important qualification. The discount may be permanent if there is an excess of exports over imports. In that case, if there are districts in which, owing to unfavourable conditions of transport or production, the price is permanently higher, the discount will replace home production by foreign products; less will be produced at home, and more will be imported. For, *ex hypothesi*, the conditions in the *importing* area are unfavourable to production. Prices are consequently equal to world price, plus the duty, and any decline in the cost of the certificate, in consequence of the excess of exports over imports as a whole, will affect demand, because such a discount is equivalent to a decline in the volume of protection afforded to the local producers. In this case, the price level over the whole area will approximate to the world price; in the exporting area, because there is a surplus over local need, in the importing area, because the discount on the certificate will stimulate imports at virtually lower prices.

§ 23. In France the opposition to the certificates arose from the protests of local producers whose position was threatened by the fall in the price of the certificates, and who argued that this discount was equivalent to a reduction in the amount of protection which the law guaranteed them. Thus, the French iron masters of the north and the wheat growers of the south were united in opposition to the system, and their opposition produced those changes which we have already described. In Germany, opposition has arisen in part from the consumers, who regard the certificates as one of the causes of high wheat prices, with perfect justice; though naturally, the producers argue that this is just the effect the system was intended to produce: whilst the economists tend to criticise the tendency which we have already explained, towards the appearance of export bounties in a concealed form.[1]

§ 24. From the standpoint of this work, the main problem has been to analyse the assumption that the certificate system only alters the distribution of the imports and the exports, and does not alter the balance; that, in other words, national production remains the same, both in quantity and in character. This is a contention which cannot be sustained. Having made this point clear, we are now in a position to pass on to an entirely fresh subject—that of export drawbacks.

---

[1] Beckmann's criticisms have already been stated. He only objects to the appearance of export bounties: that the system should permanently raise the internal price above the world price is not a defect in the system to him, but its justification. A different point is emphasised by Von Tyszka, "Das Welt wirtschaftliche Problem der Modernen Industrie-Staaten," who argues that the system has made Germany more and not less dependent on foreign countries, by stimulating export after the harvest, and thus reducing the stocks in hand towards the end of the crop year.

CHAPTER X.—*Continued.*

DRAWBACKS.

THE drawback is a method of evading the consequences of the protectionist régime (in so far as this raises prices and therefore impedes sale in competition with foreign producers), by refunding, in whole or in part, the duties on the raw materials which have been employed in the manufacturing of the commodity. Or, in the case of taxation imposed on the finished article, by refunding this if the commodity has been originally imported, and, lacking sale, has been re-exported, or by exempting the article altogether if it was domestically produced, and the tax is one on domestic consumption. It seems at first sight as if the system of drawbacks were the ideal system. It avoids the administrative difficulties of manufacture under bond: it does not occasion the dangers of the improvement trade, that articles may not be re-exported at all, and thus the customs authorities be deprived of part of their revenue. It allows the manufacturer all possible liberty and yet places him on the same level as his competitors by refunding the duty on the goods exported.

Nevertheless, the drawback system is in practice not devoid of difficulties of its own, and these we must next proceed to discuss. In any case, it must be pointed out that no drawback system can avoid the inconveniences arising from the locking up of capital in duties which are afterwards refunded. If the duties are not paid, but bond only is given, there is no true drawback system, but only a variety of improvement trade, or of manufacture under bond.

There are three fundamental questions about any drawback system—

(1) To what articles shall it be applied? Are all articles into which a dutiable material enters to be allowed drawback on exportation, or only selected articles?

(2) What shall be the amount of the drawback? Is the whole of the duty accruing on that portion of the imported

material embodied in the product to be exported, to be repaid, or only a portion?

(3) How shall the amount of the dutiable material contained in the exported article be ascertained?

It is the third of these problems which in practice has occasioned most trouble, because of the opportunities offered by a lax interpretation to the emergence of export bounties. A simple illustration will make this clear. If the milling industry imports wheat to be made into flour, the amount of the drawback must be governed by the amount of wheat which a given amount of flour represents, for the duty was paid on the wheat, and what is exported is flour. Suppose the ratio upon which drawback is actually paid is such that the amount of wheat which is actually milled from the wheat is greater than the official ratio, what is the effect?

The effect is to create concealed export bounties. For the drawback is supposed to be a repayment of the duty actually paid in the first instance; consequently, if the improvement in the milling industry is such that more is milled than the law allows for, this refund is equivalent to paying the same drawback on a smaller quantity of wheat, whereas the duty in the smaller quantity of wheat would be less than the drawback actually paid. It follows that if the article exported is subject to drawback, and this drawback is paid on a conventional scale, then every improvement in the processes of manufacture will increase the bounty actually received. It follows also that drawback legislation, unless it only provides for drawback on the exact amount of the material used, or a drawback which is less than the proportionate amount of duty on the material actually used, may easily become itself an encouragement to exportation, and not a mere removal of a hindrance to exportation. The most celebrated instance of drawbacks becoming export bounties is provided in the case of the beet sugar drawbacks which the European sugar producing States granted when the domestic sugar, subject to internal excise duties, was exported; bounties which were only swept away in the case of some of the States, by the provision for the manufacture of sugar in bond contained in the Brussels Convention of 1903.

The second and third of our questions are, it will be seen, really linked up with one another, in consequence of the danger just alluded to. The first question, whether drawbacks ought to be granted to all articles or to selected articles only, requires attention in consequence of the difficulties which arise if the principle of universal applicability of drawbacks is accepted or rejected.

If the duty on all materials is to be drawn back when the articles are exported, then the system becomes cumbersome, owing to the presence of mixed articles, in which the several components may only be present in small and varying quantities, so that the drawback legislation may become extremely complicated in its working. If the principle of selected commodities only is adopted, then the system can be denounced as unfair to those whose goods happen to be excluded. In any case, the system does not apply to those who have bought domestic raw materials whose prices have been raised in consequence of protection having been granted to the producers thereof, these domestically produced materials not being subject to an internal excise duty. Thus, if imported wheat is subject to duty, and a drawback system is in force, the flour made out of this imported wheat may be subject to drawback. A miller whose flour is wholly made of domestic wheat cannot claim drawback, in spite of the fact that the presence of the import duty will probably affect the price of his raw material, and thus hamper his competitive efficiency.

The manner in which drawback legislation actually works can best be studied from illustrative material. In the following paragraphs we shall examine some drawback legislation, and we will begin with that of the United States :—[1]

The position is thus—

(*a*) Articles exported under original conditions of import. If the goods have been warehoused, they may remain in bond for three years, and if re-exported within that time are entitled to a drawback of 99 per cent. of the duties paid. Articles which have been entered for consumption are similarly entitled to drawback, if the entry duties are 50 dollars or more and the goods are "exported directly from the uninterrupted custody of officers of the customs."

The further conditions for the receipt of drawback are—

Goods must be re-exported in their original packages (except in a few cases, drugs, medicines, chemical preparations,

---

[1] Customs Regulations of the U.S.A., §§ 836-889, Tariff Act of 1913, paragraph O of Part IV.

and unrefined sugar) "without diminution or change of quantity, quality, or value, unavoidable wastage or damage excepted."

(*b*) Goods manufactured from dutiable materials. Paragraph O of the 1913 Act enacts that a drawback of 99 per cent. is payable in such cases. The following conditions are enacted by the said sections :—

1. ". . . Where a principal product and a by-product result from the manipulation of the imported material, and only the by-product is exported, the proportion of the drawback distributed to such by-product shall not exceed the duty assessable under this Act on a similar by-product if imported into the United States." If there is no duty on the by-product there is no drawback on the exported by-product so manufactured, but in that case the principal product, if exported, shall receive the whole duty less 1 per cent. as drawback.

2. When the articles exported are of mixed content, "the imported materials or the parts of the articles manufactured from such materials shall so appear in the completed articles that the quantity or measure thereof be ascertained."

3. " . . . that the imported materials used in the manufacture or production of articles entitled to drawback of customs duties when exported shall, in all cases where drawback of duties on such materials is claimed, be identified, the quantity of such materials used and the amount of duties paid thereon shall be ascertained, the facts of the manufacture or production of such articles in the United States and their exportation therefrom shall be determined, and the drawback due thereon shall be paid to the manufacturer, producer, or exporter, to the agent of either, or to the person to whom such manufacturer, producer, exporter, or agent shall, in writing, order such drawback paid, under such regulations as the Secretary of the Treasury shall prescribe."

Notice of intent to export must be filed with the collector, and the inspecting officer must be furnished with such notice, which must be signed by him. All shipments must be inspected, though failure to get goods inspected is not always a bar to the receipt of drawback (Art. 861). The drawback claims must be completed within one year, unless the failure to complete is due to accident, inadvertence, or other good cause, in which case the department may, on application, grant an extension of six months. Non-completion within this period of twelve or eighteen months respectively is regarded as an abandonment of the claims.

If the goods are exported by the manufacturer, and made from materials imported by him, the customs requires a certificate from him, setting forth a sworn statement of imported materials used. If the goods are manufactured from materials not imported by the manufacturer, no drawback is allowable unless there is also filed "a certificate of delivery of imported merchandise" setting forth a sworn statement of the importer: if the goods were not directly sold by the importer to the manufacturer, every intermediate transfer must be separately noted on the certificate by a sworn statement.

If the goods have been purchased for export, the purchaser must swear to certain particulars, instead of the manufacturer doing so (that the goods were manufactured from the materials mentioned in the certificate annexed, that the materials are duty paid, that the duties so paid have not been previously refunded, that the particulars are correct, and that the goods are not intended to be relanded in the U.S.A.). Where the materials used have passed through "some process of manufacture before delivery, and the partly or completely finished article is used in the manufacture of some other article for exportation or where completely manufactured articles are purchased for exportation without further manipulation, a certificate of manufacture and delivery shall be filed." This must be sworn by the manufacturer in so far as it is intended that he reserves the drawback for himself. In addition to the usual description of the goods and their contents, it contains a sworn affirmation of the delivery of the goods, to the person named in the document. A second form of certificate is provided by the same article (872), for those cases in which the exporter reserves the drawback and not the manufacturer. By Article 876, evidence of landing must be furnished, such certificate to be furnished by the consignee, the foreign revenue officer, or the ships' agent at the place of landing. If the drawback exceeds 100 dollars, and payment is required before the certificate is received, bond must be given by the party desiring the drawback.[1]

[1] "Where the exportation is by sea, and the drawback does not exceed $100 on an entry, and where the merchandise is exported by land and the drawback is not in excess of $25, no landing certificate is required."

In *Sweden* Article 11 of the Preliminary Disposition of the Tariff lays down the general principle that "duty properly charged and paid shall not be refunded even if the goods are re-exported."

But this does not apply—

(1) To articles containing poison in excess of the limits laid down by the law, and re-exported.

(2) The cases where there was apparent cause for exemption of duty in virtue of Article 8 (which deals with the improvement trade), where the articles are exported three months after importation, and there appears to be no reasonable doubt as to the identity of the imported and exported goods.

(3) To the construction, alteration, and repair of ships. The duty shall be refunded in respect of "dutiable materials used therefor, if imported from abroad, including articles of household furniture firmly fixed on the vessel, which cannot be separated therefrom without losing their utility, or which are shown by special and durable marks to be exclusively intended for use on such vessel, or in case duty has not been paid," but, it is also provided, that if bond only has been given, such bonded goods are to be exempted from final payment of duty. For the conditions under which the rule holds, see Article 12. Completion must be within three years.

(4) Article 13 provided for specific drawbacks on refined loaf, candy, or cake sugar: cocoa in powder, coffee, burned or roasted, but not ground: bread, macaroni or vermicelli, of wheat, rice, starch, manufactured tobacco, manufactures of paper, for woollen, linen and silk tissues, "if exported by sea from a Swedish staple town . . . when manufactured in Sweden from foreign materials."

The conditions are that a minimum export of 25 kilos. take place: the export declaration must be accompanied by a sworn statement of the exporter, attested by two witnesses, that the goods have been manufactured in Sweden of fully paid raw material, the fact of exportation must be verified by the port authorities at the port of arrival, legalised by the Swedish consular authorities, if there are any.

In addition, drawbacks are allowed to—

1. Owners of mills on the exportation by sea of the following:—Fine flour of wheat, rye or barley, and groats of wheat or barley: the drawback being the amount of duty

paid by the millers on the corresponding quantity of unground cereals of the same kind, imported directly from abroad. The equivalents are fixed by the law itself.

The conditions are—the intention to grind for re-export with drawback must be stated on importation, import and export must take place at the same customs office, at least 2,000 kilos. must be exported at one time: the shipment must be accompanied by a sworn statement attested by two witnesses that the goods are the products of the exporter's own mills: the raw materials must have been imported within six months of the shipment, the customs authorities must verify the weight of the exports, seal the sacks, and supervise the loading, the authorities must also keep accounts. In order to receive drawback, a monthly request must be made by the person concerned, accompanied by "extracts from the balance accounts of the customs house, and by receipts for the customs duties in respect of the quantities of unground cereals entered in the balance sheets."

2. The same facilities are granted to the owners of rice mills, on the export of rice ground from grain, whether cleaned, whole, or crushed, "provided it was imported by the mill-owner directly from abroad or from a free port or removed from bond." Certain equivalents are fixed in this case also, but the previous importation is extended to twelve months. These drawbacks are also payable if the products are exported by land to Norway, if exported under the appropriate regulations.[1]

In *Australia* [2] "drawback of the full amount of duty paid shall be allowed on all imported goods (other than spirits, including perfumes, wine, beer, tobacco, cigars, cigarettes, and opium) which are exported in the original packages in which they were imported, or in packages packed in the presence of an officer. Provided that drawback shall not be allowed in respect of goods which are exported in other than original packages, unless the goods are exported within three years from date of payment of duty.

As to articles manufactured in Australia, drawback may be allowed on the actual quantity of imported material used in their manufacture, to the extent of the duty paid on

---

[1] See Kelly, *op. cit.*, p. 614, col. 1.

[2] § 168, *et seq.*, of the Customs Act. Arts. 129-147 of the Regulations under the Customs Act.

original importation. Drawback under this regulation shall only be allowed in respect of such material as the minister specifies by Gazette notice, and under the conditions and restrictions prescribed in the notice." [1]

Goods which have been used after first importation are not entitled to drawback: the packing of goods for export on which drawback is to be claimed must take place under the superintendence of customs officers, after due notice given, and payment must be made for the services of the inspecting officer.

In the *United Kingdom* the general rule is that only those goods are subject to drawback for which specific authority has been given.

Thus, tea is not subject to drawback, nor are the various other compounds, nor playing cards, nor dried fruit, among other possible illustrations. On the other hand, the commodities taxable under § 12 of the Finance (No. 2) Act, 1915 (motor cars, motor accessories, and component parts, musical instruments, and accessories, and component parts thereof, clocks, watches, and component parts, cinematograph films), are all subject to drawback under § 13 (1) of the said Act.[2]

The next point which requires mention is that the amount of drawback is not usually equal to the amount of duty originally imposed, as can easily be seen by comparing the rates of duty imposed on tobacco and spirits, sugar, and sugar derivatives, with the rates of drawback.

By § 119 of the Customs Consolidation Act the limit of time for the payment of drawback is two years from the date of shipment of the goods. The drawbacks are made conditional—(i) on the certification by the collector or other proper officer of the entry outwards of the goods on the debenture which is required, " and so soon as the same (goods) shall have been duly exported, and a notice containing the particulars of the goods shall have been delivered by the

---

[1] Regs., Arts. 129-130. The regulations governing the drawback on sugar used in making jam and other goods and with regard to oils lay down in greater detail the procedure to be followed. Arts. 131-132.

[2] " If it is proved to the satisfaction of the Commissioners of Customs and Excise that a new import duty has been duly paid in respect of any article, and that the article has not been used in Great Britain or Ireland, a drawback equal to the amount of duty shall be allowed on that article if exported as merchandise."

exporter to the export officer, the shipment and exportation thereof shall be certified upon such debenture by the export officer, and the debenture shall thereupon be computed and passed with all convenient despatch " (Customs Consolidation Act, § 117 (2)). The person entitled to any drawback on any goods duly exported or his agent authorised by him for that purpose shall make and subscribe upon the debenture that the goods mentioned therein have been actually exported, and have not been relanded, and are not intended to be relanded in any part of the United Kingdom, and that such person at the time of entry and shipping was and continued to be entitled to the drawback thereon, and the name of such person shall be stated in the debenture, which shall then be delivered to such person or his agent, and the receipt of such person on the debenture, countersigned by the holder of such debenture, if the same shall have been transferred in the meantime, shall be the discharge for such drawback when paid." Failure to comply with the requirement to export, or not to re-import, is punishable with the confiscation of the goods, " together with any ship, boat, or craft which may have been used in so unshipping, relanding, landing, or carrying such goods from the ship in which the same were shipped for exportation," together with a fine of the master of the ship, or other responsible person, equal to a minimum of £100, or a sum equal to treble the duty paid value of such goods.[1]

§ 25. It is natural that in countries in which the improvement trade system has obtained a firm hold, the question of drawbacks should have relatively small rôle to play, for the drawback and the free entry of goods under the conditions of the improvement trade are rival methods. If at the same time, those articles which are subject to internal excise duties are manufactured in bond, so that the revenue authorities are fully conversant with the facts of the case, the area which is left to the drawback is really restricted to those cases in which the right to free entry for improvement trade purposes is, for one reason or another, impossible. Hence, drawback legislation plays only a subordinate rôle in the legislation of such countries as France and Belgium.

---

[1] § 14 of the Customs and Inland Revenue Act, 1879, quoted Highmore, *op. cit.*, p 107.

§ 26. We have now passed under review the principal methods by which the necessity of having regard to the competitive efficiency of countries in international trade leads to mitigation of the protectionist régime. In all cases the object is the same. The goods intended for internal consumption, directly or indirectly, are made subject to duty, whilst those which are intended for re-export are either freed from duty altogether, or have the volume of duty which they have paid returned on re-export, whether in their original or a more finished state.

NOTE I. TO CHAPTER X.

On Some Difficulties Connected with Changes in the Rate of Duty.

In § 14 of the foregoing chapter reference was made to the difficulty which arose in deciding at what rate dutiable goods should be rated on clearance from warehouse, should the rate of duty have changed. Analogous to this is the problem of how to rate goods, the passage of which through the customs is incomplete at a time the rates are changed. This, it will be noted, is a different problem to the constitutional one of deciding whether it is desirable to rate goods before the legal changes associated with an alteration of customs duty are complete—whether, in other works, a higher rate is to be levied by mere resolution of the legislature. What we are dealing with are the effects of changes in the rate, whatever the sanction, on warehoused goods, or on goods in process of clearance.

At the same time another point requires examination—*i.e.*, the treatment of re-imported goods: ought these to pay duty, or ought they to be free?

(1) **Warehoused Goods and Goods in process of Importation.**

In the case of the United Kingdom we have to consider the effect of the following legal dispositions :—

(*a*) Customs Consolidation Act, § 19. "All goods deposited in any warehouse or place of security under any Act for the warehousing of goods without payment of duty upon the first warehousing, or which may be imported, and on board ship, shall, upon being entered for home consumption, be subject to such and the like duties as may at the time of passing such entry be due and payable on the like sort of goods under any Customs Act at the time of passing such entry, save and except in cases where special provision shall be made by such Act to the contrary."

(*b*) Finance Act, 1900, 63 and 64 Vict., c. 7, § 9. "The duty to be paid on goods or commodities deposited in a customs or excise warehouse is hereby declared to be the duty chargeable at the date of the actual removal of those goods or commodities from the warehouse, and if before that date any sums shall have been paid in respect of duty, the difference (if any) between the sums so paid and the actual duty chargeable shall be paid or repaid, as the case may be."

This gives us four cases—

(i) Change between date of warehousing and date of entry for home consumption, duty leviable at the rates in force on time of entry.

(ii) Change of duty between date of entry for home consumption and "actual removal of those goods or commodities from the warehouse," duty in force on date of actual removal.

(iii) In the case of imported goods the date of entry fixes the rate of duty payable, whether there has been a change in the rate between the date of import and the date of entry, or a change of duty between the date of entry and the date of clearance or not.

(For definition of date of importation, see § 40 of the C.C.A., and its amendment by the Finance Act, 1901, § 7 (2) in Highmore, p. 45.)

In **India,** by § 115 of the Sea Customs Act, "If, after any goods entered for warehousing have been assessed under § 87 and alteration is made in the duty leviable upon such goods, or in the tariff valuation (if any) applicable thereto, such goods shall be re-assessed in accordance with (such alteration)."

In **South Africa,** § 66 of the Customs Management Act, "warehoused goods . . . shall, after being entered for home consumption, be subject and liable to such and the like duties as may at the time of passing such entry be due and payable upon goods of the like kind under any law in force when such entry was passed."

In **France,** warehoused goods cleared for consumption are dutiable at the rates in force at the time of clearance, except in the case of colonial products originating from a country which at the moment of entry for warehousing enjoyed the French minimum tariff. Goods under these conditions continue to enjoy the lower rate, even, if at the time of entry for consumption, the country from which they originate should have lost the benefit of the lower rates. But the lower rates then granted are those of the minimum tariff at the time of clearance, and not the rates of the time of entry for warehousing.[1]

(2) Re-Importation of Goods.

United Kingdom.—The regulations contained in C.C.A, § 63, were repealed by 42 and 43 Vict., c. 21, § 6. As things now stand, goods are to be treated as foreign if liable to customs duty, and subject to the same regulations as foreign goods, unless re-imported within five years and proven to be British goods, provided that any drawback goods shall be treated as foreign unless specially exempted by the Commissioner of Customs,[2] and on payment of such drawbacks: all foreign goods re-imported, whether duty paid or not, are to be treated as if imported for the first time: trade marked re-imported British goods may be re-admitted on proof that they are British by consent of proprietor or on proof, to the satisfaction of the customs authorities, that they are British.

For plain British spirits re-imported, see § 59 of the Spirits Act, 1880 (43 and 44 Vict., c. 24).

Commonwealth of Australia.—§ 151 of the Customs Act, and item 446 of the C.T., 1908-11. § 111 of the regulations under the Customs Act, Stat. Rules, 1913, No. 346.

Goods other than Samples of Duty Paid Goods.—Goods must be brought back within two years from date of exportation: drawback of excise duty must not have been paid: the character of the goods must in no way have been changed: the collector must be satisfied that the goods are the same by reference to the export entry or by statutory declaration: if free entry is claimed, proof must be given that customs duty has once been paid: finally, "the minister must be satisfied that the re-importation or bringing of the goods will not unfairly disturb the market for similar goods in Australia generally or in the place where the goods are proposed to be landed."

---

[1] Pallain, *op. cit.*, vol. i., p. 522, note 1.

[2] The articles dutiable under the Finance (No. 2) Act, 1915, are exempted, subject to the conditions set out in § 13 of that Act.

United States.—Customs regulations, Art. No. 234: T.A., 1913, § 1, paras. 404 and 642.

Art. 234. Dutiable merchandise imported and afterwards exported, although it may have paid duty on the first importation, is liable to duty on every subsequent importation into the United States; but this does not apply to wearing apparel, personal and household effects taken abroad and brought back by a returning resident of the United States. Neither does it apply to iron or steel drums of domestic or foreign manufacture used for the shipment of acids or other chemicals which shall have been exported from the United States, nor to articles exported from the United States for repairs, which may be returned upon payment of a duty upon the value of the repairs at the rate at which the article itself would be subject if imported.

Tariff Act of 1913.—

No. 404 of the *Free List*—" Articles, the growth, produce, or manufacture of the United States, when returned after having been exported, without having been advanced in value or improved in condition by any process of manufacture or other means . . ." (the other section of the paragraph refers to containers and articles exported for repairs not falling under this head).

Notes.—1. This paragraph shall not apply to any article upon which an allowance of drawback has been made, the re-importation of which is hereby prohibited except upon payment of duties equal to the drawbacks allowed; or to any article manufactured in bonded warehouses and exported under any provision of law.

Switzerland.—Customs Law, Art. 3, sub-sec. (*p*) (freed from import duty).

" Goods and cattle of Swiss origin which return to Switzerland within the period of time laid down in the regulations in consequence of their being refused by the consignee, or in consequence of impossibility of sale abroad.

" The customs department is further empowered to exempt from customs duty in other than the above-mentioned cases, goods of Swiss origin, which return to the consignor within a period of time to be determined by the administration, if the Swiss origin of the goods and their export is appropriately proven."

Cf. Art. 151 of the V.V.Z. which adds to the cases enumerated that of foreign goods which have been exported from the Swiss customs area, and on whose account customs duty has therefore been paid.

To obtain free re-import a special entry has to be made, accompanied by a notarial or official proof of the local or customs authorities as to the origin, destination, and date of dispatch of the goods, based upon the inspection of the commercial books and the correspondence relating to the shipment.

Appeal may be made in these cases in which free re-entry having been refused the goods have paid duty.

In the cases of special exemption the period is limited to two years, and the decision left to the Federal Authorities.

Article 152 covers the case of goods which have paid duty on import, but which, in consequence of refusal to accept them on the part of the addresse or on other grounds, are re-exported abroad.

The duty is repayable under the following conditions:— The returning package must correspond in nature and weight with the imported, must be consigned to the original consignor, which must be confirmed to the exporting bureau by the production of the original bill of lading in order to facilitate comparison with the export bill of lading.

2. The export bill of lading must be made out by the Swiss consignor direct to the address of the recipient.

3. The export must take place within two months, reckoned from the date of import.

4. The demand for repayment of the import duty is to be handed in at the time of export, accompanied by a statement of the grounds of refusal at the exporting bureau, which is to send them on to the Gebiets-direktion with a report as to the state of the goods on survey. (Revisionsbefund.) The latter office will then decide the matter itself, or, if it is not competent to do so, will forward the documents to the Oberzoll-direktion.

In **Germany,** § 113 of the Federal Customs Law lays it down that "products of the Federal Area, which apart from fair and market traffic, have been sent abroad on order, for inspection, to public exhibitions, on consignment or for temporary use, and which return from thence, may be exempted from duty, in so far as no doubt exists that the same goods are being imported as were exported."

The fair and market traffic is separately regulated by § 112 of the Act, which lays it down that—

" In order to encourage the use of foreign fairs and markets, the duty-free importation of goods of Federal origin which have remained unsold, may be permitted.

" There may also be allowed to foreign merchants and industrials, who frequent domestic fairs and markets, the import duty on their unsold goods on their re-export."

It is laid down by the Federal decision of 5th July, 1888, that " re-imported goods, which have been exported abroad against drawback, may be re-imported free of duty on the repayment of the drawback given.

" Goods of foreign origin which have undergone an improvement process in the interior under reservation of customs duty may be re-imported as return goods (§ 113) on resumption of the customs obligation noted at the time of entry for improvement."

CHAPTER XI.

Commercial and Tariff Treaties.[1]

§ 1. We may define a commercial treaty as an instrument regulating for a period of time (which may be fixed by the instrument or may be indefinite, as depending on the will of the parties themselves), the commercial relations of two or more States. This instrument must be assented to by the Executives of the States in question, with or without the further assent of the legislatures. Such an instrument differs from an autonomous regulation of such relationship—for two States may accord each other privileges by the device of legislative enactments or executive decree without the conclusion of a treaty—by the fact that a treaty is always bi-lateral in origin; there is always a co-contractant, whether the benefits are reciprocal or not, whereas this is not the case with a domestic law or regulation.

For our purposes we are more particularly concerned with those aspects of commercial treaties which deal with importation and exportation, and, in still narrower definition, with the tariff treatment of imports and exports, together with those formalities and processes which attend import and export as commercial and fiscal phenomena. The growing importance of these aspects of commercial intercourse between States has led to the emergence of that particular class of commercial treaties which is, somewhat loosely, known as the Tariff Treaty. No rigid line of distinction can be drawn between the genus and the species, but to the older technical terms of "Treaties of Commerce and Navigation," or "Friendship, Commerce, and Navigation," or "Friendship and Alliance," there must now be added "Treaty of Commerce, Customs, and Navigation." This is not to imply that tariff treaties, in the sense of treaties regulating and fixing customs duties are a

[1] In this chapter, the letters M.F.N. will be used as a convenient abbreviation of Most-Favoured-Nation.

new invention of the recent past: it is only an indication of the fact that such matters are now of such importance as to lead to inclusion among the technical titles of the instrument employed. In truth, however, the phrase tariff treaty is an expression of economic rather than diplomatic importance, and the connotation of the phrase being loose, it is descriptive rather than logical in import.

§ 2. The objects with which commercial and tariff treaties are concluded are, of course, very numerous. But the detailed content is capable of subsumption [1] under very much less complicated categories as soon as we ask what the detailed regulations are in every case intended to effect. Here we meet with two aims: the contracting States may attempt to—

(1) Make the position as between themselves at least as favourable as it is between one of them and any other State.

(2) Make the position of the States as between themselves better than it is between one of them and any other State.

Here we are looking at the matter from the standpoint of advantage: in the first case the States attempt to obtain a condition of equality with that of other or more favoured States: in the second case they attempt to obtain a position of preference as compared to other States.

The technical problem which presents the greatest logical interest is whether these two positions are capable of being reconciled. It looks at first sight as if they were totally opposed, but this is not the case. Two contracting States may quite logically agree to treat one another at least as well as either of them treats any third State, and may at the same time agree to give one another concessions which they have not given to any other third State with which they have been concluding treaties in the past. The problem really becomes difficult when States enter into a series of agreements, because then they have to reconcile the different treaties into which they have entered with each other. If State A enters into a series of agreements with States B, C, and D, in each of which it promises to treat the contractant at least as well as any other

[1] Compare the classification in Grunzel, "Handelspolitik."

State, and at the same time gives special advantages to each of its co-contractants, are the others entitled to demand those concessions, or are they not? To this question we can give no definite answer at this stage, for the facts of international intercourse yield two divergent interpretations. All that we need do is to indicate the problem which we have thus raised: it is the problem of "Most-Favoured-Nation" treatment, in many ways the most important of all the problems which commercial treaties raise. Its detailed consideration must for the moment be postponed.

A moment's reflection will show that the promise of most-favoured-nation treatment, however we may define this, is not necessarily the best standard when we are dealing only with the position of two States *inter se*. The standard of comparison may be shifted from the concessions granted to any third State to the rights of the citizens of the grantee State. In this way we obtain a second standard of comparison, that which is usually known as "National Treatment," or "Inland Parity" as compared to "Foreign Parity." In this case the two contracting States promise one another that as concerns certain subjects, they will treat the citizens or goods of the other at least as well as the goods and the persons of their own citizens.

Though these two standards are distinct, yet they are connected by the network of treaties, for the simple reason that if two States promise one another national treatment, and then promise other States most-favoured-nation treatment, then these latter States may quite legitimately claim that they are also entitled to be treated on a national basis, for otherwise they are not being treated as favourably as the most-favoured-nation, assuming that there is a material difference in treatment as a result of the different promises made.

Of course, such a claim could only be preferred if the promise of most-favoured-nation treatment in the one case and national treatment in the other covered the same ground. The simplest way of avoiding difficulties on this ground is to adhere to a uniform practice—that is, to separate the matters in which national treatment is given from those in which most-favoured-nation treatment is given, and at the same time never to give one State national treatment in matters in which other States have only been given favoured nation status. To some extent such a division of the field arises "naturally." National treatment is extended in those cases in which, granted a desire to extend most favourable treatment in the absolute sense of the word, the standard of estimating what is most favourable treatment is afforded by the rights of the nationals of the contracting States. Thus, as regards the rights of settlement, the acquisition of property, the treatment before the courts of law, and so forth, the national standard is obviously the best basis. But in other cases, also assuming an equal desire for the most favourable treatment absolutely, no national standard is possible. Such a case is presented for instance by the treatment of consular officers.

But though the practical problem of discrimination between two nations may be avoided by uniformity of practice, it must not be overlooked that the national standard and the most favoured standard may be *conflicting* standards. That is, the cases in which one or the other can be adopted are by no means small in number, and it must not be assumed that in practice, where choice is possible, the national standard is the one adopted, where that would lead to the greater rights being obtained by the foreigner. It is true that in some cases where differentiation could easily be practised between the national and the foreigner, no differentiation is in fact practised, as, for instance, discrimination between imports on the ground of the nationality of the importer; though discrimination on the ground of the nationality of the ship is by no means so frowned upon. The choice between the two standards is in fact very largely a matter of feeling at different times, and a period of anti-foreign feeling will reduce the number of matters in which national treatment is granted, whilst periods of more "cosmopolitan" sentiment will increase them. The tendency at the moment is distinctly in the direction of restriction, whilst in the 19th century the most usual matter in which national treatment might have been possible, and was in fact not granted, was the reservation of the coasting trade.[1]

---

[1] For an easy method of comparison of these two grants, see Cd. 3395, "Return of Most-Favoured-Nation Clauses," and Cd. 3396, "Return of National Treatment Clauses," both referring to the Treaties between the U.K. and Foreign Powers in force on the 1st January, 1907. For exclusion of the coasting trade, see, *e.g.*, Treaties with Austria-Hungary, 30/4/68, Art. 2; Colombia, 16/2/66, Art. 9; Egypt, 29/10/89, Art. 5; Roumania, 31/11/05, Art. 10; Uruguay, 13/11/85, Art. 3; on the other hand, the coasting trade is specifically included in the category of

§ 3. Quite different from the questions hitherto discussed is the question whether national treatment is ever justified. The opponent of the policy can say that the issue of justice hardly arises : that so long as no foreigner is more privileged than another, there is no question of discrimination, and all that justice requires is that all foreigners should be equal in competition with one another. To make their position equal to that of the national is to forget that charity begins at home.

We may leave the question of justice on one side, and deal with the matter from a purely utilitarian standpoint. The fact is that national treatment where the objective circumstances make it possible—where, in other words, there is a real opportunity of choice between the two principles—can be defended on the ground that its absence interferes with the possibility of the maximum volume of trade. If we suppose

---

"National Treatment" in the Treaties with Greece, 10/11/86, Art. 7 ; Salvador, 24/19/62, Art. 3.

In some treaties the two forms will be found, not as rival, but as complementary choices, combined in the same clause, *cf.* the following :—

U.K., Switzerland, 6/9/55, Art. 8 : "In all that relates to the importation into, the warehousing in, the transit through, and the exportation from, their respective territories, of any article of lawful commerce, the two contracting parties engage that their respective subjects and citizens shall be placed upon the same footing as subjects and citizens of the country, or as the subjects and citizens of the most-favoured-nation in any case where the latter may enjoy an exceptional advantage not granted to natives." Japan, 16/7/94, Art. 3 : "They shall have liberty freely to come with their ships and cargoes to all places, ports, and rivers in the dominions and possessions of the other, which are or may be opened to foreign commerce, and shall enjoy, respectively, the same treatment in matters of commerce and navigation as native subjects, or subjects or citizens of the most-favoured-nation, without having to pay taxes, imposts, or duties, of whatever nature, or under whatever denomination, levied in the name or for the profit of the Government, public functionaries, private individuals, corporations, or establishments of any kind, other or greater than those paid by native subjects, or subjects or citizens of the most-favoured-nation, subject always to the Laws, Ordinances, and Regulations of each country."

On the question of the appropriateness of the two standards in different cases, see Grunzel, "Economic Protectionism," p. 171, *et seq.*, who, however, exaggerates the degree to which the most-favoured standard must be adopted, when he says, "it affects only such measures of economic policy as relate exclusively to foreign goods and foreign persons, such as regulations regarding duties and customs administration, the admission of consuls, etc." In fact, were customs duties and regulations differentiated according to the *nationality* of the importer as a general rule, the protection afforded by the most-favoured-nation rule would be small. Tacitly or specifically, national treatment is applied in such cases.

On the other hand, see *op. et loc. cit.* for an admirable discussion on the difficulty of enforcing national treatment in the case of railway rates, a matter which falls outside the scope of this work.

a State in which habitually there is effective discrimination between foreigners and nationals in the courts of law, to the disadvantage of the former, then it will be obvious that, other things equal, foreigners will avoid trading with the nation in question, that prices will rise in consequence of the smaller volume of trade, a rise which the individual will justify on the ground that he is entitled to "compensation for risk." Hence, the granting of national treatment can be justified in general on perfectly "business principles," quite apart from the possible chances of retaliation which may rob the venture of all hope of being profitable in the case of countries which have wide interests in foreign countries.

There are, of course, exceptions to every rule: and it is perfectly possible to defend discrimination on grounds of public safety and the like, though such grounds should not easily be assumed. Ultimately, however, the deciding factor is very largely nationalist sentiment, which leads to changes of policy which it is hard to justify on rational grounds.

§ 4. The question of national *versus* most favoured treatment has taken us rather away from our subject. It has been necessary to deal with it at some length because there is some danger of the importance of the "national treatment" principle being overlooked. Discussion turns largely upon what is meant by the "most-favoured-nation clause," rather overlooking that this is, in those cases in which national treatment is possible, the less valuable principle.

It is now possible for us to turn again to the question of treaties, and the first question which arises is the form of the treaty. We have already seen in a previous chapter that on the continent of Europe two main types of tariff have arisen—the maximum-minimum and the conventional. On this basis, and adding the most-favoured-nation clause we get the following classifications :—

(A) Dealing with the whole range of possible commercial treaties, which, of course, includes tariff treaties, Grunzel's classification can be adopted—[1]

(1) Treaties without M.F.N. clauses and without tariff rates.

[1] *Op. cit.*, p. 447.

(2) Treaties without M.F.N. clauses and with tariff rates.

(3) Treaties with M.F.N. clauses and with tariff rates.

(4) Treaties with M.F.N. clauses and without tariff rates.

(B) For our purpose this classification is insufficient, since we are more particularly concerned with the forms which tariff treaties can assume. Here we get the following possibilities :—

(1) Most-favoured-nation treatment only—

(2) (*a*) Grant of part of minimum tariff only.
(*b*) Grant of whole of minimum tariff only.
(*c*) Grant of whole of minimum tariff *and* conventionalisation of—
(1) Some rates.
(2) All rates.
(*d*) Grant of special concessions by way of convention only.
(*e*) Grant of special concessions by way of convention, and the grant simultaneously of all other conventionalised rates.

(3) Combination of most-favoured-nation treatment (1) with some of the forms under (2).

§ 5. We must now deal with these possibilities in more detail.

(*a*) *Most Favoured Treatment Only.*—In this case no particular rate is granted; the only condition which the treaty lays down is that the co-contracting party shall not be treated worse in this respect than the most-favoured-nation. Whether this allows the grantor State to insist upon compliance with possible conditions—that is, whether the grant of most-favoured-nation treatment can be conditional is a matter we must take up separately in a later section. In regard to the alteration of rates, whether in an upward or downward direction, the grantor State retains full autonomy. All that the grant conveys is a promise that *discrimination* will not be practised.

(*b*) *Group* 2.—It will be noted that this group can again be sub-divided into minor groups, and that these sub-groups can have reference to those specific forms of the bi-lateral tariff which were discussed in Chapter III. The first sub-group comprises items *a*, *b*, and *c* above, and we must discuss the differences between them.

Sub-group i.—If a part only of the minimum tariff is granted —an instance in point is the Franco-American agreement of 1911—all that the State contracts to do is to grant the minimum rates in its tariff at the moment of the signature of the treaty. It does not bind itself not to raise these rates, though it may pledge itself to give notice of its intention to do so ; it does not pledge itself in any way with regard to other articles, in regard to which the co-contracting State has no claim. Nor has the co-contracting State the right to demand concessions accorded to other States unless these lower rates have been autonomously fixed, for, as it is not in possession of the most-favoured-nation guarantee, a conventional concession is outside its rights.

If the whole of the minimum tariff is granted, the position is only altered in so far as the co-contracting State enjoys the advantage of subsequent autonomous reductions in the rates of duty on all articles.

The rights of the co-contracting State receive a distinct increase when the treaty binds the grantor State not to alter the rate as laid down by the treaty for a given period of time. But, so long as the grantee does not enjoy most-favoured-nation treatment, the grant does not convey the right to enjoy concessions of still lower rates which may be made to other States later on. That is, *discrimination* is still possible, but *stability* is secured.

In the event of such a treaty being concluded, wherein, it may be asked, does it differ from a conventional treaty of the type referred to under (*e*)? In form, it no longer differs at all, but the process by which it comes into existence is very different. To arrive at the conventionalised rates by a process of diplomatic bargaining is surely a very different thing to incorporating into a treaty a series of rates already previously determined upon.

Sub-group ii.—When we turn to (*d*) and (*e*) the grantor State bargains with the grantee, and accords certain concessions on the general tariff which are embodied specifically in the tariff. The concessions which, in a similar way, have been granted to other States, in the absence of the favoured nation clause, may or may not be extended, but the grantor has no claim to future favours, whether in regard to the wider or narrower form of the treaty. Again there is *stability*, but no guarantee against *discrimination*.

All this follows from what has been said in Chapter III., but the form of the treaty is really profoundly affected when it is attempted to combine the most-favoured-nation provision with any of the sub-groups with which we have just been dealing. In so far as group 2 by itself is concerned, we are really dealing with particular forms of what may broadly be called reciprocity treaties. When we come to combine these groups with the M.F.N. clause, we get a "mixed" form of treaty, the true nature of which depends upon the extent to which the M.F.N. clause modifies, and is modified by, the technical nature of the bargain in the reciprocal clauses of the treaty.

We must, consequently, study the various interpretations which may be placed upon the M.F.N. clause itself. Since, in the last fifty or sixty years the M.F.N. clause has played a leading rôle in the treaty history of tariffs, this is a matter of the preatest possible consequence.

§ 6. In general,[1] the grant of M.F.N. treatment implies a promise that the grantee State shall not, with reference to the subject matter to which, given the context or explicitly, the clause refers, be treated worse than any third State possessing the greater or greatest privileges: or, positively put, that any advantages granted to a third State which, in respect to the matters at issue, represents the most favoured State, shall also be extended to the grantee.

§ 7. The M.F.N. clause can thus be formulated positively and negatively. Much more important from our point of

[1] For general discussions of the M.F.N. Clause, see particularly, Hornbeck, "The M.F.N. Clause" in 3 American J. of Int. Law, 1909, p. 395, *et seq.*, p. 619, *et seq.*, p. 797, *et seq.* (bibliography, p. 396); Glier, "Die Meistbegünstigungsklausel, 1905"—the most thorough historical study of the more formal aspects of the problem; Moore's "Digest of Int. Law," vol. v., pp. 257-319; U.S.A. Tariff Commission Report on Reciprocity and Commercial Treaties, 1919, Pt. ii., pp. 389-456: Lippert, "Internationales Finanzrecht," § 28, pp. 131-180. For other references, see this and the following sections, passim. So far as I am aware, there is no systematic English treatise on the problems raised by the M.F.N. Clause, a remarkable instance of the deplorable influence exercised by acquiescence in the superficial dogmas of political parties.

view, however, are three possible divergencies in the *material* shaping of the clause.

(1) The promise may be one- or two-sided—*i.e.*, *non-reciprocal* or *reciprocal*. In the first case the grantor State is not given the same privileges in return, in the second case it is.

(2) The promise may be *limited* or *unlimited*. When the M.F.N. clause is limited, certain exceptions to the general grant are made. But it is important to be quite clear as to what is meant. The exception must refer to the matter in hand. It may be true to say that the M.F.N. clause in a treaty between two given countries may be limited to a certain portion of the total of all conceivable matters to which the clause might refer in other treaties, but it would not follow from this that the clause in the treaty in question would be technically "limited." It would only be limited if certain portions of the particular field of reference were expressly or impliedly excluded thereform.

(3) The promise may be *conditional* or *unconditional*. This distinction refers not to the content or subject matter of the clause, but to the qualifications subject to which the grant, whether limited or unlimited, reciprocal or non-reciprocal is made.

§ 8. Here, then, we have 3 conditions which can be combined with one another in the following ways :—

M.F.N.	Conditional	Reciprocal	Limited, . . .	(1)
			Unlimited, . .	(2)
		Non-reciprocal	Limited, . . .	(3)
			Unlimited, . .	(4)
	Unconditional	Reciprocal	Limited, . . .	(5)
			Unlimited, . .	(6)
		Non-reciprocal	Limited, . . .	(7)
			Unlimited, . .	(8)

Here we have eight *possible* forms: we might add to the number. If, in other words, it were considered that a promise implying that in addition to the M.F.N. privileges having to be unconditionally extended, they should also be *immediately* extended to the other contracting party, created a sub-class. Each of the above classes could be sub-divided into immediately extensible and those where this requirement was not laid down : thus giving us 16 forms in all.[1]

Other schemes of classification [2] have been suggested, but from our point of view it is more important to proceed to give illustrations of these various forms.

§ 9. *Form* 1—**Conditional, Reciprocal, and Limited**—

U.S.A.-Brazil, 12th December, 1828, Article II. :—

> "The United States of America and His Majesty the Emperor of Brazil . . . engage mutually not to grant any particular favour to other nations, in respect of commerce and navigation, which shall not immediately become common to the other party, *who shall enjoy the same freely, if the concession was freely made, or on allowing the same compensation if the concession was conditional.* It is understood, however, that the relations and conventions which now exist, or may hereafter exist, between

---

[1] *E.g.*, Zollverein-Belgium, 1865, Art. 2: "Every favour, every immunity, every reduction of import duties that one of the high contracting parties shall give to a third party shall be *immediately* and unconditionally extended to the other party."

The U.S.A. Report takes the standpoint that the insertion of the requirement of immediacy creates a "type which may be looked upon either as distinct or as a mere variation." As a matter of fact, in its own classification, the "immediacy" requirement is only considered in the case of unconditional M.F.N. Clauses, but it is also possible to accommodate the requirement to the circumstances of the conditional forms, as in the Brazilian Treaty quoted later on. But in the case of the conditional forms, the requirement of immediacy means only that the concession must be extended as soon as the qualifying conditions have been complied with, and this, it must be noted, is not the same thing as saying that a willingness to comply with the conditions has to be immediately followed by an acceptance of the offer to comply—such an offer has in fact been implicitly refused by the U.S.A. in the case of the Hawaii Treaty of 30/1/1875, which in the words of the report just quoted, meant that "the latter country was no longer free to extend to Great Britain even the opportunity to purchase concessions," *op. cit.*, 418-9. The true ground for denying the "immediately and unconditionally" clause the character of a true subclass lies to my mind in the fact that the stipulation adds nothing to the content of the unconditionality of the clause, for to insist on a time-lag would be to infringe either the unconditionality of the clause or its freedom from limitations.

[2] The following may be cited :—

(*a*) *Glier* (*op. cit.*, p. 5, n. 1).

(1) Conditional and unconditional.
(2) Limited and unlimited.
(3) "Clean" M.F.N. treatment, "if it is neither conditional nor limited."
(4) M.F.N. treatment *pro praeterito* denotes "the concession of advantages which a third state at the moment of the concession already enjoys, which are, therefore, derived from former treaties,

Brazil and Portugal, shall form an exception to this article." [1]

Form 2—**Conditional, Reciprocal, and Unlimited**—

U.K.-Liberia, 21st November, 1848, Article VII. :—

" It being the intention of the two contracting parties to bind themselves by the present treaty to treat each other on the footing of the most-favoured-nation, it is hereby agreed between them that any favour, privilege, or immunity whatever, in matters of commerce and navigation, which either contracting party has actually granted, or may hereafter grant, to the subjects or citizens of the other contracting party, *gratuitously, if the concession in favour of that other State shall have been gratuitous, or in return for a compensation as nearly as possible of proportionate value and effect, to be adjusted by mutual agreement, if the concession shall have been conditional.*"

---

whilst M.F.N. treatment *pro futuro* concerns those advantages which derive from treaties to be concluded later."

(*b*) *Hornbeck* (*op. cit.*, pp. 403-5).

(1) Simple transfer " which grants a privilege without reciprocity or condition."
(2) Specialised reciprocal " which applies only to favours mentioned in the treaty."
(3) Simple reciprocal—that is, general in scope, and mutual.
(4) The imperative or unconditional form.
(5) The qualified, or conditional, reciprocal form.

(*c*) U.S.A. Tariff Commission Report (*op. cit.*, p. 445).

I. *Unconditional Forms.*

A. Unilateral (*i.e.*, non-reciprocal).
1. Unilateral and unlimited.
2. Unilateral and limited.
B. Reciprocal and unlimited (general), but not expressly immediate and unconditional.
C. Reciprocal, unlimited, and expressly immediate and unconditional.
D. Reciprocal and limited.

II. *Conditional Forms.*

A. Unilateral and unlimited, but expressly conditional.
B. Reciprocal and unlimited, but expressly conditional.
C. Reciprocal and limited, but expressly conditional.

This classification only differs from that in the text by introducing immediacy as a basis of division in the first group, *and* omitting the possible case of a conditional, non-reciprocal, but limited M.F.N. clause.

[1] Cited, Report on Reciprocity, etc., p. 450.

U.S.A.-France, 6th February, 1778, Article II. :—

"The Most Christian King and the U.S. engage mutually not to grant any particular favour to other nations, in respect of commerce and navigation, which shall not immediately become common to the other party, *who shall enjoy the same favour freely, if the concession was freely made, or on allowing the same compensation if the concession was conditional.*"

Greece and Austria-Hungary, 2nd March, 1835 :—

"The raw and manufactured products of both States whose importation into the other State is legally allowed shall not be subjected to any higher or other imposts of whatever sort than those articles which come from other countries, either at present or in the future with this exception : *that where a concession is given in return for certain advantages, such concessions shall be given to the other of the parties to this treaty if a similar compensation or a similar equivalent is assured.* But in each case a special convention must be made between the two parties to the treaty."

Form 3—**Conditional, Non-Reciprocal, and Limited**—

This form, though logically possible, does not seem to occur in practice, though there is nothing inherently difficult in it. A country might be prepared to grant a conditional non-reciprocal group of favours and exclude certain points from the grant, which would make the clause at once non-reciprocal, conditional, and limited.

Form 4—**Conditional, Non-Reciprocal, and Unlimited**—

U.S.A-Korea, 22nd May, 1882, Article XIV. :—

"The High Contracting Powers hereby agree that, should at any time the King of Chosen grant to any nation or to the merchants or citizens of any nation, any right, privilege, or favour, connected either with navigation, commerce, political, or other intercourse, which is not conferred by this treaty, such right, privilege, and favour shall freely inure to the benefit of the United States, its public officers, merchants, and citizens, provided always, that whenever such right, privilege, or favour is accompanied by any condition or equivalent concession granted by the other nation interested, the United States, its officers, and people shall only be entitled to the benefit of such right, privilege, or favour upon complying with the conditions or concessions connected therewith."

Form 5—**Unconditional, Reciprocal, and Limited**—

The original Cobden Treaty, U.K.-France, of 23rd January, 1860, Article XIX. was worded as follows :—

> " Each of the two high contracting parties binds itself to give to the other party every favour, every privilege or decrease in import duties *on the articles mentioned in the present treaty*, which one of the parties may grant to a third power."

U.K.-Austria-Hungary, 5th December, 1876, Articles III. and IV. :—

> " Every reduction in the tariff of import and export duties, as well as every favour or immunity that one of the contracting parties grants to the subjects and commerce of a third power, shall be participated in simultaneously and unconditionally by the other.
>
> " The stipulations of the foregoing Articles I. to III., relative to the reciprocal treatment on the footing of the M.F. third country, shall not apply " (hereupon follow the exceptions).

Form 6—**Unconditional, Non-Reciprocal, and Unlimited**—

U.K.-Greece, 19th December, 1886, Article IX. :—

> " The contracting parties agree that, in all matters relating to commerce and navigation, any privilege, favour, immunity whatever which either contracting party has actually granted or may hereafter grant to the subjects or citizens of any other State shall be extended immediately and unconditionally to the subjects or citizens of the other contracting party ; it being their intention that the trade and navigation of each country shall be placed in all respects by the other on the footing of the most-favoured-nation." [1]

---

[1] Also Italy, 15/6/1883 ; Japan, 16/7/1894, Art. ix, etc.

Form 7—**Unconditional, Non-Reciprocal, and Limited**—

U.K.-Japan, 14th October, 1854, Article V. :—

"In the ports of Japan, either now open or which may hereafter be opened to the ships or subjects of any foreign nation, British ships and subjects shall be entitled to admission and to the enjoyment of an equality of advantages with those of the M.F. nation, always excepting the advantages accruing to the Dutch and Chinese from the existing relations with Japan."

Form 8—**Unconditional, Non-Reciprocal, and Unlimited**—[1]

U.K.-Siam, 18th April, 1855, Article X. :—

"The British Government and its subjects will be allowed free and equal participation in any privileges that may have been, or may hereafter, be granted by the Siamese Government to the Government or subjects of any other nation."

§ 10. As soon as one passes from a mere description of the possible and actual forms of the M.F.N. clause and enters upon the task of analysing meaning, the real difficulties appear. It is possible to throw light upon the clause by an examination of the predominant forms at different *periods of time:* to analyse the situation *historically*. It is possible to ask what are the functions of the clause at present—this would give one a functional analysis : it is possible to investigate the working of the clause from the standpoint of its material content : that is, to compare the terms of treaties and to note what is and is not accepted by the diplomatic practice of nations as consistent with the terms of the clause.

There is a certain attractiveness about "beginning at the beginning" and dealing with the clause historically before dealing with it functionally. But there are also difficulties. In the first place, though from the European standpoint the clause has passed through three distinct periods,

---

[1] And see particularly the recent treaties of Peace with Germany (Cmd. 153), Part x., Arts. 264-7, 269, and 280, and Austria (Cmd. 400), Part x., Arts. 217-220, 223, and 232. Here we have (1) unlimited M.F.N. for a period of five years, or such time as the League of Nations may otherwise decide ; (2) the enforcement of certain minimum rates, not exceeding the most favourable of 31/7/14 or 28/7/14 respectively, for a defined time and for a defined group.

this is only true so far as the practice of European States is concerned. The U.S.A. has consistently adhered to one form of the clause—the conditional, whilst the practice of South American States has been equivocal. It seems to me, therefore, best to begin by discussing the functions of the M.F.N. clause in relation to its form.

We saw in a previous section (see § 2) that one of the objects with which States conclude treaties is to prevent themselves from being treated worse than other States are being treated. Hence, the first purpose of the M.F.N. clause is to prevent discrimination: but how achieve this? It is easy enough to demand the concessions *already* granted, but this will only guarantee equality at the moment of the grant. States have a future as well as a present, and, therefore, we must postulate that discrimination must be interpreted as applying *pro futuro* as well as *pro praeterito*.

Now let us see exactly what this involves. In addition to being interested in obtaining the concessions which have already been granted to other states previously, a state will certainly not object to being given *greater* concessions than these. This at once creates inequality again—an inequality which can only be removed by conferring on the previous treaty-making States the advantages which have been conferred on the later treaty making States. But this last member of the series will be as interested as the earlier members in any future additions to the list, the later desire to gain at least as much as the earlier members, the earlier desire to gain all the new advantages (if any) which may exceed those they have already.

Now let us add one other point. The concessions obtained have generally to be exchanged or "bought:" consequently it may be argued that if bigger concessions are granted, bigger concessions will have to be given. Taking into account (*a*) the desire of *all* the States to prevent discrimination, (*b*) the universal practice of bargaining, two possible methods of operating the clause arise—the conditional and the unconditional.

1. The conditional form emphasises the factor of bargaining or reciprocity. It is desirable to avoid discrimination, but it would be unfair to give any State all the advantages for which another State may have had to pay. Consequently it lays down the principle that future concessions must be paid for, and on approximately the same terms for all the contracting States,

and should only be freely granted to any one State if they have been freely granted to all. In effect, the promise implied by the conditional M.F.N. clause is that no State willing to pay the price shall be deprived of the right to obtain the concession. "In the American view," say the latest American commentators, "its proper function is to safeguard against the denial of opportunities — that is, to prevent discrimination."[1]

2. The unconditional form wants, as a matter of fact to do exactly the same thing, to prevent discrimination, but, say the Americans, "in the European view the function of the clause is automatically to distribute advantages." This is only equivalent to saying that the unconditional form does not make the distinction between "concessions freely made," and concessions not freely made, or gratuitous and non-gratuitous advantages, though in the past this distinction has been made. In view of the apparent absurdity involved in granting all round the concessions which one State has had to buy, we must here endeavour to find some justification for this attitude.

The justification for the "European view" lies in the fact that what people find to be economical, they will in the long run also find to be equitable. In other words, the defence of the unconditional M.F.N. clause consists in the great economy of effort which it brings about. It enables the diplomatists of two countries to concentrate on the special points in which those two areas considered *in vacuo* for the moment have the greatest interest. If the contracting States had to take into account not only the special points in which they were more particularly interested, *but had also to review the whole of the previous concessions* in striking a tariff bargain, it is probable that no conventional tariff would, under modern circumstances, ever come into existence. For the whole of the range of possible concessions granted to all the co-contractants would have to be reviewed by each single one of them, and, in view of the enormous number of articles which it is possible to bargain upon, the debate would never come to an end. Consequently we must regard the "automatic distribution of advantages" as inseparable from the system of conventional tariffs under modern conditions of complexity. This is, in

---

[1] *Op. cit.*, p. 394.

fact, recognised by Americans when they argue[1] that the conditional form of the M.F.N. clause is inevitable if the single line tariff of America is to be adhered to. The most economical form of clause for the U.S.A. is just the conditional. For, desiring at one and the same time to maintain simplicity of tariff form, *and* to obtain concessions from foreign countries, the U.S.A. is inevitably driven to devise a list of articles on which it is prepared to reduce the rates. The desire to limit the degree of interference with the protection accorded to home industries works in the same direction. The result is that it *can* quite clearly represent to the co-contractant what the equivalents are, for the price paid to each foreign country is the same, and hence it is easy to work out the counter concession also. Under the conventional system, the concessions asked for and the price paid depend on the special interests in each particular case, and there is consequently no single, clear, and universal measuring rod by which to judge the relative demands. Country A wants concessions on wine, and is willing to give concessions on steel goods: country B wants concessions on cotton goods, and is willing to give counter concessions on woollen goods. If the whole of the other concessions which do not in the first instance interest any particular country, have also to be paid for, an impossible task will be thrust upon the negotiators.[2], [3]

The two-line conventional tariff is, of course, not the only form which European practice reveals. We must also deal with the two forms of the autonomous tariff—the single line autonomous tariff and the maximum-minimum, and, finally, with the single line conventional tariff.

(1) In the case of the single line conventional tariff, dis-

---

[1] Hornbeck, *op. cit.*, p. 818, "No nation in the position of the United States and with a high protective, single-schedule tariff, could, with due regard to economic circumstances, give most-favoured-nation concessions under other than the United States interpretation, nor has the United States ever meant to do so."

[2] Fontana-Russo, discussing the strategy of tariff-treaty-making, supports the idea of a simultaneous negotiation of treaties in order to prevent the watering down of concessions through the knowledge that some other country is offering a particular concession in return for a given reduction of rates which would then accrue automatically to all the others. But secrecy and simultaneity cannot prevent experts from telling pretty accurately the points which will interest the other countries and in obtaining concessions for those of the articles of the countries they represent in which there is least competition.

[3] It is often overlooked that retaliation against the United States has in the past been difficult in consequence of the nature of her exports. See below, § 15.

crimination is really impossible without an abandonment of the form of tariff chosen: and a policy of conventional concessions which are afterwards generalised, which would conserve the form of the tariff, is inconsistent with autonomy. Consequently, as the State in question cannot bargain against bargain, does not discriminate, and hence treats all States on a footing of equality, it is States possessing this form of tariff which are logically bound to oppose that form of M.F.N. clause which makes the receipt of favours conditional. For it is not possible for such a State to make the receipt of its own concessions conditional, and it will, therefore, suffer if other States make the receipt of their favours conditional, since it itself can only pay the price at the expense of its freedom, and cannot discriminate easily; whilst not being able to bargain, it is in constant danger of being discriminated against.

This analysis will serve as an explanation of the traditional attitude of British statesmen towards the M.F.N. clause in the later portion of the 19th century, when the reaction against the clause was already setting in elsewhere.

(2) When we turn to the maximum-minimum tariff, however, the problem is complicated by the fact that in this case a policy of discrimination is possible: for the State can refuse to extend to others the benefits of the minimum tariff without counter-concessions being obtained. This means that it is in a better position to bargain, but, as it desires to retain its full right of altering the tariff as and when it wishes, the conditional form of tariff is unsuitable to it. For, since it refuses to bind itself, the co-contractant will not as a rule be willing to give the necessary price without security, so that the unconditional form represents for the autonomous State a method of conserving its freedom. At the same time, if the clause is reciprocally conditional, the autonomous State must part with its freedom, for it can only buy the concessions at the expense of its freedom. Hence, if it retains the unconditional interpretation, it benefits from the reductions made by others, and need not itself reduce its rates to obtain these reductions. It is, however, true that, possessing in the two-line tariff an instrument of coercion, such a State is much better able to dispense with the M.F.N. clause altogether as compared with the country with a single line autonomous tariff, for if it is discriminated against, it can inflict damage

itself by withdrawing the benefits of the lower rates, and this it can do at any time, since it does not tie its rates.[1]

(3) We are left with the case of the State which—like Belgium—incorporates the conventional rates in its "general" tariff in order to retain the single line tariff. This procedure is in fact the logical consequence of an acceptance of the unconditional form of the M.F.N. clause, and this again of the fact that a single line tariff is inconsistent with a policy of discrimination.[2]

§ 11. It is now possible to see more closely, than if we had begun with an historical sketch, the tendency for there to be a relation between the tariff form, the trade circumstances of a country and the choice it will make between the conditional and the unconditional M.F.N. clauses. The U.S.A. have adhered consistently to one form of the clause because in the main they have had to deal with the same set of circumstances as far as form of tariff and the nature of their export interests are concerned. It is only now that the United States are becoming a great manufacturing exporting country that the satisfaction with the traditional form of their M.F.N. clauses has become so far modified as to permit of a critical study of the possibilities of change. The tariff instruments

---

[1] The history of the reciprocity treaties of the United States brings out both the positive and negative aspects of this autonomous and yet not defenceless tariff policy. For the United States found it relatively easy to use the various reciprocity clauses to obtain the lowest rates in force in various European countries, but, on the other hand, found it very difficult to obtain the M.F.N. clause, so that the history of reciprocity is full of the difficulties occasioned by the precise rights of the American Government. Thus it was fairly easy to obtain concessions, but not easy to get the larger European States to tie themselves *vis-a-vis* the reluctance of the United States to tie its rates in formal treaties. It is also significant that the success of the United States with France was less than with other States, largely, it seems to me, because the French policy is very like the American in some respects. The United States was, however, successful in obtaining M.F.N. treatment in the formal sense from Spain (1/8/1906, Art. 2) and Portugal (12/6/1900, Art. 2, but only on some articles). In the case of most other countries the concessions were the minimum rates in force, but with no guarantee for the future.

The American policy was, of course, complicated by the practice of only offering concessions on a few articles, the traditional refusal to diverge from the conditional interpretation, the desire for high protection, and the antipathy to treaties which has marked American legislatures. But this emphasises the reluctance of States to grant America a cheque on the future in the shape of M.F N. treatment rights. The autonomous policy of France has at least been modified by a willingness to retain the unconditional clause, which, as already explained above, is a cheap form of insurance for the autonomous State.

[2] On the whole of the preceding, *cf.* Report, p. 439.

and the tariff aims of European countries have changed more than once and with them the M.F.N. clause. Of course, one must make allowance for the fact that it is only in the recent past that the adaptation of means to ends in commercial matters has been capable of exerting much influence in shaping the technical instruments employed to achieve given ends, and that the ends themselves are not necessarily always clearly apprehended: but it is fairly obvious that the form of the instrument should at all times stand in some relation to the end envisaged. The result is that in studying the history of the M.F.N. clause one is faced by the task of disentangling the occasions when an altered end has altered the instrument, and the occasions when the end being more or less the same, increased recognition of the unsuitable nature of the instrument has led to a change in the latter. Such a task is one for the historian of tariff policy, and cannot be attempted here. But some mention of the changes in European policy in these respects must be made.

The history of the M.F.N. clause in Europe divides into three periods [1]:—

(1) From the 17th century to the second and third decades of the 19th century, when the unconditional form of the clause obtained.

(2) A period which begins with the American use of the conditional clause, but is only prominent later among European countries, when the conditional clause is the usual form, which period for Europe ends again with the year 1860.

(3) From 1860 to the outbreak of the European War, when the European clause was the unconditional, whilst the American clause was still the conditional. But in the later years of the period a growing dissatisfaction with the unconditional form is manifest, which requires us to discuss not only the past of the clause, but also its future.

The fact that *when* a clause is used it is of a particular type is of course no guarantee of the frequency of its use. Thus,

[1] The main authority here is Glier, especially the chronological table appended to his work; but see also Hornbeck, *op. cit.*, pp. 398-402, who follows Glier in part, but refers also to Cavaretta and Visser.

of the 29 treaties which Glier gives as having been concluded between 1703 and 1800, 6 were reciprocity treaties, 7 were tariff treaties without M.F.N. clauses, and 16 contained the M.F.N. clause in one or other form. It is significant that Adam Smith should have confined himself to a very meagre description of the Methuen, a reciprocity treaty of the most pronounced and exclusive kind.[1] But that the 17th century M.F.N. clauses were already of the unconditional type (though not necessarily of the unlimited character) is to be easily seen from the treaties concluded by Great Britain and various Foreign States.[2]

It requires more ingenuity of mind to explain why the unconditional form should ever have been abandoned, once it had been discovered, than why it was originally invented. At the time of concluding a commercial treaty, it seems the "natural" process to ensure to oneself not only all the rights secured by others at that particular moment, but also the rights which others may secure in the future. The reason for the change may have been what Bowring describes as a "strong feeling in France . . . that England had some sinister purpose to serve by desiring to enter into a commercial treaty with France, and that the undoubted consequences of such an arrangement would be the sacrifice of French

---

1 "Wealth of Nations," Book iv., Chap. vi.

2 See, *e.g.*, the Treaties with Denmark of 1660/1, Art. xiii., and 1670, Art. xl.; Spain, of 1667, Art. xxxviii., 1713 (13/7/13), Art. ix., and treaties of 9/12/1713, 14/12/1715, 5/10/1750; Sweden, Treaties of 11/4/1654, Art. iv., 1656, Art. viii., 1661, Art. iv., 5/2/1766, Art. ii. (limited M.F.N.); Portugal, 1642, Art. xiii., 1654, Art. xi.

We may quote one of these clauses, Art. iv. of the 1654 Treaty with Sweden: "That either of the aforesaid confederates, their people and subjects, may, without any safe conduct, freely and securely go and enter by land or sea, on and to the kingdoms, countries, and provinces, lands, islands, cities, villages, towns, whether walled or unwalled, fortified or otherwise, havens, and whatsoever dominions of the other, and there stay, and from thence return or pass through; and in the same places, upon just prices to procure, and provision of victuals, for their use and sustenance, and to be used with all friendly offices; and that either confederate, their people and subjects, may trade and have commerce, in all places where commerce hath hitherto been exercised, in what goods and merchandises they please, and may freely import and export the same, paying the customs which are due; and conforming themselves to the laws and ordinances of the said commonwealth and kingdom, whether the same respect, trade, or any other right; *which presupposed, the people, subjects, and inhabitants of both confederates shall have and enjoy in each other's kingdoms, countries, lands, and dominions, as large and ample privileges, relaxations, liberties, and immunities, as any other foreigner at present doth, or hereafter shall, enjoy there.*"

industry."[1] For the unconditional form would certainly have availed the more advanced industrial nation by giving it all the advantages of reductions without necessarily emperilling the agricultural protection which the political situation at home still made necessary. It is also true that as compared with the exclusive commercial treaty of the Methuen type, the reciprocity treaty with the conditional clause represented a distinct advance—it at least gave other nations the opportunity of acquiring the same rights on giving the same price, so that, if there was retrogression from one point of view there was advance from another. Nor was the swing over to the conditional form complete, as Hornbeck points out.[2]

The reason for the universal adoption of the unconditional form of the M.F.N. clause after 1860 can be in part associated with the autonomous tariff policy which had by that time attained such a hold upon political and economic circles in this country that the whole policy of treaty making had to meet with the bitter attacks of the more " orthodox " free traders, represented by writers like M'Culloch and politicians of the school of Lowe, the two great bugbears of Sir Louis Mallet and his distinguished diplomatic friend Sir Robert Morier.[3]

---

[1] First Report on the Commercial Relations between England and France, 1834, p. 6. See also List, " National System of Political Economy," English translation, p. 260, when, discussing the feasibility of inter-European treaties based on mutual concessions, he says, " What they all have to fear at this time is solely the preponderating competition of England." Peel's famous statement in 1846 that " wearied with our long and unavailing efforts to enter into satisfactory commercial treaties with other nations, we have resolved at length to consult our own interests, etc.," is a tribute to the suspicion that prevailed.

[2] *Op. cit.*, p. 620.

We have already quoted the Liberian Treaty, in which the U.K. Treaty used the conditional form. See also Treaties with Portugal, 19/2/1810, Art. 2 : Nether lands, 27/10/37/ Art. 1 ; Austria, 3/7/1838, Art. 11 ; Portugal, 3/7/1842, Art. 4 ; Russia, 11/1/43, Art. 11 ; Kingdom of the Two Sicilies, 29/4/1845, Art. 6 : Uruguay, 26/7/42, Art. 3. On the other hand, the treaty with Rio de la Plata, 2/2/1825, Art. 4, and that with Mexico, 26/12/26, Art. 4, as also that with the Peru-Bolivian Confederation, 5/6/1837, contain the unconditional form. None of these treaties " conventionalise " rates, and their conclusion by no means invalidates the correctness of Peel's argument quoted in Note 1 above.

[3] For M'Culloch's views on the Cobden Treaty, see his edition of Adam Smith, Note xiv., p. 546, " it (the treaty) is alike degrading and injurious, whether it is considered in a political or an economical point of view," and so on. For Morier on M'Culloch, see the " Memoirs and Letters of the Rt. Hon. Sir Robert Morier," vol. ii., p. 135, *et seq.*, for Morier's attack on Lowe, his anonymous " Commercial Treaties : Free Trade and Internationalism," by a Disciple of Richard Cobden, first published in the *Manchester Examiner*, and republished by the Cobden Club in 1870. See also Sir B. Mallet's Memoir of his father. The feeling of the anti-

The British Government wished to extend the reductions embodied in the Cobden Treaty freely to all nations; it was, therefore, impossible for this country, in view of the declared policy of the British Government of the day, to agree to the conditional clause, because this would have implied that France was "paying" for what other countries would get for nothing. On the other hand, the political position on the Continent was such as to encourage the conclusion of similar treaties by other countries with France—thus, Prussia saw in the clause a means of avoiding the inclusion of Austria in the Zollverein. Finally, we must not forget that the sixties provided an intellectual atmosphere favourable to free trade—it was the era in which the "Manchester School" dominated economic thought not only in this country but to a considerable extent abroad—and though the M.F.N. clause in the unconditional form is separable from the idea of free trade, there is no doubt that an *era* of economic liberalism found the unconditional form a convenient instrument. The inclusion of the unconditional form as Article XI. of the Treaty of Frankfort meant that there was, even after 1870, a fixed point in the European treaty system upon which the unconditional form could rest, and this in part explains why the clause continued to be used until the outbreak of the War of 1914. Even without this buttress, there were solid grounds for the continued use of the clause, the essential factor being the division of labour which

---

treaty school that conventional tariffs were fatal to autonomy shows how easy it is to reproduce on both sides of the struggle between Free Trade and Protection essentially the same arguments, for there is not much difference *au fond* between the attitude of these men and the opponents of conventional treaties in France. It appears to me that Mr. Hornbeck overlooked this anti-treaty attitude of certain free-traders when he argued that under "the Utopian system (of free trade), the clause would have no value, as it would be absolutely redundant" (*op. cit.*, p. 818). The only reference given in support of this opinion is to Morley's "Life of Cobden," vol. ii., p. 342. The whole argument seems to overlook the advantage afforded by the clause in giving, not only a guarantee that discrimination will not be practised at the moment, but that a formal notice is required before it can be practised in the future. Equally ill-considered seems to me to be his idea (*op. et loc. cit.*) that "logically the universal acceptance of that form and interpretation of the clause which would satisfy the 'unconditional' school would eventually lead, whether that be its object or not, to absolute free trade." On the contrary, a system of autonomous nations, all guaranteeing each other unconditional M.F.N. treatment, would prevent discrimination. but would not lead to free trade, unless they autonomously reduced their tariffs. On the other hand, even the conditional form would lead to universal free trade if there were reciprocal bargaining, provided it were effective, or if there were a series of "concessions" freely granted, as there would be if the nations in question all reduced their tariffs autonomously.

it permitted, but there is also no doubt that as the century wore to a close the voices raised against the clause grew more and more powerful.

Of the influence which produced this revulsion of feeling, it is only necessary here to mention two, the continued ill-feeling between France and Germany, which in part produced the movement in favour of the autonomous double tariff in France, and the general resentment which was felt on the continent at the tariff policy of the United States. This resentment produced a reaction against the clause especially in Germany, where the clause found a powerful opponent in Glier and others. A third factor was the actual practice of European States in reducing the value of the clause by various devices which will require separate mention later, a feature of the situation which Austrian economists especially have emphasised as showing the gradual deliquescence of the belief in the clause.[1]

§ 12. Having dealt with the nature of conditional and unconditional clauses, we must now say a word as to the reciprocal element. The absence of reciprocity is such an obvious mark of lack of bargaining power that we find non-reciprocal clauses only in treaties with weak States, such as China, Siam, and the like, or with States which have been vanquished on the field of battle, and even in the case of China these concessions represent successful military intervention as much as ecomonic weakness. Such non-reciprocal clauses have been incorporated in the series of peace treaties which concluded the late War, but in this case they are for a limited period of time only, and certainly mark the position of inferiority of the Central Powers.

---

[1] Article xi. has been spoken of above as unconditional, but this is not the same thing as saying that it was unlimited, though in fact the limitation of the effects of the clause to the countries named in the Article had no practical effect so long as there was a network of treaties. For concessions granted to one of the States not named in the Treaty by one of the States actually named had to be conceded to the contracting powers in virtue of the unconditional M.F.N. clause. Concessions made by either France or Germany to one of the States not named in the treaty had to be extended to the States named in the treaty so long as the M.F.N. treaties continued, and had, therefore, to be extended to France also, if the concession were made by Germany, or to Germany if the concession were made by France. In the same way, so long as the European treaties with the United States contained the M.F.N. clause, the concessions made to third parties owing to the network had to go to the U.S.A. also, for to all except the first recipient the concession was freely made.

§ 13. Much more important is the division into limited and unlimited M.F.N. clauses, to which we now turn. The importance of such limitations has been much canvassed in recent discussion, and the whole matter is one of great interest.

The easiest way of dealing with the problem is to detail some of the more usual limitations, and then to go on to ask what are the disputed points in this connection. It is as well to remember that what we are concerned with is not the value of the clause, but the concessions to which no claim can be made even by a State in possession of the grant of M.F.N. treatment. Nor are we concerned here with the question of whether the clause be conditional or unconditional. We are asking, what is excluded from the content of the concessions conveyed by the grant.

(1) The first of these limitations [1] concerns the frontier trade and the improvement trade, which is excluded from a very large number of treaties. Thus, Article 2 of the treaty of 6th December, 1891, between Germany and Austria-Hungary, which excludes "such advantages as are granted by one of the contracting parties to a neighbouring State for certain stretches of frontier and for the inhabitants of certain areas."

So also in the Austrian Treaties with Italy, 6th December, 1891, Art. 2, Switzerland, 10th December, 1891, and Belgium, 6th December, 1891. See also Art. 6 of the Franco-Roumanian Treaty of 6th March, 1907: France-Japan, 19th August, 1911, Art. 18 (1).

(2) The second exception is afforded by the exclusion of concessions made as a result of the contracting parties entering into a Customs Union, or other preferential arrangements. Thus, Art. 18 (2) of the Franco-Japanese Treaty, Art. 11 of the Russo-German Treaty of 1894; Art. 11 (2) of the Swedish-German Treaty of 2nd May, 1911; the treaties concluded between Egypt and the U.K., 29th October, 1889, Art. 13, Germany, 19th July, 1892, and France,

---

[1] A convenient summary of the exceptions in the German treaties will be found in the detailed index, *s.v.* "Meistbegünstigung," "(*c*) Auschluss von der Meistbegüngstigung," of the two volumes "Die Handelsverträge des Deutschen Reichs." See in this connection esp. Lippert, *op. cit.*, from whom my illustrations are partly derived.

26th November, 1902, Art. 22, which respectively reserve the relations between Egypt and other portions of the Ottoman Empire, Egypt, and Persia, and Egypt and the Soudan. Final Protocol to the Anglo-Portuguese Treaty of 1914, and Art. 17, " it is understood that the provisions of this treaty which secure in Portugal M.F.N. treatment to British goods and vessels shall not apply to the special favours which Portugal accords or may hereafter accord to the goods or vessels of Spain or Brazil." So also in the Treaty of Spain and the U.S.A. of 1st August, 1906, whereby Spain reserves the preference to Portugal, and the U.S.A. those to Cuba. The Russo-Swedish Treaty of 27th July, 1906, excludes " the special privileges which shall be granted by Sweden to Norwegian subjects, commercial and financial companies, as well as to Norwegian products, so long as these privileges shall not be extended also to the subjects, companies, or products of another State. 2. The arrangements which regulate or shall regulate the trade of Russia with the neighbouring States and areas of Asia."

The same restriction occurs in the Treaties with South American States, thus, the German Treaty with Nicaragua, 4th February, 1896, Art. 32, and Protocol to the Treaty with Guatemala, (*ad* Art. 33), of 26th June, 1888: " the special concessions, which are extended or shall be extended by the State of Guatemala to the other four Central American States or any of them, shall not be claimed by Germany on the basis of the M.F.N. treatment granted in the present treaty, so long as such concessions are also denied to all other third States."

(3) Exclusions based on sanitary grounds, or on grounds of internal safety. Thus, Art. 5 of the Franco-Roumanian Treaty of 6th March, 1907, excludes from the M.F.N. clause—

1. Exclusions arising from exceptional circumstances as regards munitions of war.
2. For reasons of the interior safety of the State.
3. For reasons of sanitary policy, or for the prevention of the spread of epidemics, or from the destruction of plants, notably by insects or harmful parasites.

The same in the Franco-Japanese Treaty of 19th August, 1911, Art. 6.

(4) The national fisheries, the coasting trade.

Germany-Japan, 24th June, 1911, Art. 6, excludes "the products of the national fisheries of the two contracting parties, nor do the concessions apply to the special customs dispositions which Japan may grant to the fish and other products of the sea caught in the territorial waters of any third neighbouring State of Japan's." Art. 13 of the Russian-German Treaty, 1894; see also the cases mentioned in § 1 of this chapter.

(5) Restriction of the M.F.N. clause to particular classes of goods, or exclusion of certain classes of goods therefrom.

Thus, the original Cobden Treaty confined the benefits of M.F.N. treatment to the goods mentioned in the present treaty; but the limitations of this kind do not seem to be very numerous. Thus, after the Spanish-Italian Tariff War of 18th November, 1905, to 23rd July, 1914, a new treaty was signed on the 30th March, 1914, but wine, with certain minor exceptions, was excluded and placed under the general tariff rates.[1]

(6) Goods directly imported, and goods nationalised in the exporting country.

(*a*) In the case of countries which impose taxes on indirect importation, the question of whether these can be reconciled with M.F.N. clauses at once arises. In the Treaty of Frankfort, as we have seen, the right of the French Government to continue to impose the Surtaxe de Pavillon was conceded. The restriction is contained in Art. 12 of the Franco-Norwegian

[1] See Schilder, "Mittel-Europa und die Meistbegünstigung," p. 31, where also the case of the Franco-Italian treaty of 4/2/1899 (silk) is given. According to Lippert, *op. cit.*, p. 152, in the Austrian treaties down to 1891, there was a special concession on Italian wines in Austria-Hungary, first granted in the Sardinian Treaty of 1846, and continued by the Treaties of 1851-1867-1878-1887, down to 1891. It was objected by France as an infringement of the M.F.N.C., an objection which was bought off for the time being by a special treaty of 1896 (20/7/96), in which Austria recognised the abolition of the capitulations in Tunis, the wine duty to continue until 1/1/1904. In the new Italian Treaty of 31/12/1903 the wine concession was given up for reductions on Southern fruits.

Treaty of 30th December, 1881, "merchandise not Swedish or Norwegian in origin imported from the Kingdoms to France, shall not be weighted by surtaxes higher than those which goods of the same kind imported into France from all other European countries otherwise than directly in French ships. The Kingdoms reserve on their part, the right to establish on goods not of French origin surtaxes equal to those which shall be levied in France on importations other than direct."

So also in the case of the Franco-Canadian Treaty of 19th October, 1907, Art. 8, the benefit of M.F.N. treatment on the articles included in the schedules of the convention is only accorded on direct transportation, or from a territory enjoying, in Canada, preferential treatment, or the advantages of the intermediate tariff, or, as regards imports into France, if the goods are directly imported or *via* a country which enjoys the French minimum tariff. Further, "these dispositions do not in any way interfere with the régime of surtaxes d'entrepôt which is or may be established in either country on indirect importation."

(*b*) The question of "nationalised" goods arises in the following way:—If one of two countries only enjoys M.F.N. treatment, are goods arriving *via* the favoured country, having paid duty there, to be treated as goods of that country, or are the higher duties which the same goods would have paid, if imported directly from their true country of origin, to be imposed? It is, of course, difficult to distinguish the case of indirect importation and the question of "nationalisation," in those cases in which there is no surtax on indirect importation, but only differential treatment of the goods of the two areas. In so far as the *cause* of the difficulty is concerned, however, the nationalisation problem in its nature is the reverse of the previous problem, for in the first case the duties are higher because of indirect importation, whereas in the second case indirect importation is frowned upon because the incidence of the tariff is less than it would have been if indirect importation had not been resorted to.

There is no uniformity of practice in these matters, but, as Lippert points out, the tendency in recent times has been to narrow the conception of what are the products and manufactures of a country. As an example of the earlier and more generous interpretation of the concept, see, for instance, the treaty between the U.K. and Paraguay of 16th October, 1884, in which M.F.N. treatment is extended to "the produce and manufacture, *as well as all goods coming from the dominions and possessions of Her Britannic Majesty*," etc. So also the Austrian Treaty of 5th December, 1876, speaks of "the produce and manufactures of, as well as all goods coming from Austria-Hungary," etc. The usual formula employed in English Treaties seems to be the following:—"The produce and manufactures of . . . *from whatever place arriving*," this is intended to give the products referred to the benefits of the lowest rates even if the country from which they come has not the benefit of the lowest rates. (See—*e.g.*, Japan, 16th July, 1894, Art. 5; Roumania, 31st October, 1905, Art. 5; Russia, 12th January, 1859, Art. 2; Italy, 15th June, 1883, Art. 2.) On the other hand, in the treaty between Brazil and Columbia of 21st August, 1908, Art. 11 expressly denies the possibility of nationalisation, similarly, a Roumanian law allows surtaxes to be imposed on goods, whether directly imported or *via* a third State, "à la suite d'une naturalisation dans un autre état."[1] The Franco-Japanese Treaty of 19th August, 1911, Art. 8, permits certificates of origin to be demanded "in those cases in which a third State

[1] Both cases cited by Lippert, *op. cit.*, p. 157.

shall not be linked with one or other contracting party by the M.F.N. clause."

(7) The next limitation is one which has occasioned a good deal of controversy in the past. This limitation concerns the imposition of the countervailing duties on bounty fed articles. In the event of the countervailing duty being imposed on the product of a country enjoying the benefits of the most favoured clause, is the latter being infringed by the special duty? [1]

The matter has been of practical importance mainly in regard to the countervailing duties upon sugar. The position of the United Kingdom in this matter has varied from time to time: in 1864 the United Kingdom was a party to the Sugar Convention, which, by Article xix., reserved to the signatory powers—France, Holland, Belgium, and the United Kingdom—the right to consider surtaxes on the imports of refined sugar from those States which did not suppress their bounties.[2] In 1880 [3] the Foreign Office took the line that such countervailing duties were an infringement of the M.F.N. clause, though it agreed to the proposal in 1887, whilst the Conservative Government, after the introduction of countervailing duties on sugar in India, opposed the Russian Government's protests, and finally became a party to the Brussels Convention of 1903, in consequence of which Act it excluded Russian sugar from the United Kingdom, an Order in Council being issued under the terms of the Sugar Convention Act, 1903, on the 11th of August, 1903. In 1902 the British Government took the line that the Russian Treaty could be denounced, if the Russian Government were dissatisfied.

The United States, also, came into conflict with the bounty paying countries over countervailing duties. In 1894, the American Executive had taken the line that such duties were a violation of the treaty obligations of the United States, but this attitude was reversed after 1897.

---

[1] On this matter, see Hornbeck, *op. cit.*, pp. 640-645; U.S.A. Report, pp. 433-5.

[2] Fuchs, "The Trade Policy of Great Britain," p. 81; text of Convention in Hertslet, xii., p. 199.

[3] Fuchs, p. 87.

The legality of the action of the United States Government was upheld by the Supreme Court of the United States in the case of Downs *v.* U.S. (187 U.S., 496).[1]

At the International Sugar Conference of 1887 [2] both the United Kingdom and Germany had supported the principle of countervailing duties, but Germany was among the European countries which protested to the United States. Finally, the Russian Government, which had quarrelled both with the United Kingdom and the United States over sugar, and with the United States over a retaliatory duty on petroleum, seems to have reversed its attitude in 1905, when it again gave the United States the benefit of certain conventional rates which it had withdrawn in 1901, in consequence, as Count Witte expressed it, " of a misunderstanding in the interpretation of the M.F.N. clause." [3]

Hornbeck, summing up the discussion, states that " international law has not yet become so established that it may be cited as either affirming or denying the right in question," but points to the fact that the clause itself was established in order to further the cause of commercial equality, which the bounty system threatened. Others regard the practice as doubtful.[4] But the United Kingdom has adhered to the interpretation it adopted at the beginning of the century, witness the Anglo-Portuguese Treaty, 1914, Art. 7, the only exceptions to the rule that prohibitions or restrictions must extend to the like articles " the produce or manufacture of any other foreign country," being, *inter alia*, " the measures applicable in either of the two countries to articles enjoying a direct or indirect bounty in the other." [5]

§ 14. We can now pass from the descriptive to the critical portion of our work. A series of questions at once arise. What is the actual restrictive effect of these various limitations? Ought the M.F.N. clause to be abandoned, or ought the condi-

[1] Cited Report, p. 434; Hornbeck, p. 643.

[2] Art. vii., Fuchs, p. 97.

[3] Cited Report, p. 435.

[4] See the quotation from Visser in Hornbeck, p. 644, n. 104.

[5] It must, however, be noted that the adherence to the right to exclude bounty-fed goods did not prevent the U.K. from modifying the terms of the Convention in 1907 and withdrawing from it in 1912.

tional clause to replace universally the unconditional, or *vice versâ?*

If we begin by discussing the actual extent to which the M.F.N. clause has suffered violation, we must admit that absolutely, the extent of such infraction is by no means inconsiderable. But we must not overlook the great tract of ground that is *not* affected by these limitations, nor must we overstress the importance of those that actually exist. Thus, there has been a tendency among recent German and Austrian writers, influenced by a desire to further the cause of the Central European Customs Union, to declare that the importance of the clause has been greatly exaggerated, and that its future is uncertain. Apart from the matters which we have already dealt with, such critics point to other features of the situation which merit a moment's notice.[1]

The importance which is assigned by these writers to the frontier arrangements, and to the recognition of preferential arrangements in the South American Treaties, for instance, arises from the fact that practical necessities forced them to find some defence for the imposition of intermediate duties between Germany and Austria. On no other ground could the scheme come into existence. But there at once arose the difficulty, that the M.F.N. clause stood in the way. Hence, if it could be successfully shown that the existing practice already recognised such preferential arrangements, the task of the defenders of the Union could be made much easier. Unfortunately for them, the existing cases are either based on political affinity, as in the case of Cuba, and other American spheres of influence, or common sovereignty, as in the case of the Empire, or historical association, as in the case of Portugal

---

[1] See particularly, Schilder, "Mittel-Europa und die Meistbegünstigung," and Schüller in Herkner's Collection of Essays, published in three parts as vol. clv. of the S.V.S.P., "Die wirtschaftliche Annäherung zwischen dem Deutschen Reiche und seinen Verbündeten." For a thorough critical study of these and most other writers on Central Europe, see Eulenburg in the W.W.A., vol. vii., p. 370, *et seq.*, vol. viii., p. 395, *et seq.*, vol. xiii., p. 305, *et seq.* On the authors cited above, Eulenburg remarks, "that an unprejudiced description of the M.F.N. clause required an emphasis of its real working in a positive sense. The exclusion from the clause of the Russian frontier districts, for instance, creates the impression that it is really unimportant for Central Europe to have the clause or not. That may be so for Austria-Hungary, because the clause really does play a minor rôle for it. But for Germany, which has to meet the competition of other industrial states, England, the U.S.A., Japan perhaps also in the future, the case is not the same. . . ."

and Brazil, or geographical contiguity, as in the case of Spain and Portugal, Russia and Sweden. It is curious to find that the last point, which might have been utilised with advantage by the supporters of the plan, seems to have escaped their notice, probably because it was felt that, in fact, its importance was not very great.

These additional criticisms do not assert that the clause *qua* clause is useless: they assert that the unpopularity of the clause has made States anxious to circumvent it. This they have done by the development of administrative protection, by such devices as the manipulation of railway rates; by veterinary regulations, which, since they must be specific in every case, fail to respond to standardisation; by refusal to recognise the analyses of "disfavoured" countries; by the rationing of imports; by the manipulation of the power to decide customs cases, and thus differentiating against a particular country; by favouring particular States by specially low autonomous rates, and thus giving them great advantages without requiring them to bargain for them:[1] by manipulation of contracts, rigid regulation of packing, and thus giving opportunity for customs complaints, and consequently holding up imports from the State so treated, and so on. It may be admitted at once that measures of this sort reduce the value of the M.F.N. clause, but what these authors do not prove is that matters in these respects would be any better if the most favoured clause were swept out of existence. It may, indeed, be argued that the clause has made importation easier than would otherwise be the case, but since the absence of the clause would cause importation to be more difficult, what we have here to deal with are devices intended to check importation, which, under the special circumstances, take the form of practicising discrimination under colour of recognising the advantages of equality. Since the argument is directed against the clause because it tends to encourage importation, these practices would only disappear, if the desire to prevent importation were as easily satisfied in other ways. It is at least as likely that the clause might disappear, leaving these administrative devices as *additional* methods of enforcing limitation of imports behind it. To prove that the M.F.N. clause, at least in its unconditional form, is the cause, as well

[1] Schüller, *op. cit.*, p. 139.

as the occasion of such practices, it should be shown that no State which does not use the unconditional form, such as the United States, makes no use of these devices. This, in my judgment, is an impossible task. But, again, admitting the truth of these allegations, it is again a matter not only of how, but of how much? The value of the M.F.N. clause may be diminished by such practices, but there is a danger that the extent to which such operations reduce its value in practice may be exaggerated.

There is one aspect of the effect of administrative technique on the value of the M.F.N. clause which deserves a moment's further attention. This is the effects of specialisation. We have already referred to this matter in our chapter on "Differentiation" above, we must now look at it from a different angle. The effect of specialisation is to restrict the value of a concession to any but the State to which it was originally granted: thus, even if any other State claims the concession under the M.F.N. clause, the advantages it draws therefrom are reduced in proportion to the degree to which the reductions in question have been adapted to the needs of the State originally obtaining them. Hence, countries which cannot bargain for themselves, and are forced to rely on the concessions which are conventionalised as the result of previous bargaining by other States, are prejudiced.

Here again, it is a question of fact as to the extent to which such specialisations seriously reduce the value of the concessions to third parties. If we take the United Kingdom especially into account, we must remember that the United Kingdom is predominantly an exporter of manufactured articles, and that even those writers who stress the fact of specialisation admit that it is far less easy to practice it successfully in the case of manufactured articles than in the case of raw materials. Schilder's argument, it is true, is based on the fact that such specialisation leads to quarrels, it "leads much more easily to quarrels with third industrial States than to success in respect to the particular country which it is intended to hit." [1] Even here, it is necessary to remark, in view of the reputed helplessness of the United Kingdom, that even if this country has no direct power of retaliation, the fact that the fear of reprisals leads to a modification of the

[1] *Op. cit.*, p. 46.

rigour of specialisation benefits her, since she gains through the M.F.N. treatment the concessions actually granted, and these are, *ex hypothesi*, less specialised than they would otherwise be. But the general argument would seem to be this: the industrial specialisation of the different countries of the world is not such a fixed and unalterable thing that no changes in the efficiency of industry are possible. Consequently, although in the first instance, a specialised concession may mean more to one country than to its competitors, it does not in the least follow that they cannot adapt their production to it in such a way as not to draw some advantage from it. It follows, therefore, that though it is certainly true that specialisation may hamper third States from gaining as much advantage from a given concession as a single State, it is not necessarily true that third States draw no advantage from it. In other words, we must again beware of exaggeration.[1]

§ 15. The preceding section has dealt with defects in the unconditional form of the M.F.N. clause which arise from the practice of administrative protection, which limits its usefulness and which, so its opponents claim, are induced by the very form of that clause. We must now investigate the complaints directly levelled against the clause itself. Here we have a large literature: nearly every writer who has handled the subject of commercial treaties has discussed this point.

Let us begin by classifying the complaints.

> (1) The clause has a value which is determined, not by the direct bargaining between two contracting powers, but between these two and the rest of the commercial world. On these latter negotiations, the original cocontractant is not in a position to exert any direct influence, and yet it is upon the result of these latter negotiations that the value of the concession depends. As v. Marschall expressed it in the Reichstag on 22nd January, 1892, " the content of M.F.N. Treaties are not

[1] Schilder even argues (*op. cit.*, p. 40) that specialisation is to this extent favourable to the continuance of the treaty system and the M.F.N. clause, in that it encourages states to enter the treaty system, which would be unwilling to conclude treaties at all, were their products in the concessionary markets open to the unrestricted competition of all other States. But this is hardly an argument which will appeal to the believers in the position that things should be what they seem, rather than seem what they are not

determined by my treaty desires (Vertragswillen) but by the treaty desires of other States." [1]

(2) The value of any concessions made are reduced by the fact that they will have to be shared with others, which reduces the willingness to conclude treaties on both sides. For one side sees the value of the concession reduced by the admission of other States to the same rights, whilst the grantor State has to grant freely the same concessions to others, which, therefore, reduces its bargaining power. Hence, the M.F.N. clause, instead of adding to the body of international agreements, detracts from them. This is an argument which has been brought forward not only by protectionists, but by free traders.[2]

(3) The unconditional makes it difficult to apply the necessary pressure to those States which, like the United States, insist upon the conditional form. In such a relationship, one side would obtain all the concessions granted by the other, whilst the other side would have to buy the concessions on the normal lines of the conditional contract.[3] It has already been stated that the practice of the United States was the occasion, if not the cause, for the revulsion against the unconditional form in the later years of last century and the opening years of this.

(4) The clause is unsuccessful in forcing "high protection" countries to reduce their tariffs, for, in so far as

---

[1] Cited, Glier, *op. cit.*, p. 353, who adds that "this explanation constitutes the strongest argument against unconditional M.F.N. treatment."

[2] Glier, *op. et loc. cit.*; Grunzel, "Handelspolitik," p. 476; Phillipovitch, "Grundriss der Pol. Oekon.," 5 edn., pp. 349-50; Pflaum, in W.W.A., vol. iii., pp. 33-4. For a free trade objection, see Farrer, "Free Trade *v.* Fair Trade," p. 281, ". . . if it is a great advantage to have duties reduced for us behind our back, and without effort on our part, by the operation of the M.F.N. clause, there is some inconvenience in having them raised behind our back by action on the part of two foreign nations with which we have nothing to do. It may also be some drawback to the value of this generally excellent clause if one nation —France for instance—should be prevented from reducing her tariff in our favour, because, if she did so, she would be compelled by the M.F.N. clause to give the same privilege to another nation—say Germany." This is a somewhat ingenuous argument; for it implies either that free traders should welcome differential tariffs, against which so much of their thunder has been directed, or that a country which is unwilling to generalise concessions is willing to extend them gratuitously to all. As *ex hypothesi*, the latter is out of the question, we are left with the first deduction.

[3] Emphasised by Schmoller, "Grundriss," pp. 619-20; Phillipovitch, *op. et loc. cit.*

> they obtain the concessions due to the sacrifices of others, they need not themselves modify their tariffs. Thus, an era of high protection *and* the adoption of the unconditional form plays into the hands of the less liberal States.[1]

The weak points of the unconditional form are, other things equal, likely to be the strong points of the conditional form. Thus the contracting States know precisely how far they commit themselves, they know that by insisting on equivalent concession for a concession of theirs they can force the hand of high protection States, or, at any rate, use against them the weapon they use against others, they know also that the other side cannot expect to be given concessions unless they themselves are ready to give concessions in return, so that the conflict of interpretations is avoided.

The conditional form seems to have the arguments so much in its favour, that at first blush the reader may be inclined to wonder that statesmen in Europe should have clung so long to the unconditional form. The demerits of the conditional clause have, as a matter of fact, received by no means so much attention as the defects of the unconditional form, and we must now even things up a little by going into these.

The main disadvantages of the conditional form seem to me to be two in number.

> (1) It presents a serious obstacle to the conclusion of tariff treaties as soon as the commercial relations between States become complex, because of the difficulty of rebargaining the whole of the concessions on the conclusion of each successive treaty. In other words, the unconditional form possesses the enormous advantage of enabling a division of labour among the treaty making powers. Let us take the contrary case and see what the result would be. Each country is interested in a very large

---

[1] Perhaps best expressed in the U.S.A. Report, pp. 442-3, "Assuming as an original condition that no discriminations exist, unconditional M.F.N. treatment will tend to preserve equality. But assuming, as has been the case, that there prevails at the outset a régime of discrimination, unconditional M.F.N. treatment may enable the balance of advantages as among States some of whose discriminatory practices are extensive and others of whose discriminatory practices are not extensive, with the former, while, on the other hand, conditional M.F.N. treatment may enable the more liberal States to reduce the extent of the discriminatory practices of the less liberal, but will in the process probably lead to an increase in the extent of such practices on the part of the former."

number of reductions, but the degree of interest varies from case to case. Consequently, it would be difficult in any case to argue that to buy the same concession the *same* counter-concession would have to be given, because the first counter-concession may have been given by a State very much more interested in the object for which that original counter-concession was given than in any other. There would consequently be an attempt to use the idea not of *identical* reductions but of *equivalent* reductions, which, as already implied, would mean the rearguing of each section with all the participants. Hence, the labour of concluding treaties would be much greater, and the number of treaties to be concluded would also rise. For, if we consider the present position, the only States which need enter directly into treaty relations with one another are those whose commercial relations represent for each of them the dominant factor in their foreign trade at any moment. With the rest of the world, simple M.F.N. Treaties will suffice, for on this basis they will at any rate enjoy the rights of other States, and yet, since the volume of trade is relatively small, they can devote their energies in bargaining to the important areas. The universal adoption of the conditional form would seem to me to make this arrangement impossible.

(2) It follows from the above that there is a danger, if the unconditional form is abandoned, that the degree of differentiation may increase, in the sense that the number of M.F.N. Treaties may decrease, and that a larger number of countries will no longer be linked together by treaties of any kind. It may be true that as between the treaty making powers still remaining, there may be greater approximation in the level of duties, but this will not in itself prevent a greater degree of differentiation than formerly between the trading nations as a whole. A smaller number than before will become entitled to the benefits of M.F.N. treatment on any terms at all.

We have already seen that it may also be argued against the unconditional form that it may prevent treaties from being concluded: consequently, we must, in summing up, decide whether we think that the existence of smaller differentiation plus the possible reluctance of some countries to conclude treaties is a greater or smaller evil than the possibility of a greater approximation in the tariff levels of some countries, coupled with more differentiation due to the smaller number of countries between which treaties are concluded. If we agree with Fontana-Russo [1] that it is not the absolute height of the tariff wall in the case of a given country that is so objectionable to the exporter to that country as the existence of differentiation in its tariffs, we shall prefer the unconditional form, if we believe that the absolute height of the wall is the greater evil, we shall, on the whole, prefer the conditional form, other things equal.

But, of course, other things are not always equal, and before we can finally dispose of the subject we must investigate the factors on which these general conclusions finally rest.

(*a*) The first of the unequal factors is the nature of the exports of the country in question. Countries which predominantly export manufactured articles are much more vulnerable to retaliation than countries which import manufactured articles and export raw materials. It is no mere coincidence that the period of the supremacy of the unconditional form in Europe should also be the period of industrial expansion. To all "manufacturing nations" differentiation is the greatest evil they have to face, and they have a collective interest in seeing that the degree of differentiation should be cut down, as well as an individual interest. But the same is by no means so true of the raw material States: the danger of retaliation is not so great to them, positively, because their export products are the basis of the manufacturing power of the industrial states, negatively, because they can inflict severe loss on the retaliating manufacturing nation by counter retaliation. Hence, it is only recently, when the United States is passing from the raw material exporting stage, to the manufacturing stage, that the desirability of the retention of the conditional form is being seriously discussed. But this matter has already been referred to in previous sections.[2]

(*b*) The second of the disturbing factors is the general belief or disbelief in the virtues of freer or more restricted

---

[1] *Op. cit.*, p. 654.

[2] See above, §§ 10, 11.

trade. That in this respect a great change has come over European nations since the era of the Cobden Treaty needs no mention, and the causes thereof fall outside the scope of this work. But it is on reflection clear that apart from the technical merits of either form, the conditional fits much better the aspirations of a protectionist régime. And this for the reason that *directly* the unconditional form seems to require a greater immediate sacrifice than the conditional. The fact that in the long run all nations benefit from the extension of trade which freer intercourse brings with it, so that the apparent sacrifice may be amply requited, is a point that is the fundamental assumption of free trade, but it is a point that is not equally attractive at all times and to all schools of thinkers.

Some of the resentment which is felt at the unconditional form is, no doubt, the result of careless thinking. It is overlooked that "two can play at the game," and that if a country imposes conditions, the co-contractants will ask conditions of it. There are but few exceptions to this general rule. The first, the nature of a country's exports, we have already examined. The second great exception is the power of a victor. He can impose any conditions on an enemy he likes, and if he imposes on his enemy the unconditional form and restricts his own counter-concession to the conditional form, he is more generous than he strictly need be, for he might have conferred nothing, and demanded the unconditional form nevertheless. But whether it is worth while even in this case to break the great principle of reciprocity is a wider question which we will leave unanswered.

The final question which demands an answer is the future of the M.F.N. clause. Here the position is uncertain. In the first place, the war has enormously stimulated the anti-foreign feeling in most countries, and this is itself unfavourable to the unconditional form. In the second place, the feeling that it is desirable that Allies should be better treated than neutrals and ex-enemies is a further factor making in the same direction. During the War itself, a good deal of ink was spilled in Germany and Austria in defending the position that in the future special concessions made to the Middle European States must be excluded from the content of the M.F.N. clause. In this way there would arise a new limiting principle, though the demand that the clause should in the future be used only in the conditional form played, so far as my knowledge goes, no rôle in these discussions. Similarly, in the United Kingdom we find the Balfour of Burleigh Commission attempting to work out a practicable scheme by which the Allies could benefit more than the neutrals. Two ideas presented themselves: the first the granting to them of concessions on those articles in which they possessed particular interests, so that, though treaties with neutral States were continued, the latter could not benefit therefrom, or only to a restricted extent. The second alternative was the denunciation of all existing treaties, and the granting of concessions *de novo* to the Allies. It is not quite clear as to whether, in the latter case, only the Allies are to be given reductions from the tariff to be established, or whether the report contemplates, as a possibility, a neutral as well as an allied tariff schedule. In any case the report came to the conclusion that any "action in the direction of preferential treatment of our Allies should be of a kind compatible with the maintenance of our existing commercial treaties—namely, the grant to such of the Allies and Neutrals as may be prepared to reciprocate, reductions from the general rates of duty in respect of such classes of goods subjected for any reason to import duties as may be of particular interest to them, those classes of goods being so selected that the reductions would be of no practical use to other States to which they might nominally be extended by virtue of the "most-favoured-nation clause." [1] Here it is clear that the difficulties of a special preference to the Allies have caused the idea to be implicitly dropped, and they are assimilated to the neutrals. But the passage also shows that the wish to limit as far as possible the value of the M.F.N. clause has by no means disappeared.

The subsequent action of the British Government in denouncing its treaties indicates that it is hoped that changes in the commercial policy of the country may be effected, but, up to the moment of writing, no practical steps have been taken to enforce a new régime, which, to be effective, would require the previous construction of a tariff for the United Kingdom.

---

[1] Cd. 9035, 1918, pars. 249-252.

APPENDIX I.

Export and Transit Duties.

§ 1. We have had occasion in previous chapters incidentally to deal with export and transit duties. In this appendix we can examine the matter more formally.

A certain prejudice attaches to export and transit duties which one does not find in the case of import duties. Thus, export duties are forbidden under the American Constitution,[1] and transit duties are prohibited by § 69 of the German Federal Customs Law.[2] It is fairly easy to see why transit taxes should not be popular, for they limit the competitive efficiency of the carrying services of a country. But export duties play a not unimportant rôle to-day, and are likely to play a more important rôle in the future.

When we investigate the cases in which export duties are levied, we find, however, that their frequency is in inverse ratio to the industrial development of the country, and in inverse ratio to the degree of finish of the article. Except in special cases—*e.g.*, opium or arms and ammunition—export duties tend to be limited to raw materials.

§ 2. The fact that it is less advanced or raw material producing countries, that tend to rely to some extent on export duties, whilst manufacturing countries do not, is to a large extent due to the differences in the general economic level of such areas. Plantation areas are not suitable for direct taxation, and export duties on the staple crops represent a substitute for land taxes, just as import duties in the same areas tend to be a substitute for income taxes.

---

[1] Art. I., § 9, clause 5, "No tax or duty shall be laid on articles exported from any State." Art. I., § 10, clause 2, "No State shall without the consent of Congress levy any imposts or duties on imports or exports except what may be absolutely necessary for executing its inspection laws." For the legal interpretations by which the meaning of exports has been limited to exports to foreign countries, see Willoughby on the Constitution, I. § 277, p. 608, *et seq.*

[2] "No duties shall be raised on transit."

When export duties are levied frankly as a substitute for direct taxation, the question of incidence hardly arises. But if the question as to who pays export duties is raised, is the answer more favourable to export duties on raw materials than to export duties on finished commodities? Who pays the export duty? The answer is that export duties are shifted on to the consumer only if his demand cannot be diverted to other sources, and when we are comparing manufactured articles with raw materials as proper objects of export taxation we cannot deal with them as classes at all. In the case of a given manufactured article for which there is only *one source of supply*, the tax tends to be borne by the consumer, whereas in the case of a raw material for which there are competing sources of supply, the tax will tend to be borne by the producer in the taxed area. There is, therefore, no essential difference in this respect.

The fact that the producer and not the consumer tends to pay the tax may be made a reason for imposing an export tax. For, if there are competing sources of supply, or substitutes, these will be preferred, and the demand for the taxed article will fall off. Hence, the local users of the commodity can obtain a cheaper article, whilst the local producers must put up with a lower price.[1] On the other hand, it may be argued that it is easier *as a general rule* to obtain manufactured articles from a rival source than it is to obtain raw materials, so that export taxes represent a greater encouragement to competition in the former than in the latter case.

§ 3. To examine in detail the technical form of export taxes would be to go over again matters already discussed in previous chapters. Thus, we find taxes levied on number or tale, on value,[2] and on quantity, just as we find the sliding scale.[3] The utmost diversity prevails as to the articles which we find in these export duty schedules: they include gold (New Zealand), coal and coke (British Columbia), timber,

---

[1] A classical instance of the divergence of interests between producers and users is to be found in the history of the English woollen industry, when the "landed interest" desired to export wool freely and the manufacturers desired prohibition of export in order to safeguard their raw material.

[2] See the interesting Peruvian Tax Law of 10/5/1911, by which india rubber and other gums "shall pay duty at the rate of 8 per cent. *ad valorem* on their market value at Liverpool, in lieu of the specific duty now leviable thereon."

[3] *E.g.*, the sliding scale imposed on rubber in the Malay States, C.I.D., 1914, Appendix vii., p. 872.

sugar, hides and skins, diamonds (South Africa), lead, copper, iron, argentiferous ores (Spain), washed and unwashed wool (Bulgaria), silk waste, seeds, articles for collection and works of art (Italy). The frequent inclusion of rags (Italy, Russia, the old Austria-Hungary) is due to the desire to conserve a supply of raw material for the local paper-making industry.

§ 4. Nor is the retaliatory duty lacking. Here is an instance from Newfoundland [1]—

> "In case of any country imposing an import duty on herrings exported from Newfoundland and imported into such country in vessels belonging to the Colony when such herrings may be imported into such country in vessels belonging to the same free of duty, the Governor-in-Council may, by proclamation, impose an export duty equal to the amount of the duty so imposed by such country aforesaid on herrings exported from Newfoundland in vessels belonging to such country when such import duty is imposed."

§ 5. In the recent past two developments are of interest. The first is the use of the export duty as a means of economic warfare. We have already had to refer to this matter in connection with the differential export tax on tropical produce. In the case of the European Peace Treaties, we find that steps have been taken to prevent the policy of export duties intended to hamper the economic position of the other States from taking effect. Thus, with regard to the Saar Basin, Art. 31 of Chapter II. of the Annex to Part III., § IV. enacts that "no export tax shall be imposed upon metallurgical products or coal exported from the said territory to Germany, nor upon German exports for the use of the industries of the territory of the Saar Basin." [2] So in the case of the transference of Upper Silesia to Poland, Art. 90 of the treaty enforces for fifteen years both the permission and the freedom of coal exports, and further enacts that "Poland agrees to take such steps as may be necessary to secure that any such products shall be available for sale to purchasers in Germany on terms as favourable as are applicable to like products sold under similar

[1] C.I.D., Appendix vii., p. 863. See No. 18 of Act 9 of 1905.

[2] This clause does not prohibit the *prohibition* of export, it will be noted.

conditions to purchasers in Poland or in any other Country." [1] So also under Art. 224 of the Austrian Treaty—

> (1) Czecho-Slovakia and Poland may not for fifteen years levy differential duties on coal going to Austria.
>
> (2) The same States undertake, pending the conclusion of reciprocal agreements for the supply of raw materials and coal, " but in no case during more than three years from the coming into force of the present treaty, that no export duty or other restrictions of any kind shall be imposed on the export to Austria of coal or lignite up to a reasonable quantity, to be fixed, failing agreement between the States concerned, by the Reparation Commission."

§ 6. The second interesting development is the use of the export tax as a means of correcting the depreciation of the exchanges. Thus in Germany, an ordinance of 20th December, 1919, " concerning control of export trade " introduces, in Art. 6, a tax on export licenses. By the Ministerial Proclamation of 8th April, 1920, Art. 9, the tax is assessable " on the total value which is put to the account of the foreign consignee . . . if the merchandise is exported unsold, the tax will be calculated according to the export value of the goods; and in the case of 'improvement trade,' according to the value of payments made in connection therewith." The Ministers for Economic Affairs and of Finance can regulate the charges to be made, and are bound to alter them on demand of the Reichsrat. By Art. 10, " if the wares are priced in foreign currency the value is to be calculated in German currency converted at the rate of exchange to be fixed " by the said Ministers, " for the purpose of computing the amount of the charge." [2] So long as the internal purchasing power of the mark was greater than its parity value in terms of foreign currency, this system represented a sharing of the profits between the foreign buyer and the German Government.

[1] It may also be noted that Art. 266 of the Treaty guarantees the Allies unlimited M.F.N. treatment as regards exportation (including internal charges): no differential charges on import or export based on frontier, kind, ownership, flag of transport, place of departure or destination, route or places of trans-shipment. No direct or indirect bounties in favour of German ports or shipping are allowed. (All Art. 323.)

[2] See *B.T.J.*, 29/4/20, pp. 590-591, and subsequent weeks: and *Economist* Berlin Correspondent), 15/5/20, p. 1004.

The value of the system becomes problematical when the internal value of the mark falls, for then no profit is to be obtained by buying German goods, and the tax operates like any other export tax as a discouragement to export.[1]

§ 7. The importance of avoiding impediments to transit is shown by the Peace Treaty with Germany; by Art. 321 national treatment is set up, and "goods in transit shall be exempt from all customs or other similar duties." The real difficulty at the present day is not open taxation of transit, but differential railway rates on goods moving inwards and outwards, so as to favour export against import. To investigate this matter would take us beyond the scope of our present work.[2]

---

[1] Discontent with the system very soon manifested itself. See *Economist*, 22/5/20, p. 1051.

[2] See Treaty of Peace with Germany, Part. XII. *Cf.* Grunzel, "Ec. Protectionism," p. 163, *et seq.*

APPENDIX II.

THE TARIFF AS A REVENUE INSTRUMENT.

§ 1. THE problems which are raised by the collection of revenue by means of customs duties are part of the general subject matter of public finance, and the questions discussed in this note have, therefore, received due attention from the accredited writers on the subject. It will not be necessary, therefore, to do more than draw attention to the salient points.[1]

§ 2. Apart from a very few "free trade" countries, such as the United Kingdom is (or was), the duties contained in any actual tariff fall into two main classes, according as they are intended primarily to raise revenue, or are intended to protect the industries of the country. It is obvious that any particular rate may in part protect the local industries from the full effect of foreign competition, and in part raise a revenue for the State, but it is also obvious that the more effective a particular duty is in keeping out foreign articles, the less revenue it is capable of bringing in. On the other hand, those rates which are most fruitful of revenue at a particular moment need not necessarily be those which offer *no* protection, for the duties may be quite high enough to encourage a local industry to rise up in their shade. Thus, duties which were originally not protective in *intention* may become so in *effect* in the course of time. But such is not the purpose of a revenue duty, and when it is found that the rates imposed are encouraging the rise of local industries, they should be supplemented by internal excise duties. For, if this is not done, the State will be deprived of part of the revenue it might otherwise

[1] For a general survey, see Bastable, "Public Finance," 3rd edn., pp. 551-73; Leroy-Beaulieu, "Science des Finances," 6th edn., vol. i., pp. 641-701; and Lotz, "Finanzwissenschaft," pp. 568-586.

have obtained—*i.e.*, that part of the demand, which is satisfied from the locally produced supplies, will not contribute its quota to the revenue. Hence it follows that the choice of revenue duties is in part determined by the very fact that no local industry exists to supply the commodity in question, though, unless substitutes are carefully watched, this does not in all cases safeguard the revenue.

But, though no clear line of distinction can be drawn between what is at any moment of time a protective and a pure revenue duty, there is a clear line of distinction between revenue duties as such and protective duties as such. Though practical necessity may compel a compromise between the necessity of raising revenue and the desire to protect local industries, the logical results to which a pure revenue tariff will lead are entirely different to those to which a pure protective tariff will conduct. In fact, however, most States desire to raise revenue as well as to protect their industries. The practical opposition is also mitigated by the fact that among those articles which yield most revenue are in a large number of cases those which have no protective effect, and that in most cases also the greater amount of revenue is derived from a relatively small number of articles. To this important fact we must later return.

§ 3. Let us first approach the matter from the customs standpoint. Here the following rule holds good :—

> (1) The fewer the dutiable articles the simpler and the less costly the customs administration. Hence, the larger will be the net return per £ of duty collected, or, in other words, the smaller the duty need be in relation to the amount of revenue which it is desired to collect.
>
> It follows that the articles must be in general demand, and also that the demand for them must be relatively inelastic.
>
> (2) The articles which are selected should be such that it is difficult to smuggle them. It follows that easily portable articles of great value in proportion to their bulk should not be selected, other things equal.
>
> (3) It is a well-known fact that equal additions to the rate add unequal amounts to the revenue. Consequently there is a limit imposed to the fewness of the

articles which can be selected: a consideration which is reinforced by the further fact that the danger of smuggling increases directly with the increase in the duties.

(4) The loss of revenue from diversion is least when the article is wholly imported, and there are available no efficient local substitutes. Where a local supply exists, it should be taxed equally with the imported supply. Hence, it follows that *any* difference between the customs and the excise duty, or any addition of the excise duty *to* the customs duty in the case of imported articles will involve loss of revenue through the diversion of demand to the locally produced and favoured supply.

§ 4. Are all articles in general demand equally suitable to be the subject of customs taxation? Here it at once becomes apparent that two sets of problems arise.

(1) The interests of trade and industry. The taxation of raw materials represents "inverse" protection, *i.e.*, a positive disadvantage to the manufacturer if he attempts to sell in competition with untaxed rivals. Hence the selection of raw material as articles of taxation involves (*a*) an elaborate system of drawbacks or (*b*) bounties upon export, or (*c*) a system of "improvement trade," or free zones. The necessity of avoiding administrative expense or administrative complexity tells against the use of raw materials as taxable objects in a tariff intended for revenue only, and results in their unpopularity even in the case of protective tariffs.

(2) The second factor is the sacrifice involved on the part of the consumer. It is an inevitable effect of taxing articles in general demand that the effects of such taxation should result in regression, for a larger part of the income of the poor will be spent on such commodities than will the incomes of the rich. This affects our problem in two distinct ways.

Firstly, "luxury" goods are more suitable than "necessaries," other things being equal. For, though it still remains true that the effect of taxing tobacco and alcoholic liquors is to produce a regressive effect (the possibility of differentiation being for the moment neglected), yet economy and equity alike suggest the desirability of exempting the food and clothing which represent the essentials of industrial efficiency; whereas in the case of tobacco and alcohol some discouragement of consumption may be regarded as a positive advantage.

Secondly, the regressive effect of indirect taxation suggests that the plan of taxing only a few articles may have positive disadvantages as well as benefits. If we assume a country in which the imposition of direct taxes is impossible, and in which most of the articles consumed by rich and poor alike are imported, then, other things equal, it will be better in such a State to collect the revenue by a very moderate taxation of those articles mainly consumed by the poor, and by differentiating heavily those articles which are mainly consumed by the rich, so that the revenue is collected from a larger number of articles than would be required for raising the same amount of taxation if incomes and consumption were more equally distributed. That is, the virtue of economy in collection may be too dearly bought, if economy accentuates the regressiveness of indirect taxation. Hence, where, as in "new" countries, a system of direct taxation is difficult to instal, a *primâ facie* case is made out for the spreading of the taxation over a large number of articles—that is, a larger number than would be required for the revenue desired were it possible to consider only the economy of collection.

§ 5. When we turn to the concrete aspects of the situation, we must illustrate two groups of facts—

(1) The distribution of the total revenue from customs duties among articles of different *types*, and the amount paid per capita of the population.

(2) The distribution of the total revenue among the *number* of articles taxable.

§ 6. *Distribution among Articles of Different Types.*—In 1909 the British Board of Trade published some useful tables showing, in the case of certain countries, the distribution among articles, and the amount paid per capita of the population—[1]

Year.	Percentage Borne by			Gross Return per Capita.
	Class 1. Food, Drink and Tobacco.	Class 2. Raw Materials.	Class 3. Manufactures.	s. d.
1890-4, . .	99·8 %	0·2 %		10/7 U.K.
1895-9, . .	99·8 %	0·2 %		10/10
1900-4, . .	99·8 %	0·2 %		15/1
1905-8, . .	99·9 %	0·1 %		15/0
1890-4, . .	71·8 %	16·9 %[2]	11·3 %	8/9 France.
1895-9, . .	67·4 %	19·8 %	12·8 %	9/0
1900-4, . .	59·4 %	23·9 %	16·7 %	8/4
1905-8, . .	55·4 %	25·6 %	19·0 %	9/2
1890-4, . .	74·1 %	4·0 %	22·0 %	7/6 Germany.
1895-9, . .	72·0 %	5·7 %	22·4 %	8/8
1900-4, . .	72·3 %	5·7 %	21·9 %	9/2
1905-8, . .	75·0 %	5·2 %	20·0 %	10/9
1890-4, . .	19·8 %	10·6 %	69·4 %	12/1 U.S.A.
1895-9, . .	32·4 %	10·0 %	57·5 %	9/7
1900-4, . .	35·7 %	12·6 %	51·5 %	13/2
1905-8, . .	29·5 %	14·8 %	55·4 %	14/3

We may add the following summary for Belgium :—[3]

	Percentage Distribution in				
	1909.	1910.	1911.	1912.	1913.
Live animals, .	2·7 %	2·3 %	1·9 %	2·5 %	1·7 %
Drink and food, .	27·0 %	28·7 %	27·6 %	27·1 %	28·4 %
Raw and semi-manufactured.	21·9 %	20·3 %	20·9 %	21·0 %	19·0 %
Manufactured, .	48·4 %	48·7 %	49·6 %	49·4 %	50·9 %

(2) Let us now turn to a comparative survey of yield per capita—

[1] Cd. 4954 of 1909 (Third Fiscal Blue-Book), p. 90, *et seq.*
[2] Includes leaf tobacco.
[3] "Tableau Général du Commerce de la Belgique," vol. i., p. 349.

Year.	Country.	Return per Capita.	Total Yield.
		In Shillings.	In Million Pounds.
1912	United Kingdom,	14·74	33·52 (net receipts).
1912	Germany, .	10·14	38·00 (exclusive of repayments on account of import certificates).
1912	France, . .	14·30	28·37 (inclusive of navigation and statistical taxes, but not the duty on salt).
1912	United States, .	13·53	65·61
1912	Belgium, . .	7·84	2·98
1912	Switzerland, .	17·86	3·42
1912	Holland, . .	4·31	1·32
1912	Argentina, .	45·10	16·58
1912	Chile, . .	26·38	4·63
1911	Canada, . .	48·60	17·50
1912	Australia, .	55·16	13·06
1912	South Africa, .	15·10	4·634
1912	New Zealand, .	62·34	3·279
1912	India, . .	0·59	7·197 (population of British India in 1911).

§ 7. From this survey two results emerge—

(1) If we deal first with the larger European countries and the United States we find that in spite of very divergent distribution among the various groups of articles, the customs revenue per head of the population tends to be very much the same. That is, protectionist countries do not necessarily raise more per head than do free trade countries.

(2) If we turn to the "new" countries, there is a tendency for the per capita return to be very much higher than in the case of European countries. It is obvious that this higher return per capita is not due to a higher ability to pay, but must in the main result from different systems of taxation—that is, the relative importance of customs duties in the revenue systems is different. But, in addition, there must be considered, in discussing this point, the influence exerted on the per capita return, by a large native population possessed of small purchasing power, which tends to reduce the amount per head, and the influence, secondly, of the legal structure of the State. If the State is a Federal State, then some of the expenses borne in a Unitary State by the central Government are

borne by the Federal States, so that the comparison is vitiated by the fact that unlike things are being compared. All this is tantamount to saying that too much reliance must not be placed on these per capita figures.[1]

§ 8. The next matter we must deal with is the concentration of the revenue among the total articles chargeable.

The *locus classicus* in this respect is the report of the select committee of 1840, which, under the chairmanship of Hume, investigated the British Tariff of the early Victorian era. It was made abundantly evident that from the revenue point of view the then existing tariff was completely unnecessary: for the greater part of the revenue was collected from a very small number of articles. As a matter of strict historical fact this had been discovered before, and both the reformer Parnell and the Statistician Porter drew attention to this aspect of the tariff problem before the select committee entered upon its labours.[2]

Before we pass over to modern illustrations, we may give again these celebrated figures.

§ 9. Out of a total of 862 articles,[3] yielding altogether £22,122,095, 147 resulted in a positive loss of £5,398.[4] So that the number of articles yielding revenue was 715, of which

9 yielded, ...	£18,575,071
10 "	1,838,630
	£20,413,701
696 "	1,713,792
	£22,127,493
Loss, ...	5,398
Revenue, ...	£22,122,095

[1] Using the figures for Gross Revenue and for Customs Revenue in Cd. 9051 of 1918, the 53rd Abstract for the several British Self-Governing Dominions, etc., the ratio of customs revenue to total revenue was for 1912:—

South Africa, .	26 per cent.	Canada (1911), .	64 per cent.
Australia, . .	58 "	New Zealand, .	28 "

Canada and Australia are Federations; the other two are Unitary States. But South Africa has a very large native population, and New Zealand a very small population.

[2] See Porter, "The Progress of the Nation," edn. of 1838, vol. ii., p. 323, *et seq.*, using the "customs house accounts," and Parnell, "On Financial Reform," 2nd edn. of 1830, p. 120, *et seq.*, quoting from the Report of the Select Committee on Finance.

[3] Report, p. 4.

[4] This loss was due to an excess of drawback.

With this may be compared Parnell's table, referring to the year 1827, the figures of the select committee of 1840 referring to the preceding year. The total number of articles contributing to the revenue was 566, and

			£	s.	d.
18	articles produced £100,000 and upwards, making	.	£17,683,445	8	8
9	articles produced £50,000 to £100,000,	.	784,415	18	6
9	,, £25,000 to £50,000,	.	370,066	17	1
20	,, £10,000 to £25,000,	.	370,402	5	1
510	,, less than £10,000,	.	585,072	6	0
566					
	Miscellaneous articles,	.	20,903	7	7
	Gross revenue,	.	£19,815,206	2	11 [1]

§ 10. What, next, were the most productive articles in 1839? The articles producing £100,000 and over were—[2]

(1) Sugar and molasses,	£4,827,018
(2) Tea,	3,658,800
(3) Tobacco,	3,495,686
(4) Rum, brandy, etc.,	2,615,443
(5) Wine,	1,849,709
(6) Timber,	1,603,194
(7) Corn,	1,098,779
(8) Coffee,	779,114
(9) Cotton wool,	416,257
(10) Silk manufactures,	247,362
(11) Butter,	213,077
(12) Currants,	189,291
(13) Tallow,	182,000
(14) Seeds,	145,323
(15) Sheep's wool,	139,770
(16) Raisins,	134,589
(17) Cheese,	110,521 [3]
	£21,700,630

§ 11. Let us now turn to modern illustrations. We may begin with Norway and Sweden.

In Norway,[4] on the average of the years 1914-17, 78 per cent. of the duties were raised from taxation of 15 articles, whilst 51·35 per cent. was raised by the taxation of 4 articles.

[1] Parnell, *op. cit.*, p. 130. The addition sum is wrongly made, which I have allowed for in this place.

[2] Report, p. 208.

[3] This is given in the Report as only £10,521, an obvious printer's error.

[4] Statistical Abstract of Norway, 1918, p. 169. (Statistik Aarbok for Kongeriket Norge.)

The total revenue was 57·714 mill. kr., and of this amount there was raised from the imports of

Sugar,	mill. kr.	11·1
Tissues,	,,	8·7
Brandy and other alcoholic drinks,	,,	3·5
Tobacco,	,,	6·3
Total,	,,	29·6

Coffee, the next item of importance, yielded 4·9. mill. kr., equal to 8·55 per cent. of the revenue.

In Sweden,[1] the total customs revenue in 1913 amounted to 69·6 mill. kr. Of this amount 43·233 millions was raised from the following articles :—

Cereals,	mill. kr.	10·994 (unmilled)
,,	,,	1·485 (milled)
Green coffee,	,,	4·090
Tobacco,	,,	6·777
Brandy,	,,	3·190
Wine,	,,	2·243
Silk tissues,	,,	1·001
Woollens,	,,	2·133
Cottons,	,,	2·135
Iron and steel manufactures,	,,	4·133
Other metals,	,,	1·683
Machines and tools,	,,	3·369
Total,	,,	43·233, or 62·3%

In the case of Belgium,[2] the total customs revenue in 1913 was 74·4 mill. fcs. Of this amount, 24·7 millions were raised from the six most productive groups of articles, viz. :—

Wood for constructional purposes,	mill. fcs.	5·4
Unmanufactured tobacco,	,,	5·1
Oats,	,,	4·2
Haberdashery and hardware,	,,	4·2
Brandy in bulk,	,,	3·4
Oranges and lemons,	,,	2·4
Total,	,,	24·7

equal to 30 per cent. approximate of the total. The next 13 articles contributed 17·6 millions, and the next three 3·1 millions. The remaining 29·0 millions were raised from 120 articles or groups.

[1] Statistical Abstract for Sweden, 1918, p. 266. (Statistik Årsbok för Sverige.)
[2] Tableau Général, 1914, vol. i., p. 356.

When we turn to France,[1] the average revenue, 1910-13, amounted to 682·2 mill. fcs. Of this amount 500·5 mill. fcs. was contributed by the first 11 most productive articles or groups. Over the years 1910-13 the revenue from these more productive articles was, in the order of relative importance—

Coffee,	mill. fcs.	151·0
Cereals,	,,	104·0 [2]
Mineral oils,	,,	70·0
Machines and tools,	,,	32·0
Cocoa,	,,	29·5
Colonial sugars,	,,	24·0
Coal,	,,	23·0
Wines,	,,	23·0
Wood,	,,	21·0
Apparatus and metals,	,,	13·0
Table fruit and fruit for distillation,	,,	10·0

In the case of the United States,[3] out of a total revenue in 1917 of $ mill. 221·5, the first 3 articles in order of importance contributed $ mill. 104·6, or nearly 47 per cent. of the total: the first 10 articles contributed $ mill. 174·4, or nearly 79 per cent. of the revenue. These articles were—

(1) Sugar and molasses,	mill. $.	55·4
(2) Tobacco and manufactures thereof,	,,	29·8
(3) Cotton manufactures,	,,	19·4
(4) Silk and silk manufactures,	,,	18·1
(5) Spirits, wines, malt liquors, and other beverages,	,,	13·6
(6) Vegetable fibres and manufactures thereof,	,,	10·4
(7) Precious and semi-precious stones,	,,	8·1
(8) Wool and manufactures thereof,	,,	7·2
(9) Chemicals, drugs, dyes, and medicines,	,,	6·5
(10) Fruits and nuts,	,,	5·9
		174·4

The rule that among the leading revenue articles are usually to be found those for which protection internally is not possible, breaks down in the case of the United States, though it tends

[1] Based upon Tableau Général du Commerce et de la Navigation, 1914, vol. i., p. 86.

[2] A very fluctuating source—*i.e.*,

1910,	mill. fcs.	52·6
1911,	,,	164·0
1912,	,,	65·3
1913,	,,	134·0

[3] Based on Commerce and Navigation of the United States, 1917, pp. 54-55, Table No. xii.

to be true of Europe. This rule is, in fact, only true where the natural conditions of the country make the production of "colonial products," such as coffee and tobacco, either difficult or impossible. In other cases competition between the imported article and a locally produced article is always *possible*, and hence the duty always has a potentially protective effect.

When we turn to Germany we find that, in 1913,[1] the amount raised from purely revenue duties—*i.e.*, duties on products not produced at home, or, if so produced, subject to an internal tax—was 236·5 million marks. The revenue from protective duties was 444·0 million marks. But from this latter amount must be deducted the cost of the import certificates, which reduced the net revenue to 275·2 million marks from protective duties. Of the gross revenue, without deduction of the repayments on account of import certificates, the revenue articles thus contributed 43 per cent., the protective duties contributed 57 per cent.

But to take the distribution among groups without further analysis is to give a misleading picture of the distribution among articles. The single article of most importance among those taxable on grounds of protection is cereals. The gross yield from this source was 270·9 million marks. The import certificate reduced this to a net amount of 102·1 million marks, or 15·5 per cent. of the net revenue. Of the protective duties, those on foodstuffs contributed 41·2 per cent. of the gross, of which amount again cereals contributed 31 per cent. If we exclude the foodstuffs group, then we find that the remaining protective duties contributed only 15·8 per cent. of the gross revenue, the most important article being wood, from which 18·4 million marks was raised. No other protective duty contributed as much as 10 million marks, or £500,000 to the revenue.

Of the revenue duties—

Unworked tobacco leaves contributed,	mill. mks.	116·4	131·0
Tobacco products,	„	14·6	
Raw coffee and coffee substitutes,	„	99·1	
Mineral oils,	„	78·5	
Wine of all kinds,	„	26·9	
Southern fruits,	„	13·5	
Raw cocoa,	„	10·2	

[1] Lotz, *op. cit.*, following the Statistisches Jahrbuch for 1915, pp. 361-363.

No other revenue duty reached the 10 million line, the articles remaining, in their order of importance, being rice (9·6 mm.), spices (4·6 mm.), tea (4·2 mm.), cocoa, chocolate, and confectionary (1·9 mm.).[1]

§ 12. It will be seen that whilst it is incorrect to assert that protective duties do not yield any revenue, it is nevertheless also true that, in order to obtain an adequate yield, such protective duties must be imposed upon articles largely of general consumption, such as wheat. They are objectionable on the ground that they have necessarily a regressive effect, though the objection that they cause an aggregate sacrifice greater than is required to raise an equal revenue *by indirect taxation* can be overcome if the corresponding article of domestic origin is subjected to taxation. In that case they cease to be protective and merely become consumption taxes, yielding a large return, but socially undesirable on the ground of their regressiveness.

---

[1] The reader will find some interesting additional details in the otherwise somewhat over-elaborated article by Manicke, "Deutschland's gegenwärtiges Zollwesen, Seine Bedeutung und Verfassung" in Finanz-Archiv, vol. xxv., esp. pp. 272-279. On the theoretical side, Dr. Manicke's article is almost worthless; on the technical side it contains some valuable information.

INDEX.

A

B

C

H

I

N

O

P

Z